T0335997

Handbook of Research on Fireworks Algorithms and Swarm Intelligence

Ying Tan
Peking University, China

A volume in the Advances in Computational
Intelligence and Robotics (ACIR) Book Series

Published in the United States of America by
IGI Global
Engineering Science Reference (an imprint of IGI Global)
701 E. Chocolate Avenue
Hershey PA, USA 17033
Tel: 717-533-8845
Fax: 717-533-8661
E-mail: cust@igi-global.com
Web site: http://www.igi-global.com

Copyright © 2020 by IGI Global. All rights reserved. No part of this publication may be reproduced, stored or distributed in
any form or by any means, electronic or mechanical, including photocopying, without written permission from the publisher.
Product or company names used in this set are for identification purposes only. Inclusion of the names of the products or
companies does not indicate a claim of ownership by IGI Global of the trademark or registered trademark.

Library of Congress Cataloging-in-Publication Data

Names: Tan, Ying, 1964- editor.
Title: Handbook of research on fireworks algorithms and swarm intelligence
 / Ying Tan, editor.
Description: Hershey, PA : Engineering Science Reference, 2020. | Includes
 bibliographical references and index. | Summary: ""This book provides
 vital research on theory analysis, improvements, and applications of
 fireworks algorithm. While highlighting topics such as convergence rate,
 parameter applications, and global optimization analysis, this
 publication explores up-to-date progress on the specific techniques of
 this algorithm"--Provided by publisher"-- Provided by publisher.
Identifiers: LCCN 2019032848 (print) | LCCN 2019032849 (ebook) | ISBN
 9781799816591 (h/c) | ISBN 9781799816607 (eISBN)
Subjects: LCSH: Fireworks--Research. | Swarm intelligence.
Classification: LCC TP300 .H363 2020 (print) | LCC TP300 (ebook) | DDC
 662/.1--dc23
LC record available at https://lccn.loc.gov/2019032848
LC ebook record available at https://lccn.loc.gov/2019032849

This book is published in the IGI Global book series Advances in Computational Intelligence and Robotics (ACIR) (ISSN:
2327-0411; eISSN: 2327-042X)

British Cataloguing in Publication Data
A Cataloguing in Publication record for this book is available from the British Library.

All work contributed to this book is new, previously-unpublished material. The views expressed in this book are those of the
authors, but not necessarily of the publisher.

For electronic access to this publication, please contact: eresources@igi-global.com.

Advances in Computational Intelligence and Robotics (ACIR) Book Series

Ivan Giannoccaro
University of Salento, Italy

ISSN:2327-0411
EISSN:2327-042X

MISSION

While intelligence is traditionally a term applied to humans and human cognition, technology has progressed in such a way to allow for the development of intelligent systems able to simulate many human traits. With this new era of simulated and artificial intelligence, much research is needed in order to continue to advance the field and also to evaluate the ethical and societal concerns of the existence of artificial life and machine learning.

The **Advances in Computational Intelligence and Robotics (ACIR) Book Series** encourages scholarly discourse on all topics pertaining to evolutionary computing, artificial life, computational intelligence, machine learning, and robotics. ACIR presents the latest research being conducted on diverse topics in intelligence technologies with the goal of advancing knowledge and applications in this rapidly evolving field.

COVERAGE

- Cognitive Informatics
- Algorithmic Learning
- Artificial Life
- Artificial Intelligence
- Adaptive and Complex Systems
- Pattern Recognition
- Computational Intelligence
- Computer Vision
- Heuristics
- Automated Reasoning

IGI Global is currently accepting manuscripts for publication within this series. To submit a proposal for a volume in this series, please contact our Acquisition Editors at Acquisitions@igi-global.com or visit: http://www.igi-global.com/publish/.

The Advances in Computational Intelligence and Robotics (ACIR) Book Series (ISSN 2327-0411) is published by IGI Global, 701 E. Chocolate Avenue, Hershey, PA 17033-1240, USA, www.igi-global.com. This series is composed of titles available for purchase individually; each title is edited to be contextually exclusive from any other title within the series. For pricing and ordering information please visit http://www.igi-global.com/book-series/advances-computational-intelligence-robotics/73674. Postmaster: Send all address changes to above address. Copyright © 2020 IGI Global. All rights, including translation in other languages reserved by the publisher. No part of this series may be reproduced or used in any form or by any means – graphics, electronic, or mechanical, including photocopying, recording, taping, or information and retrieval systems – without written permission from the publisher, except for non commercial, educational use, including classroom teaching purposes. The views expressed in this series are those of the authors, but not necessarily of IGI Global.

Titles in this Series

For a list of additional titles in this series, please visit:
http://www.igi-global.com/book-series/advances-computational-intelligence-robotics/73674

Smart Systems Design, Applications, and Challenges
João M.F. Rodrigues (Universidade do Algarve, Portugal & LARSyS, Institute for Systems and Robotics, Lisbon, Portugal) Pedro J.S. Cardoso (Universidade do Algarve, Portugal & LARSyS, Institute for Systems and Robotics, Lisbon, Portugal) Jânio Monteiro (Universidade do Algarve, Portugal & INESC-ID, Lisbon, Portugal) and Célia M.Q. Ramos (Universidade do Algarve, Portugal & CIEO, ortugal)
Engineering Science Reference • © 2020 • 459pp • H/C (ISBN: 9781799821120) • US $245.00

Deep Learning Applications and Intelligent Decision Making in Engineering
Karthikrajan Senthilnathan (VIT University, India) Balamurugan Shanmugam (Quants IS & CS, India) Dinesh Goyal (Poornima Institute of Engineering and Technology, India) Iyswarya Annapoorani (VIT University, India) and Ravi Samikannu (Botswana International University of Science and Technology, Botswana)
Engineering Science Reference • © 2020 • 335pp • H/C (ISBN: 9781799821083) • US $245.00

Implementing Computational Intelligence Techniques for Security Systems Design
Yousif Abdullatif Albastaki (Ahlia University, Bahrain) and Wasan Awad (Ahlia University, Bahrain)
Information Science Reference • © 2020 • 332pp • H/C (ISBN: 9781799824183) • US $195.00

Managerial Challenges and Social Impacts of Virtual and Augmented Reality
Sandra Maria Correia Loureiro (Business Research Unit (BRU-IUL), Instituto Universitário de Lisboa (ISCTE-IUL), Lisboa, Portugal)
Engineering Science Reference • © 2020 • 318pp • H/C (ISBN: 9781799828747) • US $195.00

Innovations, Algorithms, and Applications in Cognitive Informatics and Natural Intelligence
Kwok Tai Chui (The Open University of Hong Kong, Hong Kong) Miltiadis D. Lytras (The American College of Greece, Greece) Ryan Wen Liu (Wuhan University of Technology, China) and Mingbo Zhao (Donghua University, China)
Engineering Science Reference • © 2020 • 403pp • H/C (ISBN: 9781799830382) • US $235.00

Avatar-Based Control, Estimation, Communications, and Development of Neuron Multi-Functional Technology Platforms
Vardan Mkrttchian (HHH University, Australia) Ekaterina Aleshina (Penza State University, Russia) and Leyla Gamidullaeva (Penza State University, Russia)
Engineering Science Reference • © 2020 • 355pp • H/C (ISBN: 9781799815815) • US $245.00

701 East Chocolate Avenue, Hershey, PA 17033, USA
Tel: 717-533-8845 x100 • Fax: 717-533-8661
E-Mail: cust@igi-global.com • www.igi-global.com

List of Contributors

Table of Contents

Section 1
Survey of FWA Studies and Applications

Section 2
Algorithm Improvements on FWA

Section 3
FWA Applications in Machine Learning

Section 4
FWA Application in Engineering

Section 5
Innovative Applications of Swarm Intelligence and Swarm Robotics

Detailed Table of Contents

Section 1
Survey of FWA Studies and Applications

Fireworks Algorithm has been proposed for almost 10 years. Because of its basic but profound collaborative searching manner and advantages of universal effectiveness, hundreds of scholars have conducted and published a wide range of work on it. This chapter serves as a background description of fireworks algorithms' developments by introducing its detailed status of researches and applications. Specifically, it gives a brief summarization and analysis of published researches on Fireworks Algorithms since 2010 to clarify characteristics of its historical progress and future trend in detailed fields like algorithms improvements, theoretical analysis, and practical applications.

Section 2
Algorithm Improvements on FWA

Fireworks algorithm (FWA) searches the global optimum by the cooperation between the firework with the best fitness named as core firework (CF) and the other non-CFs. Loser-out tournament-based fireworks algorithm (LoTFWA) uses competition as a new manner of interaction. If the fitness of a firework cannot catch up with the best one, it is considered a loser and will be reinitialized. However, its independent selection operator may prevent non-CFs from aggregating to CF in the late search phase if they fall into different local optima. This chapter proposes a last-position, elimination-based fireworks algorithm which allocates more fireworks in the initial process to search. Then for every fixed number of generations, the firework with the worst fitness is eliminated and its sparks is reallocated to other fireworks. In the final stage of search, only CF survives with all the budget of sparks and thus the aggregation of non-CFs to CF is ensured. Experimental results performed show that the proposed algorithm significantly outperforms most of the state-of-the-art FWA variants.

Chapter 3

Jun Yu, JSPS Research Fellow, Kyushu University, Japan
Hideyuki Takagi, Kyushu University, Japan

This chapter briefly reviews the basic explosion mechanism used in the fireworks algorithm (FWA) and comprehensively investigates relevant research on explosion operations. Since the explosion mechanism is one of the most core operations directly affecting the performance of FWA, the authors focus on analyzing the FWA explosion operation and highlighting two novel explosion strategies: a multi-layer explosion strategy and a scouting explosion strategy. The multi-layer explosion strategy allows an individual firework to perform multiple explosions instead of the single explosion used in the original FWA, where each round of explosion can be regarded as a layer; the scouting explosion strategy controls an individual firework to generate spark individuals one by one instead of generating all spark individuals within the explosion amplitude at once. The authors then introduce several other effective strategies to further improve the performance of FWA by full using the information generated by the explosion operation. Finally, the authors list some open topics for discussion.

Section 3
FWA Applications in Machine Learning

Chapter 4

Daniel C. Lee, Simon Fraser University, Canada
Katherine Manson, British Columbia Institute of Technology, Canada

The Fireworks Algorithm (EFWA) is studied as a method to optimize the noise covariance parameters in an induction motor system model to control the motor speed without a speed sensor. The authors considered a system that employs variable frequency drives (VFDs) and executes an extended Kalman filter (EKF) algorithm to estimate the motor speed based on other measured values. Multiple optimizations were run, and the authors found that the EFWA optimization provided, on average, better solutions than the Genetic Algorithm (GA) for a comparable number of parameter set trials. However, EFWA parameters need to be selected carefully; otherwise, EFWA's early performance advantage over GA can be lost.

Chapter 5

Sreeja N. K., PSG College of Technology, India

Learning a classifier from imbalanced data is one of the most challenging research problems. Data imbalance occurs when the number of instances belonging to one class is much less than the number of instances belonging to the other class. A standard classifier is biased towards the majority class and therefore misclassifies the minority class instances. Minority class instances may be regarded as rare events or unusual patterns that could potentially have a negative impact on the society. Therefore, detection of such events is considered significant. This chapter proposes a FireWorks-based Hybrid ReSampling (FWHRS) algorithm to resample imbalance data. It is used with Weighted Pattern Matching based classifier (PMC+) for classification. FWHRS-PMC+ was evaluated on 44 imbalanced binary datasets. Experiments reveal FWHRS-PMC+ is effective in classification of imbalanced data. Empirical results were validated using non-parametric statistical tests.

Chapter 6

Shoufei Han, Nanjing University of Aeronautics and Astronautics, China
Kun Zhu, Nanjing University of Aeronautics and Astronautics, China

The Dynamic Search Fireworks Algorithm (dynFWA) is an effective algorithm for solving optimization problems. However, dynFWA is easy to fall into local optimal solutions prematurely and it also provides a slow convergence rate. To address these problems, an improved dynFWA (IdynFWA) is proposed in this chapter. In IdynFWA, the population is first initialized based on opposition-based learning. The adaptive mutation is proposed for the core firework (CF) which chooses whether to use Gaussian mutation or Levy mutation for the CF according to the mutation probability. A new selection strategy, namely disruptive selection, is proposed to maintain the diversity of the algorithm. The results show that the proposed algorithm achieves better overall performance on the standard test functions. Meanwhile, IdynFWA is used to optimize the Extreme Learning Machine (ELM), and a virtual machine fault warning model is proposed based on ELM optimized by IdynFWA. The results show that this model can achieve higher accuracy and better stability to some extent.

Chapter 7

Yu Xue, Nanjing University of Information Science and Technology, China

As a recently developed swarm intelligence algorithm, fireworks algorithm (FWA) is an optimization algorithm with good convergence and extensible properties. Moreover, it is usually able to find the global solutions. The advantages of FWA are both optimization accuracy and convergence speed which endue the FWA with a promising prospect of application and extension. This chapter mainly focuses on the application of FWA in classification problems and the improvement of FWA. Many prior studies around FWA have been produced. The author here probes improvement of FWA and its application in classification. The chapter studies FWA around: (1) Application of FWA in classification problems; (2) Improvement of FWA's candidate solution generation strategy (CSGS), including the employment of self-adaptive mechanisms; (3) Improved SaFWA and classification model. For each part, the author conducts research through theory, experimentation, and results analysis.

Chapter 8

Sarat Chandra Nayak, CMR College of Engineering and Technology, Hyderabad, India
Subhranginee Das, KIIT University, Bhubaneswar, India
Bijan Bihari Misra, Silicon Institute of Technology, India

Financial time series are highly nonlinear and their movement is quite unpredictable. Artificial neural networks (ANN) have ample applications in financial forecasting. Performance of ANN models mainly depends upon its training. Though gradient descent-based methods are common for ANN training, they have several limitations. Fireworks algorithm (FWA) is a recently developed metaheuristic inspired from the phenomenon of fireworks explosion at night, which poses characteristics such as faster convergence, parallelism, and finding the global optima. This chapter intends to develop a hybrid model comprising FWA and ANN (FWANN) used to forecast closing prices series, exchange series, and crude oil prices time series. The appropriateness of FWANN is compared with models such as PSO-based ANN, GA-based ANN, DE-based ANN, and MLP model trained similarly. Four performance metrics, MAPE, NMSE, ARV, and R2, are considered as the barometer for evaluation. Performance analysis is carried out to show the suitability and superiority of FWANN.

Chapter 9

    Juan Barraza, Tijuana Institute of Technology, Mexico
    Fevrier Valdez, Tijuana Institute of Technology, Mexico
    Patricia Melin, Tijuana Institute of Technology, Mexico
    Claudia I. Gonzalez, Tijuana Institute of Technology, Mexico

This chapter presents Interval Type 2 Fuzzy Fireworks Algorithm for clustering (IT2FWAC). It is an optimization method for finding the optimal number of clusters based on the centroid features which uses the Fireworks Algorithm (FWA), but with a dynamic adjustment of parameters using an Interval Type 2 Fuzzy Inference System (IT2FIS). Three variations of the IT2FWAC are proposed to find the optimal number of clusters for different datasets: IT2FWAC -I, IT2FWAC -II, and IT2FWAC –III. They are explained in detail.

Section 4
FWA Application in Engineering

Chapter 10

    Tingjun Lei, Mississippi State University, USA
    Chaomin Luo, Mississippi State University, USA
    John E. Ball, Mississippi State University, USA
    Zhuming Bi, Purdue University, Fort Wayne, USA

In recent years, computer technology and artificial intelligence have developed rapidly, and research in the field of mobile robots has continued to deepen with development of artificial intelligence. Path planning is an essential content of mobile robot navigation of computing a collision-free path between a starting point and a goal. It is necessary for mobile robots to move and maneuver in different kinds of environment with objects and obstacles. The main goal of path planning is to find the optimal path between the starting point and the target position in the minimal possible time. A new firework algorithm (FWA) integrated with a graph theory, Dijkstra's algorithm developed for autonomous robot navigation, is proposed in this chapter. The firework algorithm is improved by a local search procedure that a LIDAR-based local navigator algorithm is implemented for local navigation and obstacle avoidance. The grid map is utilized for real-time intelligent robot mapping and navigation. In this chapter, both simulation and comparison studies of an autonomous robot navigation demonstrate that the proposed model is capable of planning more reasonable and shorter, collision-free paths in non-stationary and unstructured environments compared with other approaches.

Chapter 11

Yuchen Zhang, School of Computer Science, Shaanxi Normal University, China
Xiujuan Lei, School of Computer Science, Shaanxi Normal University, China
Ying Tan, Peking University, China

Fireworks Algorithm (FWA) has been applied to many fields in recent years, showing a strong ability to solve optimization problems. In this chapter, FWA is applied to some research hotspots in bioinformatics, such as biclustering of gene expression data, disease-gene prediction, and identification of LncRNA-protein interactions. This chapter briefly introduces some backgrounds of bioinformatics and related issues. Through corresponding bioinformatics' problems to optimization problems, some specific optimization functions are constructed and solved by the Fireworks Algorithm. The simulation results illustrate that the fireworks algorithm shows high performance and potential application value in the field of bioinformatics.

Chapter 12

David Roch-Dupré, Comillas Pontifical University, Spain
Tad Gonsalves, Sophia University, Japan

This chapter proposes the application of a discrete version of the Fireworks Algorithm (FWA) and a novel PSO-FWA hybrid algorithm to optimize the energy efficiency of a metro railway line. This optimization consists in determining the optimal configuration of the Energy Storage Systems (ESSs) to install in a railway line, including their number, location, and power (kW). The installation of the ESSs will improve the energy efficiency of the system by incrementing the use of the regenerated energy produced by the trains in the braking phases, as the ESSs will store the excess of regenerated energy and return it to the system when necessary. The results for this complex optimization problem produced by the two algorithms are excellent and authors prove that the novel PSO-FWA algorithm proposed in this chapter outperforms the standard FWA.

Chapter 13

Saad Mohammad Abdullah, Islamic University of Technology (IUT), Bangladesh
Ashik Ahmed, Islamic University of Technology (IUT), Bangladesh

In this chapter, a hybrid bare bones fireworks algorithm (HBBFWA) is proposed and its application in solving the load flow problem of islanded microgrid is demonstrated. The hybridization is carried out by updating the positions of generated sparks with the help of grasshopper optimization algorithm (GOA) mimicking the swarming behavior of grasshoppers. The purpose of incorporating GOA with bare bones fireworks algorithm (BBFWA) is to enhance the global searching capability of conventional BBFWA for complex optimization problems. The proposed HBBFWA is applied to perform the load flow analysis of a modified IEEE 37-Bus system. The performance of the proposed HBBFWA is compared against the performance of BBFWA in terms of computational time, convergence speed, and number of iterations required for convergence of the load flow problem. Moreover, standard statistical analysis test such as the independent sample t-test is conducted to identify statistically significant differences between the two algorithms.

Information protection in computers is gaining a lot of importance in real world applications. To secure the private networks of businesses and institutions, a firewall is installed in a specially designated computer separate from the rest of the network so that no incoming packet can directly get into the private network. The system monitors and blocks the requests from illegal networks. The existing methods of packet filtering algorithms suffer from drawbacks in terms of search space and storage. To overcome the drawbacks, a Fireworks-based approach of packet filtering is proposed in this chapter. Termed Fireworks-based Packet Filtering (FWPF) algorithm, the sparks generated by the fireworks makes a decision about the rule position in the firewall ruleset matching with the incoming packet. The advantage of FWPF is that it reduces the search space when compared to the existing packet filtering algorithms.

A new report on childhood obesity is published every so often. The bad habits of food and the increasingly sedentary life of children in a border society has caused an alarming increase in the cases of children who are overweight or obese. Formerly, it seemed to be a problem of countries with unhealthy eating habits, such as the United States or Mexico in Latin America, where junk food is part of the diet in childhood. However, obesity is a problem that we already have around the corner and that is not so difficult to fight in children. In the present research the development of an application that reduces the problem of the lack of movement in the childhood of a smart city is considered a future problem which it is the main contribution, coupled with achieving an innovative way of looking for an Olympic sport without the complexity of physically moving to a space with high maintenance costs and considering the adverse weather conditions.

With the advancement of technology, power demand is increasing day-by-day. Energy deficiency problem and increasing petroleum/diesel cost have resulted in severe impacts to many technical facts. Introduction of non-conventional energy sources such as wind and photovoltaic energy, which is clean and copiously present in nature, can be possible solutions to these problems. This chapter presents optimization of a Hybrid power system, with one of swarm intelligent algorithms named as particle swarm optimization (PSO). The hybrid system uses PID controllers for controlling its output. It has been done by studying various combinations of diesel engine generator, wind turbine generator, aqua electrolyzer, fuel cell, and battery. With the optimized system parameters, high-quality power supply can be delivered to the load and the frequency fluctuations can also be minimized.

Applying swarm intelligence techniques to software engineering problems has appealed to both researchers and practitioners in the software engineering community. This chapter describes issues and challenges of its application to formal verification, which is one of the core research fields in software engineering. Formal verification, which explores how to effectively verify software products by using mathematical technique, often suffers from two open problems. One is the so-called state explosion problem that verification tools need too many computational resources to make verification feasible. The other problem is that the results of verification have often too much complexity for users to understand. While a number of research projects have addressed these problems in the context of traditional formal verification, recent researches demonstrate that Swarm Intelligence is a promising tool to tackle the problems. This chapter presents how Swarm Intelligence can be applied to formal verification, and surveys the state-of-the-art techniques.

Chapter 18

Object-oriented intelligent modeling, model management, etc. are difficult problems in the designing and development of underwater platform combat deduction system. The command and control description model based on OODA loop depicted the business process of underwater platform combat deduction using service-oriented and agent modeling technology and established an underwater platforms deduction system architecture, effectively solving the problem of intelligence, reusing, and extensibility in combat deduction modeling. The chapter has reference value in the designing and development of underwater platforms deduction systems.

Preface

As we know, explosion is a common phenomenon in nature. From the explosion behavior widely existing in nature, we think of fireworks explosion in real life. Generally-speaking, fireworks rise into the night sky and explode to generate a cluster of sparks, lighting a local area; many fireworks explode in different forms, which can illuminate the whole night sky. This explosion phenomenon is able to be abstracted as an explosive search operator, resulting in a new swarm intelligence optimization algorithm, so-called fireworks algorithm (FWA) to be put forward innovatively in terms of establishing a cooperative mechanism among multiple fireworks. Since the fireworks algorithm (FWA) was put forward in 2010 by Ying Tan et.al., it has quickly become a research hotspot and attracted a number of researchers to follow, the number of papers related to FWA has increased rapidly and the number of citations of the original paper of FWA has increased rapidly, and furthermore, a variety of applications are also emerging in an endless stream.

After years of research, the efficiency and validity of fireworks algorithm has made great progress. In one hand, FWA and its variants have made significant progress in solving for single-mode and multimode objective functions. On the other hand, in the IEEE-CEC13 benchmark test function set, the latest version of FWA, i.e., LOT-FWA, can beat all other classic algorithms including standard PSO, artificial bee colony, DE and CMA-ES to achieve the best performance. Compared with other algorithms, LOT-FWA has obvious advantages in multi-mode functions and composite functions. Therefore, the excellent performance of FWA has been unanimously recognized in the communities of swarm intelligence (SI) and intelligent optimization computation.

This book is intended as a timely summary of recent researches of FWA and some related work in swarm intelligence. We collected the latest results of some influential experts and active researchers in FWA and SI to show the research status and cutting edges in those fields and how they do innovative works.

The first chapter gives a comprehensive survey of FWA in all directions since its invention in 2010. Then there are chapters that contain typical algorithm improvements of FWA or hybrid methods. In the following chapters, the most typical work of meta-heuristic researches are also provided, which give one or several improved algorithms for a practical problem. After that, some chapters address FWA's applications in machine learning and some specific engineering problems. Finally, a few chapters address some innovative applications in the fields of swarm intelligence and swarm robot system.

The collection and combination of all chapters in this handbook truly reflects the current research status and cutting edges of FWA and related SI because they were conducted and written by active researchers and experts who are in the research front-edges of FWA and SI. This handbook serves as an important summary of researches on FWA and its related SI at the critical time when swarm intelligence optimization methods shows great value and FWA receives wide attentions.

The book is intended to the academic researchers, postgraduates and some professionals in the fields of FWA and swarm intelligence; it is also suitable for readers who are interested in intelligent computing approaches. Specifically, experienced researchers could learn about the recent research progress and status in this field, while beginners could learn some research innovations in FWA, and touch the souls or ideas in the applications of FWA and its related technologies.

The full content of this handbook is able to be divided into following parts:

SURVEY OF FWA STUDIES AND APPLICATIONS

In Chapter 1, the author gives a comprehensive description of all the publications regarding to FWA, including algorithm improvements, theoretical analysis, applications and implementation methods. By introducing all kinds of researches on FWA, this chapter can help readers completely understanding the current status and trends of this promising field, and show a panorama of FWA researches and developments.

ALGORITHM IMPROVEMENTS ON FWA

In Chapter 2, the authors introduced their latest development on the FWA's improvement. In their Last-position Elimination-based FWA, a new fireworks cooperation strategy with adaptive firework size is proposed based on the framework of LoT-FWA. They also showed how a sufficient theoretical and experimental analysis is conducted in such kind of study.

In Chapter 3, the authors focused on the explosion operator of FWA and made two novel explosion strategies to enhance its performance. In the multi-layer explosion strategy, some of the sparks generated by fireworks also explode to conduct a more delicate local search. In the scouting explosion strategy, sparks of each firework are generated one by one, each in the local area of its previous one. Once a spark is worse than the firework, the next one will be generated around the firework. Both strategies make the explosion operator more flexible and achieved significant improvements in experiments.

FWA APPLICATIONS IN MACHINE LEARNING

In Chapter 4, the authors give a very detailed description of the problem, algorithm and experiments for speed control of a three-phase induction motor model by optimizing the noise covariance parameters. They also conducted in-depth study of the effects of various parameters' setting of EFWA on efficiency.

In Chapter 5, the authors applied FWA to a classic machine learning problem. For the classification with imbalanced data, a hybrid re-sampling algorithm (with FWA) was proposed for weighted pattern matching based classifier (PMC+). Instead of using FWA for a certain optimization problem, they introduced the principle idea of FWA to design the re-sampling algorithm.

Chapter 6 also gives an application in machine learning. The authors improved the dynamic search FWA and applied it to the training of extreme learning machine which is finally used to predict virtual machine fault. A large number of experimental results on the improved algorithm and its application efficiency are shown in detail.

In Chapter 7, the authors considered the general optimization method for classification based on a linear model. They introduced FWA and proposed a self-adaptive FWA, SaFWA, for short, for this problem. And further they improved the SaFWA and the classification model. Overall, the authors gave series of research ideas and progress on this issue in this chapter.

In Chapter 8, the authors intended to apply FWA to artificial neural network for financial time series forecasting. A two-layer neural network was designed for time series predicting and FWA was used to optimize its parameters. This method is also compared to multi-layer perceptron (MLP) and neural networks trained by other EC or SI algorithms.

In Chapter 9, the authors combined FWA with type-2 fuzzy method for clustering. Based on the framework of FWA, the proposed IT2FWAC used interval type-2 fuzzy inference system to decide its parameters dynamically.

FWA APPLICATION IN ENGINEERING

In Chapter 10, the authors introduced their application of FWA on robot path planning. Like most classic practical optimization researches, they gave a mathematical model to describe the problem and novel FWA variant was proposed for this specific problem. The obtained solutions were analyzed and explained in detail.

In Chapter 11, the authors introduced several kinds of applications of FWA in bio-informatics. Here, FWA is used as a bi-clustering method, prediction method and identification method. In all these studies, the exact optimization problems are described. It provides a very typical idea of their related application researches.

In Chapter 12, FWA was applied to the optimization of the electrical infrastructure of a railway line. Instead of improving FWA on the specific problem, they combined FWA and PSO together to obtain a new hybrid algorithm to address this specific problem.

In Chapter 13, the authors solved load flow optimization of islanded micro-grid by using a hybrid algorithm of grasshopper optimization algorithm and bare-bone FWA, expecting to maximize the advantages of both algorithms.

In Chapter 14, FWA was introduced and used to efficient packet filtering in firewall. In their proposed algorithm termed fireworks based packet filtering (FWPF), each spark was used to make a decision about the rule position in the firewall rule-set matching with the incoming packet. According to their experiments and analysis, the proposed algorithm is able to reduce the search space dramatically when compared to the existing method.

In Chapter 15, the authors introduced an interesting application in a Wii game of a collaborative sport to a society in a smart city for children education. FWA was applied to tune some parameters of the designed system.

INNOVATIVE APPLICATIONS OF SWARM INTELLIGENCE AND SWARM ROBOTICS

In Chapter 16, a practical application of PSO was introduced. The hybrid power system was a small set of co-operating units generating electricity or heat with diversified primary energy carriers. A PID controller optimization algorithm based on PSO was proposed with a detailed explanation of its efficiency.

In Chapter 17, a detailed survey of software verification techniques was given. The authors introduced GA, ACO and PSO in detail, and listed plenty of researches based on them. They also summarized a few of future directions of their studies.

In Chapter 18, the authors designed a combat deduction function of underwater platform to simulate the real process in the field of swarm robotics. Their system contains service-oriented agents, an overall architecture and the service agent management process. Experimental results show that it provides a feasible technical approach and important reference value for further studies.

Although I am unable to include all the latest research progress of the researches on FWA and SI due to time constraints and limited space, the content already included here can also reflect the main highlights in this field. I hope the publication of this handbook can bring some positive effects to the research on FWA and SI, and strengthen its impact to SI community in the coming years. As a matter of fact, I wish this handbook can be regarded as a platform to share the latest research results and show their recent progress in the field. For researchers or practitioners who are interested in firework algorithms or related approaches, I hope this handbook can show the research methods and application ideas in this field and help reader understanding the main points of research and usage of related technologies.

Ying Tan
Peking University, China

Acknowledgment

First of all, I would appreciate all the contributors of each chapter for their great work that consists of the primary parts of this book. Further, I also would like to thank the reviewers for their strict comments and constructive suggestions which guarantee such a high-quality book in hand.

Secondly, I am graceful to my PhD student, Mr. Yifeng Li who gave me a strong assistance in helping to coordinate the authors and experts timely.

Thirdly, I want to thank Lindsay Wertman (née Johnston), managing director, and Ms. Jordan Tepper, development coordinator, of IGI Global publisher, for their kind coordination and suggestions.

Fourthly, I want to thank my family to support me with love and encouragement.

While working on the topics of this handbook, I was supported by the Natural Science Foundation of China (NSFC) under grant no. 61673025 and supported by Beijing Natural Science Foundation (4162029), and partially supported by National Key Basic Research Development Plan (973 Plan) Project of China under grant no. 2015CB352302, and also supported by Science and Technology Innovation 2030 - "New Generation Artificial Intelligence" Major Project (Grant Nos.: 2018AAA0102301, 2018AAA0100302).

Ying Tan
Peking University, China

Section 1
Survey of FWA Studies and Applications

Chapter 1
Recent Developments of Fireworks Algorithms

Ying Tan
Peking University, China

ABSTRACT

Fireworks Algorithm has been proposed for almost 10 years. Because of its basic but profound collabora-tive searching manner and advantages of universal effectiveness, hundreds of scholars have conducted and published a wide range of work on it. This chapter serves as a background description of fireworks algorithms' developments by introducing its detailed status of researches and applications. Specifically, it gives a brief summarization and analysis of published researches on Fireworks Algorithms since 2010 to clarify characteristics of its historical progress and future trend in detailed fields like algorithms improvements, theoretical analysis, and practical applications.

INTRODUCTION

Optimization is an everlasting topic in science and engineering. However, traditional mathematic tools for optimization have failed on many situations due to the significant complexity in modern optimiza-tion problems. As an example, the most commonly applied method, gradient-decent or the Newton's method, seems always inevitably trapped in local optimal for complex multi-modal problems, let alone it can be scarcely possible to be implemented in gradient-free or discontinuous objective functions. New mathematical tools have been invented but they are still too fragile for high dimensional, sophisticated constrains or other requirements. Decades ago, evolutionary computation was proposed and developed, which is flexible and robust for all kinds of optimization problems. Nowadays, evolutionary computation has become one of the most active subfield of artificial intelligence.

Swarm Intelligence Optimization Algorithms (SIOAs) is a new class of algorithms that is available and effective for general optimization problems. Like many evolutionary algorithms, SIOAs subtly controls a group of individuals moving or evolving in the search space, each represents a solution of the objective problem. However, SIOAs focus on the collaborative behaviors between individuals to improve the whole population instead of simply eliminating bad ones. Classic algorithms like Particle

DOI: 10.4018/978-1-7998-1659-1.ch001

Copyright © 2020, IGI Global. Copying or distributing in print or electronic forms without written permission of IGI Global is prohibited.

Swarm Optimization (PSO) (Eberhart & Kennedy,1995) and Ant Colony Optimization (ACO) (Dorigo & Di Caro, 1999) have been used in a large number of engineering problems.

Fireworks Algorithm (FWA) is a new type of swarm intelligence optimization algorithms proposed since 2010 (Tan & Zhu, 2010). Different from other SIOAs, FWA maintains multiple groups of individuals which independently searching their local area and the global optimization is enhanced by the collaboration of strategies. Fireworks algorithm have received extensive attention because of its simplicity and effectiveness. In recent years, there are hundreds of work on fireworks algorithms published in international journals or conferences. Here, we are going to summarize and introduce some important results on fireworks algorithms since it is proposed, and try to expose its development trends and promising research directions.

FIREWORKS ALGORITHMS

Motivation and Principle

Fireworks and firecrackers are one of the traditional events for Chinese festivals, especially for New Year's Eve. In the night, fireworks rise and explode, bursting with plenty of sparks to light up the sky. Plenty of fireworks explode in different ways which form a distribution of sparks over the night sky. Such a process has much in common with the optimization process. And this is how fireworks algorithm been inspired and proposed at 2010 by Prof. Tan and Zhu (Tan & Zhu, 2010).

Figure 1. Fireworks in the night sky

Most meta-heuristic algorithms designed delicate local optimization mechanisms to accelerate population convergence. However, the behavior of fireworks illustrates a different perspective for global optimization, that is, to manage several simple local search process conducted by sub-groups of individuals and enhance global optimization by collaboration between each group.

So the population of fireworks algorithms are composed of several individual called fireworks and each firework corresponds to plenty of individuals called sparks. In each iteration of the optimization, each firework simply generates certain number of sparks around itself. However, the distribution and allocation of sparks are carefully designed with considering of cooperation between fireworks. With proper collaboration method, fireworks algorithms are able to achieve stable global exploration and fast local exploitation with very basic search method for each firework. The framework of fireworks algorithms can also be viewed as cooperation of several simultaneous local optimization process, thus could be easily combined with other methods.

Practically, fireworks algorithms simply scatter sparks with uniform distribution or normal distribution around itself. For fireworks with better fitness (objective value), more sparks are usually generated within closer range. For fireworks with worse fitness, less sparks are usually generated within farther range. The process of generating sparks for each firework is called explosion. And the next generation of fireworks are selected from current fireworks and sparks.

Framework of Fireworks Algorithm

Fireworks algorithms are performed according to following flowchart.

Figure 2. Flowchart of fireworks algorithm

Specifically, nodes in the flowchart represent following steps:

1. **Initialization:** Initialize a certain number of fireworks in the feasible space.
2. **Generation:** Generate sparks for each firework.
3. **Selection:** Select certain number of fireworks from current generation of fireworks or sparks.
4. **Termination:** Decide whether the algorithm should be stopped.

This overall framework of fireworks algorithm is the same with most evolutionary optimization algorithms. Most versions of fireworks algorithms can be summarized as combinations of following components:

1. **Initialization:** Distribute and evaluate several random fireworks in the search space.
2. **Explosion:** Distribute and evaluate explosion sparks for each firework.
3. **Mutation:** Distribute mutation sparks to enhance optimization with information obtained from explosion sparks.
4. **Selection:** Select next generation of fireworks from current fireworks and sparks.
5. **Mapping Rule:** Mapping rule is used to map infeasible individuals back into the search space during the individual generation process.
6. **Communication Strategy:** Plenty of strategies are introduced in recent variants of FWA to make overall control of fireworks in order to enhance communication.

Here, explosion and mutation operators make up most of the individual generation process, and represents the main characteristics of fireworks algorithms. We are going to give detailed explanations of classic implementations of those operators in the next subsection.

Comparing with Classic Algorithms

Fireworks algorithms is commonly considered as a swarm intelligence algorithm, but its framework also contains features from evolutionary algorithm.

In typical swarm intelligence algorithms, the population size is usually fixed (for example, in PSO and ACO), or 'almost' fixed (like ABC (Karaboga & Basturk2007)). And swarm in them are improved through cooperation, which usually manifests in poor individuals' learning from good ones. However, fireworks algorithms generate much more offspring (sparks) than current generation (fireworks), and it improves by selecting better individuals into next generation. From this point of view, fireworks algorithms are more similar to evolutionary algorithms.

Fireworks algorithms do resemble many evolutionary algorithms. If we consider each firework and its explosion amplitude as parameters of a Gaussian distribution, fireworks algorithm is quite the same as a EDA (Estimation of Distribution Algorithm (Larrañaga & Lozano, 2001)) with the mixture of Gaussian distribution. However, the principle idea of fireworks algorithm is that multiple fireworks interact and cooperate to accomplish efficient global optimization. Therefore, it is considered as a developmental (evolutionary) swarm intelligence algorithm by some researches (Shi, 2014).

Fireworks algorithms also seem to be closely related to the co-evolutionary approach as a sub-field of evolutionary computation. But actually, coevolution mainly studies interactive behaviors between different types of species. Instead, in fireworks algorithms, homogeneous individuals automatically perform grouping and grouped collaboration during the optimization.

OVERALL DEVELOPMENT OF FIREWORKS ALGORITHMS

Since fireworks algorithm was introduced in 2010, it has received extensive attention and become an increasingly important method in swarm intelligent optimization algorithms. As more and more researchers or engineers would like to apply fireworks algorithm as their optimization tool or comparison method, the number of citations of the original papers of fireworks algorithm is increasing faster and faster. Currently, it has 589 citations in Google Scholar and there are plenty more related studies as far as we know.

Published works on fireworks algorithms mainly includes following five categories:

1. **Theory Analysis:** In those works, theoretical analysis of fireworks algorithm is conducted to illustrate or prove some features or properties. For example, proof of swarm convergence and converge rate analysis are commonly theoretical analysis conducted for swarm intelligent optimization algorithms.

2. **Algorithm Improvement:** Those works propose new version of fireworks algorithm which have improved optimization efficiency. Researches on fireworks algorithm itself are most important for its further development. Plenty of methods have been applied to improve fireworks algorithm. Some researches adjust certain operators of fireworks algorithm. Some researches combine fireworks

algorithm with other optimization algorithm to obtain better hybrid method. And some researches even make improvements on the fireworks algorithm's framework.

3. **Application:** Those works usually apply modified fireworks algorithms to practical optimization problems. As a universal optimization algorithm, fireworks algorithms can be efficient for most types of problems in areas like researching, engineering, investing and etc.

4. **Implementation:** Those works consider how fireworks algorithms could be implemented efficiently on specific computation platforms. For example, some work studies how to implement firework algorithm on GPU to accelerate optimization time.

5. **Others:** Other works related with fireworks algorithms include survey, algorithm comparison and so on.

The chart below shows the number of different types of research on fireworks algorithms publish until 2018:

Figure 3 Bar plot of published researches on FWA

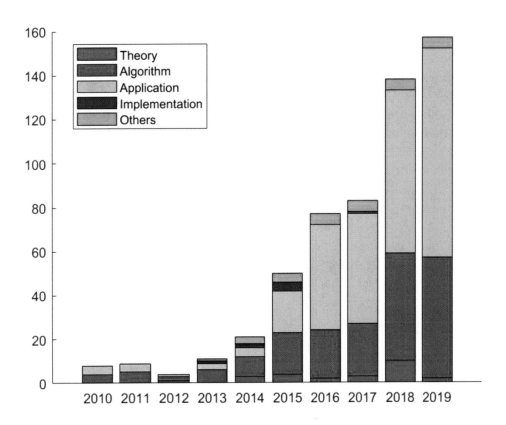

As we can see, publications of fireworks algorithm have been increasing rapidly, especially in recent years. Among them, publications on algorithm improvements and practical applications are particularly prominent, which shows that the fireworks algorithms have sufficient development potential and theoretical value to attract researches on itself, and its actual optimization efficiency is also good enough for various practical problems.

Fireworks algorithms related studies are frequently published in top journals like IEEE Transactions on Evolutionary Computation and IEEE Transactions on Cybernetics, or important international conference on evolutionary computation like IEEE World Congress on Computational Intelligence, IEEE Conference on Evolutionary Computation and conference on swarm intelligence like the International Conference on Swarm Intelligence.

In the following sections, we are going to introduce specific researches of each types since FWA is proposed. There is an introduction (Tan, Yu, Zheng & Ding, 2013) and a monograph (Tan, 2015) published in by Tan et al in 2013 and 2015 respectively. And a comprehensive review (Li & Tan, 2019) of literature of FWA before 2018 is published recently. While in this paper, we are going to introduce the most important and latest works of FWA to illustrate its trends from 2010 to 2019, instead of giving a complete introduction of all published researches.

Algorithm Improvements

In this section, we are going to introduce the literature of algorithmic researches that improved fireworks algorithms itself, including improvements of certain operators (or introduce new operators), hybridizations of FWA with other algorithms, and adaptations of FWA for special types of optimization problems. As plenty of work combines improvements in several directions which are highly correlated, we are going to introduce each variant of FWA mainly in chronological order.

Operator Improvements

Here, we introduce improvements on operators of FWA algorithms, which is also the main content of FWA research. First, we are going to introduce basic improvements on FWA's operators, including explosion operator, mutation operator, selection operator and mapping rule. Later, we will introduce new methods designed based on elite strategy and mechanisms used to enhance interaction between fireworks. Finally, we introduce some other research.

Basic Improvements

The basic improvements of FWA's operator improvements contains researches that make fundamental changes on the explosion mechanism. Most of those works proposed new explosion amplitude strategy or spark number allocation strategy. Some proposed new explosion method, or studied the mutation method and mapping rule.

The enhanced fireworks algorithm (EFWA, (Zheng, Janecek, & Tan, 2013, June)) is proposed in 2013 as the first stable variant of FWA. In this research, a comprehensive analysis on the original FWA is conducted and many operators are improved.

1. **Explosion Spark Generation:** In the explosion operator of original FWA, the displacement e is the same in each dimension for a certain spark, which limit the exploration ability of explosion seriously. Therefore, the displacement takes different random values in each direction in EFWA.
2. **Explosion Amplitudes:** According to the linear method in original FWA, amplitude for the best firework is actually 0, which stopped the search in the best local area. Therefore, a minimal explosion amplitude threshold is proposed to prevent it being too small, which decreases with the number of evaluations.
3. **Mutation Operator and Mapping Rule:** In the original FWA, both mutation operator and mapping rule inclined to distribute individuals near the origin point, which can be misleading and harmful for more general objective problems. They are both corrected in EFWA.
4. **Selection Operator:** The density-based selection is time-consuming, especially for large population. A simple but efficient method called elitism-random selection is proposed in EFWA.

With above corrections, EFWA achieved better performance and efficiency than the original FWA. It has been used as the basis and benchmark for later research and has also been applied to a wide range of practical problems. Most later variants of FWA are based on EFWA.

Liu, Zheng & Tan (2013, June) pointed out that directly using fitness values to linearly decide A_i and n_i can be unstable for general problems. They proposed improved fireworks algorithm (IFWA), in which a rank-based transfer function is applied to calculate the weight of each firework for deciding amplitudes and spark numbers in equation (2) and (3). Si & Ghosh (2015, March) further improved the transfer function in IFWA by considering both the ranks and the differences between fireworks' fitness. The proposed algorithm called FWA-ATF outperforms the original FWA, EFWA and IFWA significantly on the benchmarks of CEC2005.

Li et al. and Zheng et al. both studied the amplitudes method of explosion operator in FWA and pointed out that the explosion amplitudes strategy in EFWA cannot adapt to the state of local optimization appropriately. They proposed adaptive FWA (AFWA (Li, Zheng, & Tan, 2014, July)) and dynamic search FWA (dynFWA (Zheng, Janecek, Li, & Tan, 2014, July)) respectively to compensate for this deficiency. Their key idea is similar, that the amplitude of a firework should be adaptively or dynamically adjusted according to information obtained from explosion sparks. When a firework is improved, its amplitude should be amplified to accelerate the local search. Otherwise, it should be reduced to increase the probability of improving. AFWA calculates amplitudes according to the distance from the best spark to the best spark which is not better than current firework. Instead, dynFWA amplify or shrink the amplitude of the core fireworks (best firework) by determined constants. Gaussian mutation is also abandoned in dynFWA. Both algorithms outperform EFWA and several PSO variants on benchmarks of CEC2013. The dynamic explosion method is extensively referenced in later variants due to its simplicity and efficiency.

Zhang, B., Zhang, M., & Zheng, Y. J. (2014, October) proposed a new mutation operator and a new selection operator in their FWA variant based on EFWA, which is called improved EFWA (IEFWA). In the mutation operator, two random individuals are chosen and a mutation spark is then generated between them. In the selection operator, q opponents are randomly selected for each individual and the individuals that win most times are kept into next generation. Later, they (Zhang, B., Zheng, Y. J., Zhang, M. X., & Chen, S. Y., 2017) hybridized the migration operator of bio-geography based optimization (BBO) (Simon, 2008) with the explosion operator in FWA and proposed FWA_EI based on IEFWA. Both algorithms outperform EFWA in experiments significantly.

Cheng, Qin, Chen, Shi & Zhang (2015). are concerned with the design of mapping rules in fireworks algorithms. They studied four different types of mapping rules, in which mapping to the boundary or mapping to limited stochastic region outperforms other methods in experiments. Yet, Li, Xu & Tan (2018, July) also explored this topic in large scale optimization and found the mirror mapping rule outperforms other methods on most test functions.

Li, Han & Gong (2017) modified and improved FWA in many aspects. 1) At the initialization step, each firework is evaluated together with its opposition solution, and only the better one is selected as a firework in the first generation. 2) Dynamic explosion amplitude strategy in dynFWA is applied except when all the fireworks are of the same fitness, their explosion amplitude will be amplified. 3) Gaussian mutation in EFWA is improved with t-distribution. 4) The opposition solution of the best firework is used as an elite individual. 5) In the selection operator, the best candidate is kept and other individuals are selected by a special roulette method, in which the candidates with top and bottom fitness are selected with higher probability than ordinary ones. The proposed algorithm is proved to be globally convergent and outperforms the original FWA, EFWA and dynFWA significantly on CEC2013 benchmarks.

Li, Han, Zhao, & Gong (2017, November) proposed a new algorithm based on AFWA which is referred to as TMSFWA. In this method, a new displacement method based on AFWA is applied. An elitism-tournament selection operation is proposed which selects the best individual and then repeatedly choose two random individual and the better one is kept into next generation. TMSFWA beats EFWA, AFWA and dynFWA significantly on the CEC2015 benchmark.

Li, Han, Zhao, Gong, & Liu (2017) improved dynFWA with an adaptive mutation operator, which using Levy distribution and Gaussian distribution in early phases and late phases respectively. The algorithm (AMdynFWA) outperforms EFWA, AFWA and dynFWA on the CEC2015 benchmark.

Yu & Takagi (2017, July) proposed a new variant based on original FWA where the amplitudes of all fireworks are the same value which decreases linearly and remains unchanged after certain phase. They also proposed a new selection method which selects offspring for each firework locally.

Li and Tan (2017) proposed a simplified algorithm called bare bones FWA (BBFWA) in which most mechanisms are eliminated. In BBFWA, only one firework is adopted with dynamic amplitude strategy from dynFWA. Thanks to its simplicity, BBFWA runs much faster than any other FWA variants and it still achieved significant performance on CEC2013 compared with EFWA, AFWA, dynFWA and CoFFWA (which we'll introduce later) and several other evolutionary algorithms. Its performance on three real-world problems from CEC2011 competition is also comparable to the champion.

Yu, Tan, & Takagi (2018, July) proposed a way to improve the explosion operator by generating new sparks one by one. Beginning from the firework, each spark is generated around the former one. Once the fitness of a new spark is worse than the former, next spark will restart around the firework. They also applied an adjusted selection method which ignores the sparks worse than corresponding firework. The proposed algorithm is compared with EFWA on benchmarks from CEC2013, the performance is improved significantly.

Cheng, Bai, Zhao, Tan & Xu (2019) studied EFWA and made several improvements. 1) They adjusted the explosion operator to generate sparks in a spherical neighborhood of each firework. 2) They revised the Gaussian mutation operator to allow mutation sparks generated directly from fireworks. 3) A deep information exchange strategy is borrowed from the Grey Wolf Optimizer (GWO) (Mirjalili, S., Mirjalili, S. M., & Lewis, 2014). The algorithm outperforms EFWA on 23 test functions.

Bejinariu, S. I., Luca, R., & Costin, H. (2016, October) adjusted the Gaussian mutation method by generating mutation spark around the middle between the best firework and a randomly selected one. Experiments on 23 test functions indicate the new algorithms outperforms EFWA and dynFWA significantly.

Yu, Takagi, & Tan (2018) developed a new explosion framework by conducting several layers of explosions. In each layer, sparks (fireworks for the first layer) from previous layer explodes further according to their fitness values. The proposed algorithm outperforms EFWA and PSO on CEC2013 benchmark functions.

Elite Mechanisms

Elite mechanisms refers to the methods that specifically utilized some of the best individuals. Usually they help to generate offspring with higher quality.

Pei, Zheng, Tan & Takagi (2012, October) introduced an elite strategy into FWA by fitness landscape approximation. In each iteration, some individuals are chosen to approximate the landscape of fitness function on each projected dimension and an elite spark is inferred. The obtained spark replaces the worst individual if it has better fitness. Experiments from 10 of the test functions from CEC2005 indicate the proposed method is effective. They (2015) further explored different approximation approaches. Experimental results show that approximation in low dimensional space with randomly chosen population performs better.

Li & Tan (2015, May) and Li, Zheng & Tan (2016) point out that the information obtained from the explosion spark is not fully applied in dynFWA. They proposed an information utilization oriented mutation operator called guiding mutation. For each firework, the difference vector from the centroid of bad sparks to the centroid of good ones. The vector shows the improving direction of each firework, and it is added to the firework to get the guiding spark, which helps both accelerating convergence and global exploration. The proposed algorithm is called guided FWA (GFWA) and it outperforms EFWA, AFWA and dynFWA on the CEC2013 test suit. And experimental results on the CEC2010 large-scale optimization benchmark indicate that GFWA can achieve competitive performance on large scale problems (1000 dimensions) compared with state-of-art methods.

Interactive Mechanisms

Interactive mechanisms means methods that are used to help the collaboration between fireworks.

Zheng, Li, Janecek & Tan (2017) conducted experiments on FWA and show that fireworks other than the best one have limited contribution to the search. This is mostly because the information of non-core fireworks is not able to inherit to the next generation using elite-random selection. For this reason, they proposed independent selection framework, in which each firework conduct selection in its own offspring. They further proposed a crowdedness-avoiding strategy to prevent non-core fireworks wasting resources in optimal firework's explosion area, which makes up for the problem of weakening synergy under independent selection.

Zhao, Li, Zuo & Tan (2017, July) proposed three improvements based on dynFWA and proposed elite-leading FWA (ELFWA). 1) The spark number of the best firework is fixed. 2) A mirror mapping rule is applied. 3) Each non-core firework could be reinitialized with a certain probability towards the best firework. ELFWA outperforms dynFWA, dynFWACM and the eddynFWA on the CEC2015 benchmark.

Lana, Del Ser & Vélez, (2017, June) implemented a similar idea by introducing a wind inertia dynamic into EFWA in order to force sparks moving towards the best firework. Experimental results on six test functions indicate that the proposed algorithm (EFWA-WID) outperforms EFWA significantly.

Li & Tan (2016, July; 2017) proposed a fireworks algorithm variant based on CoFFWA, which accomplished efficient cooperation for global optimization through competition. The proposed interactive mechanism is called Loser-out tournament, in which each non-core firework's potential is estimated. If a firework is not improving fast enough to beat the best solution before the search ended, it would be reinitialized at a random location. The proposed loser-out-tournament-based FWA (LoTFWA) is tested on benchmark of CEC2013 and it shows significant performance on multi-modal test functions compared with EFWA, AFWA, dynFWA, CoFFWA, GFWA and evolutionary algorithms like IPOP-CMAES.

Yu, Takagi & Tan (2018, June) also proposed an elite strategy based on EFWA which is called convergence point estimation method. For each firework, a gradient-like vector is computed as an estimation of the improving direction. Then, the convergence point of those vectors are computed, which joins the population replacing the worst individual if it has better fitness value. The proposed algorithm outperforms EFWA significantly on 20 of CEC2013 test functions.

Zhang & Li (2019, July) proposed a last-point elimination-based FWA (LEFWA) based on LoTFWA. During its optimization process, the worst firework is eliminated one by one, and its sparks are allocated to remaining fireworks. By this way, optimization resource (sparks) will concentrate to the core firework. Experimental results on both CEC2013 and CEC2015 benchmarks show that the proposed algorithm significantly outperforms most of the state-of-the-art FWA variants.

Other Work

Zheng, Yu, Li, & Tan (2015, May) discovered in experiments that with fewer explosion dimensions, the explosion sparks in dynFWA have a greater chance to surpass the firework. Based on this principle, they proposed ed-dynFWA by reducing the number of explosion dimensions by a certain coefficient after every certain number of generations. They tested the proposed algorithm on CEC2015 benchmark, but no comparison was made.

Chen, Yang, Ni, Xie, & Cheng (2015, May) proposed a new variant of FWA utilizing landscape information to balance exploration and exploitation. If the coverage of sparks is large, the sparks are generated randomly in the next generation. If the coverage is middle, sparks are generated utilizing landscape information. Otherwise, sparks are generated by the original method. Experimental results on eight test functions indicate the proposed algorithm outperforms original FWA and EFWA.

Kumar, Chhabra, & Kumar (2015) evaluated original FWA on six test functions and obtained optimal parameter setting on these problems.

Barraza, Melin, Valdez, & González (2016), Barraza et al. (2017), and Barraza, Melin, Valdez, Gonzalez, & Castillo (2017) applied fuzzy logic to dynamically allocate explosion sparks and adjust amplitudes. During different stage of optimization, explosion amplitudes and spark numbers are subject to different membership functions. The proposed algorithm IFFWA outperforms original FWA significantly. Later, they (Barraza et al, 2017) introduced a new input for the fuzzy system called sparks dispersion measure. The proposed algorithm DPIFFWA is tested on 14 test functions with different shift values and outperforms IFFWA significantly.

Gong (2016, June; 2019; 2020) introduced chaotic maps into AFWA which controls the amplification coefficient. The proposed algorithm called CAFWA is tested on 12 shifted test functions and outperforms original FWA, AFWA, EFWA and several swarm intelligence algorithms.

Zhang, Zhu, & Zhou (2017, July) proposed resampling-based FWA for noisy optimization problems. Their core idea is to enlarge the number of top sparks resampled while reducing the number of resampling times during the search process. The proposed algorithm FWA-NO outperforms CoFFWA and its simple resampling version on benchmark from CEC2015.

Han, Zheng, Wang, Zheng & Wang (2019) proposed an improved fireworks algorithm based on original FWA by dynamic search and tournament selection. The iteration number of current generation is introduced to decide explosion amplitudes, and a minimal amplitude is defined. New generation is composed by best individual of several randomly chosen ones. The proposed algorithm is tested on six benchmark function and a practical application, and it shows significant efficiency over original FWA.

Zhao, Zhang & Ning improved dynFWA based on the idea of utilizing information from the exploiting updating of the core firework (CF). The proposed algorithm amplifies the explosion range on the direction on which CF is updated and distributes more sparks along this update direction. The algorithm is compared and analyzed with plenty other methods, and shows outstanding optimization ability.

Li, Yu, Takagi, & Tan (2019, July) introduced weight-based guiding spark strategy and generate more weighted guiding sparks instead of explosion sparks when a firework is not improved. The new algorithm achieved significant improvements over GFWA on CEC2013 benchmarks.

Li (2019) introduced a mutation operator which is similar with Gaussian mutation in EFWA but added controlled learning factor. This method is tested on 28 benchmark functions of CEC2013.

Hybrid Methods

Fireworks algorithms can be easily combined with other optimization methods. The most common way is to use operators from other algorithms as mutation methods to generate additional sparks after explosion.

(Yu, Kelley, Zheng & Tan, 2014, July; Yu, Li & Tan, 2014, October) introduced differential evolution (DE) method as a mutation method in EFWA. The proposed algorithm FWA-DM outperforms EFWA significantly on CEC2014 benchmarks.

Zheng, Xu, Ling & Chen (2015) proposed an improved version of hybrid algorithm of FWA and DE. The DE operation is conducted upon μ individuals selected from best sparks or fireworks using roulette. And the generated solutions will replace the original ones if they have better fitness, which become fireworks of the next generation. The proposed algorithm beats FWA and DE on eight test functions.

(Yu & Tan, 2015, May; Yu, Kelley & Tan, 2015, May; Yu, Kelley & Tan, 2016, July) introduced a covariance mutation inspired from CMA-ES into AFWA, dynFWA and CoFFWA. The proposed algorithm FWA-CM based on AFWA outperforms AFWA significantly on CEC2015 benchmark.

Gao & Li (2015) introduced opposition-learning and quantum computing into FWA and proposed OQFWA, which outperforms original FWA significantly on five test functions.

Bacanin, Tuba & Beko (2015) proposed a mutation operator into original FWA inspired from the search manner in firefly algorithm. The algorithm outperforms original FWA and several PSO variants on six test functions. Wang, Peng, Deng, Li & Zheng (2018, October) also introduced explosion operator into firefly algorithm to improve local search. This hybrid algorithm outperforms FWA and variants of firefly algorithms on CEC2013 benchmarks.

Gong (2016) combined AFWA with opposition-based learning and proposed opposition-based FWA (OAFWA). In the initialization step, both the fireworks and their opposition solutions are evaluated, and the better ones are chosen as fireworks in the first generation. During the optimization, the quasi opposites of randomly selected fireworks are evaluated and would replace the fireworks if they have better fitness. OAFWA outperforms AFWA significantly on 12 test functions.

Sun, Wang & Song (2016) introduced the grouping strategy from shuffled frog leaping algorithm (SFLA) (Eusuff, Lansey, & Pasha, 2006) into the original FWA. The hybrid algorithm outperforms both the original FWA and SFLA on four test functions.

Ye & Wen (2017, December) applied the simulated annealing method on the minimal explosion amplitude strategy of EFWA. The proposed algorithm is test on five functions from CEC2013 and three functions from CEC2014 and it outperforms the double elite co-evolutionary genetic algorithm and the differential evolution algorithm based on self-adapting mountain-climbing operator.

Chen, Liu, Wei & Guan (2018) proposed a hybrid algorithm of PSO and FWA, where the PSO operator is applied for exploration, while FWA are applied for exploitation. The proposed algorithm PS-FWA outperforms PSO and original FWA on 22 test functions.

Barraza, Rodríguez, Castillo, Melin, & Valdez (2018) proposed a hybrid algorithm of GWO and FWA, where the explosion operation is conducted for initialization. The proposed algorithm shows effective performance on 22 test functions with low dimensions.

Zhang, B., Zhang, M. X., & Zheng (2014, July) proposed a hybrid algorithm of BBO and FWA, where operators of BBO or FWA are executed by a certain probability in each iteration. While Farswan and Bansal (2019) also combined BBO and FWA, but they use operators from two algorithms alternately in each iteration.

Hao (2019, October) introduced the idea of fireworks algorithm into estimation of distribution algorithm (EDA), and proposed FMEDA for multi-model optimization. In this method, several probabilistic models are maintained and they generate different number of solutions just like fireworks in FWA.

Chen, Li, Zhao, Xiao, Wu & Tan (2019) combined harmony search (HS) with fireworks algorithm and proposed simplified hybrid fireworks algorithm (SHFWA). The improvisation of harmony in HS is introduced into FWA as mutation operator in order to explore new search space. SHFWA is compared with GFWA, GPSO, DE and other methods on 40 test functions. Experimental results show significant improvements of the hybrid method.

Guo, Liu W, Liu M & Zheng (2019) proposed a hybrid algorithm of EFWA and DE. Instead of using DE operator as a mutation method, they divide the population into two groups and each evolves according to different ways. Elite individuals in each sub-population are exchanged for communication. The proposed algorithm outperforms some state-of-the-art FWA variants on most testing functions.

Adaptations on Complex Problems

Dynamic Optimization

Pekdemir & Topcuoglu (2016, July) proposed two variants of EFWA for dynamic optimization problems. In EFWA-D1, sparks numbers and amplitudes of explosion of all fireworks are changed by rates 1.1 and 0.9 respectively. Independent selection is applied and not mutation operator is used. In EFWA-D2, a simple adaptive amplitude strategy is applied based on EFWA-D1. Both algorithms have better performance measured by offline error compared with previous dynamic optimization techniques like hyper-mutation, random immigrants, memory search and self-organization scouts.

Multi-Objective Optimization

Liu, Zheng & Tan (2015, May) proposed a multi-objective FWA based on S-metric called S-MOFWA. Compared with original FWA, the proposed algorithm keeps the candidates with largest S-metrics as fireworks of the next generation. An external archive is also adopted to maintain a best solution set, which updates in each generation by removing solutions with smallest S-metrics one by one. S-MOFWA outperforms NSFA-II, SPEA-2 and PESA-2 on six multi-objective problems.

Bejinariu, Costin, Rotaru, Luca, & Niţă (2016) extended FWA for multi-objective problems by two different approaches. 1) Multi-objective optimization problem is transformed into a single-objective problem with weighted sum of original objective functions. 2) Random selection of non-dominated solutions into next generation. The proposed algorithms are tested on a multi-objective problem, but no comparison is made.

Chen, Shi, Zhou, Xu & Wu (2018, November) introduced operators in FWA into MOEA/D framework (Zhang & Li, 2007). In the proposed algorithm, explosion operator and Gaussian mutation are used to generate offspring. It outperforms several MOEA/D variants on 19 test functions.

Taowei, Yiming, Kun, & Duan (2018, October) combined membrane computing and fireworks algorithm to solve multi-objective optimization problems. The proposed membrane fireworks algorithm (MFWA) applies explosion operator in FWA to improve local searching ability and the elite opposition-based learning mechanism for global optimization. Experimental results on six ZDT and DTLZ series test functions show that MFWA is feasible and effective.

Niching Problem

Jun, Takagi, & Ying (2019, June) improved fireworks algorithm to solve niching problem. In order to find out multiple global/local optima, the worse one of two fireworks whose search space overlap is re-initialized according to the opposite-based generation strategy. Experimental results on the CEC2015 multi-niche benchmark test suite show that the proposed algorithm can converge to multiple different optima.

Theoretical Analysis

Research on the theory of fireworks algorithms is very limited, mainly because of the significant complexity of swarm-based optimization analysis. Existing research conducts analysis on simplified optimization process, and give explanations on the convergence characteristics of the algorithm.

Liu, Zheng, & Tan (2014, July) considered FWA as a Markov stochastic process and use it to analyze convergence and time complexity of FWA. They pointed out that FWA is globally convergent because of the global random mutation operator. And they gave an estimation of FWA's convergence time.

Li, Han & Gong (2017) also gave proof of global convergence of their improved FWA using a similar procedure as (Liu, Zheng & Tan, 2014, July). While Hongyuan, Yanan, & Chenwan (2018) analyzed FWA in a different way and proved that the populations probability density function would be closely concentrated near the objective function's global optimal after sufficient iterations.

Li, Zheng & Tan (2016) analyzed the properties of the guiding mutation operator of GFWA on a simple two-dimensional objective function. They proved several advantages of guiding mutation method: 1) the length of guiding vector on irrelevant direction is relatively short, so the direction is accurate. 2) the length of the guiding vector is adaptive according to the distance to the local optimum.

Li & Tan (2018) gave a set of sufficient conditions of local convergence of BBFWA. They also mentioned that the sufficient conditions can be relaxed when an amplification coefficient is adopted. They also proved that generating more sparks is helpful for avoiding premature convergence.

Applications

Different versions of FWA variants have been applied to all kinds of practical fields. Here, we give a summarization of applications published before 2019, and give some detailed introduction of the most recent works after 2019.

Machine Learning

Wang et al. (2019, September) improved fireworks algorithm to optimize back-propagation neural network, which is used for financial early warning. Similar work was done by (Zhang, J., & Zhang, H., 2018, July) for short-time traffic flow forecasting. Suo, Song, Dou & Cui (2019, November) use fireworks algorithm to tune the hyper-parameters of XGBoost for multi-dimensional short-term load forecasting task. FWA is also used to train the hyper-parameters of random forest model for container cloud task classification (Qiu, Xie, Tao, Xu & Liu). Barraza, J., Valdez, F., Melin, P., & González, C. (2020) used fireworks algorithm to find the optimal cluster number of given data set. WANG, Kai, HE, YUAN & ZHANG (2018) applied a hybrid method GA-FWA to optimize parameters of SVM model for prediction of sintering burning through point. Similarly, Luo (2019) proposed a quantum fireworks algorithm to train SVM model for financial problems with big data on Spark platform, and Tuba et al. (2019, June) used BBFWA for feature selection and SVM optimization. Messaoudi & Kamel (2019) proposed an improved fireworks algorithm for community detection of social networks. (Liu, Gao, He, & Qi) proposed a soft sensor modelling method of acrolein conversion based on the hidden Markov model with principle component analysis (PCA) and fireworks algorithm. Ren, Ren, Zhang, & Zheng (2019) used fireworks algorithm to optimize parameters of an extreme learning machine combined with k-nearest neighbor method. Lu, Gui & Su (2019) designed a FWA with a dual population strategy to train their MM* model for system-level fault diagnosis.

Design and Control

Manson, Lee, Bloemink & Palizban (2018, November) used enhanced fireworks algorithm (EFWA) to optimize an extended Kalman filter, which is applied in speed estimation of an induction motor drive system. Xiong, Cheng, Gao, Wang, Liu & Yang (2019, June) proposed a design method of Linear Parameter Varying (LPV) control system for flight control, and used fireworks algorithm to optimize the PID controller. (Athar, Pooya, Ziaei, & Goudarzi, 2019) applied Bare-Bone fireworks algorithm to optimize the optimal setting of individual and networks of wind farm. (Lahcen, Mustapha, Ali, Saida & Adel, 2019) used fireworks algorithm to reduce peak-to-average power ratio of OFDM system. (Gao, Zhang, Lu & Ma, 2019, February) applied FWA for calculation in their game based SBCA cloud resource

Table 1 Applications of fireworks algorithm

Supervised Learning	Spam detection (He, Mi & Tan, 2013, June), palm-print and finger-vein identification (Zheng & Tan, 2013, March), de novo motif prediction (Hasoon & Hassan, 2019), gamma-ray spectrum analysis (Alamaniotis & Tsoukalas, 2018), feature subset optimization (Gonsalves; Ma & Niu, 2016; Sreeja, 2019), support vector machine parameters optimization (Duan, Qu, Gao & Chen, 2017, July; Lei, Fang, Gao, Jia & Pan, 2018, October; Tuba E, Tuba M & Beko, 2016, June; Zhang, Yuan, Wang & Cheng, 2018), artificial neural network training (Bolaji, Ahmad, & Shola, 2018; Dutta, Karmakar, & Si, 2016; Gonsalves, 2016; Khuat & Le, 2016; Khuat & Le, 2017; Salman, Ucan, Bayat & Shaker, 2018; Suksri & Kimpan, 2016, December; Tung & Loan, 2016; Zhang & Zhang, 2018, July), linear model training (Xue, Zhao & Ma, 2016, October; Xue, Zhao, Ma & Liu, 2018; Xue, Zhao, Ma & Pang, 2018), prediction of values of the dynamic signature features (Zalasiński, Łapa & Cpałka, 2018), Gaussian process regression model training (Tao, & Zhao, 2018)
Unsupervised Learning	Clustering (Karimov & Ozbayoglu, 2015, October; Liu, Xiao, Li & Cai, 2018, June; Mattos, Barreto, Horstkemper & Hellingrath, 2017, June; Tuba E, Jovanovic, Hrosik, Alihodzic & Tuba M, 2018, June; Yang & Tan, 2014, October), web information retrieval (Bouarara, Hamou, Amine & Rahmani, 2015), grammatical evolution (Si, 2016), community detection (Guendouz, Amine & Hamou, 2017; Ma & Xia, 2017, October)
Scheduling Routing	Fertilization in oil crop production (Zheng, Song & Chen, 2013), power system reconfiguration (Ali, Ejaz, Lee & Khater, 2018; Ikegami & Mori, 2018; Imran & Kowsalya, 2014; Imran, Kowsalya & Kothari, 2014; Lenin, Reddy & Kalavathi, 2015; Mori & Ikegami, 2017, July; Neagu, Ivanov & Gavrilaş, 2017, October; Niu, Ding & Liang, 2015, August; Zhang, Liu, Zhou, Guo & Tang), vehicle routing (Abdulmajeed & Ayob,2014; Cai, Qi, Chen, Cai & Hejlesen, 2018; Yang & Ke, 2019), portfolio optimization [12] (Bacanin & Tuba, 2015; Zhang & Liu, 2017), multi-satellite control resource scheduling (Liu, Feng & Ke, 2015, May), RFID network planning (Strumberger, Tuba, Bacanin, Beko & Tuba, 2018, July; Tuba M, Bacanin & Beko, 2015, April; Tuba V, Alihodzic & Tuba M, 2017, March), thermal unit commitment (Panwar, Reddy & Kumar, 2015; Reddy, Panwar, Kumar & Panigrahi, 2016; 2016, March; 2018; Saravanan, Kumar & Kothari, 2016), data-intensive service mashup (Yang, Zhang & Mu, 2015), wireless sensor network (Arsic, Tuba, & Jordanski, 2016; Liu, Zhang & Zhu, 2017, April; Tuba et al., 2018, March; Tuba E, Tuba M & Beko, 2016, September; Tuba E, Tuba M & Simian, 2016, September; Wei et al., 2018, June; Xia et al., 2018, October), tourist route planning (Ding, Ke & Geng, 2016, July), assembly sequence planning (Li & Lu, 2016; Lu & Li, 2017) satellite link scheduling (Liu, Feng & Ke, 2016, June; Zhang et al., 2016, July), load balancing for cloud-fog network (Shi, Ren & He, 2016, September), UAV path planning (Alihodzic, 2016) (Alihodzic, Hasic & Selmanovic, 2018; Wang, Zhang & Zheng, 2017, July), economic dispatch (Jadoun, Pandey, Gupta, Niazi & Swarnkar, 2018; Pandey, Jadoun, Gupta, Niazi & Swarnkar, 2018), aircraft mission planning (Xue, Wang, Li & Xiao, 2016, June), heat exchanger networks synthesis (Pavão, Costa, Ravagnani & Jiménez, 2017), warehouse scheduling (Ye et al., 2017), economic/environmental operation management (Wang, Zhu, Huang & Yang, 2017), multimodal transportation (Mnif & Bouamama, 2017), flow-shop scheduling (Fu, Ding, Wang, H., & Wang, J., 2018; Ting, Ming & Hua, 2018, July), fault current limiter placement (Bahramian-Habil, Azad-Farsani, Vahidi, Askarian-Abyaneh & Gharehpetian, 2017), software project scheduling (Guo et al, 2019), multi-core processor scheduling (Jingmei, Lanting, Jiaxiang, & He, 2018, February)
Numerical Calculation	Nonnegative matrix factorization (Janecek & Tan, 2011; 2011, June; 2011, July; 2015), numerical optimization (Zheng, Liu, Yu, Li & Tan, 2014, October), parameter estimation of chaotic systems (Li, Bai, Xue, Zhu & Zhang, 2015, June), fitting of Bezier curves/ surfaces (Reddy, Mandal, Verma & Rajamohan, 2016), numerical integration (GUAN, SU, Li & Yu, 2016), conditional nonlinear optimal perturbation (Mu, Zhao, Yuan & Yan, 2016, May)
Design / Control	Digital filters design (Gao & Diao, 2011), truss/frame structure optimization (Gholizadeh & Milany, 2018; Pholdee & Bureerat, 2014), selective harmonic elimination in PWN inverter (Rajaram, Palanisamy, Ramasamy & Ramanathan, 2014), laser machining process (Goswami & Chakraborty, 2015), ultrasonic machining process (Goswami & Chakraborty, 2015), parameter extraction of two diode solar PV model (Babu, Ram, Sangeetha, Laudani & Rajasekar, 2016)., PID parameter optimization (Łapa & Cpałka, 2016; Su et al., 2016; Su, Tsou, Wang, Hoang & Pin, 2016; Su et al., 2016; Xue et al, 2016; Yin, Li, Liu & Wang, 2017, July), antenna design (BouDaher & Hoorfar, 2018; Tang, Lang, Hu & Zhu, 2018, July), supplementary damping controller design (de Vargas Fortes, Macedo, Martins & Miotto, 2017), maximum power point tracking in PV systems (Manickam, Raman, G. P., Raman, G. R., Ganesan & Chilakapati, 2016; Sangeetha, Babu & Rajasekar, 2016), parameter identification of concrete dams (Dou et al, 2017), critical slip surface locating (Xiao, Tian & Lu, 2019), design of nonlinear OFDM (Amhaimar, Ahyoud, Elyaakoubi, Kaabal, Attari, & Asselman, 2018; Basílio, 2018; Guerreiro, Beko, Dinis & Montezuma, 2017, September), control of hypersonic vehicles (Wei, Liu, Wang & Yang, 2018; Yin, Wei, Liu & Wang, 2018), optimization of energy harvesting cognitive radio (Hongyuan, Yanan & Chenwan, 2018), determination of Johnson-Cook material model parameters (Karkalos & Markopoulos, 2018), improvement of the crashworthiness of subway vehicles (Xie, Li, Yang & Yao, 2018), design of a spiral inductor (Jeronymo, Leite, Mariani, dos Santos Coelho & Goudos, 2018, May), optimization of the ascent path of multistage launch vehicles (Pallone, Pontani & Teofilatto, 2018)
Image Processing	Multilevel image thresholding (Chen, Deng, Yan & Ye, 2017; Chen et al. 2018; Liu et al, 2018; Tuba M, Bacanin & Alihodzic, 2015, April), privacy preserving through image perturbation (Rahmani, Amine, Hamou, Rahmani & Bouarara, 2015), cells tracking (Shi, Xu, Zhu & Lu, 2016, October; Shi et al., 2015, October), image registration (Bejinariu et al, 2016; Tuba et al., 2018, May; Tuba E, Tuba M & Dolicanin, 2017), image fusion [25], image compression (Tuba E, Jovanovic, Beko, Tallón-Ballesteros & Tuba M, 2018, November; Tuba E, Tuba M, Simian & Jovanovic, 2017, June), image retrieval (Wang, Wu, Yan, Zhou & Cai, 2018, September)
Others	Seismic waveform inversion (Chen, Wang & Zhang, 2017; Ding, Chen, Wang & Tan, 2015, May), estimation of thermal and optical properties of molten salt (Ren et al., 2016), set covering problem (Crawford, Soto, Astudillo, Olguín & Misra, 2016, July), maximal covering location problem (Tuba E, Dolicanin, & Tuba M, 2017, July), travelling salesman problem (Luo, Xu & Tan, 2018, July; Taidi, Benameur & Chentoufi, 2017), knapsack problem (Xue, Wang & Xiao, 2017), inverse scattering of a conducting cylinder (Lee, 2017; 2018), nonlinear modeling (Łapa, 2017, September; Łapa, Cpałka & Rutkowski, 2018), slope stability analysis (Xiao, Tian & Lu, 2019), minefield attack decision (Yan, Handong & Wei, 2019), capacitated p-median problem (Tuba E, Strumberger, Bacanin & Tuba M, 2018, June), mobile robot odor source localization (Miao, Ma, Jin & Lu, 2018, July), task-oriented satellite agent team formation (Chen, Yang, Li & Jing, 2018)

adjustment method. Qiao, Ke, Wang & Lu (2019, June) used a multi-agent architecture and fireworks algorithm to conduct signal controlling of urban traffic network. SUN & WU used FWA for distribution system reconfiguration. FWA is applied in (Wang, Liu, & Qian, 2019) as optimizer for a new modeling approach for the probability density distribution function of wind power fluctuation.

Scheduling and Routing

(BAO, ZHANG, YIN, & CAI, 2019) implemented a discrete fireworks algorithm to optimize the selection path of stacking machines in the case of semi-tray out of the automated warehouse. Zheng, Wang & Xi (2018, August) introduced explosion operator of FWA into their improved Ant Colony Algorithm for multi-agent path planning in dynamic environment. Hasoon et al. [77] applied fireworks algorithm to traditional Job Shop Scheduling Problem. Lyu et al. (2019) proposed a hybrid simulated annealing discrete fireworks algorithm, and applied it in a multi-node charging planning algorithm. Song, Gao, Chen & Gao (2019) proposed enhanced fireworks algorithm for auto disturbance rejection control (EFWA-ADRC) for path tracking of robot fish in unknown waters. Qian & Hu (2019, March) introduced FWA into their GIS platform with multi-system data, in order to select optimal path for fault repair. Tian, Liu & Jiang (2019, May) used a cloud task scheduling FWA for space-based satellite mission in cloud computing environment. Zhang & Hu (2019, June) combined FWA with artificial bee colony algorithm (ABC) to solve their mathematical model for multi-constrained routing optimization. A discrete FWA is applied for path planning of welding robot by Zhou, Zhao & Zhang (2019, July), and FWA is also combined with Wolf Swarm Algorithm for path planning of mobile robot by (Chen, Zhang, Li & Huang, 2019, May). He, Li, Zhang & Cao (2019) proposed a discrete multi-objective fireworks algorithm for flow shop scheduling with sequence-dependent setup time.

Image Processing

Bejinariu, S. I., Rotariu, C., Costin, H., & Luca, R. (2019, March) implemented a chaos enhanced fireworks algorithm for features-based image registration. Tuba E, Jovanovic & Tuba M (2020) applied Bare Bone FWA on multispectral satellite image classification. They (2019, July) also applied BBFWA for Lymphoblastic Leukemia Cell Detection.

Others

Liu et al. (2019) applied fireworks algorithm for protein-ligand docking, which is of great significance to drug designing. Wang, Pan, Tang & Ding (2019) applied fireworks algorithm to construct and analysis chaotic S-box. Zhang & Wang (2019, June) presented a non-cooperative game Nash equilibrium algorithm and applied an improved fireworks algorithm for spectrum allocation problem. Huang & Yu (2019, April) provided a general wireless sensor network high-precision positioning platform. They applied fireworks algorithm to obtain the optimal approximation results. Liao, Fu & Mung'onya (2019, May) combined the weighted subspace fitting (WSF) algorithm and the pseudo-random noise resampling (PR) with modified FWA for two-dimensional direction of arrival (DOA) estimation. Wang & Liu (2019, June) proposed a sparse FWA for gene regulatory network reconstruction based on fuzzy cognitive maps. Dou, Li, & Kang (2019) improved FWA with RBF-based surrogate model for health diagnosis of concrete dams.

IMPLEMENTATIONS

Basic Implementations

The Matlab experiment code of most important variants of FWA is provided on the official forum of FWA (Tan, 2019). The python implementation of several FWA variants can be found on Github (Tan, 2019). Baidoo (2017) also implemented a Java version of FWA with a simple user interface.

Parallelization

Ding, Zheng & Tan (2013, July) first implemented the parallel framework of FWA on GPU. They also proposed an attract-repulse mutation operator in the GPU-FWA to enhance optimization performance. Without frequently exchange of information, the proposed framework could achieve 200 times speedup. At the same time, GPU-FWA outperforms both original FWA and PSO. Later, Ding and Tan (2015) further improved GPU-FWA by introducing the dynamic explosion amplitude and a Cauchy mutation operator.

Ludwig & Dawar (2015) implemented EFWA with MapReduce platform. They found EFWA could achieve a better speedup rate on MapReduce than PSO.

DISCUSSION

As we mentioned before, there are more and more published articles on fireworks algorithm. These are also more developments in 2019 than 2018. Finally, we separately analyze what changes and trends FWA have shown in different direction.

Algorithm Improvements

After 2018, there are still a considerable amount of work focused on the firework algorithm itself. But the main content of those research has changed.

In the early stage of research on FWA, most work has focused on the adjustment of explosion methods and parameters, or the design of efficient mutation operators. Papers in this direction have decreased in recent years. On the one hand, work in this area is already quite adequate. On the other hand, BBFWA and LoTFWA have proved that FWA can be rather efficient without communication in explosion operator. However, many interesting algorithms that proposed which applied new explosion methods, new mutation methods, or global elite strategies.

Interactive mechanisms have become an important topic of FWA, especially for research based on LoTFWA. Although many related works are not classified in this type, quite a lot of FWA variants tried new mechanisms to help interact between local searches.

There are no obvious changes in the study of hybrid methods. Most research concentrates on introducing new mechanisms as mutation operator. Some interesting work combines different frameworks or maintains several populations. There are also work introduced explosion operator into other algorithms.

Research on the application of FWA to complex optimization problems has been relatively weak. Now, FWA has been proved effective for dynamic optimization, multi-objective optimization and niching problem. Among them, multi-objective optimization has made new progress in recent years. And niching problem was solved by FWA shortly for the first time. Research in this area has great potential.

It is worth mentioning that many outstanding improvements on FWA are proposed in application research. These works are worthy of reference and development for algorithm researchers.

Theoretical Analysis

Theoretical analysis on FWA has been relatively limited. Traditional analysis about proof of convergence, convergence time, and proof of global optimization ability is given very early. Recently, some analysis of FWA is provided as the publishing of GFWA and BBFWA. As the framework of FWA change a lot with independent selection, more theoretical work is needed now.

Applications

A great number of application works are done with FWA in 2019. Its main application areas are still parameters tuning in machine learning, design and control, or scheduling and routing. There have been a number of research on numerical calculation, but less work has been done in recent years.

In most application research, new variant of FWA is designed for the specific problem. This is really important because different problem backgrounds always require different optimization algorithms. But those studies always rely on early variants of FWA and they have almost no continuity. It would be of great help to the development of FWA's applications if those issues get noticed.

Implementations

Implementations of FWA have made some progress in recent years, but there are still many directions that need improvement. For example, more stable and efficient algorithm implementation that is capable of adapting to different application problems is needed. There are also no available parallel computing implementation or convenient user software interface.

ACKNOWLEDGMENT

This research was supported by the Natural Science Foundation of China (NSFC) [grant number 61673025].

REFERENCES

Abdulmajeed, N. H., & Ayob, M. (2014). A firework algorithm for solving capacitated vehicle routing problem. *International Journal of Advancements in Computing Technology*, *6*(1), 79.

Alamaniotis, M., Choi, C. K., & Tsoukalas, L. H. (2015). Application of fireworks algorithm in gamma-ray spectrum fitting for radioisotope identification. [IJSIR]. *International Journal of Swarm Intelligence Research*, *6*(2), 102–125. doi:10.4018/IJSIR.2015040105

Alamaniotis, M., & Tsoukalas, L. H. (2018). Assessment of Gamma-Ray-Spectra Analysis Method Utilizing the Fireworks Algorithm for Various Error Measures. In *Critical Developments and Applications of Swarm Intelligence* (pp. 155–181). IGI Global. doi:10.4018/978-1-5225-5134-8.ch007

Ali, H. M., Ejaz, W., Lee, D. C., & Khater, I. M. (2018). Optimising the power using firework-based evolutionary algorithms for emerging IoT applications. *IET Networks*, *8*(1), 15–31. doi:10.1049/iet-net.2018.5041

Alihodzic, A. (2016, November). Fireworks algorithm with new feasibility-rules in solving UAV path planning. In *2016 3rd International Conference on Soft Computing & Machine Intelligence (ISCMI)* (pp. 53-57). IEEE. 10.1109/ISCMI.2016.33

Alihodzic, A., Hasic, D., & Selmanovic, E. (2018, August). An Effective Guided Fireworks Algorithm for Solving UCAV Path Planning Problem. In *International Conference on Numerical Methods and Applications* (pp. 29-38). Cham, Switzerland: Springer.

Amhaimar, L., Ahyoud, S., Elyaakoubi, A., Kaabal, A., Attari, K., & Asselman, A. (2018). PAPR Reduction Using Fireworks Search Optimization Algorithm in MIMO-OFDM Systems. *Journal of Electrical and Computer Engineering*, *2018*. doi:10.1155/2018/3075890

Arsic, A., Tuba, M., & Jordanski, M. (2016, July). Fireworks algorithm applied to wireless sensor networks localization problem. *Proceedings 2016 IEEE Congress on Evolutionary Computation (CEC)* (pp. 4038-4044). IEEE. 10.1109/CEC.2016.7744302

Athar, H., Pooya, S., Ziaei, D., & Goudarzi, N. (n.d.). Artificial Intelligence for Optimal Sitting of Individual and Networks of Wind Farms. In *ASME 2019 Power Conference*. American Society of Mechanical Engineers Digital Collection.

Babu, T. S., Ram, J. P., Sangeetha, K., Laudani, A., & Rajasekar, N. (2016). Parameter extraction of two diode solar PV model using Fireworks algorithm. *Solar Energy*, *140*, 265–276. doi:10.1016/j.solener.2016.10.044

Bacanin, N., & Tuba, M. (2015, May). Fireworks algorithm applied to constrained portfolio optimization problem. *Proceedings 2015 IEEE Congress on Evolutionary Computation (CEC)* (pp. 1242-1249). IEEE. 10.1109/CEC.2015.7257031

Bacanin, N., Tuba, M., & Beko, M. (2015). Hybridized fireworks algorithm for global optimization. *Mathematical Methods and Systems in Science and Engineering*, 108-114.

Bahramian-Habil, H., Azad-Farsani, E., Vahidi, B., Askarian-Abyaneh, H., & Gharehpetian, G. B. (2017). Fault Current Limiter Placement Using Multi-Objective Firework Algorithm. *Electric Power Components and Systems*, *45*(17), 1929–1940. doi:10.1080/15325008.2017.1405466

Baidoo, E. (2017). Fireworks Algorithm for Unconstrained Function Optimization Problems. *Applied Computer Science, 13*.

Bao, S., Zhang, M., Yin, J., & Cai, Z. (2019). A Research on the Order Picking Optimization for Stacker's Composite Operation of Semi-tray out of the Automated Warehouse. *Industrial Engineering Journal*, *22*(1), 90.

Barraza, J., Melin, P., Valdez, F., & González, C. (2017). Fireworks algorithm (FWA) with adaptation of parameters using fuzzy logic. In *Nature-Inspired Design of Hybrid Intelligent Systems* (pp. 313–327). Cham, Switzerland: Springer. doi:10.1007/978-3-319-47054-2_21

Barraza, J., Melin, P., Valdez, F., & Gonzalez, C. (2017). Fuzzy fireworks algorithm based on a sparks dispersion measure. *Algorithms*, *10*(3), 83. doi:10.3390/a10030083

Barraza, J., Melin, P., Valdez, F., & Gonzalez, C. I. (2016, July). Fuzzy FWA with dynamic adaptation of parameters. *Proceedings 2016 IEEE Congress on Evolutionary Computation (CEC)* (pp. 4053-4060). IEEE. 10.1109/CEC.2016.7744304

Barraza, J., Melin, P., Valdez, F., Gonzalez, C. I., & Castillo, O. (2017, July). Iterative fireworks algorithm with fuzzy coefficients. *Proceedings 2017 IEEE International Conference on Fuzzy Systems (FUZZ-IEEE)* (pp. 1-6). IEEE.

Barraza, J., Rodríguez, L., Castillo, O., Melin, P., & Valdez, F. (2018). A new hybridization approach between the fireworks algorithm and grey wolf optimizer algorithm. *Journal of Optimization, 2018*.

Barraza, J., Valdez, F., Melin, P., & González, C. (2020). Optimal Number of Clusters Finding Using the Fireworks Algorithm. In *Hybrid Intelligent Systems in Control, Pattern Recognition, and Medicine* (pp. 83–93). Cham, Switzerland: Springer. doi:10.1007/978-3-030-34135-0_7

Basílio, D. F. F. (2018). *Approaching the Optimal Performance of Nonlinear OFDM With FWA Techniques* (Doctoral dissertation).

Bejinariu, S. I., Costin, H., Rotaru, F., Luca, R., & Niţă, C. (2016). Fireworks algorithm based single and multi-objective optimization. *Bulletin of the Polytechnic Institute of Jassy. Automatic Control and Computer Science Section*, *62*(3), 19–34.

Bejinariu, S. I., Costin, H., Rotaru, F., Luca, R., Niţă, C. D., & Lazăr, C. (2016, August). Fireworks algorithm based image registration. In *International Workshop Soft Computing Applications* (pp. 509-523). Cham, Switzerland: Springer.

Bejinariu, S. I., Luca, R., & Costin, H. (2016, October). Nature-inspired algorithms based multispectral image fusion. *Proceedings 2016 International Conference and Exposition on Electrical and Power Engineering (EPE)* (pp. 010-015). IEEE. 10.1109/ICEPE.2016.7781293

Bejinariu, S. I., Rotariu, C., Costin, H., & Luca, R. (2019, March). Image Registration using Fireworks Algorithm and Chaotic Sequences. *Proceedings 2019 11th International Symposium on Advanced Topics in Electrical Engineering (ATEE)* (pp. 1-4). IEEE. 10.1109/ATEE.2019.8725020

Bolaji, A. L. A., Ahmad, A. A., & Shola, P. B. (2018). Training of neural network for pattern classification using fireworks algorithm. *International Journal of System Assurance Engineering and Management*, *9*(1), 208–215. doi:10.100713198-016-0526-z

Bouarara, H. A., Hamou, R. M., Amine, A., & Rahmani, A. (2015). A fireworks algorithm for modern web information retrieval with visual results mining. [IJSIR]. *International Journal of Swarm Intelligence Research*, *6*(3), 1–23. doi:10.4018/IJSIR.2015070101

BouDaher, E., & Hoorfar, A. (2016, June). Fireworks algorithm: A new swarm intelligence technique for electromagnetic optimization. *Proceedings 2016 IEEE International Symposium on Antennas and Propagation (APSURSI)* (pp. 575-576). IEEE. 10.1109/APS.2016.7695996

Cai, Y., Qi, Y., Chen, H., Cai, H., & Hejlesen, O. (2018, May). Quantum Fireworks Evolutionary Algorithm for Vehicle Routing Problem in Supply Chain with Multiple Time Windows. In *2018 2nd IEEE Advanced Information Management, Communicates, Electronic, and Automation Control Conference (IMCEC)* (pp. 383-388). IEEE. 10.1109/IMCEC.2018.8469677

Chen, H., Deng, X., Yan, L., & Ye, Z. (2017, December). Multilevel thresholding selection based on the fireworks algorithm for image segmentation. *Proceedings 2017 International Conference on Security, Pattern Analysis, and Cybernetics (SPAC)* (pp. 175-180). IEEE. 10.1109/SPAC.2017.8304271

Chen, H., Yang, S., Li, J., & Jing, N. (2018). Exact and Heuristic Methods for Observing Task-Oriented Satellite Cluster Agent Team Formation. *Mathematical Problems in Engineering, 2018*, 2018. doi:10.1155/2018/2103625

Chen, J., Yang, Q., Ni, J., Xie, Y., & Cheng, S. (2015, May). An improved fireworks algorithm with landscape information for balancing exploration and exploitation. *Proceedings 2015 IEEE Congress on Evolutionary Computation (CEC)* (pp. 1272-1279). IEEE. 10.1109/CEC.2015.7257035

Chen, S., Liu, Y., Wei, L., & Guan, B. (2018). PS-FW: A hybrid algorithm based on particle swarm and fireworks for global optimization. *Computational Intelligence and Neuroscience, 2018*, 2018. doi:10.1155/2018/6094685 PMID:29675036

Chen, X., Shi, C., Zhou, A., Xu, S., & Wu, B. (2018, November). A Hybrid Replacement Strategy for MOEA/D. *Proceedings International Conference on Bio-Inspired Computing: Theories and Applications* (pp. 246-262). Springer, Singapore. 10.1007/978-981-13-2826-8_22

Chen, X., Zhang, Y., Li, K., & Huang, B. (2019, May). Path Planning of Mobile Robot Based on Improved Wolf Swarm Algorithms. *Proceedings 2019 IEEE 8th Joint International Information Technology and Artificial Intelligence Conference (ITAIC)* (pp. 359-364). IEEE. 10.1109/ITAIC.2019.8785503

Chen, Y., Li, L., Zhao, X., Xiao, J., Wu, Q., & Tan, Y. (2019). Simplified hybrid fireworks algorithm. *Knowledge-Based Systems, 173*, 128–139. doi:10.1016/j.knosys.2019.02.029

Chen, Y., Wang, Y., & Zhang, Y. (2017). Crustal velocity structure of central Gansu Province from regional seismic waveform inversion using firework algorithm. *Earth Science, 30*(2), 81–89. doi:10.100711589-017-0184-5

Chen, Y., Yang, W., Li, M., Hao, Z., Zhou, P., & Sun, H. (2018). Research on Pest Image Processing Method Based on Android Thermal Infrared Lens. *IFAC-PapersOnLine, 51*(17), 173–178. doi:10.1016/j.ifacol.2018.08.083

Cheng, R., Bai, Y., Zhao, Y., Tan, X., & Xu, T. (2019). Improved fireworks algorithm with information exchange for function optimization. *Knowledge-Based Systems, 163*, 82–90. doi:10.1016/j.knosys.2018.08.016

Cheng, S., Qin, Q., Chen, J., Shi, Y., & Zhang, Q. (2015). Analytics on fireworks algorithm solving problems with shifts in the decision space and objective space. [IJSIR]. *International Journal of Swarm Intelligence Research, 6*(2), 52–86. doi:10.4018/IJSIR.2015040103

Crawford, B., Soto, R., Astudillo, G., Olguín, E., & Misra, S. (2016, July). Solving Set Covering Problem with Fireworks Explosion. *Proceedings International Conference on Computational Science and Its Applications* (pp. 273-283). Cham, Switzerland: Springer. 10.1007/978-3-319-42085-1_21

Ding, H., Ke, L., & Geng, Z. (2016, July). Route planning in a new tourist recommender system: A fireworks algorithm based approach. *Proceedings 2016 IEEE Congress on Evolutionary Computation (CEC)* (pp. 4022-4028). IEEE. 10.1109/CEC.2016.7744300

Ding, K., Chen, Y., Wang, Y., & Tan, Y. (2015, May). Regional seismic waveform inversion using swarm intelligence algorithms. *Proceedings 2015 IEEE Congress on Evolutionary Computation (CEC)* (pp. 1235-1241). IEEE. 10.1109/CEC.2015.7257030

Ding, K., & Tan, Y. (2015). Attract-repulse fireworks algorithm and its CUDA implementation using dynamic parallelism. [IJSIR]. *International Journal of Swarm Intelligence Research, 6*(2), 1–31. doi:10.4018/IJSIR.2015040101

Ding, K., Zheng, S., & Tan, Y. (2013, July). A GPU-based parallel fireworks algorithm for optimization. *Proceedings of the 15th annual conference on Genetic and evolutionary computation* (pp. 9-16). ACM. 10.1145/2463372.2463377

Dorigo, M., & Di Caro, G. (1999, July). Ant colony optimization: a new meta-heuristic. *Proceedings of the 1999 congress on evolutionary computation-CEC99 (Cat. No. 99TH8406)* (Vol. 2, pp. 1470-1477). IEEE. 10.1109/CEC.1999.782657

Dou, S., Li, J., & Kang, F. (2017). Parameter identification of concrete dams using swarm intelligence algorithm. *Engineering Computations, 34*(7), 2358–2378. doi:10.1108/EC-03-2017-0110

Dou, S. Q., Li, J. J., & Kang, F. (2019). Health diagnosis of concrete dams using hybrid FWA with RBF-based surrogate model. *Water Science and Engineering, 12*(3), 188–195. doi:10.1016/j.wse.2019.09.002

Duan, J., Qu, Q., Gao, C., & Chen, X. (2017, July). BOF steelmaking endpoint prediction based on FWA-TSVR. *Proceedings 2017 36th Chinese Control Conference (CCC)* (pp. 4507-4511). IEEE. 10.23919/ChiCC.2017.8028067

Dutta, R. K., Karmakar, N. K., & Si, T. (2016). Artificial neural network training using fireworks algorithm in medical data mining. *International Journal of Computers and Applications, 137*(1), 1–5. doi:10.5120/ijca2016908726

Eberhart, R., & Kennedy, J. (1995, November). Particle swarm optimization. *Proceedings of the IEEE International Conference on Neural Networks* (Vol. 4, pp. 1942-1948). 10.1109/ICNN.1995.488968

Eusuff, M., Lansey, K., & Pasha, F. (2006). Shuffled frog-leaping algorithm: A memetic meta-heuristic for discrete optimization. *Engineering Optimization, 38*(2), 129–154. doi:10.1080/03052150500384759

Farswan, P., & Bansal, J. C. (2019). Fireworks-inspired biogeography-based optimization. *Soft Computing, 23*(16), 7091–7115. doi:10.100700500-018-3351-2

Fortes, E., Macedo, L. H., Martins, L. F. B., & Miotto, E. L. (2017, March). A fireworks metaheuristic for the design of PSS and TCSC-POD controllers for small-signal stability studies. In *Latin American Congress on Generation, Transmission, and Distribution (CLAGTEE)* (pp. 1-6).

Fu, Y., Ding, J., Wang, H., & Wang, J. (2018). Two-objective stochastic flow-shop scheduling with deteriorating and learning effect in Industry 4.0-based manufacturing system. *Applied Soft Computing*, *68*, 847–855. doi:10.1016/j.asoc.2017.12.009

Gao, H., & Diao, M. (2011). Cultural firework algorithm and its application for digital filters design. *International Journal of Modelling Identification and Control*, *14*(4), 324–331. doi:10.1504/IJMIC.2011.043157

Gao, H., & Li, C. (2015). Opposition-based quantum firework algorithm for continuous optimisation problems. *International Journal of Computing Science and Mathematics*, *6*(3), 256–265. doi:10.1504/IJCSM.2015.069747

Gao, Y., Zhang, B., Lu, M., & Ma, A. (2019, February). Game Based SBCA Cloud Resource Adjustment Method. *Proceedings 2019 21st International Conference on Advanced Communication Technology (ICACT)* (pp. 47-51). IEEE. 10.23919/ICACT.2019.8702050

Gholizadeh, S., & Milany, A. (2018). An improved fireworks algorithm for discrete sizing optimization of steel skeletal structures. *Engineering Optimization*, *50*(11), 1829–1849. doi:10.1080/0305215X.2017.1417402

Gong, C. (2016). Opposition-based adaptive fireworks algorithm. *Algorithms*, *9*(3), 43. doi:10.3390/a9030043

Gong, C. (2016, June). Chaotic adaptive fireworks algorithm. *Proceedings International Conference on Swarm Intelligence* (pp. 515-525). Cham, Switzerland: Springer.

Gong, C. (2019). Dynamic search fireworks algorithm with chaos. *Journal of Algorithms & Computational Technology*, *13*. doi:10.1177/1748302619889559

Gong, C. (2020). Dynamic Search Fireworks Algorithm with Adaptive Parameters. [IJACI]. *International Journal of Ambient Computing and Intelligence*, *11*(1), 115–135. doi:10.4018/IJACI.2020010107

Gonsalves, T. (2016). Two diverse swarm intelligence techniques for supervised learning. In *Psychology and mental health: Concepts, methodologies, tools, and applications* (pp. 849–861). IGI Global. doi:10.4018/978-1-5225-0159-6.ch034

Gonsalves, T. (n.d.). Feature Subset Optimization through the Fireworks Algorithm. *Studies*, *8*, 12.

Goswami, D., & Chakraborty, S. (2015). A study on the optimization performance of fireworks and cuckoo search algorithms in laser machining processes. *Journal of The Institution of Engineers (India): Series C, 96*(3), 215-229.

Goswami, D., & Chakraborty, S. (2015). Parametric optimization of ultrasonic machining process using gravitational search and fireworks algorithms. *Ain Shams Engineering Journal*, *6*(1), 315–331. doi:10.1016/j.asej.2014.10.009

Guan, J. X., Su, Q. H., Li, W., & Yu, C. (2016). A Numerical Integration Method Based on Fireworks Algorithm. DEStech Transactions on Computer Science and Engineering, (aita).

Guendouz, M., Amine, A., & Hamou, R. M. (2017). A discrete modified fireworks algorithm for community detection in complex networks. *Applied Intelligence*, *46*(2), 373–385. doi:10.100710489-016-0840-9

Guerreiro, J., Beko, M., Dinis, R., & Montezuma, P. (2017, September). Using the Fireworks Algorithm for ML Detection of Nonlinear OFDM. *Proceedings 2017 IEEE 86th Vehicular Technology Conference (VTC-Fall)* (pp. 1-5). IEEE. 10.1109/VTCFall.2017.8287944

Guo, J., & Liu, W. (2018, October). Enhanced Fireworks Algorithm with an Improved Gaussian Sparks Operator. *Proceedings International Symposium on Intelligence Computation and Applications* (pp. 38-49). Springer, Singapore.

Guo, J., Liu, W., Liu, M., & Zheng, S. (2019). Hybrid fireworks algorithm with differential evolution operator. *International Journal of Intelligent Information and Database Systems*, *12*(1-2), 47–64. doi:10.1504/IJIIDS.2019.102326

Guo, Y., Ji, J., Ji, J., Gong, D., Cheng, J., & Shen, X. (2019). Firework-based software project scheduling method considering the learning and forgetting effect. *Soft Computing*, *23*(13), 5019–5034. doi:10.100700500-018-3165-2

Han, X., Zheng, L., Wang, L., Zheng, H., & Wang, X. (2019). Fireworks algorithm based on dynamic search and tournament selection. *International Journal of Computers and Applications*, 1–12. doi:10.1080/1206212X.2019.1590034

Hao, L. (2019, October). A Fireworks-inspired Estimation of Distribution Algorithm. [IOP Publishing.]. *IOP Conference Series. Materials Science and Engineering*, *631*(5). doi:10.1088/1757-899X/631/5/052053

Hasoon, J. N., & Hassan, R. (2019). Solving Job Scheduling Problem Using Fireworks Algorithm. *Journal of Al-Qadisiyah for Computer Science and Mathematics, 11*(2), 1-8.

He, L., Li, W., Zhang, Y., & Cao, Y. (2019). A discrete multi-objective fireworks algorithm for flowshop scheduling with sequence-dependent setup times. *Swarm and Evolutionary Computation*, *51*, 100575. doi:10.1016/j.swevo.2019.100575

He, W., Mi, G., & Tan, Y. (2013, June). Parameter optimization of local-concentration model for spam detection by using fireworks algorithm. *Proceedings International Conference in Swarm Intelligence* (pp. 439-450). Berlin, Germany: Springer. 10.1007/978-3-642-38703-6_52

Hongyuan, G. A. O., Yanan, D. U., & Chenwan, L. I. (2018). Quantum fireworks algorithm for optimal cooperation mechanism of energy harvesting cognitive radio. *Journal of Systems Engineering and Electronics*, *29*(1), 18–30. doi:10.21629/JSEE.2018.01.02

Huang, M., & Yu, B. (2019, April). Demo Abstract: RPTB: Range-based Positioning TestBed for WSN. *Proceedings IEEE INFOCOM 2019-IEEE Conference on Computer Communications Workshops (INFOCOM WKSHPS)* (pp. 999-1000). IEEE.

Ikegami, H., & Mori, H. (2018). Development of discrete CoFFWA for distribution network reconfigurations. *Electrical Engineering in Japan*, *205*(3), 55–62. doi:10.1002/eej.23151

Imran, A. M., & Kowsalya, M. (2014). A new power system reconfiguration scheme for power loss minimization and voltage profile enhancement using fireworks algorithm. *International Journal of Electrical Power & Energy Systems, 62*, 312–322. doi:10.1016/j.ijepes.2014.04.034

Imran, A. M., Kowsalya, M., & Kothari, D. P. (2014). A novel integration technique for optimal network reconfiguration and distributed generation placement in power distribution networks. *International Journal of Electrical Power & Energy Systems, 63*, 461–472. doi:10.1016/j.ijepes.2014.06.011

Jadoun, V. K., Pandey, V. C., Gupta, N., Niazi, K. R., & Swarnkar, A. (2018). Integration of renewable energy sources in dynamic economic load dispatch problem using an improved fireworks algorithm. *IET Renewable Power Generation, 12*(9), 1004–1011. doi:10.1049/iet-rpg.2017.0744

Jadoun, V. K., Shah, M. K., Pandey, V. C., Gupta, N., Niazi, K. R., & Swarnkar, A. (2016). Multi-Area Dynamic Economic Dispatch Problem with Multiple Fuels Using Improved Fireworks Algorithm.

Janecek, A., & Tan, Y. (2011). Swarm intelligence for non-negative matrix factorization. [IJSIR]. *International Journal of Swarm Intelligence Research, 2*(4), 12–34. doi:10.4018/jsir.2011100102

Janecek, A., & Tan, Y. (2011, July). Iterative improvement of the multiplicative update nmf algorithm using nature-inspired optimization. *Proceedings 2011 Seventh International Conference on Natural Computation* (Vol. 3, pp. 1668-1672). IEEE. 10.1109/ICNC.2011.6022356

Janecek, A., & Tan, Y. (2011, June). Using population-based algorithms for initializing nonnegative matrix factorization. *Proceedings International Conference in Swarm Intelligence* (pp. 307-316). Berlin, Germany: Springer. 10.1007/978-3-642-21524-7_37

Janecek, A., & Tan, Y. (2015). Swarm Intelligence for Dimensionality Reduction: How to Improve the Non-Negative Matrix Factorization with Nature-Inspired Optimization Methods. In Emerging Research on Swarm Intelligence and Algorithm Optimization (pp. 285-309). IGI Global.

Jeronymo, D. C., Leite, J. V., Mariani, V. C., dos Santos Coelho, L., & Goudos, S. K. (2018, May). Spiral inductor design based on fireworks optimization combined with free search. *Proceedings 2018 7th International Conference on Modern Circuits and Systems Technologies (MOCAST)* (pp. 1-4). IEEE. 10.1109/MOCAST.2018.8376558

Jingmei, L., Lanting, L., Jiaxiang, W., & He, L. (2018, February). A CMP Thread Scheduling Strategy Based on Improved Firework Algorithm. *Proceedings 2018 4th International Conference on Computational Intelligence & Communication Technology (CICT)* (pp. 1-6). IEEE. 10.1109/CIACT.2018.8480208

Jun, Y. U., Takagi, H., & Ying, T. A. N. (2019, June). Fireworks Algorithm for Multimodal Optimization Using a Distance-based Exclusive Strategy. *Proceedings 2019 IEEE Congress on Evolutionary Computation (CEC)* (pp. 2215-2220). IEEE.

Karaboga, D., & Basturk, B. (2007). A powerful and efficient algorithm for numerical function optimization: Artificial bee colony (ABC) algorithm. *Journal of Global Optimization, 39*(3), 459–471. doi:10.100710898-007-9149-x

Karimov, J., & Ozbayoglu, M. (2015, October). High-quality clustering of big data and solving empty-clustering problem with an evolutionary hybrid algorithm. *Proceedings 2015 IEEE International Conference on Big Data (Big Data)* (pp. 1473-1478). IEEE. 10.1109/BigData.2015.7363909

Karkalos, N. E., & Markopoulos, A. P. (2018). Determination of Johnson-Cook material model parameters by an optimization approach using the fireworks algorithm. *Procedia Manufacturing, 22*, 107–113. doi:10.1016/j.promfg.2018.03.017

Khuat, T. T., & Le, M. H. (2016). An effort estimation approach for agile software development using fireworks algorithm optimized neural network. [IJCSIS]. *International Journal of Computer Science and Information Security, 14*(7).

Khuat, T. T., & Le, M. H. (2017). An application of artificial neural networks and fuzzy logic on the stock price prediction problem. *JOIV: International Journal on Informatics Visualization, 1*(2), 40–49. doi:10.30630/joiv.1.2.20

Kumar, V., Chhabra, J. K., & Kumar, D. (2015). Optimal choice of parameters for fireworks algorithm. *Procedia Computer Science, 70*, 334–340. doi:10.1016/j.procs.2015.10.027

Lahcen, A., Mustapha, H., Ali, E., Saida, A., & Adel, A. (2019). Peak-to-Average Power Ratio Reduction Using New Swarm Intelligence Algorithm in OFDM Systems. *Procedia Manufacturing, 32*, 831–839. doi:10.1016/j.promfg.2019.02.291

Lana, I., Del Ser, J., & Vélez, M. (2017, June). A novel fireworks algorithm with wind inertia dynamics and its application to traffic forecasting. *Proceedings 2017 IEEE Congress on Evolutionary Computation (CEC)* (pp. 706-713). IEEE. 10.1109/CEC.2017.7969379

Łapa, K. (2017, September). Population-Based Algorithm with Selectable Evolutionary Operators for Nonlinear Modeling. In *International Conference on Information Systems Architecture and Technology* (pp. 15-26). Cham, Switzerland: Springer.

Łapa, K., & Cpałka, K. (2016). On the application of a hybrid genetic-firework algorithm for controllers structure and parameters selection. *Information Systems Architecture and Technology: Proceedings of 36th International Conference on Information Systems Architecture and Technology–ISAT 2015–Part I* (pp. 111-123). Cham, Switzerland: Springer.

Łapa, K., Cpałka, K., & Rutkowski, L. (2018). New Aspects of Interpretability of Fuzzy Systems for Nonlinear Modeling. In *Advances in Data Analysis with Computational Intelligence Methods* (pp. 225–264). Cham, Switzerland: Springer. doi:10.1007/978-3-319-67946-4_9

Larrañaga, P., & Lozano, J. A. (Eds.). (2001). *Estimation of distribution algorithms: A new tool for evolutionary computation* (Vol. 2). Springer Science & Business Media.

Lee, K. C. (2017). Inverse scattering of a conducting cylinder in free space by modified fireworks algorithm. *Progress in Electromagnetics Research, 59*, 135–146. doi:10.2528/PIERM17061101

Lee, K. C. (2018). Microwave imaging of a conducting cylinder buried in a lossless half space by modified fireworks algorithm. *Microwave and Optical Technology Letters*, *60*(6), 1374–1381. doi:10.1002/mop.31159

Lei, C., Fang, B., Gao, H., Jia, W., & Pan, W. (2018, October). Short-term power load forecasting based on Least Squares Support Vector Machine optimized by Bare Bones Fireworks algorithm. *Proceedings 2018 IEEE 3rd Advanced Information Technology, Electronic, and Automation Control Conference (IAEAC)* (pp. 2231-2235). IEEE. 10.1109/IAEAC.2018.8577212

Lenin, K., Reddy, B. R., & Kalavathi, M. S. (2015). Reduction of Real Power Loss by Upgraded Fireworks Algorithm. *International Journal of Advanced Engineering and Science*, *4*(2), 1.

Li, H., Bai, P., Xue, J. J., Zhu, J., & Zhang, H. (2015, June). Parameter estimation of chaotic systems using fireworks algorithm. *Proceedings International Conference in Swarm Intelligence* (pp. 457-467). Cham, Switzerland: Springer. 10.1007/978-3-319-20472-7_49

Li, J. (2019). (Preprint). A random dynamic search algorithm research. *Journal of Computational Methods in Sciences and Engineering*, 1–14.

Li, J., & Tan, Y. (2015, May). Orienting mutation-based fireworks algorithm. *Proceedings 2015 IEEE Congress on Evolutionary Computation (CEC)* (pp. 1265-1271). IEEE. 10.1109/CEC.2015.7257034

Li, J., & Tan, Y. (2016, July). Enhancing interaction in the fireworks algorithm by dynamic resource allocation and fitness-based crowdedness-avoiding strategy. *Proceedings 2016 IEEE Congress on Evolutionary Computation (CEC)* (pp. 4015-4021). IEEE. 10.1109/CEC.2016.7744299

Li, J., & Tan, Y. (2017). Loser-Out Tournament-Based Fireworks Algorithm for Multimodal Function Optimization. *IEEE Transactions on Evolutionary Computation*, *22*(5), 679–691. doi:10.1109/TEVC.2017.2787042

Li, J., & Tan, Y. (2018). The bare bones fireworks algorithm: A minimalist global optimizer. *Applied Soft Computing*, *62*, 454–462. doi:10.1016/j.asoc.2017.10.046

Li, J., & Tan, Y. (2019). A Comprehensive Review of the Fireworks Algorithm. [CSUR]. *ACM Computing Surveys*, *52*(6), 121.

Li, J., Zheng, S., & Tan, Y. (2014, July). Adaptive fireworks algorithm. *Proceedings 2014 IEEE Congress on evolutionary computation (CEC)* (pp. 3214-3221). IEEE. 10.1109/CEC.2014.6900418

Li, J., Zheng, S., & Tan, Y. (2016). The effect of information utilization: Introducing a novel guiding spark in the fireworks algorithm. *IEEE Transactions on Evolutionary Computation*, *21*(1), 153–166. doi:10.1109/TEVC.2016.2589821

Li, J. Y., & Lu, C. (2016). Assembly sequence planning with fireworks algorithm. *International Journal of Modeling and Optimization*, *6*(3), 195–198. doi:10.7763/IJMO.2016.V6.526

Li, X., Han, S., Zhao, L., & Gong, C. (2017, November). Adaptive fireworks algorithm based on two-master sub-population and new selection strategy. *Proceedings International Conference on Neural Information Processing* (pp. 70-79). Cham, Switzerland: Springer. 10.1007/978-3-319-70093-9_8

Li, X. G., Han, S. F., & Gong, C. Q. (2017). Analysis and improvement of fireworks algorithm. *Algorithms*, *10*(1), 26. doi:10.3390/a10010026

Li, X. G., Han, S. F., Zhao, L., Gong, C. Q., & Liu, X. J. (2017). Adaptive mutation dynamic search fireworks algorithm. *Algorithms*, *10*(2), 48. doi:10.3390/a10020048

Li, Y., Yu, J., Takagi, H., & Tan, Y. (2019, July). Accelerating Fireworks Algorithm with Weight-based Guiding Sparks. *Proceedings International Conference on Swarm Intelligence* (pp. 257-266). Springer, Cham. 10.1007/978-3-030-26369-0_24

Liao, Y., Fu, C., & Mung'onya, E. M. (2019, May). 2D DOA Estimation of PR-WSF Algorithm Based on Modified Fireworks Algorithm. *Proceedings International Conference on Artificial Intelligence for Communications and Networks* (pp. 210-224). Springer, Cham. 10.1007/978-3-030-22968-9_19

Lihu, A., & Holban, Ş. (2015). De novo motif prediction using the fireworks algorithm. [IJSIR]. *International Journal of Swarm Intelligence Research*, *6*(3), 24–40. doi:10.4018/IJSIR.2015070102

Liu, F. Z., Xiao, B., Li, H., & Cai, L. (2018, June). Discrete Fireworks Algorithm for Clustering in Wireless Sensor Networks. *Proceedings International Conference on Swarm Intelligence* (pp. 273-282). Cham, Switzerland: Springer. 10.1007/978-3-319-93815-8_27

Liu, J., Zheng, S., & Tan, Y. (2013, June). The improvement on controlling exploration and exploitation of firework algorithm. *Proceedings International Conference in Swarm Intelligence* (pp. 11-23). Berlin, Germany: Springer. 10.1007/978-3-642-38703-6_2

Liu, J., Zheng, S., & Tan, Y. (2014, July). Analysis on global convergence and time complexity of fireworks algorithm. *Proceedings 2014 IEEE Congress on Evolutionary Computation (CEC)* (pp. 3207-3213). IEEE. 10.1109/CEC.2014.6900652

Liu, L., Zheng, S., & Tan, Y. (2015, May). S-metric based multi-objective fireworks algorithm. *Proceedings 2015 IEEE Congress on Evolutionary Computation (CEC)* (pp. 1257-1264). IEEE. 10.1109/CEC.2015.7257033

Liu, S., Gao, X., He, H., & Qi, W. (n.d.). Soft Sensor Modelling of Acrolein Conversion Based on Hidden Markov Model of Principle Component Analysis and Fireworks Algorithm. *The Canadian Journal of Chemical Engineering, 97*(12), 3052-3062.

Liu, W., Shi, H., He, X., Pan, S., Ye, Z., & Wang, Y. (2018). An application of optimized Otsu multi-threshold segmentation based on fireworks algorithm in cement SEM image. *Journal of Algorithms & Computational Technology, 13*.

Liu, X., Zhang, X., & Zhu, Q. (2017, April). Enhanced Fireworks Algorithm for Dynamic Deployment of Wireless Sensor Networks. *Proceedings 2017 2nd International Conference on Frontiers of Sensors Technologies (ICFST)* (pp. 161-165). IEEE. 10.1109/ICFST.2017.8210494

Liu, Z., Feng, Z., & Ke, L. (2015, May). Fireworks algorithm for the multi-satellite control resource scheduling problem. *Proceedings 2015 IEEE Congress on evolutionary computation (CEC)* (pp. 1280-1286). IEEE. 10.1109/CEC.2015.7257036

Liu, Z., Feng, Z., & Ke, L. (2016, June). A modified fireworks algorithm for the multi-resource range scheduling problem. *Proceedings International Conference on Swarm Intelligence* (pp. 535-543). Cham, Switzerland: Springer. 10.1007/978-3-319-41000-5_53

Liu, Z., Jiang, D., Zhang, C., Zhao, H., Zhao, Q., & Zhang, B. (2019). A Novel Fireworks Algorithm for the Protein-Ligand Docking on the AutoDock. *Mobile Networks and Applications*, 1–12. doi:10.100711036-018-1136-6

Lu, C., & Li, J. Y. (2017). Assembly sequence planning considering the effect of assembly resources with a discrete fireworks algorithm. *International Journal of Advanced Manufacturing Technology*, *93*(9-12), 3297–3314. doi:10.100700170-017-0663-9

Lu, Q., Gui, W., & Su, M. (2019). A Fireworks Algorithm for the System-Level Fault Diagnosis Based on MM* Model. *IEEE Access: Practical Innovations, Open Solutions*, *7*, 136975–136985. doi:10.1109/ACCESS.2019.2942336

Ludwig, S. A., & Dawar, D. (2015). Parallelization of enhanced firework algorithm using MapReduce. [IJSIR]. *International Journal of Swarm Intelligence Research*, *6*(2), 32–51. doi:10.4018/IJSIR.2015040102

Luo, H., Xu, W., & Tan, Y. (2018, July). A Discrete Fireworks Algorithm for Solving Large-Scale Travel Salesman Problem. *Proceedings 2018 IEEE Congress on Evolutionary Computation (CEC)* (pp. 1-8). IEEE. 10.1109/CEC.2018.8477992

Luo, T. (2019). Research on financial network big data processing technology based on fireworks algorithm. *EURASIP Journal on Wireless Communications and Networking*, *2019*(1), 122. doi:10.118613638-019-1443-z

Lyu, Z., Wei, Z., Lu, Y., Wang, X., Li, M., Xia, C., & Han, J. (2019). Multi-Node Charging Planning Algorithm With an Energy-Limited WCE in WRSNs. *IEEE Access: Practical Innovations, Open Solutions*, *7*, 47154–47170. doi:10.1109/ACCESS.2019.2909778

Ma, T., & Niu, D. (2016). Icing forecasting of high voltage transmission line using weighted least square support vector machine with fireworks algorithm for feature selection. *Applied Sciences (Basel, Switzerland)*, *6*(12), 438. doi:10.3390/app6120438

Ma, T., & Xia, Z. (2017, October). A Community Detection Algorithm Based on Local Double Rings and Fireworks Algorithm. *Proceedings International Conference on Intelligent Data Engineering and Automated Learning* (pp. 129-135). Cham, Switzerland: Springer. 10.1007/978-3-319-68935-7_15

Manickam, C., Raman, G. P., Raman, G. R., Ganesan, S. I., & Chilakapati, N. (2016). Fireworks enriched P&O algorithm for GMPPT and detection of partial shading in PV systems. *IEEE Transactions on Power Electronics*, *32*(6), 4432–4443. doi:10.1109/TPEL.2016.2604279

Manson, K., Lee, D., Bloemink, J., & Palizban, A. (2018, November). Enhanced Fireworks Algorithm to Optimize Extended Kalman Filter Speed Estimation of an Induction Motor Drive System. *Proceedings 2018 IEEE 9th Annual Information Technology, Electronics, and Mobile Communication Conference (IEMCON)* (pp. 267-273). IEEE. 10.1109/IEMCON.2018.8614914

Mattos, C. L., Barreto, G. A., Horstkemper, D., & Hellingrath, B. (2017, June). Metaheuristic optimization for automatic clustering of customer-oriented supply chain data. *Proceedings 2017 12th International Workshop on Self-Organizing Maps and Learning Vector Quantization, Clustering, and Data Visualization (WSOM)* (pp. 1-8). IEEE. 10.1109/WSOM.2017.8020025

Messaoudi, I., & Kamel, N. (2019). Community Detection Using Fireworks Optimization Algorithm. *International Journal of Artificial Intelligence Tools, 28*(03). doi:10.1142/S0218213019500106

Miao, Y., Ma, X., Jin, X., & Lu, H. (2018, July). Mobile Robot Odor Source Localization Based on Modified FWA. *Proceedings 2018 IEEE 8th Annual International Conference on CYBER Technology in Automation, Control, and Intelligent Systems (CYBER)* (pp. 854-860). IEEE. 10.1109/CYBER.2018.8688288

Mirjalili, S., Mirjalili, S. M., & Lewis, A. (2014). Grey wolf optimizer. *Advances in Engineering Software, 69*, 46–61. doi:10.1016/j.advengsoft.2013.12.007

Mnif, M., & Bouamama, S. (2017). Firework algorithm for multi-objective optimization of a multimodal transportation network problem. *Procedia Computer Science, 112*, 1670–1682. doi:10.1016/j.procs.2017.08.189

Mori, H., & Ikegami, H. (2017, July). *An advanced fireworks algorithm for distribution network reconfigurations. Proceedings 2017 IEEE Power & Energy Society General Meeting* (pp. 1–5). IEEE.

Mu, B., Zhao, J., Yuan, S., & Yan, J. (2017, May). Parallel dynamic search fireworks algorithm with linearly decreased dimension number strategy for solving conditional nonlinear optimal perturbation. *Proceedings 2017 International Joint Conference on Neural Networks (IJCNN)* (pp. 2314-2321). IEEE. 10.1109/IJCNN.2017.7966136

Neagu, B. C., Ivanov, O., & Gavrilaş, M. (2017, October). A comprehensive solution for optimal capacitor allocation problem in real distribution networks. *Proceedings 2017 International Conference on Electromechanical and Power Systems (SIELMEN)* (pp. 565-570). IEEE. 10.1109/SIELMEN.2017.8123388

Niu, S., Ding, Y., & Liang, Z. (2015, August). Study on Distribution Network Reconfiguration with Various DGs. *Proceedings International Conference on Materials Engineering and Information Technology Applications (MEITA 2015)*. Atlantis Press. 10.2991/meita-15.2015.140

Pallone, M., Pontani, M., & Teofilatto, P. (2018). Performance evaluation methodology for multistage launch vehicles with high-fidelity modeling. *Acta Astronautica, 151*, 522–531. doi:10.1016/j.actaastro.2018.06.012

Pandey, V. C., Jadoun, V. K., Gupta, N., Niazi, K. R., & Swarnkar, A. (2018). Improved Fireworks algorithm with chaotic sequence operator for large-scale non-convex economic load dispatch problem. *Arabian Journal for Science and Engineering, 43*(6), 2919–2929. doi:10.100713369-017-2956-6

Panwar, L. K., Reddy, S., & Kumar, R. (2015). Binary fireworks algorithm based thermal unit commitment. [IJSIR]. *International Journal of Swarm Intelligence Research, 6*(2), 87–101. doi:10.4018/IJSIR.2015040104

Pavão, L. V., Costa, C. B. B., Ravagnani, M. A. D. S. S., & Jiménez, L. (2017). Large-scale heat exchanger networks synthesis using simulated annealing and the novel rocket fireworks optimization. *AIChE Journal. American Institute of Chemical Engineers, 63*(5), 1582–1601. doi:10.1002/aic.15524

Pei, Y., Zheng, S., Tan, Y., & Takagi, H. (2012, October). An empirical study on influence of approximation approaches on enhancing fireworks algorithm. *Proceedings 2012 IEEE International Conference on Systems, Man, and Cybernetics (SMC)* (pp. 1322-1327). IEEE. 10.1109/ICSMC.2012.6377916

Pei, Y., Zheng, S., Tan, Y., & Takagi, H. (2015). Effectiveness of approximation strategy in surrogate-assisted fireworks algorithm. *International Journal of Machine Learning and Cybernetics, 6*(5), 795–810. doi:10.100713042-015-0388-8

Pekdemir, H., & Topcuoglu, H. R. (2016, July). Enhancing fireworks algorithms for dynamic optimization problems. Proceedings 2016 IEEE congress on evolutionary computation (CEC) (pp. 4045-4052). IEEE. doi:10.1109/CEC.2016.7744303

Pholdee, N., & Bureerat, S. (2014). Comparative performance of meta-heuristic algorithms for mass minimisation of trusses with dynamic constraints. *Advances in Engineering Software, 75*, 1–13. doi:10.1016/j.advengsoft.2014.04.005

Qian, Z., & Hu, C. (2019, March). Optimal Path Selection for Fault Repair Based on Grid GIS Platform and Improved Fireworks Algorithm. *Proceedings 2019 IEEE 3rd Information Technology, Networking, Electronic, and Automation Control Conference (ITNEC)* (pp. 2452-2456). IEEE. 10.1109/ITNEC.2019.8729359

Qiao, Z., Ke, L., Wang, X., & Lu, X. (2019, June). Signal Control of Urban Traffic Network Based on Multi-Agent Architecture and Fireworks Algorithm. *Proceedings 2019 IEEE Congress on Evolutionary Computation (CEC)* (pp. 2199-2206). IEEE.

Qiu, M., Xie, X., Tao, X., Xu, K., & Liu, Y. (n.d.). Research on Container Cloud Task Classification Algorithm based on Improved Random Forest. doi:10.1109/CEC.2019.8790300

Rahmani, A., Amine, A., Hamou, R. M., Rahmani, M. E., & Bouarara, H. A. (2015). Privacy preserving through fireworks algorithm-based model for image perturbation in big data. [IJSIR]. *International Journal of Swarm Intelligence Research, 6*(3), 41–58. doi:10.4018/IJSIR.2015070103

Rajaram, R., Palanisamy, K., Ramasamy, S., & Ramanathan, P. (2014). Selective harmonic elimination in pwm inverter using firefly and fireworks algorithm. [IJIRAE]. *International Journal of Innovative Research in Advanced Engineering, 1*, 55–62.

Reddy, K. S., Mandal, A., Verma, K. K., & Rajamohan, G. (2016). Fitting of Bezier curves using the fireworks algorithm. *International Journal of Advances in Engineering and Technology, 9*(3), 396.

Reddy, K. S., Mandal, A., Verma, K. K., & Rajamohan, G. (2016). Fitting of Bezier surfaces using the fireworks algorithm. *International Journal of Advances in Engineering and Technology, 9*(3), 421.

Reddy, K. S., Panwar, L., Panigrahi, B. K., & Kumar, R. (2018). Low carbon unit commitment (LCUC) with post carbon capture and storage (CCS) technology considering resource sensitivity. *Journal of Cleaner Production, 200*, 161–173. doi:10.1016/j.jclepro.2018.07.195

Reddy, K. S., Panwar, L. K., Kumar, R., & Panigrahi, B. K. (2016). Binary fireworks algorithm for profit based unit commitment (PBUC) problem. *International Journal of Electrical Power & Energy Systems*, *83*, 270–282. doi:10.1016/j.ijepes.2016.04.005

Reddy, K. S., Panwar, L. K., Kumar, R., & Panigrahi, B. K. (2016). Distributed resource scheduling in smart grid with electric vehicle deployment using fireworks algorithm. *Journal of Modern Power Systems and Clean Energy*, *4*(2), 188–199. doi:10.100740565-016-0195-6

Reddy, S., Panwar, L. K., Panigrahi, B. K., & Kumar, R. (2016, March). Optimal demand response allocation in resource scheduling with renewable energy penetration. *Proceedings 2016 IEEE 6th International Conference on Power Systems (ICPS)* (pp. 1-6). IEEE.

Ren, J., Ren, B., Zhang, Q., & Zheng, X. (2019). A Novel Hybrid Extreme Learning Machine Approach Improved by K Nearest Neighbor Method and Fireworks Algorithm for Flood Forecasting in Medium and Small Watershed of Loess Region. *Water (Basel)*, *11*(9), 1848. doi:10.3390/w11091848

Ren, Y. T., Qi, H., He, M. J., Ruan, S. T., Ruan, L. M., & Tan, H. P. (2016). Application of an improved firework algorithm for simultaneous estimation of temperature-dependent thermal and optical properties of molten salt. *International Communications in Heat and Mass Transfer*, *77*, 33–42. doi:10.1016/j.icheatmasstransfer.2016.06.012

Salman, I., Ucan, O., Bayat, O., & Shaker, K. (2018). Impact of metaheuristic iteration on artificial neural network structure in medical data. *Processes (Basel, Switzerland)*, *6*(5), 57. doi:10.3390/pr6050057

Sangeetha, K., Babu, T. S., & Rajasekar, N. (2016). Fireworks algorithm-based maximum power point tracking for uniform irradiation as well as under partial shading condition. In *Artificial Intelligence and Evolutionary Computations in Engineering Systems* (pp. 79–88). New Delhi, India: Springer. doi:10.1007/978-81-322-2656-7_8

Saravanan, B., Kumar, C., & Kothari, D. P. (2016). A solution to unit commitment problem using fire works algorithm. *International Journal of Electrical Power & Energy Systems*, *77*, 221–227. doi:10.1016/j.ijepes.2015.11.030

Shi, C., Ren, Z., & He, X. (2016, September). Research on Load Balancing for Software Defined Cloud-Fog Network in Real-Time Mobile Face Recognition. *Proceedings International Conference on Communications and Networking in China* (pp. 121-131). Cham, Switzerland: Springer. Academic Press.

Shi, J., Xu, B., Zhu, P., & Lu, M. (2016, October). Multi-task firework algorithm for cell tracking and contour estimation. *Proceedings 2016 International Conference on Control, Automation, and Information Sciences (ICCAIS)* (pp. 27-31). IEEE. 10.1109/ICCAIS.2016.7822430

Shi, J., Xu, B., Zhu, P., Lu, M., Zhang, W., Xu, L., & Zhang, J. (2015, October). Multiple cells tracking by firework algorithm. *Proceedings 2015 International Conference on Control, Automation, and Information Sciences (ICCAIS)* (pp. 508-511). IEEE.

Shi, Y. (2014). Developmental swarm intelligence: Developmental learning perspective of swarm intelligence algorithms. [IJSIR]. *International Journal of Swarm Intelligence Research*, *5*(1), 36–54. doi:10.4018/ijsir.2014010102

Si, T. (2016). Grammatical Evolution Using Fireworks Algorithm. *Proceedings of Fifth International Conference on Soft Computing for Problem Solving* (pp. 43-55). Springer, Singapore.

Si, T., & Ghosh, R. (2015, March). Explosion sparks generation using adaptive transfer function in firework algorithm. *Proceedings 2015 3rd International Conference on Signal Processing, Communication, and Networking (ICSCN)* (pp. 1-9). IEEE. 10.1109/ICSCN.2015.7219917

Simon, D. (2008). Biogeography-based optimization. *IEEE Transactions on Evolutionary Computation, 12*(6), 702–713. doi:10.1109/TEVC.2008.919004

Song, X., Gao, S., Chen, C., & Gao, Z. (2019). Enhanced Fireworks Algorithm-Auto Disturbance Rejection Control Algorithm for Robot Fish Path Tracking. *International Journal of Computers, Communications, & Control, 14*(3), 401–418. doi:10.15837/ijccc.2019.3.3547

Sreeja, N. K. (2019). A weighted pattern matching approach for classification of imbalanced data with a fireworks-based algorithm for feature selection. *Connection Science, 31*(2), 143–168. doi:10.1080/09540091.2018.1512558

Strumberger, I., Tuba, E., Bacanin, N., Beko, M., & Tuba, M. (2018, July). Bare bones fireworks algorithm for the RFID network planning problem. *Proceedings 2018 IEEE Congress on Evolutionary Computation (CEC)* (pp. 1-8). IEEE. 10.1109/CEC.2018.8477990

Su, T. J., Li, T. Y., Wang, S. M., Hoang, V. M., & Chen, Y. F. (2016). A novel method for controller design in engineering education. *World Trans. Eng. Technol. Educ, 14*(2), 288–294.

Su, T. J., Tsou, T. Y., Wang, S. M., Hoang, V. M., & Pin, K. W. (2016). A hybrid control design of FOPID and FWA for inverted pendulum systems.

Su, T. J., Wang, S. M., Li, T. Y., Shih, S. T., & Hoang, V. M. (2016). Design of hybrid sliding mode controller based on fireworks algorithm for nonlinear inverted pendulum systems. *Advances in Mechanical Engineering, 9*(1).

Suksri, S., & Kimpan, W. (2016, December). Neural Network training model for weather forecasting using Fireworks Algorithm. *Proceedings 2016 International Computer Science and Engineering Conference (ICSEC)* (pp. 1-7). IEEE.

Sun, L., & Wu, Z. (n.d.). Distribution System Reconfiguration Based on FWA and DLF with DGs. doi:10.1109/ICSEC.2016.7859952

Sun, Y. F., Wang, J. S., & Song, J. D. (2016). An improved fireworks algorithm based on grouping strategy of the shuffled frog leaping algorithm to solve function optimization problems. *Algorithms, 9*(2), 23. doi:10.3390/a9020023

Suo, G., Song, L., Dou, Y., & Cui, Z. (2019, November). Multi-dimensional Short-Term Load Forecasting Based on XGBoost and Fireworks Algorithm. *Proceedings 2019 18th International Symposium on Distributed Computing and Applications for Business Engineering and Science (DCABES)* (pp. 245-248). IEEE. 10.1109/DCABES48411.2019.00068

Taidi, Z., Benameur, L., & Chentoufi, J. A. (2017). A fireworks algorithm for solving travelling salesman problem. *International Journal of Computational Systems Engineering*, *3*(3), 157–162. doi:10.1504/IJCSYSE.2017.086740

Tan, Y. (2015). *Fireworks Algorithm*. Heidelberg, Germany: Springer. doi:10.1007/978-3-662-46353-6

Tan, Y. (2019). Python implementation of fireworks algorithms. Retrieved from https://github.com/cilatpku/firework-algorithm

Tan, Y. (2019). *Forum of fireworks algorithms*. Retrieved from https://www.cil.pku.edu.cn/fwa/index.htm

Tan, Y., Yu, C., Zheng, S., & Ding, K. (2013). Introduction to fireworks algorithm. [IJSIR]. *International Journal of Swarm Intelligence Research*, *4*(4), 39–70. doi:10.4018/ijsir.2013100103

Tan, Y., & Zhu, Y. (2010, June). Fireworks algorithm for optimization. *Proceedings International Conference in Swarm Intelligence* (pp. 355-364). Berlin, Germany: Springer.

Tang, P., Lang, L., Hu, F., & Zhu, D. (2017, July). The design of two-fold redundancy linear arrays in aperture synthesis radiometers. *Proceedings 2017 IEEE International Symposium on Antennas and Propagation & USNC/URSI National Radio Science Meeting* (pp. 149-150). IEEE. 10.1109/APUSNCURSINRSM.2017.8072117

Tao, Y., & Zhao, L. (2018). A novel system for WiFi radio map automatic adaptation and indoor positioning. *IEEE Transactions on Vehicular Technology*, *67*(11), 10683–10692. doi:10.1109/TVT.2018.2867065

Taowei, C., Yiming, Y., Kun, Z., & Duan, Z. (2018, October). A Membrane-Fireworks Algorithm for Multi-Objective Optimization Problems. *Proceedings 2018 11th International Congress on Image and Signal Processing, BioMedical Engineering and Informatics (CISP-BMEI)* (pp. 1-6). IEEE. 10.1109/CISP-BMEI.2018.8633082

Tian, G., Liu, C., & Jiang, H. (2019, May). Scheduling Strategy of Space-based Satellite Based on Fireworks Algorithm under Cloud Computing. *Proceedings of the 2019 4th International Conference on Big Data and Computing* (pp. 91-96). ACM. 10.1145/3335484.3335511

Ting, D. X., Ming, L. C., & Hua, H. Z. (2018, July). Fireworks Explosion Algorithm for Hybrid Flow Shop Scheduling and Optimization Problem1. [IOP Publishing.]. *IOP Conference Series. Materials Science and Engineering*, *382*(3). doi:10.1088/1757-899X/382/3/032005

Tuba, E., Dolicanin, E., & Tuba, M. (2017, July). Guided Fireworks Algorithm Applied to the Maximal Covering Location Problem. *Proceedings International Conference on Swarm Intelligence* (pp. 501-508). Cham, Switzerland: Springer. 10.1007/978-3-319-61824-1_55

Tuba, E., Jovanovic, R., Beko, M., Tallón-Ballesteros, A. J., & Tuba, M. (2018, November). Bare Bones Fireworks Algorithm for Medical Image Compression. *Proceedings International Conference on Intelligent Data Engineering and Automated Learning* (pp. 262-270). Cham, Switzerland: Springer. 10.1007/978-3-030-03496-2_29

Tuba, E., Jovanovic, R., Hrosik, R. C., Alihodzic, A., & Tuba, M. (2018, June). Web Intelligence Data Clustering by Bare Bone Fireworks Algorithm Combined with K-Means. *Proceedings of the 8th International Conference on Web Intelligence, Mining, and Semantics* (p. 7). ACM. 10.1145/3227609.3227650

Tuba, E., Jovanovic, R., & Tuba, M. (2020). Multispectral Satellite Image Classification Based on Bare Bone Fireworks Algorithm. In *Information and Communication Technology for Sustainable Development* (pp. 305–313). Singapore: Springer. doi:10.1007/978-981-13-7166-0_30

Tuba, E., Strumberger, I., Bacanin, N., Jovanovic, R., & Tuba, M. (2019, June). Bare bones fireworks algorithm for feature selection and SVM optimization. *Proceedings 2019 IEEE Congress on Evolutionary Computation (CEC)* (pp. 2207-2214). IEEE. 10.1109/CEC.2019.8790033

Tuba, E., Strumberger, I., Bacanin, N., & Tuba, M. (2018, June). Bare bones fireworks algorithm for capacitated p-median problem. *Proceedings International Conference on Swarm Intelligence* (pp. 283-291). Cham, Switzerland: Springer. 10.1007/978-3-319-93815-8_28

Tuba, E., Strumberger, I., Bacanin, N., Zivkovic, D., & Tuba, M. (2019, July). Acute Lymphoblastic Leukemia Cell Detection in Microscopic Digital Images Based on Shape and Texture Features. *Proceedings International Conference on Swarm Intelligence* (pp. 142-151). Springer, Cham. 10.1007/978-3-030-26354-6_14

Tuba, E., Strumberger, I., Zivkovic, D., Bacanin, N., & Tuba, M. (2018, May). Rigid Image Registration by Bare Bones Fireworks Algorithm. *Proceedings 2018 6th International Conference on Multimedia Computing and Systems (ICMCS)* (pp. 1-6). IEEE. 10.1109/ICMCS.2018.8525968

Tuba, E., Tuba, I., Dolicanin-Djekic, D., Alihodzic, A., & Tuba, M. (2018, March). Efficient drone placement for wireless sensor networks coverage by bare bones fireworks algorithm. *Proceedings 2018 6th International Symposium on Digital Forensic and Security (ISDFS)* (pp. 1-5). IEEE. 10.1109/ISDFS.2018.8355349

Tuba, E., Tuba, M., & Beko, M. (2016, June). Support vector machine parameters optimization by enhanced fireworks algorithm. *Proceedings International Conference on Swarm Intelligence* (pp. 526-534). Springer, Cham. 10.1007/978-3-319-41000-5_52

Tuba, E., Tuba, M., & Beko, M. (2016, September). Node localization in ad hoc wireless sensor networks using fireworks algorithm. *Proceedings 2016 5th International Conference on Multimedia Computing and Systems (ICMCS)* (pp. 223-229). IEEE. 10.1109/ICMCS.2016.7905647

Tuba, E., Tuba, M., & Dolicanin, E. (2017). Adjusted fireworks algorithm applied to retinal image registration. *Studies in Informatics and Control*, *26*(1), 33–42. doi:10.24846/v26i1y201704

Tuba, E., Tuba, M., & Simian, D. (2016, September). Wireless sensor network coverage problem using modified fireworks algorithm. *Proceedings 2016 International Wireless Communications and Mobile Computing Conference (IWCMC)* (pp. 696-701). IEEE. 10.1109/IWCMC.2016.7577141

Tuba, E., Tuba, M., Simian, D., & Jovanovic, R. (2017, June). JPEG quantization table optimization by guided fireworks algorithm. *Proceedings International Workshop on Combinatorial Image Analysis* (pp. 294-307). Springer, Cham. 10.1007/978-3-319-59108-7_23

Tuba, M., Bacanin, N., & Alihodzic, A. (2015, April). Multilevel image thresholding by fireworks algorithm. *Proceedings 2015 25th International Conference Radioelektronika (RADIOELEKTRONIKA)* (pp. 326-330). IEEE. 10.1109/RADIOELEK.2015.7129057

Tuba, M., Bacanin, N., & Beko, M. (2015, April). Fireworks algorithm for RFID network planning problem. *Proceedings 2015 25th International Conference Radioelektronika (RADIOELEKTRONIKA)* (pp. 440-444). IEEE. 10.1109/RADIOELEK.2015.7129049

Tuba, V., Alihodzic, A., & Tuba, M. (2017, March). Multi-objective RFID network planning with probabilistic coverage model by guided fireworks algorithm. *Proceedings 2017 10th International Symposium on Advanced Topics in Electrical Engineering (ATEE)* (pp. 882-887). IEEE. 10.1109/ATEE.2017.7905125

Tung, K. T., & Loan, N. T. B. (2016). Applying Artificial Neural Network Optimized by Fireworks Algorithm for Stock Price Estimation. *ICTACT Journal on Soft Computing, 6*(3).

Wang, D. D., Kai, Y., He, Z. J., Yuan, Y. Q., & Zhang, J. (2018). Application Research Based on GA-FWA in Prediction of Sintering Burning Through Point. DEStech Transactions on Computer Science and Engineering, (ccme).

Wang, C., Wang, Y., Yan, L., Ye, Z., Cai, W., & Wu, P. (2019, September). Financial Early Warning of Listed Companies Based on Fireworks Algorithm Optimized Back-Propagation Neural Network. *Proceedings 2019 10th IEEE International Conference on Intelligent Data Acquisition and Advanced Computing Systems: Technology and Applications (IDAACS)* (Vol. 2, pp. 927-932). IEEE. 10.1109/IDAACS.2019.8924376

Wang, C., Wu, P., Yan, L., Zhou, F., & Cai, W. (2018, September). Image retrieval based on fireworks algorithm optimizing convolutional neural network. In *2018 IEEE 4th International Symposium on Wireless Systems within the International Conferences on Intelligent Data Acquisition and Advanced Computing Systems (IDAACS-SWS)* (pp. 53-56). IEEE. 10.1109/IDAACS-SWS.2018.8525760

Wang, J., Pan, B., Tang, C., & Ding, Q. (2019). Construction Method and Performance Analysis of Chaotic S-Box Based on Fireworks Algorithm. *International Journal of Bifurcation and Chaos in Applied Sciences and Engineering, 29*(12). doi:10.1142/S021812741950158X

Wang, L., Liu, J., & Qian, F. (2019). A New Modeling Approach for the Probability Density Distribution Function of Wind power Fluctuation. *Sustainability, 11*(19), 5512. doi:10.3390u11195512

Wang, X., Peng, H., Deng, C., Li, L., & Zheng, L. (2018, October). An Improved Firefly Algorithm Hybrid with Fireworks. *Proceedings International Symposium on Intelligence Computation and Applications* (pp. 27-37). Springer, Singapore.

Wang, Y., & Liu, J. (2019, June). A Sparse Fireworks Algorithm for Gene Regulatory Network Reconstruction based on Fuzzy Cognitive Maps. *Proceedings 2019 IEEE Congress on Evolutionary Computation (CEC)* (pp. 1188-1194). IEEE. 10.1109/CEC.2019.8790068

Wang, Y., Zhang, M. X., & Zheng, Y. J. (2017, July). A hyper-heuristic method for UAV search planning. *Proceedings International Conference on Swarm Intelligence* (pp. 454-464). Springer, Cham. 10.1007/978-3-319-61833-3_48

Wang, Z., Zhu, Q., Huang, M., & Yang, B. (2017). Optimization of economic/environmental operation management for microgrids by using hybrid fireworks algorithm. *International Transactions on Electrical Energy Systems, 27*(12). doi:10.1002/etep.2429

Wei, X., Liu, L., Wang, Y., & Yang, Y. (2018). Reentry trajectory optimization for a hypersonic vehicle based on an improved adaptive fireworks algorithm. *International Journal of Aerospace Engineering, 2018*, 2018. doi:10.1155/2018/8793908

Wei, Z., Wang, L., Lyu, Z., Shi, L., Li, M., & Wei, X. (2018, June). A multi-objective algorithm for joint energy replenishment and data collection in wireless rechargeable sensor networks. *Proceedings International Conference on Wireless Algorithms, Systems, and Applications* (pp. 497-508). Springer, Cham. 10.1007/978-3-319-94268-1_41

Xia, C., Wei, Z., Lyu, Z., Wang, L., Liu, F., & Feng, L. (2018, October). A novel mixed-variable fireworks optimization algorithm for path and time sequence optimization in WRSNs. *Proceedings International Conference on Communications and Networking in China* (pp. 24-34). Springer, Cham.

Xiao, Z., Tian, B., & Lu, X. (2019). Locating the critical slip surface in a slope stability analysis by enhanced fireworks algorithm. *Cluster Computing, 22*(1), 719–729. doi:10.100710586-017-1196-6

Xie, S., Li, H., Yang, C., & Yao, S. (2018). Crashworthiness optimisation of a composite energy-absorbing structure for subway vehicles based on hybrid particle swarm optimisation. *Structural and Multidisciplinary Optimization, 58*(5), 2291–2308. doi:10.100700158-018-2022-3

Xiong, J., Cheng, Z., Gao, J., Wang, Y., Liu, L., & Yang, Y. (2019, June). Design of LPV Control System Based on Intelligent Optimization. *Proceedings 2019 Chinese Control and Decision Conference (CCDC)* (pp. 2160-2165). IEEE. 10.1109/CCDC.2019.8832439

Xue, J., Wang, Y., & Xiao, J. (2017). Uncertain bilevel knapsack problem and its solution. *Journal of Systems Engineering and Electronics, 28*(4), 717–724. doi:10.21629/JSEE.2017.04.11

Xue, J. J., Wang, Y., Li, H., Meng, X. F., & Xiao, J. Y. (2016). Advanced fireworks algorithm and its application research in PID parameters tuning. *Mathematical Problems in Engineering, 2016*, 2016. doi:10.1155/2016/2534632

Xue, J. J., Wang, Y., Li, H., & Xiao, J. Y. (2016, June). Discrete fireworks algorithm for aircraft mission planning. *Proceedings International Conference on Swarm Intelligence* (pp. 544-551). Springer, Cham. 10.1007/978-3-319-41000-5_54

Xue, Y., Zhao, B., & Ma, T. (2016, October). Classification based on fireworks algorithm. *Proceedings International Conference on Bio-Inspired Computing: Theories and Applications* (pp. 35-40). Springer, Singapore.

Xue, Y., Zhao, B., Ma, T., & Liu, A. X. (2018). An evolutionary classification method based on fireworks algorithm. *IJBIC, 11*(3), 149–158. doi:10.1504/IJBIC.2018.091747

Xue, Y., Zhao, B., Ma, T., & Pang, W. (2018). A self-adaptive fireworks algorithm for classification problems. *IEEE Access: Practical Innovations, Open Solutions, 6*, 44406–44416. doi:10.1109/ACCESS.2018.2858441

Yan, M., Handong, Z., & Wei, Z. (2019). Research on Intelligent Minefield Attack Decision Based on Adaptive Fireworks Algorithm. *Arabian Journal for Science and Engineering, 44*(3), 2487–2496. doi:10.100713369-018-3159-5

Yang, W., & Ke, L. (2019). An improved fireworks algorithm for the capacitated vehicle routing problem. *Frontiers of Computer Science*, *13*(3), 552–564. doi:10.100711704-017-6418-9

Yang, W., Zhang, C., & Mu, B. (2015). Data-intensive service mashup based on game theory and hybrid fireworks optimization algorithm in the cloud. *Informatica (Vilnius)*, *39*(4).

Yang, X., & Tan, Y. (2014, October). Sample index-based encoding for clustering using evolutionary computation. *Proceedings International Conference in Swarm Intelligence* (pp. 489-498). Springer, Cham. 10.1007/978-3-319-11857-4_55

Ye, S., Ma, H., Xu, S., Yang, W., & Fei, M. (2017). An effective fireworks algorithm for warehouse-scheduling problem. *Transactions of the Institute of Measurement and Control*, *39*(1), 75–85. doi:10.1177/0142331215600047

Ye, W., & Wen, J. (2017, December). Adaptive fireworks algorithm based on simulated annealing. *Proceedings 2017 13th International Conference on Computational Intelligence and Security (CIS)* (pp. 371-375). IEEE. 10.1109/CIS.2017.00087

Yet, X., Li, J., Xu, B., & Tan, Y. (2018, July). Which Mapping Rule in the Fireworks Algorithm is Better for Large Scale Optimization. *Proceedings 2018 IEEE Congress on Evolutionary Computation (CEC)* (pp. 1-8). IEEE.

Yin, X., Li, X., Liu, L., & Wang, Y. (2017, July). Improved fireworks algorithm and its application in PID parameters tuning. *Proceedings 2017 36th Chinese Control Conference (CCC)* (pp. 9841-9846). IEEE. 10.23919/ChiCC.2017.8028926

Yin, X., Wei, X., Liu, L., & Wang, Y. (2018). Improved hybrid fireworks algorithm-based parameter optimization in high-order sliding mode control of hypersonic vehicles. *Complexity*, *2018*, 2018. doi:10.1155/2018/9098151

Yu, C., Kelley, L., Zheng, S., & Tan, Y. (2014, July). Fireworks algorithm with differential mutation for solving the CEC 2014 competition problems. *Proceedings 2014 IEEE Congress on Evolutionary Computation (CEC)* (pp. 3238-3245). IEEE. 10.1109/CEC.2014.6900590

Yu, C., Kelley, L. C., & Tan, Y. (2015, May). Dynamic search fireworks algorithm with covariance mutation for solving the CEC 2015 learning based competition problems. *Proceedings 2015 IEEE Congress on Evolutionary Computation (CEC)* (pp. 1106-1112). IEEE. 10.1109/CEC.2015.7257013

Yu, C., Kelley, L. C., & Tan, Y. (2016, July). Cooperative framework fireworks algorithm with covariance mutation. *Proceedings 2016 IEEE Congress on Evolutionary Computation (CEC)* (pp. 1196-1203). IEEE. 10.1109/CEC.2016.7743923

Yu, C., Li, J., & Tan, Y. (2014, October). Improve enhanced fireworks algorithm with differential mutation. *Proceedings 2014 IEEE International Conference on Systems, Man, and Cybernetics (SMC)* (pp. 264-269). IEEE. 10.1109/SMC.2014.6973918

Yu, C., & Tan, Y. (2015, May). Fireworks algorithm with covariance mutation. *Proceedings 2015 IEEE Congress on Evolutionary Computation (CEC)* (pp. 1250-1256). IEEE. 10.1109/CEC.2015.7257032

Yu, J., & Takagi, H. (2017, July). Acceleration for fireworks algorithm based on amplitude reduction strategy and local optima-based selection strategy. *Proceedings International Conference on Swarm Intelligence* (pp. 477-484). Springer, Cham. 10.1007/978-3-319-61824-1_52

Yu, J., Takagi, H., & Tan, Y. (2018). Multi-layer Explosion Based Fireworks Algorithm. *J Swarm Intel Evol Comput*, 7(173), 2.

Yu, J., Takagi, H., & Tan, Y. (2018, June). Accelerating the Fireworks Algorithm with an Estimated Convergence Point. *Proceedings International Conference on Swarm Intelligence* (pp. 263-272). Springer, Cham. 10.1007/978-3-319-93815-8_26

Yu, J., Tan, Y., & Takagi, H. (2018, July). Scouting strategy for biasing fireworks algorithm search to promising directions. *Proceedings of the Genetic and Evolutionary Computation Conference Companion* (pp. 99-100). ACM. 10.1145/3205651.3205740

Zalasiński, M., Łapa, K., & Cpałka, K. (2018). Prediction of values of the dynamic signature features. *Expert Systems with Applications*, *104*, 86–96. doi:10.1016/j.eswa.2018.03.028

Zhang, B., Zhang, M., & Zheng, Y. J. (2014, October). Improving enhanced fireworks algorithm with new gaussian explosion and population selection strategies. *Proceedings International Conference in Swarm Intelligence* (pp. 53-63). Springer, Cham. 10.1007/978-3-319-11857-4_7

Zhang, B., Zhang, M. X., & Zheng, Y. J. (2014, July). A hybrid biogeography-based optimization and fireworks algorithm. *Proceedings 2014 IEEE Congress on Evolutionary Computation (CEC)* (pp. 3200-3206). IEEE. 10.1109/CEC.2014.6900289

Zhang, B., Zheng, Y. J., Zhang, M. X., & Chen, S. Y. (2017). Fireworks algorithm with enhanced fireworks interaction. [TCBB]. *IEEE/ACM Transactions on Computational Biology and Bioinformatics*, *14*(1), 42–55. doi:10.1109/TCBB.2015.2446487 PMID:28182542

Zhang, J., & Li, W. (2019, July). Last-Position Elimination-Based Fireworks Algorithm for Function Optimization. *Proceedings International Conference on Swarm Intelligence* (pp. 267-275). Springer, Cham. 10.1007/978-3-030-26369-0_25

Zhang, J., & Zhang, H. (2018, July). An Improved Back Propagation Neural Network Forecasting Model Using Variation Fireworks Algorithm for Short-time Traffic Flow. *Proceedings 2018 13th World Congress on Intelligent Control and Automation (WCICA)* (pp. 1085-1090). IEEE. 10.1109/WCICA.2018.8630368

Zhang, J., & Zhang, H. (2018, July). An Improved Back Propagation Neural Network Forecasting Model Using Variation Fireworks Algorithm for Short-time Traffic Flow. *Proceedings 2018 13th World Congress on Intelligent Control and Automation (WCICA)* (pp. 1085-1090). IEEE. 10.1109/WCICA.2018.8630368

Zhang, J., Zhu, S., & Zhou, M. (2017, July). From Resampling to Non-resampling: A Fireworks Algorithm-Based Framework for Solving Noisy Optimization Problems. *Proceedings International Conference on Swarm Intelligence* (pp. 485-492). Springer, Cham. 10.1007/978-3-319-61824-1_53

Zhang, L., & Wang, C. (2019, June). A Spectrum Allocation Algorithm Based on Non-cooperative Game. [IOP Publishing.]. *Journal of Physics: Conference Series*, *1213*(3). doi:10.1088/1742-6596/1213/3/032026

Zhang, M., Yuan, Y., Wang, R., & Cheng, W. (2018). Recognition of mixture control chart patterns based on fusion feature reduction and fireworks algorithm-optimized MSVM. *Pattern Analysis & Applications*, 1–12.

Zhang, Q., & Li, H. (2007). MOEA/D: A multiobjective evolutionary algorithm based on decomposition. *IEEE Transactions on Evolutionary Computation, 11*(6), 712–731. doi:10.1109/TEVC.2007.892759

Zhang, T., Ke, L., Li, J., Li, J., Li, Z., & Huang, J. (2016, July). Fireworks algorithm for the satellite link scheduling problem in the navigation constellation. *Proceedings 2016 IEEE Congress on Evolutionary Computation (CEC)* (pp. 4029-4037). IEEE. 10.1109/CEC.2016.7744301

Zhang, T., & Liu, Z. (2017). Fireworks algorithm for mean-VaR/CVaR models. *Physica A, 483*, 1–8. doi:10.1016/j.physa.2017.04.036

Zhang, X., & Hu, Y. (2019, June). Multiconstrained routing based on artificial bee colony algorithm and dynamic fireworks algorithm. [IOP Publishing.]. *Journal of Physics: Conference Series, 1237*(2). doi:10.1088/1742-6596/1237/2/022058

Zhang, Y., Liu, J., Zhou, H., Guo, K., & Tang, F. (n.d.). Intelligent Reconfiguration for Distributed Power Network with Multivariable Renewable Generation. *Proceedings* 2018 *Asian Conference on Energy, Power, and Transportation Electrification (ACEPT)* (pp. 1-5). IEEE. 10.1109/ACEPT.2018.8610870

Zhao, H., Zhang, C., & Ning, J. (n.d.). A core firework updating information guided dynamic fireworks algorithm for global optimization. *Soft Computing*, 1-27.

Zhao, X., Li, R., Zuo, X., & Tan, Y. (2017, July). Elite-Leading Fireworks Algorithm. *Proceedings International Conference on Swarm Intelligence* (pp. 493-500). Springer, Cham.

Zheng, S., Janecek, A., Li, J., & Tan, Y. (2014, July). Dynamic search in fireworks algorithm. *Proceedings 2014 IEEE Congress on evolutionary computation (CEC)* (pp. 3222-3229). IEEE. 10.1109/CEC.2014.6900485

Zheng, S., Janecek, A., & Tan, Y. (2013, June). Enhanced fireworks algorithm. *Proceedings 2013 IEEE Congress on evolutionary computation* (pp. 2069-2077). IEEE. 10.1109/CEC.2013.6557813

Zheng, S., Li, J., Janecek, A., & Tan, Y. (2017). A cooperative framework for fireworks algorithm. [TCBB]. *IEEE/ACM Transactions on Computational Biology and Bioinformatics, 14*(1), 27–41. doi:10.1109/TCBB.2015.2497227 PMID:26552094

Zheng, S., Liu, L., Yu, C., Li, J., & Tan, Y. (2014, October). Fireworks algorithm and its variants for solving ICSI2014 competition problems. *Proceedings International Conference in Swarm Intelligence* (pp. 442-451). Springer, Cham. 10.1007/978-3-319-11897-0_50

Zheng, S., & Tan, Y. (2013, March). A unified distance measure scheme for orientation coding in identification. *Proceedings 2013 IEEE Third international conference on information science and technology (ICIST)* (pp. 979-985). IEEE. 10.1109/ICIST.2013.6747701

Zheng, S., Yu, C., Li, J., & Tan, Y. (2015, May). Exponentially decreased dimension number strategy based dynamic search fireworks algorithm for solving CEC2015 competition problems. *Proceedings 2015 IEEE Congress on Evolutionary Computation (CEC)* (pp. 1083-1090). IEEE. 10.1109/CEC.2015.7257010

Zheng, Y., Wang, L., & Xi, P. (2018, August). Improved Ant Colony Algorithm for Multi-Agent Path Planning in Dynamic Environment. *Proceedings 2018 International Conference on Sensing, Diagnostics, Prognostics, and Control (SDPC)* (pp. 732-737). IEEE. 10.1109/SDPC.2018.8664885

Zheng, Y. J., Song, Q., & Chen, S. Y. (2013). Multiobjective fireworks optimization for variable-rate fertilization in oil crop production. *Applied Soft Computing*, *13*(11), 4253–4263. doi:10.1016/j.asoc.2013.07.004

Zheng, Y. J., Xu, X. L., Ling, H. F., & Chen, S. Y. (2015). A hybrid fireworks optimization method with differential evolution operators. *Neurocomputing*, *148*, 75–82. doi:10.1016/j.neucom.2012.08.075

Zhou, X., Zhao, Q., & Zhang, D. (2019, July). Discrete Fireworks Algorithm for Welding Robot Path Planning. [IOP Publishing.]. *Journal of Physics: Conference Series*, *1267*(1). doi:10.1088/1742-6596/1267/1/012003

Section 2
Algorithm Improvements on FWA

Chapter 2
Last-Position Elimination-Based Fireworks Algorithm for Function Optimization

JunQi Zhang
Tongji University, China

JianQing Chen
Tongji University, China

WeiZhi Li
Tongji University, China

ABSTRACT

Fireworks algorithm (FWA) searches the global optimum by the cooperation between the firework with the best fitness named as core firework (CF) and the other non-CFs. Loser-out tournament-based fireworks algorithm (LoTFWA) uses competition as a new manner of interaction. If the fitness of a firework cannot catch up with the best one, it is considered a loser and will be reinitialized. However, its independent selection operator may prevent non-CFs from aggregating to CF in the late search phase if they fall into different local optima. This chapter proposes a last-position, elimination-based fireworks algorithm which allocates more fireworks in the initial process to search. Then for every fixed number of generations, the firework with the worst fitness is eliminated and its sparks is reallocated to other fireworks. In the final stage of search, only CF survives with all the budget of sparks and thus the aggregation of non-CFs to CF is ensured. Experimental results performed show that the proposed algorithm significantly outperforms most of the state-of-the-art FWA variants.

DOI: 10.4018/978-1-7998-1659-1.ch002

Copyright © 2020, IGI Global. Copying or distributing in print or electronic forms without written permission of IGI Global is prohibited.

INTRODUCTION

Optimization problems play an important role in a scientific research field. In the past two decades, many stochastic and population-based optimization algorithms based on Swarm Intelligence (SI) (Dong & Zhou, 2016) (Gu, Yu & Hu, 2017) (Han et al., 2015) (Mareda, Gaudard & Romerio, 2017) were proposed. These algorithms have shown great success for solving optimization problems in many applications. Most of SI algorithms are inspired by some intelligent colony behaviors in nature like particle swarm optimization (PSO) (Eberhart, R., & Kennedy, J., 1995, October). Different from these algorithms, fireworks algorithm (FWA) proposed by Tan & Zhu (2010, June), as a rising SI optimization algorithm, is inspired by the explosion process of fireworks in the sky. In this algorithm, the explosion process of a firework can be considered as a search by the sparks in the local area around a specific point where the firework is set off. In order to balance exploration and exploitation, the better a firework's fitness is, the more sparks it generates and the smaller its explosion amplitude is, and vice versa. In recent years, many improved versions of FWA have been presented. Zheng, Janecek & Tan (2013, June) propose an enhanced fireworks algorithm (EFWA) with five modifications to FWA. Among these improvements, the selection operator is widely adopted. It employs an elitism-random selection method to select the candidate with the best fitness as a firework at first, and then chooses the rest randomly among all the individuals in current population. This operator decreases the time complexity while maintaining the performance similar to that of the original one. Based on the work of EFWA, Zheng, Janecek, Li & Tan (2014, July) propose the dynamic search fireworks algorithm (dynFWA). In it, the firework with best fitness in each generation is called core firework (CF) and others are called non-core fireworks (non-CFs). It uses a dynamic explosion amplitude for CF, while non-CFs use the same strategy as that in EFWA. Li, Zheng & Tan (2014, July) present an adaptive fireworks algorithm (AFWA) by using adaptive amplitude. In AFWA, explosion amplitude is calculated according to the already evaluated fitness of individuals adaptively. Li, Zheng & Tan (2016) propose a guided fireworks algorithm (GFWA) by introducing a novel guiding spark to improve FWA performance. Its idea is to use the objective function information acquired by explosion sparks to construct a guiding vector with a promising direction and adaptive length, and to generate an elite solution called a guiding spark by adding the guiding vector to the position of each firework.

Although many FWA variants are developed from EFWA, its dependent selection operator makes CF absorb non-CFs into its search range quickly and may result in premature convergence. To overcome this limitation, Zheng, Li, Janecek & Tan (2017) propose a cooperative framework for fireworks algorithm (CoFFWA) which can greatly enhance the exploitation ability of non-CFs by using an independent selection operator and increase the exploration capacity by a crowdness-avoiding cooperative strategy among the fireworks. Li & Tan (2017) propose a loser-out tournament-based fireworks algorithm (LoTFWA) which also utilizes an independent selection operator to select fireworks for the next generation. In LoT-FWA, fireworks compete with each other and the losers will be forced to restart from a new location. The competitive mechanism is based on the anticipation of fireworks' fitness. If the fitness of a firework cannot catch up with the best one with its current progress rate, then this firework is considered a loser and will be reinitialized to avoid wasting resources on searching unpromising areas.

From aforementioned algorithms, LoTFWA is a novel variant characterized by using competition as a new manner of interaction. Benefit from this mechanism, LoTFWA achieves better performance than other fireworks algorithms. However, its independent selection operator may prevent non-CFs from aggregating to CF in the late evolutionary stage. This chapter proposes a novel Last-position Elimination-based fireworks algorithm (LEFWA). At first, it allocates more fireworks at the initial phase to search and locate scattered local optima. Then for every G($>$1) generations, the firework with the worst fitness is eliminated and its budget of sparks is reallocated to other fireworks. At the final stage of optimization, only CF survives with all the budget of sparks and thus the aggregation of non-CFs to CF is guaranteed. This elimination mechanism reinforces exploitation by eliminating unpromising areas along with an evolution process and reveals where the true global optimum locates.

The rest of this chapter is organized as follows. Section RELATED WORK introduces the related work. Section PROPOSED ALGORITHM describes and analyzes the proposed algorithm in detail. Section EXPERIMENTS presents the experimental settings and results. Conclusions are given in Section CONCLUSION.

BACKGROUND

In this section, Loser-out Tournament Based Fireworks Algorithm (LoTFWA) is introduced in detail from following aspects: explosion operation, mutation operation, selection mechanism and loser-out tournament.

Explosion Operation

The explosion operation is the key operation in FWA. Certain numbers of explosion sparks will be generated around the fireworks within certain explosion amplitudes in each generation.

In LoTFWA, at first, it uses a new formula to calculate the number of explosion sparks for each firework which can allocate the resource more efficiently. The number of sparks for each firework depends on the ranking of its fitness value rather than the fitness value itself, it is calculated as follows:

$$S_i = M \cdot \frac{r_i^{-\alpha}}{\sum_{i=1}^{n} r_i^{-\alpha}} \tag{1}$$

where r_i is the fitness ranking of firework i, α is a parameter to control the shape of the distribution. The larger α is, the more explosion sparks good fireworks generate. M and n represent the total number of sparks and fireworks, respectively.

Secondly, LoTFWA adopts a dynamic amplitude update strategy for each firework which is first introduced in the dynFWA (Zheng, Janecek, Li & Tan, 2014, July).

$$A_i(t) = \begin{cases} A_i(t-1) \cdot \rho^+ & \text{if} f(X_i(t)) - f(X_i(t-1)) < 0 \\ A_i(t-1) \cdot \rho^- & \text{if} f(X_i(t)) - f(X_i(t-1)) \geq 0 \end{cases} \tag{2}$$

where $X_i(t)$ and $A_i(t)$ are the position and the amplitude of i-th firework at generation t, respectively. ρ^+ and ρ^- are the coefficients of amplification and reduction, respectively. Finally, the explosion sparks are generated uniformly within a hypercube. The radius of the hypercube is the explosion amplitude and the center of the hypercube is the position of the firework. Algorithm 1 shows how the explosion sparks are generated for each firework.

Algorithm 1. Generating explosion sparks for X_i
    1: **for** $j = 1$ to S_i **do**
    2: **for** $d = 1, 2, D$ **do**
    3: $s_{i,j}^d = X_i^d + A_i \cdot rand(-1,1)$
    4: **if** $s_{i,j}^d < B_L$ **or** $s_{i,j}^d > B_U$ **then**
    5: $s_{i,j}^d = B_L + (B_U - B_L) \cdot rand(0,1)$
    6: **end if**
    7: **end for**
    8: **end for**
    9: **return** all the $s_{i,j}$

Mutation Operation

LoTFWA utilizes a recently proposed guiding spark (Li, Zheng & Tan, 2016) as the mutation operator which is simple and efficient. Algorithm 2 shows how the guiding sparks are generated for each firework. σ is a parameter to control the proportion of adopted explosion sparks. Note that only one guiding spark is generated for each firework.

Algorithm 2. Generating the guiding spark for X_i
    1: Sort the sparks by their fitness values $f(s_{i,j})$ in the ascending order
    2 $\Delta_i = X_i + \dfrac{1}{\sigma S_i}(\sum_{j=1}^{\sigma S_i} s_{i,j} - \sum_{j=S_i - \sigma S_i + 1}^{S_i} s_{i,j})$
    3: $gs_i = X_i + \Delta_i$
    4: **return** gs_i

Selection Mechanism

LoTFWA adopts an independent selection operator to enhance the exploitation ability of non-CFs. In LoTFWA, each firework and its sparks are regarded as a group. The best candidate x_i^* in group i in the current generation is selected as a new firework for the next generation.

Loser-out Tournament

The search manner of the conventional fireworks algorithm is based on the cooperation of several fireworks. While in LoTFWA, the competition becomes a new manner of interaction, in which the fireworks are compared with each other not only according to their current status but also according to their progress rate. The progress rate of the i-th firework in generation g is calculated as follows:

$$\delta_i^g = f(X_i^{g-1}) - f(X_i^g) \geq 0 \tag{3}$$

The prediction of its fitness in the final generation g_{max} is calculated as follows:

$$f(X_l^{\widetilde{g_{max}}}) = f(X_i^g) - \delta_i^g(g_{max} - g) \ . \tag{4}$$

The *i*-th firework is considered as a loser and will be reinitialized if the prediction is worse than the current best one, i.e., $f(\widetilde{X_i^{g_{max}}}) > min_j f(X_j^g)$. Algorithm 3 shows how the loser-out tournament mechanism works in every generation.

Algorithm 3. Loser-out tournament
    1: **for** i = 1 to n **do**
    2: **if** $f(X_i^{g-1}) - f(X_i^g) \geq 0$ **then**
    3: $\delta_i^g = f(X_i^{g-1}) - f(X_i^g)$
    4: **end if**
    5: **if** $f(X_i^g) - \delta_i^g(g_{max} - g) > min_j(f_j^g)$ **then**
    6: reinitialize the i-th firework
    7: **end if**
    8: **end for**

Integrating the above mechanisms, the main process of LoTFWA is described in Algorithm 4.

Algorithm 4. LoTFWA
    1: Initialize n fireworks and evaluate their fitness
    2: **while** (stopping criterion not met) **do**
    3: **for** i = 1 to *n* **do**
    4: Calculate the number of sparks using (1)
    5: Calculate explosion amplitude using (2)
    6: Generate explosion sparks using Algorithm 1
    7: Generate the guiding spark using Algorithm 2
    8: Evaluate all the sparks
    9: Select the new firework independently
    10: **end for**
    11: Perform the loser-out tournament using Algorithm 3
    12: **end while**

PROPOSED ALGORITHM

In order to solve the problem of LoTFWA that non-CFs cannot aggregate to CF in the final stage, this work proposes LEFWA which adopts a last-position elimination mechanism based on LoTFWA. The description and analysis of the proposed algorithm are given in this section.

LEFWA

At the initial phase, LEFWA initializes *n* fireworks randomly in a search space and evaluates their fitness. At each generation, same as LoTFWA, the number of sparks and explosion amplitude of each firework are calculated. After each firework generates its explosion sparks and the guiding spark, the independent selection operator and loser-out tournament strategy are adopted. Then, the last-position elimination mechanism is introduced in the proposed LEFWA. For every $G(>1)$ generations, the firework with the worst fitness is eliminated and G is calculated as follows:

$$G = \frac{(F_{max} - n) / M}{n} \tag{5}$$

where F_{max} is the maximum number of fitness evaluations, M is the total number of sparks and n is the initial number of fireworks. $(F_{max} - n)/M$ calculates a rough total number of generations. Because of the initialization of n fireworks at the beginning of the algorithm, n should be subtracted from F_{max}. Then the total number of generations is divided into n segments and each contains roughly G generations. For every G generations, the current number of fireworks ň is updated as:

$$ň = ň - 1 \tag{6}$$

The budget of sparks of the eliminated firework is reallocated to other better fireworks. At the final stage of evolution, only CF survives with all the budget of sparks and thus the aggregation of non-CFs to CF is guaranteed. This elimination mechanism enhances the exploitation ability by giving up unpromising areas gradually and reveals where the true global optimum locates. The procedure of LEFWA is shown in Algorithm 5.

Algorithm 5. LEFWA

    1: Initialize n fireworks and evaluate their fitness
    2: Calculate G using (5)
    3: **while** (stopping criterion not met) **do**
    4: **if** current generation is divisible by G and ň > 1 **then**
    5: Eliminate the worst firework
    6: Update ň using (6)
    7: **end if**
    8: **for** i = 1 to *ň* **do**
    9: Calculate the number of sparks using (1)
    10: Calculate explosion amplitude using (2)
    11: Generate explosion sparks using **Algorithm 1**
    12: Generate the guiding spark using **Algorithm 2**
    13: Evaluate all the sparks
    14: Select the new firework independently
    15: **end for**
    16: Perform the loser-out tournament using **Algorithm 3**
    17: **end while**

Analysis of LEFWA

The diversity of population decreases gradually due to the last-position elimination mechanism in LEFWA. To solve this problem, LEFWA needs to initialize more fireworks than LoTFWA. This work utilizes the average distance between each candidate and the center of whole population to measure the diversity of population, which is calculated as follows:

$$diversity = \frac{\sum_{i=1}^{n+M}(\|x_i - x^c\|)}{n+M} \tag{7}$$

where x_c is the center of all candidates and $x_i - x^c$ represents the distance between the i-th candidate and x_c. For the fourth function of CEC2013 benchmark (Liang, Qu, Suganthan & Hernández-Díaz, 2013), Fig.1 shows the diversity curves of LEFWA as compared to LoTFWA's in two cases, one with the same initial number of fireworks, and the other with a different number. n_0(LEFWA) and n_0(LoTFWA) are the initial number of fireworks in LEFWA and LoTFWA, respectively. We calculate the diversity of population for every 100 evaluations. In each subfigure, X-axis represents the number of calculations and Y-axis represents the diversity of population.

Figure 1. The diversity curve of LEFWA and LoTFWA

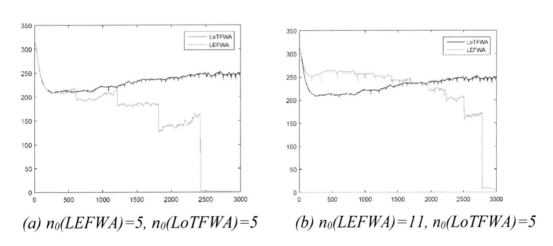

(a) n_0(LEFWA)=5, n_0(LoTFWA)=5   *(b) n_0(LEFWA)=11, n_0(LoTFWA)=5*

As shown in Figure 1(a), the diversity of population in LEFWA decreases obviously for every G generations as caused by the last-position elimination mechanism. As a result, the exploration capability of LEFWA is worse than that of LoTFWA. In Figure 1(b), LEFWA has higher diversity than LoTFWA in the early evolutionary stage because of more initial fireworks. Although the diversity of population in LEFWA decreases along with an evolution process, LEFWA has better capability of exploration at the early evolutionary phase and better exploitation ability at the late evolutionary stage than LoTFWA respectively, which are exactly a feature that evolutionary algorithms should own. In addition, Figure 1 shows that LoTFWA still maintains a high diversity at the late evolutionary stage, indicating that non-CFs cannot aggregate to CF in the final stage. It is worth mentioning that the reinitialization triggered by the loser-out tournament mechanism makes the diversity of LoTFWA increase at the late stage.

EXPERIMENTS

Experimental Settings

To show the performance of LEFWA, total 28 functions in CEC2013 benchmark (Liang, Qu, Suganthan & Hernández-Díaz, 2013) and total 15 functions in CEC2015 benchmark (Liang, Qu, Suganthan & Chen, 2014) are used, which contain unimodal, multimodal, hybrid and composition functions. For convenience, F1-F28 and F29-F43 represent functions in CEC2013 and CEC2015 benchmark, respectively. For each function, dimension D is set to 30, and the maximum number of fitness evaluations is 10000D. For a comprehensive comparison, EFWA (Zheng, Janecek & Tan, 2013, June), dynFWA (Zheng, Janecek, Li & Tan, 2014, July), CoFFWA (Zheng, Li, Janecek & Tan, 2017), GFWA (Li, Zheng & Tan, 2016) and LoTFWA (Li & Tan, 2017) are also tested. Their parameter configurations are the same as those in the corresponding references. Each algorithm is run for 51 times independently on each function. At the end of each run, it outputs the error that is defined as $f(X^*) - f^*$, where X^* represents the best solution found by it and f^* is the global optimal fitness of a function. Finally, for all algorithms, the means and standard deviations of errors are given.

In LEFWA, all parameter configurations are the same as in LoTFWA. However, as mentioned above, because of the elimination mechanism, the initial number of fireworks in LEFWA n is higher than those in LoTFWA, as listed in Table 1. To be fair, the total number of fitness evaluations in all algorithms is set to the same value, i.e., 10000D.

Table 1. Parameter Configurations

Algorithms	Parameter Settings
EFWA	n = 5, M = 50, Â = 40
dynFWA	n = 5, M = 150, Â = 40, $A_C(1)$ = 200, ρ^+ = 1.2, ρ^- = 0.9
CoFFWA	n = 5, M = 150, Â = 40, $A_C(1)$ = 200, ρ^+ = 1.2, ρ^- = 0.9
GFWA	n = 1, M = 200, σ= 0.2, Â = 40, $A_C(1)$ = 200, ρ^+ = 1.2, ρ^- = 0.9
LoTFWA	n = 5, M = 300, σ= 0.2, α=0, $A_i(1)$ = 200, ρ^+ = 1.2, ρ^- = 0.9
LEFWA	n = 11, M = 300, σ= 0.2, α=0, $A_i(1)$ = 200, ρ^+ = 1.2, ρ^- = 0.9

Experimental Results

The statistical results on CEC2013 and CEC2015 benchmarks are listed in Tables 2 and 3, which represent the accuracy of each algorithm. The best result among those obtained from all contenders is presented in a bold face. "Mean" and "Std." are the mean results and standard deviations of 51 independent runs, respectively. *AR* represents the average rank of an algorithm which is calculated by the sum of ranking values on functions divided by the number of functions. Naturally, the less the average rank, the better the performance.

Besides, a Wilcoxon rank sum test is conducted between each algorithm and LEFWA. It tests whether performances of two algorithms are significantly different (with confidence level 95%). The result of such test is shown in Table 4 and presented as a+/b/c-, which means LEFWA is significantly better than/ not significantly different from/significantly worse than the corresponding algorithm on a/b/c functions.

In CEC2013, LEFWA outperforms all the contenders. As shown in Table 2, its average ranks of mean error and standard deviation are 1.96 and 2.21, both of which rank the best and obviously better than the other algorithms. The Wilcoxon rank sum test shows that LEFWA significantly outperforms EFWA on 26 functions and dynFWA on 21 functions in a total of 28 functions. Compared to CoFFWA and GFWA, LEFWA significantly outperforms on 22 and 19 functions, respectively. Additionally, LEFWA significantly outperforms LoTFWA on 10 functions and is significantly worse than it on 3 functions.

This result indicates that LEFWA has better performance than LoTFWA's.

In CEC2015, LEFWA also outperforms all algorithms. In Table 3, the average rank of mean error and standard deviation of LEFWA are 1.60 and 2.13, which are obviously better than the second place. The Wilcoxon rank sum test shows that LEFWA significantly outperforms EFWA on 12 functions and dynFWA on 13 functions in total 15 functions. Besides, LEFWA significantly outperforms CoFFWA on 13 functions and GFWA on 12 functions. Additionally, compared with LoTFWA, LEFWA outperforms on 4 functions and is significantly worse on no function.

These results demonstrate that LEFWA significantly outperforms other state-of-the-art FWA variants.

CONCLUSION

This chapter reviews LoTFWA that utilizes an independent selection operator and points out its possible slow convergence as caused by non-core fireworks falling into local optima at the late optimization stage. In order to overcome this limitation, this chapter introduces an elimination mechanism into LoTFWA, resulting LEFWA. The proposed algorithm eliminates the firework with the worst fitness for every $G(>1)$ generations and thus guarantees the aggregation of non-CFs to CF. This last-position elimination mechanism enhances the algorithm's exploitation ability by giving up unpromising areas gradually and reveals where the true global optimum may locate. Extensive experiments demonstrate the superiority of the proposed algorithm over LoTFWA. LEFWA outperforms all representative FWA variants significantly on different types of functions.

FUTURE RESEARCH DIRECTIONS

In the future, we intend to design a more adaptive elimination mechanism by using learning automaton (LA) (Zhang, Wang & Zhou, 2014; Zhang, Wang, Zang & Zhou, 2015) or optimal computing budget allocation (OCBA) (Zhang, Zhang, Wang & Zhou, 2016; Zhang, Li, Wang, Zang & Zhou, 2016), e.g., an adaptive instead of fixed G. Moreover, we plan to apply this framework to optimization problems subject to indeterminate environments, e.g., noisy environment (Zhang, Xu, Li, Kang & Zhou, 2014,

Table 2. Statistical results on CEC2013 benchmark

	EFWA		dynFWA		CoFFWA		GFWA		LoTFWA		LEFWA	
	Mean	Std.	Mean	Std.	Mean	Std.	Mean	Std.	Mean	Std.	Mean	Std.
1	8.99E-02	1.34E-02	4.46E-13	1.28E-13	6.20E-13	2.09E-13	2.67E-14	7.40E-14	1.60E-13	1.05E-13	0.00E+00	0.00E+00
2	5.77E+05	2.08E+05	7.44E+05	3.38E+05	1.02E+06	4.62E+05	6.87E+05	2.64E+05	8.51E+05	3.41E+05	7.38E+05	3.43E+05
3	1.08E+08	2.02E+08	6.97E+07	8.33E+07	9.37E+07	1.32E+08	3.51E+07	6.36E+07	1.88E+07	1.46E+07	1.17E+07	1.53E+07
4	1.18E+00	3.44E-01	1.10E+01	5.15E+00	1.96E+03	1.68E+03	5.56E-05	7.62E-05	2.19E+03	9.19E+02	6.76E+02	3.62E+02
5	8.56E-02	1.18E-02	5.39E-04	7.88E-05	7.39E-04	1.18E-04	1.36E-04	3.19E-05	1.56E-03	1.88E-04	1.38E-03	1.72E-04
6	3.05E+01	2.61E+01	2.67E+01	2.46E+01	3.35E+01	2.74E+01	3.17E+01	2.63E+01	1.41E+01	7.94E+00	1.06E+01	5.92E+00
7	1.32E+02	3.77E+01	9.97E+01	2.69E+01	9.17E+01	1.77E+01	7.35E+01	2.75E+01	6.28E+01	1.71E+01	6.83E+01	1.53E+01
8	2.10E+01	5.19E-02	2.09E+01	7.18E-02	2.09E+01	9.18E-02	2.10E+01	8.32E-02	2.09E+01	6.12E-02	2.09E+01	7.75E-02
9	3.08E+01	4.32E+00	2.35E+01	3.29E+00	2.35E+01	4.18E+00	1.94E+01	3.50E+00	1.52E+01	2.96E+00	1.61E+01	2.49E+00
10	8.68E-01	5.99E-02	4.13E-02	2.55E-02	5.11E-02	2.63E-02	6.05E-02	2.95E-02	4.74E-03	5.44E-03	6.14E-03	6.38E-03
11	4.47E+02	8.10E+01	9.97E+01	2.59E+01	9.78E+01	.56E+012	8.37E+01	2.45E+01	6.56E+01	1.21E+01	6.99E+01	1.30E+01
12	6.29E+02	1.28E+02	1.54E+02	4.86E+01	1.54E+02	5.20E+01	1.30E+02	4.68E+01	7.10E+01	1.26E+01	7.17E+01	1.27E+01
13	4.59E+02	7.97E+01	2.44E+02	5.22E+01	.48E+022	5.25E+01	2.18E+02	5.31E+01	1.51E+02	2.37E+01	1.42E+02	1.98E+01
14	4.06E+03	5.59E+02	2.88E+03	5.54E+02	2.85E+03	5.20E+02	2.87E+03	5.52E+02	.73E+032	4.40E+02	2.65E+03	4.15E+02
15	4.08E+03	6.39E+02	3.72E+03	7.71E+02	3.47E+03	6.11E+02	3.74E+03	7.09E+02	2.88E+03	3.93E+02	2.76E+03	.19E+023
16	6.11E-01	2.43E-01	4.51E-01	2.74E-01	4.30E-01	2.95E-01	1.36E-01	1.64E-01	6.30E-02	2.05E-02	9.37E-02	3.89E-02
17	3.17E+02	6.98E+01	1.45E+02	3.11E+01	1.17E+02	2.00E+01	1.11E+02	2.46E+01	9.65E+01	9.84E+00	1.01E+02	1.34E+01
18	1.74E+02	4.03E+01	1.85E+02	5.83E+01	1.72E+02	3.43E+01	1.02E+02	2.80E+01	9.56E+01	1.18E+01	9.64E+01	1.16E+01
19	1.18E+01	3.65E+00	6.87E+00	1.95E+00	6.41E+00	2.17E+00	5.52E+00	1.75E+00	3.61E+00	5.70E-01	3.57E+00	5.29E-01
20	1.46E+01	1.44E-01	1.31E+01	1.21E+00	1.30E+01	1.15E+00	1.30E+01	1.28E+00	1.34E+01	9.89E-01	1.36E+01	1.02E+00
21	3.21E+02	8.21E+01	3.21E+02	8.31E+01	2.13E+02	6.06E+01	3.07E+02	7.92E+01	1.98E+02	3.13E+01	1.94E+02	4.20E+01
22	5.51E+03	9.33E+02	3.39E+03	6.12E+02	3.46E+03	5.70E+02	3.11E+03	7.06E+02	3.60E+03	4.49E+02	3.44E+03	4.73E+02
23	5.88E+03	8.46E+02	4.57E+03	8.71E+02	4.44E+03	6.86E+02	4.58E+03	8.31E+02	3.57E+03	4.55E+02	3.58E+03	4.15E+02
24	3.24E+02	5.49E+01	2.73E+02	1.34E+01	2.72E+02	2.15E+01	2.60E+02	1.46E+01	2.21E+02	2.25E+01	2.23E+02	2.62E+01
25	3.56E+02	2.52E+01	2.94E+02	1.18E+01	2.95E+02	1.28E+01	2.84E+02	1.15E+01	2.71E+02	1.82E+01	2.74E+02	1.24E+01
26	3.37E+02	8.55E+01	2.64E+02	8.04E+01	2.12E+02	4.15E+01	2.45E+02	7.05E+01	1.96E+02	8.87E+00	1.98E+02	6.83E+00
27	1.27E+03	1.27E+02	9.47E+02	9.84E+01	8.74E+02	2.03E+02	8.38E+02	8.75E+01	4.93E+02	1.43E+02	5.86E+02	1.77E+02
28	4.16E+03	2.18E+03	3.64E+02	2.78E+02	3.08E+02	1.74E+02	3.42E+02	2.10E+02	2.73E+02	6.93E+01	2.57E+02	8.31E+01
AR.	5.54	4.89	4.25	3.96	4.00	4.21	3.14	3.46	2.11	2.25	**1.96**	**2.21**

Table 3. Statistical results on CEC2015 benchmark

	EFWA		dynFWA		CoFFWA		GFWA		LoTFWA		LEFWA	
	Mean	Std.	Mean	Std.	Mean	Std.	Mean	Std.	Mean	Std.	Mean	Std.
29	1.20E+06	4.37E+05	1.06E+06	4.55E+05	1.01E+06	4.86E+05	1.03E+06	5.35E+05	8.16E+05	3.28E+05	7.29E+05	3.42E+05
30	1.32E+05	2.58E+04	3.36E+03	3.51E+03	3.99E+03	3.94E+03	3.41E+03	3.33E+03	3.69E+02	5.92E+02	1.83E+02	2.57E+02
31	2.02E+01	3.42E-02	2.00E+01	4.26E-06	2.00E+01	2.46E-03	2.00E+01	2.36E-06	2.00E+01	1.42E-05	2.00E+01	2.49E-05
32	3.97E+02	8.97E+01	1.42E+02	3.48E+01	1.36E+02	3.53E+01	1.10E+02	3.89E+01	7.39E+01	1.22E+01	7.63E+01	1.33E+01
33	4.07E+03	6.48E+02	3.49E+03	7.21E+02	3.10E+03	5.39E+02	3.22E+03	6.36E+02	2.41E+03	3.69E+02	2.37E+03	4.04E+02
34	5.26E+04	3.16E+04	5.68E+04	3.28E+04	5.78E+04	3.42E+04	3.59E+04	2.21E+04	2.51E+04	1.30E+04	2.18E+04	1.10E+04
35	2.38E+01	2.32E+01	1.72E+01	1.38E+01	1.38E+01	2.33E+00	1.75E+01	1.63E+01	1.01E+01	1.44E+00	1.02E+01	1.30E+00
36	2.98E+04	1.67E+04	3.89E+04	2.08E+04	4.52E+04	2.27E+04	4.08E+04	2.40E+04	1.82E+04	9.45E+03	1.66E+04	8.62E+03
37	1.94E+02	1.87E+02	1.23E+02	7.01E+01	1.12E+02	3.63E+01	1.20E+02	5.47E+01	1.04E+02	3.00E-01	1.04E+02	2.92E-01
38	4.56E+04	1.76E+04	5.12E+04	2.51E+04	6.45E+04	3.23E+04	3.07E+04	1.64E+04	4.07E+04	1.88E+04	3.91E+04	1.87E+04
39	1.03E+03	4.66E+02	6.86E+02	2.65E+02	3.91E+02	1.94E+02	5.20E+02	1.99E+02	3.04E+02	7.81E-01	2.93E+02	5.32E+01
40	1.09E+02	1.20E+00	1.11E+02	2.01E+00	1.08E+02	9.77E-01	1.10E+02	1.81E+00	1.09E+02	9.98E-01	1.09E+02	9.17E-01
41	1.88E+02	1.00E+02	1.28E+02	5.94E+00	1.28E+02	5.50E+00	1.26E+02	5.38E+00	1.21E+02	5.06E+00	1.21E+02	4.22E+00
42	3.48E+04	2.44E+03	3.36E+04	1.67E+03	2.93E+04	9.76E+03	3.30E+04	1.51E+03	2.71E+04	1.05E+04	2.28E+04	1.41E+04
43	1.00E+02	1.07E-02	1.00E+02	6.75E-12	1.00E+02	6.30E-12	1.00E+02	1.28E-13	1.00E+02	5.25E-09	1.00E+02	2.33E-09
AR.	5.40	4.80	4.53	4.20	3.80	4.00	3.60	3.47	2.07	2.40	**1.60**	**2.13**

Table 4. Wilcoxon test between each algorithm and LEFWA

Benchmark	EFWA	dynFWA	CoFFWA	GFWA	LoTFWA
CEC2013	26+/0/2-	21+/4/3-	22+/4/2-	19+/5/4-	10+/15/3-
CEC2015	12+/3/0-	13+/1/1-	13+/0/2-	12+/1/2-	4+/11/0-
Total	38+/3/2-	34+/5/4-	35+/4/4-	31+/6/6-	14+/26/3-

October) and dynamic one (Pekdemir & Topcuoglu, 2016, July; Wang, Xia, Meng & Li, 2017; Wang, Ding, Jiang, Zhou & Zheng, 2015; Tian, Ren & Zhou, 2016; Tian, Zhou, Li, Zhang & Jia, 2016; Tian, Zhou, Chu, Qiang & Hu, 2014; Tian, Zhou & Chu, 2013).

REFERENCES

Dong, W., & Zhou, M. (2016). A supervised learning and control method to improve particle swarm optimization algorithms. *IEEE Transactions on Systems, Man, and Cybernetics Systems*, *47*(7), 1135–1148. doi:10.1109/TSMC.2016.2560128

Eberhart, R., & Kennedy, J. (1995, October). A new optimizer using particle swarm theory. *MHS'95 Proceedings of the Sixth International Symposium on Micro Machine and Human Science* (pp. 39-43). IEEE. 10.1109/MHS.1995.494215

Gu, W., Yu, Y., & Hu, W. (2017). Artificial bee colony algorithmbased parameter estimation of fractional-order chaotic system with time delay. *IEEE/CAA Journal of Automatica Sinica, 4*(1), 107-113.

Han, W., Xu, J., Zhou, M., Tian, G., Wang, P., Shen, X., & Hou, E. (2015). Cuckoo search and particle filter-based inversing approach to estimating defects via magnetic flux leakage signals. *IEEE Transactions on Magnetics, 52*(4), 1–11. doi:10.1109/TMAG.2015.2498119

Li, J., & Tan, Y. (2017). Loser-Out Tournament-Based Fireworks Algorithm for Multimodal Function Optimization. *IEEE Transactions on Evolutionary Computation, 22*(5), 679–691. doi:10.1109/TEVC.2017.2787042

Li, J., Zheng, S., & Tan, Y. (2014, July). Adaptive fireworks algorithm. *Proceedings 2014 IEEE Congress on evolutionary computation (CEC)* (pp. 3214-3221). IEEE. 10.1109/CEC.2014.6900418

Li, J., Zheng, S., & Tan, Y. (2016). The effect of information utilization: Introducing a novel guiding spark in the fireworks algorithm. *IEEE Transactions on Evolutionary Computation, 21*(1), 153–166. doi:10.1109/TEVC.2016.2589821

Liang, J. J., Qu, B. Y., Suganthan, P. N., & Chen, Q. (2014). Problem definitions and evaluation criteria for the CEC 2015 competition on learning-based real-parameter single objective optimization. Technical Report201411A, Computational Intelligence Laboratory, Zhengzhou University, China and Technical Report, Nanyang Technological University, Singapore, 29, 625-640.

Liang, J. J., Qu, B. Y., Suganthan, P. N., & Hernández-Díaz, A. G. (2013). Problem definitions and evaluation criteria for the CEC 2013 special session on real-parameter optimization. Computational Intelligence Laboratory, Zhengzhou University, China and Nanyang Technological University, Singapore. *Technical Report, 201212*(34), 281–295.

Mareda, T., Gaudard, L., & Romerio, F. (2017). A parametric genetic algorithm approach to assess complementary options of large scale windsolar coupling. *IEEE/CAA Journal of Automatica Sinica, 4*(2), 260-272.

Pekdemir, H., & Topcuoglu, H. R. (2016, July). Enhancing fireworks algorithms for dynamic optimization problems. *Proceedings 2016 IEEE congress on evolutionary computation (CEC)* (pp. 4045-4052). IEEE.

Tan, Y., & Zhu, Y. (2010, June). Fireworks algorithm for optimization. *Proceedings International conference in swarm intelligence* (pp. 355-364). Springer, Berlin, Germany.

Tian, G., Ren, Y., & Zhou, M. (2016). Dual-objective scheduling of rescue vehicles to distinguish forest fires via differential evolution and particle swarm optimization combined algorithm. *IEEE Transactions on Intelligent Transportation Systems, 17*(11), 3009–3021. doi:10.1109/TITS.2015.2505323

Tian, G., Zhou, M., & Chu, J. (2013). A chance constrained programming approach to determine the optimal disassembly sequence. *IEEE Transactions on Automation Science and Engineering, 10*(4), 1004–1013. doi:10.1109/TASE.2013.2249663

Tian, G., Zhou, M., Chu, J., Qiang, T., & Hu, H. (2014). Stochastic cost-profit tradeoff model for locating an automotive service enterprise. *IEEE Transactions on Automation Science and Engineering, 12*(2), 580–587. doi:10.1109/TASE.2013.2297623

Tian, G., Zhou, M., Li, P., Zhang, C., & Jia, H. (2016). Multiobjective optimization models for locating vehicle inspection stations subject to stochastic demand, varying velocity and regional constraints. *IEEE Transactions on Intelligent Transportation Systems, 17*(7), 1978–1987. doi:10.1109/TITS.2016.2514277

Wang, B., Xia, X., Meng, H., & Li, T. (2017). Bad-scenario-set robust optimization framework with two objectives for uncertain scheduling systems. *IEEE/CAA Journal of Automatica Sinica, 4*(1), 143-153.

Wang, P., Ding, Z., Jiang, C., Zhou, M., & Zheng, Y. (2015). Automatic web service composition based on uncertainty execution effects. *IEEE Transactions on Services Computing, 9*(4), 551–565. doi:10.1109/TSC.2015.2412943

Zhang, J., Li, Z., Wang, C., Zang, D., & Zhou, M. (2016). Approximate simulation budget allocation for subset ranking. *IEEE Transactions on Control Systems Technology, 25*(1), 358–365. doi:10.1109/TCST.2016.2539329

Zhang, J., Wang, C., Zang, D., & Zhou, M. (2015). Incorporation of optimal computing budget allocation for ordinal optimization into learning automata. *IEEE Transactions on Automation Science and Engineering, 13*(2), 1008–1017. doi:10.1109/TASE.2015.2450535

Zhang, J., Wang, C., & Zhou, M. (2014). Fast and epsilon-optimal discretized pursuit learning automata. *IEEE Transactions on Cybernetics, 45*(10), 2089–2099. doi:10.1109/TCYB.2014.2365463 PMID:25415995

Zhang, J., Xu, L., Li, J., Kang, Q., & Zhou, M. (2014, October). Integrating particle swarm optimization with learning automata to solve optimization problems in noisy environment. *Proceedings 2014 IEEE International Conference on Systems, Man, and Cybernetics (SMC)* (pp. 1432-1437). IEEE. 10.1109/SMC.2014.6974116

Zhang, J., Zhang, L., Wang, C., & Zhou, M. (2016). Approximately Optimal Computing Budget Allocation for Selection of the Best and Worst Designs. *IEEE Transactions on Automatic Control, 62*(7), 3249–3261. doi:10.1109/TAC.2016.2628158

Zheng, S., Janecek, A., Li, J., & Tan, Y. (2014, July). Dynamic search in fireworks algorithm. *Proceedings 2014 IEEE Congress on evolutionary computation (CEC)* (pp. 3222-3229). IEEE. 10.1109/CEC.2014.6900485

Zheng, S., Janecek, A., & Tan, Y. (2013, June). Enhanced fireworks algorithm. *Proceedings 2013 IEEE Congress on evolutionary computation* (pp. 2069-2077). IEEE. 10.1109/CEC.2013.6557813

Zheng, S., Li, J., Janecek, A., & Tan, Y. (2017). A cooperative framework for fireworks algorithm. *IEEE/ACM Transactions on Computational Biology and Bioinformatics (TCBB), 14*(1), 27-41.

Chapter 3
Explosion Operation of Fireworks Algorithm

Jun Yu

 https://orcid.org/0000-0001-5029-0294

JSPS Research Fellow, Kyushu University, Japan

Hideyuki Takagi

Kyushu University, Japan

ABSTRACT

This chapter briefly reviews the basic explosion mechanism used in the fireworks algorithm (FWA) and comprehensively investigates relevant research on explosion operations. Since the explosion mechanism is one of the most core operations directly affecting the performance of FWA, the authors focus on analyzing the FWA explosion operation and highlighting two novel explosion strategies: a multi-layer explosion strategy and a scouting explosion strategy. The multi-layer explosion strategy allows an individual firework to perform multiple explosions instead of the single explosion used in the original FWA, where each round of explosion can be regarded as a layer; the scouting explosion strategy controls an individual firework to generate spark individuals one by one instead of generating all spark individuals within the explosion amplitude at once. The authors then introduce several other effective strategies to further improve the performance of FWA by full using the information generated by the explosion operation. Finally, the authors list some open topics for discussion.

INTRODUCTION

The fireworks algorithm (FWA) (Tan & Zhu, 2014) is a population-based meta-heuristic optimization algorithm that simulates the explosion process of real fireworks repeatedly in order to find the global optimum. Although it is a young member of the family of algorithms in the evolutionary computation (EC) community, it attracts a lot of attention from practitioners owing to its huge potential due to its e.g. ease of use, robustness, efficiency, parallelism, and other characteristics. With the rapid increase

DOI: 10.4018/978-1-7998-1659-1.ch003

Copyright © 2020, IGI Global. Copying or distributing in print or electronic forms without written permission of IGI Global is prohibited.

in its popularity and real-world applications, development of FWA is booming and it has become an important branch in EC algorithms.

Since the basic FWA was first proposed in 2010, researchers have frequently proposed many effective strategies to further improve its performance. For example, Zheng et al. modified five operations used in FWA to develop a more efficient version, enhanced FWA (EFWA) (Zheng, 2013). Yu et al. used the explosion information to calculate a convergence point that has a high possibility to locate in the global optimal area and used it as an elite individual to accelerate the convergence of FWA (Yu, Tan & Takagi, 2018). Pei et al. adopted different sampling methods to approximate the fitness landscape to accelerate the FWA search (Pei, 2012). Some work focuses on developing powerful hybrid algorithms by introducing operations from other EC algorithms into FWA to inherit their strengths, such as differential mutation (Yu & Kelley, 2014), covariance mutation (Yu & Tan, 2015), the gravitational search operator (Zhu, 2016), chaotic systems (Gong, 2016), and the firefly algorithm (Wang, 2019). Additionally, FWA has also been applied to solve various types of optimization problems, such as multimodal optimization (Yu, 2019), multi-objective optimization (Zhan, 2018), constrained optimization (Bacanin, 2015), dynamic optimization (Pekdemir, 2016), and large-scale optimization (Pandey, 2018).

FWA has not only flourished in an academic setting, but also appeared frequently in the industry in recent years. For example, FWA successfully solved the network reconfiguration required to reduce power loss and improve voltage distribution (Mohamed, 2014); it was also used to design the coefficients of a digital filter (Gao, 2011). Actually, FWA has also perfectly solved many other complex real-world problems, such as retinal image registration (Tuba, 2017), wireless sensor network coverage (Tuba, 2016), distributed resource scheduling (Reddy, 2016), image segmentation (Misra, 2017), capacitated vehicle routing problem (Yang, 2019), and others (Zhang, 2019).

The main objective of this chapter is to comprehensively analyze the explosion operation, one of FWA's three core operations, to thoroughly understand FWA and to highlight two effective new explosion strategies in detail. The second one is to introduce several strategies for accelerating FWA search by fully using the information generated by the explosion operation. Finally, the authors point out several potential research topics for discussion.

Explosion Operation

FWA was created by observing the explosion phenomenon of real fireworks and believing that an explosion can be thought of as corresponding to a local search centered on a particular point. Based on this inspiration, FWA simulates an explosion operation repeatedly and, through cooperation among firework individuals, gradually evolves to the global optimal area. Similar to other EC algorithms, FWA randomly generates multiple firework individuals to form an initial population, and then each firework individual is adaptively assigned an explosion amplitude and a number of generated spark individuals according to its fitness before the explosion operation is performed. Usually, a firework individual with better fitness generates many spark individuals within a small explosion amplitude for exploitation, while a poor firework individual generates a few spark individuals within a large explosion amplitude for exploration. FWA also employs mutation operations to increase individual diversity, and spark individuals generated in this way are referred to as mutation spark individuals. Next, a selection operation is used to select firework individuals in the next generation from all current individuals, including current firework individuals, explosion spark individuals, and mutation spark individuals. The above three operations - the explosion operation, the mutation operation, and the selection operation - are repeated until a termination condition is satisfied. Figure 1 illustrates the general optimization framework of a basic FWA.

Figure 1. The search process of the basic FWA. (a) initial firework individuals (black five-pointed stars) are randomly generated, (b), spark individuals (red solid circles) are generated around each firework individual by performing the explosion operation; mutation spark individuals (irregular blue points) are also generated by Gaussian mutation, (c) new firework individuals in the next generation are selected from all individuals in step (b). Steps (b) and (c) are iterated until a termination condition is satisfied.

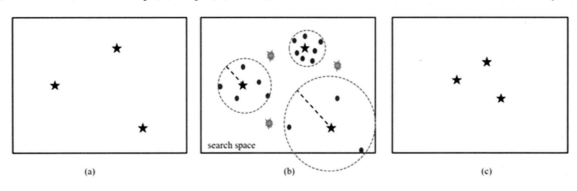

(a)   (b)   (c)

Let us begin by defining symbols to describe the implementation of an explosion operation in detail. Suppose the population size is set to N, $\widehat{A}$ and $\widehat{M}$ represent the maximum explosion amplitude and the total number of spark individuals generated by explosion operations of all firework individuals. For a given i-th firework individual, x_i, Equation (1.1) and (1.2) are used to determine its explosion amplitude, A_i, and the number of spark individuals, M_i, generated by the explosion operation for that individual. Note that we explain operations and algorithms using minimization problems in this Chapter, and they can be easily rewritten for maximization problem. The spark individuals and a firework individual are FWA's own terms and mean solution candidates of optimization.

$$A_i = \widehat{A} * \frac{f(x_i) - y_{min} + \xi}{\sum_{i=1}^{N} \left(f(x_i) - y_{min} \right) + \xi} \tag{1}$$

$$M_i = \widehat{M} * \frac{y_{max} - f(x_i) + \xi}{\sum_{i=1}^{N} \left(y_{max} - f(x_i) \right) + \xi} \tag{2}$$

where $f(x_i)$ returns the fitness of the i-th firework individual, and y_{min} and y_{max} are respectively the best and worst fitness found by the current population. ξ is the smallest constant in the computer to avoid a division-by-zero error.

To avoid the i-th firework individual generating too many or too few spark individuals, Equation (3) is used to limit the number of spark individuals generated by the explosion operation.

$$= \begin{cases} round(a * \mathrm{M}_i), & if \ \mathrm{M}_i < a * M_i \\ round(b * \mathrm{M}_i), & if \ b * \mathrm{M}_i < M_i \\ M_i, & others \end{cases} \tag{3}$$

where $round()$ is a rounded function, a and b are constant parameters ($0 < a < b < 1$).

The next problem is how a firework individual can generate multiple diverse spark individuals. The i-th firework individual randomly selects some dimensions, and a spark individual may undergo the effect of the explosion operation from these affected dimensions with the same random displacement. This process is repeated M_i times to generate M_i spark individuals. Thus, each firework individual performs its explosion operation according to the process described in Algorithm 1. When all firework individuals have performed the explosion operation, Gaussian mutation operations are activated to generate diverse mutation spark individuals, and a selection strategy is then adopted to select firework individuals for the next generation.

Researchers have proposed many effective strategies to improve the performance of the explosion operation. For example, enhanced FWA (EFWA) (Zheng, 2013) proposed a new check strategy to limit the minimum explosion amplitude and a new operator to generate spark individuals through the explosion operation. Dynamic search (Zheng, 2014) is integrated into EFWA to further improve its performance by adaptively increasing or decreasing the explosion amplitude of a firework individual according to the search process. Yu et al. proposed a non-linear decreasing strategy to balance exploration and exploitation capabilities by controlling the explosion amplitude regardless of their fitness (Yu & Takagi, 2017). Li et al. proposed a new technique of guiding spark individuals using the information generated by the explosion operations to direct evolution more effectively (Li, 2017), and weight-based guiding spark individuals (Li, 2019) are proposed to make more efficient use of local information and guide evolution, where spark individuals are given different weights according to their different scenarios. Their explosion operation is effective and has been succeeded by many related studies. The authors extend this operator from a new perspective and introduce two new explosion strategies in this Chapter.

Algorithm 1. The explosion process of an i-th firework individual. D: Dimension; s_j is the j-th spark individual generated by the i-th firework individual.

  1. $count = 0$;

  2. while $count < \mathrm{M}_i$ do

  3. $z = round(D * rand(0,1))$;

  4. Randomly select z dimensions of the i-th firework individual;

  5. Randomly generate a displacement, $h = \mathrm{A}_i * rand(-1,1))$;

  6. for each affected k-th dimension do

  7. $s_j^k = x_i^k + h$

  8. end for

  9. if a generated spark individual, s_j, is outside the search area then

  10. use a mapping rule to bring back to the search area.

  11. end if

  12. $count ++;$

  13. end while;

Multi-Layer Explosion Strategy

A fireworks festival often attracts many people to enjoy the visual feast of various fascinating firework explosions. The explosive patterns formed by real fireworks are not only simple spheres, but also many customized explosive effects, e.g. several explosion shapes such as circle, heart, fan, star, or willow, single or multiple explosion stages, and their combinations. Through the observation and review of these explosion patterns, Yu et al. creatively proposed a multi-layer explosion strategy (Yu, Takagi & Tan, 2018) to fully exploit the local fitness landscape instead of the single-layer spherical explosion strategy used normally in FWA, where each round of explosions can be considered as a layer. Although the maximum number of explosion layers can theoretically be set to any positive integer, it should be set reasonably according to the characteristics of the optimization problem and calculation cost, e.g. the total number of fitness evaluations and CPU consumption time. Figure 2 illustrates the overall optimization process of the multi-layer explosion strategy.

Figure 2. The general framework of a multi-layer explosion strategy. (a) a few spark individuals (colored four-pointed stars) are generated by a firework individual (a black five-pointed star) in the first layer, (b) these generated spark individuals, rather than the firework individual, individually trigger the next round of explosion operations and generate new spark individuals in the subsequent layer, and the newly generated spark individuals continue to perform the next layer of explosion operations until a maximum predefined number of layers is reached.

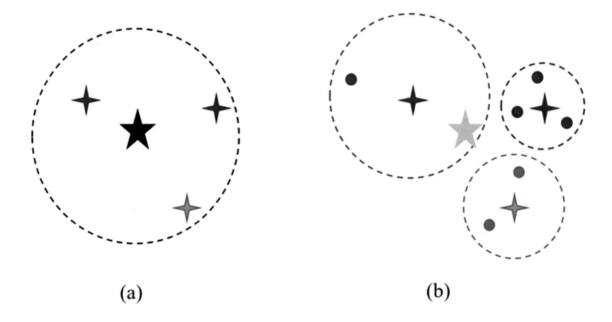

(a)   (b)

First Layer Explosion

An explosion operation is determined by two parameters: the number of generated spark individuals and the explosion amplitude. Similar to basic FWA, Equation (1) is used to adaptively determine the explosion amplitude of a firework individual according to its fitness.

However, the difference here is that all firework individuals generate the same number of few spark individuals in the first layer regardless of their fitness. Since this strategy does not focus on how to generate a spark individual, Algorithm 1 or any other method can be employed to generate the spark individuals in the first layer. Suppose the number of spark individuals generated by the i-th firework individual is set to $m_i^{(1)}$, all spark individuals generated in the first layer, $m_i^{(1)} * n$, instead of the firework individuals start the next round of explosion operations.

Subsequent Layer Explosion

Suppose the number of firework individuals in set to N, and m_i is the total number of spark individuals in all layers under the i-th firework individual, i.e. $\widehat{M} = \sum_{i=1}^{N} m_i$. The maximum number of explosion layers of each firework individual is set to L, and $m_i^{(k)}$ represents the number of generated spark individuals in the k-th explosion layer ($k < L$) and $m_i = \sum_{i=1}^{L} m_i^{(k)}$.

To perform explosion operations in subsequent layers smoothly, the first problem to be solved is how to allocate the remaining assignable spark individuals, $\widehat{M} - m_i^{(1)} * N$. Since the i-th firework individual and m_i spark individuals form a subgroup, the number of spark individuals in subsequent layers, $m_i - m_i^{(1)}$, is dynamically assigned to each subgroup according to the fitness of its initial firework individual using the Equation (2). Next, each subsequent layer in the i-th subgroup is evenly allocated a number of spark individuals, i.e. the number of spark individuals in the k-th layer is set to $\frac{m_i - m_i^{(1)}}{L-1}$.

The other key problem is to decide on the setting of the two parameters, the number of spark individuals and the explosion amplitudes, for spark individuals in the $(k-1)$ layer to trigger the k-th round of explosions. These two parameters are also dynamically determined by the fitness of the spark individuals in the $(k-1)$ layer using Equation (1) and (2), and then this layer explosion is repeated until the explosions have been repeated $(L-1)$ times. Here, the Algorithm 2 summarizes the overall optimization process of a multi-layer explosion strategy.

Algorithm 2. The general framework of a multi-layer explosion strategy
1.   for $i = 0$; $i <$ N; $i++$ do
2.   Decide the number of spark individuals, $m_i^{(1)}$, in the first layer for the i-th firework individual;
3.   Decide an explosion amplitude for the i-th firework individual;
4.   end for
5.   Perform the first layer explosion for all firework individuals to generate spark individuals;
6.   while the number of explosions does not reach a predefined L layer do
7.   Perform the next round of explosion operations for each spark individual in the previous layer described in the sub-section **Subsequent Layer Explosion**.
8.   end while
9.   end of the multi-layer explosion.

The multi-layer explosion strategy does not need to change the optimization framework of the basic FWA or add additional fitness calculations, and can be combined with any other FWA variants easily by replacing their explosion operation. Its core idea is to fully use the characteristics of the local fitness landscape to generate promising spark individuals by exploding layer by layer. Additionally, because spark individuals are derived from both firework individuals and spark individuals in previous layers, the diversity of the population is greatly increased. Thus, this strategy can explore local landscape information deeply and not easily fall into local minima, especially useful for some complex multi-modal problems.

Although the maximum number of explosion layers can be set to any positive number, the authors do not recommend setting it too large. When the number of layers is greater than 2, each spark individual can only generate one new individual because the total number of spark individuals in subsequent layers is equally distributed. To overcome this limitation, practitioners can use a non-equal method to assign the number of spark individuals in subsequent layers, or develop an adaptive version to tune the maximum number of explosion layers according to the optimization process. Additionally, some poor spark individuals can be forbidden from exploding again to save resources and transfer this part of the resources to promising spark individuals to explore their local areas. In short, there is still a lot of room and value to further improve this strategy.

A set of control experiments was carefully designed in the reference (Yu, Takagi & Tan, 2018) to compare (EFWA + the proposed strategy) with particle swarm optimization and guided FWA to evaluate their performance. The experimental results confirmed that the proposal could improve the performance of the FWA significantly by using the local fitness landscape information efficiently, especially for complex cases, and the acceleration effect became more obvious as the dimension increases. The authors also investigated the effect of the number of spark individuals generated in the first layer on the performance. Although it does not have a large impact on the performance of the proposed strategy, a lot of resources, i.e. spark individuals, should be avoided in the first layer, appropriate parameter settings should be designed based on the characteristics of optimization problems and computational costs.

Scouting Explosion Strategy

There is a phenomenon that often occurs during a large fireworks festival where real fireworks can explode repeatedly in some specific directions rather than spreading everywhere. Inspired by these observations, the scouting explosion strategy (Yu, Tan & Takagi, 2018) is introduced into the FWA to increase local search capabilities and bias toward promising areas by generating spark individuals one by one instead of generating them all at once. Figure 3 illustrates the general explosion effect of a firework individual when adopting a scouting strategy.

Since this strategy also focuses on generating spark individuals in a more efficient way without modifying the overall optimization framework of FWA, the only difference is that it gradually generates spark individuals to track promising areas, which gives the appearance of a scout looking for a safe direction forward in an unknown environment.

Take the i-th firework individual as an example; the following explosion operation replaces the original operation used in the FWA to develop a new FWA version. First, only one spark individual is generated at a time and compared with the i-th firework individual. If the spark individual is worse, the i-th firework individual generates a new spark individual randomly again until a better spark individual emerges. The better spark individual becomes the center of the next explosion operation to generate a new spark individual. This process is repeated until the $(j+1)$-th spark individual is worse than the j-th spark individual, then the current continuous scouting stops and a new scouting starts from the

Figure 3. An instance of a scouting explosion strategy for a firework individual. A black five-pointed star and red solid points represent respectively a firework individual and its generated spark individuals. Solid arrows indicate that the current direction is promising and continues to be tracked, whereas dotted arrows indicate that the continuous scouting stops here and new scouting starts from the initial point.

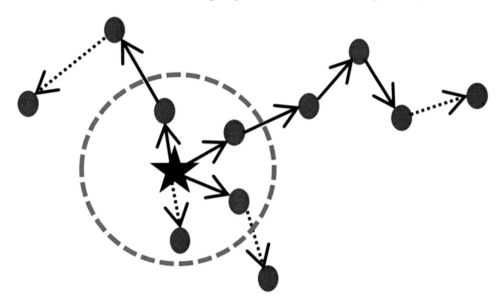

initial firework individual. Since an explosion operation only generates one spark individual, the i-th firework individual repeats M_i times to generate multiple spark individuals. Finally, all firework individuals perform the scouting explosion strategy described in the Algorithm 3 in turn to generate spark individuals.

Algorithm 3. A scouting explosion strategy is used for the i-th firework individual to generate M_i spark individuals

    1.   Determine the total number of spark individual, M_i, generated by the i-th firework individual;

    2.   Determine the explosion amplitude, A_i, of the i-th firework individual;

    3.   *count* = 0 ;

    4.   while *count* is less than M_i do

    5.   Randomly generate a spark individual within A_i and evaluate it.

    6.   *count* = *count* + 1;

    7.   if the spark individual is worse than the i-th firework individual then

    8.   Go to step 5;

    9.   end if

    10. while the subsequent spark individual is better than previous one (firework or spark individual) do

    11. Generate a new spark individual randomly around the previous individual rather than the i-th firework individual within the explosion amplitude, A_i;

    12. *count* = *count* + 1;

13. end while
14. end while.

The scouting explosion strategy calculates the number of generated spark individuals, M_i, and explosion amplitude, A_i, for the i-th firework individual in the same way as in basic FWA; i.e. according to Equation (1) and (2). However, it generates spark individuals one by one to dig deeper into local directions with high potential instead of randomly exploring within an explosion amplitude; this allows it to make better use of the local fitness landscape to speed up the FWA search because more resources (fitness evaluations) are allocated to areas of high potential. Since many promising spark individuals have an opportunity to generate their offspring individuals, population diversity is greatly enriched, avoiding the population becoming tracked in local areas. Obviously, this strategy can be easily combined with other FWA variants and only requires that they replace their explosion operations without any tedious modification. This strategy can thus be said to be a *low-cost, high-reward* strategy.

Although a single point tracking method is used to explore the local information, other tracking methods are acceptable, too. For example, practitioners can try to use a multi-point tracking or tree tracking method to further reduce the risk of falling into a locally optimal area. Additionally, how to adaptively tune an explosion amplitude during the process of a tracking search is also a promising topic for future exploration.

A set of control experiments was designed to evaluate the performance of the proposed scouting explosion strategy in the reference (Yu, Tan & Takagi, 2018). The experimental results showed that the proposed strategy could accelerate the convergence process of FWA significantly, especially for high dimensional problems. This is because the proposed strategy can quickly find some potential directions and track these directions to generate diverse potential spark individuals. Besides, extracting more hidden information from these directions is also one of the effective approaches to accelerate FWA convergence. For example, the number of consecutive explosions in a direction can be used to roughly evaluate the potential of the direction. Thus, obtaining more accurate the information of local fitness landscape is an effective way to speed up FWA search.

Improvements on Explosion Operation

The explosion operation is one of the core factors directly affecting FWA performance. The operation has two parameters that control the generation of the many spark individuals that are used to achieve a local search. However, this raises a problem in that many spark individuals are destroyed quickly after only participating in the selection operations; this is a great waste of limited resources (fitness evaluations) and the approach does not make reasonable use of the spark individuals. Here, the authors list two efficient strategies for controlling the parameters and making full use of existing spark individuals to better guide evolution than a random search.

Amplitude Reduction Strategy

The basic FWA dynamically determines the explosion amplitudes of firework individuals according to their fitness in order to balance well both exploration and exploitation; the better the firework individual, the smaller the explosion amplitudes. Since firework individuals become similar with the process of convergence while the maximum explosion amplitude, $\widehat{A}$, is fixed in each generation, all firework individuals will share the same maximum amplitude, $\widehat{A}$, equally. This results in the exploitation ability not being highlighted, which makes it difficult for FWA to converge. An amplitude reduction strategy (Yu & Takagi, 2017) is introduced to nonlinearly reduce the explosion amplitude of firework individuals regardless of their fitness. This means that all firework individuals are treated equally and their explosion amplitude are determined by Equation (1.4). Figure 4 illustrates the process by which the explosion amplitudes are changed throughout the whole search period.

Figure 4. Changes in explosion amplitudes of firework individuals throughout the whole search period

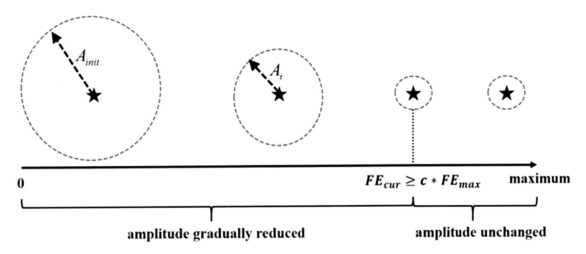

$$\begin{cases} \widehat{A} * \left(1 - \dfrac{FE_{cur}}{FE_{max}}\right), & if \ FE_{cur} < c * FE_{max} \\ \widehat{A} * (1 - c) & Others \end{cases} \tag{4}$$

where FE_{cur} and FE_{max} are the current and maximum number of fitness evaluations, respectively; and c is a constant to avoid an explosion amplitude becoming too small ($0 < c < 1$).

This strategy emphasizes the exploration ability of all firework individuals in the early stages of the search process to quickly find potential areas. According to the population convergence, this ability becomes weaker gradually, while its exploitation ability becomes stronger gradually to improve convergence accuracy in the later stages of search process. Its core is to switch between two different abilities during different search stages. Obviously, applying appropriate methods for controlling explosion amplitudes is a key factor affecting its performance, so developing other methods is a potential research direction. The experimental results (Yu & Takagi, 2017) also show that this strategy can balance exploration and exploitation well and improve the performance of FWA significantly.

Synthetic Spark Individuals

A firework individual usually generates multiple spark individuals within its explosion amplitude. Although these spark individuals can carefully search local areas, it is difficult for them all to survive to the next generation and most of them are abandoned after the selection operation is performed. To improve the efficiency of local fitness information utilization, a new type of individual, the synthetic spark individual (Yu, Tan & Takagi, 2018), is proposed.

A firework individual and its generated spark individuals are considered to belong to the same sub-area, and each sub-area can thus calculate a synthetic spark individual by fully using these spark individuals. Take any given i-th firework individual as an example. The first step is to construct M_i vectors from the i-th firework individual to each spark individual. If an offspring individual (spark) is better than the parent individual (firework), this direction is considered to have potential. Otherwise, its opposite direction is considered to be potential and involved in the calculation of a synthetic spark individual. Next, the absolute value of the fitness difference between the endpoint and the start point of a vector is employed to evaluate the potential of these vectors even if the opposite direction is used, i.e. the larger the fitness difference, the higher the weight of the vector. Finally, a synthetic spark individual is calculated by weighting these vectors using Equation (5); Figure 5 illustrates the construction of a synthetic spark individual.

$$v_i = \sum_{j=1}^{M_i} \frac{f(x_i) - f(s_j)}{\sum_{j=1}^{M_i} \left\| f(x_i) - f(s_j) \right\|} * (s_j - x_i) + x_i \tag{5}$$

where s_j is the j-th generated spark individual or antipodal individual in the i-th sub-group, and v_i is the i-th synthetic spark individual.

Since a synthetic spark individual reuses multiple spark individuals, it has good anti-noise properties and a high possibility to find a better potential direction - although it does require an additional fitness evaluation. To avoid additional fitness costs, the reverse symmetry points of poor spark individuals are not evaluated but participate in the calculation, and the fitness difference of the original vector is roughly used to evaluate a used antipodal direction. However, these factors may cause the accuracy of synthetic spark individuals to decrease. One of the key tasks in the future is to further improve accuracy from the cost-performance point of view. For example, gradient information can replace the fitness difference of vectors to evaluate their weights more objectively.

The original intention of this strategy is to construct moving vectors to estimate a convergence point that can be used as an elite individual and replace the worst firework individual with it to accelerate the convergence. The results showed that this strategy did help to improve the accuracy of an estimated convergence point and significantly improve the performance of FWA. Besides, how to effectively use synthetic spark individuals to accelerate FWA is also a task that is worth solving in the near future.

SUMMARY

This chapter focuses on analyzing the effects of the FWA's explosion operation. The basic explosion operation is first reviewed in detail, and two novel explosion strategies are demonstrated to accelerate FWA search. Attention is next focused on introducing some interesting strategies by which FWA performance could be further enhanced by controlling parameters or reusing existing information efficiently. Although all of these strategies have achieved satisfactory results, the authors finally introduce some other topics worthy of further study and discussion.

Figure 5. A synthetic spark individual is calculated from a firework individual (black five-pointed star) and its generated spark individuals (the red solid points). The presence of a red hollow circle means that the antipode has been used. The purple solid point is the synthetic spark individual obtained by weighting these vectors.

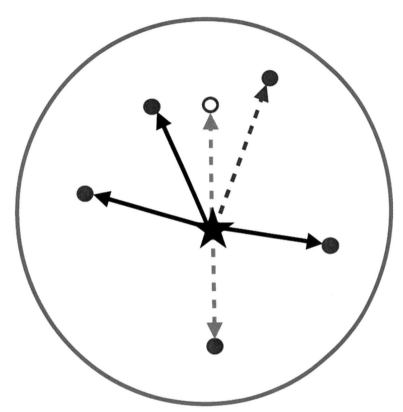

- How can diverse spark individuals be generated from a firework individual? Since the relationship between parent individuals (fireworks) and offspring individuals (sparks) is one-to-many, i.e. lots of spark individuals are derived from a few firework individuals, it is difficult to generate diverse spark individuals when all firework individuals have become similar. It also means that once we have become trapped in a local minimum, it is difficult to jump out. How to increase the diversity of the population is thus one of the problems that need to be solved.

- How can the many generated spark individuals be used most efficiently? As described above, all spark individuals are involved in the selection operation, but only a few survive to the next generation. It is a great waste of limited resources, especially in expensive problems. Thus, it is an effective approach to accelerate FWA convergence by mining more hidden information from these spark individuals.

- How can resources be allocated appropriately to achieve a stronger performance? Due to the limitations of any real-world implementation, the maximum number of fitness evaluations often cannot be set too large. Furthermore, different optimization problems have different characteristics. Thus, balancing resource allocation between firework individuals and spark individuals as well as setting suitable parameters to solve various problems is also an important topic.

ACKNOWLEDGMENT

This work was supported in part by Grant-in-Aid for Scientific Research (17H06197, 18K11470, 19J11792).

REFERENCES

Bacanin, N., & Tuba, M. (2015). Fireworks algorithm applied to constrained portfolio optimization problem. *Proceedings of 2015 IEEE Congress on Evolutionary Computation* (pp. 1242-1249). Sendai, Japan. 10.1109/CEC.2015.7257031

Gao, H., & Diao, M. (2011). Cultural firework algorithm and its application for digital filters design. *International Journal of Modelling, Identification, and Control, 14*(4), 324–331. doi:10.1504/IJMIC.2011.043157

Gong, C. (2016). Chaotic adaptive fireworks algorithm. *Proceedings of the Seventh International Conference on Swarm Intelligence* (pp. 515-525). Bali, Indonesia. Academic Press.

Li, J. Z., Zheng, S. Q., & Tan, Y. (2017). The Effect of Information Utilization: Introducing a Novel Guiding Spark in the Fireworks Algorithm. *IEEE Transactions on Evolutionary Computation, 21*(1), 153–166. doi:10.1109/TEVC.2016.2589821

Li, Y. H., Yu, J., Takagi, H., & Tan, Y. (2019) Accelerating Fireworks Algorithm with Weight-based Guiding Sparks. *Proceedings of 10th International Conference on Swarm Intelligence* (pp. 257-266). Chiang Mai, Thailand. 10.1007/978-3-030-26369-0_24

Misra, P. R., & Si, T. (2017). Image segmentation using clustering with fireworks algorithm. *Proceedings of 11th International Conference on Intelligent Systems and Control* (pp. 97-102). Coimbatore, India. 10.1109/ISCO.2017.7855961

Mohamed Imran, A., & Kowsalya, M. (2014). A new power system reconfiguration scheme for power loss minimization and voltage profile enhancement using Fireworks Algorithm. *International Journal of Electrical Power & Energy Systems, 62*, 312–322. doi:10.1016/j.ijepes.2014.04.034

Pandey, V. C., Jadoun, V. K., Gupta, N., Niazi, K. R., & Swarnkar, A. (2018). Improved Fireworks Algorithm with Chaotic Sequence Operator for Large-Scale Non-convex Economic Load Dispatch Problem. *Arabian Journal for Science and Engineering, 43*(6), 2919–2929. doi:10.100713369-017-2956-6

Pei, Y., Zheng, S. Q., Tan, Y., & Takagi, H. (2012). An empirical study on influence of approximation approaches on enhancing fireworks algorithm. *Proceedings of 2012 IEEE International Conference on Systems, Man, and Cybernetics* (pp. 1322-1327). Seoul, Korea. 10.1109/ICSMC.2012.6377916

Pekdemir, H., & Topcuoglu, H. R. (2016). Enhancing fireworks algorithms for dynamic optimization problems. *Proceedings of 2016 IEEE Congress on Evolutionary Computation* (pp. 4045-4052). Vancouver, Canada. 10.1109/CEC.2016.7744303

Reddy, K. S., Panwar, L. K., Kumar, R., & Panigrahi, B. K. (2016). Distributed resource scheduling in smart grid with electric vehicle deployment using fireworks algorithm. *Journal of Modern Power Systems and Clean Energy, 4*(2), 188–199. doi:10.100740565-016-0195-6

Tan, Y., & Zhu, Y. C. (2010). Fireworks algorithm for optimization. *Proceedings of The First International Conference on Swarm Intelligence* (pp. 355-364). Beijing, China.

Tuba, E., Tuba, M., & Dolicanin, E. (2017). Adjusted fireworks algorithm applied to retinal image registration. *Studies in Informatics and Control, 26*(1), 33–42. doi:10.24846/v26i1y201704

Tuba, E., Tuba, M., & Simian, D. (2016). Wireless sensor network coverage problem using modified fireworks algorithm. *Proceedings of 2016 International Wireless Communications and Mobile Computing Conference* (pp. 696-701). Cyprus. 10.1109/IWCMC.2016.7577141

Wang, X., Peng, H., Deng, C., Li, L., & Zheng, L. (2019). An improved firefly algorithm hybrid with fireworks. *Proceedings of 10th International Symposium on Intelligence Computation and Applications* (pp. 27-37). Jiujiang, China. 10.1007/978-981-13-6473-0_3

Yang, W., & Ke, L. (2019). An improved fireworks algorithm for the capacitated vehicle routing problem. *Frontiers of Computer Science, 13*(3), 552–564. doi:10.100711704-017-6418-9

Yu, C., Kelley, L., Zheng, S., & Tan, Y. (2014). Fireworks algorithm with differential mutation for solving the CEC 2014 competition problems. *Proceedings of 2014 IEEE Congress on Evolutionary Computation* (pp. 3238-3245). Beijing, China. 10.1109/CEC.2014.6900590

Yu, C., & Tan, Y. (2015). Fireworks algorithm with covariance mutation. *Proceedings of 2015 IEEE Congress on Evolutionary Computation* (pp. 1250-1256). Sendai, Japan. 10.1109/CEC.2015.7257032

Yu, J., & Takagi, H. (2017) Acceleration for Fireworks Algorithm Based on Amplitude Reduction Strategy and Local Optima-based Selection Strategy. *Proceedings of the Eighth International Conference on Swarm Intelligence* (pp. 477-484). Fukuoka, Japan. 10.1007/978-3-319-61824-1_52

Yu, J., Takagi, H., & Tan, Y. (2018). Multi-layer Explosion-Based Fireworks Algorithm. *International Journal of Swarm Intelligence and Evolutionary Computation, 7*(3), 1–9. doi:10.4172/2090-4908.1000173

Yu, J., Takagi, H., & Tan, Y. (2019). Fireworks Algorithm for Multimodal Optimization Using a Distance-based Exclusive Strategy. *Proceedings of 2019 IEEE Congress on Evolutionary Computation* (pp. 2216-2221). Wellington, New Zealand. 10.1109/CEC.2019.8790312

Yu, J., Tan, Y., & Takagi, H. (2018). Accelerating Fireworks Algorithm with an Estimated Convergence Point. *Proceedings of the Ninth International Conference on Swarm Intelligence* (pp. 263-272). Shanghai, China. 10.1007/978-3-319-93815-8_26

Yu, J., Tan, Y., & Takagi, H. (2018). Scouting Strategy for Biasing Fireworks Algorithm Search to Promising Directions. *Proceedings of the genetic and evolutionary computation conference companion* (pp. 99-100). Kyoto, Japan. 10.1145/3205651.3205740

Zhan, D., & Xie, C. (2018). An Improved Multi-Objective Fireworks Algorithm. *Proceedings of 9th International Symposium on Intelligence Computation and Applications* (pp. 204-218). Guangzhou, China.

Zhang, T., Yue, Q., Zhao, X., & Liu, G. (n.d.). An improved firework algorithm for hardware/software partitioning. Applied Intelligence, 49(3), 950–962.

Zheng, S., Janecek, A., & Tan, Y. (2013). Enhanced fireworks algorithm. *Proceedings of 2013 IEEE Congress on Evolutionary Computation* (pp. 2069-2077). Cancun, Mexico. 10.1109/CEC.2013.6557813

Zheng, S. Q., Janecek, A., Li, J. Z., & Tan, Y. (2014). Dynamic search in fireworks algorithm. *Proceedings of 2014 IEEE Congress on Evolutionary Computation* (pp. 3222-3229). Beijing, China. 10.1109/CEC.2014.6900485

Zheng, S. Q., Janecek, A., & Tan, Y. (2013). Enhanced Fireworks Algorithm. *Proceedings of 2013 IEEE Congress on Evolutionary Computation* (pp. 2069-2077). Cancun, Mexico. 10.1109/CEC.2013.6557813

Zhu, Q. B., Wang, Z. Y., & Huang, M. (2016). Fireworks algorithm with gravitational search operator. *Kongzhi yu Juece/Control and Decision, 31*(10), 1853-1859. (in Chinese).

Section 3
FWA Applications in Machine Learning

Chapter 4
EFWA as a Method of Optimizing Model Parameters:
Example of an Expensive Function Evaluation

Daniel C. Lee
Simon Fraser University, Canada

Katherine Manson
British Columbia Institute of Technology, Canada

ABSTRACT

The Fireworks Algorithm (EFWA) is studied as a method to optimize the noise covariance parameters in an induction motor system model to control the motor speed without a speed sensor. The authors considered a system that employs variable frequency drives (VFDs) and executes an extended Kalman filter (EKF) algorithm to estimate the motor speed based on other measured values. Multiple optimizations were run, and the authors found that the EFWA optimization provided, on average, better solutions than the Genetic Algorithm (GA) for a comparable number of parameter set trials. However, EFWA parameters need to be selected carefully; otherwise, EFWA's early performance advantage over GA can be lost.

INTRODUCTION

In industrial applications, it is often desired to set the values of design variables to optimize performance. However, the quantitative relationship between a performance criterion and design variables may not be well known. In many applications, the exact mathematical expression of the quantitative performance measure of interest as a function of design variables is unknown, and the numerical value of the performance measure for a given set of design variables can only be estimated through simulation or experimentation. Evaluating performance for the purpose of optimization can be costly because this type of experimentation can be expensive and the simulation may require a large amount of computational resources. Therefore, in order to employ an evolutionary algorithm for such an application,

DOI: 10.4018/978-1-7998-1659-1.ch004

Copyright © 2020, IGI Global. Copying or distributing in print or electronic forms without written permission of IGI Global is prohibited.

one of the primary concerns is to obtain a good solution after a small number of function evaluations. In this chapter, the authors intend to exhibit use of the enhanced fireworks algorithm (EFWA) for such optimization (Tan, 2015; Zheng, 2013). The authors will present EFWA's performance for optimally choosing model parameters for controlling the speed of an induction motor. Industry uses induction motors (IMs) extensively to drive mechanical loads, so the optimization problem presented is a concrete, real-life example. Due to the high cost of evaluating the performance function, the focus of the chapter will be on how fast the algorithm improves the best candidate solution's performance as the number of function evaluations increases, rather than convergence to the optimal solution.

In order to convey the nature of the optimization problem, the speed control system for the induction motor will be explained for general audiences in the following section. The objective of speed control is to match the actual speed of the motor to the speed command schedule. When speed sensors are used, feedback control schemes can be employed; however, having speed sensors in the system has its disadvantages, and speed sensors are not installed in the example application being studied. Instead of measuring speed, it is estimated based on other measured values. The extended Kalman filter (EKF), a well-known technique to estimate the speed, was used for this purpose (Crassidis & Junkins, 2011). To apply the extended Kalman filter, the covariance values of the process and measurement noise are required for computation. These statistics are not known a priori, but they can be determined through experimentation or simulation as model parameters prior to the actual operation of the motor.

In the application to be presented in this chapter, the performance measure is the mean-square error in the motor speed estimate. To be specific, the performance objective function is the expected value of the square of the difference between the speed of the motor at a given time and the estimation of that speed computed by the estimator, which is a part of the system. Note that the speed of the motor is a randomly time-varying signal, and the mean-square error, as a function of the model parameters, is not known and can only be approximately evaluated through extensive simulation or experimentation. A natural method of estimating the performance value corresponding to a set of parameter values is to take the time average of the square of the difference between the actual speed and the estimator's estimation of the speed. Time averaging requires collection of many samples of the actual speed through experimentation or simulation, and this process can be costly. The next section will present more details on this point.

In earlier work, other researchers used a genetic algorithm (GA) to optimize covariance values as model parameters through simulation and experimentation (Shi et al., 2002). The objective of the authors' research was to gain more knowledge about the EFWA's performance for optimizing the model parameters for the induction motor's speed estimation.

It was found, as expected, that the best candidate solution's performance (the mean square error of motor speed for the example problem studied in this chapter) in the EFWA tends to eventually converge to the value to which the GA converges as the number of generations increases. An interesting observation was that for many different sets of algorithm parameter values, the EFWA's best performing solution tended to improve more quickly, in the initial few generations, than the GA's. The early improvement is important for applications with high function evaluation cost. In the following sections, detailed results are presented from the accumulated data obtained and the statistical significance of EFWA's faster improvement observed at early generations of the algorithms is analyzed.

BACKGROUND

Three-Phase Induction Motor Model and Speed Control

The author's studied a common industrial application, which was to estimate the rotor speed of the three-phase induction motor for the purpose of controlling the speed. The mathematical model of how the three-phase induction motor works is briefly presented in this section. Most induction motors have a stator, which is a non-moving part, and a rotor, which rotates. In the three-phase induction motor, the stator and rotor each have three windings of connecting coils. Three windings in each part are physically arranged so that their angular positions are 120 degrees apart from each other. Sinusoidal electric power is supplied to the stator's three windings with a phase difference of 120 degrees which creates a rotating magnetic field. The field induces electric currents in the rotor's three windings, and electromagnetic force is produced that can cause the rotor to rotate.

The relationship between voltages and electric currents though the three windings can be derived from electromagnetic theory. We will use indices a,b,c to refer to the three windings. We denote by V_{as}, V_{bs}, V_{cs} the voltage applied to windings a,b,c of the stator, respectively. We denote by i_{as}, i_{bs}, i_{cs} the current flowing through windings a,b,c of the stator, respectively. We denote by $\lambda_{as}, \lambda_{bs}, \lambda_{cs}$ the magnetic flux linkages of windings a,b,c of the stator, respectively. We denote by R_s the resistance of each stator winding. Then the mathematical relation between those time-varying variables are:

$$i_{as} R_s + \frac{d}{dt}\lambda_{as} = V_{as}; \quad i_{bs} R_s + \frac{d}{dt}\lambda_{bs} = V_{bs}; \quad i_{cs} R_s + \frac{d}{dt}\lambda_{cs} = V_{cs} \tag{1}$$

Likewise, we have the following relationships among rotor variables

$$i_{ar} R_r + \frac{d}{dt}\lambda_{ar} = 0; \quad i_{br} R_r + \frac{d}{dt}\lambda_{br} = 0; \quad i_{cr} R_r + \frac{d}{dt}\lambda_{cr} = 0 \tag{2}$$

where i_{ar}, i_{br}, i_{cr} denote currents in the three rotor windings, $\lambda_{ar}, \lambda_{br}, \lambda_{cr}$ denote flux linkages of the three rotor windings, and R_r denotes the resistance of each rotor winding. Note that the voltages of rotor windings V_{ar}, V_{br}, V_{cr} are each 0, as there is no external voltage source in these windings. These relations and variables can be expressed more concisely by using matrix notations,

$$\mathbf{i}_{abcs} \equiv \left(i_{as}, i_{bs}, i_{cs}\right)^T; V_{abcs} \equiv \left(V_{as}, V_{bs}, V_{cs}\right)^T; »_{abcs} \equiv \left(\lambda_{as}, \lambda_{bs}, \lambda_{cs}\right)^T \tag{3}$$

$$\mathbf{i}_{abcr} \equiv \left(i_{ar}, i_{br}, i_{cr}\right)^T; \mathbf{v}_{abcr} \equiv \left(v_{ar}, v_{br}, v_{cr}\right)^T; »_{abcr} \equiv \left(\lambda_{ar}, \lambda_{br}, \lambda_{cr}\right)^T \tag{4}$$

The above two equations can be expressed as

$$\mathbf{R}_s \mathbf{i}_{abcs} + \frac{d}{dt} »_{abcs} = \mathbf{V}_{abcs}; \quad \mathbf{R}_r \mathbf{i}_{abcr} + \frac{d}{dt} »_{abcr} = \mathbf{V}_{abcr} = \mathbf{0} \tag{5}$$

Also, the relation between electrical currents and flux linkages can be modelled as the following linear relation (Krause et al., 2013)

$$\begin{pmatrix} \lambda_{abcs} \\ \lambda_{abcr} \end{pmatrix} = \begin{pmatrix} \mathbf{L}_s & \mathbf{L}_{sr} \\ \left(\mathbf{L}_{sr}\right)^T & \mathbf{L}_r \end{pmatrix} \begin{pmatrix} \mathbf{i}_{abcs} \\ \mathbf{i}_{abcr} \end{pmatrix}, \tag{6}$$

$$\mathbf{L}_s = \begin{pmatrix} L_{ls} + L_{ms} & -\dfrac{L_{ms}}{2} & -\dfrac{L_{ms}}{2} \\ -\dfrac{L_{ms}}{2} & L_{ls} + L_{ms} & -\dfrac{L_{ms}}{2} \\ -\dfrac{L_{ms}}{2} & -\dfrac{L_{ms}}{2} & L_{ls} + L_{ms} \end{pmatrix}, \quad \mathbf{L}_r = \begin{pmatrix} L_{lr} + L_{mr} & -\dfrac{L_{mr}}{2} & -\dfrac{L_{mr}}{2} \\ -\dfrac{L_{mr}}{2} & L_{lr} + L_{mr} & -\dfrac{L_{mr}}{2} \\ -\dfrac{L_{mr}}{2} & -\dfrac{L_{mr}}{2} & L_{lr} + L_{mr} \end{pmatrix},$$

$$\mathbf{L}_{sr} = L_{sr} \begin{pmatrix} \cos\theta_r & \cos\left(\theta_r + \dfrac{2\pi}{3}\right) & \cos\left(\theta_r + \dfrac{4\pi}{3}\right) \\ \cos\left(\theta_r + \dfrac{4\pi}{3}\right) & \cos\theta_r & \cos\left(\theta_r + \dfrac{2\pi}{3}\right) \\ \cos\left(\theta_r + \dfrac{2\pi}{3}\right) & \cos\left(\theta_r + \dfrac{4\pi}{3}\right) & \cos\theta_r \end{pmatrix}, \tag{7}$$

where L_{ls} is the leakage inductance of a stator winding, L_{ms} is the magnetizing-inductance of the stator windings, L_{lr} is the leakage inductance of a rotor winding, L_{mr} is the magnetizing-inductance of the rotor windings, L_{sr} is the peak value of the stator-to-rotor mutual inductance, θ_r is the angular position of the rotor with the stator windings' position as the reference.

In the study of power systems, mathematical transforms (Ong, 1997) are often used to facilitate the solutions of difficult equations with time-varying coefficients or to refer all variables to a common reference frame. For the three-phase induction motor the $qd0$ transform is used (Krause et al., 2013), denoted as a 3×3 matrix $T(\theta)$. It is typically used to transform the vector variables with coordinates a,b,c to vector variables with coordinates named q (quadrature), d (direct), 0; namely,

$$\left(f_q, f_d, f_0\right)^T = T(\theta)\left(f_a, f_b, f_c\right)^T \tag{8}$$

where the superscript T denotes matrix transpose and

$$T(\theta) = \frac{2}{3}\begin{pmatrix} \cos\theta & \cos\left(\theta - \dfrac{2\pi}{3}\right) & \cos\left(\theta - \dfrac{4\pi}{3}\right) \\ \sin(\theta) & \sin\left(\theta - \dfrac{2\pi}{3}\right) & \sin\left(\theta - \dfrac{4\pi}{3}\right) \\ \dfrac{1}{2} & \dfrac{1}{2} & \dfrac{1}{2} \end{pmatrix}, \quad T(\theta)^{-1} = \begin{pmatrix} \cos\theta & \sin(\theta) & 1 \\ \cos\left(\theta - \dfrac{2\pi}{3}\right) & \sin\left(\theta - \dfrac{2\pi}{3}\right) & 1 \\ \cos\left(\theta - \dfrac{4\pi}{3}\right) & \sin\left(\theta - \dfrac{4\pi}{3}\right) & 1 \end{pmatrix} \tag{9}$$

Variables f_q, f_d, f_0 in $\left(f_q, f_d, f_0\right)^T = T(\theta)\left(f_a, f_b, f_c\right)^T$ can be interpreted as in a new reference frame (qd0). Parameter θ in transformation can be interpreted as the angle between the qd0 reference frame and the abc reference frame. Often, the variables of the motor system are expressed in a rotating qd0 reference frame (time varying θ). Note that the inverse transformation $T(\theta)^{-1}$ exists, so the variables in the abc reference frame can be recovered back from the variables in a qd0 reference frame. We can apply the $qd0$ transformation $T(\theta)$ to the voltage, current, and flux linkage variables:

$$\mathbf{i}_{qd0s} = T(\theta)\mathbf{i}_{abcs}; \qquad V_{qd0s} = T(\theta)V_{abcs}; \qquad \lambda_{qd0s} = T(\theta)\lambda_{abcs}$$
$$\mathbf{i}_{qd0r} = T(\theta-\theta_r)\mathbf{i}_{abcr}; \quad V_{qd0r} = T(\theta-\theta_r)V_{abcr}; \quad \lambda_{qd0r} = T(\theta-\theta_r)\lambda_{abcr}$$

(10)

where

$$\mathbf{i}_{qd0s} \equiv \left(i_{qs},i_{ds},i_{0s}\right)^{T}; V_{qd0s} \equiv \left(V_{qs},V_{ds},V_{0s}\right)^{T}; \lambda_{qd0s} \equiv \left(\lambda_{qs},\lambda_{ds},\lambda_{0s}\right)^{T}$$
$$\mathbf{i}_{qd0r} \equiv \left(i_{qr},i_{dr},i_{0r}\right)^{T}; V_{qd0r} \equiv \left(V_{qr},V_{dr},V_{0r}\right)^{T}; \lambda_{qd0r} \equiv \left(\lambda_{qr},\lambda_{dr},\lambda_{0r}\right)^{T}$$

and θ_r is the angular position of the rotor. Then, the relation between the voltage, current, and flux linkage in equations (5) can be expressed in terms of the variables of the qd0 reference frame:

$$R_s\mathbf{i}_{qd0s} + T(\theta)\frac{d}{dt}T(\theta)^{-1}\lambda_{qd0s} = V_{qd0s}; \; R_r\mathbf{i}_{qd0r} + T(\theta-\theta^r)\frac{d}{dt}T(\theta-\theta^r)^{-1}\lambda_{qd0r} = V_{qd0r}$$

which in turn result in

$$R_s\mathbf{i}_{qd0s} + T(\theta)\frac{dT(\theta)^{-1}}{dt}\lambda_{qd0s} + \frac{d\lambda_{qd0s}}{dt} = V_{qd0s}; \; R_r\mathbf{i}_{qd0r} + T(\theta-\theta^r)\frac{dT(\theta-\theta^r)^{-1}}{dt}\lambda_{qd0r} + \frac{d\lambda_{qd0r}}{dt} = V_{qd0r}$$

(11)

The relationship between the flux linkages and current (6), (7) can be expressed as

$$\lambda_{qd0s} = T(\theta)\mathbf{L}_s T(\theta)^{-1}\mathbf{i}_{qd0s} + T(\theta)\mathbf{L}_{sr}T(\theta-\theta_r)^{-1}\mathbf{i}_{qd0r},$$

$$\lambda_{qd0r} = T(\theta-\theta_r)\left(\mathbf{L}_{sr}\right)^{T}T(\theta)^{-1}\mathbf{i}_{qd0s} + T(\theta-\theta_r)\mathbf{L}_r T(\theta-\theta_r)^{-1}\mathbf{i}_{qd0r},$$

and the following mathematical equivalence can be algebraically shown:

$$T(\theta)\mathbf{L}_s T(\theta)^{-1} = \begin{pmatrix} L_{ls}+\dfrac{3}{2}L_{ms} & 0 & 0 \\ 0 & L_{ls}+\dfrac{3}{2}L_{ms} & 0 \\ 0 & 0 & L_{ls} \end{pmatrix}$$

$$T\left(\theta-\theta_r\right)\mathbf{L}_r T\left(\theta-\theta_r\right)^{-1} = \begin{pmatrix} L_{lr}+\dfrac{3}{2}L_{mr} & 0 & 0 \\ 0 & L_{lr}+\dfrac{3}{2}L_{mr} & 0 \\ 0 & 0 & L_{lr} \end{pmatrix},$$

$$T\left(\theta\right)\mathbf{L}_{sr} T\left(\theta-\theta_r\right)^{-1} = \begin{pmatrix} \dfrac{3}{2}L_{sr} & 0 & 0 \\ 0 & \dfrac{3}{2}L_{sr} & 0 \\ 0 & 0 & 0 \end{pmatrix},$$

It is noteworthy that $T(\theta)\mathbf{L}_s T(\theta)^{-1}$, $T(\theta-\theta_r)\mathbf{L}_r T(\theta-\theta_r)^{-1}$, and $T(\theta)\mathbf{L}_s T(\theta-\theta_r)^{-1}$ are invariant of θ and θ_r. In summary, in the qd0 frame, we have equations

$$\begin{bmatrix} V_{qs} \\ V_{ds} \\ V_{0s} \end{bmatrix} = \begin{bmatrix} \dfrac{d\lambda_{qs}}{dt}+\omega\lambda_{ds}+R_s i_{qs} \\ \dfrac{d\lambda_{ds}}{dt}-\omega\lambda_{qs}+R_s i_{ds} \\ \dfrac{d\lambda_{0s}}{dt}+R_s i_{0s} \end{bmatrix}; \quad \begin{bmatrix} V_{qr} \\ V_{dr} \\ V_{0r} \end{bmatrix} = \begin{bmatrix} \dfrac{d\lambda_{qr}}{dt}+\left(\omega-\omega_r\right)\lambda_{ds}+R_r i_{qr} \\ \dfrac{d\lambda_{dr}}{dt}-\left(\omega-\omega_r\right)\lambda_{qr}+R_r i_{dr} \\ \dfrac{d\lambda_{0r}}{dt}+R_r i_{0r} \end{bmatrix} \tag{12}$$

$$\begin{bmatrix} \lambda_{qs} \\ \lambda_{ds} \\ \lambda_{0s} \end{bmatrix} = \begin{pmatrix} L_{ls}+\dfrac{3}{2}L_{ms} & 0 & 0 \\ 0 & L_{ls}+\dfrac{3}{2}L_{ms} & 0 \\ 0 & 0 & L_{ls} \end{pmatrix} \begin{bmatrix} i_{qs} \\ i_{ds} \\ i_{0s} \end{bmatrix} + \begin{pmatrix} \dfrac{3}{2}L_{sr} & 0 & 0 \\ 0 & \dfrac{3}{2}L_{sr} & 0 \\ 0 & 0 & 0 \end{pmatrix} \begin{bmatrix} i_{qr} \\ i_{dr} \\ i_{0r} \end{bmatrix}, \tag{13}$$

$$\begin{bmatrix} \lambda_{qr} \\ \lambda_{dr} \\ \lambda_{0r} \end{bmatrix} = \begin{pmatrix} \dfrac{3}{2}L_{sr} & 0 & 0 \\ 0 & \dfrac{3}{2}L_{sr} & 0 \\ 0 & 0 & 0 \end{pmatrix} \begin{bmatrix} i_{qs} \\ i_{ds} \\ i_{0s} \end{bmatrix} + \begin{pmatrix} L_{lr}+\dfrac{3}{2}L_{mr} & 0 & 0 \\ 0 & L_{lr}+\dfrac{3}{2}L_{mr} & 0 \\ 0 & 0 & L_{lr} \end{pmatrix} \begin{bmatrix} i_{qr} \\ i_{dr} \\ i_{0r} \end{bmatrix}, \tag{14}$$

where $\omega_r \equiv \dfrac{d\theta_r}{dt}$ is the angular velocity of the rotor and $\omega \equiv \dfrac{d\theta}{dt}$ is the angular velocity of the rotating qd0 frame.

In a balanced three-phase system, the sinusoidal voltages applied to the three stator windings $V_{as}(t), V_{bs}(t), V_{cs}(t)$ have the same amplitude and different phases so that the sum $V_{as}(t)+V_{bs}(t)+V_{cs}(t)=0$. Therefore, $V_{0s}(t)=\{V_{as}(t)+V_{bs}(t)+V_{cs}(t)\}/3$, the 0-coodinate in the qd0 reference frame is 0. Also, three-phase systems are often wye (Y) connected without a neutral conductor, and in such a system the current sum $i_{as}(t) + i_{bs}(t) + i_{cs}(t)$ is 0 and thus $i_{0s}(t)$ is 0. (Krause, 2012) In short, the 0-coordinate in the qd0 reference frame need not be considered in a balanced system. The result is the following equations:

$$V_{qs} = \frac{d\lambda_{qs}}{dt} + \omega\lambda_{ds} + R_s i_{qs}; \qquad V_{ds} = \frac{d\lambda_{ds}}{dt} - \omega\lambda_{qs} + R_s i_{ds} \tag{15}$$

$$0 = \frac{d\lambda_{qr}}{dt} + (\omega - \omega_r)\lambda_{dr} + R_r i_{qr}; \quad 0 = \frac{d\lambda_{dr}}{dt} - (\omega - \omega_r)\lambda_{qr} + R_r i_{dr} \tag{16}$$

$$\lambda_{qs} = \left(L_{ls} + \frac{3}{2}L_{ms}\right)i_{qs} + \frac{3}{2}L_{sr}i_{qr}; \quad \lambda_{ds} = \left(L_{ls} + \frac{3}{2}L_{ms}\right)i_{ds} + \frac{3}{2}L_{sr}i_{dr} \tag{17}$$

$$\lambda_{qr} = \frac{3}{2}L_{sr}i_{qs} + \left(L_{lr} + \frac{3}{2}L_{mr}\right)i_{qr}; \quad \lambda_{dr} = \frac{3}{2}L_{sr}i_{ds} + \left(L_{lr} + \frac{3}{2}L_{mr}\right)i_{dr} \tag{18}$$

The angular velocity ω of the qd0 reference frame can be set to any value for mathematical convenience, and in this analysis it is set it to 0—i.e, the 0-reference frame. The following notations are used:

$$L_s \equiv L_{ls} + \frac{3}{2}L_{ms} \text{ (stator inductance)}; \quad L_r \equiv L_{lr} + \frac{3}{2}L_{mr} \text{ (rotor inductance)} \tag{19}$$

to simplify the mathematical expressions. Then results are as follows:

$$V_{qs} = \frac{d\lambda_{qs}}{dt} + R_s i_{qs}; \qquad V_{ds} = \frac{d\lambda_{ds}}{dt} + R_s i_{ds} \tag{20}$$

$$0 = \frac{d\lambda_{qr}}{dt} - \omega_r\lambda_{dr} + R_r i_{qr}; \quad 0 = \frac{d\lambda_{dr}}{dt} + \omega_r\lambda_{qr} + R_r i_{dr} \tag{21}$$

$$\lambda_{qs} = L_s i_{qs} + \frac{3}{2}L_{sr}i_{qr}; \quad \lambda_{ds} = L_s i_{ds} + \frac{3}{2}L_{sr}i_{dr} \tag{22}$$

$$\lambda_{qr} = \frac{3}{2}L_{sr}i_{qs} + L_r i_{qr}; \quad \lambda_{dr} = \frac{3}{2}L_{sr}i_{ds} + L_r i_{dr} \tag{23}$$

The variables $V_{qs}, V_{ds}, V_{qr}, V_{dr}, i_{qs}, i_{ds}, i_{qr}, i_{dr}, \lambda_{qs}, \lambda_{ds}, \lambda_{qr}, \lambda_{dr}, \omega_r$ are used in eight equations. From this system of eight equations, we can eliminate four variables $i_{qs}, i_{ds}, \lambda_{qs}, \lambda_{ds}$ and express the system evolution by the following four equations. To eliminate rotor current variables and stator flux variables (all four variables), we use equations (22) (23) above. From (23) we have

$$i_{qr} = \frac{1}{L_r} \lambda_{qr} - \frac{3}{2} L_{sr} \frac{1}{L_r} i_{qs}; \quad i_{dr} = \frac{1}{L_r} \lambda_{dr} - \frac{3}{2} L_{sr} \frac{1}{L_r} i_{ds} \tag{24}$$

and plugging these in (22) results in

$$\lambda_{qs} = L_s i_{qs} + \frac{3}{2} L_{sr} \left[\frac{1}{L_r} \lambda_{qr} - \frac{3}{2} L_{sr} \frac{1}{L_r} i_{qs} \right] = \frac{3}{2} L_{sr} \frac{1}{L_r} \lambda_{qr} + \left[L_s - \left(\frac{3}{2} L_{sr} \right)^2 \frac{1}{L_r} \right] i_{qs}$$

$$\lambda_{ds} = L_s i_{ds} + \frac{3}{2} L_{sr} \left[\frac{1}{L_r} \lambda_{dr} - \frac{3}{2} L_{sr} \frac{1}{L_r} i_{ds} \right] = \frac{3}{2} L_{sr} \frac{1}{L_r} \lambda_{dr} + \left[L_s - \left(\frac{3}{2} L_{sr} \right)^2 \frac{1}{L_r} \right] i_{ds}$$

To simplify the description, this notation is used:

$$K_l = L_s - \left(\frac{3}{2} L_{sr} \right)^2 \frac{1}{L_r} \tag{25}$$

Therefore, we have

$$\lambda_{qs} = \frac{3}{2} L_{sr} \frac{1}{L_r} \lambda_{qr} + K_l i_{qs}; \quad \lambda_{ds} = \frac{3}{2} L_{sr} \frac{1}{L_r} \lambda_{dr} + K_l i_{ds} \tag{26}$$

Substituting i_{qr}, i_{dr} of (24) and $\lambda_{qs}, \lambda_{ds}$ in (26) in (21), results in:

$$\frac{d\lambda_{qr}}{dt} = -\frac{R_r}{L_r} \lambda_{qr} + \omega_r \lambda_{dr} + \frac{3}{2} L_{sr} \frac{R_r}{L_r} i_{qs}; \quad \frac{d\lambda_{dr}}{dt} = -\omega_r \lambda_{qr} - \frac{R_r}{L_r} \lambda_{dr} + \frac{3}{2} L_{sr} \frac{R_r}{L_r} i_{ds} \tag{27}$$

Plugging (26) into (20), provides:

$$V_{ds} = \frac{3}{2} L_{sr} \frac{1}{L_r} \left[-\omega_r \lambda_{qr} - \frac{R_r}{L_r} \lambda_{dr} + \frac{3}{2} L_{sr} \frac{R_r}{L_r} i_{ds} \right] + K_l \frac{d}{dt} i_{ds} + R_s i_{ds},$$

$$V_{qs} = \frac{3}{2} L_{sr} \frac{1}{L_r} \left[-\frac{R_r}{L_r} \lambda_{qr} + \omega_r \lambda_{dr} + \frac{3}{2} L_{sr} \frac{R_r}{L_r} i_{qs} \right] + K_l \frac{d}{dt} i_{qs} + R_s i_{qs},$$

or equivalently,

$$\frac{d}{dt}i_{ds} = -\frac{1}{K_l}\left[R_s + \frac{1}{L_r}\left(\frac{3}{2}L_{sr}\right)^2\frac{R_r}{L_r}\right]i_{ds} + \frac{3}{2}L_{sr}\frac{1}{K_lL_r}\frac{R_r}{L_r}\lambda_{dr} + \frac{3}{2}L_{sr}\frac{\omega_r}{K_lL_r}\lambda_{qr} + \frac{V_{ds}}{K_l}$$

$$\frac{d}{dt}i_{qs} = -\frac{1}{K_l}\left[R_s + \frac{1}{L_r}\left(\frac{3}{2}L_{sr}\right)^2\frac{R_r}{L_r}\right]i_{qs} - \frac{3}{2}L_{sr}\frac{\omega_r}{K_lL_r}\lambda_{dr} + \frac{3}{2}L_{sr}\frac{1}{K_lL_r}\frac{R_r}{L_r}\lambda_{qr} + \frac{V_{qs}}{K_l} \tag{28}$$

To simplify the description, the following notation is used:

$$K_r \equiv R_s + \frac{1}{L_r}\left(\frac{3}{2}L_{sr}\right)^2\frac{R_r}{L_r}; \qquad L_m \equiv \frac{3}{2}L_{sr} \tag{29}$$

Then, (28) is expressed as

$$\frac{d}{dt}i_{ds} = -\frac{K_r}{K_l}i_{ds} + \frac{L_m}{K_lL_r}\frac{R_r}{L_r}\lambda_{dr} + L_m\frac{\omega_r}{K_lL_r}\lambda_{qr} + \frac{V_{ds}}{K_l} \tag{30}$$

$$\frac{d}{dt}i_{qs} = -\frac{K_r}{K_l}i_{qs} - L_m\frac{\omega_r}{K_lL_r}\lambda_{dr} + L_m\frac{1}{K_lL_r}\frac{R_r}{L_r}\lambda_{qr} + \frac{V_{qs}}{K_l} \tag{31}$$

Equations (27) (30) (31) can be concisely written by the following vector differential equation:

$$\frac{d}{dt}\begin{bmatrix} i_{ds} \\ i_{qs} \\ \lambda_{dr} \\ \lambda_{qr} \end{bmatrix}(t) = \begin{bmatrix} -\dfrac{K_r}{K_l} & 0 & \dfrac{L_m}{K_lL_r}\dfrac{R_r}{L_r} & \dfrac{L_m\omega_r(t)}{K_lL_r} \\ 0 & -\dfrac{K_r}{K_l} & -\dfrac{L_m\omega_r(t)}{K_lL_r} & \dfrac{L_m}{K_lL_r}\dfrac{R_r}{L_r} \\ L_m\dfrac{R_r}{L_r} & 0 & -\dfrac{R_r}{L_r} & -\omega_r(t) \\ 0 & L_m\dfrac{R_r}{L_r} & \omega_r(t) & -\dfrac{R_r}{L_r} \end{bmatrix}\begin{bmatrix} i_{ds}(t) \\ i_{qs}(t) \\ \lambda_{dr}(t) \\ \lambda_{qr}(t) \end{bmatrix} + \begin{bmatrix} \dfrac{V_{ds}(t)}{K_l} \\ \dfrac{V_{qs}(t)}{K_l} \\ 0 \\ 0 \end{bmatrix} \tag{32}$$

The electrical torque that the motor exerts on the load at time t is proportional to $\lambda_{dr}(t)i_{qr}(t) - \lambda_{qr}(t)i_{dr}(t)$, and the total torque (the motor's electrical torque and the load torque) at time t can be expressed as a function of $i_{ds}(t), i_{qs}(t), \lambda_{dr}(t), \lambda_{qr}(t)$ and the load torque. The instantaneous acceleration of the rotor's angle, $\frac{d\omega_r}{dt}(t)$ is equal to the instantaneous torque. Therefore, (32) with the torque-acceleration equation describes the time evolution of the five state variables $i_{ds}(t), i_{qs}(t), \lambda_{dr}(t), \lambda_{qr}(t), \omega_r(t)$.

Equation (32) was derived for the two-pole machine, which means that each winding has two magnetic poles (north and south). The system dynamics of the P-pole machine, which means that each winding has P magnetic poles, can be derived in a similar manner with more complexity. The state evolution can be expressed as:

$$\frac{d}{dt}\begin{bmatrix} i_{ds} \\ i_{qs} \\ \lambda_{dr} \\ \lambda_{qr} \end{bmatrix}(t) = \begin{bmatrix} -\dfrac{K_r}{K_l} & 0 & \dfrac{L_m}{K_l L_r}\dfrac{R_r}{L_r} & \dfrac{P}{2}\dfrac{L_m \omega_{rm}(t)}{K_l L_r} \\ 0 & -\dfrac{K_r}{K_l} & -\dfrac{P}{2}\dfrac{L_m \omega_{rm}(t)}{K_l L_r} & \dfrac{L_m}{K_l L_r}\dfrac{R_r}{L_r} \\ L_m\dfrac{R_r}{L_r} & 0 & -\dfrac{R_r}{L_r} & -\dfrac{P}{2}\omega_{rm}(t) \\ 0 & L_m\dfrac{R_r}{L_r} & \dfrac{P}{2}\omega_{rm}(t) & -\dfrac{R_r}{L_r} \end{bmatrix}\begin{bmatrix} i_{ds}(t) \\ i_{qs}(t) \\ \lambda_{dr}(t) \\ \lambda_{qr}(t) \end{bmatrix} + \begin{bmatrix} \dfrac{V_{ds}(t)}{K_l} \\ \dfrac{V_{qs}(t)}{K_l} \\ 0 \\ 0 \end{bmatrix} \qquad (33)$$

where $\omega_{rm}(t)$ is the angular speed of the rotor. Note that equation (32) is identical to (33) if $\omega_r(t) = \frac{P}{2}\omega_{rm}(t)$. In motor literature, quantity $\omega_r(t)$ is referred to as the rotor speed in electrical radians/sec, and $\omega_{rm}(t)$ is referred to as the rotor speed in mechanical radians/sec. Finally, to include in the model the random noise, the following model for the system evolution is used:

$$\frac{d}{dt}\begin{bmatrix} i_{ds} \\ i_{qs} \\ \lambda_{dr} \\ \lambda_{qr} \end{bmatrix}(t) = \begin{bmatrix} -\dfrac{K_r}{K_l} & 0 & \dfrac{L_m}{K_l L_r}\dfrac{R_r}{L_r} & \dfrac{P}{2}\dfrac{L_m \omega_{rm}(t)}{K_l L_r} \\ 0 & -\dfrac{K_r}{K_l} & -\dfrac{P}{2}\dfrac{L_m \omega_{rm}(t)}{K_l L_r} & \dfrac{L_m}{K_l L_r}\dfrac{R_r}{L_r} \\ L_m\dfrac{R_r}{L_r} & 0 & -\dfrac{R_r}{L_r} & -\dfrac{P}{2}\omega_{rm}(t) \\ 0 & L_m\dfrac{R_r}{L_r} & \dfrac{P}{2}\omega_{rm}(t) & -\dfrac{R_r}{L_r} \end{bmatrix}\begin{bmatrix} i_{ds}(t) \\ i_{qs}(t) \\ \lambda_{dr}(t) \\ \lambda_{qr}(t) \end{bmatrix} + \begin{bmatrix} \dfrac{V_{ds}(t)}{K_l} \\ \dfrac{V_{qs}(t)}{K_l} \\ 0 \\ 0 \end{bmatrix} + W(t) \qquad (34)$$

Random signal $W(t)$ can represent the inexactness of the model and the random noise present in the physical system. Equation (34) and the rotor acceleration equation together can be viewed as a nonlinear dynamic system (Luenberger, 1979), with $V_{ds}(t)$ and $V_{qs}(t)$ as control variables and $i_{ds}(t), i_{qs}(t), \lambda_{dr}(t),$ $\lambda_{qr}(t), \omega_{rm}(t)$ as state variables.

Controlling the speed of the motor is a practical problem. As, the stator currents can be measured, feedback control can be exercised. If the system has a motor speed sensor, the measured speed would be valuable feedback information for controlling the motor speed. However, having mechanical speed sensors has its disadvantages too, and the authors focus on controlling the speed without speed sensors. The approach is to estimate the rotor speed from the measurements of stator currents and use that estimation in deciding the value of the control variables.

For a linear system with additive noise, the Kalman filter (Kalman, 1960; Grewal, 2001; Gallager, 2013) is a well-known estimator. With $i_{ds}(t), i_{qs}(t), \lambda_{dr}(t), \lambda_{qr}(t), \omega_{rm}(t)$ as state variables, (34) is a nonlinear system. This chapter considers the extended Kalman filter (Crassidis & Junkins, 2011) as the state estimator of the nonlinear system. In order to run the extended Kalman filter, the system parameters like the noise covariance are needed. This chapter focuses on optimizing the noise covariance so that the mean-square error of the speed estimation is minimized.

Discrete-Time Model

For implementing the state estimator on a microcontroller, a discrete-time model is required. (Hilairet et al., 2009). A discrete-time model can be derived by time-sampling the continuous-time system. If we denote the sampling period by M for deriving discrete-time models, then each variable in continuous time, $f(t)$, is replaced with $f(Mn)$, and $\frac{df}{dt}(t)$ with $\frac{f(Mn+M)-f(Mn)}{M}$. In the discrete-time model, the nth sampled value shall be simply denoted as $f(n)$ in this chapter. If the sampling period M is sufficiently small, the rotor acceleration between time Mn and at time $M(n+1)$ is close to 0, and for the purpose of speed estimation by the extended Kalman filter, rotor speed acceleration can be approximately modelled as

$$\omega_{rm}(n+1) = \omega_{rm}(n) \tag{35}$$

Then, the resulting discrete-time dynamic system has the following form (Shi et al, 2002) and (Marino et al, 2010):

$$\begin{aligned}
\mathbf{x}(n+1) &= \mathbf{A}(n)\mathbf{x}(n) + \mathbf{B}(n)\mathbf{u}(n) + \mathbf{w}(n) \\
\mathbf{y}(n) &= \mathbf{C}(n)\mathbf{x}(n) + \mathbf{v}(n)
\end{aligned} \tag{36}$$

where $\mathbf{x}(n) = \left[i_{ds}(n), i_{qs}(n), \lambda_{dr}(n), \lambda_{qr}(n), \omega_{rm}(n) \right]^T$ is the state vector, $\mathbf{u}(n) = \left[V_{ds}^n, V_{qs}^n \right]^T$ represents the inputs, $\mathbf{y}(n) = \left[i_{ds}^n, i_{qs}^n \right]^T$ represents the measured values, and

$$\mathbf{A}(n) = \begin{bmatrix}
1 - \dfrac{K_r}{K_l}M & 0 & \dfrac{L_m R_r}{L_r^2 K_l}M & \dfrac{PL_m \omega_{rm}(n)}{2L_r K_l}M & 0 \\[2ex]
0 & 1 - \dfrac{K_r}{K_l}M & -\dfrac{PL_m \omega_{rm}(n)}{2L_r K_l}M & \dfrac{L_m R_r}{L_r^2 K_l}M & 0 \\[2ex]
\dfrac{L_m R_r}{L_r}M & 0 & 1 - \dfrac{R_r}{L_r}M & -\dfrac{P\omega_{rm}(n)}{2}M & 0 \\[2ex]
0 & \dfrac{L_m R_r}{L_r}M & \dfrac{P\omega_{rm}(n)}{2}M & 1 - \dfrac{R_r}{L_r}M & 0 \\[2ex]
0 & 0 & 0 & 0 & 1
\end{bmatrix} \tag{37}$$

$$\mathbf{B}(n) = \begin{bmatrix} \dfrac{M}{K_l} & 0 \\[2ex] 0 & \dfrac{M}{K_l} \end{bmatrix} \text{ and } \mathbf{C}(n) = \begin{bmatrix} 1 & 0 & 0 & 0 & 0 \\ 0 & 1 & 0 & 0 & 0 \end{bmatrix}.$$

Vector sequences $\mathbf{w}(n), \mathbf{v}(n)$ are discrete-time random sequences representing the process noise and the measurement noise, respectively. These noise terms are assumed to have zero mean and can represent both the random noise physically present in the system and the modelling inexactness. Recalling that the discrete-time model (36) and (37) has approximate relation (35) without considering noise terms, we note that the discrete-time dynamic system model (36) (37) is mainly used for the purpose of estimating the rotor speed, not for predicting the motor's behavior through these equations.

For speed estimation based on observation sequence $y(n)$, the values of noise covariance matrices are required. As the noise terms $w(n), v(n)$ include modeling inaccuracy, the noise covariance values are not available a priori, and these values can be considered as modeling parameters to be tuned. This chapter focuses on optimizing the noise covariance so that the mean-square error of the speed estimation is minimized. It is assumed that random vector sequence $w(n)$ and $v(n)$ are uncorrelated across difference times and so can be denoted as the following:

$$E\left[w(n+k)w(n)^T \right] = Q\delta(k) \;, E\left[v(n+k)v(n)^T \right] = R\delta(k) \tag{38}$$

where $\delta(k)$ denotes the Kronecker delta function, and Q and R are the covariance matrices of $w(n)$ and $v(n)$, respectively. Then, the performance (the mean-square error of speed estimation) resulting from using modelling parameter values Q and R can be denoted by a function $f(Q,R)$. A major issue addressed by this research was to minimize the function $f(Q,R)$. A major goal of this research was to analyze the performance of the enhanced fireworks (EFWA) algorithm for this optimization. This research focused on the system that used the extended Kalman filter (EKF) as the state estimator.

The Extended Kalman Filter

The induction motor (IM) state-space model is a nonlinear dynamic system because matrix A contains the fifth state variable, ω_r. However, the dynamic system contains only a few nonlinear (in fact bilinear) terms, so it can be considered as being close to a linear system. As such, the extended Kalman filter is a good candidate for dealing with the nonlinearity. Indeed, the extended Kalman filter is often discussed in literature for induction motor state estimation (Hussain & Abid Bazaz, 2016; Lee, 2016a; Lee, 2016b; Li, et al., 2016; Lin, et al., 2014; Alsofyani, et al., 2012; Alonge & D'Ippolio, 2010; Shi, et al., 2002; Shi, et al., 2000; Hilairet, et al., 2009; Kim, 1994; Salvatore, et al., 1993). The basic idea of the extended Kalman filter is to linearize the state transition function by using the Jacobian matrix of the transition function.

The Jacobian Matrix

The state transition functions are provided in equations 39 and 40 (Shi et al., 2002).

Denote $x(n+1) = f(x(n), u(n))$, where

$$f\big(\mathbf{x}(n),\mathbf{u}(n)\big) = \begin{bmatrix} \left(1-\dfrac{K_r}{K_l}M\right)i_{ds} + \dfrac{L_m R_r}{L_r^2 K_l}M\lambda_{dr} + \dfrac{PL_m\omega_{rm}}{2L_r K_l}M\lambda_{qr} + \dfrac{M}{K_l}V_{ds} \\[2ex] \left(1-\dfrac{K_r}{K_l}M\right)i_{qs} - \dfrac{PL_m\omega_{rm}}{2L_r K_l}M\lambda_{dr} + \dfrac{L_m R_r}{L_r^2 K_l}M\lambda_{qr} + \dfrac{M}{K_l}V_{qs} \\[2ex] \dfrac{L_m M}{T_r}i_{ds} + \left(1-\dfrac{M}{T_r}\right)\lambda_{dr} - \dfrac{P\omega_{rm}}{2}M\lambda_{qr} \\[2ex] \dfrac{L_m M}{T_r}i_{qs} + \dfrac{P\omega_{rm}}{2}\lambda_{dr} - \left(1-\dfrac{M}{T_r}\right)\lambda_{qr} \\[2ex] \omega_{rm} \end{bmatrix} \qquad (39)$$

where $T_r \equiv L_r/R_r$. The basic idea of the discrete-time EKF is to linearize the state transition function, $f(\cdot)$, at each time step, by differentiating by x. The result is called the Jacobian matrix, and for the IM it is as follows (Shi et al., 2002).

$$\frac{\partial \mathbf{f}}{\partial \mathbf{x}} = \begin{bmatrix} \left(1-\dfrac{K_r}{K_l}M\right) & 0 & \dfrac{L_m R_r}{L_r^2 K_l}M & \dfrac{PL_m\omega_{rm}}{2L_r K_l}M & \dfrac{PL_m}{2L_r K_l}M\lambda_{qr} \\[2ex] 0 & \left(1-\dfrac{K_r}{K_l}M\right) & -\dfrac{PL_m\omega_{rm}}{2L_r K_l}M & \dfrac{L_m R_r}{L_r^2 K_l}M & -\dfrac{PL_m}{2L_r K_l}M\lambda_{dr} \\[2ex] \dfrac{L_m}{T_r}M & 0 & 1-\dfrac{M}{T_r} & -\dfrac{P\omega_{rm}}{2}M & \dfrac{P}{2}M\lambda_{qr} \\[2ex] 0 & \dfrac{L_m}{T_r}M & -\dfrac{P\omega_{rm}}{2}M & 1-\dfrac{M}{T_r} & \dfrac{P}{2}M\lambda_{dr} \\[2ex] 0 & 0 & 0 & 0 & 1 \end{bmatrix} \qquad (40)$$

Predict and Filter Cycles

The EKF estimation process is an iterative process. Each iteration has two cycles: the predict cycle and the filter cycle. Initially the estimated value of the state matrix, $\hat{\mathbf{x}}(n|n)$, is all zeros. The hat on top of the variable $\mathbf{x}$ means that it is an estimate. For the variables in brackets, the first letter n means the value at the nth iteration, and the second letter n means the results from the first n iterations are known. Therefore, the meaning can be summarized as the value of the estimates of the state variables (x-hat) at the nth iteration, given the results from the first n iterations.

The error covariance matrix, $\mathbf{P}(n|n)$, is a measure of the joint variability of the errors in the state variables at the nth step, given the first n iterations. Initially the error covariance matrix of the process noise, $\mathbf{P}(n|n)$, is assumed to be a unit matrix. The values in this matrix are updated with each iteration of the model, based on the state Jacobian matrix and the system process covariance.

In the two-step estimation process, inputs, $\mathbf{u}(n)$, are applied to the system and as a result the measurements, $\mathbf{y}(n)$, are produced. The same inputs are applied to the EKF predict cycle along with the previous state, $\hat{\mathbf{x}}(n|n)$, to find the a priori prediction of the state, $\hat{\mathbf{x}}(n+1|n)$. The prediction of the error covariance matrix, $\mathbf{P}(n|n+1)$, is found using the following equation (Shi et al., 2002).

$$P(n+1\,|\,n) = \frac{\partial \mathbf{f}}{\partial \mathbf{x}}\bigg|_{x=x(nn)} P(nn)\frac{\partial \mathbf{f}}{\partial \mathbf{x}}^{T}\bigg|_{x=x(nn)} + \mathbf{G}(n)\mathbf{Q}(n)\mathbf{G}(n)^{T}\big| \tag{41}$$

where the variable $\mathbf{G}(n)$ is the weighting matrix of noise.

The filter cycle uses the measurements and predictions to compute the Kalman gain that will minimize the difference between these values. The Kalman gain is calculated so that when the measurement noise is smaller, the measurement is weighted more heavily in determining the best estimate. If the process noise is small, the a priori estimate is more heavily weighted (Matlab/Simulink website, 2019). The optimal estimate is the mean of the pdf.

Steps to Calculate Gain and Update Prediction

The steps to calculate the Kalman gain are described in this section. The matrix, $\mathbf{H}$, is called the measurement function. It is denoted by $\mathbf{H}(x(n)) = \mathbf{C}(n)\mathbf{x}(n)$, giving the following result (Shi et al, 2002).

$$\mathbf{H}(\mathbf{x}(n)) = \begin{bmatrix} 1 & 0 & 0 & 0 & 0 \\ 0 & 1 & 0 & 0 & 0 \end{bmatrix} \begin{bmatrix} i_{ds} \\ i_{qs} \\ \lambda_{dr} \\ \lambda_{qr} \\ \omega_{r} \end{bmatrix} = \begin{bmatrix} i_{ds} \\ i_{qs} \end{bmatrix} \tag{42}$$

The measured values are used to correct the estimate. Another matrix, $\mathbf{C}$, is used, derived as follows (Shi et al, 2002).

$$\frac{\partial \mathbf{H}}{\partial \mathbf{x}} = \begin{bmatrix} 1 & 0 & 0 & 0 & 0 \\ 0 & 1 & 0 & 0 & 0 \end{bmatrix} = \mathbf{C}(n) \tag{43}$$

This matrix is used to identify which of the state values are actually measured, which in this case are the components of the current.

The Kalman gain, $\mathbf{K}(n)$, is computed to improve convergence of the estimate to actual values. It's calculated using error covariance, $\mathbf{P}$, and the measurement noise covariance matrix, $\mathbf{R}$. Note that a superscript, T, means transpose (Shi et al., 2002).

$$\mathbf{K}(n+1) = \mathbf{P}(n\,|\,n+1)\mathbf{C}(n)^{T}\left[\mathbf{C}(n)\mathbf{P}(n\,|\,n+1)\mathbf{C}(n)^{T} + \mathbf{R}(n)\right]^{-1} \tag{44}$$

The proof for the Kalman filter gain equation is provided in Shi et al, (2002) and is based on conditional probability.

The updated state estimate is as follows (Shi et al., 2002):

$$\hat{\mathbf{x}}(n+1\,|\,n+1) = \hat{\mathbf{x}}(n\,|\,n+1) + \mathbf{K}(n)\left[\mathbf{y}(n) - \mathbf{C}(n)\hat{\mathbf{x}}(n\,|\,n+1)\right] \tag{45}$$

where the portion of the equation inside square brackets indicates the error or difference between the measured and estimated values. The updated error covariance matrix is calculated as follows (Shi et al, 2002).

$$\mathbf{P}(n+1\,|\,n+1) = \mathbf{P}(n\,|\,n+1) - \mathbf{K}(n)\mathbf{C}(n)\mathbf{P}(n+1\,|\,n) \tag{46}$$

The algorithm repeats with each iteration, but only needs the previous time step, and so is recursive. These steps are implemented in a function block in Matlab/Simulink in the manner described in Figure 1.

Figure 1. Simulink implementation of EKF showing predict and filter cycles

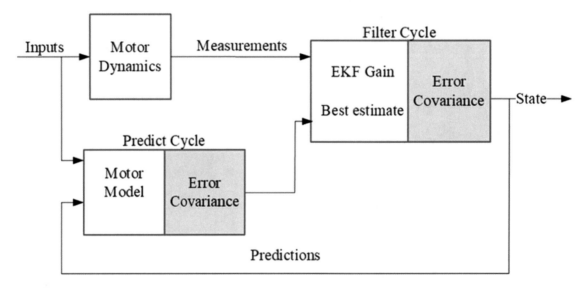

State of the Art

Several different approaches have been taken for EKF speed sensing covariance optimization. Adaptive tuning with a fuzzy logic controller has been successfully used with an EKF to combine different measurements (Loebis et al, 2004) and (Hussain and Abid Bazaz 2016). Particle swarm optimization (PSO) was considered but with less successful results, because it did not fully explore the space before termination (Lin, Jing and Liu, 2014). In recent papers, good results were reported with classical PSO (Rayyam and Zazi, 2018). Improved PSO, which includes GA, is used in speed estimation for field-oriented control of an IM with good results (Lin, Jing and Liu, 2014). Modified PSO (MPSO) is successfully implemented in (Song, Xu and Xu, 2018). The recent results from PSO, IPSO and MPSO look promising; however, the performance was not compared to other optimization algorithms such as GA.

The fireworks algorithm (FWA) is a particle swarm algorithm which mimics fireworks explosions to find a good solution (Tan, 2015). Swarm intelligence has the advantage of moving the population towards "good" locations with favourable results and away from those with poor results. This improves the search by reducing the time to find a solution. The enhanced fireworks algorithm (EFWA) is a relatively new iteration of the FWA, which implements many significant improvements to the original algorithm (Tan, 2015).

In this research, an EFWA is implemented as part of a speed-sensorless drive to optimize the EKF covariance matrices, which is a new approach. The algorithm is modified for this purpose by setting the number of fireworks, number of explosion sparks, and minimum and maximum number of sparks per iteration, as well as by establishing a minimum spark amplitude. The results demonstrate that the EFWA optimization provides good results with fewer iterations, compared to the best alternative GA optimization with different variations of EFWA and IM parameters. This advantage may be desirable for applications in adaptive sensorless drives with EKF, where a quick solution is required for online tuning of controllers.

A major issue in this research was to optimize the performance measure, the mean square error of the speed estimation error as a function of modeling parameters $\mathbf{Q}$ and $\mathbf{R}$, (the noise covariance matrices in the application of this research). A practical challenge of this problem is that the explicit, closed-form expression of this function is not available, and the function value at each combination of independent variables can only be evaluated through simulation or experimentation.

As the function evaluation is costly, an important issue to be considered in selecting an evolutionary algorithm is that the algorithm produce a good solution with a small number of function evaluations. In this research, we analyzed the performance of the enhanced fireworks algorithm (EFWA).

THE FIREWORKS ALGORITHM

The family of particle swarm algorithms, which include the fireworks algorithm (FWA), use "intelligence" created by the cooperative nature of swarms. In some applications, swarm intelligence can help to improve optimization results by finding an acceptable solution in fewer iterations.

Principles of FWA

The FWA randomly generates individual fireworks which represent candidate solutions to the given optimization problem. These fireworks are tested and given a fitness score. If the fitness level is strong, the firework will generate many sparks and the distance the sparks travel will be small. This allows the algorithm to exploit the general area around a successful candidate solution. If the fitness level of an individual candidate solution is poor, the firework will generate fewer sparks and the distance the sparks travel will tend to be greater. Fewer sparks means that the algorithm avoids unnecessary computing of candidate solutions in a poor region and allows the algorithm to explore a larger solution space. Figure 2 provides the conceptual idea of FWA (Tan, 2015).

FWA Equations for Minimizing a Cost Function

Two key equations are used in the FWA: the number of sparks and the amplitude of sparks. The number of sparks is calculated as follows (Tan, 2015):

Figure 2. Basic Principle of Fireworks Algorithm Showing the Results from Good and Bad Fitness Scores

Good fitness score

Bad fitness score

$$S_i = m \frac{Y_{max} - f(x_i) + \varepsilon}{\sum_{i=1}^{N}(Y_{max} - f(x_i)) + \varepsilon} \qquad (47)$$

Where S_i is the number of sparks associated with the firework indexed by i, N is the number of fireworks, Y_{max} is the cost function value (a measure of fitness) for the worst firework, $f(x_i)$ is the cost function value for the current firework, m is the total number of sparks, and ε is a value used to avoid dividing by zero (Tan, 2015).

The amplitude of the sparks is found using the following equation (Tan, 2015):

$$A_i = \widehat{A} \frac{f(x_i) - Y_{min} + \varepsilon}{\sum_{i=1}^{N}(f(x_i) - Y_{min}) + \varepsilon} \qquad (48)$$

where A_i is the amplitude for the current firework, N is the number of fireworks, Y_{min} is the smallest cost function value in the population (the cost function value of the firework with best fitness, $f(x_i)$ is the fitness value for the current firework, $\widehat{A}$ is a constant to control explosion amplitudes, and ε is a value used to avoid dividing by zero (Tan, 2015).

Issues With FWA

Researchers identified issues with the original FWA. Some concerns are associated with the amplitudes, which represent the distance the sparks travel from the firework, and other problems related to mapping and mutation.

In the FWA, the calculated spark amplitude could be very small for fireworks with good scores, which means that the algorithm may converge prematurely around a good solution, instead of continuing to search for a better one. As well, the FWA applies the calculated spark amplitude equally to all dimensions of the search space, which leads to poor search diversity (Zheng et al., 2013).

Another issue with the FWA is related to the mutation operator. It tends to move solutions towards the origin (0,0) of the search space (Tan, 2015; Zheng et al., 2013). This tendency may not be desirable for applications where the best solutions exist at locations other than the origin.

A third issue is that if a solution lands outside of the boundaries of the feasible search space, the FWA moves the infeasible candidate solution into a feasible set of the optimization problem. The mapping is based on using a modulus operator to provide a new value when a spark travels outside of the bounds. This modulus operator has the tendency to move candidate solutions towards the origin. Once again, this may not be the best approach for all systems (Tan, 2015; Zheng et al, 2013).

Lastly, the original FWA's strategy for selecting candidate solutions for passing onto the next generation is computationally expensive, and it was not found to improve the results significantly over random selection (Tan, 2015; Zheng et al., 2013).

Improvements in the Enhanced Fireworks Algorithm

The enhanced fireworks algorithm (EFWA) was developed due to concerns identified with the original FWA (Zheng et al., 2013). Amplitude, mapping, and selection issues are addressed in the EFWA.

A minimum amplitude is introduced in the EFWA, which linearly decreases with each generation, to mitigate the issue of small amplitudes in the FWA. As well, a different random displacement of the amplitude is applied to each dimension, to improve search diversity (Zheng et al., 2013).

As for the mutation operation, the Gaussian operation is modified to randomly move the candidate solution by the amount of a Gaussian random variable from their original location along the line connecting the current location and the location of the current best candidate solution (Zheng et al., 2013). This modification keeps the algorithm from tending to move towards the origin, as was the case with the FWA.

In the EFWA, a random mapping function was introduced in place of the modulus operator to keep solutions within the search space (Zheng et al., 2013). Solutions that fall outside the boundary are moved to a random new location inside the search space, without the tendency to move towards the origin, as in the FWA. This helps to support search diversity.

The EFWA uses "elitism-randomism" to select solutions, instead of the distance-based selection strategy of the FWA. The top candidate solution is chosen for the next generation (iteration) and the rest of the group in the next generation (iteration) is selected randomly from the current generation's candidate solutions (Zheng et al., 2013).

According to Tan (2015) and Zheng et al. (2013), the EFWA modifications produced beneficial results in many applications, so the authors decided to use the EFWA in this research.

EFWA Pseudocode

Algorithm 1 summarizes the pseudocode implemented for the EFWA based on Tan (2015) and Zheng et al. (2013).

Algorithm 1. EFWA pseudocode
1. Set the lower and upper bounds of the search space
2. Set the number of fireworks, mutant sparks, generations, and max number of sparks, max amplitude, and dimensions of the search space
3. Set initial and final minimum amplitude
4. Generate first set of fireworks randomly within the specified bounds
5. Run the simulation with each of the fireworks to get fitness values
6. Find the best and the worst firework and associated fitness value
7. Use the results from step 6 to calculate the number of sparks for each firework
8. Adjust for limitations on number of sparks
9. Use results from step 6 to calculate the amplitude for each firework
10. Adjust amplitudes to within upper and lower bounds
11. Randomly choose dimensions and adjust amplitude
12. Generate mutant sparks
13. Map any spark outside of search space back inside boundary
14. Find fitness value for all sparks
15. Find firework or spark with best fitness value
16. Pass optimum solution (best firework or spark) to next generation of fireworks
17. Randomly select the rest of the fireworks
18. Loop back and repeat steps 6-17 for the rest of the generations

IMPLEMENTATION OF THE SIMULATION

In optimizing the performance function $f(Q,R)$ of modelling parameters (Q,R) through an evolutionary algorithm, the function value must be computed for multiple candidate solutions (Q,R). As mentioned before, the function evaluation $f(Q,R)$ requires simulation or experimentation. This research resorted to simulation for function evaluation. In this section, how this function was evaluated for each candidate solution is discussed.

In this research, the EFWA optimization was applied to a simple system that comprises the induction motor (IM), a simple speed controller called a closed-loop voltage per hertz controller, and the extended Kalman filter (EKF). The diagram in Figure 3 illustrates this system. The voltage per hertz controller exerts control action to change the motor speed by varying the voltage magnitude and frequency applied to the IM stator. The speed of the IM rotor depends on the applied frequency. The magnitude of the applied voltage must be varied in proportion to the frequency in order to maintain a constant flux, hence the name, voltage per hertz. This controller can be implemented in a commercial power electronics device called a variable frequency drive (VFD). The basic components of a VFD are a controller, a diode bridge rectifier, a capacitor and a controllable invertor.

The applied voltage and the resulting stator currents are transformed to $qd0$ components and provided as input to the EKF, which estimates the state of the IM including the rotor speed based on the mathematical model previously discussed and the noise covariances (Q,R). The difference between the estimated speed and the set point is fed back to the controller through a proportional-integrative feedback loop. Thus, a feedback speed control loop for an IM is accomplished without a speed sensor.

In order to evaluate the mean-square difference, $f(Q,R)$, between the estimated rotor speed and the actual rotor speed for a candidate solution (Q,R), the system illustrated in Figure 3 should be in operation for a period of time and the actual rotor speed and the rotor speed estimation produced by the EKF must be sampled so that the mean-square error between them is computed. This research resorted to simulation, so both the actual speed and the EKF-estimated speed were computed by the simulator.

The actual rotor speed used for EKF optimization was calculated based on mathematical equations for calculating the speed of the induction motor rotor given the stator voltages and the mechanical load (torque). These equations are based on the equivalent T-circuit for an induction motor (Krause, et. al., 2012) and use parameters determined from the blocked-rotor and no load test.

To simulate operation of the system in Figure 3, the induction motor (IM) system is assumed to start from zero initial conditions. Each single simulation consists of the following speed reference profile:

Figure 3. Kalman Gain Feedback Loop Block Diagram Showing The IM State Variables Vector and State Variable Matrix

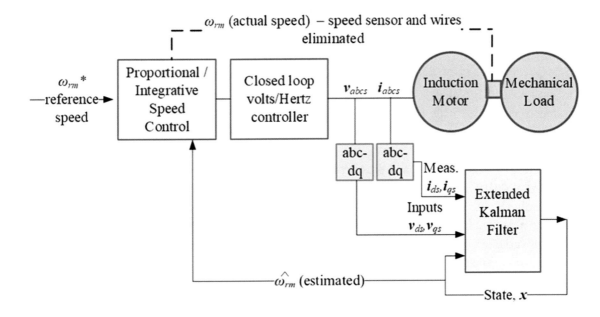

$$\omega_{rm}^{\cdot} = \begin{cases} 0 \sim 120 rad \, / \, s, & \text{if } 0s < t \le 1.5s \\ 120 rad \, / \, s, & \text{if } 1.5s < t \le 3s \\ 120 \sim 20 rad \, / \, s, & \text{if } 3s < t \le 4.25s \\ 20 rad \, / \, s, & \text{if } 4.25 < t \le 5s \end{cases} \qquad (49)$$

To compare and evaluate the candidate solutions that are obtained by different methods, the performance is assessed iteratively using the mean square error (MSE) calculated as follows:

$$MSE = \frac{\sum_{i=1}^{i=N} \left(\omega_{act,rm}(i) - \hat{\omega}_{rm}(i) \right)^2}{N} \qquad (50)$$

where N represents the number of samples, $\omega_{act,rm}$ is the actual speed, and $\hat{\omega}_{rm}$ is the estimated speed. The goal of optimizing the EKF parameters is to reach the lowest *MSE* value. For consistency of comparison among different methods, the sampling time is set to be 1×10^{-4} seconds for all simulations. Profiles (49) were chosen because that is commonly accepted in the induction motor community – e.g., (Shi et al., 2002), and using the same speed profile facilitates comparison with existing research (Shi et al., 2002).

Simulink Model

The speed estimation control system illustrated in Figure 3 is implemented in a commercial tool called Matlab/Simulink. Matlab is a programming environment used for scientific and mathematical problem solving based on the Matlab language. Simulink, one of the tools in the Matlab environment, allows block diagram-based modelling, simulation and analysis of dynamic systems (Matlab/Simulink website, 2019)

The Simulink model composed for this research has the following blocks: Proportional/Integrative (PI) speed controller, volts/Hertz (V/Hz) variable frequency drive (VFD) controller, induction motor (IM) and the extended Kalman filter (EKF) estimator. The PI control module is a feedback control mechanism that combines proportional and integral control and is widely used. An automatic controller typically compares the actual value of the controlled (plant) variable with the reference (command) input to determine the deviation, and the control action is taken to reduce the deviation to zero or a small value. (Ogata, 2010). It is intuitive to set value of the control variable, which causes the control action, proportional to the deviation perceived by the controller; this type of control action is called the proportional control action. In order to reduce the oscillation of the controlled variable, the controller can make the control variable proportional to the time integral of the past deviation; this type of control action is called the proportional control action. The Proportional/Integrative (PI) refers to the controller that takes into account both instantaneous and integrative deviation to decide the value of the control variable.

The output of the PI speed control module in Figure 3 can be mathematically described as

$$\omega_{rm}^{\cdot}(t) + K_i \int_0^t e(\tau) d\tau, \quad t > 0 \,,$$

where $e(\tau) \equiv \omega_{rm}^{*}(\tau) - \hat{\omega}_{rm}(\tau)$ is the difference (deviation) between the referenced (specified) command speed, $\omega_{rm}^{*}(\tau)$, of the motor at time τ, and the estimated speed, $\hat{\omega}_{rm}(\tau)$, at time τ, and K_i is the parameters of the control system.

The V/Hz (volt-per-hertz) controller uses the output of the PI speed control module to determine the stator voltage and frequency to apply to the induction motor required to obtain the specified speed. Basically, the V/Hz (volt-per-hertz) controller make the frequency of the sinusoidal stator voltages (input voltages) to the output of the PI speed control module while maintaining the ratio of the input voltage amplitude to the frequency constant in order to keep the flux linkage constant.

The calculation to determine the stator voltage depends on the output of the PI controller and can be mathematically described as:

$$V_{qs} = \left(\frac{\sqrt{2} * V_{base}}{\omega_{base}} * \frac{P}{2} \right) * \omega_{PI}; \qquad V_{ds} = 0$$

where ω_{PI} is the output of the PI controller, P is the number of poles,, V_{base} is the base (rated) root-mean-square value of the voltage of the system, ω_{base} is the base (rated) frequency of the system, and V_{qs} is the q component of the voltage to be applied to the stator. The speed of the rotor of an induction motor is proportional to the frequency of the voltage applied to the stator. By adjusting the frequency of the stator voltage, one can control the speed of the rotor. In the V/Hz controller the output, V_{qs}, sets the rotor speed established by its frequency. The output, V_{qs}, also sets the magnitude of the voltage. The magnitude is determined using the ratio of the base voltage magnitude and base frequency to maintain the ratio of volts per hertz constant over the full range of speeds. This ratio must be kept constant in order to maintain constant flux in the induction motor. This prevents the motor from overheating. This is why this type of control is called volts per Hertz control. The outputs of the V/Hz controller are the q and d components of the stator voltages. These values are transformed back to abc components before being applied to the induction motor Simulink block.

The inputs to the induction motor (IM) Simulink block are the abc stator voltages. The voltages are transformed to $qd0$ components. The $qd0$ voltages are used to determine all of the states of the IM ($qd0$ currents, torque and speed) using fundamental Simulink blocks such as the integrator and gain blocks to implement the basic motor equations derived from the IM equivalent T circuit (Krause et. al., 2013). The speed from the IM block is denoted as the actual speed and it is compared to the speed estimated by the EKF.

The Simulink model is shown in Figure 4. Each block in the diagram is a subsystem within the main model. All blocks are built using fundamental Simulink components as opposed to using pre-built Simscape/Power Systems blocks, for increased accuracy and faster response times. A Matlab parameter file contains the values for the constant terms used in the Simulink model. The parameters used were determined using the blocked rotor and no load test. These parameters and others used in the Simulink model, such as the mechanical load inertia and sample time, are provided in Appendix.

Figure 4. Simulink Model of Speed Estimation Control System used to Optimize Noise Covariance Matrices

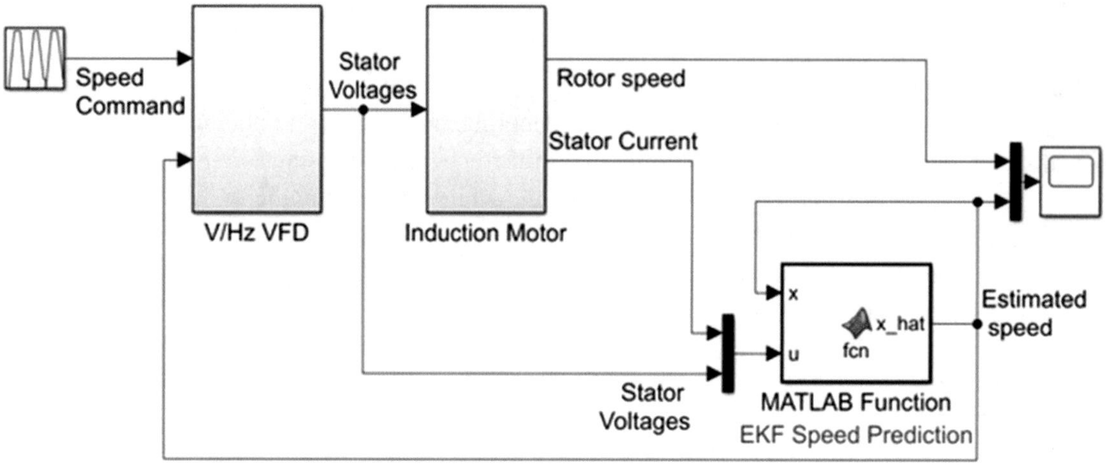

EKF Speed Estimation Block

A Matlab function block is used in Simulink to implement the EKF. The EKF code is executed for each iteration of the simulation. Pseudocode for the EKF estimator implements the equations previously derived and is provided in *Algorithm 2*.

Algorithm 2. Pseudocode for EKF estimator Matlab function block
1. Assign motor and system parameters
2. Assign error covariance matrix to be a 5x5 unit matrix
3. Assign sample time
4. Repeat the following steps with each iteration
   a. Read and assign inputs (voltages, currents and last state)
   b. Calculate Jacobian matrix at current state
   c. Predict next state
   d. Estimate error covariance matrix
   e. Calculate Kalman gain
   f. Update the error covariance matrix
   g. Update the prediction of the next state

RESEARCH RESULTS

The EFWA has configurable parameters, such as the number of sparks and fireworks and the amplitude constant which can influence the outcome of the optimization. In this section, these parameters are explored to determine good parameter values to use for optimizing the induction motor speed control model. Then, for a set of good EFWA parameter values found, the authors compare the EFWA performance

Figure 5. Number of fireworks varied with resulting MSE versus number of function calls – results from 20 independent optimizations using amplitude of 100, nominal population of 100, 10 mutated sparks

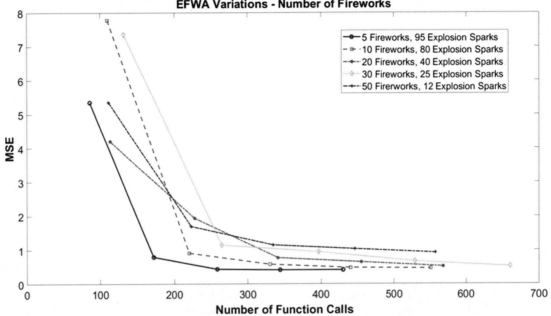

with the GA, using approximately equivalent GA parameters. The optimization problem considered is to minimize the MSE for the induction motor speed profile.

Exploring EFWA Parameters

The authors studied the effect of varying one parameter at a time in the EFWA on performance to determine optimal parameter values for the induction motor application. The parameters considered were the number of fireworks and sparks in a population and explosion amplitude. The optimization performance criterion considered for the application of motor speed control is the mean square error (MSE).

Multiple runs were necessary due to the random nature of the algorithms, hence, each of the data sets in the following study represents the average value from twenty independent runs with the same parameters.

Number of Fireworks

In each iteration (in each generation of the evolutionary algorithm), the fireworks are generated first and tested for fitness to determine the amplitude and number of sparks. Values of 5, 10, 20, 30 and 50 fireworks were considered, and EFWA algorithms were run using each of these values for 20 iterations. The effect of the number of fireworks on the speed of performance (mean square error of estimation error) improvement is shown in Figure 5. The other parameters used were, a nominal number of 100 explosion sparks, amplitude constant of 100, and 10 mutation sparks. Based on these results, in this particular application and setting, the optimal number of fireworks appears to be 5 - 10.

Figure 6. Magnified view of number of fireworks varied with resulting MSE versus number of function calls using amplitude of 100, nominal population of 100, 10 mutated sparks

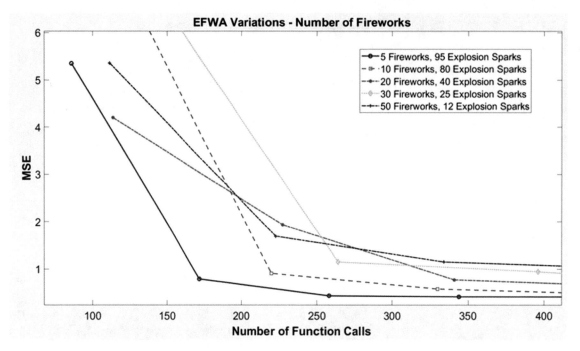

Figure 7. Nominal number of sparks varied with resulting MSE versus number of function calls using amplitude of 100, nominal population of 100, 10 mutated sparks

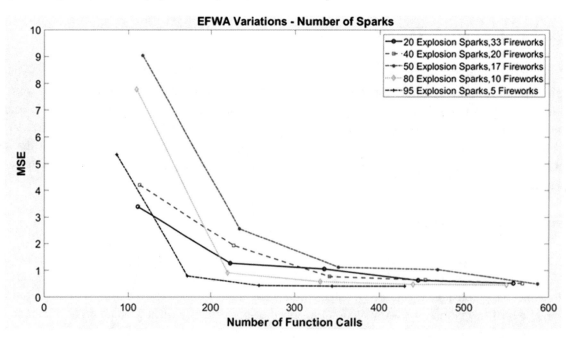

Figure 8. Magnified view of number of sparks varied with resulting MSE versus number of function calls using amplitude of 100, nominal population of 100, 10 mutated sparks

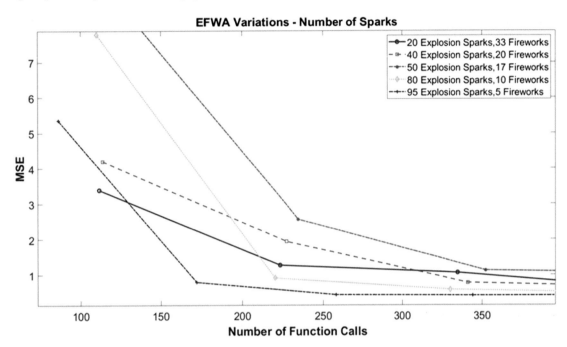

The magnified view of the results for the maximum number of fireworks is shown in Figure 6. This graph indicates that, assigning 5-10% of the population to be fireworks provide acceptable results for this application and population size.

Nominal Number of Explosion Sparks

Fireworks generate sparks, each one representing one candidate solution from the specified range. The nominal number of explosion sparks is a parameter that is specified in the algorithm and used to determine the number of sparks allocated to each firework. The nominal number of sparks is indeed a nominal value. The total number of explosion sparks actually generated in each iteration of EFWA can be different from the nominal value specified as an algorithm parameter and can vary from iteration to iteration. The reason for this is that the EFWA, in allocating the numbers of sparks to fireworks, imposes the minimum and maximum number of sparks a firework can generate in each iteration.

The authors compared the performance of EFWA for the following nominal numbers of explosion sparks: 20, 40, 50, 80 and 95. The other parameters used are amplitude constant of 100 and 10 mutation sparks. In Figure 7 the effect of changing the nominal number of sparks on the progress in the best mean square error attained by EFWA is shown. Based on the results, in this particular application and using the settings specified, the best EFWA performance among the parameter values tried was shown for the case of nominal number of sparks being 80 or 95.

In Figure 8, a magnified view of the results is presented for varying the maximum number of sparks. This graph verifies the previous conclusion that 80-95 sparks showed the fastest improvement of MSE as the total number of function calls increases for this application.

Figure 9. Amplitude varied with resulting MSE versus number of function calls using 10 fireworks, 90 explosion sparks, 10 mutated sparks

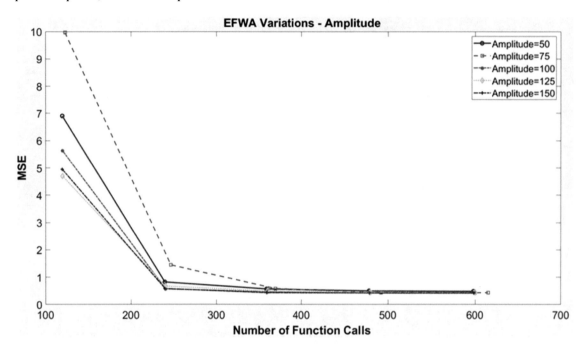

Amplitude Constant

As previously described, the amplitude constant, $\hat{A}$ in equation 48, is used to determine the distance away from the original firework that the sparks travel. The effect of changing the amplitude constant on the mean square error of the best result for each generation is shown in Figure 9. The different amplitude constants considered, as shown in the legend, are 50, 75, 100, 125 and 150. As can be seen in the graph, in this application the optimizations with higher values (100-150) provide the best results. The other parameters used are 10 fireworks, 90 nominal number of sparks and 10 mutation sparks.

In Figure 10 a magnified view of Figure 9 is presented. This graph confirms that higher values of amplitude constants provide good results. With the magnification it can be seen that a value of 100, 125 or 150 is the best choice in this application.

PERFORMANCE COMPARISON BETWEEN EFWA AND GA

This section will compare the performance of EFWA and GA for the induction motor application presented.

Setting EFWA and GA Parameters with the Objective of Obtaining Equal Number of Function Calls for Both

In the GA, the number of individuals in a population for each generation is fixed, whereas in the EFWA, the number of individuals can vary from generation to generation due to the enforcement of the maximum

Figure 10. Magnified view of amplitude varied with resulting MSE versus number of function calls using 10 fireworks, 90 explosion sparks, 10 mutated sparks

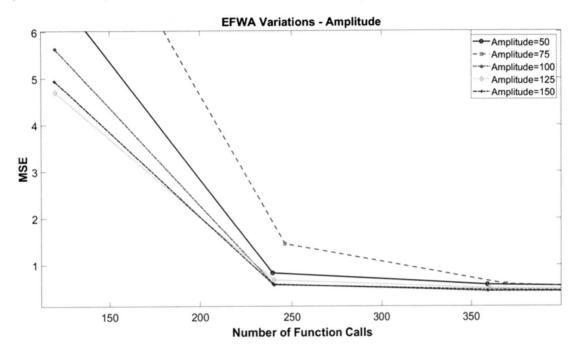

and minimum number of explosion sparks for each firework. Each EFWA generation (iteration) is comprised of both fireworks and sparks. The number of fireworks in each iteration, the number of mutation fireworks, and the nominal number of explosion sparks are set as EFWA parameters. If the maximum and minimum number of explosion sparks for each firework were not enforced, the number of function calls in each iteration of EFWA would be the sum of the number of fireworks, the number of explosion sparks, and the number of mutation sparks. However, because there are a minimum and maximum number of sparks per firework, the actual number of sparks varies per generation. For comparing EFWA with GA, the authors set the algorithm parameters with the intention of making the number of function calls per iteration (generation) and the total number of function calls in each simulation equal for both EFWA and GA. In order to make the number of function calls per generation approximately the same for both algorithms, a counter was used to track the number of function calls in EFWA.

In each optimization run of EFWA, the authors obtained the total number of function calls and divided it by the total number of iterations, which is denoted by G. The result of this division is the average number of function calls per iteration in each run of EFWA. The authors set the population size of GA to this number in order to compare EFWA's performance against GA's performance. In short, the GA's population size, N_{GA}, was obtained from the following equation.

$$N_{GA} = \frac{1}{G} \sum_{i=1}^{G} n_{EFWA}(i)$$

(51)

where $n_{EFWA}(i)$ denotes the number of EFWA function calls at the ith iteration.

Fitness Function

As was described in an earlier section, equation 50 is used to calculate the MSE to evaluate the fitness of each candidate firework and spark. The best solution is the one which results in the lowest MSE.

After running a few trial studies, using EFWA optimization, the MSE is typically reduced to less than 0.5 within five generations, using the parameters described in the previous section. The following optimized matrices, which were obtained after only four generations, provide a fitness score of 0.4212:

$$Q = Diag[0.07067, 0.03550, 0.01908, 0.01618, 0.02413] \text{ and } R = Diag[0.1723, 0.01618].$$

Comparison of EFWA with GA

To compare performance of EFWA with GA, the authors collected simulation data from twenty independent runs of each algorithm. The MSE of the best performing candidate solutions found up to each generation in those twenty simulation runs were averaged. The algorithm parameters used are described in the next section.

Parameters Used for Comparison

In comparing EFWA and GA, the following input parameters were used. The GA parameters are similar to those used in (Shi et al, 2002), and EFWA parameters were chosen to make a fair comparison using equation 51. Table 1 shows EFWA and Table 2 shows GA parameters.

Table 1. Parameters for EFWA

EFWA Parameters	
Number of fireworks	**10**
Nominal number of sparks	**100**
Constant used to determine min number of sparks	**0.1**
Constant used to determine max number of sparks	**0.3**
Amplitude constant	**100**
Initial minimum amplitude of sparks	**0.1**
Final minimum amplitude of sparks	**1.00E-06**
Elite count	**1**
Number of mutation sparks per generation	**10**
Population initial range of each variable	**[0-0.1]**

Table 2. GA parameters

GA Parameters	
Population size	**115**
Elite count	**1**
Crossover rate	**0.9**
Population initial range of each variable	**[0-0.1]**

Result of Comparison

Twenty independent runs of each optimization method, EFWA and GA, were conducted, and the average *MSE* was calculated for each generation, with the results provided in Figure 11. The graph shows that the GA results start with a high *MSE* and take about 10 generations to reduce to a MSE less than 0.5 (*MSE* = 0.4348 after 10 generations). The EFWA tends to start with a much better solution in the first generation and reaches a good solution of MSE, less than 0.5, after just a few generations (*MSE* = 0.4212 after 4 generations).

Figure 11. Average MSE per generation for twenty independent runs each of EFWA and GA optimizations with 95% confidence interval

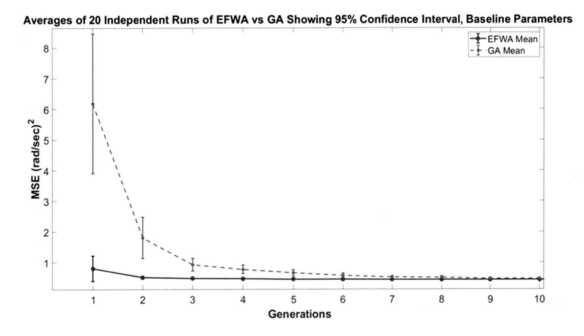

This graph represents the average *MSE* for each generation from 20 independent optimization runs. The graph shows the 95% confidence interval lines associated with average MSEs for both the EFWA and the GA. The confidence intervals do not overlap until 7 generations have passed.

Sample Speed Profile Comparison of EFWA and GA

Figure 12 illustrates the EKF speed estimation for the closed-loop IM system, with the covariance matrices optimized by the EFWA, trial-and-error, and GA methods for the comparison. Figure 13 shows a magnified view of the comparison. The EKF provides accurate speed tracking for increasing, decreasing, and constant speed conditions and good results with respect to the actual speed.

Figure 12. Illustration of EFWA Optimized Speed Estimate Simulation for One Solution (where the actual speed is from the Simulink IM model)

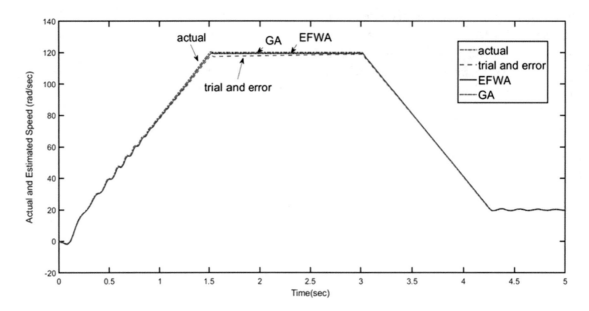

Figure 13. Magnified view of illustration of EFWA optimized speed estimate simulation for one solution (where the actual speed is from the Simulink IM model)

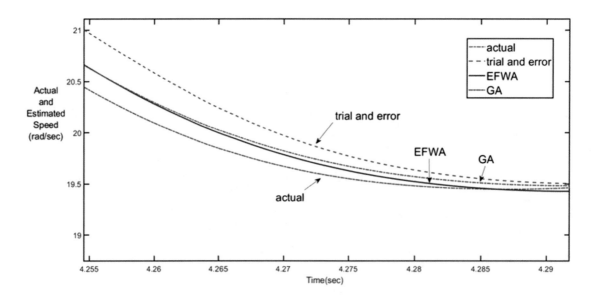

The EFWA method provides as good accuracy as GA; however, it became obvious after many optimization runs that the real improvement with the EFWA was that it was able to find an acceptable solution with fewer function calls. Typically, it was found that the *MSE* was reduced to less than 0.5 within five generations given a population size of approximately 100.

CONCLUSION

The authors conducted research on using the EFWA (enhanced fireworks algorithm) to optimally tune the model parameters for the purpose of controlling the induction motor without a speed sensor. This research considered a conventional volts-per-hertz induction motor (IM) drive with an extended Kalman filter (EKF) speed estimator. The system and measurement noise covariance matrices of the IM required to implement the EKF are typically unknown. The optimal system and noise covariances for an IM can be found using trial and error or using an optimization algorithm. The objective of either method is to minimize the error or difference between the estimated speed and the speed determined by a model of the IM. It was proposed that using a new algorithm; the enhanced fireworks algorithm (EFWA), for the purpose of optimizing the noise covariances, may improve results.

To compare the different optimization methods, a model was built to simulate the IM and VFD using Simulink fundamental blocks. The EKF estimator was implemented using a Matlab function block. The IM model was built in Simulink using induction motor (IM) equations and the function block was created using EKF equations. A genetic algorithm (GA) was implemented to optimize noise covariances for use with the EKF. The resulting mean-square-error between IM model and EKF estimator block were compared to results from similar studies, to verify the model and function block.

After verifying the model, the parameters of the EFWA were investigated. Different values for each of the number of fireworks and sparks were compared, for example, the amplitude constant and number of mutations. These results proved to be interesting and helpful in terms of choosing parameters for this particular application. Next, a study of twenty independent runs using a comparable sample space and number of function evaluations for both the GA and the EFWA was completed. The 95% confidence interval of the data was also calculated. In this study, it was found that the EFWA found a good solution in fewer iterations than the GA.

The objective of this research was to find whether the Enhanced Fireworks algorithm (EFWA) is a good choice for determining the noise covariance matrix values of the induction motor model for the purpose of speed estimation. The research results indicate that the EFWA is adequately competitive in finding good parameter values efficiently.

FUTURE RESEARCH DIRECTIONS

The future research direction in EKF speed sensorless control is to explore optimization algorithms with the objective of finding one that provides good results with fewer iterations than the current benchmark. If less iterations are required, then the amount of time and cost to find a good solution is reduced and the optimization can be run more frequently, or online. This emerging trend is called "adaptive optimization." In the authors' research it was found that using the EFWA for optimization in this application provided good results in fewer iterations than the GA. EFWA has many detailed algorithmic parameters, such as the number of mutation sparks, the parameters that confine the number of explosion sparks associated with each firework (Zheng et. Al, 2013), the initial minimal amplitude of explosion, in addition to the ones focused in this chapter (the number of fireworks, the nominal number of explosion sparks, and the amplitude constant). The space of these EFWA parameters values in fact poses a challenge in optimally configuring the EFWA. Good tuning of other EFWA parameters may further improve performance of the algorithm. To this end, other EFWA parameter selection should be rigorously explored.

Along with research into parameter selection, the performance of the EFWA should also be compared against other trending optimization algorithms for the application presented in this chapter Particle swarm optimization (PSO) is a particularly interesting choice for comparison with the EFWA for this application because the optimization in this application is continuous. Much research has been written about on PSO results compared against improved and modified versions of the PSO algorithm, but none are made with the EFWA for this particular application. It is important to have these comparisons, to make decisions for implementation, and for the overall evolution of the EFWA, other algorithms and EKF speed sensorless control.

REFERENCES

Alonge, F., & D'Ippolio, F. (2010). Extended Kalman Filter for Sensorless Control of Induction Motors. *Proceedings IEEE First Symposium on Sensorless Control for Electronic Drives*, pp. 107–113. 10.1109/SLED.2010.5542796

Alsofyani, I. M., Idris, N., Sutikno, T., & Alamri, Y. A. (2012). An optimized Extended Kalman Filter for speed sensorless direct torque control of an induction motor. *Proceedings 2012 IEEE International Conference on Power and Energy (PECon)*, pp. 319–324. Kota Kinabalu. 10.1109/PECon.2012.6450230

Chan, T., & Shi, K. (2011). *Applied Intelligent Control of Induction Motor Drives*. Singapore: Wiley. doi:10.1002/9780470825587

Chang, E., & Zak, S. (1996). *An Introduction to Optimization*. New York, NY: Wiley.

Crassidis, J. L., & Junkins, J. L. (2012). *Optimal Estimation of Dynamic Systems* (2nd ed.). Boca Raton, FL: CRC Press.

Gallager, R. (2013). *Stochastic Processes Theory for Application*. Cambridge, UK: Cambridge University Press. doi:10.1017/CBO9781139626514

Grewal, M. (2001). *Kalman Filtering: theory and practice using Matlab*. New York: John Wiley.

Hilairet, M., Auger, F., & Berthelot, E. (2009). Speed and rotor flux estimation of induction machines using a two-stage extended Kalman filter. *Automatica*, 5(8), 1819–1827. doi:10.1016/j.automatica.2009.04.005

Hussain, S., & Abid Bazaz, M. (2016). Sensorless control of PMSM drive using extended Kalman filter and fuzzy logic controller. *International Journal of Industrial Electronics and Drives*, 3(1), 12–19. doi:10.1504/IJIED.2016.077677

Kalman, R. (1960). *A New Approach to Linear Filtering and Prediction Problems*. Baltimore, MD: Research Institute for Advanced Study. doi:10.1115/1.3662552

Kim, Y. (1994, September). Speed Sensorless Vector Control of Induction Motor Using Extended Kalman Filter. *IEEE Transactions on Industry Applications*, 30(5).

Krause, P. C., Wasynczuk, O., & Pekarek, S. (2012). *Electromechanical Motion Devices* (2nd ed.). Piscataway, NJ: IEEE Press. doi:10.1002/9781118316887

Krause, P. C., Wasynczuk, O., & Sudhoff, S. (2013). *Analysis of Electric Machinery and Drive Systems* (3rd ed.). Piscataway, NJ: IEEE Press. doi:10.1002/9781118524336

Lee, D. C. (2016a). Designing an extended Kalman filter for estimating speed and flux of an induction motor with unknown noise covariance. *Proc. IEEE Canadian Conference on Electrical and Computer Engineering*, June. 10.1109/CCECE.2016.7726654

Lee, D. C. (2016b). Gradient-based methods of tuning noise covariance for an induction motor model. *Proc. IEEE Canadian Conference on Electrical and Computer Engineering*, June. 10.1109/CCECE.2016.7726630

Lewis, F. (1992). *Applied Optimal Control & Estimation*. New York: Prentice Hall.

Li, J., Zhang, L.-H., Niu, Y., & Ren, H.-P. (2016). Model predictive control for extended Kalman filter-based speed sensorless induction motor drives. *Proc. IEEE Applied Power Electronics Conference and Exposition (APEC)*, pp. 2770–2775. 10.1109/APEC.2016.7468256

Lin, G., Jing, Z., & Liu, Z. (2014). Tuning of Extended Kalman Filter using Improved Particle Swarm Optimization for Sensorless Control of Induction Motors. *Journal of Computer Information Systems*, 10.

Loebis, D., Sutton, R., Chudley, J., & Naeem, W. (2004, December). Adaptive tuning of a Kalman filter via fuzzy logic for an intelligent AUV navigation system. *Control Engineering Practice*, *12*(12), 1531–1539. doi:10.1016/j.conengprac.2003.11.008

Luenberger, D. G. (1979). *Introduction to Dynamic Systems*. John Wiley & Sons.

Marino, R., Tomei, P., & Verrelli, C. M. (2010). *Induction Motor Control Design*. Rome, Italy: Springer. doi:10.1007/978-1-84996-284-1

Matlab/Simulink website: https://www.mathworks.com/videos/series/understanding-kalman-filters.html. (2019).

Ogata, K. (2010). *Modern Control Engineering, 5*. Upper Saddle River, NJ: Prentice Hall.

Ong, C.-M. (1997). *Dynamic Simulation of Electric Machinery*. Prentice Hall.

Rayyam, M., & Zazi, M. (October 2018). Particle Swarm Optimization of a Non Linear Kalman Filter for Sensorless Control of Induction Motors. *Proceedings 7th International Conference on Renewable Energy Research and Applications*, pp. 1016-1020. Paris, France.

Salvatore, L., Stasi, S., & Tarchioni, L. (1993, October). A new EKF-based algorithm for flux estimation in induction machines. *IEEE Transactions on Industrial Electronics*, *40*(5), 496–504. doi:10.1109/41.238018

Shi, K., Chan, T., Wong, Y., & Ho, S. (2000). Speed Estimation of an Induction Motor Drive Using an Extended Kalman Filter. *2000 IEEE Power Engineering Society Winter Meeting, Conference Proceedings (Cat. No.00CH37077)*, 1, pp. 243–248, Singapore, 2000. 10.1109/PESW.2000.849963

Shi, K., Chan, T., Wong, Y., & Ho, S. L. (2002, February). Speed Estimation of an Induction Motor Drive Using an Optimized Extended Kalman Filter. *IEEE Transactions on Industrial Electronics*, *49*(1), 124–133. doi:10.1109/41.982256

Song, B., Xu, J., & Xu, L. (2018, July). PSO-based Extended Kalman Filtering for Speed Estimation of an Induction Motor. *Proceedings of the 37th Chinese Control Conference*, Wuhan, China, pp. 3803-3807. 10.23919/ChiCC.2018.8482581

Tan, Y. (2015). *Fireworks Algorithm: A Novel Swarm Intelligence Optimization*. New York: Springer. doi:10.1007/978-3-662-46353-6

Zheng, S., Janecek, A., & Tan, Y. (2013). Enhanced Fireworks Algorithm. *Proceedings 2013 IEEE Congress on Evolutionary Computation*, Cancún, México. 10.1109/CEC.2013.6557813

KEY TERMS AND DEFINITIONS

Arbitrary Reference Frame: Axis used as reference rotating at a chosen speed.

Covariance: Measure of the joint variability of two random variables.

Electro-Motive Force: Measurement of the energy that causes a current to flow in a circuit.

Error: Difference between estimated value and the measured value.

Extended Kalman Filter: A variant of the Kalman filter used to estimate states of a non-linear system.

Flux: Measurement of the total magnetic field that passes through an area.

Flux Linkages: The number of turns multiplied by the flux for a given coil.

Inductance: Physical property of a coil that represents EMF generated in a coil to oppose a change in current.

Kalman Filter: An algorithm that uses a series of measurements over time to estimate the unknown states of a system.

Kalman Gain: In a closed loop system, the error is multiplied by this value in order to improve convergence.

Leakage Flux: Flux that is generated by one set of windings that does not pass through the second set of magnetically coupled windings.

Leakage Inductance: Inductive component of leakage flux.

Magnetically Coupled: Two windings, with no physical contact, affect each other through magnetic fields.

Magnetic Flux: Flux that is generated by one set of windings that passes through the second set of magnetically coupled windings.

Mutual Inductance: The measure of interaction of the flux of two coils.

Phase: An ac voltage waveform.

Proportional Integrative Control: A type of feedback control that responds to the error proportionally and also to the integral of the error.

Reluctance: Magnetic equivalent of resistance; depends on the properties of the material.

Root Mean Square: Square root of the sum of the squares of a sinusoidal waveform.

Rotor: Rotating winding – part of induction motor.

Self-Inductance: Induction of the coil voltage when current flows in the coil.

Slip: The difference between the rotor speed and the stator speed.

Squirrel-Cage Induction Motor: IM motor with rotor bars shorted together.

Stationary Reference Frame: Reference axis that are stationary (speed=0).

Stator: Stationary winding – part of the induction motor.

Synchronous Speed: The speed of the electrical system, i.e., 60 Hz.

Three-Phase AC Power: Three separate ac voltages applied to a load, each voltage shifted by 120 degrees.

Variable Frequency Drive: Electronic device which provides variable RMS voltage and frequency output to allow speed control of an induction motor.

APPENDIX

Simulation Parameters

The parameters are based on an original EKF paper which used a GA to optimize the noise and process covariances (Shi et al, 2002). The parameters are provided in Tables 3 and 4.

Table 3. Induction motor parameters used for simulation

Parameter	Description	Value	Unit
R_s	Stator resistance	0.288	Ω/phase
R_r	Rotor resistance	0.161	Ω/phase
X_{ls}	Stator leakage reactance	0.512	Ω/phase
X_{lr}	Rotor leakage reactance*	0.218	Ω/phase
X_M	Magnetizing reactance	14.82	Ω/phase

Table 4. Simulink Parameters

Symbol	Value/Equation	Description
Vrated (V_{base})	220	Rated phase voltage in V
Poles (P)	6	Number of magnetic poles in IM
frated	60	Rated frequency in Hz
wb (ω_{base})	2*pi*frated	Base electrical frequency in rad/sec
wbm	2*wb/Poles	Base mechanical frequency in rad/sec
Tb	60	Base torque in Nm
J1	0.4	Rotor inertia in kg*m^2
J2	0.4	Load inertia in kg*m^2
J	J1+J2	Total inertia
tau_reg (K_i)	0.1*(J*wb)/(P*Tb)	Time constant used in PI controller
Ts (M)	1e-4	Sample time in sec

Chapter 5
Learning From Class Imbalance:
A Fireworks-Based Resampling for Weighted Pattern Matching Classifier (PMC+)

Sreeja N. K.

PSG College of Technology, India

ABSTRACT

Learning a classifier from imbalanced data is one of the most challenging research problems. Data imbalance occurs when the number of instances belonging to one class is much less than the number of instances belonging to the other class. A standard classifier is biased towards the majority class and therefore misclassifies the minority class instances. Minority class instances may be regarded as rare events or unusual patterns that could potentially have a negative impact on the society. Therefore, detection of such events is considered significant. This chapter proposes a FireWorks-based Hybrid ReSampling (FWHRS) algorithm to resample imbalance data. It is used with Weighted Pattern Matching based classifier (PMC+) for classification. FWHRS-PMC+ was evaluated on 44 imbalanced binary datasets. Experiments reveal FWHRS-PMC+ is effective in classification of imbalanced data. Empirical results were validated using non-parametric statistical tests.

INTRODUCTION

Despite intense research in the field of Machine learning, learning from imbalanced data still remains a challenging problem. Class imbalance is a phenomenon in which the number of instances belonging to one class (majority class) is much more than the instances belonging to the other class (minority class). Minority class instances may be regarded as rare events or unusual patterns in daily life which are difficult to detect. Although rare, they are considered important and require immediate response.

Developments in learning from imbalanced data have been motivated by numerous real-life applications involving such rare events. Data for forecasting natural disasters (Hong et al.,2013), fraudulent credit card transactions (Panigrahi et al., 2009), target identification from satellite radar images (Kubat et

DOI: 10.4018/978-1-7998-1659-1.ch005

Copyright © 2020, IGI Global. Copying or distributing in print or electronic forms without written permission of IGI Global is prohibited.

al., 1998), classifying biological anomalies (Choe et al.,1998), computer-assisted medical diagnosis and treatment (Mazurowski, et al., 2008) exhibit class imbalance. Conventional classifiers are designed to work with balanced class distributions and therefore they are biased towards the majority class distribution. Therefore, conventional classifiers do not predict rare events. The extent of imbalance in a dataset is determined by the imbalance ratio. It is defined as the ratio of the number of instances belonging to the majority class to the number of instances belonging to the minority class.

The problem of class imbalance may be addressed in three ways: (i) Data level approaches that aim to rebalance the class distributions using over-sampling, under-sampling or hybrid techniques, (ii) Cost-sensitive approaches that introduces penalty for every misclassification and (iii) Ensemble approaches that model multiple classifiers for better classification.

Resampling techniques are data level approaches that aim at restoration of the balance in the dataset. Cost sensitive approaches considers different numeric costs for different misclassification types during model building. However, this method requires a cost matrix to be defined. Ensemble classifiers combine several classifiers thereby improving the classifier performance. Ensemble classifiers are time consuming as they build several base classifiers. Among these, the most common and an effective technique to tackle class imbalance is to rebalance the data using data level approaches. Many times, resampling methods are combined with a base classifier for better performance (Alberto et al., 2013).

Classifiers like Weighted Data Gravitation based classification (DGC+), Weighted Pattern Matching based Classification (PMC+) and Imbalanced DGC (IDGC) were also proposed for classification of imbalanced data. These classifiers do not use resampling or cost sensitive method for tackling the class imbalance.

This chapter proposes a FireWorks-based Hybrid ReSampling (FWHRS) algorithm to restore the balance in the dataset. The proposal is used with Weighted Pattern Matching based classifier (PMC+) for classification. Experiments have been performed on 44 imbalanced binary datasets collected from the KEEL repository (Alcalá-Fdez et al., 2011). The experiments consider various problem domains, number of instances and imbalanced ratio. Experiments indicate the competitive nature of the proposed FWHRS-PMC+ algorithm obtaining significantly better results in terms of Cohen's kappa rate and Area Under the Curve (AUC). Statistical analysis like Iman and Davenport test and Bonferroni-Dunn post hoc test was performed to evaluate whether there are significant differences in the results of the classifiers.

RELATED WORK

Class imbalance is a common scenario encountered in the field of machine learning and pattern recognition. Methods that handle class imbalance are categorized into Data level approaches, Cost sensitive approaches and ensemble approaches. Resampling is a data level approach that artificially inflates the minority class instances or reduces the number of majority class instances. Cost sensitive approaches introduces penalty for each misclassification. Ensemble classifiers constructs several classifiers and combine them to obtain a new classifier that outperforms the individual ones.

Data Level Approaches: Resampling

Data level approaches preprocesses the original imbalanced dataset to balance the class distribution. Thus, the base classifier need not be modified. It is empirically proved that these methods are a useful solution for class imbalance (Batista et al., 2004; Batuwita & Palade, 2010; Fernández et al., 2010; Fernández et al., 2008). Resampling methods are categorized into over-sampling and under-sampling.

Over-sampling eliminates the effect of skewed distribution by increasing the number of minority class instances in the dataset. Synthetic Minority Over-sampling TEchnique (SMOTE) (Chawla, Bowyer, Hall, & Kegelmeyer, 2002) is a well-known method for oversampling. SMOTE generates many synthetic minority class instances through learning several neighbors of the minority class thereby restoring the balance of the dataset. SMOTE achieves a good balance between the majority and minority class instances and is usually combined with other classifiers. However, in some cases, SMOTE deteriorates the classifier performance (Xuan, Dang, Osamu, & Kenji, 2015). Oversampling increases the likelihood of over fitting since the minority class instances are replicated.

Under-sampling techniques reduces the number of majority class instances to balance to dataset. Random Undersampling (RUS) is a non-heuristic, yet an effective method that eliminates some of the majority class instances at random (Batista et al., 2004). Tomek Link (TL) (Tomek, 1976) is another under-sampling technique that obtains a set of instances belonging to spaces near the decision boundaries. Under-sampling might exclude potentially useful information for the learning process during training. Resampling methods are generally combined with a base classifier. C4.5-RUS (Wilson & Martinez, 2000) constructs decision trees using C4.5 for classification of the data preprocessed using RUS. C4.5-SMOTE (Batista et al., 2004) generates synthetic minority instances using SMOTE and then constructs decision trees using C4.5.

Hybrid methods combine over-sampling and under-sampling methods. SMOTE-TL (Batista et al., 2004) is a hybrid method that uses SMOTE for oversampling and TL for undersampling. C4.5-SMOTE-TL (Tomek, 1976) preprocesses the dataset using SMOTE to create synthetic minority class instances and uses TL to remove the instances near the decision boundaries. Finally, decision trees are constructed using C4.5 algorithm from the transformed data.

Cost Sensitive Learning

Cost sensitive methods modifies the classifier by considering varying costs for different misclassifications thereby using a cost matrix during model building. The cost matrix is provided by domain experts or they may be learned using other approaches (Sun et al., 2007; Sun et al., 2009). Cost sensitive learners aim at minimizing the total cost rather than minimizing the error rate thereby guiding the classifier to highlight the minority class instances. Cost sensitive learners are categorized in to three. The first type modifies the decision thresholds or assigns weight to the instances according to the cost matrix during resampling. The transformed dataset is biased towards the minority class and aids in better classification of imbalanced data (Zadrozny, Langford, & Abe, 2003).

The second type changes the learning process to build a cost sensitive classifier (Domingos, 1999). Conventional classifiers like C4.5 and Artificial Neural Networks have been modified using this. C4.5-CS (Ting, 2002) is a decision tree classifier that weights the instances of the dataset to consider the associated costs from imbalanced classification. Zhou and Liu (2006) proposed NN-CS and have shown that the sampling and thresholding have been effective for problems involving class imbalance. CSVM-CS (Tang et al., 2009) considers the cost associated with the class distribution and builds an SVM model for classification. The third type is based on Bayes decision theory. They incorporate the cost matrix into bayes-based decision boundary and assigns each instance to the class with the lowest risk (Zadrozny & Elkan, 2001). Performance of cost sensitive classifiers are highly dependent on the misclassification costs assigned. However, assignment of misclassification costs for real world problems is practically infeasible (Sun et al., 2007).

Ensemble Classifiers

Ensemble classifiers combines several base classifiers that outperform every independent one, thereby increasing the classifier performance. Bagging (Quinlan, 1996) and Boosting (Mikel, Fernandez, Barrenechea, Bustince, & Herrera, 2012; Quinlan, 1996) are the commonly used ensemble techniques. Some of the ensemble methods used for classification of imbalanced data include SMOTEBoost (Chawla, Lazarevic, & Hall, 2003), Balance Cascade (Liu, Wu, & Zhou, 2009), RUSBoost (Seiffert, Khoshgoftaar, Van Hulse, & Napolitano, 2010) and SMOTEBagging (Wang & Yao, 2009). ADAC2 (Sun et al., 2007) is a boosting algorithm that constructs an ensemble of decision trees using C4.5 algorithm. Every instance in the dataset has an associated cost. ADAC2-CS increases the weight of the minority class instances during each iteration of boosting. This may be achieved using a resampling procedure after the weight update. Ensemble methods consume more time than resampling and cost sensitive approaches (Khoshgoftaar et al., 2011). Also, error diversity is the key element in creating accurate ensembles. Brown, Wyatt, Harris, & Yao (2005) have stated that the concept of error diversity is ill defined for classification problems.

Other Classifiers for Imbalanced Data

In recent years, researchers have focused on classifiers that do not use resampling or cost sensitive methods. Alberto et al. (2013) proposed a Weighted Data Gravitation based classifier (DGC+) for classification of standard and imbalanced data. The approach uses a weight matrix to weight the distance between the instances and considers both global and local information especially in the decision boundaries. The method shows better performance in terms of AUC and Cohen's Kappa rate. Peng et al., (2014) proposed a specific data gravitation model named Imbalanced DGC (IDGC). It computes amplified gravitation coefficient to compute the gravitation and rebalances the gravitational field strength disparity between the majority and minority classes. Although IDGC is effective in classifying imbalanced data, its computational complexity is relatively high with respect to the weight optimization procedure, consuming more time for large datasets (Peng et al., 2014). Sreeja (2019) proposed weighted Pattern Matching based classifier (PMC+) for classification of imbalanced data. The algorithm uses a simple classification procedure with weights for classification. PMC+ shows high performance when compared to other classifiers.

WEIGHTED PATTERN MATCHING BASED CLASSIFIER (PMC+)

Consider a dataset with K instances, n features and Q classes. Each instance in the dataset is represented as $X_p = (X_{p1}, X_{p2}, ..., X_{pn}, Cl_i)$ where $X_{p1}, X_{p2},...,X_{pn}$ represents the features of the instance X_p and Cl_i denotes the class to which X_p belongs with p=1,2,..,K and i=1,2,...,Q.

Given an unknown instance x = {x1, x2, ..., xn}, PMC+ classifies the unknown instance in the following manner.

1. Compute the number of instances in the dataset belonging to each class Cl_i.

2. Find the absolute difference between each selected feature value of the instances in the dataset and the corresponding feature value of the unknown instance.
3. Count the number of features in each instance whose absolute difference in feature values is less than or equal to an arbitrary weight. This denotes the attribute match count.
4. The instances in the dataset having the maximum value of attribute match count are grouped.
5. The unknown instance belongs to the class that occurs maximum number of times in the group.
6. If there are more than one majority class label in the group, the probability of occurrence of each majority class label is found and the unknown instance belongs to the class with highest probability.

Figure 1 shows the pseudocode of PMC+ (Sreeja, 2019). PMC+ uses a Feature and Weight selection for PMC+ (FWPMC+) algorithm to find an optimal subset of features and weight relevant for classifica-

Figure 1. Pseudocode of PMC+

```
Procedure PMC+ (x, DS[X₁,₂..ₖ], s, w)
//x denotes the unlabeled instance, s is the features selected, w is the weight and Q is the number of classes in DS
begin
for i=1 to Q
```
$$C_i = Count(X_p \in Cl_i)$$
```
//Xp denotes the instances in the dataset DS
end;
for p=1 to K
for j=1 to |s|
if (abs(Xpj-xj))≤ w) then
amc(Xp)=amc(Xp) +1;
endif;
end;
end;
G={φ} // G is an empty set
for p= 1 to K
if amc(Xp) = max(amc(Xp))
    G=G ∪{Xp}
endif;
end;
for each class Cli in G
    Countclass(Cli) = count (Xp ∈ G) ∀ Xp ∈ Cli  //Number of instances in G with class Cli
end;
class label(x) = Class (Xp ∈ G) for which Countclass(Cli) =max(Countclass(Cli))
if there are more than one majority class label in G then
for i = 1 to Q
P(Cli)= countclass(Cli)/ Ci;
end;
class label(x)= Class (Xp ∈ G) for which P(Cli)= max(P(Cli));
  endif;
```

tion. FWPMC+ is an embedded feature selection method. Embedded feature selection techniques (Lal, Chapelle, Western, & Elisseeff, 2006) are specific to a classifier and therefore the learning part and the feature selection part cannot be separated.

HYBRID RESAMPLING USING FIREWORKS ALGORITHM

This section details a hybrid resampling method based on fireworks algorithm. Termed FireWorks based Hybrid ReSampling (FWHRS) algorithm, the proposal is used with Weighted Pattern Matching based Classifier (PMC+) for classification.

Fireworks Algorithm

Inspired by the explosion of fireworks, Ying and Yuanchun (2010) proposed Fireworks algorithm for global optimization of complex functions. The working of Fireworks algorithm is shown in Figure 2 (Ying & Yuanchun, 2010).

According to this algorithm, Fireworks are initialized at n locations in the search space and exploded. The explosion may be considered as a search in the local space where the firework was set. Each location in the local space is evaluated and the algorithm chooses an optimal location in the local space and the search proceeds in a similar way until an optimal solution in the search space is found.

The success of fireworks algorithm lies in the good design of the explosion process and proper method of selecting the locations (Ying and Yuanchun, 2010). Fireworks algorithm is capable of processing linear, nonlinear and multi model test functions. The algorithm can be parallelized to handle complex problems. It has good convergence properties and finds a good optimal solution.

Fireworks Based Hybrid Resampling Algorithm for PMC+

FireWorks based Hybrid ReSampling (FWHRS) algorithm generates a resampled dataset which may be used with PMC+ for classification. The algorithm has a storage pool and a solution pool. The storage pool stores all instances in the dataset. The instances in the storage pool is divided in to two mutually exclusive subsets, one consisting of the majority class instances (majority set) and the other consisting of the minority class instances (minority set). The solution pool stores the resampled instances, the number of instances selected from the majority class and the Kappa statistic. The global value stores the resampled instances and the Kappa statistic. Initially the solution pool and the global value are empty. The algorithm has a variable R that denotes the number of instances to be selected from the majority class. The algorithm chooses a value for R at random in the range [1, number of majority class instances/2]. In addition, the algorithm has another binary variable called resampling status which may take values 0 or 1. A resampling status of 1 indicates that a new value for variable R is selected for the current iteration. A resampling status of 0 indicates that the algorithm retains the value of R in the previous iteration.

During the first iteration, the value of resampling status is 1. Therefore, the algorithm chooses a random number in the range [1, number of majority class instances/2] for the variable R. To determine the instances to be selected, a group of fireworks are placed at random positions in each subset in the storage pool and exploded. The sparks from each firework fall at different locations in each subset. Depending upon the value of the variable R, sparks at different positions are chosen at random from majority set.

Figure 2. Flowchart of fireworks algorithm

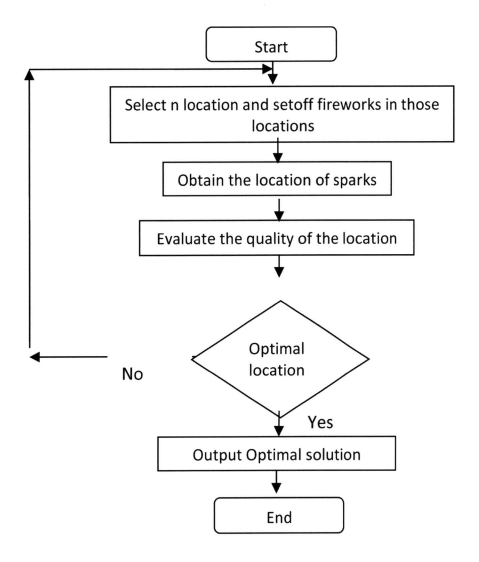

The majority class instances at positions other than the chosen positions are grouped together. Similarly, depending upon the value of R, sparks at different locations are chosen at random from the minority set. The minority class instances at these positions are replicated and grouped along with the instances in the minority set. The grouped majority and minority class instances together form the new resampled dataset and is stored in the solution pool along with the value of R. The size of the resampled dataset is same as the original dataset. If the value of R is greater than the number of instances in the minority set, some of the minority instances chosen at random are replicated again until the total number of instances selected from the minority class is R. The quality of the location of the spark for each firework is evaluated by finding the kappa statistic of PMC+ for the features and weight already chosen for the dataset in Sreeja (2019) using leave-one out method. The kappa statistic for the current iteration is also stored in the solution pool. After the first iteration, the storage pool contains the original dataset and the solution pool contains the resampled dataset, R value and the kappa rate of the iteration. The global value is updated with the resampled dataset and the Kappa rate of the current iteration.

In the second iteration, the value of the resampling status is updated. If the value of the resampling status is 1, a new value for R is selected. Otherwise, the algorithm retains the value of R in the previous iteration. Fireworks are exploded in the majority and minority set in the storage pool. Depending upon the value of R, a group of sparks for each firework are chosen at random from the majority and minority set. As in the previous iteration, a set of instances are chosen from the majority and minority set. The quality of the location of the sparks for each firework is evaluated by finding the Kappa statistic of PMC+ algorithm for the features and weight already chosen for the dataset using leave-one out method. If the quality of the location for the current iteration is greater than or equal to the previous iteration, then the solution pool is updated with the new set of instances, R value and the kappa statistic of the current iteration. If the Kappa statistic in the solution pool is greater than the global value, the global value is updated with the set of instances and the Kappa statistic in the solution pool. If the quality of the location for the current iteration is less than the previous iteration, the chosen instances are ignored. The algorithm is repeated for 10 iterations if the imbalance ratio of the dataset is less than 9 and otherwise, for 50 iterations. Finally, the set of instances in the global value denotes the dataset obtained after resampling. The pseudocode of FWHRS algorithm is shown in Figure 3.

EXPERIMENTAL STUDY

This section describes the experiments performed on 44 imbalanced datasets to evaluate the capabilities of the proposal. The performance of the algorithm on different problem domain was studied and nonparametric statistical tests are used to evaluate the proposal.

Problem Domain

The imbalanced datasets used for experiments were collected from KEEL repository (Alcalá- Fdez et al., 2011). Experiments have been carried out for imbalance ratio ranging between 1.82 and 129.44. Table 1 summarizes the characteristics of the datasets used.

The datasets were partitioned using stratified fivefold cross-validation (Refaeilzadeh, Tang, & Liu, 2008) to ensure the presence of minority class instances in every test dataset.

Performance Measure

Classifiers are evaluated based on various performance measures based on the classification subfield problem (Gu et al., 2009, Sokolova and Lapalme, 2009). Different behaviors may be observed from different measures, increasing the strength of empirical study (Fernández et al., 2010; Galar et al., 2011). Accuracy is a standard performance measure for classification problems. Accuracy may give misleading results especially in datasets with class imbalance as high accuracy is obtained due to all-positive or all-negative classification. Since, most of the real-world datasets are imbalanced, evaluation of the model has to be based on some other performance criteria.

Figure 3. Pseudocode of FWHRS algorithm

```
Procedure FWHRS (DS[X₁,₂..ₖ], ma, mi)
//DS denotes the dataset, ma and mi are the number of majority and minority instances respectively
begin
   IR = ma/mi
   if IR < 10 then
      P = 10
   else
      P = 50
   endif;
   Storage_pool = { DS = Xma U Xmi }
                  // Xma denote the majority class instances,  Xmi denote the minority class instances
   Solution_pool = { φ }
   Global_value = { φ }
   Resampling_status = 1
   for  j = 1 to P
      if Resampling_status = 1 then
         Rj =  random (1 to ma/2)
      else
         Rj = Rj-1
      endif;
      S1 = Rj instances from Xma picked at random
      S2 = Rj instances from Xmi picked at random
      Replicate S2 and store in S2
      Resampledj = { DS - S1 } U { S2 }
      for i = 1 to K
              PMC+(i, Resampledj, s, w)
      end;
      Kappaj =Cohen's Kappa rate (PMC+)
      Solution_pool = {Resampledj, Rj, Kappaj}
      if Kappaj ≥ Kappa in the Global_value then
              Global_value = { Resampledj, Kappaj }
      Resampling_status = Random { 0, 1}
      endif;
   end;
end FWHRS;
```

Cohen's Kappa rate (Ben David 2008a, 2008b) is a good measure to evaluate the merit of the classifier as it compensates for the random hits. Kappa value ranges between [-1,1]. A value -1 indicates total disagreement, 1 indicates total agreement and 0 indicates random classification. A low Kappa value indicates that the classifier fails to classify imbalance data (Li, Fong, & Zhuang, 2015). Kappa penalizes all positive or all negative predictions in imbalance problems (Alberto et al., 2013). Kappa values are obtained from the confusion matrix using equation (1)

Table 1. Imbalanced datasets

Data Set	Number of Instances	Number of Features	Imbalance Ratio
Abalone19	4174	8	129.44
Abalone9-18	731	8	16.4
Ecoli-0-1-3-7 vs 2-6	281	7	39.14
Ecoli-0 vs 1	220	7	1.86
Ecoli1	336	7	3.36
Ecoli2	336	7	5.46
Ecoli3	336	7	8.6
Ecoli4	336	7	15.8
Glass-0-1-2-3 vs 4-5-6	214	9	3.2
Glass-0-1-6 vs 2	192	9	10.29
Glass-0-1-6 vs 5	184	9	19.44
Glass0	214	9	2.06
Glass1	214	9	1.82
Glass2	214	9	11.59
Glass4	214	9	15.47
Glass5	214	9	22.78
Glass6	214	9	6.38
HabermanImb	306	3	2.78
Iris0	150	4	2
New-Thyroid1	215	5	5.14
New_Thyroid2	215	5	5.14
Page-Blocks-1-3 vs 4	472	10	15.86
Page-Blocks0	5472	10	8.79
PimaImb	768	8	1.87
Segment0	2308	19	6.02
Shuttle-C0 vs C4	1829	9	13.87
Shuttle-C2 vs C4	129	9	20.5
Vehicle0	846	18	3.25
Vehicle1	846	18	2.9
Vehicle2	846	18	2.88
Vehicle3	846	18	2.99
Vowel0	988	13	9.98
WisconsinImb	683	9	1.86
Yeast-0-5-6-7-9 vs 4	528	8	9.35
Yeast-1-2-8-9 vs 7	947	8	30.57
Yeast-1-4-5-8 vs 7	693	8	22.1
Yeast-1 vs 7	459	7	14.3
Yeast-2 vs 4	514	8	9.08
Yeast-2 vs 8	482	8	23.1
Yeast1	1484	8	2.46
Yeast3	1484	8	8.1
Yeast4	1484	8	28.1
Yeast5	1484	8	32.73
Yeast6	1484	8	41.4

$$Kappa = \frac{K \sum_{i=1}^{Q} x_{ii} - \sum_{i=1}^{Q} x_{i.} \, x_{.i}}{K^2 - \sum_{i=1}^{Q} x_{i.} \, x_{.i}} \qquad (1)$$

where xii denotes the number of instances along the main diagonal of the confusion matrix, K is the total number of instances, Q is the number of classes, x.i and xi. are the column and row total counts, respectively.

Another common measure to evaluate the model for imbalanced data is the Area Under Receiver Operating Characteristic (ROC) curve (AUC) (Bradley,1997; Huang & Ling, 2005). The ROC curve is a graphical illustration of the trade-off between the specificity and sensitivity (Fernández, del Jesus, & Herrera, 2010). The curve depicts the behavior of the classifier ignoring the class distribution. AUC values are also computed from the confusion matrix using equation (2).

$$AUC = \frac{1 + \dfrac{TP}{TP + FN} - \dfrac{FP}{FP + TN}}{2} \qquad (2)$$

where TP denotes the number of minority (positive) instances that are correctly classified, FP is the number of majority (negative) instances that are incorrectly classified as positive samples, TN is the number of majority instances that are correctly classified and FN is the number of minority instances that are incorrectly classified as negative samples.

David (2009) has stated that AUC is fundamentally incoherent in terms of misclassification cost. Hanczar (2010) states that ROC curves should be used with extreme caution unless the sample size is large. The unreliability of ROC was proved by Hanczar (2010) using resampling techniques.

Statistical Tests

The empirical results obtained were validated using various nonparametric statistical tests (García, Molina, Lozano, & Herrera, 2009; García et al., 2010) like Iman and Davenport test and Bonferroni-Dunn post hoc test. Iman and Davenport test is performed to determine if there are significant differences in the results of the classifiers. Friedman test (Friedman, 1937; Friedman, 1940), a nonparametric equivalent for ANOVA, ranks the classifiers on each dataset separately with tied ranks shared equally. If there are A classifiers and B datasets, Friedman test ranks each classifier in the B datasets. The Friedman statistic is found using equation (3).

$$x_F^2 = \frac{12B}{A(A+1)} \left(\sum_{j=1}^{A} Rank_j^2 - \frac{A(A+1)^2}{4} \right) \qquad (3)$$

where $Rank_j$ is the average rank of a classifier given by equation (4).

$$Rank_j = \frac{\sum_{i=1}^{B} r_i^j}{B} \qquad (4)$$

where r_i^j is the rank of the classifier j on the ith dataset with i=1,2,...,B and j = 1,2,...,A.

Iman and Davenport (1980) showed that the test statistic proposed by Friedman (1937) is undesirably conservative and derived a better statistic for comparison of classifiers, the Iman Davenport correction as in equation (5).

$$F_F = \frac{(B-1)x_F^2}{B(A-1)-x_F^2}$$

(5)

which is distributed according to the F-distribution with (A-1) and (A-1)(B-1) degrees of freedom.

If the Iman and Davenport test indicates the results are significantly different, Bonferonni-Dunn post hoc test (Dunn, 1961; Seshkin, 2007) was performed to check the quality of classifiers in multiple comparisons. The performance of the classifiers is significantly different if the corresponding average ranks obtained by the classifiers differ by at least a critical difference value (Demsar, 2006) given in equation (6).

$$CriticalDifference = Q_a\sqrt{\frac{k(k+1)}{6N}}$$

(6)

where Q_α is the critical difference for α=0.05, k is the number of algorithms and N is the number of datasets.

EXPERIMENTAL RESULTS

This section presents the empirical results on 44 imbalanced datasets. The AUC and Cohen's Kappa rate of FWHRS-PMC+ was compared with the values obtained for other classifiers like PMC+, DGC+, ADAC2-CS, CSVM-CS, C4.5-CS, C4.5 RUS, C4.5-SMOTE and C4.5-SMOTE-TL. The results obtained were validated using statistical tests.

Area Under the Curve

The average values of AUC for PMC+ obtained from 5-fold cross-validation was compared with other classifiers using the results reported in Alberto et al., (2013). Table 2 shows the results of AUC obtained by different classifiers for various datasets. It may be observed from Table 2 that FWHRS-PMC+ obtains first best results for 22 datasets. It can be observed from Table 2 that FWHRS-PMC+ obtains highest AUC for highly imbalanced datasets like Abalone19, Ecoli-0-1-3-7_vs_2-6, Ecoli4, Glass-0-1-6_vs_2, Glass2, Glass4, Glass5, Shuttle-C0-vs-C4, Shuttle-C2-vs-C4, Vowel0, Yeast-0-5-6-7-9_vs_4, Yeast-1-2-8-9_vs_7, Yeast4 and Yeast6. It may be noted that FWHRS-PMC+ shows remarkable performance for the dataset Abalone19 whose imbalance ratio is 129.44. FWHRS-PMC+ obtains an AUC of 1 for the datasets Vowel0, Iris0, Shuttle-C0-vs-C4 and Shuttle-C2-vs-C4 and remains a perfect model for classification of these datasets like PMC+. The proposal obtains the highest average AUC and average rank among the other classifiers for imbalanced data.

Table 2. AUC results of imbalanced data

Dataset	FWHRS-PMC+	PMC+	DGC+	ADAC2-CS	CSVM-CS	C4.5-CS	C4.5-RUS	C4.5-SMOTE	C4.5 – SMOTE-TL
Abalone19	**0.9303**	0.5000	0.6609	0.5085	0.7615	0.5701	0.6248	0.5719	0.5663
Abalone9-18	0.8581	0.6421	0.8124	0.7172	**0.8740**	0.6655	0.6892	0.7892	0.7022
Ecoli-0-1-3-7_vs_2-6	**0.8627**	0.8553	0.8427	0.8154	0.8500	0.8281	0.7900	0.7318	0.8172
Ecoli-0_vs_1	**0.9931**	0.9870	0.9799	0.9692	0.9671	0.9832	0.9796	0.9832	0.9761
Ecoli1	0.9090	0.8860	0.8804	0.8763	0.9062	**0.9114**	0.8852	0.8926	0.8801
Ecoli2	**0.9493**	0.9449	0.9378	0.8845	0.5000	0.8905	0.8693	0.8906	0.8979
Ecoli3	0.8700	0.8505	**0.8713**	0.8478	0.7925	0.8326	0.8453	0.8645	0.8502
Ecoli4	**0.9567**	0.9484	0.9092	0.9280	0.9529	0.8636	0.8613	0.9513	0.8449
Glass-0-1-2-3_vs_4-5-6	**0.9635**	0.9583	0.9215	0.9033	0.8445	0.8777	0.8811	0.9023	0.9102
Glass-0-1-6_vs_2	**0.874**	0.6177	0.6350	0.5400	0.5000	0.6155	0.6500	**0.7869**	0.6895
Glass-0-1-6_vs_5	0.9884	**0.9886**	0.8363	0.8800	0.5000	**0.9886**	0.9429	0.9157	0.9243
Glass0	0.9012	**0.9018**	0.8650	0.8101	0.5074	0.8212	0.8206	0.7754	0.8039
Glass1	**0.8497**	0.8220	0.7496	0.7866	0.6264	0.7160	0.7153	0.7434	0.7711
Glass2	**0.7761**	0.7226	0.7134	0.7099	0.5953	0.6416	0.6663	0.7112	0.7172
Glass4	**0.9840**	0.9615	0.8869	0.8706	0.9126	0.8431	0.8347	0.8452	0.9151
Glass5	**0.9924**	0.9420	0.8093	0.9732	0.9732	0.9427	0.9366	0.9756	0.8634
Glass6	**0.9546**	0.9310	0.9091	0.8923	0.8725	0.8896	0.8824	0.8923	0.8965
HabermanImb	0.6259	0.6141	0.6213	0.5604	0.5382	0.5752	0.6423	**0.6539**	0.6203
Iris0	1	1	1	0.9900	1	0.9900	0.9900	0.9900	0.9900
New-Thyroid1	0.9832	0.9829	**0.9939**	0.9464	0.9687	0.9746	0.9159	0.9492	0.9718
New-Thyroid2	0.9744	0.9714	**0.9916**	0.9575	0.9829	0.9802	0.9071	0.9579	0.9440
Page-Blocks-1-3_vs_4	0.9633	0.9609	0.9395	**0.9978**	0.8566	0.9789	0.9436	0.9888	0.9774
Page-Blocks0	0.9195	0.9223	0.9412	0.8816	0.9254	**0.9458**	0.9448	0.9395	0.9388
PimaImb	0.7310	0.7241	**0.7394**	0.7114	0.7289	0.7125	0.7235	0.7134	0.6948
Segment0	0.9957	**0.9965**	0.9927	0.9826	**0.9965**	0.9919	0.9788	0.9914	0.9914
Shuttle-C0-vs-C4	1	1	0.9975	0.9997	1	0.9997	1	0.9994	0.9997
Shuttle-C2-vs-C4	1	1	0.9743	0.9500	1	1	0.9840	0.9588	1
Vehicle0	**0.9743**	0.9735	0.9460	0.9438	0.9493	0.9289	0.9357	0.9274	0.9281
Vehicle1	**0.7667**	0.7593	0.7585	0.7531	0.7546	0.7013	0.6820	0.6814	0.7422
Vehicle2	0.9815	**0.9852**	0.9487	0.9729	0.9571	0.9434	0.9326	0.9556	0.9507
Vehicle3	0.6859	0.6711	0.7516	0.7345	**0.7904**	0.7283	0.7005	0.7112	0.7463
Vowel0	1	1	0.9879	0.9706	0.8461	0.9422	0.9438	0.9722	0.9850
WisconsinImb	0.9712	0.9709	0.9668	0.9653	**0.9719**	0.9636	0.9522	0.9579	0.9627
Yeast-0-5-6-7-9_vs_4	**0.8375**	0.7423	0.7857	0.7610	0.5000	0.7243	0.7858	0.8308	0.7548
Yeast-1-2-8-9_vs_7	**0.9167**	0.6167	0.6416	0.6376	0.5000	0.6769	0.6050	0.5966	0.5755
Yeast-1-4-5-8_vs_7	0.5333	0.5167	0.5806	0.5426	0.5000	0.5540	0.5739	**0.5913**	0.5270
Yeast-1_vs_7	0.6786	0.6667	**0.7594**	0.7049	0.5000	0.6139	0.6603	0.6871	0.6994
Yeast-2_vs_4	0.9052	0.8889	0.9103	0.9172	0.5000	0.8866	0.8856	0.8810	**0.9309**
Yeast-2_vs_8	0.8092	0.7739	0.7706	0.6218	0.7664	0.8652	0.7347	0.8415	**0.8686**
Yeast1	0.6611	0.6573	**0.7183**	0.6604	0.6749	0.6779	0.7161	0.7112	0.6809
Yeast3	0.8502	0.8460	**0.9202**	0.9108	0.8951	0.9117	0.9073	0.9119	0.9148
Yeast4	**0.8484**	0.6394	0.8252	0.7204	0.8155	0.7222	0.8194	0.7420	0.7838
Yeast5	0.9174	0.8939	0.9498	0.8833	0.9656	0.9330	0.9375	0.9517	**0.9712**
Yeast6	**0.9107**	0.8102	0.8530	0.7163	0.8758	0.8082	0.8113	0.8309	0.8462
Average AUC	**0.8876**	0.8419	0.8520	0.8252	0.7885	0.8321	0.8293	0.8443	0.8414
Average rank	**2.6932**	4.5114	3.8750	6.1364	5.6364	5.6136	6.2159	5.1477	5.1705

Iman and Davenport test was performed to evaluate whether there are significant differences in the results of algorithms. The test established a F distribution of 1.97 for a significance level $\alpha = 0.05$. The Iman and Davenport test statistic for AUC (distributed according to the F-distribution with 8 and 344 degrees of freedom) was found to be 9.0455. Thus, the test rejects the null hypothesis and therefore it may be concluded that there are significant differences in the AUC values of the classifiers.

Bonferroni-Dunn post hoc test was performed on AUC with $\alpha = 0.05$ and critical difference 1.5905. The application of Bonferroni–Dunn's test to AUC with $\alpha = 0.05$ is summarized in Figure 4. The X-axis represents the classifiers for imbalanced data and the Y axis represents the average rank obtained by each classifier for AUC. The thick horizontal line indicates the critical difference. The classifiers whose average rank for AUC falls beyond the line performs significantly worse than FWHRS-PMC+. It may be noted from Figure 4 that all classifiers except DGC+ performs worse than FWHRS-PMC+.

Since, Hanzar et al., (2010) has proved that AUC is unreliable and David (2009) has stated that AUC is incoherent in terms of misclassification costs, the performance of the proposal with respect to Kappa is emphasized.

Figure 4. Bonferroni-Dunn test for AUC of imbalanced data

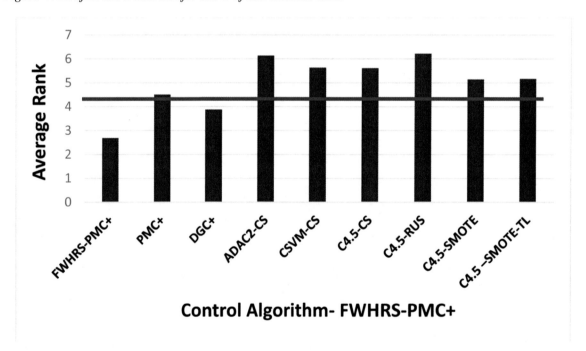

Cohen's Kappa Rate

The average values of Cohen's Kappa rate for PMC+ obtained from 5 fold cross-validation was compared with the kappa values of other classifiers using the results reported in Alberto et al., (2013). Table 3 shows the results of kappa obtained by different classifiers for various datasets. It may be observed from Table 3 that FWHRS-PMC+ obtains the highest kappa rate for 33 datasets. It may be noted from Table 3 that the proposal shows phenomenal performance for the datasets Abalone9, Abalone9-18, Glass-0-1-6_vs_5,

Table 3. Kappa results of imbalanced data

Dataset	FWHRS-PMC+	PMC+	DGC+	ADAC2-CS	CSVM-CS	C4.5-CS	C4.5-RUS	C4.5-SMOTE	C4.5 – SMOTE-TL
Abalone19	**0.7909**	0	0.0185	0.0052	0.0339	0.037	0.0092	0.0465	0.0375
Abalone9-18	**0.7010**	0.4206	0.3652	0.3284	0.4341	0.2958	0.1167	0.3554	0.2325
Ecoli-0-1-3-7_vs_2-6	**0.7681**	0.7638	0.6221	0.3632	0.7317	0.5114	0.1509	0.2839	0.2665
Ecoli-0_vs_1	**0.9896**	0.9799	0.9652	0.9305	0.9479	0.9695	0.9598	0.9695	0.9504
Ecoli1	**0.8180**	0.7789	0.6783	0.6815	0.6926	0.7577	0.6843	0.7082	0.6881
Ecoli2	0.8845	**0.8968**	0.8505	0.6581	0	0.6803	0.6862	0.6874	0.6871
Ecoli3	0.7331	**0.7584**	0.5613	0.4968	0.3783	0.5136	0.4597	0.5685	0.5466
Ecoli4	**0.9362**	0.9183	0.7221	0.7065	0.6951	0.5525	0.3312	0.6905	0.5230
Glass-0-1-2-3_vs_4-5-6	**0.9230**	0.9105	0.8141	0.7976	0.7441	0.7295	0.7373	0.7958	0.7858
Glass-0-1-6_vs_2	**0.6166**	0.359	0.2049	0.0868	0	0.1914	0.1170	0.3853	0.2581
Glass-0-1-6_vs_5	**0.8456**	0.807	0.5764	0.6259	0	0.8289	0.4545	0.5164	0.6081
Glass0	**0.7940**	0.767	0.7037	0.5812	0.0181	0.5942	0.5942	0.5113	0.5431
Glass1	**0.6937**	0.6636	0.4774	0.5323	0.2139	0.4131	0.4181	0.4468	0.5059
Glass2	**0.5100**	0.4988	0.3039	0.3251	0.0303	0.2171	0.0904	0.2380	0.3188
Glass4	**0.9680**	0.9575	0.6921	0.4202	0.5595	0.3244	0.3912	0.4019	0.5872
Glass5	**0.9154**	0.884	0.5256	0.7205	0.7181	0.8394	0.4092	0.6200	0.3958
Glass6	**0.9408**	0.9153	0.8257	0.7412	0.7704	0.7154	0.5907	0.7406	0.7972
HabermanImb	**0.3385**	0.2886	0.1977	0.0946	0.0840	0.111	0.2614	0.2627	0.1787
Iris0	1	1	1	0.9846	1	0.9846	0.9846	0.9846	0.9846
New-Thyroid1	0.9588	**0.9659**	0.9648	0.8351	0.9477	0.9191	0.6985	0.8504	0.9061
New-Thyroid2	0.9680	0.9651	0.9648	0.8923	0.9658	0.9496	0.7129	0.8337	0.7686
Page-Blocks-1-3_vs_4	0.9124	0.9066	0.8725	**0.9645**	0.7707	0.9578	0.5443	0.8431	0.7248
Page-Blocks0	0.8422	**0.8446**	0.7481	0.4374	0.6402	0.8254	0.7302	0.7382	0.6814
PimaImb	0.4841	**0.4851**	0.4504	0.3878	0.4551	0.3976	0.4266	0.4064	0.3486
Segment0	**0.9935**	0.9929	0.9827	0.9662	0.9843	0.9788	0.8953	0.967	0.9670
Shuttle-C0-vs-C4	1	1	0.9965	0.9958	1	0.9958	1	0.9916	0.9958
Shuttle-C2-vs-C4	1	1	0.8803	0.9297	1	1	0.8575	0.6780	1
Vehicle0	**0.9294**	0.9261	0.8442	0.8493	0.8896	0.8419	0.8092	0.8186	0.7773
Vehicle1	**0.4961**	0.4806	0.4281	0.4241	0.4350	0.358	0.3019	0.3248	0.3978
Vehicle2	0.9521	**0.9603**	0.8671	0.9358	0.8943	0.8700	0.8369	0.8838	0.8626
Vehicle3	0.3577	0.3433	0.3901	0.3920	0.4816	**0.399**	0.3229	0.3496	0.3909
Vowel0	1	1	0.9768	0.9475	0.7627	0.8170	0.7252	0.8708	0.9006
WisconsinImb	**0.9400**	0.939	0.9230	0.9233	0.9392	0.9114	0.8918	0.9104	0.9113
Yeast-0-5-6-7-9_vs_4	**0.6894**	0.5469	0.4028	0.3442	0	0.3655	0.3684	0.4471	0.3591
Yeast-1-2-8-9_vs_7	**0.9029**	0.3708	0.0905	0.1427	0	0.1821	0.0417	0.0843	0.0632
Yeast-1-4-5-8_vs_7	**0.1081**	0.0619	0.0600	0.0604	0	0.0809	0.0481	0.0636	0.0184
Yeast-1_vs_7	0.3995	**0.4831**	0.3169	0.1875	0	0.2081	0.1135	0.2388	0.2077
Yeast-2_vs_4	**0.8551**	0.8362	0.7310	0.6773	0	0.6510	0.6118	0.6115	0.7178
Yeast-2_vs_8	**0.7375**	0.6775	0.4780	0.2435	0.5404	0.6652	0.1453	0.4415	0.4932
Yeast1	0.3709	0.3642	0.3888	0.2443	0.3078	0.2834	**0.3989**	0.3849	0.2998
Yeast3	**0.7450**	0.7334	0.6824	0.6176	0.6094	0.7110	0.6047	0.6999	0.6763
Yeast4	**0.7010**	0.3213	0.2670	0.2333	0.2363	0.2632	0.1735	0.2865	0.2872
Yeast5	**0.7997**	0.7708	0.6577	0.7537	0.4475	0.6901	0.4168	0.6504	0.6137
Yeast6	**0.7779**	0.6291	0.4042	0.2124	0.2446	0.3669	0.0162	0.3423	0.3663
Average Kappa	**0.7747**	0.7085	0.6108	0.5609	0.4910	0.5899	0.4804	0.5666	0.5598
Average rank	**1.5341**	2.4432	4.4659	5.9773	5.9773	5.3182	7.5227	5.6591	6.1023

Shuttle-c2-vs-c4, Yeast-1-4-5-8_vs_7, Glass5, Yeast-2_vs_8, Yeast4, Yeast-1-2-8-9_vs_7, Yeast5, Ecoli-0-1-3-7_vs_2-6 and Yeast6 with high imbalance ratio. The Cohen's Kappa rate of the datasets Iris0, Vowel0, Shuttle-c2-vs-c4 and Shuttle-c0-vs-c4 is 1 as that of PMC+. FWHRS-PMC+ obtains the highest average kappa and average rank among the other classifiers for imbalanced data.

Iman and Davenport test was performed to evaluate whether there are significant differences in the results of algorithms. The test established a F distribution of 1.97 for a significance level $\alpha = 0.05$. The Iman and Davenport test statistic for kappa rate (distributed according to the F-distribution with 8 and 344 degrees of freedom) was found to be 39.852. Thus, the test rejects the null hypothesis and therefore it may be concluded that there are significant differences in the kappa values of the classifiers.

Bonferroni-Dunn post hoc test was performed on the Kappa rate with $\alpha = 0.05$ and critical difference 1.5905. Figure 5 summarizes the application of Bonferroni-Dunn's test on Kappa with $\alpha = 0.05$. The X-axis represents the classifiers for imbalanced data and the Y axis represents the average rank obtained by each classifier for Kappa rate. The thick horizontal line indicates the critical difference. The classifiers whose average rank for kappa falls beyond the line performs significantly worse than FWHRS-PMC+. It may be noted from Figure 5 that all classifiers except PMC+ performs worse than FWHRS-PMC+.

Figure 5. Bonferroni-Dunn test for Kappa rate of imbalanced data

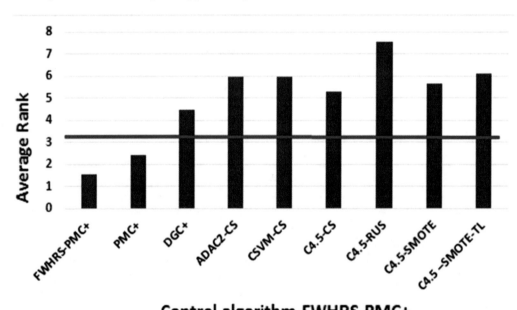

DISCUSSION

This section discusses the results of experiments performed on 44 imbalanced datasets. FWHRS-PMC+ obtains first best results for 22 datasets and second-best results for 8 datasets for AUC. The proposal also obtains first best results for 33 datasets and second-best results for 6 datasets for Kappa rate. FWHRS-PMC+ obtains the highest average value and rank for AUC and Kappa. It may be noted from Table 2 and Table 3 that the AUC and Kappa values of FWHRS-PMC+ for highly imbalanced datasets like

Abalone19, Yeast-1_2_8_9_vs_7, Yeast4, Glass-0_1_6_vs_2, is much higher than the other classifiers. The proposal obtains an AUC and Kappa of 1 for the datasets Iris0, Shuttle-C0-vs-C4, Shuttle-C2-vs-C4 and Vowel0 making it a perfect model for classification of such datasets. Since the disadvantage of AUC has been discussed earlier, the performance of the proposal is evaluated based on the Cohen's Kappa rate. It is apparent from Figure 5 that the performance of FWHRS-PMC+ is significant compared to the other classifiers. It may be noted from Table 3 that the Kappa rate of the datasets Ecoli2, Newthyroid1, Pageblocks0, PimaImb, Vehicle2, Yeast-1_vs_7 is slightly lesser than that of PMC+. This marginal decrease in Kappa values is due to the elimination of certain useful majority class instances by the FWHRS algorithm.

CONCLUSION

This chapter proposes a FireWorks based Hybrid ReSampling (FWHRS) algorithm for resampling imbalanced data. The algorithm is used with Weighted Pattern Matching Classifier (PMC+) for classification. According to FWHRS algorithm, fireworks are exploded at random locations in the search space (dataset) and the sparks fall at different locations. The algorithm performs hybrid resampling on the original dataset by increasing the number of minority instances and decreasing the number of majority instances based on the location of sparks chosen at random. PMC+ is then employed to classify the resampled instances. Experimental results indicate the remarkable performance of FWHRS-PMC+ algorithm in terms of Cohen's Kappa rate and Area Under the Curve (AUC). Empirical results were validated using non-parametric statistical tests to prove the performance of the proposal.

REFERENCES

Alcalá-Fdez, J., Fernandez, A., Luengo, J., Derrac, J., García, S., Sánchez, L., & Herrera, F. (2011). KEEL data-mining software tool: Data set repository, integration of algorithms and experimental analysis framework, J. Mult.-. *Valued Log. Soft Comput.*, *17*, 255–287.

Batista, G., Prati, R., & Monard, M. (2004). A study of the behavior of several methods for balancing machine learning training data. *SIGKDD Explorations*, *6*(1), 20–29. doi:10.1145/1007730.1007735

Batuwita, R., & Palade, V. (2009). AGm: a new performance measure for class imbalance learning. application to bioinformatics problems. *Proceedings of the 8th International Conference on Machine Learning and Applications (ICMLA 2009)*, pp. 545–550. 10.1109/ICMLA.2009.126

Ben-David, A. (2008a). Comparison of classification accuracy using Cohen's weighted kappa. *Expert Systems with Applications*, *34*(February (2)), 825–832. doi:10.1016/j.eswa.2006.10.022

Ben-David, A. (2008b). About the relationship between ROC curves and Cohen's kappa. *Engineering Applications of Artificial Intelligence*, *21*(September (6)), 874–882. doi:10.1016/j.engappai.2007.09.009

Bradley, A. P. (1997). The use of the area under the ROC curve in the evaluation of machine learning algorithms. *Pattern Recognition*, *30*(7), 1145–1159. doi:10.1016/S0031-3203(96)00142-2

Brown, G., Wyatt, J., Harris, R., & Yao, X. (2005). Diversity creation methods: A survey and categorization. *Information Fusion, 6*(1), 5–20. doi:10.1016/j.inffus.2004.04.004

Cano, A., Zafra, A., & Ventura. S. (2013). Weighted data gravitation classification for standard and imbalanced data. *IEEE Trans. Cybern. 43,* December (6).

Cao, H., Li, X.-L., Woon, D. Y.-K., & Ng, S.-K. (2013). Integrated oversampling for imbalanced time series classification. *IEEE Transactions on Knowledge and Data Engineering, 25*(12), 2809–2822. doi:10.1109/TKDE.2013.37

Chawla, N. V., Bowyer, K. W., Hall, L. O., & Kegelmeyer, W. P. (2002). SMOTE: Synthetic minority over-sampling technique. *Artificial Intelligence Research, 16*(1), 321–357. doi:10.1613/jair.953

Chawla, N. V., Lazarevic, A., & Hall, L. O. (2003). SMOTEBoost: improving prediction of the minority class in boosting. *Proceedings of the 7th European Conference on Principles of Data Mining and Knowledge Discovery*, pp. 107–119. 10.1007/978-3-540-39804-2_12

Choe, W., Ersoy, O. K., & Bina, M. (2000). Neural network schemes for detecting rare events in human genomic DNA. *Bioinformatics (Oxford, UK), 16*(12), 1062–1072. doi:10.1093/bioinformatics/16.12.1062 PMID:11159325

Dang, X. T., Tran, D. H., Hirose, O., & Satou, K. (2015). SPY: A Novel Resampling Method for Improving Classification Performance in Imbalanced Data. *Proceedings Seventh International Conference on Knowledge and Systems Engineering (KSE)*. 10.1109/KSE.2015.24

Demsar, J. (2006). Statistical comparisons of classifiers over multiple data sets. *Journal of Machine Learning Research, 7*, 1–30.

Domingos, P. (1999). MetaCost: a general method for making classifiers cost-sensitive. *Proceedings of the 5th ACM SIGKDD International Conference of Knowledge Discovery and Data Mining*, pp. 155–164. San Diego, CA. 10.1145/312129.312220

Dunn, O. J. (1961). Multiple comparisons among means. *Journal of the American Statistical Association, 56*(March(293)), 52–64. doi:10.1080/01621459.1961.10482090

Fernández, A., del Jesus, M. J., & Herrera, F. (2010). On the 2-tuples-based genetic tuning performance for fuzzy rule-based classification systems in imbalanced data-sets. *Inf. Sci., 180*(8), 1268–1291. doi:10.1016/j.ins.2009.12.014

Fernández, A., García, S., Luengo, J., Bernado-Mansilla, E., & Herrera, F. (2010). Genetics-based machine learning for rule induction: State of the art, taxonomy, and comparative study. *IEEE Transactions on Evolutionary Computation, 14*(December (6)), 913–941. doi:10.1109/TEVC.2009.2039140

Fernández, S., García, S., del Jesus, M. J., & Herrera, F. (2008). A study of the behaviour of linguistic fuzzy rule-based classification systems in the framework of imbalanced data-sets. *Fuzzy Sets and Systems, 159*(18), 2378–2398. doi:10.1016/j.fss.2007.12.023

Friedman, M. (1937). The use of ranks to avoid the assumption of normality implicit in the analysis of variance. *Journal of the American Statistical Association, 32*(200), 675–701. doi:10.1080/01621459.1 937.10503522

Friedman, M. (1940). A comparison of alternative tests of significance for the problem of m rankings. *Annals of Mathematical Statistics, 11*(1), 86–92. doi:10.1214/aoms/1177731944

Galar, M., Fernández, A., Barrenechea, E., Bustince, H., & Herrera, F. (2011). An overview of ensemble methods for binary classifiers in multi-class problems: Experimental study on one-vs-one and one-vs-all schemes. *Pattern Recognition, 44*(August (8)), 1761–1776. doi:10.1016/j.patcog.2011.01.017

Galar, M., Fernandez, A., Barrenechea, E., Bustince, H., & Herrera, F. (2012). A Review on Ensembles for the Class Imbalance Problem: Bagging-, Boosting-, and Hybrid-Based Approaches. *IEEE Transactions on Systems, Man and Cybernetics. Part C, Applications and Reviews, 42*(4), 463–484. doi:10.1109/TSMCC.2011.2161285

García, S., Fernández, A., Luengo, J., & Herrera, F. (2010). Advanced nonparametric tests for multiple comparisons in the design of experiments in computational intelligence and data mining: Experimental analysis of power. *Inf. Sci., 180*(May(10)), 2044–2064. doi:10.1016/j.ins.2009.12.010

García, S., Molina, D., Lozano, M., & Herrera, F. (2009). A study on the use of non-parametric tests for analyzing the evolutionary algorithms' behaviour: A case study. *Journal of Heuristics, 15*(December (6)), 617–644. doi:10.100710732-008-9080-4

Gu, Q., Zhu, L., & Cai, Z. (2009). Evaluation measures of the classification performance of imbalanced data sets. *Communications in Computer and Information Science, 51*(1), 461–471. doi:10.1007/978-3-642-04962-0_53

Hanczar, B., Hua, J., Sima, C., Weinstein, J., Bittner, M., & Dougherty, E. R. (2010). Small-sample precision of ROC-related estimates. *Bioinformatics, 26*(6), 822-830.

Hand, D. J. (2009). Measuring classifier performance: a coherent alternative to the area under the ROC curve, Mach Learn 77, pp. 103–123.

Huang, J., & Ling, C. X. (2005). Using AUC and accuracy in evaluating learning algorithms. *IEEE Transactions on Knowledge and Data Engineering, 17*(3), 299–310. doi:10.1109/TKDE.2005.50

Iman, R. L., & Davenport, J. M. (1980). Approximations of the critical region of the Friedman statistics. *Communications in Statistics. Theory and Methods, 9*(6), 571–595. doi:10.1080/03610928008827904

Khoshgoftaar, T. M., Hulse, J. V., & Napolitano, A. (2011). Comparing boosting and bagging techniques with noisy and imbalanced data. *IEEE Transactions on Systems, Man, and Cybernetics. Part B, Cybernetics, 41*(3), 552–568. doi:10.1109/TSMCA.2010.2084081

Kubat, M., Holte, R. C., & Matwin, S. (1998). Machine learning for the detection of oil spills in satellite radar images. *Machine Learning, 30*(2-3), 195–215. doi:10.1023/A:1007452223027

Lal, T. N., Chapelle, O., Western, J., & Elisseeff, A. (2006). Embedded methods. *Stud. Fuzziness Soft Comput., 207*(1), 137–165. doi:10.1007/978-3-540-35488-8_6

Li, J., Fong, S., & Zhuang, Y. (2015). Optimizing SMOTE by metaheuristics with neural network and decision tree. *Proceedings 2015 3rd International Symposium on Computational and Business Intelligence (ISCBI)*. IEEE.

Liu, X. Y., Wu, J., & Zhou, Z. H. (2009). Exploratory undersampling for classimbalance learning. *IEEE Transactions on Systems, Man, and Cybernetics. Part B, Cybernetics*, *39*(2), 539–550. doi:10.1109/TSMCB.2008.2007853 PMID:19095540

Mazurowski, M. A., Habas, P. A., Zurada, J. M., Lo, J. Y., Baker, J. A., & Tourassi, G. D. (2008). Training neural network classifiers for medical decision making: The effects of imbalanced datasets on classification performance. *Neural Networks: Off. J. Int. Neural Network Soc.*, *21*(2-3), 427–436. doi:10.1016/j.neunet.2007.12.031 PMID:18272329

Panigrahi, S., Kundu, A., Sural, S., & Majumdar, A. K. (2009). Credit card fraud detection: A fusion approach using Dempster–Shafer theory and Bayesian learning. *Information Fusion, 10*, pp. 354-363.

Peng, L., Zhang, H., Yang, B., & Chen, Y. (2014). A new approach for imbalanced data classification based on data gravitation. *Information Sciences, 288*, pp. 347-373.

Quinlan, J. R. (1996). Bagging, boosting, and C4. 5, AAAI/IAAI, 1.

Refaeilzadeh, P., Tang, L., & Liu, H. (2008). *Cross-Validation*. Arizona State University.

Seiffert, C., Khoshgoftaar, T. M., Van Hulse, J., & Napolitano, A. (2010). Rusboost: A hybrid approach to alleviating class imbalance. *IEEE Trans. Syst. Man Cybern. Part A*, *40*(1), 185–197. doi:10.1109/TSMCA.2009.2029559

Sheskin, D. J. (2007). *Handbook of Parametric and Nonparametric Statistical Procedures*. London, UK: Chapman & Hall.

Sokolova, M., & Lapalme, G. (2009). A systematic analysis of performance measures for classification tasks. *Information Processing & Management*, *45*(4), 427–437. doi:10.1016/j.ipm.2009.03.002

Sreeja, N. K. (2019). A weighted pattern matching approach for classification of imbalanced data with a fireworks-based algorithm for feature selection. *Connection Science*, *31*(2), 143–168. doi:10.1080/09540091.2018.1512558

Sun, Y., Kamel, M., Wong, A., & Wang, Y. (2007). Cost-sensitive boosting for classification of imbalanced data. *Pattern Recognition*, *40*(12), 3358–3378. doi:10.1016/j.patcog.2007.04.009

Sun, Y., Wong, A. K. C., & Kamel, M. S. (2009). Classification of imbalanced data: A review. *International Journal of Pattern Recognition and Artificial Intelligence*, *23*(4), 687–719. doi:10.1142/S0218001409007326

Tan, Y., & Zhu, Y. (2010). Fireworks Algorithm for Optimization. *Proc. First International Conference of Advances in Swarm Intelligence, ICSI 2010*, June 12-15.Beijing, China.

Tang, Y., Zhang, Y. Q., & Chawla, N. (2009). SVMS modeling for highly imbalanced classification. *IEEE Transactions on Systems, Man, and Cybernetics. Part B, Cybernetics*, *39*(1), 281–288. doi:10.1109/TSMCB.2008.2002909 PMID:19068445

Ting, K. M. (2002). An instance-weighting method to induce cost-sensitive trees. *IEEE Transactions on Knowledge and Data Engineering*, *14*(3), 659–665. doi:10.1109/TKDE.2002.1000348

Tomek, I. (1976). Two modifications of CNN. *IEEE Transactions on Systems, Man, and Cybernetics. Part B, Cybernetics, 6*(11), 769–772.

Wang, S., & Yao, X. (2009). Diversity analysis on imbalanced data sets by using ensemble models. *Proceedings of IEEE Symposium Series on Computational Intelligence and Data Mining (IEEE CIDM 2009),* pp. 324–331. 10.1109/CIDM.2009.4938667

Wilson, D. R., & Martinez, T. R. (2000). Reduction techniques for instance-based learning algorithms. *Machine Learning, 38*(3), 257–286. doi:10.1023/A:1007626913721

Zadrozny, B., & Elkan, C. (2001). Learning and making decisions when costs and probabilities are both unknown. *Proceedings of the 7th International Conference on Knowledge Discovery and Data Mining (KDD01),* pp. 204–213. 10.1145/502512.502540

Zadrozny, B., Langford, J., & Abe, N. (2003). Cost-sensitive learning by cost-proportionate example weighting. *Proceedings of the 3rd International Conference of Data Mining,* pp. 435–442. Melbourne, FL. 10.1109/ICDM.2003.1250950

Zhou, Z. H., & Liu, X. Y. (2006). Training cost-sensitive neural networks with methods addressing the class imbalance problem. *IEEE Transactions on Knowledge and Data Engineering, 18*(1), 63–77. doi:10.1109/TKDE.2006.17

Chapter 6
An improved Dynamic Search Fireworks Algorithm Optimizes Extreme Learning Machine to Predict Virtual Machine Fault

Shoufei Han

Nanjing University of Aeronautics and Astronautics, China

Kun Zhu

Nanjing University of Aeronautics and Astronautics, China

ABSTRACT

The Dynamic Search Fireworks Algorithm (dynFWA) is an effective algorithm for solving optimization problems. However, dynFWA is easy to fall into local optimal solutions prematurely and it also provides a slow convergence rate. To address these problems, an improved dynFWA (IdynFWA) is proposed in this chapter. In IdynFWA, the population is first initialized based on opposition-based learning. The adaptive mutation is proposed for the core firework (CF) which chooses whether to use Gaussian mutation or Levy mutation for the CF according to the mutation probability. A new selection strategy, namely disruptive selection, is proposed to maintain the diversity of the algorithm. The results show that the proposed algorithm achieves better overall performance on the standard test functions. Meanwhile, IdynFWA is used to optimize the Extreme Learning Machine (ELM), and a virtual machine fault warning model is proposed based on ELM optimized by IdynFWA. The results show that this model can achieve higher accuracy and better stability to some extent.

INTRODUCTION

Fireworks Algorithm (FWA) (Tan & Zhu, 2010) is a new intelligent optimization algorithm which has been proposed in recent years. Different from other intelligent algorithms, the main idea of FWA is to simulate the fireworks explosion to search the feasible space of the function to be optimized. Up to now,

DOI: 10.4018/978-1-7998-1659-1.ch006

Copyright © 2020, IGI Global. Copying or distributing in print or electronic forms without written permission of IGI Global is prohibited.

FWA have been applied to many real-world optimization problems (Tan, 2015) including the decomposition of non-negative matrices (Janecek & Tan, 2011), filter design (Gao & Diao, 2011), spam parameter optimization (He, Mi, & Tan, 2013), network reconstruction (Imran,, Kowsalya, & Kothari, 2014) truss mass minimization (Pholdee & Bureerat, 2014), chaotic system parameter estimation (Li, Bai, Xue, Zhu, & Zhang, 2015), resource scheduling (Liu, Feng, & Ke, 2015), etc.

However, similar to other intelligent optimization algorithms, FWA also have the disadvantages of slow convergence and low convergence accuracy. Therefore, researchers have proposed many improved algorithms to solve these problems. Based on the analysis of the explosion operator, mutation operator, selection strategy and mapping rules of fireworks algorithm, an enhanced fireworks algorithm (EFWA) is proposed (Zheng, Janecek, & Tan, 2013). The Adaptive Fireworks Algorithm (AFWA) was proposed for the fireworks algorithm to self-adjust the explosion amplitude (Zheng, Li, & Tan, 2014) which depends on the distance between the current individual with the best individual. A dynamic search fireworks algorithm (dynFWA) was proposed (Zheng & Tan, 2014) in which divided the fireworks into core firework and non-core fireworks according to the fitness value and adaptive adjustment of explosion amplitude for the core firework. Due to simplicity and efficiency, dynFWA has attracted the attention of more and more researchers. However, dynFWA has some problems such as easy to fall into local optimal solution and slow convergence.

In order to solve these problems and further improve its performance, an improved dynFWA (IdynFWA) is proposed in this chapter. In IdynFWA, firstly, the opposition-based learning is adopted to generate initial population. Then, the Gaussian mutation or Levy mutation is chosen alternately for the core firework (CF) according to mutation probability. Finally, a novel selection strategy is proposed to maintain the diversity of the population. Experimental results show that the proposed algorithm has better overall performance on the test functions.

Extreme Learning Machine (ELM) is a new single hidden layer forward feedback neural network (Huang, Zhu, & Siew, 2006), ELM has the advantages such as fast learning speed and good generalization performance, so it is used to solve various real-world problems. ELM has demonstrated superior performance over traditional methods in some areas including face recognition (Zong & Huang, 2011), text classification (Zheng, Qian, & Lu, 2013), medical diagnosis (Wang, Yu, Kang, Zhao, & Qu, 2014), image classification (Cao, Bo, & Dong, 2013), etc. However, the input weights and offsets of the ELM are randomly generated, which can cause instability of the model. In order to maintain the stability and obtain higher accuracy, IdynFWA is used to optimize ELM which is applied to predict virtual machine fault in this chapter. Experimental results show that proposed algorithm can achieve higher accuracy and better stability.

The main contribution of this paper is shown in three aspects.

1. An improved dynFWA (IdynFWA) is proposed in this chapter.
2. By comparing the performance with FWA variants and some classic intelligent optimization algorithms on CEC2013 standard functions, the proposed algorithm can improve the overall performance.
3. The IdynFWA is applied to optimize ELM to maintain the stability and obtain higher accuracy.
4. The optimized ELM is used to predict virtual machine fault.

The remainder of this chapter is organized as follows. Section II introduces framework of dynFWA and ELM. Our proposed algorithm is presented and discussed in Section III. Section IV presents experimental results. The proposed algorithm optimizes ELM and constructing virtual machine fault warning model is presented in Section V. The conclusion is made in Section VI.

BACKGROUND

Dynamic Search Fireworks Algorithm

In this section, we will briefly introduce the framework and the operators of the dynFWA for further discussion.

Without loss of generality, consider the following minimization problem:

$$\min f(x) \tag{1}$$

the object is to find an optimal x with minimal evaluation (fitness) value.

In dynFWA, for each firework X_i, the number of explosion sparks is calculated as follows:

$$S_i = m \times \frac{y_{max} - f(X_i) + \varepsilon}{\sum_{i=1}^{N} (y_{max} - f(X_i)) + \varepsilon} \tag{2}$$

where y_{max} is the maximum fitness value, m is a constant to control the number of explosion sparks.

In order to ensure that each firework can produce a certain amount of sparks, its scope is defined as.

$$S_i = \begin{cases} round(a \times m), & S_i < a \times m \\ round(b \times m), & S_i > b \times m \\ round(S_i), & otherwise \end{cases} \tag{3}$$

where a and b are fixed constant parameters that confine the range of the population size.

In dynFWA, based on fitness value, the fireworks are divided into two types: non-core fireworks and core firework, in which core firework (CF) is the firework with the smallest fitness value, and the remaining fireworks belong to non-core fireworks.

The non-core fireworks' explosion amplitudes (except for CF) are calculated as follows:

$$A_i = A \times \frac{f(X_i) - y_{min} + \varepsilon}{\sum_{i=1}^{N} (f(X_i) - y_{min}) + \varepsilon} \tag{4}$$

where y_{min} is the smallest fitness value, A is a constant to control he explosion amplitude.

But for the CF, its explosion amplitude is adjusted according to the search results in the last generation:

$$A_{CF}(t) = \begin{cases} A_{CF}(1) & t = 1 \\ C_r A_{CF}(t-1) & f(X_{CF}(t)) = f(X_{CF}(t-1)) \\ C_a A_{CF}(t-1) & f(X_{CF}(t)) < f(X_{CF}(t-1)) \end{cases} \tag{5}$$

where $A_{CF}(t)$ is the explosion amplitude of the CF in generation t.

Algorithm 1 describes the process of the explosion operator in dynFWA:

Algorithm 1. Generating explosion sparks

```
Calculate the number of explosion sparks S_i
Calculate the non-core fireworks of explosion amplitude A_i
Calculate the core firework of explosion amplitude A_CF
Set z = rand(1,d)
For k = 1:d do
  If k∈z then
    If X_j^k is core firework then
      X_j^k=X_j^k + rand(0,A_CF)
    Else
      X_j^k=X_j^k + rand(0,A_i)
    If X_j^k out of bounds
      Randomly take a value from [LB, UB]
    End if
  End if
End for
```

Extreme Learning Machine

Extreme Learning Machine (ELM) is a neural network algorithm, which is proposed by Huang, ELM biggest feature is for the traditional neural network, especially the single hidden layer feed forward neural network, ELM faster than the traditional learning algorithm and has better generalization performance.

For N arbitrary samples (x_i, y_i), and $x_i = [x_{i1}, x_{i2}, ..., x_{in}]^T \epsilon R^n$, $y_i = [y_{i1}, y_{i2}, ..., y_{in}]^T \epsilon R^n$. The output of the feed forward neural network with L hidden layer nodes and the stimulus function $g(x)$ can be expressed as:

$$\sum_{i=1}^{N} \beta_i \cdot g(w_i \cdot x_j + a_i) = O_j, j = 1, 2, ..., N, \tag{6}$$

where w_i is the single hidden layer input weight, O_i is the single hidden layer output weight, and a_i is the single hidden layer bias.

The purpose of neural network training is to minimize the error of the output value:

$$\sum_{i=1}^{N} \|O_j - T_i\| = 0, \tag{7}$$

From the Equation (7), it can be seen that there are β_i, w_i, a_i so that make the following formula set up.

$$\sum_{i=1}^{N} \beta_i \cdot g(w_i \cdot x_j + a_i) = T_j, j = 1, 2, ..., N ,$$

(8)

The above formula can be expressed simply as:

$$H\beta = T,$$

(9)

In the extreme learning machine algorithm, once the input weight w_i and the hidden layer bias a_i are randomly determined, the output matrix H of the hidden layer is uniquely determined. Then the training single hidden layer neural network is transformed into solving a linear equation $H\beta=T$, and the output weights can be determined $\beta=H^{-1}T$.

AN IMPROVED DYNAMIC SEARCH FIREWORKS ALGORITHM

Opposition-Based Learning Population Initialization

Opposition-based learning (OBL) is first proposed by Tizhoosh (Tizhoosh & H, 2005). OBL simultaneously considers a solution and its opposite solution, and then choosing the top N solutions from all solutions (normal solutions and opposite solutions).

Here, OBL was add to dynFWA to initialize population. For each firework X_i, its opposite solution OX_i is calculated as follows:

$$OX_i = LB + UB - X_i$$

(10)

In the population initialization, both a random solution P and an opposite solution OP are considered to obtain fitter starting candidate solutions.

Algorithm 2 is performed for opposition-based population initialization as follows.

Algorithm 2. Opposition-based population initialization
Initialize fireworks P with a size of N randomly
Calculate an opposite fireworks OP by Equation (10)
Assess 2 × N fireworks' fitness
Choose the top N individuals from P and OP as initial fireworks

Adaptive Mutation for Core Firework

The mutation operation is an important step in swarm intelligence algorithm, which can help to jump out the local optimum. dynFWA is easy to fall into local optima, thus, Levy mutation is introduced into dynFWA to solve this problem, which enhances the exploration ability. Meanwhile, the Gaussian mutation is also introduced into dynFWA to enhance the exploitation ability. Thus, combine Gaussian mutation with Levy mutation is an effective way to improve the exploitation and exploration of dynFWA.

For the core firework, two mutation schemes are alternative to be conducted based on a probability *p*. The new mutation strategy is defined as follows:

$$X_{CF}' = \begin{cases} X_{CF} + X_{CF} \times Gaussian(), & if \ E < p \\ X_{CF} + X_{CF} \times Levy(), & Otherwise \end{cases} \tag{11}$$

where *p* is a probability parameter, X_{CF} is the core firework in the current population. *Gaussian()* is a random number generated follows the normal distribution with mean parameter *mu* = 0 and standard deviation parameter *sigma* = 1. *Levy()* is a random number generated follows the levy distribution, and it can be calculated as with parameter $\beta = 1.5$, the value of *E* varies dynamically with the evolution of population, with reference to the annealing function of the simulated annealing algorithm, the value of *E* is expected to change exponentially, and it is calculated as follows:

$$E = e^{-(2t/T_{max})^2} \tag{12}$$

where *t* is the current function evaluations, and T_{max} is the maximum number of function evaluations.

Algorithm 3 shows the process of generating mutation seeds for CF.

Algorithm 3. Generating mutation sparks
    Set mutation probability p
    Find out the core firework XCF in current population
    Calculate E by Equation (12)
    Generate mutation spark by Equation (11)

A Novel Selection Strategy: Disruptive Selection

In dynFWA, the core idea of selection strategy is: the CF is always kept, and the remaining fireworks is selected randomly. Due to randomness, this selection strategy cannot maintain the diversity of the population. Thus, a novel selection strategy, namely disruptive selection, is proposed in this chapter, in which the CF is also kept, but the remaining fireworks is selected based on selection probability p_i which is calculated as follows:

$$p_i = \frac{|Y_i - Y_{avg}|}{\sum\limits_{n=1}^{SN} Y_n} \tag{13}$$

where Y_i is the fitness value of the objective function, Y_{avg} is the mean of all fitness values of the population in generation *t*, *SN* is the set of all fireworks.

Algorithm 4 demonstrates the complete framework of the IdynFWA.

Algorithm 4. Complete framework of AMdynFWA
    Generate an initial population by Algorithm 2
    Assess their fitness
    Repeat
    Produce explosion sparks by Algorithm 1
    Produce mutation sparks by Algorithm 3
    Assess all sparks' fitness
    Retain the best spark as a firework
    Select other m-1 fireworks by Equation (13)
    Until termination condition is satisfied
    Return the best fitness and a firework location

EXPERIMENTS AND ANALYSES

Parameters Setting

In IdynFWA, the number of fireworks is set to 5, the number of mutation sparks is also set to 5, and the maximum number of sparks is set to 150. Others parameters setting follow the suggestion in (Zheng & Tan, 2014) .

In the experiment, the function of each algorithm is repeated 51 times, and the final results after the $1000D$ function evaluations are presented, where D is the dimension of the test function and set to 30. In order to verify the performance of the algorithm proposed in this paper, we use the CEC2013 test set (Liang, Qu, Suganthan, & Hernandez-Diaz, 2013), including 28 different types of test functions, which are listed in Table 1.

Comparison of IdynFWA With Different *p*

In this section, the performance of IdynFWA with different p is discussed. In this experiment, p is set to 0.1, 0.3, 0.5, 0.7, and 0.9, respectively. The mean value and average rankings are shown in Table 2. It can be seen that the performance of IdynFWA with $p = 0.3$ is the best, and p is set to 0.3 in the following experiments.

Comparison of IdynFWA With FWA Variants

To show the performance of IdynFWA, EFWA, AFWA and dynFWA are compared on the test functions. The mean errors and the number of rank 1 are presented in Table 3. It can be seen that the IdynFWA has better performance than EFWA, AFWA and dynFWA.

The results of t-test are shown in Figure 1. '+' indicates the rejection of the null hypothesis at the 5% significance level, and '-' indicates accept the null hypothesis at the 5% significance level. The results indicate that the IdynFWA performs the best among them.

Table 1. CEC2013 test set

	Function number	Function name	Optimal value
Unimodal Functions	1	Sphere function	-1400
	2	Rotated high conditioned elliptic function	-1300
	3	Rotated bent cigar function	-1200
	4	Rotated discus function	-1100
	5	Different powers function	-1000
Basic Multimodal Functions	6	Rotated rosenbrock's function	-900
	7	Rotated schaffers F7 function	-800
	8	Rotated Ackley's function	-700
	9	Rotated weierstrass function	-600
	10	Rotated griewank's function	-500
	11	Rastrigin's function	-400
	12	Rotated rastrigin's function	-300
	13	Non-continuous rotated rastrigin's function	-200
	14	Schewefel's function	-100
	15	Rotated schewefel's function	100
	16	Rotated katsuura function	200
	17	Lunacek Bi_Rastrigin function	300
	18	Rotated Lunacek Bi_Rastrigin function	400
	19	Expanded griewank's plus rosenbrock's function	500
	20	Expanded scaffer's F6 function	600
Composition Functions	21	Composition function 1(N=5)	700
	22	Composition function 2(N=3)	800
	23	Composition function 3(N=3)	900
	24	Composition function 4(N=3)	1000
	25	Composition function 5(N=3)	1100
	26	Composition function 6(N=5)	1200
	27	Composition function 7(N=5)	1300
	28	Composition function 8(N=5)	1400

Comparison of IdynFWA With Other Swarm Intelligence Algorithms

In order to verify the performance of the proposed algorithm, it is compared with other intelligent optimization algorithms including ABC (Karaboga, 2007), DE (Storn & Storn, 1997), CMA-ES (Hansen, 1996) and SPSO2011 (Zambrano-Bigiarini, Clerc, & Rojas, 2013). The mean errors and ranks are presented in Table 4, and the average rankings are shown at the bottom of Table 4.

From the results, ABC beats other algorithms on 12 functions (some differences are not significant), but performs poorly on other functions. CMA-ES performs well on unimodal functions, but suffers from premature convergence on others. In terms of average rankings, IdynFWA ranked the first. IdynFWA

Table 2. Mean value and average rankings achieved by IdynFWA with different p on test functions

Functions	p=0.1	p=0.3	p=0.5	p=0.7	p=0.9
	Mean	Mean	Mean	Mean	Mean
f1	**-1.40E+03**	**-1.40E+03**	**-1.40E+03**	**-1.40E+03**	**-1.40E+03**
f2	**3.76E+05**	3.84E+05	4.56E+05	3.96E+05	4.13E+05
f3	1.01E+08	8.32E+07	**5.56E+07**	7.16E+07	6.69E+07
f4	-1.10E+03	-1.10E+03	**-1.10E+03**	-1.10E+03	-1.10E+03
f5	-1.00E+03	-1.00E+03	-1.00E+03	-1.00E+03	**-1.00E+03**
f6	-8.70E+02	**-8.76E+02**	-8.76E+02	-8.75E+02	-8.75E+02
f7	-7.14E+02	-7.11E+02	**-7.14E+02**	-7.13E+02	-7.03E+02
f8	**-6.79E+02**	-6.79E+02	-6.79E+02	-6.79E+02	-6.79E+02
f9	**-5.79E+02**	-5.77E+02	-5.78E+02	-5.77E+02	-5.77E+02
f10	**-5.00E+02**	-5.00E+02	-5.00E+02	-5.00E+02	-5.00E+02
f11	-3.05E+02	-3.02E+02	-3.07E+02	**-3.11E+02**	-3.10E+02
f12	-1.65E+02	**-1.75E+02**	-1.64E+02	-1.74E+02	-1.55E+02
f13	-3.20E+01	**-3.64E+01**	-3.57E+01	-3.07E+01	-3.23E+01
f14	2.62E+03	**2.54E+03**	2.68E+03	2.59E+03	2.70E+03
f15	**3.66E+03**	3.97E+03	3.89E+03	3.95E+03	3.72E+03
f16	2.00E+02	2.00E+02	2.00E+02	**2.00E+02**	3.00E+02
f17	4.38E+02	4.26E+02	4.26E+02	**4.24E+02**	4.28E+02
f18	5.83E+02	5.78E+02	5.79E+02	5.76E+02	**5.74E+02**
f19	5.07E+02	5.07E+02	5.07E+02	5.07E+02	**5.06E+02**
f20	6.13E+02	6.13E+02	**6.13E+02**	6.14E+02	6.13E+02
f21	1.05E+03	1.05E+03	**1.02E+03**	1.04E+03	1.05E+03
f22	**3.87E+03**	3.93E+03	4.11E+03	4.06E+03	4.03E+03
f23	5.40E+03	5.57E+03	5.52E+03	5.60E+03	**5.34E+03**
f24	1.26E+03	1.27E+03	1.27E+03	1.27E+03	**1.26E+03**
f25	1.39E+03	**1.39E+03**	1.39E+03	1.39E+03	1.39E+03
f26	**1.41E+03**	1.41E+03	1.42E+03	1.41E+03	1.41E+03
f27	2.20E+03	2.19E+03	2.19E+03	2.19E+03	**2.18E+03**
f28	1.81E+03	1.76E+03	**1.71E+03**	1.77E+03	1.83E+03
Average Ranking					
	2.93	2.82	2.86	3.07	2.93

Table 3. Mean errors and total number of rank 1 achieved by IdynFWA and FWA variants

Functions	EFWA	AFWA	dynFWA	IdynFWA
	Mean error / Rank	Mean error / Rank	Mean error / Rank	Mean error / Rank
f1	7.82E-02 / 2	**00E+00 / 1**	**00E+00 / 1**	**00E+00 / 1**
f2	5.43E+05 / 2	8.93E+05 / 4	7.87E+05 / 3	**3.84E+05 / 1**
f3	1.26E+08 / 2	1.26E+08 / 2	1.57E+08 / 3	**8.32E+07 / 1**
f4	1.09E+00 / 2	1.15E+01 / 3	1.28E+01 / 4	**2.02E-02 / 1**
f5	7.90E-02 / 4	6.04E-04 / 3	5.42E-04 / 2	**1.86E-04 / 1**
f6	3.49E+01 /4	2.99E+01 / 2	3.15E+01 / 3	**2.39E+01 / 1**
f7	1.33E+02 / 4	9.19E+01 / 2	1.03E+02 / 3	**8.85E+01 / 1**
f8	2.10E+01 /2	**2.09E+01 / 1**	**2.09E+01 / 1**	**2.09E+01 / 1**
f9	3.19E+01 / 4	2.48E+01 / 2	2.56E+01 / 3	**2.28E+01 / 1**
f10	8.29E-01 / 4	4.73E-02 / 3	4.20E-02 / 2	**3.18E-02 / 1**
f11	4.22E+02 / 4	1.05E+02 / 2	1.07E+02 / 3	**9.75E+01 / 1**
f12	6.33E+02 / 4	1.52E+02 / 2	1.56E+02 / 3	**1.25E+02 / 1**
f13	4.51E+02 / 4	2.36E+02 / 2	2.44E+02 / 3	**1.63E+02 / 1**
f14	4.16E+03 / 4	2.97E+03 / 3	2.95E+03 / 2	**2.64E+03 / 1**
f15	4.13E+03 / 4	3.81E+03 / 2	**3.71E+03 / 1**	3.87E+03 / 3
f16	5.92E-01 / 4	4.97E-01 / 3	4.77E-01 / 2	**3.4E-01 / 1**
f17	3.10E+02 / 4	1.45E+02 / 2	1.48E+02 / 3	**1.25E+02 / 1**
f18	**1.75E+02 / 1**	**1.75E+02 / 1**	1.89E+02 / 3	1.77E+02 / 2
f19	1.23E+01 / 4	6.92E+00 / 3	6.87E+00 / 2	**6.55E+00 / 1**
f20	1.46E+01 / 2	**1.30E+01 / 1**	**1.30E+01 / 1**	**1.30E+01 / 1**
f21	3.24E+02 / 3	3.16E+02 / 2	**2.92E+02 / 1**	3.51E+2 / 4
f22	5.75E+03 / 4	3.45E+03 / 3	3.41E+03 / 2	**3.12E+03 / 1**
f23	5.74E+03 / 4	4.70E+03 / 3	**4.55E+03 / 1**	4.67E+03 / 2
f24	3.37E+02 / 4	2.70E+02 / 2	2.72E+02 / 3	**2.65E+02 / 1**
f25	3.56E+02 / 4	2.99E+02 / 3	2.97E+02 / 2	**2.87E+02 / 1**
f26	3.21E+02 / 4	2.73E+02 / 3	2.62E+02 / 2	**2.12E+02 / 1**
f27	1.28E+03 / 4	9.72E+02 / 2	9.92E+02 / 3	**8.87E+02 / 1**
f28	4.34E+02 / 3	4.37E+02 / 4	**3.40E+02 / 1**	3.62E+02 / 2
	total number of rank 1			
	1	4	**7**	23

Figure 1. T-test results of IdynFWA vs EFWA, AFWA and dynFWA

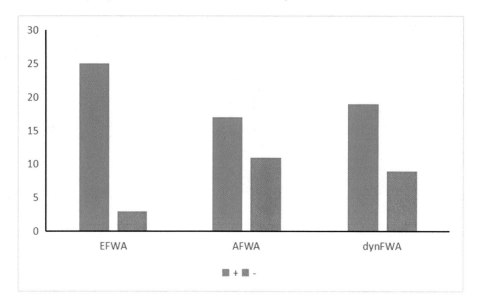

performs the best among these 5 algorithms on test functions due to its stability. DE and ABC take the second place and the third place respectively. The performances of CMA-ES and the SPSO2011 are comparable.

OPTIMIZATION FOR EXTREME LEARNING MACHINE WITH PROPOSED ALGORITHM TO PREDICT VIRTUAL MACHINE FAULT

Mathematical Model of Virtual Machine Fault Based on Extreme Learning Machine

In the previous section, the ELM was described in detail. This section mainly uses ELM to construct the model of virtual machine fault.

The ELM can be simply expressed by a matrix as:

$$H(w_1,...,w_L;b_1,...,b_L;x_1,...,x_L) = \begin{bmatrix} g(w_1 x_1 + b_1) & \cdots & g(w_L x_1 + b_L) \\ \vdots & \vdots & \vdots \\ g(w_1 x_N + b_1) & \cdots & g(w_L x_N + b_L) \end{bmatrix}_{N \times L} \tag{14}$$

Now, the performance index values are collected from each virtual machine, and the data set (x, y) is obtained through preprocessing, where x is the performance index value of the virtual machine at a certain moment, and y is the performance indicator value of the virtual machine at next moment.

Table 4. Mean error, rank and average rankings of five algorithms

Functions	ABC	DE	CMA-ES	SPSO2011	IdynFWA
f1	**0.00E+00 / 1**	1.89E-03 / 2	**0.00E+00 / 1**	**0.00E+00 / 1**	**0.00E+00 / 1**
f2	6.20E+06 / 5	5.52E+04 / 2	**0.00E+00 / 1**	3.38E+05 / 3	3.84E+05 / 4
f3	5.74E+08 / 5	2.16E+06 / 2	**1.41E+01 / 1**	2.88E+08 / 4	8.32E+07 / 3
f4	8.75E+04 / 5	1.32E-01 / 3	**0.00E+00 / 1**	3.86E+04 / 4	**2.02E-02 / 2**
f5	**0.00E+00 / 1**	2.48E-03 / 4	**0.00E+00 / 1**	5.42E-04 / 3	1.86E-04 / 2
f6	1.46E+01 / 3	7.82E+00 / 2	**7.82E-02 / 1**	3.79E+01 / 5	2.39E+01 / 4
f7	1.25E+02 / 5	4.89E+01 / 2	**1.91E+01 / 1**	8.79E+01 / 3	8.85E+01 / 4
f8	**2.09E+01 / 1**	**2.09E+01 / 1**	2.14E+01 / 2	**2.09E+01 / 1**	**2.09E+01 / 1**
f9	3.01E+01 / 4	**1.59E+01 / 1**	4.81E+01 / 5	2.88E+01 / 3	2.28E+01 / 2
f10	2.27E-01 / 4	3.42E-02 / 3	**1.78E-02 / 1**	3.40E-01 / 5	3.18E-02 / 2
f11	**00E+00 / 1**	7.88E+01 / 2	4.00E+02 / 5	1.05E+02 / 4	9.75E+01 / 3
f12	3.19E+02 / 4	**8.14E+01 / 1**	9.42E+02 / 5	1.04E+02 / 2	1.25E+02 / 3
f13	3.29E+02 / 4	**1.61E+02 / 1**	1.08E+03 / 5	1.94E+02 / 3	1.63E+02 / 2
f14	**3.58E-01 / 1**	2.38E+03 / 2	4.94E+03 / 5	3.99E+03 / 4	2.64E+03 / 3
f15	3.88E+03 / 3	5.19E+03 / 5	5.02E+03 / 4	**3.81E+03 / 1**	3.87E+03 / 2
f16	1.07E+00 / 3	1.97E+00 / 5	**5.42E-02 / 1**	1.31E+00 / 4	3.40E-01 / 2
f17	**3.04E+01 / 1**	9.29E+01 / 2	7.44E+02 / 5	1.16E+02 / 3	1.25E+02 / 4
f18	3.04E+02 / 4	2.34E+02 / 3	5.17E+02 / 5	**1.21E+02 / 1**	1.77E+02 / 2
f19	**2.62E-01 / 1**	4.51E+00 / 3	3.54E+00 / 2	9.51E+00 / 5	6.55E+00 / 4
f20	1.44E+01 / 4	1.43E+01 / 3	1.49E+01 / 5	1.35E+01 / 2	**1.30E+01 / 1**
f21	**1.65E+02 / 1**	3.20E+02 / 3	3.44E+02 / 4	3.09E+02 / 2	3.51E+02 / 5
f22	**2.41E+01 / 1**	1.72E+03 / 2	7.97E+03 / 5	4.30E+03 / 4	3.12E+03 / 3
f23	4.95E+03 / 3	5.28E+03 / 4	6.95E+03 / 5	4.83E+03 / 2	**4.67E+03 / 1**
f24	2.90E+02 / 4	**2.47E+02 / 1**	6.62E+02 / 5	2.67E+02 / 3	2.65E+02 / 2
f25	3.06E+02 / 4	2.89E+02 / 2	4.41E+02 / 5	2.99E+02 / 3	**2.87E+02 / 1**
f26	**2.01E+02 / 1**	2.52E+02 / 3	3.29E+02 / 5	2.86E+02 / 4	2.12E+02 / 2
f27	**4.16E+02 / 1**	7.64E+02 / 4	5.39E+02 / 2	1.00E+03 / 5	8.87E+02 / 3
f28	**2.58E+02 / 1**	4.02E+02 / 4	4.78E+03 / 5	4.01E+02 / 3	3.62E+02 / 2
	Average rankings				
	2.71	2.57	3.32	3.11	**2.35**

Therefore, the mathematical model of virtual machine fault can be expressed as:

$$\beta = \begin{bmatrix} \dfrac{1}{g(w_1 \bullet x_1 + b_1)} & \cdots & \dfrac{1}{g(w_1 \bullet x_N + b_1)} \\ \vdots & \cdots & \vdots \\ \dfrac{1}{g(w_L \bullet x_1 + b_L)} & \cdots & \dfrac{1}{g(w_L \bullet x_N + b_L)} \end{bmatrix}_{L \times N} \times \begin{bmatrix} y_1 \\ \vdots \\ y_N \end{bmatrix}_{N \times 1} \tag{15}$$

In summary, the mathematical model of virtual machine fault based on ELM is:

$$\beta = \begin{bmatrix} \sum\limits_{k=1}^{N} \dfrac{y_k}{g(w_1 \bullet x_k + b_1)} \\ \vdots \\ \sum\limits_{k=1}^{N} \dfrac{y_k}{g(w_L \bullet x_k + b_L)} \end{bmatrix} \tag{16}$$

From the above formula, it can be seen that the parameters input layer weight w and offset b have a great influence on the model, but in ELM, the parameters are randomly generated, which causes the instability of model. In order to improve the stability of ELM, the proposed algorithm is applied to optimize the ELM (IdynFWA-ELM), which can help choose the best input weight and offset.

The Proposed Algorithm Optimizes Virtual Machine Fault Model

In this section, the proposed algorithm is used to optimize the virtual machine fault model based on ELM, that is, making use of the proposed algorithm choose the suitable input weight and offset so that the model is more stable. The steps of the IdynFWA-ELM are as follows:

Step 1: Set the initial parameters of the ELM, including the number of hidden layer nodes L and the stimulus function $g(x)$.

Step 2: Initialize the parameters of the IdynFWA

Step 3: Initialize the fireworks population, randomly generate the initial solution. The dimension of each solution is $L \times (n + 1)$ (n is the number of neurons). $L \times n$ dimension is the input weight, and the remaining L dimension is the offset.

Step 4: Perform the IdynFWA to find the optimal solution, and the root mean square error (RMSE) or classification accuracy calculated from the training data is taken as the fitness function of the IdynFWA.

Step 5: Determine whether the IdynFWA has reached the maximum number of iterations, and if it is satisfied, go to step 6. Otherwise return to step 4.

Step 6: The optimal input weight and the offset can be obtained by the returned optimal solution.

Experimental Simulation

The data used in this section is the one-day data provided by a research institute (one sample is collected every 5 minutes). Finally, there are 200 samples by preprocessing. The 133 samples are randomly selected as training set, and the remaining 67 samples were used as test set.

The performance of IdynFWA-ELM is compared with ELM, PSO-ELM, BA-ELM, EFWA-ELM and GA-ELM on the dataset. In our experiments, we set the the number of hidden layer nodes $L=20$ and set the stimulus function as 'sigmoid', and the experimental results are the average of the algorithm running 10 times.

Comparison of Each Performance Indicators

Comparison of CPU Performance Indicator

The RMSE of CPU performance indicator is shown in Table 5. It can be seen that the ELM-based model has the shortest training time, but the error is the biggest and the stability is the worst. The performances of EFWA-ELM, PSO-ELM, GA-ELM and BA-ELM are moderate and the RMSE are similar. In addition, we can see that the IdynFWA-ELM is the best in training time, RMSE and stability.

Table 5. Comparison of CPU performance indicator

Algorithm	Training Time/s	RMSE	Dev
ELM	0.0234	0.0721	0.0215
EFWA-ELM	14.6563	0.0658	0.0114
PSO-ELM	13.4145	0.0689	0.0199
GA-ELM	14.1181	0.0658	0.0152
BA-ELM	13.4457	0.0636	0.0188
IdynFWA-ELM	13.3577	0.0444	0.0094

Comparison of Hard Disk Usage Indicator

The RMSE of hard disk usage performance indicator is shown in Table 6. It can be seen that the ELM-based model has the shortest training time, but the error is the biggest and the stability is the worst. The RMSE of EFWA-ELM, PSO-ELM, GA-ELM and BA-ELM are compared. And the IdynFWA-ELM performs well among them.

Table 6. Comparison of hard disk usage performance indicator

Algorithm	Training Time/s	RMSE	Dev
ELM	0.002	0.0895	0.0252
EFWA-ELM	14.7624	0.0864	0.0156
PSO-ELM	13.5471	0.0655	0.0241
GA-ELM	14.1540	0.0818	0.0130
BA-ELM	13.6392	0.0751	0.0229
IdynFWA-ELM	13.5184	0.0572	0.0102

Comparison of Memory Usage Indicator

The RMSE of memory usage performance indicator is shown in Table 7. It can be seen that the ELM-based model has the shortest training time, but the error is the biggest and the stability is the worst. The IdynFWA-ELM has better performance than EFWA-ELM, PSO-ELM, GA-ELM and BA-ELM.

Table 7. Comparison of memory usage performance indicator

Algorithm	Training Time/s	RMSE	Dev
ELM	0.0016	0.0432	0.0093
EFWA-ELM	14.8568	0.0371	0.0101
PSO-ELM	13.5674	0.0380	0.0091
GA-ELM	14.1680	0.0361	0.0094
BA-ELM	13.2336	0.0369	0.0095
IdynFWA-ELM	13.1303	0.0303	0.0116

Comparison of Network Usage Indicator

The RMSE of network usage performance indicator is shown in Table 8. It can be seen that the ELM is the worst. The PSO-ELM has the better stability. The IdynFWA-ELM performs the best among EFWA-ELM, PSO-ELM, GA-ELM and BA-ELM.

Table 8. Comparison of network usage performance indicator

Algorithm	Training Time/s	RMSE	Dev
ELM	0.0047	0.0897	0.0152
EFWA-ELM	14.8786	0.0856	0.0127
PSO-ELM	13.5066	0.0702	0.0105
GA-ELM	14.2304	0.0698	0.0115
BA-ELM	13.4442	0.0576	0.0136
IdynFWA-ELM	14.0049	0.0485	0.0109

Comparison of Performance Indicators Fusion

In this section, we combine the above four performance indicators into one indicator and use this indicator to predict virtual machine fault. The fusion indicator is calculated as follows:

$$T = 0.25 \times (A_1 + A_2 + A_3 + A_4) \tag{17}$$

where A_1 is CPU usage, A_2 is hard disk usage, A_3 memory usage and A_4 is network usage.

The RMSE based on the fusion indicator is shown in Table 9. It can be seen that the IdynFWA-ELM has the smallest RMSE, the shortest training time, and the smallest deviation. The results indicate that the IdynFWA-ELM is the bset model among them.

Table 9. Comparison of six algorithms with fusion indicator

Algorithm	Training Time/s	RMSE	Dev
ELM	0.1997	0.0395	0.0958
EFWA-ELM	23.812	0.0057	0.0069
PSO-ELM	19.4908	0.0032	0.0015
GA-ELM	19.5688	0.0326	0.0986
BA-ELM	18.6172	0.0027	0.0013
IdynFWA-ELM	18.1818	0.0020	0.0013

CONCLUSION

In order to further improve the performance of dynFWA, an improved dynamic search fireworks algorithm (IdynFWA) is proposed. The proposed algorithm firstly uses opposition-based learning to initialize the population, then introduces adaptive mutation to help balance exploitation and exploration ability. Finally, a new selection strategy is proposed to maintain the diversity of the population. Experiments show that the proposed algorithm is superior to the dynFWA in performance. Meanwhile, a virtual machine fault model based on the proposed algorithm to optimize ELM is proposed and verifying the validity of the model on the collected real data sets, the results show that the virtual machine fault model based on IdynFWA-ELM has better performance than other five algorithms.

REFERENCES

Cao, F., Bo, L., & Dong, S. P. (2013). Image classification based on effective extreme learning machine. *Neurocomputing, 102*(2), 90–97. doi:10.1016/j.neucom.2012.02.042

Gao, H., & Diao, M. (2011). Cultural Firework Algorithm and its Application for Digital Filters Design. *International Journal of Modelling Identification & Control, 14*(4), 324–331. doi:10.1504/IJMIC.2011.043157

Hansen, N. (1996). Adapting arbitrary normal mutation distributions in evolution strategies: The covariance matrix adaptation. In *Proceedings of the 1996 IEEE International Conference on Evolutionary Computation*, pp. 312-317. Nagoya, Japan. 10.1109/ICEC.1996.542381

He, W., Mi, G., & Tan, Y. (2013). Parameter Optimization of Local-Concentration Model for Spam Detection by Using Fireworks Algorithm. In *Proceedings of the 4th International Conference on Swarm Intelligence* (2013, pp. 439-450). Harbin, China. 10.1007/978-3-642-38703-6_52

Huang, G. B., Zhu, Q. Y., & Siew, C. K. (2006). Extreme learning machine: Theory and applications. *Neurocomputing, 70*(1-3), 489–501. doi:10.1016/j.neucom.2005.12.126

Imran, A. M., Kowsalya, M., & Kothari, D. P. (2014). A novel integration technique for optimal network reconfiguration and distributed generation placement in power distribution networks. *International Journal of Electrical Power & Energy Systems, 63*(371), 461–472. doi:10.1016/j.ijepes.2014.06.011

Janecek, A., & Tan, Y. (2011). Using population-based algorithms for initializing nonnegative matrix factorization. In *Proceedings of International Conference on Advances in Swarm Intelligence* (2011, pp. 307-316). Springer-Verlag.

Karaboga, D., & Basturk, B. (2007). A powerful and efficient algorithm for numerical function optimization: Artificial bee colony (ABC) algorithm. *Journal of Global Optimization*, *39*(3), 459–471. doi:10.100710898-007-9149-x

Li, H., Bai, P., Xue, J. J., Zhu, J., & Zhang, H. (2015). *Parameter Estimation of Chaotic Systems Using Fireworks Algorithm. Advances in Swarm and Computational Intelligence*. Springer International Publishing.

Liang, J., Qu, B., Suganthan, P., & Hernandez-Diaz, A.G. (2013). Problem Definitions and Evaluation Criteria for the CEC 2013 Special Session on Real-Parameter Optimization. Technical Report 201212 (2013). Zhengzhou University, China.

Liu, Z., Feng, Z., & Ke, L. (2015). Fireworks algorithm for the multi-satellite control resource scheduling problem. In *Proceedings of the 2015 IEEE Congress on Evolutionary Computation* (2015, pp. 1280-1286). Sendai, Japan. 10.1109/CEC.2015.7257036

Pholdee, N., & Bureerat, S. (2014). Comparative performance of meta-heuristic algorithms for mass minimisation of trusses with dynamic constraints. *Advances in Engineering Software*, *75*(3), 1–13. doi:10.1016/j.advengsoft.2014.04.005

Storn, R., & Price, K. (1997). Differential evolution–a simple and efficient heuristic for global optimization over continuous spaces. *Journal of Global Optimization*, *11*(4), 341–359. doi:10.1023/A:1008202821328

Tan, Y. (2015). Fireworks algorithm introduction. China/Beijing State: Science Press.

Tan, Y., & Zhu, Y. (2010). Fireworks Algorithm for Optimization. *Proceedings of International Conference on Advances in Swarm Intelligence* (2010, pp. 355-364). Springer-Verlag. 10.1007/978-3-642-13495-1_44

Tizhoosh, H. R. (2005). Opposition-Based Learning: A New Scheme for Machine Intelligence. In *Proceedings of International Conference on Computational Intelligence for Modelling, Control & Automation, & International Conference on Intelligent Agents, Web Technologies, & Internet Commerce*. Vienna, Austria. Academic Press.

Wang, Z., Yu, G., Kang, Y., Zhao, Y., & Qu, Q. (2014). Breast tumor detection in digital mammography based on extreme learning machine. *Neurocomputing*, *128*(5), 175–184. doi:10.1016/j.neucom.2013.05.053

Zambrano-Bigiarini, M., Clerc, M., & Rojas, R. (2013). Standard particle swarm optimization 2011 at CEC2013: a baseline for future PSO improvements. In *Proceedings of the 2013 IEEE Congress on Evolutionary Computation*, pp. 2337-2344, Cancun, Mexico. 10.1109/CEC.2013.6557848

Zheng, S., Janecek, A., & Tan, Y. (2013). Enhanced fireworks algorithm. In *Proceedings of the 2013 IEEE Congress on Evolutionary Computation* (2013, pp. 2069-2077). Cancun, Mexico. 10.1109/CEC.2013.6557813

Zheng, S., Li, J., & Tan, Y. (2014). Adaptive fireworks algorithm. In *Proceedings of the 2014 IEEE Congress on Evolutionary Computation* (2014, pp. 3214-3221). Beijing, China.

Zheng, S., & Tan, Y. (2014). Dynamic search in fireworks algorithm. In *Proceedings of the 2014 IEEE Congress on Evolutionary Computation* (2014, pp. 3222-3229). Beijing, China. 10.1109/CEC.2014.6900485

Zheng, W., Qian, Y., & Lu, H. (2013). Text categorization based on regularization extreme learning machine. *Neural Computing & Applications*, *22*(3-4), 447–456. doi:10.100700521-011-0808-y

Zong, W., & Huang, G. B. (2011). Face recognition based on extreme learning machine. *Neurocomputing*, *74*(16), 2541–2551. doi:10.1016/j.neucom.2010.12.041

ADDITIONAL READING

Ahila, R., Sadasivam, V., & Manimala, K. (2015). An integrated pso for parameter determination and feature selection of elm and its application in classification of power system disturbances. *Applied Soft Computing*, *32*, 23–37. doi:10.1016/j.asoc.2015.03.036

Maulik, U., & Bandyopadhyay, S. (2000). Genetic algorithm-based clustering technique. *Pattern Recognition*, *33*(9), 1455–1465. doi:10.1016/S0031-3203(99)00137-5

Trelea, I. C. (2003). The particle swarm optimization algorithm: Convergence analysis and parameter selection. *Information Processing Letters*, *85*(6), 317–325. doi:10.1016/S0020-0190(02)00447-7

Wang, Z., Yang, F., & Yu, Y. L. (1998). Gaussian mutation in evolution strategies. *Proceedings of the Society for Photo-Instrumentation Engineers*, *3390*(4), 308–311. doi:10.1117/12.304815

Yang, X.-S. (2010). A new metaheuristic bat-inspired algorithm. *Computer Knowledge & Technology*, *284*, 65–74.

Yang, Xin-She., & Deb, Suash. (2010). Cuckoo search via levy flights. *Mathematics*, 210 - 214. Hill, W. G. (2013). Disruptive selection. *Brenners Encyclopedia of Genetics*, 333-334.

Zheng, S., Li, J., Janecek, A., & Tan, Y. (2015). A cooperative framework for fireworks algorithm. *IEEE/ACM Transactions on Computational Biology and Bioinformatics*, *14*(1), 27–41. doi:10.1109/TCBB.2015.2497227 PMID:26552094

Chapter 7
A Classification Model Based on Improved Self–Adaptive Fireworks Algorithm

Yu Xue

Nanjing University of Information Science and Technology, China

ABSTRACT

As a recently developed swarm intelligence algorithm, fireworks algorithm (FWA) is an optimization algorithm with good convergence and extensible properties. Moreover, it is usually able to find the global solutions. The advantages of FWA are both optimization accuracy and convergence speed which endue the FWA with a promising prospect of application and extension. This chapter mainly focuses on the application of FWA in classification problems and the improvement of FWA. Many prior studies around FWA have been produced. The author here probes improvement of FWA and its application in classification. The chapter studies FWA around: (1) Application of FWA in classification problems; (2) Improvement of FWA's candidate solution generation strategy (CSGS), including the employment of self-adaptive mechanisms; (3) Improved SaFWA and classification model. For each part, the author conducts research through theory, experimentation, and results analysis.

THE APPLICATION OF FWA IN CLASSIFICATION PROBLEMS

Classification Problems

Classification problems have been researched for several decades. The purpose of classification is to correctly predict the classification labels of unseen instances according to the characteristics of these instances. This issue is divided into two categories, i.e., unsupervised clustering and supervised classification. Clustering is an important research topic and it has been applied in many fields (Yu Xue, Zhao, & Ma, 2016). The main methods for solving clustering problems including K-means (Zhao, Chen, & Chen, 2017), Fuzzy c-means (FCM) (Manimala, David, & Selvi, 2015) and evolutionary computation (Y. Xue, Zhuang, Meng, & Zhang) (EC). K-means and FCM have been widely researched. However,

DOI: 10.4018/978-1-7998-1659-1.ch007

Copyright © 2020, IGI Global. Copying or distributing in print or electronic forms without written permission of IGI Global is prohibited.

both K- means and FCM are sensitive to the initial clustering centers. Thus, the solutions of K-means or FCM algorithms often easily fall into local optima. Furthermore, the parameter value of clustering centers should be given in advance. Therefore, EC techniques, which can solve the optimization problems without much information, are employed to overcome these defects in clustering methods and the evolutionary clustering methods have better performance for solving the clustering problems.

Classification methods, such as support vector machine (SVM) (Martins, Costa, Frizera, Ceres, & Santos, 2014), artificial neural network (ANN) (Oong & Isa, 2011), k-nearest neighbor (KNN) (Peterson, 2009) have become hot research topics in the past several decades. However, most of them are deterministic, they might easily be trapped into local optima. Different from the situation in clustering research field, EC techniques have been only used to improve the accuracy of the classifiers either by optimizing their parameters and structures, or by pre-processing their inputs.

As a recently developed swarm intelligence algorithm, Fireworks Algorithm (FWA) (Ying & Zhu, 2010) is an optimization algorithm with good convergence and extensible properties. Moreover, it is usually able to find the global solutions. The advantages of FWA are both optimization accuracy and convergence speed which endue the FWA with a promising prospect of application and extension. It has been proven that FWA is efficient in dealing with optimization problems. The purpose of this chapter is to investigate the feasibility of solving classification problems by EC techniques through an evolutionary optimization classification model and investigate the performance of FWA when it is employed to solve the classification problems (Yu, Binping, Tinghuai, & X., 2018). We firstly convert the classification problem into an optimization problem, then employ the FWA to solve the optimization problem. Moreover, Particle Swarm Optimization (PSO) (Tanweer, Suresh, & Sundararajan, 2015) is used as a comparison algorithm. Because PSO is a commonly used algorithm.

Evolutionary Optimization Classification Model

Give a dataset $D= \{x_1,x_2,\ldots,x_m\}$ and a training set $T= \{(x_1,y_1),\ldots,(x_m,y_m)\}$, where (x_i,y_i) is the ith example, $x_i = x_{i1},x_{i2},\ldots,x_{id} \in X = R^d$ is the ith sample, $y_i \in Y= \{1,2,\ldots,l\}(1,2,\ldots,m)$ is the label of the ith sample. The task of classification problem is to learn a model $f(x): X \rightarrow Y$ from the training set T.

The examples of a training dataset can be written as:

$$\begin{bmatrix} x_{11} & x_{12} & \cdots & x_{1d} & y_1 \\ x_{21} & x_{22} & \cdots & x_{2d} & y_2 \\ \cdots & \cdots & \cdots & \cdots & \cdots \\ x_{m1} & x_{m2} & \cdots & x_{md} & y_m \end{bmatrix} \tag{1}$$

First, we introduce a weight vector $W= (w_1,w_2,\ldots,w_d)$ and let:

$$\begin{cases} w_1x_{11} + w_2x_{12} + \ldots + w_dx_{1d} = y_1 \\ w_1x_{21} + w_2x_{22} + \ldots + w_dx_{2d} = y_2 \\ \ldots + \ldots + \ldots + \ldots = \ldots \\ w_1x_{m1} + w_2x_{m2} + \ldots + w_dx_{md} = y_m \end{cases} \tag{2}$$

By observing equation (2), we can see that if we could find a vector W which can satisfy all the equations, we could use this vector to predict the label of xi. So we transform the classification problem into solving a linear equation set problem. Generally speaking, this kind of problems can be solved by EC techniques. But, if these equations are uncorrelated and the number of the equations is much larger than the number of the weights, this problem will be a so-called inconsistent equation. So there is no exact solution for these linear equations and there is no exact method for solving such a problem. Fortunately, it is not necessary to find the exact solution for the equations. In fact, for a classification problem, it is enough to find the approximate solutions for the following equations:

$$AW^T \approx b \cong \begin{cases} w_1x_{11} + w_2x_{12} + ... + w_dx_{1d} \approx y_1 \\ w_1x_{21} + w_2x_{22} + ... + w_dx_{2d} \approx y_2 \\ ... + ... + ... + ... \approx .... \\ w_1x_{m1} + w_2x_{m2} + ... + w_dx_{md} \approx y_m \end{cases} \tag{3}$$

Obviously, EC techniques can be employed to solve this kind of problems. The objective function can be defined as follow:

$$\min(f(W) = \sqrt{\sum_{i=1}^{m}\sum_{j=1}^{d}(w_j \cdot x_{ij} - y_i)^2}) \tag{4}$$

This is a continuous numerical optimization problem. Many EC techniques can be employed to solve this problem.

Moreover, the following model can be used in the prediction process. In this process, we can predict the label of x_i belong to y_i if $y_i - \delta \le w_1x_{i1} + w_2x_{i2} + ... + w_dx_{id} < y_i + \delta$.

$$\begin{cases} y_1 - \delta \le w_1x_{11} + w_2x_{12} + ... + w_dx_{1d} < y_1 + \delta \\ y_2 - \delta \le w_1x_{21} + w_2x_{22} + ... + w_dx_{2d} < y_2 + \delta \\ ... \le ... + ... + ... + ... < ... \\ y_m - \delta \le w_1x_{m1} + w_2x_{m2} + ... + w_dx_{md} < y_m + \delta \end{cases} \tag{5}$$

There are many methods to ensure lower boundary and upper boundary of w_i, i=1,2,3,...,d In this chapter, we estimate the lower boundary and upper boundary through the following equations:

$$\pm\sigma \frac{\sum_{i=1}^{N} y_i}{\sum_{i=1}^{N}\sum_{j=1}^{d} x_{ij}} \tag{6}$$

where σ is used to control the range of the boundaries.

Experiments

Datasets

Ten different datasets were used in the experiments. The datasets were chosen from the UCI Machine learning repository (Frank & Asuncion, 2018). The detail information of all the datasets is present in Table 1. The datasets comprise of a various number of features, classes and samples. For each dataset, examples are randomly divided into two sections: 70% of them are used as the training sets and the rest are used as the test sets.

Table 1. Description of datasets

Datasets	NoE	NoF	NoC
Biodegradation	1,055	41	2
Climatemodel	540	20	2
Fertility	100	9	2
German	1,000	24	2
Indianliver	583	10	2
Ionosphere	351	33	2
Iris	150	4	3
Thyroid	215	5	3
Spectheart	267	44	2
WBCD	569	30	2

Note: NOE, NoF and NoC are abbreviations of number of examples, number of features and number of classes.

Parameter Settings

FWA was employed to find W to minimize $\sqrt{\sum_{i=1}^{m}\left(\sum_{j=1}^{d} w_j x_{xj} - y_i\right)^2}$ on each dataset. For the FWA and PSO algorithm, run time is set to 26 and the maximum number of iterations is setup to 5,000. Twenty-six run time can guarantee the randomness of the experimental results.

The other settings of FWA: n = 8, m =64, a = 0.04, b = 0.8, $\hat{A}$ = 2 and $\hat{m}$ = 8, which is applied in all the comparison experiments. For PSO, we set c1 and c2 to 2.8 and 1.3 and ω to 1. PSO is widely used to solve optimization problems and its performance has been proved since it was proposed. In our paper, PSO algorithm is applied in the experiment for comparison as its advantages of high accuracy and fast convergence.

After W is found, we calculate classification accuracy for each training sets. For each example (x_i, y_i), if $-0.5 \leq \left(W^T x_i - y_i\right) < +0.5$, then we deem the class of (x_i, y_i) is correct. So the classification accuracy can be calculated by this method.

Results and Discussions

The experimental results of the classification accuracy over 26 independent runs are listed in Tables 2 and 3, in terms of minimum value (min), maximum value (max), mean values (mean) and standard deviations (std). The best results in terms of mean values are typed in bold. To investigate the robustness of the two algorithms on the training sets and test sets, their box plots on the training sets and test sets are shown in Figures 1 and 2, respectively. Moreover, Figure 3 illustrates the convergence characteristics of the two algorithms on the training sets in terms of classification accuracy.

Table 2. Classification accuracy of PSO and FWA on the training sets

Datasets	PSO Min. Mean Std.				FWA Min. Mean Std.			
	Max.	*Min.*	*Mean*	*Std.*	*Max.*	*Min.*	*Mean*	*Std.*
Biodegradation	79.3%	57.645%	72.25%	2.615E–1	81.6%	77.943%	79.7%	4.514E–2
Climatemodel	93.39%	84.126%	90.78%	8.047E–2	92.86%	89.947%	91.2%	3.357E–2
Fertility	94.29%	82.857%	87.8%	1.388E–1	94.29%	85.7142%	88.63%	1.0969E–1
German	72.29%	65.142%	69.8%	9.891E–2	74.86%	71.1428%	73.3%	4.6961E–2
Indianliver	65.2%	58.578%	62.77%	7.860E–2	67.65%	63.48%	65.87%	5.4647E–2
Ionosphere	79.67%	34.552%	67.96%	4.971E–1	78.86%	71.5447%	75.8%	1.0881E–1
Iris	98.1%	94.285%	96.08%	4.916E–2	98.1%	94.2857%	95.97%	4.7251E–2
Thyroid	81.46%	67.549%	76.85%	1.452E–1	82.78%	70.8609%	78.27%	1.5783E–1
Spectheart	82.89%	75.401%	79.12%	7.913E–2	81.82%	75.9358%	79.23%	8.1344E–2
WBCD	82.16%	75.879%	79.32%	7.159E–2	83.67%	78.3919%	80.7%	7.1333E–2

Notes: 'Min.' and 'max.' means the minimum and maximum value of classification accuracy, 'mean' and 'std.' denote the average and standard deviation of the corresponding classification accuracy obtained over 26 runs.

Computational Results and Comparison on Training Sets

Table 2 shows that the training classification accuracy of FWA can reach to more than 79% on most training sets. Besides, the classification performance of FWA is better than that of PSO algorithm on nine datasets and worse a little than that of PSO on only one dataset. This means that the FWA performs better than PSO on most training sets.

In order to investigate the stability of the two algorithms, their box plots on the ten training sets are shown in Figure 1. It is observed that the robustness of the FWA is better than that of PSO on eight datasets, similar to that of PSO on one dataset and worse than that of PSO on one dataset. This means that FWA is more robust than PSO algorithm. By observing the column 'max', the maximum value of classification accuracy obtained by FWA is usually higher than that obtained by PSO. Thus, FWA can obtain higher classification accuracy and has much better robustness than PSO in most cases. On the whole, it is possible and reliable to solve classification problems through EC techniques by using the classification optimization model and FWA has high classification accuracy.

Table 3. Classification accuracy of PSO and FWA on the test sets

Datasets	PSO				FWA			
	Max.	Min.	Mean	Std.	Max.	Min.	Mean	Std.
Biodegradation	83.86%	55.696%	72.07%	3.074E–1	82.91%	75.316%	79.05%	9.876E–2
Climatemodel	95.06%	85.802%	90.60%	1.142E–1	95.06%	88.271%	92.14%	7.835E–2
Fertility	96.67%	66.666%	85.77%	3.318E–1	93.33%	73.3333%	86.79%	2.5595E–1
German	72%	63.666%	69.06%	1.209E–1	76.33%	68.3333%	71.97%	1.0603E–1
Indianliver	74.86%	60.571%	64.4%	1.593E–1	69.71%	59.4285%	64.44%	1.3359E–1
Ionosphere	80%	35.128%	66.89%	5.736E–1	79.05%	63.8095%	72.49%	1.912E–1
Iris	100%	91.111%	96.15%	1.239E–1	100%	91.1111%	96.07%	1.1464E–1
Thyroid	85.94%	70.312%	78%	1.86E–1	87.5%	64.0625%	77.28%	3.1809E–1
Spectheart	88.75%	71.25%	80.05%	1.849E–1	87.5%	73.75%	79.81%	1.9014E–1
WBCD	83.04%	72.514%	78.18%	1.296E–1	85.38%	74.269%	80.05%	1.6629E–1

Computational Results and Comparison on Test Sets

It can be observed from Table 3 that the test classification accuracy of FWA arrival at more than 80% on most test sets. Besides, the test classification accuracy of FWA is higher than that of PSO on seven datasets, similar to that of PSO on the rest three datasets. In order to observe the robustness of the two algorithms, the box plots are shown in Figure 2, from which it is observed that the robustness of FWA is much better than that of PSO on five datasets, similar to that of PSO on three datasets and worse than that of PSO on two datasets. Overall, the performance of FWA is better than that of PSO algorithm on the test sets in terms of classification accuracy and stability. On the whole, the results obtained by FWA are better than those obtained by PSO.

Convergence Performance of All the Algorithms on the Training Sets

Figure 3 illustrates the convergence characteristics of the two algorithms on the ten training sets in terms of classification accuracy. By comparing the convergence curves of these algorithms, it can be observed that all the algorithms have similar performance at the initial stage because the same initial method is used for all the algorithms. At the beginning stage of evolution, on most of training datasets, PSO algorithm usually converges faster than FWA on most datasets. However, at the later stages, although the convergence performance of all the algorithms decreases significantly, the classification accuracy obtained by FWA is higher than that of PSO on most datasets. Moreover, the curves fluctuate during all the evolution processes on almost all the datasets.

Thus, FWA has a better diversity property instead of stagnating into a local optimum.

Conclusion

Data classification is a classical problem in machine learning and data mining research fields. Many excellent methods have been proposed to solve the unsupervised and supervised classification problems. However, they easily be trapped into local search. In this paper, we propose a new optimization classification model. This model can be solved by most EC techniques easily and directly. In the experi-

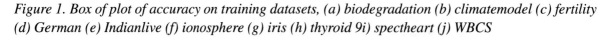

Figure 1. Box of plot of accuracy on training datasets, (a) biodegradation (b) climatemodel (c) fertility (d) German (e) Indianlive (f) ionosphere (g) iris (h) thyroid 9i) spectheart (j) WBCS

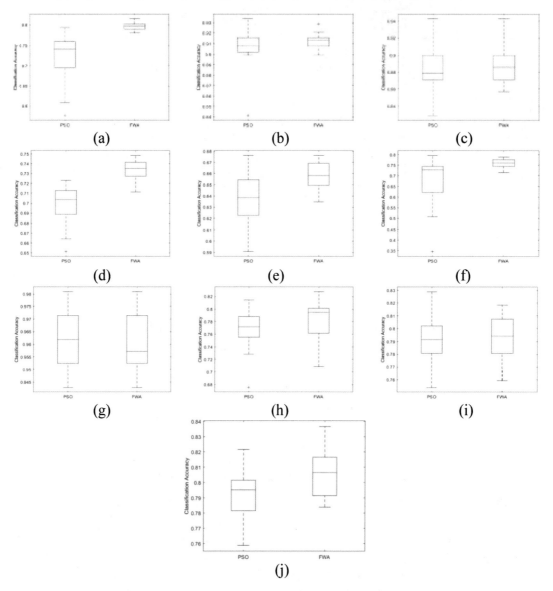

ments, ten different datasets have been employed and the results show that it is possible and reliable to solve classification problems by EC techniques through this classification optimization model. The performance of EC technique on the classification problems indicates that it is a promising technique to directly solve classification problems by EC techniques. Moreover, the performance of FWA is better than PSO. One of our further works is to improve the optimization model and FWA. Another work is to employ different datasets which have high dimensions and more classes. Besides, the structure of optimization classification model will be also taken into account.

Figure 2. Box plot of accuracy on test datasets, (a) biodegradation (b) climatemodel (c) fertility (d) German (e) Indianliver (f) ionosphere (g) iris (h) thyroid (i) spectheart (j) WBCD

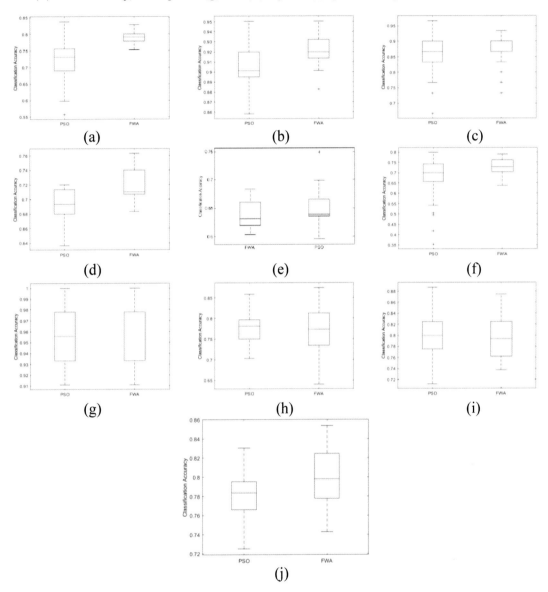

THE IMPROVEMENT OF FWA'S CANDIDATE SOLUTION GENERATION STRATEGY INCLUDING THE EMPLOYMENT OF SELF-ADAPTIVE MECHANISMS

Existing Problems

We have proposed an optimization model for classification problems, and they used fireworks algorithm (FWA) to solve the optimization classification problem. The work before has proved that EC techniques can be used to solve classification problems directly. However, the number of datasets is limited, and the

Figure 3. Curves of convergence on the training sets, (a) biodegradation (b) climatemodel (c) fertility (d) German (e) Indianliber (f) ionosphere (g) iris (h) thyroid (i) spectheart (j) WBCD

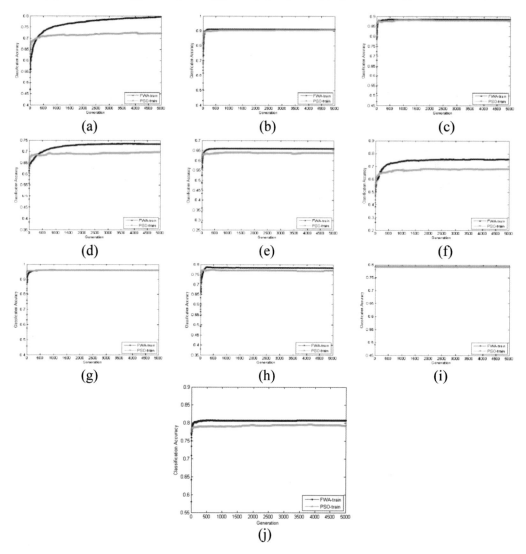

employed EC algorithm is relatively simple. In addition, FWA is not very ñexible, in particular, it does not utilize more information about other good solutions in the swarm. In other words, the individuals are not well-informed by the whole swarm. Thus, many researchers have designed different methods to improve the performance of FWA. However, in the existing research work, the performance of FWA is improved usually by modifying its parameters or operators. The new algorithm increases the degree of information sharing among the fireworks and sparks, and diversifies the search process. Self-adaptive mechanism is useful for developing EC techniques, and many effective self-adaptive EC techniques have been proposed in recent years. Many researchers have introduced self-adaptive mechanisms into EC techniques and they have achieved better results. EC techniques with self-adaptive mechanism have usually achieved excellent performance. Inspired by the powerful ability of self-adaptive mechanism, we introduce this mechanism into FWA for optimization classification problems in this paper (Y. Xue, Zhao, Ma, & Pang, 2018).

Self-Adaptive Fireworks Algorithm

Self-Adaptive Mechanism

Obviously, a fireworks algorithm with only single CSGS cannot meet demands of solving a wide range of practical problems because different problems have their specific characteristics. Meanwhile, many existing EC methods may still suffer from the problems of getting trapped into local optima. Moreover, it is time-consuming to select a suitable EC method manually for a classification problem. Thus, a self-adaptive mechanism and several CSGSs are employed in (Self-adaptive Fireworks Algorithm) SaFWA. Different CSGSs are suitable for different problems, and they can also increase the diversity of solutions. The self-adaptive mechanism can dynamically choose the best CSGS for the corresponding problem during the search process of optimization classification problems, which can improve the universality and robustness of the algorithm.

The process of self-adaptive mechanism is described as follows: Four CSGSs are used in a strategy pool, and each CSGS has its selection probability value (P). straNum represents the number of CSGSs. It is noted that different number of CSGSs may be used depending on problem characteristics. At the initialization phase, the selection probability value (P) for each CSGS is the same, and it is set to be the reciprocal of straNum (1/4). Each individual is assigned a CSGS, which is chosen from the strategy pool randomly. The strategy which is selected from the strategy pool is denoted as curStra. The new individual, which is produced using curStra, will be evaluated. Then, the new individual and the previous one are compared against each other. If the fitness of the new individual is better than that of the previous one, the strategy ñag success matrix (straFlagS) of curStra will be updated. Otherwise, the strategy ñag failure matrix (straFlagF) will be updated. At the beginning of each iteration, the straFlagS and straFlagF of all the strategies are set to 0. The information stored in straFlagS and straFlagF will be counted in total ñag success matrix (totalFlagS) and total ñag failure matrix (totalFlagF), respectively. Moreover, both straFlagS and straFlagF are initialized to 0 for the next generation. When the number of iteration reaches the learning period (LP), new P of each CSGS will be produced based on Equations (7) and (8),

$$
P_q = \begin{cases} \sum_{n=1}^{LP} totalFlagS_n \Big/ \left(\sum_{n=1}^{LP} totalFlagS_n + \sum_{n=1}^{LP} totalFlagF_n \right), & \sum_{n=1}^{LP} totalFlagS_n \neq 0 \\ \left(\sum_{n=1}^{LP} totalFlagS_n + \varepsilon \right) \Big/ \sum_{n=1}^{LP} totalFlagF_n, & \sum_{n=1}^{LP} totalFlagS_n = 0 \end{cases}
\tag{7}
$$

$$
P = P_q \Big/ \sum_{q=1}^{straNum} P_q
\tag{8}
$$

where $q \in \{1,2,\ldots,straNum\}$, ε represents a small constant closed to 0, $\sum_{n=1}^{LP} totalFlagS_n$ and $\sum_{n=1}^{LP} totalFlagF_n$ represent the number of successful and failed operation during the evolutionary process, P is the new selection probabilities of all strategies.

Candidate Solution Generation Strategies (CSGSs)

The CSGSs greatly affect the efficiency of SaFWA. 4 CSGSs are used in the strategy pool. These strategies are the most popular DE strategy variants, and all of them have achieve great performance evidenced by previous applications (Jiang, Xue, Ma, & Chen, 2018; Li, Ma, & Hu; Wang, Li, & Yang, 2017).

1) DE/rand/1 (CSGS1): The new mutation vector is generated by using a random individual and a difference vector that mutates two random individuals.

$$V_i^{G+1} = X_{r_1}^G + F\left(X_{r_2}^G - X_{r_3}^G\right) \tag{9}$$

2) DE/rand/2 (CSGS2): The new mutation vector is generated by using a random individual and a difference vector that mutates four random individuals.

$$V_i^{G+1} = X_{r_1}^G + F\left(X_{r_2}^G - X_{r_3}^G\right) + F\left(X_{r_4}^G - X_{r_5}^G\right) \tag{10}$$

3) DE/best/2 (CSGS3): The new mutation vector is generated by using the best individual of the current generation and a difference vector that mutates four random individuals.

$$V_i^{G+1} = X_{best}^G + F\left(X_{r_1}^G - X_{r_2}^G\right) + F\left(X_{r_3}^G - X_{r_4}^G\right) \tag{11}$$

4) DE/current-to-best/2 (CSGS4): The new mutation vector is generated by using the current individual and a difference vector that mutates the best individual of the current generation, the current individual, and four random individuals.

$$V_i^{G+1} = X_i^G + F\left(X_{best}^G - X_i^G\right) + F\left(X_{r_1}^G - X_{r_2}^G\right) + F\left(X_{r_3}^G - X_{r_4}^G\right) \tag{12}$$

In the above four equations (Equations 9 - 12), G is the number of current generation, G+1 is the next generation, X_{r_1}, X_{r_2}, X_{r_3}, X_{r_4} are different individuals, parameter F∈[-1,1]. X_i^G is the current individual, and V_i^{G+1} is the newly produced individual. X_{best} is the individual with the best fitness value.

According to the strategy selection probability P, one strategy can be chosen through the roulette wheel algorithm during evolutionary process. At first, the selection probability value (P) for each CSGS is the same, and it is set to the reciprocal of straNum. After that, the strategy which achieves better performance will be selected with higher possibility by the self-adaptive mechanism. This can greatly improve the ability of SaFWA when solving different kinds of problems.

The details of SaFWA is described in Algorithm 1.

Experiments

Datasets

Eight different datasets were used in the experiments. The datasets were chosen from the UCI Machine Learning Repository. The detailed information of all the datasets is presented in Table 4. The datasets have various numbers of features, classes and samples. For each dataset, examples were randomly divided into two sections: 70% of them were used as the training sets and the rest were used as the test sets.

Table 4. Description of datasets

Datasets	NoE	NoF	NoC
Biodegradation	1,055	41	2
Climatemodel	540	20	2
Fertility	100	9	2
German	1,000	24	2
Ionosphere	351	33	2
Iris	150	4	3
Spectheart	267	44	2
WBCD	569	30	2

Parameter Settings

Eight different algorithms were chosen for experiments. They were standard FWA, FWA with CSGS1 (FWA-CSGS1), FWA with CSGS2 (FWA-CSGS2), FWA with CSGS3 (FWA-CSGS3), FWA with CSGS4 (FWA-CSGS4), SaFWA, DE and PSO.

Algorithm 1. SaFWA

Input: Set parameter values including max number of fitness evaluations (*MaxFES*), current number of fitness evaluations (*fitCount* = 0), *straNum*, P_q = 1/*straNum* for each $q \in straNum$,

Output: the best location

1. Randomly initialize n locations to set off fireworks and evaluate their fitness;
2. while *fitCount* < *MaxFES* do
3. **for each** *firework* x_i do
4. Calculate the number of sparks that the firework yields;
5. Obtain locations of $s\hat{}i$ sparks of the firework xi;
6. $nsFlag_{i,q}$=1;
7. **end**
8. **for each** $i < n + s_1 + \ldots + s_n$ do
9. Select one CSGS for current solution x_i from the strategy pool by roulette wheel selection method based on $p_1, p_2, \ldots, p_{straNum}$. *curStra* is selected. Generate a new solution x_i^{new} by the selected CSGS, and calculate its fitness value;

10. **if** $f(x_i^{new})$ is better than $f(x_i)$ **then**

11. $straFlagS_{i,curStra} = 1$;

12. Replace x_i with x_i^{new} ;

13. **else**

14. $straFlagF_{i,curStra} = 1$;

15. **end**

16. $fitCount=fitCount+1$;

17. **end**

18. $curIter=curIter+1$;

19. Update the *totalFlagS* and *totalFlagF* with the sum of all the rows in *straFlagS* and *straFlagF*, and reset *straFlagS* and *straFlagF* to be all-zero matrix;

20. **if** $(curIter - flagIter) = LP$ **then**

21. $flagIter = curIter$;

22. Update $\{p_1, p_2, ..., p_{curaNum}\}$ based on *totalFlagS* and *totalFlagF*;

23. Reset *totalFlagS* and *totalFlagF*;

24. **end**

25. Evaluate each location and store the best location and its fitness value;

26. Select the best location and n -1 locations by the roulette wheel algorithm and keep them for the next generation according to the probability;

27. end

All the algorithms were employed to find W to minimize $\sqrt{\sum_{i=1}^{m}\left(\sum_{j=1}^{d}w_j x_{xj} - y_i\right)^2}$ on each dataset. For SaFWA, standard FWA and FWA variants with single CSGS, each algorithm ran 26 times on each dataset, and the maximum number of fitness evaluations (NFE) was set up to 100,000. The other parameter settings of FWA were: n = 10, m = 90, a = 0.04, b = 0.8, $\hat{A}$ = 2, $\hat{m}$ = 8. LP = 10, and straNum = 4.

After W was found, we calculated the classification accuracy for each example as follow: (x_i, y_i), if $-0.5 \le (W^T x_i - y_i) < + 0.5$, then we deemed the class label of (x_i, y_i) was correctly predicted. So, the classification accuracy for the whole data set can be calculated by counting the number of the examples which had the correct results.

Results and Discussions

The experimental results of all the algorithms on the training sets and test sets over 26 independent trials are listed in Tables 5 and 6 in terms of mean values (Mean) and standard deviations (Std). We compared SaFWA with PSO, DE, standard FWA, FWA-CSGS1, FWA-CSGS2, FWA-CSGS3 and FWA-CSGS4. To investigate the robustness of the eight algorithms on the training sets or test sets, their box plots on the 8 datasets are shown in Figures 4 and 5. Moreover, Figure 6 illustrates the convergence characteristics of SaFWA, standard FWA, PSO, and DE on both the 8 training datasets in terms of the fitness values as opposed to the corresponding objective functions. The best results in terms of mean values are typed in bold.

Computational Results and Analysis on Training Sets

By observing Table 5, we can see that the following results: SaFWA has better performance than DE on 7 datasets, and worse performance than DE on 1 dataset. SaFWA has better performance than PSO on all the datasets. SaFWA has better performance than standard FWA on 5 datasets, similar performance on 2 datasets, and worse performance than standard FWA on 1 dataset. SaFWA has better performance than FWA-CSGS1 on 5 datasets, similar performance on 1 dataset, and worse performance than FWA-CSGS1

Table 5. Classification accuracies of eight algorithms on training sets

Datasets	DE	PSO	FWACSGS1	FWACSGS2	FWACSGS3	FWACSGS4	FWA	SaFWA
	Mean±Std	Mean±Std	Mean±Std	Mean±Std	Mean±Std	Mean±Std	Mean±Std	Mean±Std
Biodegradation	0.624±0.252	0.483±1.100	0.804±0.0487	0.804±0.042	0.804±0.045	0.804±0.038	0.757±0.071	0.805±0.049
Climate model	0.910±0.024	0.773±0.767	0.913±0.032	0.914±0.041	0.915±0.039	0.914±0.045	0.915±0.041	0.916±0.038
Fertility	0.871±0.000	0.668±1.394	0.881±0.116	0.889±0.088	0.884±0.102	0.899±0.115	0.890±0.115	0.892±0.115
German	0.682±0.144	0.465±0.902	0.730±0.061	0.732±0.056	0.731±0.056	0.729±0.052	0.713±0.060	0.732±0.053
Ionosphere	0.362±0.415	0.507±1.233	0.754±0.117	0.758±0.107	0.749±0.112	0.761±0.108	0.760±0.123	0.741±0.140
Iris	0.962±0.000	0.700±1.858	0.963±0.058	0.963±0.060	0.932±0.051	0.963±0.053	0.960±0.052	0.965±0.052
Spect heart	0.802±0.082	0.739±0.459	0.799±0.081	0.793±0.082	0.796±0.074	0.794±0.094	0.798±0.095	0.793±0.074
WBCD	0.797±0.020	0.714±0.711	0.806±0.058	0.803±0.060	0.806±0.058	0.807±0.006	0.804±0.072	0.803±0.073

on 2 datasets. SaFWA has better performance than FWA-CSGS2 on 6 datasets, similar performance on 1 dataset, and worse performance than FWA-CSGS2 on 1 dataset. SaFWA has better performance than FWA-CSGS3 on 5 datasets, similar performance on 2 datasets, and worse performance than FWA-CSGS3 on 1 dataset. SaFWA has better performance than FWA-CSGS4 on 5 datasets, similar performance on 1 dataset, and worse performance than FWA-CSGS4 on 2 datasets. This means that SaFWA performs better than other algorithms on most training sets. To examine stability of the eight algorithms, the box plots of the eight algorithms on the 8 training datasets are shown in Figure 4, from which it is observed that the robustness of SaFWA is better than that of the other algorithms on 4 datasets, similar to that of the other algorithms on 3 datasets, and worse than that of the other algorithms on 1 dataset. This means that SaFWA is more robust than the other algorithms. Thus, SaFWA obtains higher classification accuracy and it has much better robustness in most cases. Overall, SaFWA performs much better than the other algorithms in terms of classification accuracy and robustness on the training datasets.

Computational Results and Analysis on Test Sets

We further compare SaFWA with DE, PSO, standard FWA, FWA-CSGS1, FWA-CSGS2, FWA-CSGS3 and FWA-CSGS4 on the corresponding 8 test sets. The results are shown in Table 7, it can be observed that SaFWA has better performance than DE on 6 datasets and worse performance than DE on 2 datasets. SaFWA has better performance than PSO on all the datasets. SaFWA has better performance than standard FWA on 5 datasets, similar performance on 1 dataset, and worse performance than standard FWA on 2 datasets. SaFWA has better performance than FWA-CSGS1 on 4 datasets, similar performance on 1 dataset, and worse performance than FWA-CSGS1 on 3 datasets. SaFWA has better performance than FWA-CSGS2 on 5 datasets, similar performance on 1 dataset, and worse performance than FWA-CSGS2

Table 6. Classification accuracies of eight algorithms on test sets

Datasets	DE	PSO	FWACSGS1	FWACSGS2	FWACSGS3	FWACSGS4	FWA	SaFWA
	Mean±Std	*Mean±Std*	*Mean±Std*	*Mean±Std*	*Mean±Std*	*Mean±Std*	*Mean±Std*	*Mean±Std*
Biodegradation	0.629±0.259	0.480±1.096	0.781±0.101	0.793±0.111	0.790±0.128	0.787±0.112	0.743±0.129	0.794±0.072
Climate model	0.912±0.042	0.804±0.818	0.919±0.075	0.918±0.097	0.915±0.091	0.915±0.105	0.915±0.095	0.913±0.088
Fertility	0.900±0.000	0.664±1.550	0.881±0.284	0.865±0.233	0.967±0.258	0.865±0.289	0.869±0.279	0.855±0.258
German	0.682±0.182	0.467±0.920	0.726±0.106	0.717±0.119	0.721±0.114	0.729±0.096	0.700±0.110	0.726±0.089
Ionosphere	0.359±0.449	0.476±1.198	0.716±0.190	0.695±0.196	0.715±0.225	0.703±0.235	0.709±0.227	0.728±0.209
Iris	0.978±0.000	0.704±1.858	0.922±0.111	0.955±0.149	0.959±0.103	0.960±0.130	0.961±0.127	0.944±0.105
Spect heart	0.760±0.163	0.720±0.380	0.782±0.189	0.796±0.191	0.790±0.173	0.795±0.219	0.785±0.222	0.797±0.173
WBCD	0.794±0.048	0.782±0.705	0.806±0.118	0.807±0.140	0.804±0.124	0.805±0.166	0.807±0.166	0.811±0.137

on 2 datasets. SaFWA has better performance than FWA-CSGS3 on 5 datasets, similar performance on 1 dataset, and worse performance than FWA-CSGS3 on 2 datasets. SaFWA has better performance than FWA-CSGS4 on 4 datasets, similar performance on 2 datasets, and worse performance than FWA-CSGS4 on 2 datasets. In order to observe the robustness of the eight algorithms, the box plots are shown in Figure 5, from which we can observe that the robustness of SaFWA is better than that of the other algorithms on 4 datasets, similar to that of the other algorithms on 3 datasets, and worse than that of the other algorithms on 1 dataset. Overall, the performance of SaFWA is better than that of the other algorithms on the test sets in terms of classiÿcation accuracy and stability. It is due to four effective SCGSs can increase the diversity of solutions and avoid trapping in local optima. Besides, the self-adaptive mechanism of SaFWA can dynamically choose the best CSGS for the corresponding problem during the search process of optimization classiÿcation problems, which can achieve better performance than other ÿxed algorithms. On the whole, it is possible and reliable to solve classiÿcation problems by EC techniques using the classiÿcation optimization model, and all the eight algorithms have high classiÿcation accuracy. Besides, the results obtained by SaFWA are better than those obtained by other algorithms.

Convergence Performance of Standard FWA and SaFWA

Figure 3 illustrates the convergence characteristics of DE, PSO, standard FWA and SaFWA on the 8 datasets in terms of fitness value. In order to make the images clearer, we convert fitness to fitness named as relevant Fitness. So the horizontal axis and vertical axis represent the corresponding evolution generations and relevant fitness, respectively. By com-paring the convergence curves of these four algorithms, it can be observed that at the beginning stage of evolution, SaFWA converges faster than other three algorithms on most datasets. Besides, at the later stages, although the convergence performance of the four algorithms decreases significantly, the value of objective function obtained by SaFWA is lower than those of the other three algorithms on most datasets. Thus, SaFWA has a better diversity property instead of stagnating into local optima. In addition to that, the convergence speed of SaFWA is faster, and the objective fitness of SaFWA is usually lower than that of DE, PSO and standard FWA.

Figure 4. Box plots of accuracy on the training sets (a) biodegradation (b) climatemodel (c) fertility (d) German (e) ionosphere (f) iris (g) spectheart (h) WBCD

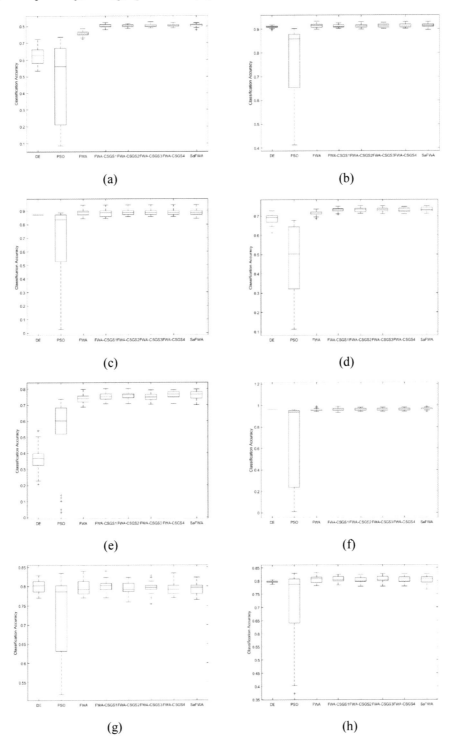

Figure 5. Box plots of accuracy on the test sets (a) biodegradation (b) climatemodel (c) fertility (d) German (e) ionosphere (f) iris (g) spectheart (h) WBCD

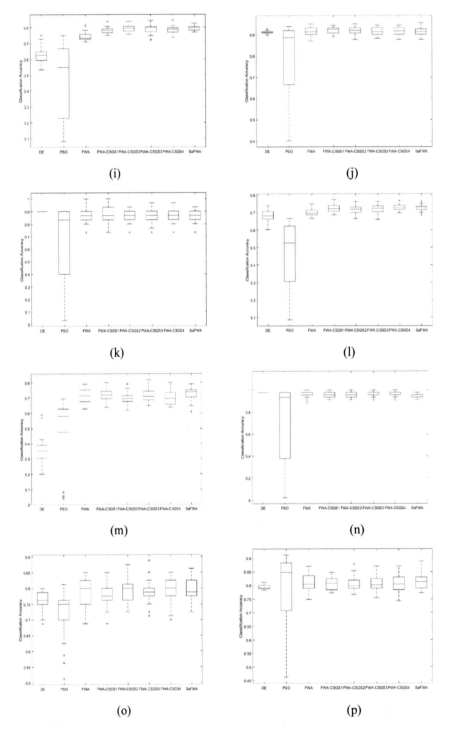

Figure 6. Curves of convergence on the eight datasets (a) biodegradation (b) climatemodel (c) fertility (d) German (e) ionosphere (f) iris (g) spectheart (h) WBCD

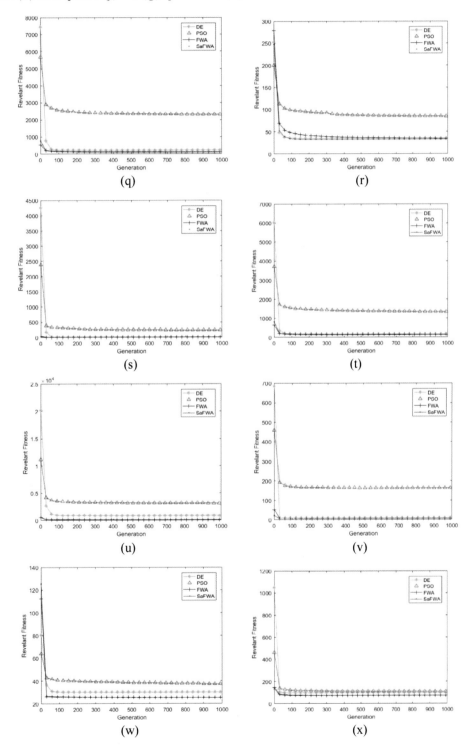

Conclusion

There are many excellent methods proposed to solve classification problems and they all have good performance for classification. In this research, we propose an optimization classification model, and it can be used to solve classification problems by most EC techniques easily and straightforwardly. Besides, SaFWA, which employed a self-adaptive mechanism and four CSGSs, has been developed. Eight different datasets have been employed in the experiments. The results show that it is possible to solve classification problems by EC techniques with this new classification optimization model, and the performance of EC technique on classification problems indicates that it is a promising technique to straightforwardly solve classification problems by EC techniques. Moreover, the performance of SaFWA is better than that of DE, PSO, standard FWA and FWA variants with single CSGS.

Our next work is to further improve the optimization classification model and SaFWA. More data sets which are of high dimensions or more classes will be tested in the experiments. Finally, we will also take the structure of optimal classification model into account and consider using non-linear models for more complicated classification tasks

IMPROVED SAFWA AND CLASSIFICATION MODEL

This chapter focuses on improving the evolutionary classification optimization model and improving one of the employed EC techniques. First of all, we propose a new objective function which is directly relate to the classification accuracy. In this model, directly maximizing the classification accuracy on each dataset is used as the objective function. Different from the old objective function, the new one can well reflect the classification accuracy on each dataset. Furthermore, this new objective function can significantly reduce the computational complexity of the algorithm. Thus, the new objective function can directly improve the classification accuracy. Secondly, an extension method has been introduced into the evolutionary classification optimization model. Finally, an improved self-adaptive fireworks algorithm (ISaFWA) has been proposed to solve the evolutionary classification optimization model. In ISaFWA, four candidate solution generation strategies (CSGSs) along with their associated adaptation parameter values are used to improve its performance. Besides, a self-adaptive search mechanism has also been used to use the four CSGSs and their associated parameters simultaneously. In this paper, seven different data sets from UCI Machine Learning Repository are employed in the experiments.

Improved Self-Adaptive Fireworks Algorithm (Parameter Adaptation)

Each CSGS has its associated control parameter F. In the conventional DE, the choice of numerical values for F highly depends on the problem under consideration, and F is closely related to the convergence speed. In ISaFWA, the number of parameter F depends on the selected CSGSs, and it is named as fNum. At first, the parameter F values (PF) for each CSGS are the same, and they are set to 0.5. After selecting a CSGS, the associated parameter F is set by a normal distribution with mean value PFcurStra and standard deviation 0.3, denoted by N(PFcurStra,0.3). A set of F values are randomly sampled from such normal distribution and applied to each CSGS in the current population. All elements of matrix PF are initialized to 0.5, and it is easy to verify that F values must fall into the range [-0.4,1.4] with the probability of 0.997. If the fitness value of the new solution is better than the previous one, the parameter F memory matrix FMemory of curStra will be updated. At the beginning of each generation, all elements of matrix FMemory of all the strategies are set to 0.5. After each iteration, the information stored in FMemory is transferred to total parameters F matrix (totalFM). Moreover, FMemory will be initialized by PF. When the iteration times reaches LP, PF values of each CSGS will also be calculated according to Equation (13).

$$PF = \sum_{h=1}^{LP} totalFM_h / LP \tag{13}$$

where $\sum_{h=1}^{LP} totalFM_h$ represents the sum of the average parameter F values of each generation. According to this method, we can balance the local exploitation capability (with small F values) and the global exploration ability (with large F values) throughout the search process. Moreover, it is time saving to adaptively determine an appropriate CSGS and its associated parameter values at different stages of evolutionary process.

Improved Evolutionary Classification Optimization Model

In this chapter, the classification problem was translated into a continuous numerical optimization problem, and obviously, EC techniques can be employed to solve this kind of problems. The objective function was defined as follow:

$$\min\left(f_1(W) = \sqrt{\sum_{i=1}^{m}(\sum_{j=1}^{D} w_j \cdot x_{ij} - y_i)^2} \right) \tag{14}$$

LSM was used in the objective function. Generally speaking, the smaller value of the objective function, the smaller differences between the class label value Y and the data obtained by $A \bullet W^T$.

From our preliminary work, the experimental results show that the classification optimization model can be solved by any EA through this model. However, the objective function has its disadvantages. Firstly, it will consume much time to calculate the fitness value of the objective function, the LSM formula was calculated in each evaluation. The more instances in the training data, the more complicated the calculation is. Secondly, the most important drawback of LSM is its high sensitivity to outliers. This is a consequence of using squares because squaring exaggerates the magnitude of differences. For example, the difference between 20 and 10 is equal to 10 but the difference between 20^2 and 10^2 is equal to 300 and therefore gives a much stronger importance to outliers. The third one, the value of objective function obtained by LMS merely represents the difference between the class labels and the data obtained by $A \bullet W^T$. There is a bias between the overall difference and the classification accuracy and the objective function value. In other words, the value of this objective function cannot well reflect the classification accuracy of the overall data. For example, given a simple training set T as follows:

$$T = \begin{bmatrix} 2 & 3 & 4 & 1 \\ 3 & 3 & 5 & 2 \\ 6 & 4 & 6 & 3 \end{bmatrix} \text{ and } A = \begin{bmatrix} 2 & 3 & 4 \\ 3 & 3 & 5 \\ 6 & 4 & 6 \end{bmatrix}, Y = \begin{bmatrix} 1 \\ 2 \\ 3 \end{bmatrix} \tag{15}$$

During the optimization process, we can always focus on the value achieved by LMS instead of classification accuracy. For two weight vector W_1 and W_2:

$$W_1 = \begin{bmatrix} -0.00078 & 0.7029 & -0.0028 \end{bmatrix} \text{ and } W_2 = \begin{bmatrix} -0.00069 & 0.6233 & -0.0028 \end{bmatrix} \tag{16}$$

the data obtained by $A \cdot W_1^T$ and $A \cdot W_2^T$ are calculated as followed:

$$A \cdot W_1^T = \begin{bmatrix} 2.0959 \\ 2.0924 \\ 2.7902 \end{bmatrix} \text{ and } A \cdot W_2^T = \begin{bmatrix} 1.8574 \\ 1.8539 \\ 2.4724 \end{bmatrix} \tag{17}$$

According to Equation (15), the difference between the class labels Y and the data obtained by $A \bullet W^T$ is $f_1(W_1) = 1.2538$ and $f_2(W_2) = 1.0348$. From the aspect of the objective function, W_1 is superior to W_2. However, the number of correct classifications of $A \cdot W_1^T$ is 2, and the number of correct classifications of $A \cdot W_2^T$ is 1. Thus, from the aspect of classification accuracy, weight vector W_1 is superior to W_2. To summarize, the classification accuracy does not match with the results achieved by LSM in some special cases.

The fourth one, in face of the large number, the small number cannot be well reflected according to the LSM when all of them are in the same class. For example, a simple training set T and two weight vector W_1 and W_2 are defined as follows:

$$T = \begin{bmatrix} 10 & 20 & 1 \\ 2 & 5 & 1 \\ 3 & 8 & 1 \end{bmatrix} \text{ and } A = \begin{bmatrix} 10 & 20 \\ 2 & 5 \\ 3 & 8 \end{bmatrix}, Y = \begin{bmatrix} 1 \\ 1 \\ 1 \end{bmatrix} \tag{18}$$

$$W_1 = \begin{bmatrix} 0.1 & 0.01 \end{bmatrix} \text{ and } W_2 = \begin{bmatrix} 0.1 & 0.1 \end{bmatrix} \tag{19}$$

the data obtained by $A \cdot W_1^T$ and $A \cdot W_2^T$ are calculated as followed:

$$A \cdot W_1^T = \begin{bmatrix} 1.2 \\ 0.25 \\ 0.38 \end{bmatrix} \text{ and } A \cdot W_2^T = \begin{bmatrix} 3.0 \\ 0.7 \\ 1.1 \end{bmatrix} \tag{20}$$

the difference between the class labels Y and the data obtained by $A \bullet W^T$ is $f_1(W_1) = 0.9934$ and $f_2(W_2) = 2.0248$. From the aspect of the objective function, W_1 is superior to W_2. However, the number of correct classifications of $A \cdot W_1^T$ is 1, and the number of correct classifications of $A \cdot W_2^T$ is 2. Thus, from the aspect of classification accuracy, weight vector W_1 is superior to W_2. This is because in the data of the same class, LSM will give priority to reducing the classification error of data with large number. The large number is sensitive to the value of the weight vector, so the data with small number cannot be well reflected in the face of the large number.

Thus, we improve the objective function by directly evaluating the classification accuracy. The new objective function can be defined as follow:

$$\max\left(f_2(W) = \frac{CorrectNum}{M} \right) \tag{21}$$

where CorrectNum is the number of the instances whose inner product with the weight fall into the scale of their label values, and M is the number of all instances in the training set.

Comparing with the old one, this new objective function reduces some calculation complexity. The result obtained by $A \cdot W_2^T$ can be directly compared with the class label value for each instance. When the difference between the value obtained by $A \cdot W_2^T$ and the label is between δ, the corresponding instance is correctly classified and will be marked. Finally, the number of successful instances will be counted. In addition, classification accuracy of all the instances are considered in this improved objective function.

Extended Evolutionary Classification Optimization Models

From Equation (3), we observed that $m \gg D$, thus this problem is an inconsistent equation set in most cases. It is impossible to find an exact solution. In order to find a more accurate solution, an extended model has been proposed, and it has been proven that the extended model is effective for increasing the classification accuracy. Thus, the extend model is used in this paper, and it is described as follows:

$$\underbrace{\{A, A, ..., A, I\}}_{k} \cdot W_E^T \approx Y \tag{22}$$

where I is a column vector including m ones, $W_E = \{w_1, w_2, ..., w_{k*D+1}\}$, k is the number of paratactic A. Here we give k times the same matrix A. The basic classification model of Equation (3) is termed as CM, and the extended models of Equation (16) is termed as CM-k-C, where k is the number of A in the model.

Experiments

Datasets

Seven different datasets, which were selected from the UCI Machine Learning Repository, were used in the experiments. Table 7 showed the detailed information of all the datasets. We used 70% of samples of each dataset as the training sets and the rest samples as the test sets.

Parameter Settings

ISaFWA was employed to optimize formula on each data. ISaFWA runs 26 times on each dataset, and the maximum number of fitness evaluations MaxFES is 300000. The other settings of parameters in ISaFWA are: n = 10, a = 0.04, b = 0.8, $\hat{A}$ =90, and $\hat{A}$ = 2. LP=10, and straNum=4, fNum=8.

Table 7. Description of data

Datasets	Examples	Features	Labels
Climate model	540	20	2
German	1000	24	2
Indian liver	583	10	2
Iris	150	4	3
Thyroid	215	5	3
Spect heart	267	44	2
WBCD	569	30	2

After W is obtained, we predict the label of each example as follows: $(\{x_i\},\{y_i\})$, if $-0.5 \leq (W^T \cdot x_i - y_i) < +0.5$, then we deem the class of $(\{x_i\},\{y_i\})$ is correct. Thus, the classification accuracy for the whole dataset is calculated by counting the number of the examples which have the correct results.

Results and Analysis

The experimental results of FWA and ISaFWA obtained on training sets and test sets with two different objective functions over 26 independent runs are listed in Tables 8 and 9, in terms of mean values (Mean), and standard deviations (Std). Moreover, Tables 10 and 11 illustrate the classification accuracy of ISaFWA with three extended evolutionary classification optimization models on both the training datasets and test datasets. A t-test is employed in the experiments. The t-test is a statistical test for checking the hypothesis on equality of means with given trust level. In our experiments DF (degree freedom)=50, and the t is equal to 2,009 (when the trust level is equal to 0.95). Therefore, the results obtained are statistically important when t is less than -2,009 or higher than +2,009. We only check two cases: IMPORTANT (+) or NOT IMPORTANT (-).

In these tables, 'CA' represents the classification accuracy. In Tables and, 'T-Sig' means there is a statistically significant difference between ISaFWA on the improved objective function and the other algorithm with original objective function. In Tables 10 and 11, 'T-Sig' means there is a statistically significant difference between CM-4-C and the other extended evolutionary classification models.

The best results in terms of mean values are typed in bold.

Performance Comparison Between FWA and ISaFWA

Tables 8 and 9 illustrate the difference between FWA and ISaFWA on both the training sets and test sets. On the training set, the performance of ISaFWA is better than FWA on 6 datasets, and the performance of ISaFWA worse than FWA on 1 dataset. On the test set, the performance of ISaFWA is better than FWA on 5 datasets and worse than FWA on 2 datasets. Besides, all the values of "Std" of ISaFWA are lower than FWA, and they are lower than 0.08. It can be concluded that ISaFWA is better than FWA in terms of classification accuracy and robustness on both training sets and test sets.

Table 8. Classification accuracy of FWA and ISaFWA on training sets based on two different objective functions (original f_1 (W), and improved f_2 (W))

Datasets	original $f_1(W)$		original $f_1(W)$		improved $f_2(W)$	
	Mean	Std.	Mean	Std.	Mean	Std.
Climate model	0.912	0.033	0.913	0	0.918	0.059
	-		-			
German	0.7134	0.0602	0.668	0.006	0.684	0.199
	-		-			
Indian liver	0.658	0.054	0.691	0.009	0.709	0.02
	+		+			
Iris	0.959	0.042	0.962	0	0.974	0.032
	+		-			
Thyroid	0.782	0.157	0.821	0	0.855	0.047
	+		+			
Spect heart	0.787	0.0813	0.801	0.068	0.789	0.061
	-		-			
WBCD	0.805	0.071	0.93	0.029	0.95	0.072
	+		-			

Notes: 'Min.' and 'max.' means the minimum and maximum value of classification accuracy, 'mean' and 'std.' denote the average and standard deviation of the corresponding classification accuracy obtained over 26 runs.

Table 9. Classification accuracy of FWA and ISaFWA on test sets based on two different objective functions (original f_1 (W), and improved f_2 (W))

Datasets	original $f_1(W)$		original $f_1(W)$		improved $f_2(W)$	
	Mean	Std.	Mean	Std.	Mean	Std.
Climate model	0.914	0.095	0.918	0	0.927	0.076
	-		-			
German	0.699	0.109	0.633	0.007	0.633	0.259
	-		-			
Indian liver	0.644	0.133	0.677	0.015	0.713	0.055
	+		+			
Iris	0.961	0.127	0.978	0	0.928	0.2
	-		-			
Thyroid	0.772	0.318	0.719	0	0.794	0.162
	-		+			
Spect heart	0.695	0.221	0.722	0.078	0.708	0.269
	-		-			
WBCD	0.807	0.166	0.904	0.078	0.934	0.153
	+		-			

The Effect of the Improved Objective Function

We further compare the performance of the improved objective function with the performance of original objective function on the corresponding 7 datasets. The results are shown in Tables 8 and 9, it can be observed that on the training sets, the performance of ISaFWA with improved objective function is better than that with original objective function on 6 datasets and worse than that with original objective function on 1 dataset. Considering the statistically significant difference on the training sets, the results obtained are statistically important between improved objective function $f_2(W)$ and original objective function $f_1(W)$ on "Indian liver" and "Thyroid" datasets, and not important between improved objective function $f_2(W)$ and original objective function $f_1(W)$ on the other training sets. On the test sets, the performance of ISaFWA with improved objective function is better than that with original objective function on 4 datasets, similar to that with original objective function on 1 dataset, and worse than that with original objective function on 2 datasets. From observing Tables 8 and 9 we can see that all the values of "Std" are lower than 0.3 and the amplitude of experimental results is small. According to the difference on the test sets, the results obtained are statistically important between improved objective function $f_2(W)$ and original objective function $f_1(W)$ on "Indian liver" and "Thyroid" datasets, and not important between improved objective function $f_2(W)$ and original objective function $f_1(W)$ on the other test sets. According to the results, we can see that the improved objective function can also increase classification accuracy on test sets and training sets.

The Effect of Extended Evolutionary Classification Optimization Models

We employ the extended evolutionary classification optimization models to solve classification problems, and compare CM-4-C with CM and CM-2-C both on training sets and test sets. The results are presented in Tables 10 and 11.

On training sets, it can be seen that the performance of CM-4-C is better than CM on 6 datasets and worse than CM on 1 dataset. The performance of CM-4-C is better than CM-2-C on 4 datasets and worse than CM-2-C on 3 datasets. Considering the statistically significant difference, the results obtained are statistically important between CM-4-C and CM on "Indian liver" and "Spect heart" datasets, and not important between CM-4-C and CM on the other training sets. The results obtained are statistically important between CM-4-C and CM-2-C on "Indian liver" and "Thyroid" datasets, and not important between CM-4-C and CM-2-C on the other training sets. On test sets, the performance of CM-4-C is better than CM on 4 datasets and worse than CM on 3 datasets. The performance of CM-4-C is better than CM-2-C on 6 datasets and worse than CM-2-C on 1 dataset. From the point of difference, the results obtained are not statistically important between CM-4-C and CM on all the test sets. The results obtained are statistically important between CM-4-C and CM-2-C on "Climate model" and "Indian liver" datasets, and not important between CM-4-C and CM-2-C on the other test sets.

According to the results, it is concluded that the classification performance on both training sets and test sets has been improved by the extended evolutionary classification optimization models. The extended method can indeed improve the classification accuracy on most of datasets while it is possible to solve the over-fitting problem.

Table 10. Classification accuracy of ISaFWA on training sets based on extended evolutionary classification optimization models

Datasets	CM		CM-2-C		CM-4-C	
	Mean	*Std.*	*Mean*	*Std.*	*Mean*	*Std.*
Climate model	0.918	0.059	0.931	0.028	0.923	0.039
	-		-			
German	0.684	0.199	0.718	0.109	0.727	0.085
	-		-			
Indian liver	0.709	0.02	0.695	0.024	0.718	0.008
	+		+			
Iris	0.974	0.032	0.982	0.037	0.978	0.038
	-		-			
Thyroid	0.855	0.047	0.861	0.03	0.843	0.023
	-		+			
Spect heart	0.782	0.061	0.805	0.1	0.836	0.122
	+		-			
WBCD	0.95	0.072	0.955	0.046	0.96	0.02
	-		-			

Table 11. Classification accuracy of ISaFWA on test sets based on extended evolutionary classification optimization models

Datasets	CM		CM-2-C		CM-4-C	
	Mean	*Std.*	*Mean*	*Std.*	*Mean*	*Std.*
Climate model	0.927	0.076	0.884	0.054	0.925	0.06
	-		+			
German	0.633	0.259	0.667	0.204	0.691	0.105
	-		-			
Indian liver	0.713	0.055	0.75	0.092	0.701	0.036
	-		+			
Iris	0.928	0.2	0.934	0.165	0.948	0.054
	-		-			
Thyroid	0.794	0.162	0.78	0.155	0.791	0.191
	-		-			
Spect heart	0.708	0.269	0.732	0.231	0.746	0.175
	-		-			
WBCD	0.934	0.153	0.939	0.081	0.946	0.053
	-		-			

CONCLUSION

Many researchers have proposed excellent methods to solve classification problems and they all have been proved with good performance. We propose an evolutionary classification optimization model, which is improved with an extended method and a new objective function. Besides, ISaFWA, which employed with a self-adaptive mechanism and four CSGSs along with adaptation parameters, has been developed. Seven different datasets have been used in the experiments. The results show that the classification performance has been improved by the extended methods, the improved objective function, and the new algorithm. Our next work is to search for an optimal extension multiplier for each dataset.

REFERENCES

Frank, A., & Asuncion, A. (2018). UC Machine Learning Repository. Retrieved from https://archive.ics.uci.edu/ml/index.php

Jiang, J., Xue, Y., Ma, T., & Chen, Z. (2018). Improved artificial bee colony algorithm with differential evolution for the numerical optimisation problems. *International Journal on Computer Science and Engineering*, *16*(1), 73–84.

Li, X., Ma, S., & Hu, J. (2017, July). Multi-search differential evolution algorithm. *Applied Intelligence*, *47*(1), 231–256. doi:10.1007/s10489-016-0885-9

Manimala, K., David, I. G., & Selvi, K. (2015). A novel data selection technique using fuzzy C-means clustering to enhance SVM-based power quality classification. *Soft Computing*, *19*(11), 3123–3144. doi:10.1007/s00500-014-1472-9

Martins, M., Costa, L., Frizera, A., Ceres, R., & Santos, C. (2014). Hybridization between multi-objective genetic algorithm and support vector machine for feature selection in walker-assisted gait. *Computer Methods and Programs in Biomedicine*, *113*(3), 736–748. doi:10.1016/j.cmpb.2013.12.005 PubMed

Oong, T. H., & Isa, N. A. M. (2011). Adaptive Evolutionary Artificial Neural Networks for Pattern Classification. *IEEE Transactions on Neural Networks*, *22*(11), 1823–1836. doi:10.1109/TNN.2011.2169426 PubMed

Peterson, L. (2009). K-nearest neighbor. Scholarpedia, *4*(2), 1883. doi:10.4249/scholarpedia.1883

Tanweer, M. R., Suresh, S., & Sundararajan, N. (2015). Self-regulating particle swarm optimization algorithm. *Information Sciences*, *294*, 182–202. doi:10.1016/j.ins.2014.09.053

Wang, S., Li, Y., & Yang, H. (2017). Self-adaptive differential evolution algorithm with improved mutation mode. *Applied Intelligence*, *47*(3), 1–15. doi:10.1007/s10489-017-0914-3

Xue, Y., Zhao, B., & Ma, T. (2016). Performance analysis for clustering algorithms. *International Journal of Computing Science and Mathematics*, *7*(5), 485. doi:10.1504/IJCSM.2016.080089

Xue, Y., Zhao, B., Ma, T., & Pang, W. (2018). A Self-Adaptive Fireworks Algorithm for Classification Problems. *IEEE Access : Practical Innovations, Open Solutions*, *6*, 44406–44416. doi:10.1109/ACCESS.2018.2858441

Xue, Y., Zhuang, Y., Meng, X., & Zhang, Y. (2013). Self-adaptive, learning-based ensemble algorithm for solving matrix eigenvalues.

Ying, T., & Zhu, Y. (2010). Fireworks Algorithm for Optimization. *Proceedings Advances in Swarm Intelligence, First International Conference, ICSI 2010, Part I*. Beijing, China, June 12-15.

Yu, X., Binping, Z., & Tinghuai, M., & X., L. A. (2018). An evolutionary classification method based on fireworks algorithm. *International Journal of Bio-inspired Computation.*

Zhao, Y., Chen, S., & Chen, T. (2017). K-means clustering method based on artificial immune system in scientific research project management in universities. *International Journal of Computing Science and Mathematics*, 8(2), 129–137. doi:10.1504/IJCSM.2017.083746

Chapter 8
Development and Performance Analysis of Fireworks Algorithm–Trained Artificial Neural Network (FWANN):
A Case Study on Financial Time Series Forecasting

Sarat Chandra Nayak

CMR College of Engineering and Technology, Hyderabad, India

Subhranginee Das

KIIT University, Bhubaneswar, India

Bijan Bihari Misra

Silicon Institute of Technology, India

AbStract

Financial time series are highly nonlinear and their movement is quite unpredictable. Artificial neural networks (ANN) have ample applications in financial forecasting. Performance of ANN models mainly depends upon its training. Though gradient descent-based methods are common for ANN training, they have several limitations. Fireworks algorithm (FWA) is a recently developed metaheuristic inspired from the phenomenon of fireworks explosion at night, which poses characteristics such as faster convergence, parallelism, and finding the global optima. This chapter intends to develop a hybrid model comprising FWA and ANN (FWANN) used to forecast closing prices series, exchange series, and crude oil prices time series. The appropriateness of FWANN is compared with models such as PSO-based ANN, GA-based ANN, DE-based ANN, and MLP model trained similarly. Four performance metrics, MAPE, NMSE, ARV, and R2, are considered as the barometer for evaluation. Performance analysis is carried out to show the suitability and superiority of FWANN.

DOI: 10.4018/978-1-7998-1659-1.ch008

Copyright © 2020, IGI Global. Copying or distributing in print or electronic forms without written permission of IGI Global is prohibited.

INTRODUCTION

The process of predicting the future data based on current and past data of a financial time series is known as financial time series forecasting. Financial time series are highly nonlinear and their movement is quite unpredictable due to economical, political, natural, and global phenomena. Accurate forecasting model design is the keen objective of researchers, financial experts, and speculators. Several conventional as well as advanced computing-based forecasting models have been developed and applied to financial domain. In early days a quite good number of mathematical as well as statistical models are suggested to model the financial time series (Contreras, Espinola, Nogales, & Conejo, 2003; Leigh, Hightower, & Modani, 2005; Swider & Weber, 2007; Kung & Yu, 2008). These models are based on the assumption of the linearity of current and previous variables and are not efficient in handling highly non-linear time series data.

With the exponential growth in computing technologies, the process of financial forecasting becomes faster and more powerful. The advancement in the electronic communication and popularity of internet technologies made the access of financial data easy. Conventional computing, i.e. hard computing requires a lot of computation time and precisely stated analytic model. However, soft computing is tolerant of imprecision, partial truth, uncertainty and approximation. It mimics the human brain as it represents ideas that seem to emulate intelligence to solve commercial problems. In soft computing the tolerance for uncertainty and imprecision is exploited to achieve tractability, lower computation cost, robustness, high machine Intelligence quotient and economy of computation. Soft computing techniques are better suited to deal with the uncertainty and irregularity involved in financial time series. Hence, they are widely used for analyzing and forecasting the financial data. They can be broadly categories as: Artificial Neural Network, Evolutionary Algorithms, and Fuzzy Logic System.

Artificial Neural Network (ANN) has the analogy with the thinking capacity of human brain and thus mimicking it. Introduction about ANN can be found in (Haykin, 2010; Kecman, 2006; Rajasekaran & Pai, 2007; Aliev, Fazlollahi & Aliev, 2004). The ANN can imitate the process of human behavior and solve nonlinear problems, which have made it popular and are widely used in calculating and predicting complicated systems. ANNs are found to be good universal approximator which can approximate any continuous function to desired accuracy. These are considered to be an effective modeling procedure for mapping input-output containing both regularities and exceptions as the case of financial time series. These advantages of ANN attract researchers to forecast financial time series with ANN based models. Dealing with uncertainty and nonlinearity associated with financial time series with ANN based forecasting method primarily involves recognition of patterns in the data and using such patterns to predict future event.

The adjustment of neuron weight and bias of ANN is the key factor of ANN training and is a crucial task. The performance of ANN based models are solely depends upon the adjustment of weight and bias vectors. To circumvent the limitations of gradient descent-based ANN training, large number of nature and bio-inspired optimization techniques are proposed and applied (N. Shadbolt). Evolutionary computing techniques are based on the behavior of nature. Normally these algorithms are motivated by biological evolution and termed as evolutionary algorithms of metaheuristic. The ideas of imitating concepts from nature have great potential in developing algorithms to solve engineering problems. In recent past, applications of these techniques have achieved popularity in wide area of engineering, computer science, medicine, economics, finance, social networks and so on. Their performance depends upon several algorithm specific control parameters and there is no single technique performing well on all problems. Evolutionary training algorithms such as GA (Goldberg, 1989), PSO (Kennedy & Eberhart, 2001), DE (Price, Storn, & Lampinen, 2005), Ant colony optimization (Dorigo & Stutzle, 2004), FWA (Tan & Zhu, 2010) etc. are capable of searching optimal solutions better than gradient descent based search techniques.

Fireworks algorithm (FWA) is a recently developed metaheuristic which simulates the phenomenon of fireworks explosion at night (Tan & Zhu, 2010). Like other nature inspired optimization it is also a population based evolutionary algorithm. It tries to find the best fit solution in the search space through the explosion of fireworks. Several applications of FWA are found in the literature for solving real data mining problems. Meantime, there are some improved and enhanced version of FWA proposed and their superiority have been established. However its application toward financial time series is limited.

The main objective of this chapter is to develop and performance analysis of FWA based ANN (FWANN) hybrid model on financial time series. We used three real financial time series such as stock closing prices series, exchange rate series and crude oil price series for evaluating FWANN. The hybrid model employed FWA to optimize the weight and bias vector of an ANN. Each location (individual) of FWA can be viewed as a possible weight and bias vector for an ANN. The FWA applies local as well as global search techniques in the form of fireworks explosion to explore the optimal weight and bias vector in the potential search space. The proposed hybrid FWANN model is evaluated in forecasting one step ahead data point of three financial time series in terms of four error statistics MAPE, NMSE, R2 and ARV. The performance of the model is compared with that of four other models such as PSO-ANN, GA-ANN, DE-ANN, and MLP trained similarly. The major contributions of this chapter are:

- A brief introduction to FWA metaheuristic
- Discussion about financial time series and their importance
- Developing hybrid model FWANN
- Developing other hybrid models using PSO, DE, GA etc.
- Designing adaptive models
- Experimenting on three financial time series such as stock closing prices, exchange rate series and crude oil price series.
- Rigorous performance analysis of the proposed hybrid models.

Fireworks Algorithm Metaheuristic

Fireworks algorithm (FWA) is a recently proposed optimization technique which simulates the explosion process of fireworks (Tan & Zhu, 2010). It tries to select certain number of locations in a search space for explosion of fireworks to produce set of sparks. Locations with qualitative fireworks are considered for the next generation. The process continues iteratively up to a desired optimum or reaching the stopping criterion. The process mainly comprises three steps: setting off N fireworks at N selected locations, obtaining the locations of sparks after explosion and evaluating them, stop on reaching optimal location or select N other locations for the next generation of explosion. An explosion of fireworks can be viewed as a search process in the local space. According to the basic FWA, for each firework x_i, the amplitude of explosion (A_i) and number of sparks (s_i) are defined as follows:

$$A_i = \hat{A} \cdot \frac{f(x_i) - f_{min} + \varepsilon}{\sum_{j=1}^{p}\left(f(x_j) - f_{min}\right) + \varepsilon} \tag{1}$$

$$s_i = \frac{m \cdot f_{max} - f(x_i) + \varepsilon}{\sum_{j=1}^{p}\left(f_{max} - f(x_j)\right) + \varepsilon} \tag{2}$$

where $\hat{A}$ is the maximum explosion amplitude. f_{max} and f_{min} are the maximum and minimum objective function values among the p fireworks. m is a controlling parameter for total number of sparks generated by a firework and ε is a constant used to avoid zero division error. Bounds are imposed on s_i to overcome the devastating effects of marvelous fireworks as follows:

$$s_i = \begin{cases} s_{max}, & \text{if } s_i > s_{max} \\ s_{min}, & \text{if } s_i < s_{min} \\ s_i, & \text{otherwise} \end{cases} \tag{3}$$

The location of each spark x_j generated by x_i is calculated by setting z directions randomly and for each dimension k setting the component x_j^k based on x_i^k, where $1 \le j \le s_i, 1 \le k \le z$.

The setting of x_j^k can be done in two ways as follows:

- For most sparks, a displacement is added to x_j^k as:

$$x_j^k = x_i^k + A_i \cdot rand(-1,1) \tag{4}$$

- To maintain diversity, for few specific sparks, an explosion coefficient based on Gaussian distribution is applied to x_j^k as:

$$x_j^k = x_i^k \cdot Gaussian(1,1) \tag{5}$$

When a new location falls out of the search space, it is mapped to the potential space as follows:

$$x_j^k = x_{min}^k + \left|x_j^k\right| \% \left(x_{max}^k - x_{min}^k\right) \tag{6}$$

where % is the modulo operator.

The next step is selection of another N location for the fireworks explosion. This step always keeps the current best location x^* for the next generation. Remaining N-1 locations are considered on the basis of their distance to other locations. The distance between a location x_i and other locations (K) can be calculated as the sum of Euclidean distance between them and as follows:

$$Distance(x_i) = \sum_{j \in K} x_i - x_j \qquad (7)$$

A location xi is selected for the next generation based on a probability value as follows:

$$prob(x_i) = \frac{Distance(x_i)}{\sum_{j \in K} Distance(x_j)} \qquad (8)$$

Based on the above concepts, the basic FWA is formulated and represented in Algorithm 1.
Algorithm 1. FA framework

Select N locations randomly for fireworks;
while (stopping criteria == false)
Set off N fireworks at N locations
for each firework x_i
Calculate number of sparks s_i using Equation3
Obtain locations of s_i sparks of firework x_i using Equation4.
end for
for k = 1: m
Select a firework x_j randomly
Generate a specific spark using Equation5.
end for
Select the best location x^* and keep it for next generation
Select remaining *N-1* locations randomly based on a probability using Equation8.
end while

Since the sparks suffer from the power of explosion, they move along z directions simultaneously. This makes FWA to achieve faster convergence. Also, it avoids the premature convergence with the two types of spark generation methods and specific location selection method (Tan & Zhu, 2010). The advantages of FWA over standard PSO and its improved variants are demonstrated in the research work (Tan & Zhu, 2010).

Financial Time Series Forecasting

A time series can be viewed as a sequence of values/data points/events separated/occurred by equal interval of time. It can be represented as a set of discrete values $\{x_1, x_2, x_3, \cdots, x_n\}$, where n is the total number of observations. A time series possess both deterministic as well as stochastic components characterized by noise interference. The forecasting process can be mathematically represented as:

$$y_{t+1} = f(y_t, y_{t-1}, y_{t-2}, \cdots, y_{t-n}) \qquad (9)$$

where y_t is the observation at time t, n is the number of past observations and y is the value to be forecasted.

However, financial time series show random fluctuations compared to ordinary time series. It is characterized with high nonlinearity, non-stationary and chaotic in nature. It is often desirable to monitor the price behavior frequently to understand the probable development of the prices in the future. Daily closing prices, exchange rates of a stock market and oil prices are few examples of financial time series. Financial time series forecasting is the process of making prediction about future performance of a stock market based on existing market behavior. Financial time series behaves like a random walk process. Due to the influence of uncertainties, financial time series forecasting is regarded as a difficult task.

Forecasting Models

The most popular statistical methods are moving averages (MA), auto-regressive integrated moving average (ARIMA), auto-regressive heteroscedastic (ARCH), generalized ARCH (GARCH) etc. (Contreras, Espinola, Nogalesn & and Conejo, 2003; Leigh, Hightower & Modani, 2005; Swider & Weber, 2007; Kung & Yu, 2008). These models are based on the assumption of the linearity of current and previous variables. However, these models are inefficient in handling highly non-linear time series data. They can't be automated easily and require expert interpretation and development at every stage. The poor capabilities of these models in capturing the nonlinearity of the financial time series forces the researchers to develop efficient models adopting soft and evolutionary computing methodologies which include artificial neural network (ANN), fuzzy neural networks, rough set theory, genetic algorithm etc.

The ANNs are applied to many areas such as data mining, stock market analysis, medical and many other fields. Some earlier use of ANN for the financial forecasting purpose can be found in the research works (Kumar & Bhattacharya, 2006; Cao, Leggio, & Schniederjans, 2005; Leigh, Hightower & Modani, 2005; Chen, Leung & Daouk, 2003; Yu, Wang, & Lai, 2009). During last few decades, the rapid growth in economical situations of developed countries has amplified the requirement of more competent and sophisticated forecasting models. In order to outperform the conventional statistical methods, several artificial intelligent systems have been developed and found to be experimentally efficient (Nayak, Misra, & Behera, 2018; Gu, Kelly, & Xiu, 2018; Board, 2017; Nayak, Misra & Behera, 2017; Guan, Dai, Zhao, & He, 2018; Nayak, Misra, & Behera, 2013; Nayak, Misra, & Behera, 2017). Authors used ANN models and linear regression models for New York stock exchange composite index (Leigh, Hightower & Modani, 2005). Results were robust and informative as to the role of trading volumes in the stock market. Group decision making models for economic interpretations are presented by the researchers in (Li, Kou & Peng, 2016; Zhang, Kou, & Peng, 2019). A survey on existing researches and methodologies on assessment and measurement of financial systemic risk combined with machine learning technologies is found in (Kou, Chao, Peng, Alsaadi, & Herrera-Viedma, 2019). Higher order and polynomial neural networks are proposed for financial time series forecasting in (Nayak, Misra, & Behera, 2016; Nayak & Misra, 2018). For improvement in forecasting accuracy of ANN based models several research works suggested for exploration and incorporation of virtual data positions in the original financial time series (Nayak, Misra, & Behera, 2017; Nayak, Misra & Behera, 2017; Nayak, Misra, & Behera, 2016). Analysis and improvement of fireworks algorithm is suggested in research work (Li, Han, & Gong, 2017). A cooperative framework for fireworks algorithm is suggested in (Zheng, Li, Janecek & Tan, 2017). An enhanced version of fireworks algorithm is proposed in for standard benchmark functions (Zheng, Janecek & Tan, 2013). Adaptive fireworks algorithm and dynamic search in fireworks algorithm are introduced by authors in (Li, Zheng, & Tan, 2014; Zheng, Janecek, Li & Tan, 2014).

Proposed FWANN Based Forecasting

The intention of this chapter is to study the suitability of FWA on searching the optimal weight and bias vector of an ANN based forecasting model. The mathematical description of ANN is beyond the scope of this chapter. We present only the description of ANN model used in this study and the forecasting process. ANN architecture with one hidden layer of neurons is used as the base neural architecture as shown in Figure 1. Since there is no rule to choose the optimal number of layer and neurons, we choose them on experimental basis.

Figure 1. FWANN based forecasting model

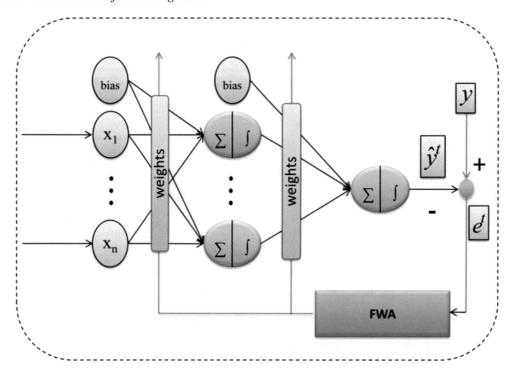

The error correction learning in this case is supervised learning, i.e. the target response for the system is presented at the output neuron. This model consists of a single output unit to estimate one-day-ahead data point in the financial time series. The neurons in the input layer use a linear transfer function, the neurons in the hidden layer and output layer use sigmoidal function as follows:

$$y_{out} = \frac{1}{1 + e^{-\lambda y_{in}}} \tag{10}$$

where yout is the output of the neuron, λ is the sigmoidal gain and yin is the input to the neuron. The first layer corresponds to the problem input variables with one node for each input variable. The second layer is useful in capturing non-linear relationships among variables. At each neuron, j in the hidden layer, the weighted output Z is calculated using Equation 11.

$$Z = f\left(B_j + \sum_{i=1}^{n} V_{ij} * O_i\right) \tag{11}$$

where O_i is the ith component of the $N \times M$ input vector, V_{ij} is the synaptic weight value between i^{th} input neuron and j^{th} hidden neuron and B_j is the bias value and f is a nonlinear activation function. The output y at the single output neuron is calculated using Equation 12.

$$y = f\left(B_0 + \sum_{j=1}^{m} W_j * Z\right) \tag{12}$$

where W_j is the synaptic weight value from j^{th} hidden neuron to output neuron, Z is the weighted sum calculated as in Equation 7, and B_0 is the output bias. This output y is compared to the target output and the error is calculated by using Equation 13.

$$Err_i = |Target_i - Estimated_i| \tag{13}$$

where Err_i is the error signal, $Target_i$ is the target signal for ith training pattern and $Estimated_i$ is the calculated output for ith pattern. The error signal $Err(i)$ and the input vector are employed to the weight update algorithm to compute the optimal weight vector. During the training, the network is repeatedly presented with the training vector and the weights as well as biases are adjusted by FWA till the desired input-output mapping occurs. The error is calculated by Equation 13 and the objective is to minimize the total error as in Equation 14 with an optimal set of weight and bias vector of the ANN.

$$Error(i) = \frac{1}{2} \sum_{i=1}^{N} Err(i)^2 \tag{14}$$

Here, the FWA is used to train the ANN model. A location (individual) of FWA can be viewed as a potential weight and bias vector for the ANN in the search space. At beginning, a set of such location is initialized and for each such location, two types of explosion are carried. The exploration as well as exploitation of the search space is achieved by these explosion methods. The locations are then evaluated in terms of error signal generation. The location with lowest error signal is considered as the best location. The selection process is then carried out with inclusion of this best location and remaining locations. The above process continues till an optimal location found and the search process then terminates. The best location is the optimal weight and bias vector for the ANN model.

CASE STUDY ON FINANCIAL TIME SERIES FORECASTING

This section performs a case study on financial time series. As we mentioned earlier, this chapter aims to develop an ANN based forecasting model trained by FWA. The proposed FWANN model is evaluated on forecasting three financial time series: (1) daily closing prices series of Bombay stock exchange, (2) exchange rate series of Indian rupees to US dollar, and (3) crude oil price series.

Description of Experimental Data

The BSE indices are collected from the source https://in.finance.yahoo.com/ for each financial day starting from 1st January 2003 to 12th September 2016. The closing prices series is shown by Figure 2. Real data from Bombay stock exchange are collected from the source www.forecasts.org. The series contains the monthly exchange rate of (Indian) Rupees against USA Dollar. The data are recorded on the first day of each month during the period 1999 to 2016 comprising 214 data points in the series. The series is presented by Figure 3. The crude oil prices (Dollars per Barrel) are retrieved from US Department of energy: Energy Information Administration web site: http://www.eia.doe.gov/ during the period Jan 02 1986 to Feb 11 2019. The crude oil price series is shown by Figure 4. The descriptive statistics from three financial time series considered are presented in Table 1.

Table 1. Descriptive statistics from three financial time series

Financial time series	Descriptive statistics						
	Minimum	**Maximum**	**Mean**	**Standard deviation**	**Skewness**	**Kurtosis**	**Jarque-Bera test statistics**
Closing price series	792.1800	1.1024e+004	4.6235e+003	2.6947e+003	0.1154	1.7908	236.0430(h=1)
Exchange rate series	39.2680	68.2400	49.5192	7.5903	1.0952	2.9765	42.7875 (h=1)
Crude oil prices series	10.4200	145.2900	42.8112	28.6656	1.0111	2.8953	1.5390e+03 (h=1)

Experimental Setup

All the experiments are carried out in MATLAB-2015 environment, with Intel ® core TM i3 CPU, 2.27 GHz processing and 2.42 GB memory size. A sliding window of fixed size is used for selecting input for the forecasting model. In this method rather than selecting all of the data seen so far, or on some sample, decision is made based only on some recent data points. On each sliding of the window, a new data point is incorporated and the oldest one is discarded. The window moves through whole financial time series and the selection of size of window is a matter of experimentation.

All the three financial time series are normalized before feeding them to the ANN model (Nayak, Misra, & Behera, 2014). The normalized data are then used to form a training bed for the network model. The model is simulated for 20 times for each training set and the average error is considered for comparative analysis of results. Since each time the sliding window moves one step ahead, only one new closing price data has been included into the training set. So there may not be significant change in nonlinearity behavior of the training data set. For that reason, instead of considering another random weight set (i.e. set of locations), we used the previously optimized weight set for the successive training. In this way, after the first training set, the number of iteration has been fixed to a small value, hence significant reduction in training time. During experimentation, different possible values for the model parameters were tested and best values are recorded. The parameters of FWA are set as suggested in (Tan & Zhu, 2010). The average performance of the models over 20 runs are considered for comparison.

Figure 2. Closing prices series of BSE

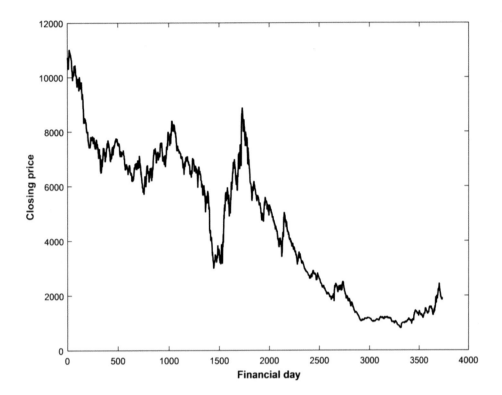

The four performance metrics used for evaluating the forecasting models are as follows:

The Mean Absolute Percentage Error (MAPE) has been considered as the first performance metric in order to have a comparable measure across experiments with different dataset. The closer the value of MAPE towards zero, the better is the prediction ability of the model. The formula for MAPE is represented by Equation 15.

$$MAPE = \frac{1}{N} \sum_{i=1}^{N} \frac{|x_i - \hat{x}_i|}{xi} \times 100\%$$ (15)

The second performance metric is the mean of squared error calculated on the normalized data sets and known as Normalized Mean Squared Error (NMSE). The closer the value of it to zero, better is the prediction ability of the model. The NMSE can be calculated as in Equation 16.

$$NMSE = \frac{1}{N} \sum_{i=1}^{N} \left(x_i - \hat{x}_i\right)^2$$ (16)

The third performance metric considered here is known as the coefficient of determination, or the coefficient of multiple determinations for multiple regressions represented as R2. R-squared is a statistical measure of how close the data are to the fitted regression line. The definition of R-squared is presented

Figure 3. Exchange rate series (Indian Rupees to US Dollar)

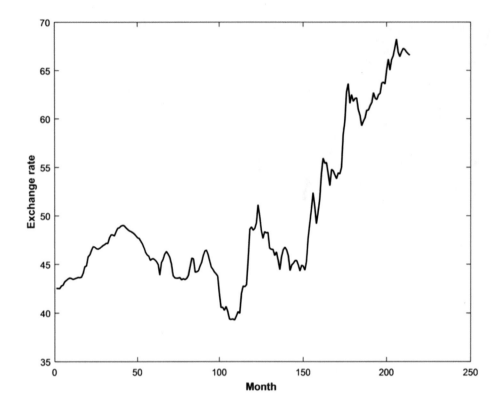

by Equation 17. The ideal value of R2 is 1(one). 0 values indicate that the model explain none of the variability of the response data around its mean whereas 1 indicates that the model explains all the variability of the response data around its mean.

$$R^2 = 1 - \frac{SS_{res}}{SS_{tot}} \tag{17}$$

where SSres is the sum of squares of residuals or residual sum of squares and represented as in Equation 18.

$$SS_{res} = \sum_{i=1}^{N} \left(x_i - \hat{x}_i \right)^2 \tag{18}$$

Similarly, SStot is the total sum of squares which is proportional to the variance of the data and calculated as in Equation 19.

$$SS_{tot} = \sum_{i=1}^{N} \left(x_i - \bar{X} \right)^2 \tag{19}$$

Figure 4. Crude oil prices series

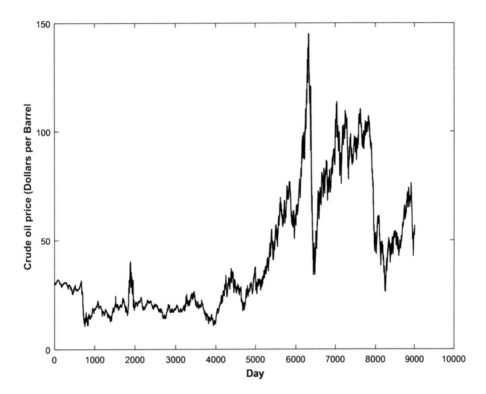

The fourth evaluation measure is the Average Relative Variance (ARV). The ARV can be calculated as in Equation 20.

$$\frac{\sum_{i=1}^{N}\left(\hat{x}_i - x_i\right)^2}{\sum_{i=1}^{N}\left(\hat{x}_i - \bar{X}\right)^2} \tag{20}$$

If the ARV value of the forecasting model is equal to 1, then it is same as considering the mean of the financial time series. The model is considered as performing worst as compared to mean if the ARV value is greater than 1. However, the model can be considered as performing better than simply calculating the mean if its ARV value is less than 1. Hence, the closer the value to 0, the forecasting model tends to be more accurate.

For all the above calculations, x_i is the observed data, $\hat{x}_i$ is the estimated data, $\bar{X}$ is the mean of observed data and N is the total number of observations.

Experimental Results and Discussion

For comparative purpose we developed another four models such as PSO-ANN, GA-ANN, DE-ANN, and MLP trained similarly. The input data for all five models are same. We conducted experiments for short term (1-step-ahead) and long term (7-step-ahead) forecasting. The results from these experiments

Figure 5. Error convergence graph of forecasting models (from closing price dataset)

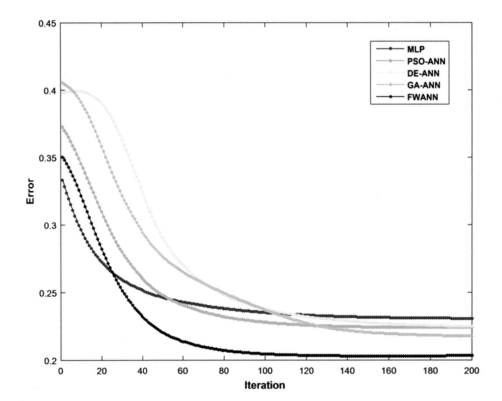

are summarized in Table 2 – 3 respectively. The error convergence graph of five forecasting models from closing price dataset is shown in Figure 5. From this curve it can be observed that the proposed FWANN model converges very fast compared to others.

As shown in Table 2, the FWANN model generated lower error signals in terms of all four metrics. Its performance is better than other models. However, in case of crude oil price prediction it shown inferior result compared to closing price and exchange rate time series. The performance of PSO-ANN, GA-ANN, and DE-ANN are acceptable but inferior to FWANN. All four hybrid models have shown better results than the MLP. To ascertain the validity of FWANN model, we also conducted experiments for long-term (7-step-ahead) forecasting and the results are summarized in Table 3. In this case also the FWANN performed better to other models. As the time step increases the error signals from the forecasting model also increases. However, in both cases the FWANN model shown lower error signals which indicates that the forecasted values are very closer to the actual values. For more clarity the estimated v/s actual values are plotted and shown by Figures 6 - 8. From Figure 6 and 7, it is observed that the estimated values by FWANN model are very close to the actual. But, in case of oil price dataset, the estimated values are slightly deviated from the actual. However, the model is capable in following the trend of the time series.

Table 2. Results from 1-step-ahead forecasting

Financial time series	Model	MAPE	NMSE	R^2	ARV
Closing price series	FWANN	0.036825	0.054783	0.937643	0.018639
	PSO-ANN	0.057547	0.085746	0.913125	0.027685
	GA-ANN	0.073648	0.082853	0.852965	0.070833
	DE-ANN	0.079900	0.058593	0.926455	0.055747
	MLP	0.108353	0.087985	0.894785	0.082845
Exchange rate series	FWANN	0.064675	0.013521	0.925400	0.047785
	PSO-ANN	0.068830	0.016468	0.903503	0.061354
	GA-ANN	0.075902	0.026863	0.873525	0.065503
	DE-ANN	0.079475	0.050522	0.901275	0.071685
	MLP	0.095355	0.065455	0.887435	0.088635
Crude oil prices series	FWANN	0.085700	0.063315	0.935427	0.085635
	PSO-ANN	0.089265	0.120127	0.900075	0.088557
	GA-ANN	0.097285	0.157500	0.846522	0.089655
	DE-ANN	0.136885	0.079822	0.890711	0.090755
	MLP	0.262384	0.095665	0.865184	0.254845

Table 3. Results from 7-step-ahead forecasting

Financial time series	Model	MAPE	NMSE	R^2	ARV
Closing price series	FWANN	0.039875	0.074478	0.920784	0.026865
	PSO-ANN	0.060754	0.089749	0.905028	0.027990
	GA-ANN	0.078004	0.088855	0.822977	0.073802
	DE-ANN	0.079985	0.070858	0.900655	0.067745
	MLP	0.178344	0.100780	0.874722	0.200285
Exchange rate series	FWANN	0.069679	0.030655	0.905372	0.054985
	PSO-ANN	0.082835	0.036465	0.883525	0.068355
	GA-ANN	0.078955	0.027986	0.833563	0.085750
	DE-ANN	0.079864	0.057505	0.900200	0.078060
	MLP	0.099384	0.216545	0.807839	0.090636
Crude oil prices series	FWANN	0.089688	0.084810	0.917542	0.088699
	PSO-ANN	0.089697	0.127225	0.917583	0.089506
	GA-ANN	0.099728	0.159204	0.840065	0.091965
	DE-ANN	0.256566	0.079974	0.832871	0.090827
	MLP	0.472385	0.295632	0.807518	0.290488

Figure 6. Actual closing price v/s estimated closing price by FWANN

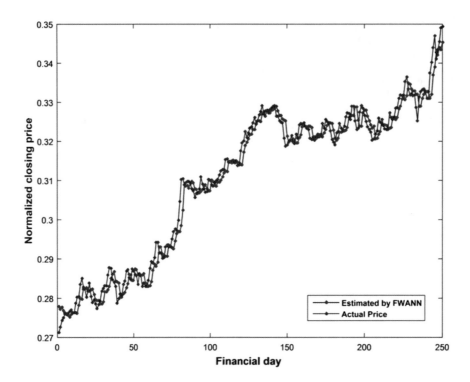

Figure 7. Actual exchange rate v/s estimated exchange rate by FWANN

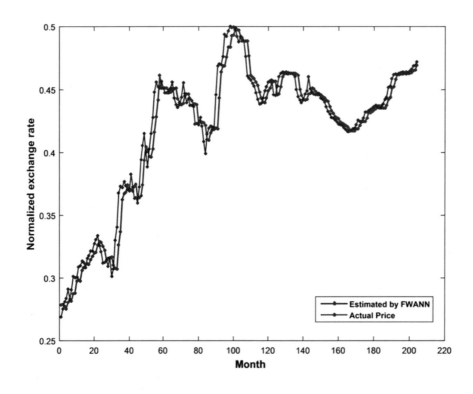

Figure 8. Actual oil price v/s estimated oil price by FWANN

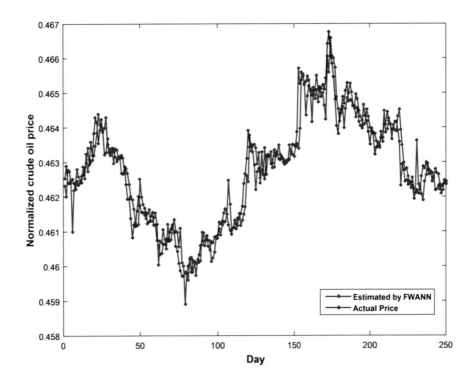

CONCLUSION

Fireworks algorithm is a recently proposed metaheuristic which simulates the explosion process of fireworks as an optimization technique. Several successful applications of FWA have been demonstrated in the literature since its inception. The adjustment of neuron weight and bias of ANN is the key factor of ANN training and is a decisive assignment. The performance of ANN based models are exclusively depends upon the adjustment of weight and bias vectors. To circumvent the limitations of gradient descent-based ANN training this chapter developed a hybrid FWANN model where the synaptic weight and bias vector of an ANN is searched with FWA. The hybrid model exhibits the better generalization capability of ANN as well as fast and efficient learning capacity of FWA, hence robust in nature. To validate the efficiency of the proposed model the chapter performed a case study on financial time series forecasting. Three financial time series such as daily closing price series, exchange rate series, and daily crude oil price time series are considered for experimentation. The proposed hybrid FWANN model is evaluated in forecasting one step ahead and seven-step-ahead data point of three financial time series in terms of four error statistics such as MAPE, NMSE, R2 and ARV. The performance of the model is compared with that of four other models such as PSO-ANN, GA-ANN, DE-ANN, and MLP trained in similar manner. From experimental studies it is observed that the FWANN model performed better to other models and competent to capture the nonlinear behavior of the financial time series. The applications of the model may be explored in other domain.

REFERENCES

Aliev, R. A., Fazlollahi, B., & Aliev, R. R. (2004). *Soft computing and its applications in business and economics* (Vol. 157). Berlin, Germany: Springer. doi:10.1007/978-3-540-44429-9

Board, F. S. (2017). Artificial intelligence and machine learning in financial services. November, available at http://www. fsb. org/2017/11/artificialintelligence-and-machine-learning-in-financialservice/ (accessed 30th January, 2018).

Cao, Q., Leggio, K., & Schniederjans, M. (2005). A comparison between Fama and French's model and artificial networks in predicting the Chinese stock market. *Computers & Operations Research*, *32*(10), 2499–2512. doi:10.1016/j.cor.2004.03.015

Chen, A., Leung, M., & Daouk, H. (2003). Application of neural networks to an emerging financial market: Forecasting and trading the Taiwan stock index. *Computers & Operations Research*, *30*(6), 901–923. doi:10.1016/S0305-0548(02)00037-0

Contreras, J., Espinola, R., Nogales, F., & Conejo, A. (2003). ARIMA models to predict next-day electricity prices. *IEEE Transactions on Power Systems*, *18*(3), 1014–1020. doi:10.1109/TPWRS.2002.804943

Dorigo, M., & Stutzle, T. (2004). *Ant colony optimization*. Cambridge: The MIT Press. doi:10.7551/mitpress/1290.001.0001

Goldberg, D. E. (1989). *Genetic algorithms in search, optimization, and machine learning*. Boston, MA: Addison-Wesley Longman Publishing.

Gu, S., Kelly, B., & Xiu, D. (2018). *Empirical asset pricing via machine learning (No. w25398)*. National Bureau of Economic Research.

Guan, H., Dai, Z., Zhao, A., & He, J. (2018). A novel stock forecasting model based on High-order-fuzzy-fluctuation Trends and Back Propagation Neural Network. *PLoS One*, *13*(2). doi:10.1371/journal.pone.0192366 PMID:29420584

Haykin, S. (2010). *Neural Networks and Learning Machine*. Upper Saddle River, NJ: Pearson Education.

Kecman, V. (2006). *Learning and Soft Computing*. Upper Saddle River, NJ: Pearson Education.

Kennedy, J., & Eberhart, R. C. (2001). *Swarm intelligence*. San Francisco, CA: Morgan Kaufmann Publishers.

Kou, G., Chao, X., Peng, Y., Alsaadi, F. E., & Herrera-Viedma, E. (2019). Machine learning methods for systemic risk analysis in financial sectors. *Technological and Economic Development of Economy*, *§§§*, 1–27.

Kumar, K., & Bhattacharya, S. (2006). Artificial neural network vs. linear discriminant analysis in credit ratings forecast. *Review of Accounting and Finance*, *5*(3), 216–227. doi:10.1108/14757700610686426

Kung, L., & Yu, S. (2008). Prediction of index futures returns and the analysis of financial spillovers-A comparison between GARCH and the grey theorem. *European Journal of Operational Research*, *186*(3), 1184–1200. doi:10.1016/j.ejor.2007.02.046

Leigh, W., Hightower, R., & Modani, N. (2005). Forecasting the New York stock exchange composite index with past price and interest rate on condition of volume spike. *Expert Systems with Applications, 28*(1), 1–8. doi:10.1016/j.eswa.2004.08.001

Leigh, W., Hightower, R., & Modani, N. (2005). Forecasting the New York stock exchange composite index with past price and interest rate on condition of volume spike. *Expert Systems with Applications, 28*(1), 1–8. doi:10.1016/j.eswa.2004.08.001

Li, G., Kou, G., & Peng, Y. (2016). A group decision making model for integrating heterogeneous information. *IEEE Transactions on Systems, Man, and Cybernetics. Systems, 48*(6), 982–992. doi:10.1109/TSMC.2016.2627050

Li, J., Zheng, S., & Tan, Y. (2014, July). Adaptive fireworks algorithm. *2014 IEEE Congress on evolutionary computation (CEC)* (pp. 3214-3221). IEEE. doi:10.1109/CEC.2013.6557813

Li, X. G., Han, S. F., & Gong, C. Q. (2017). Analysis and improvement of fireworks algorithm. *Algorithms, 10*(1), 26. doi:10.3390/a10010026

Nayak, S. C., & Misra, B. B. (2018). Estimating stock closing indices using a GA-weighted condensed polynomial neural network. *Financial Innovation, 4*(1), 21. doi:10.118640854-018-0104-2

Nayak, S. C., Misra, B. B., & Behera, H. S. (2013, September). Hybridzing chemical reaction optimization and artificial neural network for stock future index forecasting. *Proceedings 2013 1st International Conference on Emerging Trends and Applications in Computer Science* (pp. 130-134). IEEE. 10.1109/ICETACS.2013.6691409

Nayak, S. C., Misra, B. B., & Behera, H. S. (2014). Impact of data normalization on stock index forecasting. *Int. J. Comp. Inf. Syst. Ind. Manag. Appl, 6,* 357–369.

Nayak, S. C., Misra, B. B., & Behera, H. S. (2016). An adaptive second order neural network with genetic-algorithm-based training (ASONN-GA) to forecast the closing prices of the stock market. [IJAMC]. *International Journal of Applied Metaheuristic Computing, 7*(2), 39–57. doi:10.4018/IJAMC.2016040103

Nayak, S. C., Misra, B. B., & Behera, H. S. (2016). Efficient forecasting of financial time-series data with virtual adaptive neuro-fuzzy inference system. *International Journal of Business Forecasting and Marketing Intelligence, 2*(4), 379–402. doi:10.1504/IJBFMI.2016.080132

Nayak, S. C., Misra, B. B., & Behera, H. S. (2017). Artificial chemical reaction optimization of neural networks for efficient prediction of stock market indices. *Ain Shams Engineering Journal, 8*(3), 371–390. doi:10.1016/j.asej.2015.07.015

Nayak, S. C., Misra, B. B., & Behera, H. S. (2017). Artificial chemical reaction optimization based neural net for virtual data position exploration for efficient financial time series forecasting. *Ain Shams Engineering Journal.*

Nayak, S. C., Misra, B. B., & Behera, H. S. (2017). Exploration and incorporation of virtual data positions for efficient forecasting of financial time series. *International Journal of Industrial and Systems Engineering, 26*(1), 42–62. doi:10.1504/IJISE.2017.083179

Nayak, S. C., Misra, B. B., & Behera, H. S. (2017). Efficient financial time series prediction with evolutionary virtual data position exploration. *Neural Computing & Applications*, 1–22.

Nayak, S. C., Misra, B. B., & Behera, H. S. (2018). ACFLN: artificial chemical functional link network for prediction of stock market index. Evolving Systems, 1-26.

Price, K., Storn, R., & Lampinen, J. (2005). *Differential evolution: a practical approach to global optimization*. Berlin, Germany: Springer.

Rajasekaran, S., & Pai, G. A. V. (2007). *Neural Networks, Fuzzy Logic and Genetic Algorithms Synthesis and Application*. Delhi, India: PHI Learning Private Limited.

Shadbolt, N. (2004). Nature-Inspired Computing. *IEEE Intelligent Systems*, *19*(1), 2–3. doi:10.1109/MIS.2004.1265875

Swider, D. J., & Weber, C. (2007). Extended ARMA Models for Estimating Price Developments on Day- ahead Electricity Markets. *Electric Power Systems Research*, *77*(5-6), 583–593. doi:10.1016/j.epsr.2006.05.013

Tan, Y., & Zhu, Y. (2010, June). Fireworks algorithm for optimization. *Proceedings International conference in swarm intelligence* (pp. 355-364). Berlin, Germany: Springer.

Yu, L., Wang, S., & Lai, K. K. (2009). A neural-network-based nonlinear metamodeling approach to financial time series forecasting. *Applied Soft Computing*, *9*(2), 563–574. doi:10.1016/j.asoc.2008.08.001

Zhang, H., Kou, G., & Peng, Y. (2019). Soft consensus cost models for group decision making and economic interpretations. *European Journal of Operational Research*.

Zheng, S., Janecek, A., Li, J., & Tan, Y. (2014, July). Dynamic search in fireworks algorithm. *Proceedings 2014 IEEE Congress on evolutionary computation (CEC)* (pp. 3222-3229). IEEE. 10.1109/CEC.2014.6900485

Zheng, S., Janecek, A., & Tan, Y. (2013, June). Enhanced fireworks algorithm. *Proceedings 2013 IEEE Congress on evolutionary computation* (pp. 2069-2077). IEEE.

Zheng, S., Li, J., Janecek, A., & Tan, Y. (2017). A cooperative framework for fireworks algorithm. [TCBB]. *IEEE/ACM Transactions on Computational Biology and Bioinformatics*, *14*(1), 27–41. doi:10.1109/TCBB.2015.2497227 PMID:26552094

Chapter 9
Interval Type 2 Fuzzy Fireworks Algorithm for Clustering

Juan Barraza

 https://orcid.org/0000-0002-1647-5102

Tijuana Institute of Technology, Mexico

Fevrier Valdez

Tijuana Institute of Technology, Mexico

Patricia Melin

 https://orcid.org/0000-0001-5798-1426

Tijuana Institute of Technology, Mexico

Claudia I. Gonzalez

 https://orcid.org/0000-0003-1631-033X

Tijuana Institute of Technology, Mexico

ABSTRACT

This chapter presents Interval Type 2 Fuzzy Fireworks Algorithm for clustering (IT2FWAC). It is an optimization method for finding the optimal number of clusters based on the centroid features which uses the Fireworks Algorithm (FWA), but with a dynamic adjustment of parameters using an Interval Type 2 Fuzzy Inference System (IT2FIS). Three variations of the IT2FWAC are proposed to find the optimal number of clusters for different datasets: IT2FWAC -I, IT2FWAC -II, and IT2FWAC –III. They are explained in detail.

INTRODUCTION

To imitate the human functions, methodologies such as fuzzy logic (Simoes, Bose & Spiegel, 1997; Zadeh, 1989), algorithms based on nature (Aladwan, Alshraideh & Rasol, 2015; Barraza, Rodríguez, Castillo, Melin, & Valdez, 2018), swarm intelligence (Melián & Moreno, 2003), physical (Can & Alatas, 2015), and/or neural networks (Soto & Melin, 2015) we are using computational science; with the

DOI: 10.4018/978-1-7998-1659-1.ch009

Copyright © 2020, IGI Global. Copying or distributing in print or electronic forms without written permission of IGI Global is prohibited.

goal of learning or solving problems the methodologies mentioned above are added into the machines or robots (Wolpert & Macready, 1997).

The optimization topic means to maximize or minimize a solution to a problem depending on a corresponding objective function; there are different mathematical problems and optimization types: single objective and multi-objective, and, the problems of clustering validation are considered as multi-objective optimization, therefore, in the proposed method IT2FWAC we apply two different clustering validations: Intra-cluster and Inter-cluster.

Speaking about clustering (Sanchez, Castillo, Castro & Melin, 2014), we know that there are clustering algorithms which, have been applied to solve classification problems such as pattern recognition, image segmentation, among other research areas with good results (Soler, Tenc´e, Gaubert & Buche, 2013).

On the other hand, Type-I Fuzzy Logic Inference Systems are unable to directly handle rule uncertainties, because they use type-1 fuzzy sets that are certain (i.e., fully described by single numeric values); on the other hand in the Interval Type 2 Fuzzy Logic Inference Systems are useful in circumstances where it is difficult to determine an exact numeric membership function, and there are measurement uncertainties.

Fireworks Algorithm (FWA)

The conventional Fireworks Algorithm (FWA) is a swarm intelligence algorithm as mentioned above, and it is composed of 4 general steps: initialization of locations, calculation of the number of sparks, calculation of the explosion amplitude for each firework and selection of the best location (Tan, 2015; Tan & Zhu, 2010).

In this Section, the main equations of the algorithm are presented:

Number of Sparks

The number of sparks is calculated with the Equations 1 and 2.

$$Minimize\ f\left(x_i\right) \in R,\ x_{i\_}min \leq x_i \leq x_{i\_}max \tag{1}$$

where $x_{imin} \leq x_i \leq x_{imax}$ represents the bounds of the search space.

$$S_i = m.\frac{y_{max} - f\left(x_i\right) + \epsilon}{\sum_{i=1}^{n}\left(y_{max)} - f\left(x_i\right)\right) + \epsilon} \tag{2}$$

In Equation 2, m is a constant parameter, y_{max} is the worst value of the objective function and ϵ is a smallest number in the computer.

Explosion Amplitude

The explosion amplitude for each firework is calculated using Equation 2:

$$A_i = \hat{A} \cdot \frac{f(x_i) - y_{\min} + f}{\sum_{i=1}^{n}\left(f(x_i) - y_{\min}\right) + f} \tag{3}$$

where $\hat{A}$ is a constant parameter that controls the maximum amplitude of each firework, $y_{min} = \min\left(f(x_i)\right)(i = 1,2,3,...,n)$, designates the minimum value (best) of the objective function among n fireworks and ϵ indicates the smallest constant in the computer, and it is utilized with the goal that an error of division by zero does not occur.

Selection of Locations

The equations that are used in this algorithm to select the best current location are Equations 4 and 5:

$$R(x_i) = \sum_{j \in K} d(x_i, x_j) = \sum_{j \in K} x_i - x_j \tag{4}$$

In Equation 4, K is the set of all current locations from both fireworks. Then the probability for selection of a location at x_i is defined as (Abdulmajeed & Ayob, 2014; Li & Z., 2014; Tan & Z., 2014; Zheng, Song & Chen, 2013; Ochoa-Zezzatti et al., 2015):

$$p(x_i) = \frac{R(x_i)}{\sum_{j \in K} R(x_j)} \tag{5}$$

Proposed Method (IT2FWAC)

In this Section, we explain in detail the modification of the conventional Fireworks Algorithm (FWA).

We implemented the Algorithm (FWA) with an adjustment of parameter (Amplitude coefficient) using Interval Type 2 Fuzzy Logic Inference System to automatically find the optimal number of clusters, and we decided to call this as Interval Type 2 Fuzzy Fireworks Algorithm for clustering and we denoted as IT2FWAC.

The proposed IT2FWAC method has four steps:

1. Select n initial locations.
2. Set off n fireworks at n locations.
3. Obtain the locations of individuals.
4. Evaluate the quality of individuals.

It is important to mention that as every algorithm, Interval Type 2 Fuzzy Fireworks Algorithm for clustering has a stopping criterion; in some cases the algorithm stopped when the solution is found (if we have an exactly value) but, for these cases the stopping criterion is the total number of function evaluations (or iterations).

The steps are described in more detail below, but before. We present these steps in a graphic way, in the following Figure 1:

The initial swarm is formed with the equation 6:

Figure 1. Flow chart of IT2FWAC

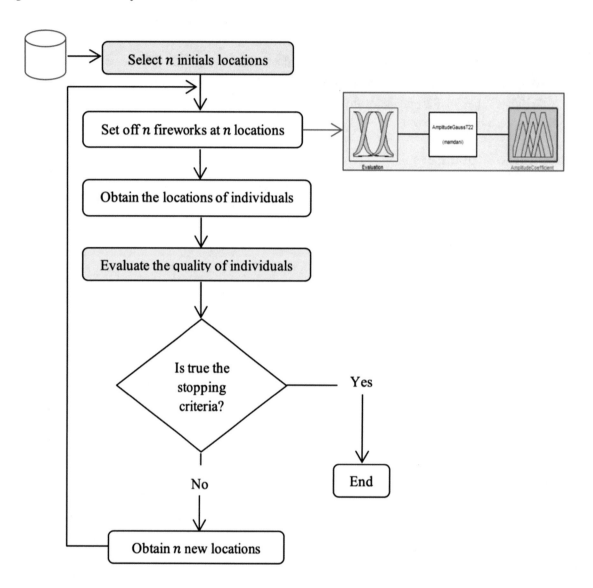

$$Swarm_{ij} = LB_j + \left(UB_j - LB_j\right) * r_{ij}, \ i = 1,2,3,...n \qquad (6)$$

With Equation 6 the first step (select n locations) is done. Where LB and UB are the lower and upper bounds for individual i in the dimension j, and r are random values between 0 and 1.

Each individual, in this algorithm, is a spark or fireworks, both are represented in a vector divided in two parts, in the following Figure 2 we illustrate an example:

In Figure 2, K is an integer number that is representing the number of centroids that one possible solution can have and the rest of the vector $(d_1, d_2, d_3, ... d_{nd} * K)$ are real numbers that are representing the features of the given data set and nd are the features per each data.

Also, we decided to introduce two statistic rules with the goal of creating bounds for the number of clusters, i.e., the rules will allow to obtain a K_{max} to help the performance of the IT2FWAC. The rules are the Square root of N and Sturges (Larson & Farber, 2003).

Figure 2. Representation of the individual in IT2FWAC

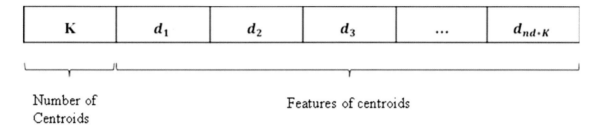

The rule of Square root of N and the rule of Sturges are expressed in Equations 7 and 8, respectively.

$$K = \sqrt{N} \tag{7}$$

$$K = 1 + 3.322 \log N \tag{8}$$

Where N is the total number of data for both rules (Sturges, 1926).

In the second step (Set off n fireworks at n locations), we implement an Interval Type 2 Fuzzy Inference System (IT2FIS) for controlling the amplitude coefficient, remember that the parameter of explosion amplitude in Equation 3 is a constant parameter, then, with the implementation of IT2FIS we are controlling the parameter in a dynamic way. The modified Equation is the following, enumerated as 9:

$$FA_i = \widehat{FA} . \frac{f(x_i) - y_{min} + \epsilon}{\sum_{i=1}^{n} \left(f(x_i) - y_{min} \right) + \epsilon} \tag{9}$$

where $\widehat{FA}$ will be in a range between 2 and 40.

The IT2FIS is shown in the Figure 3:

The Interval Type 2 fuzzy rules for controlling the amplitude explosion parameter are shown in Figure 4:

To evaluate the quality of individuals, we decided to use the two clustering validations: Intra-cluster and Inter-cluster, as we mentioned earlier. Equations 9 and 10 show the mathematical expressions for the clusters validation using Intra-cluster, and Inter-cluster, respectively.

$$Intra = \sum_{i=1}^{n} dist(c_i, C) \tag{9}$$

where c_i is the data that belong to centroid C (L. Telescaa, M. Bernardib and C. Rovellib, 2005).

Figure 3. Graphic representation of the IT2FIS

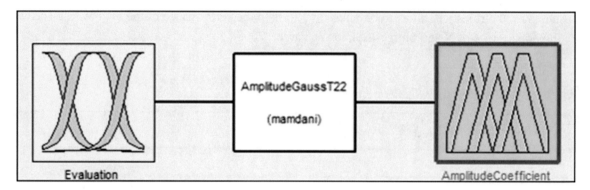

Figure 4. Fuzzy rules of the IT2FIS

1. If (**Evaluation** is **Low**)   then (**AmplitudeCoefficient** is **Big**)
2. If (**Evaluation** is **Medium**) then (**AmplitudeCoefficient** is **Medium**)
3. If (**Evaluation** is **High**)   then (**AmplitudeCoefficient** is **Small**)

$$Inter = \sum_{\substack{i,j=1, \\ i \neq j}}^{k} dist\left(C_i, C_j\right) \tag{10}$$

In Equation 10, i and j are the number of the centroids, C_i and C_j are different centroids and k is the maximum number of centroids (Wu, 2006). It is important to mention that, we are using the minimum and maximum distance because the problem is to find the optimal number of clusters (centroids) and it is not to find the location of centroids (Chena, Liua, Chena, Zhangb & Zhangb, 2012).

VARIATIONS OF THE INTERVAL TYPE 2 FUZZY FIREWORKS ALGORITHM

To test the performance of the IT2FWAC we have made three variations in the same, the variations consists in modifying the membership functions of the Interval Type 2 Fuzzy Inference Systems (IT2FIS), in concrete, the membership functions of the input and output variables (Bonabeau, Dorigo & Theraulaz, 1999), below, the three different membership functions are explained.

Triangular

In the first variation of the IT2FIS we used Triangular membership functions and for this variation, we denoted as IT2FWAC-I; in Figures 5 and 6, we show the input and output variables, and the ranges for each variable and membership function in IT2FWAC-I.

Figure 5. Input variable for IT2FWAC-I

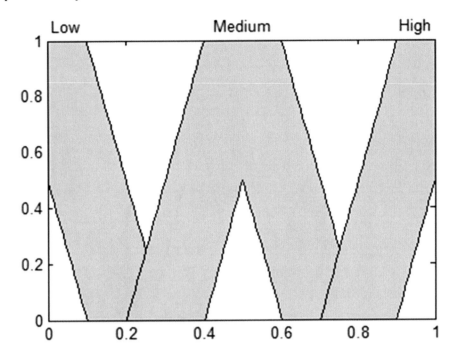

The linguistic variables, and parameters for each partition in the input variable in IT2FWAC-I are the following: Low [-0.3, -0.1, 0.1, -0.1, 0.1 and 0.3], Medium [0.2, 0.4, 0.6, 0.4, 0.6 and 0.8] and High [0.7, 0.9, 1.2, 0.9, 1.1 and 1.4] are the three partitions of the Input Variable in IT2FWAC-I.

The three partitions of the Output Variable are: Small [-15, -0.5, 10, -10, 4.5 and 15], Medium [11, 18.5, 26, 16, 23.5 and 31] and Big [27, 38.5, 45, 32, 43.5 and 50].

Gaussian

In Figures 7 and 8 the second variation of the IT2FIS is presented.

The parameters of the Gaussian membership functions for IT2FWAC-II in the input are: Low [0.1, -0.1 and 0.1], Medium [0.1, 0.4 and 0.6] and High [0.1, 0.9 and 1.1] and for the output variable are: Small [5, -5 and 5], Medium [5, 16 and 26] and Big [5, 36 and 46].

Trapezoidal

For the third variation, we implemented trapezoidal membership functions in the variables of the IT2FIS, and this variation was denoted as IT2FWAC-III.

In Figures 9 and 10 the parameters of the membership functions for the input and output variables are shown.

Low [-0.4, -0.1, 0.01, 0.3, -0.3, 0.01, 0.1, 0.4 and 0.9], Medium [0.01, 0.3, 0.5, 0.8, 0.1, 0.4, 0.6, 0.9 and 0.9] and High [0.5, 0.8, 1.01, 1.3, 0.6, 0.9, 1.1, 1.4 and 0.9] are the partitions and parameters for the input variable in IT2FWAC-III using Trapezoidal membership functions.

Figure 6. Output variable for IT2FWAC-I

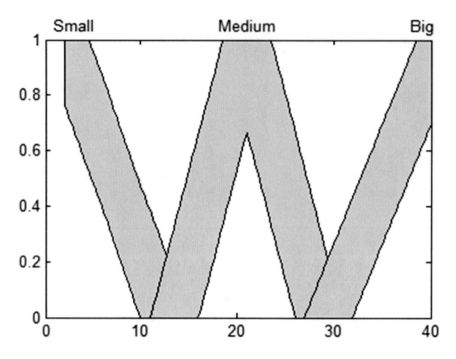

Figure 7. Input variable for IT2FWAC-II

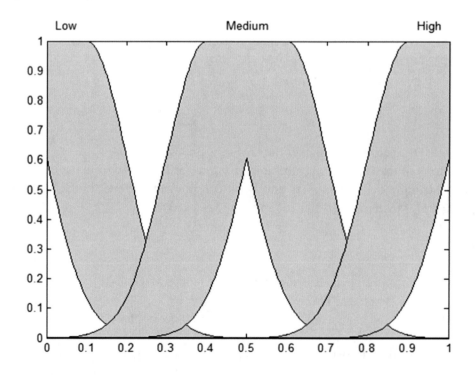

Figure 8. Output variable for IT2FWAC-I

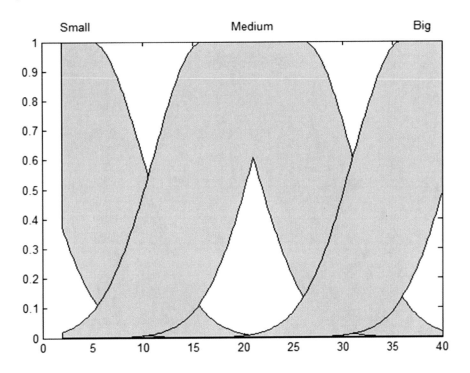

Figure 9. Input variable for IT2FWAC-III

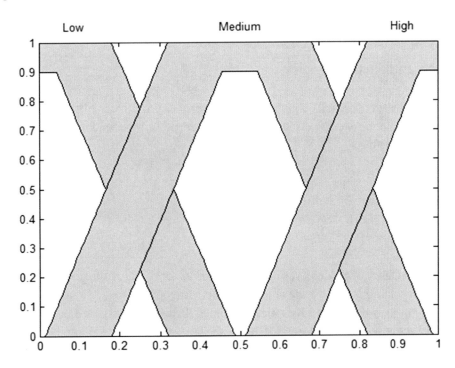

Figure 10. Output variable for IT2FWAC-III

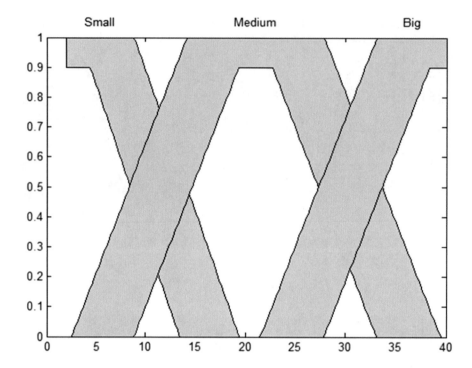

The output variable in IT2FWAC-III has the following partitions and ranges: Small [-11.6, -3.6, 3.3, 13, -7.2, -3.1, 8.8, 19 and 0.9], Medium [2.5, 14, 21, 33, 8, 20, 27, 39 and 0.9] and Big [21, 33, 40, 52, 27, 39, 46, 58 and 0.9].

Experiments and Results

In this section, we present the results obtained by the experiments realized with the Interval Type 2 Fuzzy Fireworks Algorithm for clustering (IT2FWAC). We perform 31 independent runs using the following parameters in the algorithm:

- Fireworks = 5.
- Amplitude Coefficient = [2, 40].
- Amplitude Sparks = 50.
- Function evaluations = 15,000.

To test the performance of the Interval Type 2 Fuzzy Fireworks Algorithm for clustering (IT2FWAC), we tested with three datasets: Iris, Wine and Wisconsin Diagnostic Breast Cancer (WDBC).

The features, number of data and K-Optimal for each data set is illustrated in Table 1.

Tables 2 and 3 show the results obtained of the average of the 31 independent runs with 15,000 function evaluations using Intra-cluster for minimum distance with square root of N and Sturges rule, respectively.

As we can see in Table 2, the better results obtained are using triangular membership functions in the Interval Type 2 Fuzzy Inference System and Sturges law as a metric of the K-optimal Cluster.

Table 1. Data sets

Data Set	Number of data	Features	*K*-Optimal
Iris	150	4	3
Wine	178	13	3
WDBC	569	30	2

In Table 3 the Interval Type 2 Fuzzy Inference System with Trapezoidal membership functions threw the best result.

In the same way as Table 2 in Table 4, the best result was obtained using Triangular membership functions in the Interval Type 2 Fuzzy Inference System and Sturges Law.

In Tables 5 to 7, we have shown the results with maximum distance using Intra-cluster as cluster validation for datasets.

Table 5 shows the better results using Gaussian membership functions, Table 6 shows the Triangular membership function as the best result and Table 7 shows that the best result obtained was using Trapezoidal membership functions in the Interval Type 2 Fuzzy Inference System.

In the following six tables (from Table 8 to 13), we are showing the results obtained using Inter-cluster as cluster validation. In Tables 8, 9 and 10, the results obtained with minimum distance for Iris, Wine, and WDBC, respectively, are presented.

In Table 9 the best result was obtained using Triangular membership functions in the Interval Type 2 Fuzzy Inference System.

On the other hand, in Tables 11, 12, and 13 we are presenting the results obtained with maximum distance.

Table 2. Results with minimum distance using intra-cluster for the iris data set

Variation	Ön		S	
of FWA	Mean	STD	Mean	STD
IT2FWAC-I	6.35	3.42	4.48	1.88
IT2FWAC-II	7.52	3.32	5	1.73
IT2FWAC-III	6.52	2.82	**4.35**	1.87

Table 3. Results with minimum distance using Intra-cluster for the wine data set

Variation	Ön		S	
of FWA	Mean	STD	Mean	STD
IT2FWAC-I	6.38	3.1	5.74	1.71
IT2FWAC-II	9.19	2.82	5.55	1.82
IT2FWAC-III	9.16	3.03	**5.29**	1.77

Table 4. Results with minimum distance using Intra-cluster for the WDBC data set

Variation	Ön		S	
of FWA	Mean	STD	Mean	STD
IT2FWAC-I	15.29	5.13	**6.11**	2.51
IT2FWAC-II	14.28	5.48	6.13	2.63
IT2FWAC-III	13.6	7.6	5.58	2.14

Table 5. Results with maximum distance using intra-cluster for the iris data set

Variation	Ön		S	
of FWA	Mean	STD	Mean	STD
IT2FWAC-I	6.71	3.07	5.03	1.8
IT2FWAC-II	7.1	2.94	**4.9**	1.99
IT2FWAC-III	7.23	3.21	5.03	1.64

Table 6. Results with maximum distance using intra-cluster for the wine data set

Variation	Ön		S	
of FWA	Mean	STD	Mean	STD
IT2FWAC-I	9.32	2.88	**4.9**	1.99
IT2FWAC-II	8.32	2.66	5.74	1.65
IT2FWAC-III	7.32	2.96	5.81	1.64

Table 7. Results with maximum distance using intra-cluster for the WDBC data set

Variation	Ön		S	
of FWA	Mean	STD	Mean	STD
IT2FWAC-I	15.1	6.5	7.13	2.06
IT2FWAC-II	17.81	4.54	7.45	2.1
IT2FWAC-III	16.42	4.63	**6.61**	2.54

Table 8. Results with minimum distance using inter-cluster for the iris data set

Variation	Ön		S	
of FWA	Mean	STD	Mean	STD
IT2FWAC-I	7.58	3.25	4.65	1.94
IT2FWAC-II	6.1	3.13	4.52	2.01
IT2FWAC-III	5.45	2.95	**4.03**	1.92

Table 9. Results with minimum distance using inter-cluster for the wine data set

Variation	Ön		S	
of FWA	Mean	STD	Mean	STD
IT2FWAC-I	9.42	2.66	**5.13**	1.98
IT2FWAC-II	8.68	3.29	5.32	2.15
IT2FWAC-III	8.29	3.48	5.16	1.98

Table 10. Results with minimum distance using inter-cluster for the WDBC data set

Variation	Ön		S	
of FWA	Mean	STD	Mean	STD
IT2FWAC-I	14.58	6.58	6.13	2.49
IT2FWAC-II	13.01	6.68	**5.35**	5.35
IT2FWAC-III	14.58	6.58	5.58	2.29

Table 11. Results with maximum distance using inter-cluster for the iris data set

Variation	Ön		S	
of FWA	Mean	STD	Mean	STD
IT2FWAC-I	4.1	1.78	3.42	1.41
IT2FWAC-II	4.29	2.18	3.19	1.17
IT2FWAC-III	4.23	2.36	**2.9**	0.98

The Interval Type 2 Fuzzy Inference System with Trapezoidal membership functions threw the best results for the Iris Data Set as we can see in Table 11 and 12. In table 13 the best result was obtained with Triangular membership functions.

Finally, to show the performance of the proposed method we have presented a comparison among all combinations we have made to test the Interval Type 2 Fuzzy Fireworks Algorithm for clustering (IT2FWAC) with your three variations IT2FWAC-I, IT2FWAC-II and IT2FWAC-III. The comparison presented in the following six Tables (from Table 14 to 19) is an absolute error obtained with the difference between the K-optimal and the Mean of each combination in IT2FWAC, the combination could be Inter-cluster plus, minimum distance plus, Square root of N, Inter-cluster plus maximum distance plus, Square root of N, Inter-cluster plus, minimum distance plus, Sturges, etc.

In Tables 14, 15, and 16, we are presenting a comparison of the absolute error among Intra-cluster versus Inter-cluster and the rules: square root of N versus Sturges with minimum distance.

Table 12. Results with maximum distance using inter-cluster for the wine data set

Variation	Ön		S	
of FWA	Mean	STD	Mean	STD
IT2FWAC-I	4.74	2.42	3.68	1.56
IT2FWAC-II	4.06	2.26	3.74	1.69
IT2FWAC-III	4.58	2.69	**3.52**	1.67

Table 13. Results with maximum distance using inter-cluster for the WDBC data set

Variation	Ön		S	
of FWA	Mean	STD	Mean	STD
IT2FWAC-I	8.1	5.49	**3.45**	1.23
IT2FWAC-II	9.35	7.35	3.84	1.86
IT2FWAC-III	8.87	6.83	4.16	2.38

Table 14. Comparison of the absolute error with minimum distance in IT2FWAC -I

Data	Optimal	Cluster	IT2FWAC-I	
Set	K	Validation	Ön	*S*
WDBC	2	Intra	13.29	**4.11**
		Inter	12.58	4.13
IRIS	3	Intra	3.35	**1.48**
		Inter	4.58	1.65
WINE	3	Intra	3.38	2.74
		Inter	6.42	**2.13**

Table 15. Comparison of the absolute error with minimum distance in IT2FWAC -II

Data	Optimal	Cluster	IT2FWAC-II	
Set	K	Validation	Ön	*S*
WDBC	2	Intra	12.28	4.13
		Inter	11.01	**3.35**
IRIS	3	Intra	4.52	2
		Inter	3.1	**1.52**
WINE	3	Intra	6.19	2.55
		Inter	5.68	**2.32**

Table 16. Comparison of the absolute error with minimum distance in IT2FWAC -III

Data	Optimal	Cluster	IT2FWAC-III	
Set	K	Validation	Ön	*S*
WDBC	2	Intra	11.6	**3.58**
		Inter	12.58	**3.58**
IRIS	3	Intra	3.52	1.35
		Inter	2.45	**1.03**
WINE	3	Intra	6.16	2.29
		Inter	5.29	**2.16**

We also made a comparison of the absolute error among Intra-cluster versus Inter-cluster and the rules: square root of N versus Sturges, but using the maximum distance in the cluster validation. The comparison mentioned above in Tables 17, 18, and 19 is presented.

The numbers in bold highlight the better result for the K-Optimal clusters with its clustering validation and rules, the results are the averages obtained of the 31 independent runs for Interval Type 2 Fuzzy Fireworks Algorithm for clustering (IT2FWAC).

Table 17. Comparison of the absolute error with maximum distance in IT2FWAC -I

Data	Optimal	Cluster	IT2FWAC-I	
Set	K	Validation	Ön	S
WDBC	2	Intra	13.1	5.13
		Inter	6.1	**1.45**
IRIS	3	Intra	3.71	2.03
		Inter	1.1	**0.42**
WINE	3	Intra	6.32	1.9
		Inter	1.74	**0.68**

Table 18. Comparison of the absolute error with maximum distance in IT2FWAC -II

Data	Optimal	Cluster	IT2FWAC-II	
Set	K	Validation	Ön	S
WDBC	2	Intra	15.81	5.45
		Inter	7.35	1.84
IRIS	3	Intra	4.1	1.9
		Inter	1.29	**0.19**
WINE	3	Intra	5.32	2.74
		Inter	1.06	**0.74**

Table 19. Comparison of the absolute error with maximum distance in IT2FWAC -III

Data	Optimal	Cluster	IT2FWAC-III	
Set	K	Validation	Ön	S
WDBC	2	Intra	14.42	4.61
		Inter	6.87	**2.16**
IRIS	3	Intra	4.23	2.03
		Inter	1.23	**0.1**
WINE	3	Intra	4.32	2.81
		Inter	1.58	**0.52**

CONCLUSION

The conclusions of this work could be divided in three parts: based on the results of Wisconsin Diagnostic Breast Cancer (WDBC) as the first part, the second part is based on the results obtained for the Iris data set and the third part for the Wine data set.

1. For the Wisconsin Diagnostic Breast Cancer (WDBC) the better results obtained are when using the combination of Inter-cluster plus, Sturges rule in IT2FWAC-II (Gaussian membership functions) when we are using the minimum distance, the absolute error obtained is 3.35. When we are using the maximum distance for WDBC the better combination is the same that we use for minimum distance, i.e., Inter-cluster plus, Sturges rule in IT2FWAC-II (Gaussian membership functions) but with a lower absolute error, which is 0.68.
2. For the second part of the conclusion, we can say that when we are testing in the Iris data set, the best result obtained is when using the minimum distance Inter-cluster validation plus, Sturges rule is combined in IT2FWAC-III (Trapezoidal membership functions); the absolute error obtained of this combination is equal to 1.03. The best absolute error obtained when the maximum distance calculated is equal to 0.52, it is important to mention that it is the same combination used in a minimum distance.
3. The results in the Wine data set for minimum or maximum distance is when we use the combination of Inter-cluster validation plus, Sturges rule, and the absolute errors are 0.52 and 2.13, respectively; the difference between minimum and maximum distance is the variation of the algorithm, i.e., for minimum distance the best variation is using Triangular membership functions (IT2FWAC-I) in the Interval Type 2 Fuzzy Inference System and for the maximum distance, the best variation is using Trapezoidal membership functions (IT2FWAC-II).

A general way to conclude this work is that we can say that the Interval Type 2 Fuzzy Fireworks Algorithm for clustering (IT2FWAC) performed well in finding the optimal number of clusters its three variations to three different datasets.

REFERENCES

Abdulmajeed, N. H., & Ayob, M. (2014). A Firework Algorithm for Solving Capacitated Vehicle Routing Problem. *International Journal of Advancements in Computing Technology, Bangi, Selangor, Malaysia*, *6*(1), 79–86.

Aladwan, F., Alshraideh, M., & Rasol, M. (2015). A Genetic Algorithm Approach for Breaking of Simplified Data Encryption Standard. *International Journal of Security and Its Applications*, *9*(9), 295–304. doi:10.14257/ijsia.2015.9.9.26

Barraza, J., Rodríguez, L., Castillo, O., Melin, P., & Valdez, F. (2018). A New Hybridization Approach between the Fireworks Algorithm and Grey Wolf Optimizer Algorithm, *Journal of Optimization, 2018*.

Barraza, J., Melin, P., & Valdez, F. (2016). *Fuzzy FWA with dynamic adaptation of parameters* (pp. 4053–4060). Vancouver, Canada: IEEE CEC. doi:10.1109/CEC.2016.7744304

Barraza, J., Melin, P., Valdez, F., & González, C. I. (2017). Fuzzy Fireworks Algorithm Based on a Sparks Dispersion Measure. *Algorithms*, *10*(3), 83. doi:10.3390/a10030083

Barraza, J., Melin, P., Valdez, F., González, C. I., & Castillo, O. (2017). Iterative fireworks algorithm with fuzzy coefficients, FUZZ-IEEE: pp. 1-6. Naples, Italy, July 9-12. doi:10.1109/FUZZ-IEEE.2017.8015524

Barraza, J., Valdez, F., Melin, P., & Gonzalez, C. (2017). *Fireworks Algorithm (FWA) with Adaptation of Parameters Using Fuzzy Logic* (pp. 313–327). Berlin, Germany: Nature-Inspired Design of Hybrid Intelligent Systems. doi:10.1007/978-3-319-47054-2_21

Bonabeau, E., Dorigo, M., & Theraulaz, G. (1999). Swarm intelligence: from natural to artificial systems. Oxford University Press.

Can, U., & Alatas, B. (2015). Physics based metaheuristic algorithms for global optimization. *American Journal of Information Science and Computer Engineering*, *1*, 94–106.

Chena, X., Liua, S., Chena, T., Zhangb, Z., & Zhangb, H. (2012). An Improved Semi-Supervised Clustering Algorithm for Multi-Density Datasets with Fewer Constraints. *Procedia Engineering*, *29*, 4325–4329. doi:10.1016/j.proeng.2012.01.665

Larson, R., & Farber, B. (2003). Elementary Statistics Picturing the World, (pp. 428-433). Pearson Education.

Li, J., & S. Z. (2014). *Adaptive Fireworks Algorithm. IEEE Congress on Evolutionary Computation (CEC)*, 3214-3221. Beijing, China.

Liu, J., Zheng, S., & Tan, Y. (2013). The improvement on controlling exploration and exploitation of firework algorithm. In Advances in Swarm Intelligence, pp. 11–23. Berlin, Germany: Springer. doi:10.1007/978-3-642-38703-6_2

M., Liu, S.H., and Mernik, (2013). Exploration and exploitation in evolutionary algorithms: A survey. *ACM Computational Survey, 45*(3), pp. 35-32. New York, NY.

Margain, L., Ochoa, A., Padilla, T., González, S., Rodas, J., Tokudded, O., & Arreola, J. (2016). Understanding the consequences of social isolation using fireworks algorithm. In Innovations in Bio-Inspired Computing and Applications (pp. 285-295). Cham, Switzerland: Springer. doi:10.1007/978-3-319-28031-8_2

Melián, B., & Moreno, J. (2003). Metaheuristics: A global vision. *Ibero-American Journal of Artificial Intelligence*, *19*, 7–28.

Nerurkar, P., Shirkeb, A., Chandanec, M., & Bhirudd, S. (2018). *A Novel Heuristic for Evolutionary Clustering*, Kurukshetra, India. *Procedia Computer Science*, *125*, 780–789. doi:10.1016/j.procs.2017.12.100

Rodriguez, L., Castillo, O., & Soria, J. (2016). *Grey Wolf Optimizer (GWO) with dynamic adaptation of parameters* (pp. 3116–3123). Vancouver, Canada: IEEE CEC.

Rodríguez, L., Castillo, O., & Soria, J. (2017). *A Study of Parameters of the Grey Wolf Optimizer Algorithm for Dynamic Adaptation with Fuzzy Logic* (pp. 371–390). Berlin, Germany: Nature-Inspired Design of Hybrid Intelligent Systems.

Rubio, E., & Castillo, O. (2017). *Interval Type-2 Fuzzy Possibilistic C-Means Optimization Using Particle Swarm Optimization* (pp. 63–78). Switzerland: Nature-Inspired Design of Hybrid Intelligent Systems. doi:10.1007/978-3-319-47054-2_4

Sanchez, M. A., Castillo, O., Castro, J. R., & Melin, P. (2014). Fuzzy granular gravitational clustering algorithm for multivariate data. *Information Science, 279*, 498–511. *Amsterdam, The Netherlands.* doi:10.1016/j.ins.2014.04.005

Simoes, M., Bose, K., & Spiegel, J. (1997). Fuzzy Logic Based Intelligent Control of a Variable Speed Cage Machine Wind Generation System. *IEEE Transactions on Power Electronics, 12*(1), 87–95. doi:10.1109/63.554173

Soler, J., Tenc'e, F., Gaubert, L., & Buche, C. (2013). Data Clustering and Similarity. *Proceedings of the Twenty-Sixth International Florida Artificial Intelligence Research Society Conference*, pp. 492-495. Academic Press.

Soto, J., & Melin, P. (2015). *Optimization of the Fuzzy Integrators in Ensembles of ANFIS Model for Time Series Prediction: The case of Mackey-Glass.* Paris, France: IFSA-EUSFLAT.

Sturges, H. A. (1926). The Choice of a Class Interval. *Journal of the American Statistical Association, 21*(153), 65–66. doi:10.1080/01621459.1926.10502161

Tan, Y. (2015). *Fireworks Algorithm* (pp. 355–364). Berlin, Germany: Springer-Verlag. doi:10.1007/978-3-662-46353-6

Tan, Y., & Zhu, Y. (2010). *Fireworks Algorithm for Optimization* (pp. 355–364). Berlin, Germany: Springer-Verlag.

Tan, Y., & Zheng, S. (2014). *Dynamic Search in Fireworks Algorithm.* Evolutionary Computation (CEC 2014), Beijing, China. Academic Press.

Telescaa, L., Bernardib, M., & Rovellib, C. (2005). *Intra-cluster and inter-cluster time correlations in lightning sequences.* Amsterdam, The Netherlands: Physica A, 356, pp. 655–661.

Wolpert, D. H., & Macready, W. G. (1997). No free lunch theorems for optimization. Evolutional Computational, pp. 67–82. Piscataway, NJ: IEEE Trans. doi:10.1109/4235.585893

Wu, B. Y. (2006). On the intercluster distance of a tree metric. Theoretical Computer Science, 369, pp. 136–141. Amsterdam, The Netherlands: Elsevier. doi:10.1016/j.tcs.2006.07.056

Zadeh, L. A. (1989). Knowledge Representation in Fuzzy Logic. *IEEE Transactions on Knowledge and Data Engineering, 1*(1). doi:10.1109/69.43406

Zheng, Y., Song, Q., & Chen, S.-Y. (2013). Multiobjective fireworks optimization for variable-rate fertilization in oil crop production. *Applied Soft Computing, 13*(11), 4253–4263. doi:10.1016/j.asoc.2013.07.004

Section 4
FWA Application in Engineering

Chapter 10
A Hybrid Fireworks Algorithm to Navigation and Mapping

Tingjun Lei
Mississippi State University, USA

Chaomin Luo
 https://orcid.org/0000-0002-7578-3631
Mississippi State University, USA

John E. Ball
Mississippi State University, USA

Zhuming Bi
Purdue University, Fort Wayne, USA

ABSTRACT

In recent years, computer technology and artificial intelligence have developed rapidly, and research in the field of mobile robots has continued to deepen with development of artificial intelligence. Path planning is an essential content of mobile robot navigation of computing a collision-free path between a starting point and a goal. It is necessary for mobile robots to move and maneuver in different kinds of environment with objects and obstacles. The main goal of path planning is to find the optimal path between the starting point and the target position in the minimal possible time. A new firework algorithm (FWA) integrated with a graph theory, Dijkstra's algorithm developed for autonomous robot navigation, is proposed in this chapter. The firework algorithm is improved by a local search procedure that a LIDAR-based local navigator algorithm is implemented for local navigation and obstacle avoidance. The grid map is utilized for real-time intelligent robot mapping and navigation. In this chapter, both simulation and comparison studies of an autonomous robot navigation demonstrate that the proposed model is capable of planning more reasonable and shorter, collision-free paths in non-stationary and unstructured environments compared with other approaches.

DOI: 10.4018/978-1-7998-1659-1.ch010

Copyright © 2020, IGI Global. Copying or distributing in print or electronic forms without written permission of IGI Global is prohibited.

INTRODUCTION

Nowadays, robot technology is one of the most promising technologies. Robots can be deployed in fields like medical, agricultural, and explore hostile, dangerous and unreachable environments (Luo, Yang, Li, & Meng, 2017). Real-time map construction and collision-free navigation of an intelligent mobile robot is one of the most crucial issues in robotics. In an environment populated with a variety of obstacles, the task of navigation and map construction is to search a feasible collision-free trajectory for the robot to move from the starting point to the final target and simultaneously build a map.

Nature-inspired algorithms are among the most used for resolving optimization problems. The common aspect of nature-inspired algorithms is given by the fact that they are inspired by the behavior of different species. For instance, ant colony optimization algorithm (ACO) is inspired by observing the way of ants finding food. Particle swarm optimization algorithm (PSO) mimics the pattern of birds flying to find food; Artificial bee colony algorithm (ABC), fish school search algorithm (FFS), and bacteria foraging optimization algorithm (BFO) are also inspired by the bee, fish and E-coli, respectively. In addition, by nature, social phenomena inspired algorithms are inspired by brainstorming process, music harmony and fireworks explosion.

Many natural-inspired models for intelligent mobile robot navigation and mapping have been proposed. Roy, Maitra, & Bhattacharya (2017) used a hybrid particle swarm optimization (PSO) and bacterial foraging optimization (BFO) algorithm to develop a robot path planner model with obstacle avoidance. Dolicanin, Fetahovic, Tuba, Capor-Hrosik, and Tuba (2018) applied brain storm optimization (BSO) for seeking the unmanned aerial vehicle optimal trajectory by considering fuel consumption and safety degree. The BSO algorithm reduces the computational time by moving the new candidate solutions to the local best position through the local search process (Cheng, Shi, Qin, Ting, & Bai, 2014). Mo & Xu (2015) proposed another method for path planning based on particle swarm optimization. In the environment with static obstacles, biogeography-based optimization hybridized by the particle swarm optimization was used to navigate a mobile robot. A new meta-heuristic grey wolf optimizer (GWO) was developed (Zhang, Zhou, Li, & Pan, 2016) to resolve the 2D robot path planning problem. The robot can seek a safe trajectory by connecting the chosen nodes of the 2D coordinates while avoiding the threats areas and costing minimum fuel. Artificial bee colony algorithm (ABC) was developed to search the mobile robot optimal trajectory based on path length and smoothness (Contreras-Cruz, Ayala-Ramirez, & Hernandez-Belmonte, 2015). ABC algorithm was designed as a global search procedure that combined with an evolutionary strategy, which was used to refine the search for feasible paths. Compared with other methods such as the probabilistic roadmap method, the ABC algorithm has a higher chance to find a suitable collision-free trajectory and takes less time.

Besides the nature-inspired methods, various other algorithms were proposed and adjusted for solving the path planning problem as well. Luo, Jan, Zhang, and Shen (2017) used a graph-based method to develop a two-level model, which is an enhanced Voronoi Diagram associated with Vector Field Histogram algorithm based on the LIDAR sensor information for real-time robot path planning. Ullah, Xu, Zhang, Zhang, and Ullah (2018) utilized two different independent modules, namely as Artificial Neural Networks and Reinforcement Learning model to obtain their best control policies and then combine the two trained modules for realizing collision avoidance and global path planning. Neural network was used to resolve path planning problem. Yang and Luo (2004) developed a biologically inspired neural network method of intelligent robot coverage navigation model in a non-stationary environment, which is extended to unknown workspace by concurrent mapping and navigation (Luo et al., 2017).

In this paper, a recent and very efficient swarm intelligence algorithm, firework algorithm (FWA) is proposed for solving mobile robot path planning issues in the 2D space with static obstacles. A LIDAR-based local navigator algorithm is implemented for local navigation and obstacle avoidance. Grid-based map representations are imposed for real-time autonomous robot navigation (Luo, Krishnan, Paulik, Cui, & Zhang, 2014).

FIREWORK ALGORITHM

Fireworks Algorithm (FWA) is a new sort of search method that simulates the phenomenon of fireworks exploding in the air to perform multiple simultaneous explosion search, which is different from other existing methods (Tan, Yu, Zheng, & Ding, 2014). Fireworks algorithm, a swarm intelligence algorithm, can be applied to various problems in search of the global optimal solution.

After fireworks' exploration, sparks in circular neighborhoods with varying radius around the fireworks themselves are formed (Tan, Tan, & Zhu, 2015). The range of different fireworks explosions varies greatly. Some are concentrated whereas some are scattered and sparse. In the real world, the fireworks with different marketing prices have different qualities, and the patterns and effects produced by the explosions are also not the same. Under normal circumstances, the number of sparks generated by good quality fireworks after explosion is obviously large. The distribution of sparks generated after the explosion of fireworks is dense, but their distribution range is small. However, the number of poor quality of the fireworks after the explosion is relatively less and the sparks generated after the fireworks explosion are sparse and the range is wide.

If the area formed after the fireworks explosion is regarded as a partial area in the potential solution space, the sparks generated by the explosion are regarded as solutions in the area. Thus, an explosion process of the fireworks may correspond to a search for the local area.

In the process of solving the optimization problem by the fireworks algorithm, the fitness function of the sparks generated by each firework and its explosion are calculated and used to evaluate its performance. If the value of the fitness function corresponding to fireworks and sparks is small, the fireworks or sparks are regarded as high-quality individuals. When selecting them, more sparks are generated by the fireworks or sparks with smaller explosion range. On the contrary, if the value of the fitness function corresponding to the fireworks and sparks is large, it means that the fireworks or sparks are consider as the low-quality individuals. When low-quality fireworks or sparks are selected as the next explosion fireworks, less sparks are produced with larger explosion range.

Number of Sparks

The number of sparks S_i generated by each firework xi is defined as follows:

$$S_i = m \frac{Y_{max} - f(x_i) + \varepsilon}{\sum_{i=1}^{N}(Y_{max} - f(x_i)) + \varepsilon} \tag{1}$$

where m is a parameter controlling the total number of sparks generated by the N fireworks. y_{max} is the maximum (worst) value of the objective function among the n fireworks. The $f(x_i)$ is the fitness value

Figure 1. Two types of firework explosion (redrawn from Tan, Tan, & Zhu, 2015) (a) Good explosion

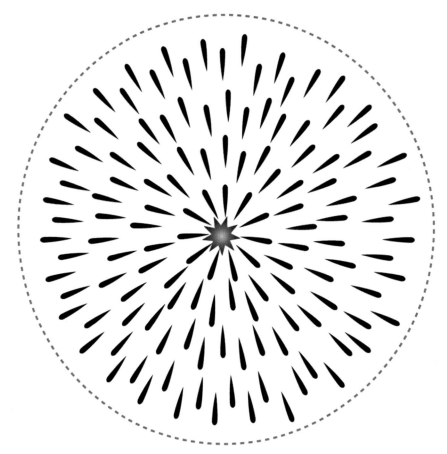

for an individual x_i. ε denotes the smallest constant in the computer utilized to avoid zero-division-error issue. To avoid overwhelming effects of splendid fireworks, bounds are defined as following:

$$\hat{S}_i = \begin{cases} round\ (a \cdot m) & S_i < am \\ round\ (b \cdot m) & S_i > bm, a < b < 1 \\ round\ (S_i) & otherwise \end{cases} \tag{2}$$

where $\hat{S}_i$ indicates the number of sparks that the i-th fireworks can generate. a and b are constant parameters.

Amplitude of Explosion

In the process of optimizing the fireworks algorithm, the explosion range of the fireworks can be decremented by the control of the explosion amplitude. It enables earlier and more efficient convergence and ultimately finds the optimal value. On the contrary, the points with poor fitness function values are often far from the optimal value. Only when such fireworks are greatly mutated, they may return

Figure 2. Two types of firework explosion (redrawn from Tan, Tan, & Zhu, 2015) (b) Bad explosion

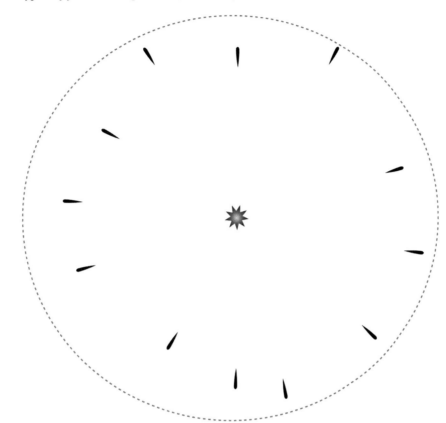

to the optimal value, as shown in Figure 1. The calculation formula of the explosion amplitude of the fireworks algorithm is

$$A_i = \hat{A} \cdot \frac{f(x_i) - y_{\min} + \varepsilon}{\sum_{i=1}^{n}(f(x_i) - y_{\min}) + \varepsilon} \tag{3}$$

where A_i gives the amplitude for an individual x_i to generate the explosion sparks and $\hat{A}$ denotes the maximum explosion amplitude. It is a constant to control the amplitudes. $y_{\min}$ is the minimum (best) fitness value of the objective function among the n fireworks. ε denotes the smallest constant in the computation utilized to avoid zero-division-error.

Generating Sparks

After determining the number of sparks generated by the fireworks explosion and the range of the explosion, it is necessary to distribute the generated sparks in a certain range by a displacement operation. A random displacement method is commonly employed to perform the displacement variation operation. The displacement operation requires displacement of each dimension of the fireworks, in which the formula is

$$\Delta x_i^k = x_i^k + rand\,(0, A_i) \tag{4}$$

x_i^k indicates the position of the i-th fireworks in the current situation; Δx_i^k indicates the position of the i-th fireworks after the displacement operation; $rand(0, A_i)$ indicates that a uniform random number is generated within the range of the explosion amplitude A_i.

Mutation Strategy

The function of the mutation operation is to further enrich the population diversity of the fireworks algorithm by introducing a Gaussian mutation step in the fireworks algorithm process. The specific operation is to randomly select one of the fireworks, before randomly selecting the dimension to perform the Gaussian mutation operation. It should be noted that the Gaussian variation occurs between the selected fireworks and the best-fitted fireworks. If the spark generated after the mutation exceeds the feasible domain, it needs to return to a new location through the mapping operation described later.

The formula for the mutation strategy is

$$x_i^k = x_i^k \cdot g \tag{5}$$

$$g = Gaussian\,(1,1) \tag{6}$$

where x_i^k represents the position of the i-th fireworks in the current situation; g is a random number of Gaussian distributions that is both mean and variance.

Mapping Strategy

Some explosion ranges of fireworks distributed beyond the boundaries of the feasible domain are likely to generate useless sparks. It obviously requires some kind of operation to return these sparks distributed outside the feasible domain to the feasible domain. These sparks could map according to the mapping rules, pulling the spark across the boundary back into the feasible domain, thus ensuring that all spark individuals remain within the feasible domain. The equation of mapping rule is

$$x_i = x_{min} + |x_i| \% (x_{max} - x_{min}) \tag{7}$$

where xi represents the positions of any sparks that lie out of bounds, while x_{max} and x_{min} stand for the maximum and minimum boundary of a spark position, respectively. The symbol % stands for the modular arithmetic operation.

Selecting Strategy

The main objective of the selection operation is to select a portion of the sparks from the sparks in the feasible domain space as the fireworks of the next explosion. The fireworks algorithm adopts the selection method based on the distance, leaving the optimal individual after each explosion and then selecting from the rest of the sparks. Among them, in order to meet the requirements of the diversity of spark populations, the spark individuals who are farther away from other individuals have a greater probability of being selected. In the fireworks algorithm, the Euclidean distance is measured between the two individuals. The formula is

$$R(x_i) = \sum_{j \in k} d(x_i, x_j) = \sum_{j \in k} \|x_i - x_j\| \tag{8}$$

where location x_i and x_j $(i \neq j)$ can be any locations and K is the set of all current locations of both fireworks and sparks. Then the selection probability of a location x_i is defined as follows

$$p(x_i) = \frac{R(x_i)}{\sum_{j \in k} R(x_j)} \tag{9}$$

$p(x_i)$ indicates the probability, in which the i-th spark individual is selected. The spark individual farther away from other spark individuals has a greater probability of becoming the next generation of fireworks, thus ensuring the diversity of the fireworks group.

FIREWORK ALGORITHM FOR NAVIGATION

Mathematical Model for Robot Path Planning

Concurrent map building and navigation are the essence of successful robot navigation under unknown environments. Map building is a fundamental task in order to achieve high levels of autonomy and robustness in robot navigation that makes it possible for autonomous robots to generate collision-free path. Therefore, in this paper, two-dimensional mobile path planning in grid-based environments with static obstacles is considered. The map is divided into equal sized grid cells. Each obstacle is represented as one or more grid cells. Environment is implemented as (x, y) matrix where 0 represent free space, which is white grid and elements 1 represent obstacles which is black grid. As a result, the environment can be modeled by a matrix E, which is composed of 1 and 0. For example, the following matrix represents the environment presented in Figure 2.

$$E = \begin{pmatrix} 0 & 0 & 0 & 1 & 1 & 0 \\ 0 & 1 & 0 & 1 & 1 & 0 \\ 0 & 1 & 0 & 0 & 0 & 0 \\ 0 & 0 & 0 & 1 & 1 & 1 \\ 0 & 0 & 0 & 1 & 1 & 1 \\ 1 & 1 & 0 & 0 & 0 & 0 \end{pmatrix} \tag{10}$$

The path is defined by the starting point S, target point T and n way points between them.

$$P = [S, wp_1, wp_2, ..., wp_n, T] \tag{11}$$

Figure 3. Environment defined by Equation 10

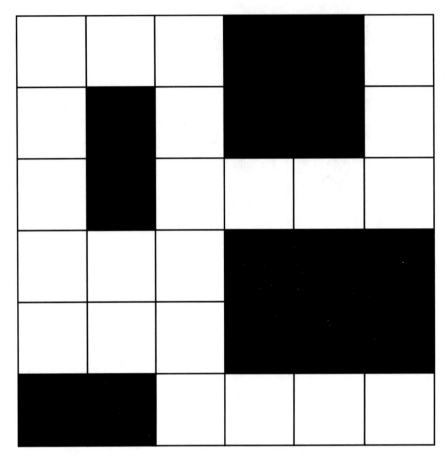

Each point is defined by its grid coordinates (x, y), Grid cell center is considered to be the grid point. The sum of Euclidean distances between two neighbor points on the path is defined as path length:

$$L(P) = \sum_{i=0}^{n} \sqrt{(x_{wp_{i+1}} - x_{wp_i})^2 + (y_{wp_{i+1}} - y_{wp_i})^2} \tag{12}$$

where wp_0 represents starting point, wp_{n+1} represents target point.

Firework Algorithm in Path Planning

In the firework algorithm, fireworks and sparks represent solutions. At the beginning, N fireworks are generated randomly. sparks are then generated by each firework x_i. To further enrich the population diversity, there are n Gaussian variation fireworks generated ($n < N$). Solutions found by the FWA are evaluated by the fitness function.

Some papers showed that fireworks algorithm has defects. The routes pass through the obstacle and fail to completely avoid the obstacle, which results in a lack of safety in the planned path. This is caused by the exploration of the fireworks. The previous generation of sparks and the next generation of sparks are not continuous. The optimization process of the fireworks algorithm has a jump, which makes the path formed between the spark with the best fitness value of the previous generation and the spark with the best fitness value of the next generation cannot take into account the existence of obstacles, resulting in incomplete obstacle avoidance.

In this paper, the authors take local search procedure into account for finding the shortest path in the map with fireworks algorithm. The proposed method integrates the local search procedure to search and find the short and reasonable trajectory with the firework exploration optimization algorithm in a graph.

The first step of seeking the optimal path is to find a feasible solution since the unfeasible ones are not realistic. In order to improve the performance of finding the optimal path through the FWA algorithm, the path is gradually constructed from the generated random points (all in free space, outside the obstacle). On the basis of Dijkstra's algorithm to find the shortest path in a graph, the path is built from the start point S and the next path point is chosen from the N randomly generated points. The same procedure is taken place for the chosen points until the final target is reached and the edges are their connections in the map. Each point is directly connected to all other points. When its connection passes an obstacle and becomes an unfeasible solution, the distance between its nodes is set to infinite to ensure that only a feasible solution can be found as the shortest path. The benefit of the local search procedure is to filter out unfeasible connection with infinite length among the nodes. The proposed algorithm for path planning is given in Figure 3.

Figure 4. Firework algorithm (FWA) for path planning

Procedure 1: Firework algorithm for Robot Navigation

Set parameters, initialize N fireworks;
while *(termination condition not met)* **do**
    Construct Solutions
    Apply Local Search
    Update Trajectroy
end
end Firework algorithm for navigation

LOCAL NAVIGATION AND MAP BUILDING

Concurrent navigation and map building are the essence of successful navigation under unknown environments. 2D grid-based map filled with equally sized grid cells, which are marked as either occupied or free, is built as the autonomous mobile robot moves towards target. Map building is a basic mission in order to achieve high levels of autonomy and robustness in autonomous robot navigation that makes it possible for autonomous robots to make decision in positioning with obstacle avoidance.

It is especially beneficial for autonomous robots to perform robust local navigation in unknown terrains, given the fact that it facilitates the utilization of global path planning algorithms, FWA, to determine the optimal trajectory. Precise estimate of the robot pose is demanded by map building so that accurate registration of the local map on the global map is able to be carried out. In this paper, the local map is dynamically built from data of on-board LIDAR. A reactive local navigation algorithm, Vector Field Histogram (VFH) is effectively integrated in mobile robot navigation and mapping (Ulrich & Borenstein, 1998). The VFH algorithm outputs a preferred target sector in light of the LIDA data for the robot to reach the final designation. The VFH algorithm provides mobile robots with a sufficiently detailed spatial representation of the environment with densely cluttered obstacles (Liu, Luo, & Shen, 2017). The recommended direction is generated from current sensor data. In the paper, heuristics have been added to overcome the issue of a back-and-forth oscillation around the curve of the structure. In this paper, this polar histogram is divided into 54 sectors as every sector is 5° and the LIDAR has a range of 270° (Liu, Luo, & Shen, 2017). The obstacles are enlarged to further eliminate the chance of the robot colliding any obstacles and to provide smoother motion for the robot. This creates a smoother path for the robot and reduces navigation time. The best sector to go through is then used to guide the robot based on a weighted formula that combines deviation from desired direction and associated obstacle densities (Liu, Luo, & Shen, 2017).

SIMULATION AND COMPARISON STUDIES

In this section, in order to validate the FWA model for robot navigation and mapping, simulation studies will be carried out to compare the proposed FWA model with other algorithms.

Parameters for the proposed methods are set empirically by conducting several pre-tests. For finding the feasible paths by the local search procedure, 50 random fireworks are generated ($N = 50$). m, the parameter controlling the total number of sparks generated by the N fireworks is set to 1. The number of Gaussian variation fireworks is 10% of N random fireworks. ε, the minimum amount of system is 10^{-8}. Maximal number of iterations is 500.

Comparison of the Proposed FWA Model with AGAACO Algorithm

The proposed firework algorithm associated with VFH local navigation is used to compare with AGAACO, GA, ACO and GA-ACO models, respectively. Recall that Chen, Xie, Li, Luo, & Feng (2015) proposed a hybrid model combining GA and ACO approaches to resolve robot motion planning issue. However, their model has not yet carried out the local navigation that is necessary for any autonomous robot navigation systems. A comparison study is described in this section to validate the efficiency of the proposed model. The proposed model compares with others in terms of the minimum trajectory length, and number of turns (Chen *et al.*, 2015).

The trajectories of robot motion planning are illustrated about the proposed model, GA-ACO, ACO and GA, respectively, in Figure 4. The workspace has a size of 20×20, which is topologically organized as a grid-based map. The final trajectory planned by the proposed FWA model is illustrated in Figure 4(e). In Table 1, comparative data may be found that the proposed model is much better than the models of AGAACO, GA-ACO, ACO, and GA, respectively, in terms of the minimum trajectory length. The comparison results show that the trajectory length by the proposed model is 0.89% shorter than AGAACO,

Table 1. Comparison of path length and turns (Figure 11 in Chen et al., 2015)

Models	Minimum Length	Number of Turns
Proposed FWA model	27.369	5
AGAACO	27.616	4
GA-ACO	29.038	7
ACO	29.524	11
GA	32.147	6

5.75% shorter than GA-ACO, 7.30% shorter than ACO, and 14.86% shorter than GA, respectively. The number of turns of proposed FWA model is 28.57% better than GA-ACO, 54.55% better than ACO, and 16.67% better than GA, respectively. However, the proposed FWA model is 25% worse than the model of AGAACO in terms of the number of turns.

Figure 5. Illustration of robot navigation with various models. (a) AGAACO model

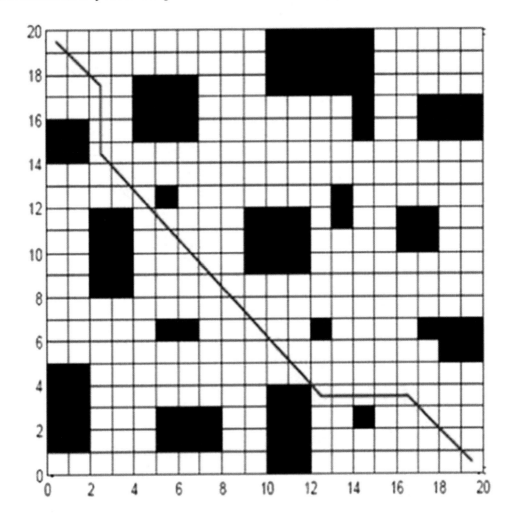

Figure 6. Illustration of robot navigation with various models. (b) GA-ACO model

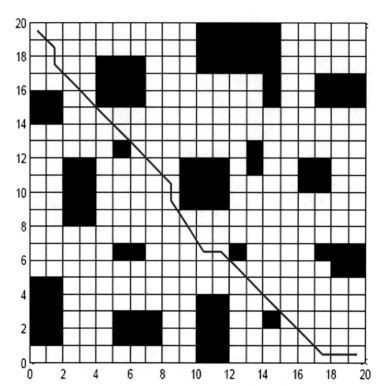

Figure 7. Illustration of robot navigation with various models. (c) ACO model

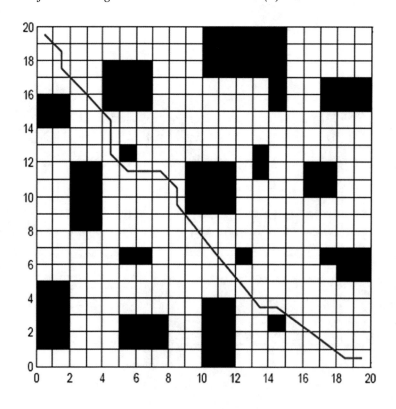

Figure 8. Illustration of robot navigation with various models. (d) GA model

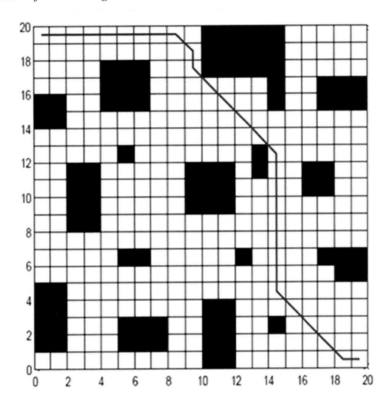

Figure 9. Illustration of robot navigation with various models. (e) The proposed FWA model

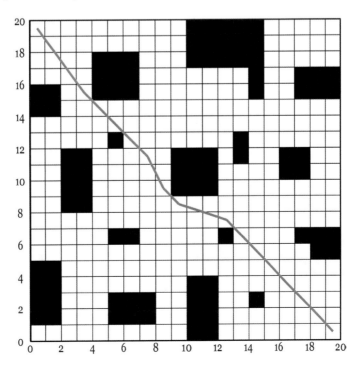

Comparison of the Proposed FWA Model With Others

The proposed model is then applied to a test scenario with populated obstacles in comparison of the test scenario identical as Figure 6 of (Nie *et al.*, 2016) shown in Figure 6(a) in this context. The workspace has a size of 20 × 20, which is topologically organized as a grip-based map.

Path length obtained by the FWA method is 27.9520. The calculated path lengths for the paths presented in (Nie *et al.*, 2016) and the obtained values were 32.0153, 30.3623 and 28.7831 obtained by basic PSO, nonlinear inertia weight PSO and simulated annealing PSO methods, respectively (which is different from the path lengths reported along with the figures). Again, the proposed FWA method found 2.89% shorter than SA-PSO, 7.94% shorter than GA-ACO, 12.69% shorter than ACO, and 14.86% shorter than GA, respectively. Described results are presented in Table 2.

Table 2. Comparison of path length and turns (Figure 6 in (Nie et al., 2016))

Models	Minimum Length	Number of Turns
Proposed FWA model	27.9520	5
SA-PSO	28.7831	9
NLI-PSO	30.3623	10
PSO	32.0153	13

Figure 10. Illustration of robot navigation with various models. (a) The proposed FWA model

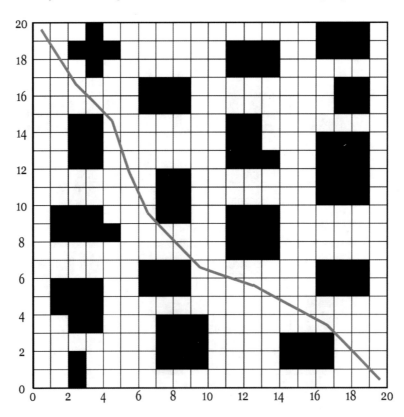

Figure 11. Illustration of robot navigation with various models. (b) Basic PSO model

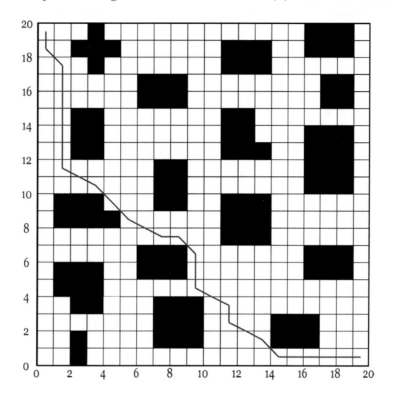

Figure 12. Illustration of robot navigation with various models. (c) Nonlinear inertia weight PSO model

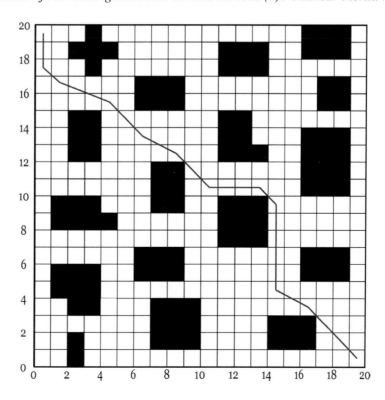

Figure 13. Illustration of robot navigation with various models. (d) Simulated annealing PSO model;

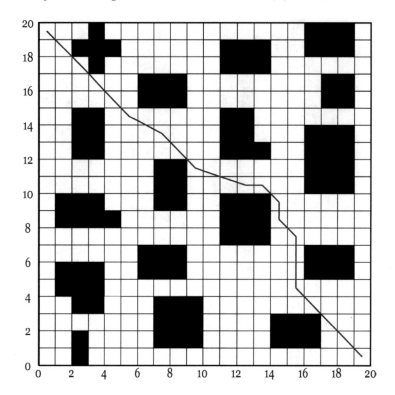

With VFH-based local navigator, the robot is able to traverse from the initial point to plan a reasonable collision-free route to reach the final designation. The green fields indicate detected obstacles, but the purple portion of image represents explored zones by the 270° LIDAR scans. The trajectory generated by the robot is shown in Figure 6(a) whereas the map built is illustrated in Figure 6(b) at the middle of the travel of the robot. In this simulation, the robot is guided in an unknown environment populated with obstacles depicted in Figure 6(c), which shows that the robot traverses from starting point to the final designation with successful obstacle avoidance. The built map while the robot moves in the unknown environment with 270° LIDAR scan is illustrated in Figure 6(d).

CONCLUSION

Mobile robot path planning problem in two-dimensional grid-based space was considered in this paper. Firework algorithm combined with the local search method was developed for real-time robot navigation and map building in this paper. A LIDAR-based local navigator algorithm was implemented for local navigation and obstacle avoidance. Path length and turns were used as objective for comparison purpose. Initial feasible solutions for the FWA were generated by local search deterministic procedure and the FWA was used to further optimize the robot trajectory. In addition to the FWA based navigation, grid-based map representations were imposed for real-time autonomous robot navigation. Simulation and comparison studies have demonstrated effectiveness of the proposed hybrid FWA approach of an autonomous mobile robot.

Figure 14. Illustration of robot navigation and mapping in various stages by the hybrid FWA model (a) trajectory generated in the middle stage

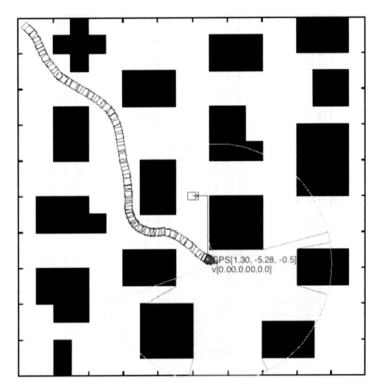

Figure 15. Illustration of robot navigation and mapping in various stages by the hybrid FWA model (b) map built in the middle stage

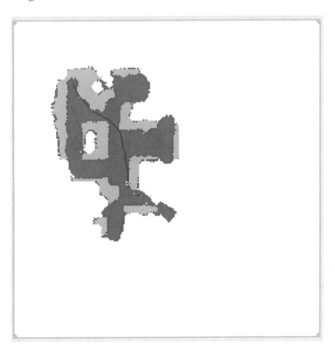

Figure 16. Illustration of robot navigation and mapping in various stages by the hybrid FWA model (c) trajectory generated at the end

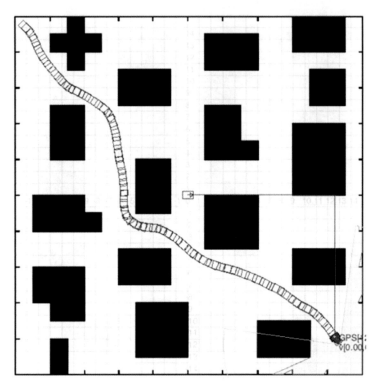

Figure 17. Illustration of robot navigation and mapping in various stages by the hybrid FWA model (d) map built at the end.

REFERENCES

Chen, J., Xie, S., Li, H., Luo, J., & Feng, K. (2015). Robot path planning based on adaptive integrating of genetic and ant colony algorithm. *International Journal of Innovative Computing, Information, & Control, 11*(3).

Cheng, S., Shi, Y., Qin, Q., Ting, T. O., & Bai, R. (2014). Maintaining population diversity in brain storm optimization algorithm. *Proceedings of the 2014 IEEE Congress on Evolutionary Computation, CEC 2014*, 3230–3237. 10.1109/CEC.2014.6900255

Contreras-Cruz, M. A., Ayala-Ramirez, V., & Hernandez-Belmonte, U. H. (2015). Mobile robot path planning using artificial bee colony and evolutionary programming. *Applied Soft Computing, 30*, 319–328. doi:10.1016/j.asoc.2015.01.067

Dolicanin, E., Fetahovic, I., Tuba, E., Capor-Hrosik, R., & Tuba, M. (2018). Unmanned combat aerial vehicle path planning by brainstorm optimization algorithm. *Studies in Informatics and Control, 27*(1), 15–24. doi:10.24846/v27i1y201802

Liu, L., Luo, C., & Shen, F. (2017). Multi-Agent formation control with target tracking and navigation. *Proceedings 2017 IEEE International Conference on Information and Automation, ICIA 2017*, (July), 98–103. 10.1109/ICInfA.2017.8078889

Luo, C., Jan, G. E., Zhang, J., & Shen, F. (2017). Boundary aware navigation and mapping for a mobile automaton. *Proceedings 2016 IEEE International Conference on Information and Automation, IEEE ICIA 2016*, (August), 561–566. Academic Press.

Luo, C., Krishnan, M., Paulik, M., Cui, B., & Zhang, X. (2014). A novel lidar-driven two-level approach for real-time unmanned ground vehicle navigation and map building. *Intelligent Robots and Computer Vision XXXI: Algorithms and Techniques, 9025*, 902503. International Society for Optics and Photonics.

Luo, C., Yang, S. X., Li, X., & Meng, M. Q. H. (2017). Neural-Dynamics-Driven Complete Area Coverage Navigation Through Cooperation of Multiple Mobile Robots. *IEEE Transactions on Industrial Electronics, 64*(1), 750–760. doi:10.1109/TIE.2016.2609838

Mo, H., & Xu, L. (2015). Research of biogeography particle swarm optimization for robot path planning. *Neurocomputing, 148*, 91–99. doi:10.1016/j.neucom.2012.07.060

Nie, Z., Yang, X., Gao, S., Zheng, Y., Wang, J., & Wang, Z. (2016). Research on autonomous moving robot path planning based on improved particle swarm optimization. *2016 IEEE Congress on Evolutionary Computation, CEC 2016*, 2532–2536. 10.1109/CEC.2016.7744104

Roy, D., Maitra, M., & Bhattacharya, S. (2017). Study of formation control and obstacle avoidance of swarm robots using evolutionary algorithms. *2016 IEEE International Conference on Systems, Man, and Cybernetics, SMC 2016 - Conference Proceedings*, 3154–3159. IEEE.

Tan, Y., Tan, Y., & Zhu, Y. (2015). *Fireworks Algorithm for Optimization Fireworks Algorithm for Optimization.* (December), 355–364.

Tan, Y., Yu, C., Zheng, S., & Ding, K. (2014). Introduction to Fireworks Algorithm. *International Journal of Swarm Intelligence Research*, *4*(4), 39–70. doi:10.4018/ijsir.2013100103

Ullah, Z., Xu, Z., Zhang, L., Zhang, L., & Ullah, W. (2018). RL- and ANN-based modular path planning controller for resource-constrained robots in the indoor complex dynamic environment. *IEEE Access: Practical Innovations, Open Solutions*, *6*, 74557–74568. doi:10.1109/ACCESS.2018.2882875

Ulrich, I., & Borenstein, J. (1998). VFH+: Reliable obstacle avoidance for fast mobile robots. *Proceedings IEEE International Conference on Robotics and Automation*, *2*, 1572–1577. doi:10.1109/ROBOT.1998.677362

Yang, S. X., & Luo, C. (2004). A Neural Network Approach to Complete Coverage Path Planning. *IEEE Transactions on Systems, Man, and Cybernetics. Part B, Cybernetics*, *34*(1), 718–725. doi:10.1109/TSMCB.2003.811769 PMID:15369113

Zhang, S., Zhou, Y., Li, Z., & Pan, W. (2016). Grey Wolf optimizer for unmanned combat aerial vehicle path planning. *Advances in Engineering Software*, *99*, 121–136. doi:10.1016/j.advengsoft.2016.05.015

Chapter 11
Application of Fireworks Algorithm in Bioinformatics

Yuchen Zhang
School of Computer Science, Shaanxi Normal University, China

Xiujuan Lei
School of Computer Science, Shaanxi Normal University, China

Ying Tan
Peking University, China

ABSTRACT

Fireworks Algorithm (FWA) has been applied to many fields in recent years, showing a strong ability to solve optimization problems. In this chapter, FWA is applied to some research hotspots in bioinformatics, such as biclustering of gene expression data, disease-gene prediction, and identification of LncRNA-protein interactions. This chapter briefly introduces some backgrounds of bioinformatics and related issues. Through corresponding bioinformatics' problems to optimization problems, some specific optimization functions are constructed and solved by the Fireworks Algorithm. The simulation results illustrate that the fireworks algorithm shows high performance and potential application value in the field of bioinformatics.

INTRODUCTION

Fireworks algorithm (FWA) (Tan & Zhu, 2010) has been applied to many research fields as a relatively new heuristic optimization algorithm proposed by Tan et al. The algorithm searches the optimal solutions of problems in solution space by simulating the explosion process of fireworks. The performance of this algorithm has also been affirmed by many scholars. For example, A power system reconstruction scheme based on FWA is proposed to minimize the power loss and voltage profile enhancement (Mohamed Imran, Kowsalya, & Systems, 2014). Milan Tuba et al. solved multilevel image threshold problem by using FWA (Tuba, Bacanin, & Alihodzic, 2015). In the large-scale non-convex economic

DOI: 10.4018/978-1-7998-1659-1.ch011

Copyright © 2020, IGI Global. Copying or distributing in print or electronic forms without written permission of IGI Global is prohibited.

load dispatch problem, the FWA with chaotic sequence operator is applied well (Pandey et al., 2018). At the same time, FWA also derived many improved versions, such as Enhanced FWA (Zheng, Janecek, & Tan, 2013) and Adaptive FWA (Li, Zheng, & Tan, 2014). Thus, FWA is a mature optimization algorithm, and its searching process follows Markova random process.

Bioinformatics, as an interdisciplinary subject of computer science, biology and mathematics, is a hot research field in recent years. Bioinformatics is mainly concerned with the collection, processing, storage, distribution, analysis and interpretation of biological information. It combines the tools and techniques of mathematics, computer science and engineering, and biology to reveal the biological secrets contained in a large number of complex biological data. Through computational methods, sequence alignment, protein complexes mining, essential proteins identification, disease-genes prediction and the relationships exploration between proteins and non-coding RNAs can be carried out. And these problems may be converted into appropriate optimization problems, which can be solved by swarm intelligence algorithm. Therefore, this chapter intends to apply FWA to bioinformatics.

With the rapid development of high-parallel and high-throughput sequencing technology, a large number of gene expression levels have been measured at the same time, thus obtaining a large number of microarray gene expression data (Xiang, Yang, Ma, & Ding, 2003). There are a lot of useful information in the unbalanced gene expression data (Eisen, Spellman, Brown, & Botstein, 1998), such as similarity of gene expression, conditional specificity of gene expression (proliferation, differentiation and canceration of cells). Therefore, data mining and machine learning technology are used widely. (Cheng & Church, 2000) Cheng et al. first applied bi-clustering analysis to gene expression data. Yang et al. combined the method of dealing miss values with the definition of biclustering based on the CC algorithm, and proposed the Flexible Overlapped BiClustering (FLOC) algorithm to obtain multiple double clusters (Yang, Wang, Wang, & Yu, 2002). According to the greedy strategy, Angiulli et al. proposed a new biclustering algorithm RWB. This algorithm utilizes the random walk strategy (Angiulli, Cesario, & Pizzuti, 2008). At the same time, heuristic intelligent algorithms have been applied to this NP-hard problem. A biclustering algorithm based on evolutionary computation is proposed (Divina & Aguilar-Ruiz, 2006). In addition, some new evaluation criteria have also been introduced (Divina, Pontes, Giráldez, Aguilar-Ruiz, & medicine, 2012). However, the new swarm intelligence optimization algorithms proposed in recent years have been applied only a few times. Some scholars found that the cuckoo optimization algorithm can solve the problem of biclustering very well (Balamurugan, Natarajan, & Premalatha, 2018). Lu Yin et al. combined cuckoos algorithms with genetic algorithms to mine submatrices (Yin, Qiu, & Gao, 2018). Therefore, based on FWA, this chapter intends to use it to carry out the study of biclustering of gene expression data.

Genes are known to be effective carriers of genetic material in DNA. Genes play important roles in today's disease research. Identifying diseases associated genes is one of the important tasks in the study of pathology in complex diseases. Although a lot of biomolecular knowledge and research methods (such as linkage analysis) (Easton, Bishop, Ford, & Crockford, 1993) related to diseases have been obtained at present, a lot of manpower and material resources have been required, and sometimes expected results are not sure to be obtained. Numerous studies have confirmed that genes related to the same or similar diseases, their functions are usually similar or related (Goh et al., 2007). This similarity or correlation may be a direct binding in the physical sense or belong to the same protein complex, or there may be an indirect interaction, such as participation in the same metabolic pathway or cellular process. This makes the development of disease-gene prediction algorithms based on molecular network become a hot topic in recent years. Kohler et al. proposed that applying the random walk with restart (RWR) model to predict disease-genes (Köhler, Bauer, Horn, & Robinson, 2008). Subsequently, a heterogeneous network was introduced and the RWRH algorithm was proposed (Li & Patra, 2010). Erten et al. proposed a data adjustment strategy to adjust the original network score of candidate genes (Erten, Bebek, Ewing, & Koyutürk, 2011). Some scholars also tend to fuse multiple methods and data. The Endeavour developed in the literature (Aerts et al., 2006) is the earliest research achievement in multi-result fusion. Ontology-based disease similarity network and gene semantic similarity network were also constructed in the literature (Le & Dang, 2016; Jiang, Gan, & He, 2011). Zhen Tian et al. integrated gene functional similarity network, protein domain similarity network and protein sequence similarity network by the similarity network fusion (SNF) model (Tian et al., 2017). In these studies, some problems require the construction of optimization functions and the use of traditional mathematical methods to solve. So, it is interesting to see whether swarm intelligence can solve these problems. This chapter will try to construct a reasonable objective function and solve it by FWA.

In addition to genes that encode proteins, a large number of non-coding RNAs play strong regulatory roles in human life. Among them, long non-coding RNAs (lncRNA), which consist of more than 200 nucleotides, have gained wide attentions because of their huge number and their essential functions. And a lot of lncRNAs are closely related to diseases (Chen, You, Yan, & Gong, 2016). However, the function of lncRNA has not been fully understood at present. In general, most lncRNAs achieve their functions by interacting with corresponding RNA binding proteins (RBPs) (Yongge, 2013). Therefore, predicting the potential interactions between lncRNAs and proteins has become a research hotspot. Like predictive studies of disease-genes, there are many computational models for predicting the interactions between lncRNAs and proteins. Ge et al. developed a two-part network propagation model LPBNI to score candidate proteins for each lncRNA (Ge, Li, & Wang, 2016). A new similarity network reconstruction method based on the linear neighborhood propagation was proposed by Wen Zhang et al. (W. Zhang, Qu, Zhang, & Wang, 2018). The HeteSim algorithm was also used to predicting lncRNA-protein interactions on heterogeneous networks (Xiao, Zhang, & Deng, 2017). Since these prediction problems are constructed based on networks, many graph theory concepts can be applied. And the swarm intelligence algorithm can also implement graph clustering to solve some of the problems (Zhu, Li, Liu, Dai, & Guo, 2019). Therefore, in this chapter, we intend to use the graph clustering model constructed by FWA to help predict the relationship of lncRNA-protein interaction.

FIREWORKS BICLUSTERING ALGORITHM FOR GENE EXPRESSION DATA

This section describes the concepts and structures of gene expression data, and introduces the concepts, structures, and types of bicluster, as well as commonly used indicators for evaluating biclustering. After that, we construct a Fireworks Biclustering (FWB) model to cluster gene expression data.

Gene Expression Data

Whether it is gene chip technology, next-generation sequencing technology or deep sequencing technology, the original experimental data can be pre-processed to obtain a gene expression data, which is usually represented by a matrix, where rows represent genes and columns represent samples or conditions. When using mathematics express gene expression data, any gene expression data can be regarded as an $n \times m$ matrix A. Each element a_{ij} in matrix A represents the expression level value of the i-th gene

Table 1. The gene expression data used in the chapter

Dataset	Name	Gene	Sample
Yeast Cycle	Yeast cell cycle (Cho et al., 1998)	2884	17
DLBDL	Diffuse large B-cell lymphoma (Alizadeh et al., 2000)	4026	96
Gasch Yeast	Yeast stress conditions (Khatri & Drăghici, 2005)	2993	173

under j-th sample. In addition, each row vector in matrix A represents the global expression pattern of the corresponding gene on the gene expression. Correspondingly, each column in matrix A represents the global expression spectrum of the corresponding sample on the gene expression data. This section selects several commonly used gene expression data, such as yeast cell cycle expression data, diffuse large B-cell lymphoma expression data and yeast stress conditions data, to study biclustering research respectively. The number of genes and the number of samples are shown in Table 1.

Definition Biclustering and Problem Description

Gene expression data contains a lot of information, and most of this information are hidden in local patterns of gene expression associated with certain conditions. However, it is uncertain as to which genes are expressed under what conditions. Therefore, it is necessary to simultaneously cluster and analysis on the rows and columns of gene expression data, which is biclustering analysis. If the cluster analysis finds that the expression patterns of some genes (or gene subsets) are similar under some conditions (conditional subsets), then the above-mentioned gene subsets and conditional subsets constitute a bicluster. A bicluster is a subset of genes I exhibited homologous properties in a gene expression pattern under the conditional subset J. Therefore, bicluster can be also defined as a k×l (k$\leq$*n*, m$\leq$*m*) submatrix B(I, J). An example of biclustering is shown in Figure 1.

In a bicluster, its elements should have similar patterns or follow certain rules. There are four types of biclusters (Yin et al., 2018): (1) bicluster with constant values, (2) bicluster with constant rows or columns, (3) bicluster with a shifting or scaling pattern, and (4) bicluster with coherent evolutions. Due to the complexity of the biclustering problems, determining a suitable bicluster quality criterion is a key step. This not only helps guide the search process of the corresponding swarm intelligence algorithm, but also helps to evaluate the performance between the different algorithms.

For a size k × l bicluster B (I, J), a_{iJ} is used to represent the average value of the gene expression values of the i-th gene in the sample set J, and a_{Ij} is the average value of the gene expression values of all the genes in the j-th condition, a_{IJ} is overall average of all gene expression values in bicluster B, Vol denotes the volume of the bicluster. The formulas are as follows:

$$a_{iJ} = \sum_{j \in J} a_{ij} / |J| \tag{1}$$

$$a_{Ij} = \sum_{i \in I} a_{ij} / |I| \tag{2}$$

Figure 1. An example of biclustering

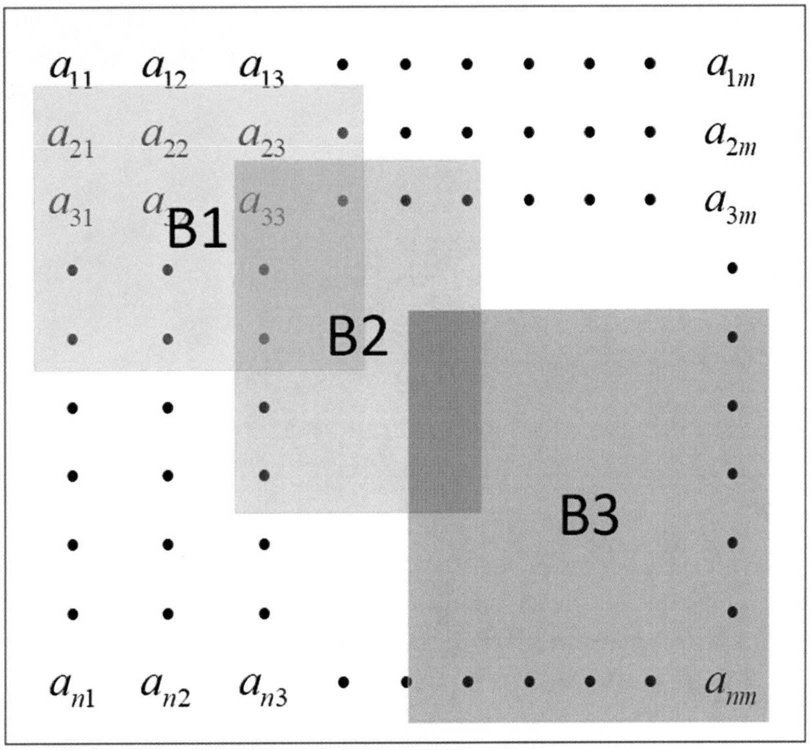

$$a_{IJ} = \sum_{i \in I, j \in J} a_{ij} / \left(|I||J| \right) \tag{3}$$

$$Vol_B = |I| \times |J| = k \times l \tag{4}$$

In addition to the above calculation, Cheng et al. also proposed Mean Squared Residue (MSR) (Cheng & Church, 2000). The definition of MSR is as follows:

$$MSR(B) = \frac{1}{Vol_B} \sum_{i=1}^{k} \sum_{j=1}^{l} (a_{ij} - a_{iJ} - a_{Ij} + a_{IJ})^2 \tag{5}$$

MSR is then widely used in various bicluster analysis algorithms. A complete bicluster satisfies MSR (B)=0. Thus, the smaller the evaluation value obtains, the better the bicluster is. In this section, the Average Correlation (AVC) is also used. The formula of AVC is as follows:

$$AVC(B) = 2 \cdot \max \left(\frac{\sum_{i=1}^{k-1} \sum_{j=1+1}^{k} |r_{ij}|}{k(k-1)}, \frac{\sum_{i=1}^{l-1} \sum_{j=1+1}^{l} |r'_{ij}|}{l(l-1)} \right) \tag{6}$$

where r_{ij} and r'_{ij} represent the Pearson Correlation Coefficient (PCC) of the i-th and j-th row vectors or i-th and j-th column vectors, respectively. Therefore, the larger the AVC value of a bicluster gains, the more relevant the expression value of the gene or sample in the bicluster is. In the other words, the quality of the bicluster is better.

Fireworks Biclustering Algorithm

Based on the characteristics of FWA, this chapter proposes a meta-heuristic biclustering analysis algorithm (Fireworks Biclustering, FWB) to solve the bicluster analysis of gene expression data.

Encoding Design

In FWB, a bicluster B(I, J) is encoded as binary string of length n+m which is

$$x_p = \left\{ g_1, g_2, \ldots g_i \ldots g_n, s_1, s_2, \ldots s_j \ldots s_m \right\},$$

$p=1,\ldots,N_p$, and N_p, is the population size (number of fireworks), As shown in Figure 2. If the i-th gene or j-th sample in the A is chosen by the B(I, J), $g_i=1$ or $s_j=1$, otherwise, $g_i=0$ or $s_j=0$. In FWB, the initial fireworks P = { $B_1, B_2, \ldots, B_{NP}$ } is composed of N_p, biclusters B_i.

Figure 2. Encoding design

1	0	1	•	•	•	•	•	0	0	1	•	•	•	0
g_1	g_2	g_3		•	•	•	•	g_n	s_1	s_2	•	•	•	s_m

Objective Function

In order to guide the search of FWB and compare with other algorithms, we used the MSR as the evaluation criteria of bicluster. Due to the imbalance of gene expression data, that is, the number of genes is often much larger than the number of conditions (samples), most of the biclustering algorithms are prone to cluster only two columns in the data. In this case, although the MSR is a small value, the bicluster is invalid. In order to avoid the meaningless biclustering with too few genes or samples, the FWB should maximize the size of the bicluster during the optimization process. Therefore, the fitness of a firework corresponding to a bicluster B in the FWB algorithm is defined as follows:

$$f(x) = f(B(I,J)) = \begin{cases} \dfrac{\delta}{MSR(B)}, MSR(B) > \delta \\ \dfrac{Vol_B}{MSR(B)+1}, otherwise \end{cases} \tag{7}$$

where δ is the MSR maximum for the bicluster on a given gene expression data A, which is the threshold. It can be imagined that FWB first searches for biclusters that satisfies the MSR constraint, which makes it cover elements as many as possible. When the MSR is similar, the larger volume of the bicluster is, the better the fitness value is. In FWB, the algorithm will search for the maximum fitness value.

Fireworks Explosion

In FWA, a firework is seen as a viable solution in the solution space of the optimization problem. Then the fireworks explosions producing a certain number of sparks are the process of searching for neighborhoods. (Note: Due to the different problems solved, all FWA involved in this chapter are different from the standard FWA, all which have improvements.) After initializing a certain number of fireworks in the solution space of the problem, the fitness of the fireworks is calculated. The fireworks with large fitness will generate more sparks in a small range. On the contrary, the fireworks with small fitness will generate less sparks in a wide range. That is, a local search for the fireworks in the better position, and a global search for the fireworks in the poor position. For a firework x_i, its explosion radius R_i, and the number of sparks produced S_i are as follows:

$$R_i = \hat{R} \times \frac{f_{max} - f(x_i) + \varepsilon}{\sum\limits_{j=1}^{NP} (f_{max} - f(x_j)) + \varepsilon} \tag{8}$$

$$S_i = M \times \frac{f(x_i) - f_{min} + \varepsilon}{\sum\limits_{j=1}^{NP} (f(x_j) - f_{min}) + \varepsilon} \tag{9}$$

where both $\hat{R}$ and M are constants used to adjust the explosion radius and number of sparks. The value of ε is set to $f_{max} - f_{min}$. In addition, considering the size of the fireworks is too large, the effect of the explosion may not be better, so the algorithm often randomly selects some elements to explode rather than all elements. At the same time, due to the imbalance of data, the rate of change p_g of gene position and the rate of change p_s of sample position may also be different.

After generating a series of sparks, in order to increase the diversity of the explosive spark population, FWA introduces a mutation operator for generating some variation sparks, that is, Gaussian variation sparks. The algorithm selects a spark x_i randomly among the generated sparks, then mutates the elements of x_i randomly. The mutation operation is as follows:

$$\hat{x}_i = x_i + \left(x_{best} - x_i\right) \times e, \quad e \sim N(0,1) \tag{10}$$

where N (0,1) represents a Gaussian distribution with mean=1 and variance=1. x_{best} is the current best firework. In the process of generating explosion sparks and Gaussian variation sparks by the explosion operator and the mutation operator, the spark generated may exceed the boundary of the feasible domain. When the k-th element of x is greater than or equal to 0.5, it is set to 1, and when the k-th element of x is less than 0.5, it is set to 0. After that, the resulting sparks are merged with the fireworks. Then we calculate their fitness values and use roulette to select N_p, i.e. optimal elements as the new fireworks of next generation. When the number of iterations reaches the maximum, the optimal solution (an optimal bicluster) of the problem will be generated. The algorithm steps are as follows:

Fireworks Biclustering Algorithm

Step 1: Parameter initializing, generating N_p fireworks.

Step 2: Calculate the fitness value, the explosion radius and the number of sparks of each firework based on Equation (7)-(9).

Step 3: Explode each firework i and generate S_i sparks. For each firework, some elements are randomly selected for explosion, the elements of the gene position are selected using a larger probability p_g, and the elements of the sample position are selected using a smaller probability p_e.

Step 4: Generate M_g Gaussian variation sparks.

Step 5: Select N_p individuals from fireworks, explosion sparks, and Gaussian variation sparks as fireworks for the next generation of iterative calculations. Then repeat steps 1-5.

Step 6: Get optimal biclustering results.

Simulation Experiment and Results

This section mainly contains comparison and analysis of biclusters. We compared FWB with the other three biclustering algorithms CC (Cheng & Church, 2000), FLOC (J. Yang et al., 2002), Bimax (Prelić et al., 2006), on three datasets. We set the initial fireworks number of FWB to 100, the radius constant $\hat{R}$ to 1, the spark constant M to 100, the Gaussian spark number M_g to 10, p_g to 0.1, and p_e to 0.05. For different datasets, we set different δ. In Yeast Cycle, DLBDL, and Gasch Yeast datasets, the δ is set to 300, 1200, and 0.5, respectively. The parameters of other algorithms use the default parameters, and the δ setting is the same as the setting in FWB. All methods were run 20 times, resulted 20 biclusters. The MSR values for the four methods are listed in Table 2. It can be seen that the MSR of the FWB is less than the threshold and is dominant in the two data sets. The clustering results of the FLOC algorithm and the Bimax algorithm are relatively poor due to cluster imbalance. Table 3 and Table 4 describe the number of genes and the number of samples in obtained biclusters, respectively. Although FWB cannot be fully dominant in the number of genes and the number of samples in obtained biclusters, the clustering results are relatively balanced. This can be seen from the clustering volume of Table 5. In the case of a small MSR, FWB obtains the largest volume of biclusters, and the biclustering coverage is high. This proves the validity of FWB.

Table 2. The MSR of comparative methods on three datasets

Database	Algorithms			
	CC	**FLOC**	**Bimax**	**FWB**
Yeast Cycle	305.21±17.25	857.57±227.15	615.57±53.39	299.3464±0.73
DLBDL	1195.7±3.56	41601.24±14312.28	22440.51±2868.99	1197.78±2.96
Gasch Yeast	0.39±0.06	0.41±0.14	0.41±0.08	0.39±0.0034

Table 3. The gene number of obtained biclusters on three datasets

Database	Algorithms			
	CC	FLOC	Bimax	FWB
Yeast Cycle	89.05±141.83	1060.6±92.27	2537.10±26.08	812.40±68.49
DLBDL	98.6±76.57	2170.50±340.98	3673.65±26.44	890.57±150.69
Gasch Yeast	578.80±532.19	1134.40±339.08	449.60±154.11	990.10±1.76

Table 4. The sample number of obtained biclusters on three datasets

Database	Algorithms			
	CC	FLOC	Bimax	FWB
Yeast Cycle	12.40±2.26	4.55±0.88	5.15±0.37	11.75±1.11
DLBDL	29.3±10.95	10.05±0.22	5.15±0.37	27.43±6.58
Gasch Yeast	24.95±41.05	12.50±7.69	5.15±0.36	173.00±1.79

Table 5. The volume of obtained biclusters on three datasets

Database	Algorithms			
	CC	FLOC	Bimax	FWB
Yeast Cycle	1104.22	4825.73	13066.07	9545.7
DLBDL	2888.9800	21813.53	18929.29	24428.33
Gasch Yeast	13692.56	14180	2572.94	171287.3

To further verify the FWB, we also used AVC for algorithm comparison on Yesat Cycle dataset, as shown in Figure 3. FWB has the highest AVC. And the correlation between the genes and samples excavated by FWB is the highest. We also implemented a gene ontology enrichment analysis for a 771×12 bicluster mined in Yeast Cycle dataset by GOTermFinder (www.yeastgenome.org/goTermFinder). Table 6 shows subsets of the bicluster with same GO, the false discovery rate (FDR) is very low (0.00) in many occasions. Furthermore, the corresponding P-value is very small (p<0.01) which shows that there is a very less probability to obtain the gene cluster in random. This shows that the double clusters excavated by FWB are biologically significant.

Section Conclusion

This section is about biclustering by FWA on gene expression data. We designed the biclustering model FWB and verified its performance. Compared with other algorithms, the biclustering results are better and biological significantly.

Figure 3. The AVC of comparative methods

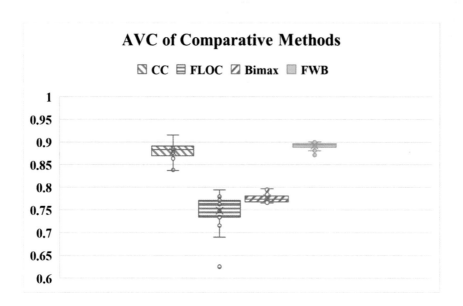

Table 6. Significant GO terms for a bicluster on Yeast Cycle data

Gene Ontology term	Cluster frequency	Genome frequency	Corrected *P*-value	FDR	False Positives
Purine nucleotide binding	122 of 771 genes, 15.8%	772 of 7166 genes, 10.8%	0.00162	0.00%	0.00
purine ribonucleoside triphosphate binding	120 of 771 genes, 15.6%	764 of 7166 genes, 10.7%	0.00271	0.00%	0.00
purine ribonucleotide binding	120 of 771 genes, 15.6%	767 of 7166 genes, 10.7%	0.00330	0.00%	0.00
anion binding	144 of 771 genes, 18.7%	966 of 7166 genes, 13.5%	0.00523	0.00%	0.00
nucleotide binding	133 of 771 genes, 17.3%	878 of 7166 genes, 12.3%	0.00539	0.00%	0.00

PREDICTING DISEASE-GENES BASED ON FIREWORKS ALGORITHM

In this section, we apply FWA to predict disease-genes (PDG-FWA). First, a gene-disease heterogeneous network is constructed, and an optimization function is designed based on the network. Then FWA is use to optimization.

Construction of Heterogeneous Network

There are complex interactions and regulatory relationships between genes. At the same time, there are phenotypic and symptomatic similarities between diseases. Therefore, in many calculating methods, the relationships between genes and diseases are often described by constructed networks. This chapter selects genes that can be expressed as proteins as research targets. Their information can be downloaded from the protein-protein interaction dataset HPRD (Human Protein Reference Database Release 9) (Peri et al., 2003). There are 9453 genes and 36867 interactions after data preprocessing. The gene network can be reprinted as an undirected graph G. Each node represents a gene, and the interactions between them were denoted by edges. Human gene-disease phenotype associations were obtained from the Online Mendelian Inheritance in Man (OMIM)database (Hamosh, Scott, Amberger, Bocchini, & McKusick, 2005). It contains 7436 pairs of gene-disease phenotypic associations. We use a bipartite graph GD to represent. The naming of diseases constitutes a complex hierarchical semantic network. Researchers can characterize the similarities between diseases through their semantic similarities. The similarities of disease phenotypes are calculated by text mining (Van Driel, Bruggeman, Vriend, Brunner, & Leunissen, 2006). The disease semantic similarity network has 5080 nodes which is denoted by D. We prune the network by taking the five nearest neighbors (5NN) of each node. Finally, we obtain 2127 gene-disease phenotype relationships with 1,351 genes and 1,657 disease phenotypes. In addition, for the effect of the subsequent method test, we extract the diseases with two known disease-genes and the corresponding genes to form a subnet, which contains 462 genes, 171 diseases and 641 pair of associations. The statistic of data in heterogeneous network is shown in Table 7.

Table 7. Statistics of data in the constructed heterogeneous network

Statistics	Values
Number of gene-disease phenotype associations	2127
Number of genes / Number of genes mapped in gene-disease phenotype associations	9,543/1,351
Number of interactions between genes	36,867
Number of disease phenotypes/ Number of phenotypes mapped in gene-disease phenotype associations	5,080/1,657
Average number of phenotypes per gene	1.5744
Average number of genes per phenotype	1.2836
Number of gene-disease phenotype associations whose mapped diseases have more than two interaction genes	641
Number of genes that have more than two interacted disease phenotypes	462
Number of disease phenotypes that have more than two interacted genes	171

Then the AdjustCD (Liu, Wong, & Chua, 2009) was used to calculate the similarities between genes. The AdjustCD can describe the similarity of network topology very well. The calculation Equation is as follows:

$$GS(i,j) = \frac{2\left|N_i \cap N_j\right| + 1}{\left|N_i\right| + \text{»}_i + \left|N_j\right| + \text{»}_j}$$

$$\text{»}_i = \max\left\{0, \frac{\sum_{x \in V}\left|N_x\right|}{\left|V\right|} - \left|N_i\right|\right\}, \text{»}_j = \max\left\{0, \frac{\sum_{x \in V}\left|N_x\right|}{\left|V\right|} - \left|N_j\right|\right\}$$

(11)

where λ_i and λ_j are used to penalize genes with very few neighbors. $|N_i|$, $|N_j|$ are degrees of gene i and gene j. $|V|$ is the number of neighbor nodes. The gene similarity network $GS_{(n \times n)}$ is constructed. Then the $GS_{(n \times n)}$, the gene-disease bipartite network $GD_{(n \times m)}$ and disease similarity network $D_{(m \times m)}$ are integrated to form a heterogeneous network which can be represented as W.

$$W = \begin{bmatrix} GS & GD \\ GD^T & D \end{bmatrix}$$

(12)

Each gene is labeled with some GO annotations to explain its function. The gene ontology can be seen as a standard for the annotation of gene products. The annotations can be linked through a directed acyclic tree, which contains two relationships, namely "is a" and "part of". These annotations are also divided into three categories to describe biological process (BP), cell composition (CC), and molecular function (MF). Here, we used the GOSemSim (Yu et al., 2010) to measure the semantic similarity among gene products. We can obtain three gene semantic similarity matrixes about GO, GS^{BP}, GS^{CC}, GS^{MF}, respectively. The range of similarity value is [0, 1]. They cover 8530 nodes, 8796 nodes and 8870 nodes in the gene network G. We set row and column elements corresponding to the nodes that are not covered to 0 in matrixes.

Description and Definition of the Problem

For a classification problem such as disease-gene prediction, it is crucial and challenging to design a reasonable optimization function. For an interested disease, an n+m dimensional vector $F = \left(f_1, f_2, \ldots f_n, f_{n+1}, \ldots f_{n+m}\right)^T$ is used to score each relational gene or disease. $f_1, f_2, \ldots f_n$ are scores of first n genes for interested disease, and $f_{n+1}, \ldots f_{n+m}$ are scores of diseases. If the f value of a gene is larger, it is more likely to be a disease-gene. This vector contains the potential pathogenicity of each gene. In the introduction, the chapter have already mentioned that the disease-genes of the unified disease have similarities. Therefore, it is reasonable to believe that their scores in F should be also similar. We suspect that there are always some nodes that are similar, and others that are independent in the development of the disease. Therefore, this chapter introduces the concept of network modularity model (Newman, 2004) to measure F. Therefore, the score F of genes and diseases should meet the constraints.

$$min_F \sum_{i=1}^{n+m} \sum_{j=1,w_{ij} \neq 0}^{n+m} (P_{ij} - P_{i.}P_{.j}) \cdot (f_i - f_j)^2$$

$$P_{ij} = W_{ij} / \sum_{i=1}^{n+m} \sum_{j=1}^{n+m} W_{ij}, \; P_{i.} = \sum_{j=1}^{n+m} W_{ij} / \sum_{i=1}^{n+m} \sum_{j=1}^{n+m} W_{ij}, \tag{13}$$

$$P_{.j} = \sum_{i=1}^{n+m} W_{ij} / \sum_{i=1}^{n+m} \sum_{j=1}^{n+m} W_{ij}$$

When $(P_{ij} - P_{i.}P_{.j})$ is large, node i and node j tend to belong to the same module in network, $(f_i - f_j)$ should also tend to a lower value. When this value is small (may be less than 0), node i and node j tend to belong to the different modules, $(f_i - f_j)$ should tend to a higher value. In addition, it is worth noting that $1/(f_i - f_j)^2$ is a degree of membership of gene i and gene j by describing F.

In addition, if both of two genes are related to a same disease, they must have similar functional annotations in GO. These two genes should have higher semantic similarity about GO, and their f values should be similar. According to this, the solution F is satisfied with the following condition:

$$min_F \sum_{k \in \Phi} \sum_{i=1}^{n} \sum_{j=1,W_{ij} \neq 0}^{n} \frac{\left[(f_i - f_j)^2 - (1 - GS^k) \right]^2}{|W|} \tag{14}$$

where |W| represents the numbers of elements in the matrix W that are not 0. $\Phi = \{BP, CC, MF\}$ is a collection of GO annotation types.

On the other hand, inspired by the network propagation algorithm, we also incorporate the stability of the propagated algorithms into the construction of the objective function. Finally, the object function of disease-gene prediction problem is:

$$Q(F) = \sum_{i=1}^{n+m} \sum_{j=1,w_{ij} \neq 0}^{n+m} (P_{ij} - P_{i.}P_{.j}) \cdot (f_i - f_j)^2$$

$$+ \sum_{i=1}^{n+m} \left[f_i - \sum_{j=1}^{n+m} W_{ij}^* \cdot f_j \right]^2 + \sum_{k \in \Phi} \sum_{i=1}^{n} \sum_{j=1,W_{ij} \neq 0}^{n} \frac{\left[(f_i - f_j)^2 - (1 - GS^k) \right]^2}{|W|} + \sum_{i=1}^{n+m} (f_i - y_i)^2 \tag{15}$$

where W* is the column normalization of W. And $Y = (y_1, y_2 \ldots y_n, y_{n+1}, \ldots y_{n+m})^T$ is the known disease-gene relationship vector. If gene i is a disease-gene of disease d, y_i is 1, otherwise it is 0. And the corresponding element y_{n+d} of disease d is also set to 1.

Predicting Disease-Genes by Fireworks Algorithm

In the process of predicting disease-genes, each firework represents a solution to the problem, and each firework is the result of a classification prediction. Through the minimize the objective function Q(F), the optimal prediction results can be found. Since F is a numerical vector, it can be manipulated using standard FWA. However, because the dimension of F is too large, if the fireworks are randomly generated, the time resources required are too large, which is not conducive to find the optimal solution. In order to solve this problem, we use the RWRH algorithm (Y. Li & Patra, 2010) to generate the initial population. An initial score vector F_0 is obtained. The method generates N_p, fireworks by adding random factors in F_0. The generation formula of initial firework i is as follows:

$$F_i = {}^3 F_0 + (1 - {}^3) \cdot rand() \tag{16}$$

where γ controls the degree of randomness. In this study, we set it to 0.9. The Gaussian variation operation is the same as that described in the first section, except that e satisfies the N(0.5, 0.5) distribution. For updating the best fireworks, this chapter use the Lévy flight model (Barthelemy, Bertolotti, & Wiersma, 2008) to randomly search. Lévy flight is a random walk in which the step-lengths are distributed according to a heavy-tailed probability distribution. The best position of fireworks is updated by (17)

$$F_g(t) = F_g(t-1) + \pm \oplus Le'vy(») \quad (1 < » \leq 3) \tag{17}$$

where α >0 is a step size which should be related to the scales of the problem. In this problem, α is set to 1. The product Å means entry-wise multiplications. Then, the algorithm selects fireworks and sparks and generates a new population, repeats the iterative process until the stop condition is met. The overall flow of the PDG-FWA algorithm is shown in Figure 4.

Simulation Experiment and Results

In order to measure the performance of algorithms in this chapter, we compared the PDG-FWA algorithm with the other five methods, namely RWR (Köhler et al., 2008), RWRH(Y. Li & Patra, 2010), DK (Köhler et al., 2008), PRINCE (Vanunu, Magger, Ruppin, Shlomi, & Sharan, 2010), PDG-FA. Among them, PDG-FA is firefly algorithm (X.-S. Yang, 2010) for predicting disease-genes. It uses the same objective function as the PDG-FWA. For PDG-FWA, the initial number of fireworks is set to 10, and Explosion radius $\widehat{R}$ takes the average value of F_0. The number of sparks and the Gaussian spark are set to 10. For RWR and RWRH, their α were set to 0.5. And the parameters α, the number of iterations were set to 0.9 and 5 in PRINCE The parameter β of DK was 0.5. And the convergence threshold of these methods is set to 10^{-9}.

In this selection, we used leave-one-out cross validation (LOOCV) (Deng et al., 2014) to measure the performance of PDG-FWA. The LOOCV is a widely used and acceptable method. In each experiment, a known disease relationship is deleted, and the residual relationship is used to predict the disease-gene relationship. If the deleted disease-gene is ranked as Top 1, one regards this to be a successful prediction. The number of successful prediction (NSP) is used as the evaluation criterion. Similarly, if the removed disease gene is ranked in the Top 5% of the test set, it can also reflect the quality of the algorithm. The mean rank ratio (MRR) is defined as the average rank ratios of all disease-genes in test sets in all validations.

In addition, the positive samples are disease-genes of one disease, the negative samples are unknown disease-genes. The chapter also used receiver operating characteristics (ROC) curve to assess the quality of PDG-FWA. The ROC curve is plotted with false positive rates (FPR or 1-specitivity) and true positive rates (TPR or sensitivity). The area under curve (AUC) of the ROC is also calculated to measure

Figure 4. The overall flow of the PDG-FWA algorithm

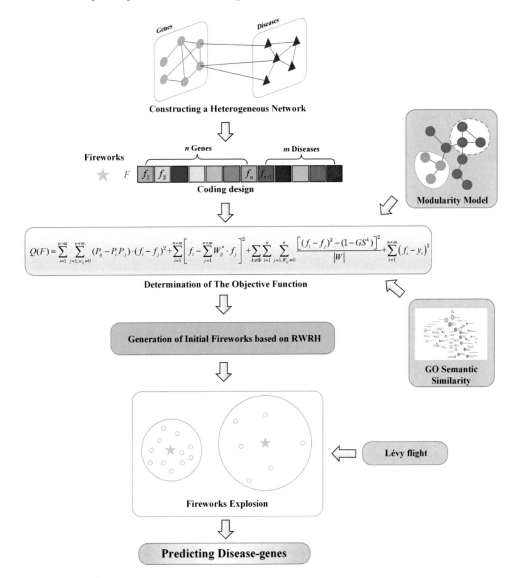

the overall performance. In addition, the precision and recall in Top-50 predicted genes are considered. We completed two experiments, one is completed for all diseases that have disease-genes, and the other is carried out on all diseases that have at least two disease-genes. We arranged the gene score column vectors for each disease into a total score matrix (e.g. 462 ×171, 1351 ×1657 matrix). Based on these matrices, we evaluated the algorithm and draw the ROC curves.

The NSP, Top 5%, MRR of comparative algorithms are shown in Table 8 and Table 9. On the data subset having two disease-genes at least, PDG-FWA has better predicting results. The NSP, Top 5%, MRR reaches the highest value in the algorithm. Although, in all disease sets, NSP of PDG-FWA are slightly lower than PDG-FA and Top 5% are slightly lower than PRINCE, the average ranking of disease gene relationships is higher than other algorithms.

Table 8. Comparative results on diseases that have at least two disease-genes

Algorithms	NSP (*Top* 1)	*Top 5%*	MRR
RWR	107	299	102.9345
RWRH	147	358	92.7816
DK	120	315	99.5117
PRINCE	131	358	88.0686
PDG-FA	**167**	356	86.9376
PDG-FWA	**167**	**359**	**83.6490**

Table 9. Comparative results on all diseases

Algorithms	NSP (*Top* 1)	*Top 5%*	MRR
RWR	85	435	469.5261
RWRH	298	1087	343.3902
DK	79	441	468.6737
PRINCE	256	**1116**	339.9196
PDG-FA	**313**	1038	344.3427
PDG-FWA	311	1053	**336.0136**

Figure 5 shows the ROC curves of the proposed algorithm and other algorithms. It can be seen that the PDG-FWA curve is above the other method curves and the AUC value is the largest no matter what data set is. It should be noted that the AUC values of the RWR and DK algorithms are less than 0.5 in all diseases. Because the two algorithms are run on a single network and cannot predict diseases with only one known disease.

Figure 5. ROC curves of PDG-FWA and other algorithms. (a) Comparison on diseases that related at least two genes, (b) Comparison on all diseases.

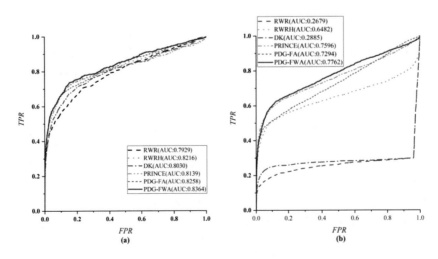

We also evaluated PDG-FWA and other methods with respect to precision, recall and f-measure. For each method, the precision, recall and f-measure of Top-k are calculated, which can help us to understand the local characteristics of these methods. As can be seen from Figures 6, 7, 8, on the diseases that related two disease-genes at least, the proposed algorithm shows the best performance. In all diseases, the algorithm is only slightly lower than the PRINCE algorithm. It can be seen that it is feasible and effective to apply the FWA to disease prediction.

Figure 6. Average precision on querying diseases of test set at each Top-k position. (a) Average precision on the diseases that related at least two disease-genes, (b) Average precision on the all diseases.

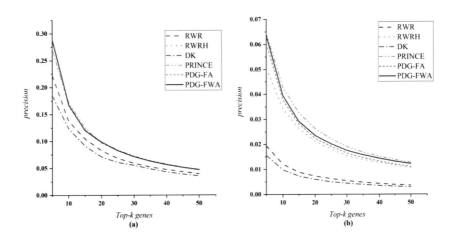

Figure 7. Average recall on querying diseases of test set at each Top-k position. (a) Average recall on the diseases that related at least two disease-genes, (b) Average recall on the all diseases.

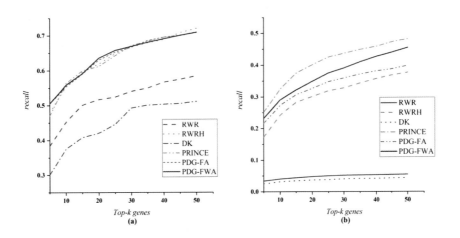

Figure 8. Average f-measure on querying diseases of test set at each Top-k position. (a) Average f-measure on the diseases that related at least two disease- genes, (b) Average f-measure on all diseases.

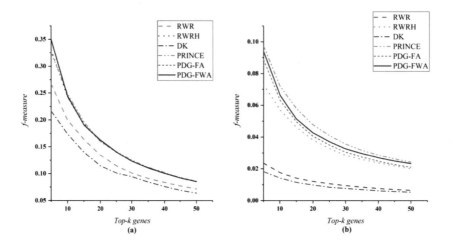

Top-k genes
(a)

Top-k genes
(b)

Section Conclusion

In the selection, we introduced the application of FWA in predicting disease-genes. It can be seen that a two-class problem can be constructed as an optimization problem and solved by the swarm intelligence algorithm. FWA can also be used to solve such problems and get good results.

IDENTIFICATION OF LNCRNA–PROTEIN INTERACTIONS BY FIREWORKS CLUSTERING ALGORITHM

Long non-coding RNAs (lncRNAs) have gained wide attentions in current years. In the section, we intend to use FWA to identify interactions between lncRNA and protein. Unlike the previous two sections, FWA in this section is designed to implement graph clustering, and to predict lncRNA-protein interactions (FWCLP) by strengthening network relationships.

Data of LncRNA–Protein Interactions

Some public databases can facilitate the study of lncRNA-protein interaction prediction. Such as, database NPinter (Hao et al., 2016), NONCODE (C. Xie et al., 2013) and SUPERFAMILY (Gough, Karplus, Hughey, & Chothia, 2001) contains a lot of lncRNAs and interactions information. Wen Zhang et al. processed the data and obtained 4158 pairs of relationships, of which 990 lncRNA and 27 proteins (W. Zhang et al., 2018). The data used in this chapter is based on their processing. The interaction profile can be described a bipartite matrix LP with n lncRNA and m proteins. If a protein p_j combines a lncRNA l_i, edge $e_{ij}=1$, otherwise, $e_{ij}=0$.

Furthermore, features of lncRNAs and proteins are also obtained from NONCODE. The human lncRNA expression data and sequence data can be downloaded. This expression profile describes the expression of lncRNA in 24 human tissues or cell types. The expression profile called by LE. For lncRNA sequences, the percentage of the four nucleotide types (A, C, G, T) in the lncRNA sequence and the percentage ratio of the 16 dinucleotide types (AA, AG, AC, ...) were calculated as the features of the sequences. The feature matrix is denoted LS. We performed a Pearson correlation analysis on the expression of each two pairs of lncRNAs in the LE matrix. For sequence features LS, we calculated the Euclidean distance before the two lncRNAs. The average of the two analysis results (LE and LS) is taken as the similarity between lncRNAs. Generate a lncRNA similarity matrix LSM and remove elements below the mean of all elements.

For proteins, we first download the protein-protein interactions (PPI) data from the STRING database (Szklarczyk et al., 2018) which is weighted for all protein relationships. Then we normalized it to get a weighted PPI network WP. Protein sequences download from SUPERFAMILY. There are three types of popular descriptors, namely, composition, transition, destruction (CTD). The "CTD" vectors of protein sequences are calculated by using the serve Profeat (Z.-R. Li et al., 2006). Obtained a "CTD" feature matrix with 27×504. Similarly, we calculate the Euclidean distance between each pair of proteins in the CTD matrix and integrate it with the weighted PPI network. After deleting the elements below the mean value, a similarity network PSM of the protein is obtained.

Fireworks Clustering for Graph

In order to enhance the lncRNA similarity relationship and protein interactions obtained in the previous step, this section used FWA to perform graph clustering. Transforming a graph clustering problem into an optimization problem.

Encoding Design

Based on our previous research (Y. Zhang, Lei, & Tan, 2017), we convert a graph clustering result into an n-dimensional vector. The FWCLP use the locus-based adjacency representation (Handl & Knowles, 2007). Each firework corresponds to a clustering result. Base on the adjacency matrix, in a fireworks X= {x1, x2...xn}, each element has a set of range values. For example, in Figure 9, the node v_1 has 3 edge with node v_2, v_4, v_9. If node j is assigned to the i-th element of a firework, there is a link between the nodes i and j. This means that the node i and node j are in the same cluster. However, there are usually a large number of single nodes as independent clusters in the network. So, we add 0 to the value range of each node. In fact, we use an n-dimensional vector to characterize several connected sub graphs. The firework is decoded into two clusters $\{v_1, v_2, v_3, v_4,\}$ and $\{v_5, v_6, v_7, v_8\}$, v_9 is an independent cluster and is excluded in Figure 9.

Objective Function

The purpose of the objective function is to calculate the fitness values for evaluating the performance of each firework (solution of problem) in the population. In the mining clusters, the solutions of the problem should satisfy the network topology of LSM and PSM (They are collectively referred to as weighted network W below). In this study, the fitness values of fireworks indicate the degree of intra-cohesion of each cluster, as well as the degree of the inter-cluster coupling of these clusters. The aim is to obtain the maximum degree of internal aggregation and the minimum degree of external coupling. We use weight sum of edges to quantify the degree. The objective function is defined as follows:

Figure 9. Encoding design of FWCPL

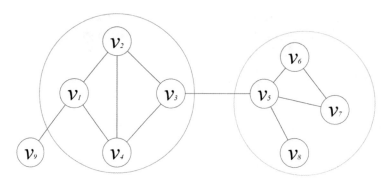

$$F\left(\left\{C^1, C^2, ..., C^k\right\}\right) = \frac{\sum_{i=1}^{k} \frac{C_{in}^i}{C_{in}^i + C_{out}^i + W_{ave} \times |C^i| \times (|C^i| - 1)/2} \times |C^i|}{\sum_{i=1}^{k} |C^i|} \qquad (18)$$

$$C_{in}^i = \sum_{p,q \in C^i} W_{pq} C_{in}^i = \sum_{p,q \in C^i} W_{pq} C_{in}^i = \sum_{p.q \in C^i} W_{pq} C_{in}^i = \sum_{p.q \in C^i} W_{pq} \qquad (19)$$

$$C_{out}^i = \sum_{p \in C^i, q \notin C^i} W_{pq} C_{out}^i = \sum_{p \in C^i, q \notin C^i} W_{pq} C_{out}^i = \sum_{p \in C^i, q \notin C^i} W_{pq} C_{out}^i = \sum_{p \in C^i, q \notin C^i} W_{pq} \qquad (20)$$

where $\{C^1, C^2, ..., C^K\}$ is a clustering result determined by a firework. Ci represents a cluster. $|C^i|$ denotes the number of proteins in a cluster. $\sum_{i=1}^{k} |C^i|$ is the total number of proteins which are found in the detected protein complexes. Wave is the average weight in the similarity network. $|C^i| \times (|C^i| - 1)/2$ is the maximum possible number of edges in the cluster C^i. C_{in}^i is the weight sum of all edge in cluster C^i. C_{out}^i is the weight sum of edges whose one endpoint is in C^i and another endpoint is not in C^i. Our goal is to find the maximum value.

Fireworks Explosion

The basic operation of this step is the same as the previous two sections. However, since the value of each element is discrete, the explosion radius is not meaningful in the FWCLP algorithm. When the explosion radius of a firework is large, it tends to move toward the globally optimal firework. And when the radius is smaller, it tends to a local search. The larger fitness value of a firework is, the more its sparks are. Experiments show that small-scale changes help to find the best clusters for the graph clustering problem.

Identification of LncRNA–Protein Interactions Based on Clusters

Using firework clustering algorithm is to cluster on lncRNA similarity network and protein similarity network, respectively. We can conclude that lncRNA or protein with high similarity are in same clusters. The interaction between a lncRNA i and a protein j can be calculated:

$$Q(i,j) = \frac{1}{2} \left(\frac{\sum\limits_{k \in V_L(i)} LSM(i,k) \cdot LP(k,j)}{|V_L(i)|} + \frac{\sum\limits_{k \in V_P(j)} PSM(k,j) \cdot LP(i,k)}{|V_P(j)|} \right) \tag{21}$$

where $V_L(i)$ denotes all lncRNAs in the clusters that contains the lncRNA i. $V_P(j)$ represents the all proteins that are in the same clusters as protein j. LP(k, j) is a correlation between lncRNA k and protein j. Figure 10 shows the relevant schematic.

In addition, the diffusion kernel (Köhler et al., 2008) was also introduced in FWCLP. Actually, it is a lazy random walk, which is defined as follows:

$$K = e^{-aS} \tag{22}$$

where S is the Laplacian matrix of LSM, S=D-LSM. Diagonal D is the degree matrix of LSM. The K(i, j) represents the probability that a lazy random walker moves from node i to node j, which is also known as the diffusion kernel distance between the two nodes. So, for a protein j, the scores of all lncRNA are:

$$\hat{Q}_{\cdot,j} = Q_{\cdot,j} + K \times Y_{\cdot,j} \tag{23}$$

where $Y_{\cdot,j}$ is a known lncRNA-protein j relationship vector. If lncRNA i is related with protein j, $y_{i,j}$ is 1, otherwise it is 0. The larger the $\hat{Q}$ value is, the more likely the corresponding lncRNA and protein are to interact.

Simulation Experiment and Results

Like the previous section, in order to verify the performance of the proposed algorithm, the FWCLP algorithm is also compared with the other five algorithms, namely RWR (Köhler et al., 2008), RWRH (Y. Li & Patra, 2010), IMC (Natarajan & Dhillon, 2014), BiRW (M. Xie, Hwang, & Kuang, 2012), PRINCE (Vanunu et al., 2010). In this algorithm, the number of fireworks is set to 50, the number of

Figure 10. Predicting lncRNA-protein interactions based on clusters

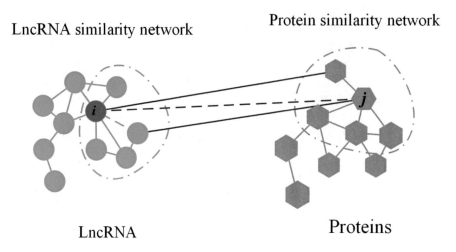

sparks is set to 100, and iteration is 1000 times. By comparing in AUC, precision, recall, f-measure, it can be found that FWCLP has better predicted results than other algorithms. And FWCLP has high accuracy for the first 50 predicted lncRNAs of each protein. This shows that clustering is a very effective role in strengthening differentiation.

Figure 11. ROC curves and AUC values of FWCLP and other algorithms

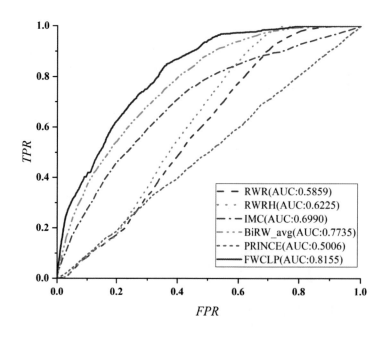

Figure 12. Average precision on querying proteins of test set at each Top-k position

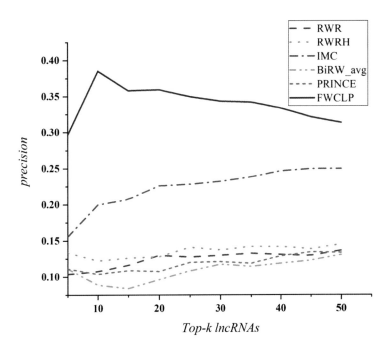

Figure 13. Average recall on querying proteins of test set at each Top-k position

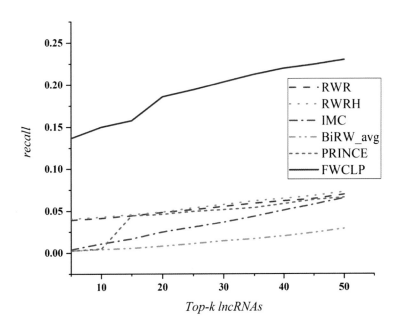

Figure 14. Average f-measure on querying proteins of test set at each Top-k position

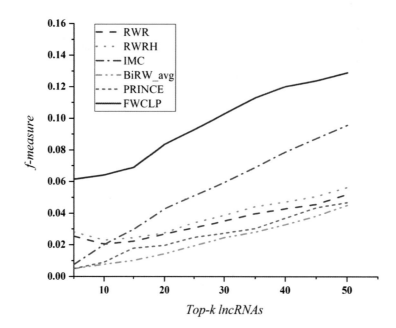

Section Conclusion

In the section, we propose a lncRNA-protein interaction recognition algorithm based on fireworks clustering. Unlike traditional relational prediction algorithms, FWCLP uses clustering to enhance the relationships between lncRNAs and proteins. And the original clustering problem is transformed into an optimization problem. It also has excellent performance.

CONCLUSION

This chapter mainly introduced the application of FWA in bioinformatics to achieve biclustering of gene expression data, design optimization function for predicting disease genes, and recognize the interactions between lncRNAs and proteins. And they all have good performance, reflecting the wide applicability of the FWA. As an emerging interdisciplinary subject, bioinformatics has received much attention in recent years. FWA, as a swarm intelligent optimization algorithm, is lack of the application to bioinformatics. However, through the research in this chapter, many unsolved prediction problems in bioinformatics can be transformed into an optimization problem to solve. This is a good inspiration for bioinformatics scholars and intelligent computing scholars. At the same time, designing a reasonable objective function and constructing a reasonable optimization model have always been challenges for this research.

ACKNOWLEDGMENT

This research was supported by the National Natural Science Foundation of China [grant numbers: 61972451, 61672334, 61902230] and the Fundamental Research Funds for the Central Universities, Shaanxi Normal University [grant numbers: GK201901010, 2018TS079].

REFERENCES

Aerts, S., Lambrechts, D., Maity, S., Van Loo, P., Coessens, B., De Smet, F., ... Hassan, B. (2006). Gene prioritization through genomic data fusion. *Nature Biotechnology*, *24*(5), 537–544. doi:10.1038/nbt1203 PMID:16680138

Alizadeh, A. A., Eisen, M. B., Davis, R. E., Ma, C., Lossos, I. S., Rosenwald, A., ... Yu, X. (2000). Distinct types of diffuse large B-cell lymphoma identified by gene expression profiling. *Nature*, *403*(6769), 503–511. doi:10.1038/35000501 PMID:10676951

Angiulli, F., Cesario, E., & Pizzuti, C. (2008). Random walk biclustering for microarray data. *Information Sciences*, *178*(6), 1479–1497. doi:10.1016/j.ins.2007.11.007

Balamurugan, R., Natarajan, A., & Premalatha, K. (2018). A New Hybrid Cuckoo Search Algorithm for Biclustering of Microarray Gene-Expression Data. *Applied Artificial Intelligence*, *32*(7-8), 644–659. doi:10.1080/08839514.2018.1501918

Barthelemy, P., Bertolotti, J., & Wiersma, D. S. (2008). A Lévy flight for light. *Nature*, *453*(7194), 495–498. doi:10.1038/nature06948 PMID:18497819

Chen, X., You, Z.-H., Yan, G.-Y., & Gong, D.-W. (2016). IRWRLDA: Improved random walk with restart for lncRNA-disease association prediction. *Oncotarget*, *7*(36), 57919. doi:10.18632/oncotarget.11141 PMID:27517318

Cheng, Y., & Church, G. M. (2000). *Biclustering of expression data*. Paper presented at the International Conference on Intelligent Systems for Molecular Biology.

Cho, R. J., Campbell, M. J., Winzeler, E. A., Steinmetz, L., Conway, A., Wodicka, L., ... Lockhart, D. J. (1998). A genome-wide transcriptional analysis of the mitotic cell cycle. *Molecular Cell*, *2*(1), 65–73. doi:10.1016/S1097-2765(00)80114-8 PMID:9702192

Deng, L., Zhang, Q. C., Chen, Z., Meng, Y., Guan, J., & Zhou, S. (2014). PredHS: A web server for predicting protein–protein interaction hot spots by using structural neighborhood properties. *Nucleic Acids Research*, *42*(W1), W290–W295. doi:10.1093/nar/gku437 PMID:24852252

Divina, F., & Aguilar-Ruiz, J. S. (2006). Biclustering of expression data with evolutionary computation. *IEEE Transactions on Knowledge and Data Engineering*, *18*(5), 590–602. doi:10.1109/TKDE.2006.74

Divina, F., Pontes, B., Giráldez, R., Aguilar-Ruiz, J. S. (2012). An effective measure for assessing the quality of biclusters. *Computers in biology and medicine*, *42*(2), 245-256.

Easton, D., Bishop, D., Ford, D., & Crockford, G. (1993). Genetic linkage analysis in familial breast and ovarian cancer: Results from 214 families. The Breast Cancer Linkage Consortium. *American Journal of Human Genetics, 52*(4), 678–701. PMID:8460634

Eisen, M. B., Spellman, P. T., Brown, P. O., & Botstein, D. (1998). Cluster analysis and display of genome-wide expression patterns. *Proc Natl Acad Sci USA*. 10.1073/pnas.95.25.14863

Erten, S., Bebek, G., Ewing, R. M., & Koyutürk, M. (2011). DADA: Degree-aware algorithms for network-based disease gene prioritization. *BioData Mining, 4*(1), 19. doi:10.1186/1756-0381-4-19 PMID:21699738

Ge, M., Li, A., & Wang, M. (2016). A bipartite network-based method for prediction of long non-coding RNA–protein interactions. *Genomics, Proteomics, & Bioinformatics, 14*(1), 62–71. doi:10.1016/j.gpb.2016.01.004 PMID:26917505

Goh, K.-I., Cusick, M. E., Valle, D., Childs, B., Vidal, M., & Barabási, A.-L. (2007). The human disease network. *Proceedings of the National Academy of Sciences of the United States of America, 104*(21), 8685–8690. doi:10.1073/pnas.0701361104 PMID:17502601

Gough, J., Karplus, K., Hughey, R., & Chothia, C. (2001). Assignment of homology to genome sequences using a library of hidden Markov models that represent all proteins of known structure. *Journal of Molecular Biology, 313*(4), 903–919. doi:10.1006/jmbi.2001.5080 PMID:11697912

Hamosh, A., Scott, A. F., Amberger, J. S., Bocchini, C. A., & McKusick, V. A. (2005). Online Mendelian Inheritance in Man (OMIM), a knowledgebase of human genes and genetic disorders. *Nucleic Acids Research, 33(suppl_1),* D514-D517.

Handl, J., & Knowles, J. (2007). An evolutionary approach to multiobjective clustering. *IEEE Transactions on Evolutionary Computation, 11*(1), 56–76. doi:10.1109/TEVC.2006.877146

Hao, Y., Wu, W., Li, H., Yuan, J., Luo, J., Zhao, Y., & Chen, R. (2016). NPInter v3. 0: An upgraded database of noncoding RNA-associated interactions. *Database (Oxford)*, 2016. PMID:27087310

Jiang, R., Gan, M., & He, P. (2011). Constructing a gene semantic similarity network for the inference of disease genes. *Proceedings BMC systems biology*. 10.1186/1752-0509-5-S2-S2

Khatri, P., & Drăghici, S. (2005). Ontological analysis of gene expression data: Current tools, limitations, and open problems. *Bioinformatics (Oxford, England), 21*(18), 3587–3595. doi:10.1093/bioinformatics/bti565 PMID:15994189

Köhler, S., Bauer, S., Horn, D., & Robinson, P. N. (2008). Walking the interactome for prioritization of candidate disease genes. *American Journal of Human Genetics, 82*(4), 949–958. doi:10.1016/j.ajhg.2008.02.013 PMID:18371930

Le, D.-H., & Dang, V.-T. (2016). Ontology-based disease similarity network for disease gene prediction. *Vietnam Journal of Computer Science, 3*(3), 197–205. doi:10.100740595-016-0063-3

Li, J., Zheng, S., & Tan, Y. (2014). Adaptive Fireworks Algorithm. *Proceedings 2014 IEEE Congress on Evolutionary Computation (CEC)*. 10.1109/CEC.2014.6900418

Li, Y., & Patra, J. C. (2010). Genome-wide inferring gene–phenotype relationship by walking on the heterogeneous network. *Bioinformatics (Oxford, England)*, *26*(9), 1219–1224. doi:10.1093/bioinformatics/btq108 PMID:20215462

Li, Z.-R., Lin, H. H., Han, L., Jiang, L., Chen, X., & Chen, Y. Z. (2006). PROFEAT: a web server for computing structural and physicochemical features of proteins and peptides from amino acid sequence. *Nucleic acids research, 34(suppl_2),* W32-W37.

Liu, G., Wong, L., & Chua, H. N. (2009). Complex discovery from weighted PPI networks. *Bioinformatics (Oxford, England)*, *25*(15), 1891–1897. doi:10.1093/bioinformatics/btp311 PMID:19435747

Mohamed Imran, A., Kowsalya, M., & Systems, E. (2014). A new power system reconfiguration scheme for power loss minimization and voltage profile enhancement using Fireworks Algorithm. *International Journal of Electrical Power*, *62*(62), 312–322. doi:10.1016/j.ijepes.2014.04.034

Natarajan, N., & Dhillon, I. S. (2014). Inductive matrix completion for predicting gene-disease associations. *Bioinformatics (Oxford, England)*, *30*(12), 60–68. doi:10.1093/bioinformatics/btu269 PMID:24932006

Newman, M. E. (2004). Fast algorithm for detecting community structure in networks. *Physical Review. E*, *69*(6). doi:10.1103/PhysRevE.69.066133 PMID:15244693

Pandey, V. C., Jadoun, V. K., Gupta, N., Niazi, K., & Swarnkar, A. (2018). Improved Fireworks algorithm with chaotic sequence operator for large-scale non-convex economic load dispatch problem. *Arabian Journal for Science*, *43*(6), 2919–2929. doi:10.100713369-017-2956-6

Peri, S., Navarro, J. D., Amanchy, R., Kristiansen, T. Z., Jonnalagadda, C. K., Surendranath, V., ... Gronborg, M. (2003). Development of human protein reference database as an initial platform for approaching systems biology in humans. *Genome Research*, *13*(10), 2363–2371. doi:10.1101/gr.1680803 PMID:14525934

Prelić, A., Bleuler, S., Zimmermann, P., Wille, A., Bühlmann, P., Gruissem, W., ... Zitzler, E. (2006). A systematic comparison and evaluation of biclustering methods for gene expression data. *Bioinformatics (Oxford, England)*, *22*(9), 1122–1129. doi:10.1093/bioinformatics/btl060 PMID:16500941

Szklarczyk, D., Gable, A. L., Lyon, D., Junge, A., Wyder, S., Huerta-Cepas, J., ... Bork, P. (2018). STRING v11: Protein–protein association networks with increased coverage, supporting functional discovery in genome-wide experimental datasets. *Nucleic Acids Research*, *47*(D1), D607–D613. doi:10.1093/nar/gky1131 PMID:30476243

Tan, Y., & Zhu, Y. (2010). Fireworks algorithm for optimization. *Proceedings International Conference in Swarm Intelligence*, (pp. 355-364). Berlin, Germany: Springer.

Tian, Z., Guo, M., Wang, C., Xing, L., Wang, L., & Zhang, Y. (2017). Constructing an integrated gene similarity network for the identification of disease genes. *Journal of Biomedical Semantics*, *8*(1), 32. doi:10.118613326-017-0141-1 PMID:29297379

Tuba, M., Bacanin, N., & Alihodzic, A. (2015, April 21-22). *Multilevel image thresholding by fireworks algorithm.* Paper presented at the 2015 25th International Conference Radioelektronika (RADIOELEKTRONIKA).

Van Driel, M. A., Bruggeman, J., Vriend, G., Brunner, H. G., & Leunissen, J. A. (2006). A text-mining analysis of the human phenome. *European Journal of Human Genetics*, *14*(5), 535–542. doi:10.1038j. ejhg.5201585 PMID:16493445

Vanunu, O., Magger, O., Ruppin, E., Shlomi, T., & Sharan, R. (2010). Associating genes and protein complexes with disease via network propagation. *PLoS Computational Biology*, *6*(1). doi:10.1371/ journal.pcbi.1000641 PMID:20090828

Xiang, Z., Yang, Y., Ma, X., & Ding, W. (2003). Microarray expression profiling: Analysis and applications. *Current Opinion in Drug Discovery & Development*, *6*(3), 384–395. PMID:12833672

Xiao, Y., Zhang, J., & Deng, L. (2017). Prediction of lncRNA-protein interactions using HeteSim scores based on heterogeneous networks. *Scientific Reports*, *7*(1), 3664. doi:10.103841598-017-03986-1 PMID:28623317

Xie, C., Yuan, J., Li, H., Li, M., Zhao, G., Bu, D., ... Zhao, Y. (2013). NONCODEv4: Exploring the world of long non-coding RNA genes. *Nucleic Acids Research*, *42*(D1), D98–D103. doi:10.1093/nar/ gkt1222 PMID:24285305

Xie, M., Hwang, T., & Kuang, R. (2012). Prioritizing disease genes by bi-random walk. *Proceedings Pacific-Asia Conference on Knowledge Discovery and Data Mining*. Berlin, Germany: Springer.

Yang, J., Wang, W., Wang, H., & Yu, P. (2002). /spl delta/-clusters: capturing subspace correlation in a large data set. *Proceedings 18th International Conference on Data Engineering*. 10.1109/ICDE.2002.994771

Yang, X.-S. (2010). *Nature-inspired metaheuristic algorithms*. Luniver Press.

Yin, L., Qiu, J., & Gao, S. (2018). Biclustering of gene expression data using Cuckoo Search and genetic algorithm. *International Journal of Pattern Recognition and Artificial Intelligence*, *32*(11). doi:10.1142/ S0218001418500398

Yongge, W. U. (2013). Function of lncRNAs and approaches to lncRNA-protein interactions. *Science China. Life Sciences*, *56*(10), 876–885. doi:10.100711427-013-4553-6 PMID:24091684

Yu, G., Li, F., Qin, Y., Bo, X., Wu, Y., & Wang, S. (2010). GOSemSim: An R package for measuring semantic similarity among GO terms and gene products. *Bioinformatics (Oxford, England)*, *26*(7), 976–978. doi:10.1093/bioinformatics/btq064 PMID:20179076

Zhang, W., Qu, Q., Zhang, Y., & Wang, W. (2018). The linear neighborhood propagation method for predicting long non-coding RNA–protein interactions. *Neurocomputing*, *273*(1), 526–534. doi:10.1016/j. neucom.2017.07.065

Zhang, Y., Lei, X., & Tan, Y. (2017). Firefly Clustering Method for Mining Protein Complexes. *Proceedings International Conference on Swarm Intelligence*. 10.1007/978-3-319-61824-1_65

Zheng, S., Janecek, A., & Tan, Y. (2013, June 20-23). Enhanced Fireworks Algorithm. *Proceedings 2013 IEEE Congress on Evolutionary Computation*. 10.1109/CEC.2013.6557813

Zhu, R., Li, G., Liu, J.-X., Dai, L.-Y., & Guo, Y. (2019). ACCBN: ant-Colony-clustering-based bipartite network method for predicting long non-coding RNA–protein interactions. *BMC Bioinformatics*, *20*(1), 16. doi:10.118612859-018-2586-3 PMID:30626319

ADDITIONAL READING

Lei, X., Ding, Y., Fujita, H., & Zhang, A. (2016). Identification of dynamic protein complexes based on fruit fly optimization algorithm. *Knowledge-Based Systems*, *105*, 270–277. doi:10.1016/j.knosys.2016.05.019

Lei, X., Fang, M., & Fujita, H. (2019). Moth–flame optimization-based algorithm with synthetic dynamic PPI networks for discovering protein complexes. *Knowledge-Based Systems*, *172*, 76–85. doi:10.1016/j.knosys.2019.02.011

Lei, X., Wang, F., Wu, F. X., Zhang, A., & Pedrycz, W. (2016). Protein complex identification through Markov clustering with firefly algorithm on dynamic protein–protein interaction networks. *Information Sciences*, *329*, 303–316. doi:10.1016/j.ins.2015.09.028

Lei, X., Yang, X., & Fujita, H. (2019). Random walk based method to identify essential proteins by integrating network topology and biological characteristics. *Knowledge-Based Systems*, *167*, 53–67. doi:10.1016/j.knosys.2019.01.012

Lei, X., & Zhang, Y. (2019). Predicting disease-genes based on network information loss and protein complexes in heterogeneous network. *Information Sciences*, *479*, 386–400. doi:10.1016/j.ins.2018.12.008

Lei, X., Zhang, Y., Cheng, S., Wu, F. X., & Pedrycz, W. (2018). Topology potential based seed-growth method to identify protein complexes on dynamic PPI data. *Information Sciences*, *425*, 140–153. doi:10.1016/j.ins.2017.10.013

Tan, Y. (Ed.). (2018). *Swarm Intelligence:Innovation, New Algorithms and Methods*. London, United Kingdom: IET.

Zhao, J., Lei, X., & Wu, F. X. (2017). Predicting protein complexes in weighted dynamic PPI networks based on ICSC. *Complexity*, *2017*, 2017. doi:10.1155/2017/4120506

KEY TERMS AND DEFINITIONS

Biclustering: A data mining technique which cluster information into a matrix by assigning the rows and columns of the matrix at the same time.

Disease-genes: Genes that are closely related during the development of the disease.

Fireworks Algorithm: Heuristic intelligent optimization algorithm by simulating fireworks explosion

Gene Expression Matrix: The rows of the gene expression matrix represent the expression of genes, and the columns represent different conditions or samples.

Gene Ontology: Gene ontology is an ontology widely used in the field of bioinformatics. It covers three aspects of biology: cellular components, molecular functions, and biological processes.

Graph Clustering: The goal of graph clustering is to find the community structure. The nodes in the same community are closely related to each other, while the nodes in different communities are relatively sparse.

Heterogeneous Networks: The nodes in the network have different kinds or properties, and they are connected to each other.

lncRNA-Protein Interactions: Mutual regulatory relationship between lncRNA and protein.

Chapter 12

Increasing Energy Efficiency by Optimizing the Electrical Infrastructure of a Railway Line Using Fireworks Algorithm

David Roch-Dupré

Comillas Pontifical University, Spain

Tad Gonsalves

Sophia University, Japan

ABSTRACT

This chapter proposes the application of a discrete version of the Fireworks Algorithm (FWA) and a novel PSO-FWA hybrid algorithm to optimize the energy efficiency of a metro railway line. This optimization consists in determining the optimal configuration of the Energy Storage Systems (ESSs) to install in a railway line, including their number, location, and power (kW). The installation of the ESSs will improve the energy efficiency of the system by incrementing the use of the regenerated energy produced by the trains in the braking phases, as the ESSs will store the excess of regenerated energy and return it to the system when necessary. The results for this complex optimization problem produced by the two algorithms are excellent and authors prove that the novel PSO-FWA algorithm proposed in this chapter outperforms the standard FWA.

1. INTRODUCTION

Most real-world optimization problems deal with a large number of decision variables. These multi-dimensional problems being NP hard cannot be solve in reasonable amount of time. In recent years, the application of metaheuristic algorithms to solve complex optimization problems has shown a great deal of success. The metaheuristic techniques differ from the mathematical programming techniques in that they do not use the gradient of the objective function. The scalability, robustness, rapid convergence, and

DOI: 10.4018/978-1-7998-1659-1.ch012

Copyright © 2020, IGI Global. Copying or distributing in print or electronic forms without written permission of IGI Global is prohibited.

domain-independence of the meta-heuristic algorithms make them an attractive choice for optimization applications in diverse field (Vasant, 2013).

Most of the meta-heuristic algorithms are nature-inspired. Rather than follow a rigid and rigorous mathematical formulation, they solve the problems by using a set of operators which are computational metaphors of natural processes. Some of the prominent metaheuristic techniques are based on Swarm Intelligence. Social insects such as ants, bees, termites, and wasps can be viewed as powerful problem-solving systems with sophisticated collective intelligence. Composed of simple interacting agents, this intelligence lies in the networks of interactions among individuals and between individuals and the environment (Bonabeau, Dorigo, Marco, Theraulaz & Théraulaz, 1999; Eberhart, Shi, & Kennedy, 2001).

Particle swarm optimization (PSO) and Fireworks Algorithm (FWA) are two robust Swarm Intelligence optimization algorithms. This chapter introduces a novel hybrid PSO-FWA algorithm designed to handle a complex engineering optimization in the railway energy sector. PSO imitates the social behavior of insects, birds, or fish swarming together to hunt for food. It is a population-based approach that maintains a set of candidate solutions, called particles, which move within the search space. In every iteration, the exploration of the search space is guided by a combination of the personal best solution of a particle (pbest) and the swarm best solution (gbest). PSO implementation is intuitive, it relies on very few external control parameters, and delivers a rapid convergence (Shi, 2001, May; Shi & Eberhart, 2001, May; Schutte & Groenwold, 2005; Clerc, 2010; Liu, Yang & Wang, 2010).

The Fireworks Algorithm (FWA) is a recent Swarm Intelligence optimization algorithm. Deriving its inspiration from the fireworks exploding in the night sky, the FWA is found to be a competitive meta-heuristic algorithm (Tan & Zhu, 2010). The FWA algorithm begins with random initial positions of N fireworks. Before the fireworks explode generating sparks, the amplitude and the number of the explosion sparks are calculated. Fireworks with higher fitness values will have a smaller explosion amplitude and a larger number of explosion sparks, while fireworks with lower fitness values will have a larger explosion amplitude and a smaller number of explosion sparks. In addition, random sparks are also generated based on a Gaussian mutation process. A new population of N fireworks is selected at the end of each iteration. This may include the original fireworks, as well as the regular and Gaussian sparks. The elitist strategy is maintained by always inserting the current best location in the new population.

The original FWA has gone through some significant changes over the years. For instance, adaptive FWA (Li, Zheng & Tan, 2014, July), dynamic search FWA (Zheng, Janecek, Li & Tan, 2014, July), guiding spark FWA (Li, Zheng & Tan, 2016), FWA with differential mutation (Yu, Kelley, Zheng & Tan, 2014, July), enhanced FWA (Zhang, Zheng, Zhang & Chen, 2015; Liu, Zhang & Zhu, 2017, April), and discrete FWA (Luo, Xu & Tan, 2018, July) are found in literature. FWA for multi-modal optimization (Li & Tan, 2017), FWA for multi-objective optimization (Mnif & Bouamama, 2017, September; Taowei, Yiming, Kun & Duan, 2018, October) biogeography-based hybrid (Zhang, Zhang & Zheng, 2014, July), hybrid FWA with differential evolution (Zheng, Xu, Ling & Chen, 2015), hybrid with Simulated Annealing (Ye & Wen, 2017, December), hybrid with Generating Set Search (Kim et al., 2017) have also been proposed. FWA optimization applications in power grid systems (Qian & Hu, 2019, March; Lei, Fang, Gao, Jia & Pan, 2018, October; Huang, Li, Zhu, Wang, Zheng & Wang, 2016, September), routing problems (Hu, Wang, Wan, Wang & Hu, 2018, October) and medical systems (Shi, Xu, Zhu, Lu, Zhang, Xu & Zhang, 2015, October; Shi, Xu, Zhu & Lu, 2016, October) are also proposed in the FWA literature.

This chapter proposes the application of a discrete version of the Fireworks Algorithm (FWA) and a novel PSO-FWA hybrid algorithm to optimize the energy efficiency of a metro railway line. The optimization consists in determining the optimal configuration of the Energy Storage Systems (ESSs) to install in a railway line, including their number, location, and power (kW). The two algorithms independently deliver the global optimal solution of the complex engineering optimization problem and the novel PSO-FWA algorithm proposed in this chapter outperforms the standard FWA.

This chapter is organized as follows: in order to give a small insight on the background in which the optimization algorithms are going to be applied, Section 2 briefly explains how installing ESSs increases the energy efficiency of railway systems. Section 3 describes the ESS optimization problem. Section 4 introduces the discrete FWA algorithm along with the variations that we have introduced. Section 5 explains our newly designed PSO-FWA hybrid algorithm. Section 6 explains the experimental design. Section 7 compares the results produced by the two algorithms, discusses their importance and relevance. The chapter closes with a short conclusion in Section 8.

2. ESSS INSTALLATION TO IMPROVE RAILWAY LINE ENERGY EFFICIENCY

As stated in (Roch-Dupré et al., 2020), increasing the efficiency of DC-electrified railway systems is crucial in the fight against climate change. There are several possibilities to increase efficiency, going from the design of more efficient trains (Kondo, 2010) to the improvement of the railway electrical infrastructure (López-López et al., 2014; Takagi, 2012; Ratniyomchai, Hillmansen, & Tricoli, 2013; Cornic, 2010, October), passing through the study of the strategies to optimize the traffic operation (Zhao et al., 2017; Fernandez-Rodriguez et al., 2015). Many of them are based on the re-utilization of the regenerated energy, generated during the braking phases by the regenerative braking system of the trains. An effective use of this regenerated energy can lead to significant reductions in energy consumption.

As explained in (Roch-Dupré et al., 2018), if there are neither Reversible Substations (RSs), nor ESSs installed in the DC-electrified railway system, the regenerated energy can only be consumed by other trains which are motoring at the same instants that the regenerated energy is being produced. In case of not being able to use part of the regenerated energy, the excess must be dissipated in the rheostats (on-board resistors), which supposes a considerable loss of energy efficiency.

Among the installation of RSs or ESSs, this book chapter will focus on the second option. The installation of the ESSs will improve the energy efficiency of the system by incrementing the use of the regenerated energy produced by the trains in the braking phases, as the ESSs will store the excess of regenerated energy (which otherwise would be lost in the rheostats) and give it back to the system when necessary (Gao et al., 2015; Lee et al., 2013; Roch-Dupré, López-López, Pecharromán, Cucala & Fernández-Cardador, 2017; Iannuzzi, Ciccarelli & Lauria, 2012; Khodaparastan, Dutta, Saleh & Mohamed, 2019).

There is some research in the literature that has studied the optimal location and sizing for the ESSs by the application of optimization algorithms. Some authors use nature-inspired optimization algorithms, in particular, (Xia, Chen, Yang, Lin & Wang, 2015) propose the Genetic Algorithm (GA), while (Calderaro, Galdi, Graber & Piccolo, 2015) proposes the PSO. There are also some authors who apply mathematical optimization models, such as the nonlinear optimization based on Lagrange multipliers (LGM) proposed by (Ratniyomchai, Hillmansen & Tricoli, 2015, June) or the mixed integer linear programming (MILP) proposed by (de la Torre, Sánchez-Racero, Aguado, Reyes & Martínez, 2014).

3. OPTIMIZATION PROBLEM

The optimization algorithms proposed will try to find the optimum ESSs configuration. Therefore, each spark contains the characteristics of a given configuration. The structure of a given spark sp_i is:

$$sp_i = \begin{bmatrix} pow_1 \cdots pow_k \cdots pow_N \end{bmatrix}$$

Where:

- pow_k is the power (kW) for the ESS installed in location k. The values of this variable are discrete, going from 0 kW (no ESS installed in location k) to 3000 kW, in steps of 500 kW.
- N is the number of potential locations for installing the ESS. For the case study line, which is a hypothetical railway line based on a real one (but with some modifications in order to make it more complex from the point of view of the decision-making of the optimization algorithms for improving the infrastructure), every location of a Traction Substation is considered as a candidate position to install the ESS. As there are 11 Traction Substations, $N = 11$.

It must be noted that the capacity of the ESS will be set to 20 kWh. This value allows not losing potential energy savings due to lack of storage capacity. It has not been included in the formulation of the optimization problem as a variable of decision because its impact is very low compared to the power. This is due to the fact that the cost associated with the power of the ESS is more than 10 times higher than the cost associated with the capacity, as can be seen when multiplying the unitary costs for power and capacity proposed by (González-Gil, Palacin & Batty, 2013) by the reasonable ranges of power and capacity sizes to install ([500-3000 kW] and [5-30 kWh], respectively).

The optimal solution is the one that raises the highest Net Present Value (NPV) of the installation. Therefore, the fitness function for a given spark sp_i is the NPV for its associated ESSs configuration. The equation of the fitness function is in (1).

$$NPV(sp_i) = \sum_{t=1}^{T} \frac{\left(E_{Raw}^{ANNUAL} - E_{ESSs}^{ANNUAL}(sp_i) \right) \cdot e_{cost}}{(1 + wacc)^t} - C_0(sp_i)$$

$$s.t \ C_0(sp_i) \leq budget \tag{1}$$

Where:

- E_{Raw}^{ANNUAL} is the annual energy consumption without any infrastructure improvement. This value is obtained from simulating the case study line without any infrastructure improvement.
- $E_{ESSs}^{ANNUAL}(sp_i)$ is the annual energy consumption obtained with the ESSs configuration determined by the spark sp_i. This value is obtained from simulating the case study line with the infrastructure improvement associated with spark sp_i.

- e_{cost} is the energy price. This parameter allows transforming the energy saving, which is computed by comparing the total energy consumption with and without infrastructure improvement $\left(E_{Raw}^{ANNUAL} - E_{ESSs}^{ANNUAL}(sp_i)\right)$, into economic cash flows.
- $C_0(sp_i)$ is the installation cost of the ESSs configuration determined by the spark sp_i.
- *wacc* is he Weighted Average Cost of Capital.
- T is the investment payback time.
- *budget* is the maximum amount of money available to undertake the infrastructure improvement.

The reason why the NPV has been selected as fitness function is that it is capable of finding a balance between what is important from the environmental point of view- the energy saving - and what is important for the railway operator - economically justifying the investment in the ESSs and obtaining benefits from it. The investment will be economically profitable provided the NPV is positive. Therefore, the optimization algorithms will try to determine the ESSs configuration with the highest NPV (the higher the NPV, the better the balance between the energy savings and the cost of the installation).

4. DISCRETE FIREWORKS ALGORITHM

The FWA used for this optimization is based on the standard FWA defined by (Tan & Zhu, 2010), but has been discretized by the application of the following rules.

Design of Fireworks Explosion

"Normal" Explosion

The original formula for the amplitude of the explosion is applied to obtain a first continuous value, Ac_i for firework i, which then will be normalized and discretized into two possible values:

- 500 kW (the smallest step for power) when the firework is within the xth percentile of the smallest continuous radius (which is equivalent to be within the x% of fireworks with the best fitness).
- 1000 kW (the next step for power) when the firework is out of the xth percentile of the smallest continuous radius (which is equivalent to be within the (100-x)% of fireworks with the worst fitness).

After this transformation from continuous to discrete, each firework j will have an associated discrete amplitude of explosion Ad_j. The algorithm to compute the displacement in location k of spark i is replaced by (2).

$$sp_i^k = fw_j^k + Ad_j \cdot randsample(-Ad_i : minimum\ step : +Ad_i) \tag{2}$$

Where:

- fw_j^k is the value for location k of firework j.

- sp_i^k is the value for location k of spark i (exploded from firework j).
- *randsample* is a logical operator that only selects one position of the vector $(-Ad_i : minimum\ step : +Ad_i)$
- *minimum step* is the smallest step allowed (500 kW for power).

"Gaussian" Explosion

The algorithm to compute the displacement in location k of spark i is replaced by (3).

while $g < 0$

$g = Gaussian\ (1,1)$

end

$$sp_i^k = round\left(fw_j^k \cdot g \Big/ minimum\ step \right) \cdot minimum\ step \tag{3}$$

Where g is the coefficient of Gaussian explosion. It must be noted that g must not be negative because the power cannot be negative, just 0 (which means no installation of an ESS in that location).

Correction of Infeasibilities

If dimension k of spark i (from "Normal" or "Gaussian" explosion) crosses the maximum or minimum limits in power, the maximum or minimum power, respectively, is set for dimension k of spark i.

If a change in dimension k of spark i violates the maximum budget constraint, the change applied is not the original one, but the maximum admissible change. This will result in reducing the ESSs' number or power, so that the ESSs configuration resulting from that change does not violate the budget constraints.

Selection of Firework Locations

The best current solution is included for the next generation of fireworks. The n-1 remaining fireworks are selected based on their distance to the other fireworks and sparks so as to keep the diversity (Tan & Zhu, 2010). The distance measure is computed according to the Manhattan distance, as this measure fits extremely well with our optimization problem, where the variables of decision have two dimensions: location and size of the ESSs to install.

5. HYBRID FWA

Just like the Fireworks algorithm, the Particle Swarm Optimization (PSO) is another metaphor in the swarm intelligence paradigm. It has become a popular meta-heuristic algorithm in the optimization domain and has been successfully applied to optimization problems ranging from business, engineering, healthcare, etc. Based on the prey-gathering behavior of swarms of bees, birds and schools of fish, PSO optimally balances exploration and exploitation. Simplicity in implementation, negligible computational overhead and rapid convergence have made it one of the outstanding swarm intelligence paradigms.

Each particle maintains a history of its flying over the search space. In every cycle of flying, the swarm also records two important pieces of information – pbest (the best position found by a particle in the course of flying) and gbest (the best position found by the swarm as a whole). These two particles act as beacons to guide the flying of the rest of the particles towards the global optimum during the search.

According to the "no free lunch" theorem, PSO also has its downsides – the tendency of the flying particles to a rapid convergence often gets them trapped in local optima. Various methods have been proposed to eject the particles from the local trap and put them on a flying trajectory towards the global optimum.

The hybrid FWA (PSO-FWA) algorithm tries to combine the PSO with the FWA in order to outperform the results obtained by the FWA. In this new algorithm, each particle carries with it a firework as a payload as it flies over the search space. Each particle ignites its payload firework from the position it has found in each iteration. Normal sparks are then generated according to the equations of the FWA. The best sparks from each firework are then recorded. In the next stage, each particle flies to the location of the best spark. The particle velocities and positions are updated according to the PSO equations. The PSO-FWA iterates through the above cycles for any desired number of times.

In the PSO-FWA hybrid proposed in this chapter, the PSO acts as a rapid explorer of the search space, while the FWA acts as an intense exploiter of the promising regions found by the PSO during every cycle of the search. The pseudo-code of the hybrid algorithms is shown below in Table 1:

Table 1.

Generate P number of particle positions *Generate particle velocities*	*Initialization*

While the termination condition is not met:
    Evaluate each particle position
    Generate S number of sparks from each particle position using FWA equations
    Evaluate the sparks
    For every particle:
        Choose the best spark from the local cluster produced by the particle
        If the best spark is better than the parent particle then
            Fly the particle to the location of the best spark
        End If
	local search

End For
Determine pbest
Determine gbest
Update particle velocities using PSO Equations
Update particle positions using PSO Equations
End while
	global search

6. EXPERIMENTAL DESIGN

Methodology

In order to find the optimal configuration, the energy saving associated with each configuration tested by the algorithms must be evaluated before transforming it into economic cash flows and computing its associated Net Present Value. The energy saving will be computed with a very realistic multi-train electrical simulator (for more details about the electrical simulator see (Roch-Dupré, Cucala, Pecharromán, López-López & Fernández-Cardador, 2018; Roch-Dupré, López-López, Pecharromán, Cucala & Fernández-Cardador, 2017; López-López, Pecharromán, Fernández-Cardador & Cucala, 2014).

As it is out of the scope of this book chapter, the multi-train electrical simulator will be considered as a "black box". The communication between the algorithms and the simulator will have the following steps:

1. The algorithm will give the configuration of the ESSs installation to be tested as the input data for the simulator.
2. After performing the electrical simulation, the simulator will give the energy saving associated with that specific configuration as the output data to the FWA.
3. The energy saving will be transformed into economic cash flows and the Net Present Value of the configuration to be tested will be computed with (1).

Criteria Used for Presenting and Comparing the Results

For presenting and comparing our results we are going to use the area within two curves:

Curve A: it is determined by the subtraction of the average of all the instances run for a specific algorithm and its standard deviation. The equation of Curve A is defined in (4).

$$Curve\ A(iter) = \mu(iter) - \sqrt{\frac{1}{no._{inst} - 1} \cdot \sum_{i=1}^{no._{inst}} | Fitness\,(iter, inst) - \mu(iter) |^2} \qquad (4)$$

Where:

- $\mu(iter)$ is the average fitness of all the instances in iteration *iter* and is defined in (5).

$$\mu(iter) = \frac{1}{no._{inst}} \cdot \sum_{i=1}^{no._{inst}} Fitness\,(iter, inst) \qquad (5)$$

- $no._{inst}$ is the total number of instances run for a specific algorithm.
- *Fitness*(*iter*, *inst*) is the fitness value obtained by the algorithm in iteration *iter* of instance *inst*.

Curve B: it is determined by the addition of the average of all the instances run for a specific algorithm and its standard deviation. The equation of Curve B is defined in (6).

$$Curve B(iter) = \mu(iter) + \sqrt{\frac{1}{no._{inst} - 1} \cdot \sum_{i=1}^{no._{inst}} | Fitness(iter, inst) - \mu(iter) |^2} \qquad (6)$$

The reason why we are not directly going to use average value is that it is extremely sensitive to outliers where the number of iterations required to achieve the optimum is very high. Therefore, using the average would create confusion about the speed of convergence of an algorithm, as it would not achieve the optimum fitness until this value had been achieved in all the instances (including the outliers with very slow convergence).

The information provided by the area between curves A and B is very complete, as it determines the normal behavior of the algorithm: the expected fitness value for a specific iteration will be inside this area. As will be seen in the different figures presented in this section, the width of the area (the distance between the two curves for a specific iteration) is reduced with the number of iterations and is only null (which means that curve A and B are the same) when all the instances (including the outliers) have achieved the optimum value.

Therefore, for analyzing the results and, more particularly, the speed of convergence of each algorithm, we must not focus on the iteration at which the area is null, but on the iteration from which the area is small enough in order to consider that the optimum is achieved in a normal situation (excluding the outliers). In order to obtain very robust results, we have established that only when the difference between both curves is less than 1% we can consider that the optimum is achieved in normal situation. The iteration from which the 1% of difference between both curves is achieved will be called Ref_{ITER}.

Scenarios Used in the Comparison and Parameters

Two main scenarios will be used for the comparisons:

- **Scenario 1: Big population.** A maximum number of 150 sparks can be set off in each iteration.
- **Scenario 2: Small population.** A maximum number of 75 sparks can be set off in each iteration. As the population has been reduced to half, this scenario will be much more demanding for the algorithms to find the optimum.

Table 2 provides the parameters used for the algorithms in each scenario for designing the fireworks explosion.

As explained previously, the velocities and positions of the particles "carrying" the fireworks in the are updated according to the PSO equations. The parameters for updating the velocities are the same in both the scenarios:

- Inertia weight (w): 0.5.
- Personal attractor (c1): 0.2.
- Global attractor (c2): 0.3.

Finally, the value of the parameters for the fitness function are the same in both scenarios and defined below:

Table 2. Parameters used for designing the fireworks explosion in the FWA and PSO-FWA

	Scenario 1	Scenario 2
Max. number of sparks	150	75
Number of locations to sett off sparks (n)	15	8
Constant parameter a of Equation (3) From (Tan & Zhu, 2010)	0.0067	0.0125
Constant parameter b of Equation (3) From (Tan & Zhu, 2010)	0.1	0.1875
x^{th} percentile for determining the radius of explosion	40	
Percentage of "normal sparks" (against total number of sparks)	93%	
Percentage of "gaussian sparks" (against total number of sparks)	7%	

- e_{cost} : 0.0642 €/kWh. This is a realistic value obtained from real market energy price and the energy tolls. For more details about the procedure to compute the energy cost, see (Roch-Dupré et al., 2017).
- $C_0(sp_i)$: this value is computed by adding the total power and capacity installed and multiplying it by their unitary costs. The unitary costs for the electrochemical double layer capacitors(EDLCs) - the storage technology chosen for the ESSs - are depicted in Table 3 and have been obtained from the range of values proposed by (González-Gil, Palacin & Batty, 2013).

Table 3. Unitary costs for power and capacity

Capital cost for energy [€/kWh]	Capital cost for power [€/kW]
270	150

- *wacc* : 2.5%.
- T :15 years. This is a very reasonable estimation for the ESSs life according to the International Renewable Energy Agency (IRENA).
- *budget* : for the case study, a budget near to €500,000 has been selected, as it is flexible enough to allow a high number of different configurations to be installed, and restrictive enough so as not to allow very expensive configurations, which are not likely to be accepted by the railway operators. For real implementation, this value must be set by the railway operators.

Criteria to Select the Number of Instances Run for Each Algorithm

The time required to run each algorithm and reach the optimum (all the algorithms have reached the optimum but with different speeds) is very considerable, going from 2 to more than 12 hours. Therefore, it is important to run each algorithm a number of instances big enough to show the representative behavior of the algorithm (especially regarding the speed of convergence) but without spending too much computation time. This balance has been found with 20 instances. The justification for selecting this number of instances is in Figure 1.

The subplots of the first column compare the area between curves A and B when running 10 and 15 instances of each algorithm in each scenario. The subplots of the second column do the same but with the results from running 15 and 20 instances. Finally, the subplots of the third column represent the value obtained for Ref_{ITER} when running 10, 15 and 20 instances of each algorithm in each scenario.

Figure 1. Influence of the number of instances

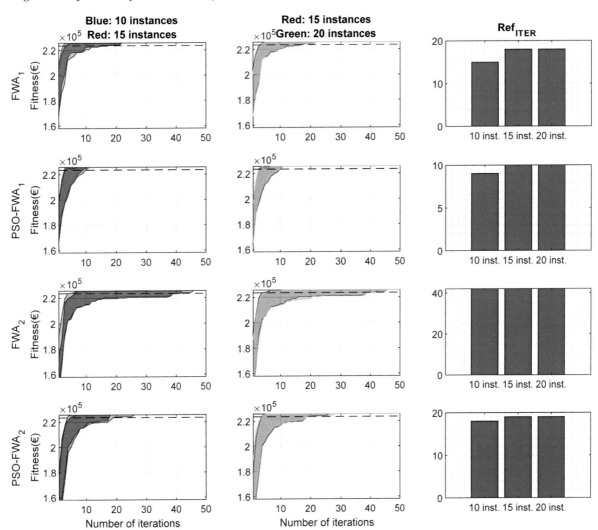

All the subplots of the same row refers to the same algorithm and scenario:

- First row: FWA in Scenario 1 (FWA1).
- Second row: PSO-FWA in Scenario 1 (PSO-FWA1).

- Third row: FWA in Scenario 2 (FWA2).
- Fourth row: PSO-FWA in Scenario 2 (PSO-FWA2).

Analyzing Figure 1, while a small difference can be appreciated between the areas obtained with 10 and 15 instances (first column of subplots), the difference is almost negligible between the results obtained with 15 and 20 instances. Furthermore, when comparing the values of Ref_{ITER}, it can be seen that there is no difference between 15 and 20 instances, while some values of Ref_{ITER} slightly differ when only 10 instances have been run.

Consequently, evaluating more than 20 instances is not significant, as the results are stabilized with this number of instances.

7. RESULTS

As previously stated, both algorithms have achieved the optimum fitness in all the instances run and in all the scenarios. This fitness corresponds to a Net Present Value of €225,814 and it is achieved when installing ESSs of 500 kW in locations 2, 3 and 6. This section will not focus on analyzing the solution itself, but on the performance of the Fireworks Algorithm (FWA) and the Hybrid Fireworks Algorithm (PSO-FWA) proposed in this book chapter.

Comparison of FWAs and PSO-FWAs in Scenario 1 (FWA1, PSO-FWA1) and Scenario 2 (FWA2, PSO-FWA2)

Figure 2 and Figure 3 shows the results of running 20 instances of the FWA and the PSO-FWA in Scenarios 1 and 2, respectively.

Figure 2. Performance of FWA and PSO-FWA in Scenario 1

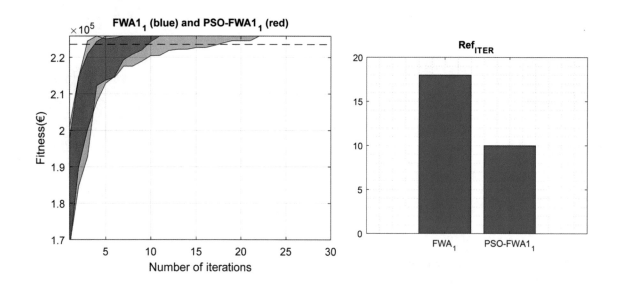

The PSO-FWA in Scenario 1 clearly outperforms the FWA, both in:

- Initial speed: the area of the PSO-FWA evolves much more vertically than the area of the FWA, achieving the optimum faster.
- Speed of convergence: determined by the value of Ref_{ITER} (18 iterations required by the FWA vs 10 iterations required by the PSO-FWA) and represented in the left subplot by the moment when the area is between the dashed black line and the maximum fitness and in the right subplot by the bar values.

The difference in the performance of the FWA and the PSO-FWA is even greater in Scenario 2, which is more demanding for the algorithms, as the number of maximum sparks to set off has been reduced to half. Specially, the big difference in the speed of convergence must be highlighted (42 iterations required by the FWA vs 19 iterations required by the PSO-FWA).

Figure 3. Performance of FWA and PSO-FWA in scenario 2

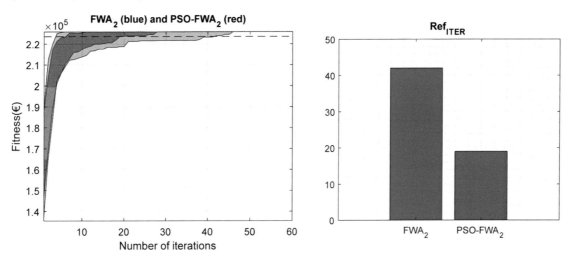

Parameter Tuning of PSO-FWA2 and Comparison With FWA1

Additionally, for the more demanding scenario (Scenario 2), some parameter tuning has been performed with the PSO-FWA, which is the main object of study of this book chapter. This parameter tuning will focus on the "Selection of Firework Locations", which is the part of the algorithm where the FWA and the PSO-FWA differs and the reason why the PSO-FWA outperforms the FWA. As stated in Section 5, the particle velocities and positions are updated according to the PSO equations. The update of the velocity is directly affected by the three parameters defined in Section 6: the inertia weight (w), the personal attractor (c1) and the global attractor (c2). The values for these parameters have been selected for our previous experience when applying the PSO to this optimization problem. Nevertheless, as stated in Section 5, there may be a tendency of the flying particles (which carry the fireworks in the PSO-FWA) to a rapid convergence and they can be trapped in local optima. In order to try to improve

Table 4. Values of w, c1 and c2 in the parameter tuning of the PSO-FWA in Scenario 2

	Name	OR	J_{2007}	LDI
	Description	Original values	Values proposed by (Jiang, M., Luo, Y. P., & Yang, S. Y., 2007)	Linear Decreasing Inertia Weight proposed by (Xin, J., Chen, G., & Hai, Y., 2009) $w = w_{max} - \dfrac{w_{max} - w_{min}}{iter_{max}} \cdot iter$
Parameters	w	0.5	0.715	$w_{max} = 0.9$ $w_{min} = 0.4$ $iter_{max} = 60$
	c_1	0.2	1.7	0.2
	c_2	0.3	1.7	0.3

the performance of the mechanism for "Selection of Firework Locations" in the PSO-FWA, we have applied some parameter tuning to w, c1 and c2 (see Table 4).

It can be seen that just using the linear decreasing inertia can slightly improve the speed of convergence of the PSO-FWA, as the value of Ref_{ITER} in Figure 4 (the PSO-FWA with the LDI parameters requires one iteration less than the PSO-FWA with the original parameters).

Figure 4. Performance of PSO-FWA in scenario 2 after the parameter tuning

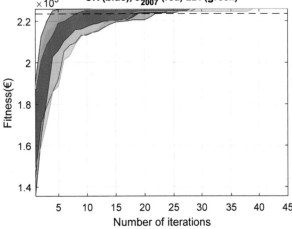
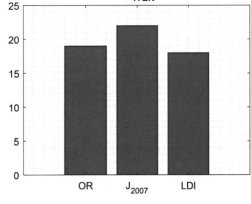

As have been already proved, the PSO-FWA clearly outperforms the FWA with the same population in different scenarios. Therefore, it is also interesting to check if the PSO-FWA with a small population also outperforms the FWA with a big population. In order to make this comparison, the PSO-FWA of Scenario 2 with the parameter tuning LDI (PSO-FWA2-LDI) and the FWA of Scenario 1 (FWA1) have been compared. The result from this comparison is shown in Figure 5.

Figure 5. Performance of FWA with big population (FWA1) and PSO-FWA with small population (PSO-FWA2-LDI)

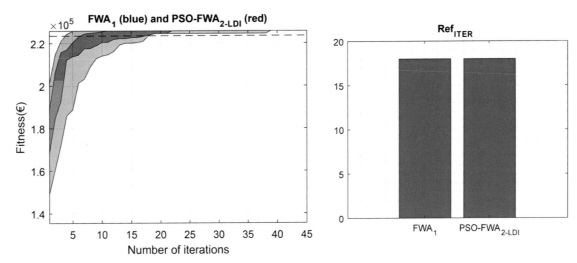

As the population of the FWA is the double of the population of the PSO-FWA, the initial speed is better in FWA1. This can be seen in area between Curves A and B of FWA1, which evolves more vertically than correspondent to PSO-FWA2-LDI. Nevertheless, the speed of convergence is very similar, indeed, the value of *Ref$_{ITER}$* is the same. This proves that the PSO-FWA is much faster than the FWA, as it achieves a speed of convergence similar to the FWA with only half of the FWA population.

8. CONCLUSION

We have verified that these two swarm intelligence algorithms, FWA and PSO-FWA hybrid are suitable for determining the optimal configuration of ESSs to install in the railway line case study. The FWA used in this chapter is based on its standard version and has been discretized in order to fit it to the optimization problem according to the indications provided in Section 4. The novel PSO-FWA proposed in Section 5 is a combination of the discrete FWA and the standard PSO. Some of the salient features of the PSO-FWA hybrid algorithm are as follows:

- PSO engages in exploration, while FWA concentrates on exploitation.
- Particles fly to the locations indicated by the best sparks.
- There is no overhead in calculating distances between pairs of sparks (as in the standard FWA).

Regarding effectiveness, there is no difference between the standard FWA and the PSO-FWA. Nevertheless, there is a big difference in terms of speed of convergence, where the PSO-FWA clearly outperforms the FWA.

- With the same population size in both the algorithms, the PSO-FWA almost doubles the speed of convergence of the standard FWA.

- The PSO-FWA presents a speed of convergence similar to that of the standard FWA with half its population.

Some of the recent variations of FWA have also been used to handle multi-objective optimization problems. As an extension to this study, we plan to design a multi-objective FWA to solve a multi-objective scenario in ESS installation.

REFERENCES

Bonabeau, E., Dorigo, M., Marco, D., Theraulaz, G., & Théraulaz, G. (1999). Swarm intelligence: from natural to artificial systems (No. 1). Oxford University Press.

Calderaro, V., Galdi, V., Graber, G., & Piccolo, A. (2015, March). Optimal siting and sizing of stationary supercapacitors in a metro network using PSO. *Proceedings 2015 IEEE International Conference on Industrial Technology (ICIT)* (pp. 2680-2685). IEEE. 10.1109/ICIT.2015.7125493

Clerc, M. (2010). *Particle swarm optimization* (Vol. 93). John Wiley & Sons.

Cornic, D. (2010, October). Efficient recovery of braking energy through a reversible dc substation. Proceedings *Electrical systems for aircraft, railway, and ship propulsion* (pp. 1–9). IEEE. doi:10.1109/ESARS.2010.5665264

de la Torre, S., Sánchez-Racero, A. J., Aguado, J. A., Reyes, M., & Martínez, O. (2014). Optimal sizing of energy storage for regenerative braking in electric railway systems. *IEEE Transactions on Power Systems*, *30*(3), 1492–1500. doi:10.1109/TPWRS.2014.2340911

Eberhart, R. C., Shi, Y., & Kennedy, J. (2001). *Swarm Intelligence (Morgan Kaufmann series in evolutionary computation)*. Morgan Kaufmann Publishers.

Fernandez-Rodriguez, A., Fernández-Cardador, A., Cucala, A. P., Domínguez, M., & Gonsalves, T. (2015). Design of robust and energy-efficient ATO speed profiles of metropolitan lines considering train load variations and delays. *IEEE Transactions on Intelligent Transportation Systems*, *16*(4), 2061–2071. doi:10.1109/TITS.2015.2391831

Gao, Z., Fang, J., Zhang, Y., Jiang, L., Sun, D., & Guo, W. (2015). Control of urban rail transit equipped with ground-based supercapacitor for energy saving and reduction of power peak demand. *International Journal of Electrical Power & Energy Systems*, *67*, 439–447. doi:10.1016/j.ijepes.2014.11.019

González-Gil, A., Palacin, R., & Batty, P. (2013). Sustainable urban rail systems: Strategies and technologies for optimal management of regenerative braking energy. *Energy Conversion and Management*, *75*, 374–388. doi:10.1016/j.enconman.2013.06.039

Hu, Y., Wang, K., Wan, J., Wang, K., & Hu, X. (2018, October). Multi-Constrained Routing Based on Particle Swarm Optimization and Fireworks Algorithm. *Proceedings IECON 2018-44th Annual Conference of the IEEE Industrial Electronics Society* (pp. 5901-5905). IEEE. 10.1109/IECON.2018.8592907

Huang, X. B., Li, H. B., Zhu, Y. C., Wang, Y. X., Zheng, X. X., & Wang, Y. G. (2016, September). Transmission line icing short-term forecasting based on improved time series analysis by fireworks algorithm. *Proceedings 2016 International Conference on Condition Monitoring and Diagnosis (CMD)* (pp. 643-646). IEEE. 10.1109/CMD.2016.7757904

Iannuzzi, D., Ciccarelli, F., & Lauria, D. (2012). Stationary ultracapacitors storage device for improving energy saving and voltage profile of light transportation networks. *Transportation Research Part C, Emerging Technologies, 21*(1), 321–337. doi:10.1016/j.trc.2011.11.002

Jiang, M., Luo, Y. P., & Yang, S. Y. (2007). Particle swarm optimization-stochastic trajectory analysis and parameter selection. *Swarm intelligence, Focus on ant and particle swarm optimization*, 179-198.

Khodaparastan, M., Dutta, O., Saleh, M., & Mohamed, A. A. (2019). Modeling and simulation of dc electric rail transit systems with wayside energy storage. *IEEE Transactions on Vehicular Technology, 68*(3), 2218–2228. doi:10.1109/TVT.2019.2895026

Kim, D. W., Park, G. J., Lee, J. H., Kim, J. W., Kim, Y. J., & Jung, S. Y. (2017). Hybridization algorithm of fireworks optimization and generating set search for optimal design of IPMSM. *IEEE Transactions on Magnetics, 53*(6), 1–4. doi:10.1109/TMAG.2017.2668608

Kondo, K. (2010). Recent energy saving technologies on railway traction systems. *IEEJ Transactions on Electrical and Electronic Engineering, 5*(3), 298–303. doi:10.1002/tee.20533

Lee, H., Jung, S., Cho, Y., Yoon, D., & Jang, G. (2013). Peak power reduction and energy efficiency improvement with the superconducting flywheel energy storage in electric railway system. *Physica. C, Superconductivity, 494*, 246–249. doi:10.1016/j.physc.2013.04.033

Lei, C., Fang, B., Gao, H., Jia, W., & Pan, W. (2018, October). Short-term power load forecasting based on Least Squares Support Vector Machine optimized by Bare Bones Fireworks algorithm. *Proceedings 2018 IEEE 3rd Advanced Information Technology, Electronic, and Automation Control Conference (IAEAC)* (pp. 2231-2235). IEEE. 10.1109/IAEAC.2018.8577212

Li, J., & Tan, Y. (2017). Loser-out tournament-based fireworks algorithm for multimodal function optimization. *IEEE Transactions on Evolutionary Computation, 22*(5), 679–691. doi:10.1109/TEVC.2017.2787042

Li, J., Zheng, S., & Tan, Y. (2014, July). Adaptive fireworks algorithm. *Proceedings 2014 IEEE Congress on evolutionary computation (CEC)* (pp. 3214-3221). IEEE. 10.1109/CEC.2014.6900418

Li, J., Zheng, S., & Tan, Y. (2016). The effect of information utilization: Introducing a novel guiding spark in the fireworks algorithm. *IEEE Transactions on Evolutionary Computation, 21*(1), 153–166. doi:10.1109/TEVC.2016.2589821

Liu, L., Yang, S., & Wang, D. (2010). Particle swarm optimization with composite particles in dynamic environments. *IEEE Transactions on Systems, Man, and Cybernetics. Part B, Cybernetics, 40*(6), 1634–1648. doi:10.1109/TSMCB.2010.2043527 PMID:20371407

Liu, X., Zhang, X., & Zhu, Q. (2017, April). Enhanced fireworks algorithm for dynamic deployment of wireless sensor networks. *Proceedings 2017 2nd International Conference on Frontiers of Sensors Technologies (ICFST)* (pp. 161-165). IEEE. 10.1109/ICFST.2017.8210494

López-López, Á. J., Abrahamsson, L., Pecharromán, R. R., Fernández-Cardador, A., Cucala, P., Östlund, S., & Söder, L. (2014). *A variable no-load voltage scheme for improving energy efficiency in dc-electrified mass transit systems.* Proceedings *2014 Joint Rail Conference.* American Society of Mechanical Engineers Digital Collection.

López-López, A. J., Pecharromán, R. R., Fernández-Cardador, A., & Cucala, A. P. (2014). Assessment of energy-saving techniques in direct-current-electrified mass transit systems. *Transportation Research Part C, Emerging Technologies, 38,* 85–100. doi:10.1016/j.trc.2013.10.011

Luo, H., Xu, W., & Tan, Y. (2018, July). A discrete fireworks algorithm for solving large-scale travel salesman problem. *Proceedings 2018 IEEE Congress on Evolutionary Computation (CEC)* (pp. 1-8). IEEE. 10.1109/CEC.2018.8477992

Mnif, M., & Bouamama, S. (2017, September). A multi-objective formulation for multimodal transportation network's planning problems. *Proceedings 2017 IEEE International Conference on Service Operations and Logistics, and Informatics (SOLI)* (pp. 144-149). IEEE. 10.1109/SOLI.2017.8120985

Qian, Z., & Hu, C. (2019, March). Optimal Path Selection for Fault Repair Based on Grid GIS Platform and Improved Fireworks Algorithm. *Proceedings 2019 IEEE 3rd Information Technology, Networking, Electronic, and Automation Control Conference (ITNEC)* (pp. 2452-2456). IEEE. 10.1109/ITNEC.2019.8729359

Ratniyomchai, T., Hillmansen, S., & Tricoli, P. (2013). Recent developments and applications of energy storage devices in electrified railways. *IET Electrical Systems in Transportation, 4*(1), 9–20. doi:10.1049/iet-est.2013.0031

Ratniyomchai, T., Hillmansen, S., & Tricoli, P. (2015, June). Energy loss minimisation by optimal design of stationary supercapacitors for light railways. *Proceedings 2015 International Conference on Clean Electrical Power (ICCEP)* (pp. 511-517). IEEE. 10.1109/ICCEP.2015.7177538

Roch-Dupré, D., Cucala, A. P., Pecharromán, R. R., López-López, Á. J., & Fernández-Cardador, A. (2018). Evaluation of the impact that the traffic model used in railway electrical simulation has on the assessment of the installation of a Reversible Substation. *International Journal of Electrical Power & Energy Systems, 102,* 201–210. doi:10.1016/j.ijepes.2018.04.030

Roch-Dupré, D., Cucala, A. P., Pecharromán, R. R., López-López, Á. J., & Fernández-Cardador, A. (2020). Simulation-based assessment of the installation of a Reversible Substation in a railway line, including a realistic model of large traffic perturbations. *International Journal of Electrical Power & Energy Systems, 115.* doi:10.1016/j.ijepes.2019.105476

Roch-Dupré, D., López-López, Á. J., Pecharromán, R. R., Cucala, A. P., & Fernández-Cardador, A. (2017). Analysis of the demand charge in DC railway systems and reduction of its economic impact with Energy Storage Systems. *International Journal of Electrical Power & Energy Systems, 93,* 459–467. doi:10.1016/j.ijepes.2017.06.022

Roch-Dupré, D., López-López, Á. J., Pecharromán, R. R., Cucala, A. P., & Fernández-Cardador, A. (2017). Analysis of the demand charge in DC railway systems and reduction of its economic impact with Energy Storage Systems. *International Journal of Electrical Power & Energy Systems*, *93*, 459–467. doi:10.1016/j.ijepes.2017.06.022

Schutte, J. F., & Groenwold, A. A. (2005). A study of global optimization using particle swarms. *Journal of Global Optimization*, *31*(1), 93–108. doi:10.100710898-003-6454-x

Shi, J., Xu, B., Zhu, P., & Lu, M. (2016, October). Multi-task firework algorithm for cell tracking and contour estimation. *Proceedings 2016 International Conference on Control, Automation, and Information Sciences (ICCAIS)* (pp. 27-31). IEEE. 10.1109/ICCAIS.2016.7822430

Shi, J., Xu, B., Zhu, P., Lu, M., Zhang, W., Xu, L., & Zhang, J. (2015, October). Multiple cells tracking by firework algorithm. *Proceedings 2015 International Conference on Control, Automation, and Information Sciences (ICCAIS)* (pp. 508-511). IEEE.

Shi, Y. (2001, May). Particle swarm optimization: developments, applications and resources. *Proceedings of the 2001 congress on evolutionary computation (IEEE Cat. No. 01TH8546)* (Vol. 1, pp. 81-86). IEEE. 10.1109/CEC.2001.934374

Shi, Y., & Eberhart, R. C. (2001, May). Fuzzy adaptive particle swarm optimization. In *Proceedings of the 2001 congress on evolutionary computation (IEEE Cat. No. 01TH8546)* (Vol. 1, pp. 101-106). IEEE. 10.1109/CEC.2001.934377

Takagi, R. (2012). Preliminary evaluation of the energy-saving effects of the introduction of superconducting cables in the power feeding network for DC electric railways using the multi-train power network simulator. *IET Electrical Systems in Transportation*, *2*(3), 103–109. doi:10.1049/iet-est.2011.0048

Tan, Y., & Zhu, Y. (2010, June). Fireworks algorithm for optimization. *Proceedings International Conference in Swarm Intelligence* (pp. 355-364). Berlin, Germany: Springer.

Taowei, C., Yiming, Y., Kun, Z., & Duan, Z. (2018, October). A Membrane-Fireworks Algorithm for Multi-Objective Optimization Problems. *Proceedings 2018 11th International Congress on Image and Signal Processing, BioMedical Engineering, and Informatics (CISP-BMEI)* (pp. 1-6). IEEE. 10.1109/CISP-BMEI.2018.8633082

Vasant, P. (2013). *Meta-heuristics optimization algorithms in engineering, business, economics, and finance*. Information Science Reference. doi:10.4018/978-1-4666-2086-5

Xia, H., Chen, H., Yang, Z., Lin, F., & Wang, B. (2015). Optimal energy management, location and size for stationary energy storage system in a metro line based on genetic algorithm. *Energies*, *8*(10), 11618–11640. doi:10.3390/en81011618

Xin, J., Chen, G., & Hai, Y. (2009, April). A particle swarm optimizer with multi-stage linearly-decreasing inertia weight. *Proceedings 2009 International Joint Conference on Computational Sciences and Optimization* (Vol. 1, pp. 505-508). IEEE. 10.1109/CSO.2009.420

Ye, W., & Wen, J. (2017, December). Adaptive fireworks algorithm based on simulated annealing. *Proceedings 2017 13th International Conference on Computational Intelligence and Security (CIS)* (pp. 371-375). IEEE. 10.1109/CIS.2017.00087

Yu, C., Kelley, L., Zheng, S., & Tan, Y. (2014, July). Fireworks algorithm with differential mutation for solving the CEC 2014 competition problems. *Proceedings 2014 IEEE Congress on Evolutionary Computation (CEC)* (pp. 3238-3245). IEEE. 10.1109/CEC.2014.6900590

Zhang, B., Zhang, M. X., & Zheng, Y. J. (2014, July). A hybrid biogeography-based optimization and fireworks algorithm. *Proceedings 2014 IEEE Congress on Evolutionary Computation (CEC)* (pp. 3200-3206). IEEE. 10.1109/CEC.2014.6900289

Zhang, B., Zheng, Y. J., Zhang, M. X., & Chen, S. Y. (2015). Fireworks algorithm with enhanced fireworks interaction. *IEEE/ACM Transactions on Computational Biology and Bioinformatics, 14*(1), 42–55. doi:10.1109/TCBB.2015.2446487 PMID:28182542

Zhao, N., Roberts, C., Hillmansen, S., Tian, Z., Weston, P., & Chen, L. (2017). An integrated metro operation optimization to minimize energy consumption. *Transportation Research Part C, Emerging Technologies, 75*, 168–182. doi:10.1016/j.trc.2016.12.013

Zheng, S., Janecek, A., Li, J., & Tan, Y. (2014, July). Dynamic search in fireworks algorithm. *Proceedings 2014 IEEE Congress on Evolutionary Computation (CEC)* (pp. 3222-3229). IEEE. 10.1109/CEC.2014.6900485

Zheng, Y. J., Xu, X. L., Ling, H. F., & Chen, S. Y. (2015). A hybrid fireworks optimization method with differential evolution operators. *Neurocomputing, 148*, 75–82. doi:10.1016/j.neucom.2012.08.075

Chapter 13

Hybrid Bare Bones Fireworks Algorithm for Load Flow Analysis of Islanded Microgrids

Saad Mohammad Abdullah

Islamic University of Technology (IUT), Bangladesh

Ashik Ahmed

Islamic University of Technology (IUT), Bangladesh

ABSTRACT

In this chapter, a hybrid bare bones fireworks algorithm (HBBFWA) is proposed and its application in solving the load flow problem of islanded microgrid is demonstrated. The hybridization is carried out by updating the positions of generated sparks with the help of grasshopper optimization algorithm (GOA) mimicking the swarming behavior of grasshoppers. The purpose of incorporating GOA with bare bones fireworks algorithm (BBFWA) is to enhance the global searching capability of conventional BBFWA for complex optimization problems. The proposed HBBFWA is applied to perform the load flow analysis of a modified IEEE 37-Bus system. The performance of the proposed HBBFWA is compared against the performance of BBFWA in terms of computational time, convergence speed, and number of iterations required for convergence of the load flow problem. Moreover, standard statistical analysis test such as the independent sample t-test is conducted to identify statistically significant differences between the two algorithms.

INTRODUCTION

Metaheuristic optimization algorithms have gained much popularity over the years in solving complex optimization problems. These algorithms work in stochastic manner which implies that there is inherent randomness in the optimization process of these algorithms. Evolutionary and swarm intelligence-based algorithms such as genetic algorithm (GA) (Holland, 1992), simulated annealing (SA) (Kirkpatrick, Gelatt, & Vecchi, 1983), particle swarm optimization (PSO) (Eberhart & Kennedy, 1995), ant colony

DOI: 10.4018/978-1-7998-1659-1.ch013

Copyright © 2020, IGI Global. Copying or distributing in print or electronic forms without written permission of IGI Global is prohibited.

optimization (ACO) (Dorigo & Birattari, 2010), imperialist competitive algorithm (ICA) (Atashpaz-Gargari & Lucas, 2007), grasshopper optimization algorithm (GOA) (Saremi, Mirjalili, & Lewis, 2017) etc. are categorized under the class of metaheuristic algorithms. Most of these algorithms are inspired from some sort of biological or natural phenomenon. Similarly, inspired by observing fireworks explosion, a novel swarm intelligence-based algorithm, named fireworks algorithm (FWA) was proposed in (Tan & Zhu, 2010). Since its inception, several modified versions of the fireworks algorithm have been proposed by different researchers over the years. The bare bones fireworks algorithm (BBFWA) is one of the modified versions of the conventional fireworks algorithm where only the essential explosion operation is kept and remaining less significant operations, i.e. mutation operations are eliminated (Li & Tan, 2018). This results in an algorithm which is easier to implement, dependent on a smaller number of parameters, and computationally less expensive. However, the absence of the mutation operator reduces the global searching capability of this algorithm. Thus, to compensate the absence of the mutation operator, the focus of this chapter will be to include the searching process involved in the grasshopper optimization algorithm (GOA) within the working steps of the BBFWA forming a hybrid bare bones fireworks algorithm (HBBFWA). This hybrid algorithm will then be applied to perform the load flow analysis of islanded microgrid considering the modified IEEE-37 bus system as a case study system. Due to the absence of slack bus, the conventional methods of load flow solution are not applicable for an islanded microgrid. Metaheuristic optimization algorithms can be good alternatives to the conventional algorithms used for load flow analysis. Considering this fact, the proposed HBBFWA will be employed to perform load flow analysis of islanded microgrids. Additionally, this will also justify the applicability of this algorithm in solving complex optimization problems. The following sub-sections include background study on the evolution of fireworks algorithm, a brief literature review on the load flow analysis of islanded microgrid and the main focus of this chapter.

Background Study on Fireworks Algorithm

Fireworks algorithm (FWA) was first introduced in the work of Tan and Zhu (2010), by mimicking the swarming behavior of sparks generated by the explosion of a firework. In conventional FWA, first of all; a certain number of solutions are randomly initialized as the locations of the fireworks. Next step is to generate the locations of sparks for each firework. The generation of sparks is analogous to the process of a stochastic search. In order to ensure diversity of sparks, a few more sparks are generated following a gaussian random process. After the generation of these two types of sparks, new set of solutions are selected from the positions of fireworks and sparks as the locations of fireworks for the next generation. Since the evolution of this new type of swarm intelligence algorithm, it gained much acceptance from different researchers. In order to improve the performance of conventional FWA, a hybrid FWA was proposed in the work of Zheng, Xu, Ling and Chen (2015), by incorporating the steps involved in Differential Evolution (DE) algorithm with the conventional FWA.

Later on, Zheng, Janecek, and Tan (2013) identified few drawbacks of the conventional FWA. This research indicated that conventional FWA works better for some particular benchmark functions which have their optimum at the origin. However, for the objective functions having significant distance between the optimum point and the origin; the performance of the conventional FWA deteriorates. To compensate these drawbacks, Zheng et al. (2013) proposed an enhanced FWA (EFWA) by introducing new ways for checking explosion amplitude and generating explosion sparks, new mapping criterion for sparks, new operator for the generation of gaussian sparks and new selection criterion for the next generation. However, Li, Zheng and Tan (2014) showed that the amplitude operator of EFWA suffered from lack of adaptability. Thus, Li et al. (2014) proposed an adaptive FWA (AFWA) by introducing a new adaptive amplitude operator replacing the original amplitude operator used in EFWA. Since then, several other modified versions of the EFWA were proposed such as dynamic search FWA (dynFWA), FWA with differential mutation (FWA-DM), and improved enhanced FWA (IEFWA) (Yu, Li, & Tan, 2014; Zhang, Zhang, & Zheng, 2014; Zheng, Janecek, Li, & Tan, 2014). In dynFWA dynamic explosion amplitude was used for the firework at the current best position, whereas in case of FWA-DM a differential mutation process was added with EFWA. A novel guided FWA (GFWA) was proposed in work of J. Li, Zheng and Tan (2016), where a guiding vector is generated based on the fitness values of the objective function obtained by the explosion sparks. The guiding vector is then added with the position of the firework to generate an improved solution called the guiding sparks. In IEFWA new processes for gaussian explosion and population selection were included to avoid local optima entrapment. In the study of Zhang, Zheng, Zhang and Chen (2017), authors focused on enhancing interaction among fireworks through development of a new gaussian mutation operator along with integration of the general explosion operator of FWA with the migration operator of biogeography-based optimization technique and utilization of a new selection operator.

A simple but efficient version of the FWA was proposed by Li and Tan (2018), entitled bare bones FWA (BBFWA). This algorithm includes only the essential exploration operators of FWA to make the algorithm simpler, faster and easier to implement. However, the authors of that work identified that due to the lack of stochastic mutation operator, the BBFWA is not globally convergent. Later on, a hybrid optimization algorithm was proposed by merging the optimization process involved in grey wolf optimizer (GWO) algorithm with the conventional FWA (Barraza, Rodríguez, Castillo, Melin, & Valdez, 2018). In another study a hybrid version of EFWA was proposed by incorporating the differential evolution (DE) operator (Guo, Liu, Liu, & Zheng, 2019). A simplified hybrid fireworks algorithm (SHFWA) was proposed by Chen et al. (2019), where the authors intended to enhance the capability of exploration and exploitation of the traditional FWA. In this work a modified search formula was designed for the core firework to improve the ability of exploitation and harmony search (HS) technique was employed in the process of generating sparks with the view to improving the ability of exploration of the search space. In another research conducted by Y. Li, Yu, Takagi and Tan (2019), in order to improve the performance of GFWA two weight-based approaches were introduced to generate the guiding sparks which resulted in significant improvement. From this brief literature review it can be observed that development of different versions of FWA has gained wide interest throughout the years.

Review on Load Flow Analysis of Islanded Microgrid

In modern time, microgrid systems have evolved as an organized and ñexible architecture comprising of distributed energy resources (DERs) which can be a potential replacement of the aging electrical infrastructure with enhanced operability, reliability and reduced CO_2 emission to alleviate the environmental change (Vandoorn, Vasquez, De Kooning, Guerrero, & Vandevelde, 2013). Microgrid has gained much acceptance due to its functionality as aggregated distributed generation (DG) unit in both islanded and grid connected mode. In grid connected mode the main grid maintains the voltage and frequency of the system, whereas in the autonomous mode the voltage and frequency are not constant. As a result, conventional load flow algorithms are not applicable for autonomous microgrids (Shuai et al., 2016). Thus, solution of the steady state operating point of an islanded microgrid through load ñow analysis still remains as a challenge. To cope up with this challenge, both conventional and non-conventional approaches are adopted by the researchers till date.

Conventional power flow methods were used in case of an islanded microgrid by treating the local bus of the generating unit with the highest power rating as the slack bus (Kamh & Iravani, 2010; Nikkhajoei & Iravani, 2007). The accuracy of these methods is limited due to the approximation of constant frequency throughout the solution. In order to compensate the shortcomings of the conventional methods, several approaches have been proposed considering the frequency as one of the power flow solution variables. In the work of Abdelaziz, Farag, El-Saadany and Mohamed (2013), a Newton-trust region method was proposed to perform the load flow analysis. Mumtaz, Syed, Al Hosani and Zeineldin (2016) later on proposed a modified Newton-Raphson method to solve the power flow problem for islanded microgrid. However, for these methods, the microgrid system model was developed in stationary reference frame considering the voltages and currents as phasors which only allowed steady state analysis of the system and failed to provide necessary information for obtaining the linearized dynamic model of the system. In the study conducted by Mueller and Kimball (2017), the system model was developed in synchronous reference frame and a quasi-Newton method was introduced to solve the load ñow analysis considering the system frequency, reference frame angles and voltage magnitudes as the load flow variables. Most of these load flow techniques use gradient-based algorithms which require evaluation of derivatives for a series of complex equations. Gradient based techniques often fail to obtain a global solution as these algorithms mostly converge on a local solution (Yang, 2014).

Multi-solution based evolutionary algorithms have better possibility of avoiding a local optimum by exploring a larger portion of the search space (Saremi et al., 2017). For droop-controlled islanded microgrid, a load flow algorithm was introduced where particle swarm optimization (PSO) technique was used to determine the droop parameters (Elrayyah, Sozer, & Elbuluk, 2014). Later on, Abedini (2016) applied hybridized ICGA algorithm for load flow analysis by incorporating imperialist competitive algorithm (ICA) with the multi-solution based genetic algorithm (GA). Fairly good performance was obtained in the aforementioned work; however, the system modeling was done in stationary reference frame.

Main Focus of the Chapter

To address the issue of global convergence in bare bones fireworks algorithm (BBFWA), the focus of this chapter will be to propose a hybrid algorithm by merging the swarm intelligence-based grasshopper optimization algorithm (GOA) with BBFWA. The inclusion of GOA is expected to compensate the absence of stochastic mutation operator of conventional BBFWA. This algorithm is expected to obtain better exploration and exploitation of the search space by updating the positions of generated sparks using the mathematical model which describes the social interactions of grasshopper swarms. Thus, the proposed hybrid BBFWA (HBBFWA) is likely to obtain a global optimum solution for complex optimization problems.

Furthermore, the intention of this chapter is to obtain a global optimum solution of the load flow problem in case of islanded microgrid by applying the proposed hybrid bare bones fireworks algorithm (HBBFWA) on a modified IEEE 37-Bus system with the system model being developed in the synchronous reference frame. Developing the system model in synchronous reference frame provides multiple advantages such as transforming the time variant quantities into time invariant ones which makes the modeling of different controllers easier. Moreover, being a non-gradient based algorithm, this proposed hybrid algorithm can be a potential alternative to the conventional gradient based methods. Load flow problem for the same case study system will be solved by BBFWA to carry out comparative performance analysis of the proposed HBBFWA.

BARE BONES FIREWORKS ALGORITHM (BBFWA)

Bare bones fireworks algorithm (BBFWA) is a simplified but efficient version of the fireworks algorithm (FWA). Only the essential explosion operation is kept in BBFWA ignoring other less important mechanisms present in different versions of fireworks algorithms. The simplicity of the BBFWA makes it very easy to implement even with low level programming languages (J. Li & Tan, 2018). The pseudo code of BBFWA is provided in Algorithm 1. The following steps are associated with the optimization process of BBFWA.

Step 1: Defining input parameters.

Step 2: This step corresponds to the random generation of the location of the firework (x) within the lower (lb) and upper (ub) boundaries of the solution variables.

Step 3: Based on the explosion amplitude (A), n number of explosion sparks are generated during each iteration within a hyper rectangle bounded by lengths ($x - A$) and ($x + A$). If any spark falls outside the boundaries, it is randomly relocated in the search space.

Step 4: If any spark attains a better fitness value compared to the firework, then the location of the firework will be updated by the location of the spark and the explosion amplitude will be updated by multiplying with an amplification coefficient $C_a > 1$. Otherwise, the location of the current firework will remain unchanged for the next iteration and a reduction coefficient $C_r < 1$ will be multiplied with the explosion amplitude.

Step 5: The termination criterion is checked in this step. If the criterion is satisfied then the location of the firework is considered as the optimum solution. Otherwise, the optimization process will be continued from step 3.

Algorithm 1. Pseudo code for BBFWA

Begin:

    Define input parameters

    Generate random location of the firework: $x \sim U(lb,ub)$

    Evaluate fitness of the firework: $f(x)$

    Calculate explosion amplitude: $A = ub - lb$

while(the stopping criterion is not satisfied)

for $i = 1$ to n

    Generate the location of ith spark: $s_i \sim U(x - A, x + A)$

    Evaluate fitness of the spark: $f(s_i)$

end

    if $\min(f(s_i)) < f(x)$

    Update the location of the firework (x) with the location of the ith spark.

    $A = C_a A$

else

$A = C_r A$

end

end

return x

End

GRASSHOPPER OPTIMIZATION ALGORITHM (GOA)

In the study conducted by Saremi et al. (2017) a new nature-inspired algorithm named the grasshopper optimization algorithm (GOA) was proposed by mathematically modeling the swarming behavior of grasshoppers in nature. Two important functions of nature-inspired optimization algorithms: exploration and exploitation are naturally present in the swarming behavior of grasshoppers. Exploration indicates the diverse movement of search agents of an optimization problem, whereas exploitation indicates the local movement of search agents. The mathematical model of swarming behavior of grasshoppers include the model for social interaction between grasshoppers. As part of the social interaction, it is considered that the individuals of the grasshopper swarm experience both attractive and repulsive forces as indicated in Figure 1. At a particular distance between two grasshoppers, the attractive and repulsive force is considered to be equal which is known as the comfort zone. At short distances, there is possibility of collision between two grasshoppers. Thus, if the distance between two grasshoppers is less than the distance of comfort zone then the repulsive force between them is considered to be higher. On the other hand, in order to form a swarm. the attractive force between two grasshoppers should be higher if the distance between them is more than the comfort zone distance (Ismael, Aleem, Abdelaziz, & Zobaa, 2018). In each iteration, the best solution is considered as the target for the next iteration which simulates the tendency of grasshoppers to move towards the source of food. While updating the positions of grasshoppers in each iteration, a deceleration coefficient is introduced to gradually obtain a balance between exploration and exploitation while chasing the target solution. The pseudo code for GOA is shown in Algorithm 2 and the steps involved in the optimization process is described as follows.

Step 1: Defining input parameters. (c_{max}, c_{min}, maximum number of iterations)

Step 2: Random initialization of the positions for n number of grasshoppers (X) within the lower (lb) and upper (ub) boundaries of the search space.

Step 3: Evaluation of the fitness values of each search agent and identification of the best one as the target solution (T).

Step 4: Calculation of the deceleration coefficient (c) based on its maximum (c_{max}) and minimum (c_{min}) values, current iteration number (l) and the maximum number of iterations (L) as indicated in equation (1).

$$c = c_{max} - l \frac{c_{max} - c_{min}}{L} \tag{1}$$

Step 5: This coefficient c is associated in updating the position of each search agent by simulating the social interaction between the grasshoppers through the social interaction function (s) which is a function of the distance between two grasshoppers ($d_{ij} = |x_j - x_i|$) as indicated in equation (2). In equation (2), f indicates the intensity of attraction and l_{att} indicates the attractive length scale. The distance between grasshoppers is normalized in the range [1,4], because the social interaction function (s) is most significant within this range for the values of $l_{att} = 1.5$ and $f = 0.5$ (Saremi et al., 2017). Based on the modeling of social interaction between grasshoppers, the positions of the grasshoppers are moved towards the target solution which imitates the movement of grasshoppers towards the food source. The position of the ith grasshopper can be updated following equation (3).

$$s(d_{ij}) = f e^{\frac{-d_{ij}}{l_{att}}} - e^{-d_{ij}} \tag{2}$$

$$X_i = c \left(\sum_{\substack{j=1 \\ j \neq i}}^{N} c \frac{ub - lb}{2} s\left(|x_j - x_i|\right) \frac{x_j - x_i}{d_{ij}} \right) + \hat{T} \tag{3}$$

Step 6: The position of the target solution will be updated by any one of the search agents if it obtains a better fitness value. Otherwise, the target solution will remain unchanged.

Step 7: If the stopping criterion is satisfied, then the position of the target solution is considered as the optimum solution. Otherwise, the process will continue from step 4 until the termination criterion is satisfied.

Figure 1. Social interaction between various grasshoppers (Saremi et al., 2017)

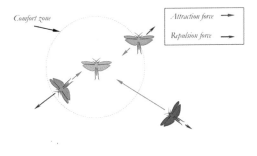

Algorithm 2. Pseudo code for GOA

Begin:

Initialize the positions of the grasshoppers: X_i ($i = 1, 2, ..., n$)

Initialize c_{max}, c_{min} and maximum number of iterations (L)

Evaluate fitness of each search agent: $f(X_i)$ ($i = 1, 2, ..., n$)

Assign, T = the best search agent

while(the stopping criterion is not satisfied)

Update deceleration coefficient (c) according to equation (1)

for $i = 1$ to n

Normalize the distance between grasshoppers in *[1,4]*

Update the position of the ith search agent (X_i) following equation (3)

Bring the search agent back if it goes outside the boundaries

end

Evaluate fitness of each search agent: $f(X_i)$ *(i = 1, 2, ..., n)*

if $\min(f(X_i)) < f(T)$

Update T with the location of the ith search agent

else

T will remain unchanged

end

$l = l+1$

end

return T

End

HYBRID BARE BONES FIREWORKS ALGORITHM (HBBFWA)

From the pseudo code of BBFWA as shown in Algorithm 1 it can be observed that the optimization process is very simple with less computational complexity. Less complexity in the optimization process makes it fast and easy to implement (J. Li & Tan, 2018). Compared to the conventional fireworks algorithm (FWA) (Tan & Zhu, 2010), the BBFWA initializes only one location of firework instead of multiple fireworks. Also, a simpler process is employed in generating the explosion sparks. The algorithm performs quite efficiently in solving optimization problems as justified by the experimental results obtained on the standard benchmark functions which were discussed in (J. Li & Tan, 2018). Though the algorithm exhibits reasonably good performance, adding diversity in the generation of explosion sparks may enhance the global searching capability of the algorithm which might assist in obtaining a faster convergence. Focusing on this goal, here, the searching process involved in GOA is incorporated with BBFWA to create diversity among the explosion sparks forming hybrid bare bones fireworks algorithm (HBBFWA). The flow chart of HBBFWA is shown in Figure 2 and the pseudo code is presented in Algorithm 3. The step by step optimization process is described as follows

Step 1: Defining input parameters.
Step 2: The location of firework (x) is randomly generated and the explosion amplitude (A) is calculated based on the pseudo code described in Algorithm 3.
Step 3: Before going to the main iterative loop, n1 number of explosion sparks ($S1$) are generated based on BBFWA (1st group of sparks). If any spark falls outside the boundaries then, it is randomly relocated in the search space.
Step 4: The n_1 number of explosion sparks generated in Step 3 are considered as the initial positions of grasshoppers and another n_1 number of sparks ($S2$) are generated following GOA (2nd group of

sparks). The location of the firework will be chosen as the target solution (T) and this 2nd group of sparks will be generated following equation (4).

$$S2_i = c\left(\sum_{\substack{j=1 \\ j \neq i}}^{N} c \frac{ub - lb}{2} s\left(\left|S2_j - S2_i\right|\right) \frac{S2_j - S2_i}{d_{ij}}\right) + \hat{T} \tag{4}$$

Step 5: The two groups of sparks will be combined to have $n = 2n_1$ number of total explosion sparks (S).

Step 6: Then, the fitness value of each of the explosion spark will be evaluated.

Step 7: If any spark attains a better fitness value compared to the firework, then the location of the firework will be updated by the location of the spark and the explosion amplitude will be updated accordingly as indicated in Algorithm 3.

Step 8: The process will terminate if the stopping criterion is satisfied. Otherwise, the positions of the 1st group of sparks ($S1$) and 2nd group of sparks ($S2$) will be modified following BBFWA and GOA respectively to generate the overall explosion sparks (S) for the next iteration. Then, the optimization process will be repeated from step 6.

Algorithm 3. Pseudocode for HBBFWA

Begin:
    Define input parameters
    Generate random location of the firework: $x \sim U(lb, ub)$
    Evaluate fitness of the firework: $f(x)$
    Calculate explosion amplitude: $A = ub - lb$
    l = 1
for $i = 1$ to n_1
    Generate the location of ith spark: $S1_i \sim U(x - A, x + A)$
end
    Initialize the positions of the grasshoppers: $S2 = S1$
    Initialize c_{max}, c_{min} and maximum number of iterations (L)
    Target Solution: $T = x$
    Calculate deceleration coefficient (c) according to equation (1)
for $i = 1$ to n_1
    Normalize the distance between grasshoppers in *[1,4]*
    Update the position of the ith search agent ($S2_i$) following equation (4)
    Bring the search agent back if it goes outside the boundaries
end
    Overall sparks: $S = \begin{bmatrix} S1 \\ S2 \end{bmatrix}$
    Overall number of sparks: $n = 2 * n_1$
    Evaluate fitness of each spark: $f(S_i)$ (*i = 1, 2, ..., n*)
if $\min(f(S_i)) < f(x)$

Figure 2. Flowchart of HBBFWA

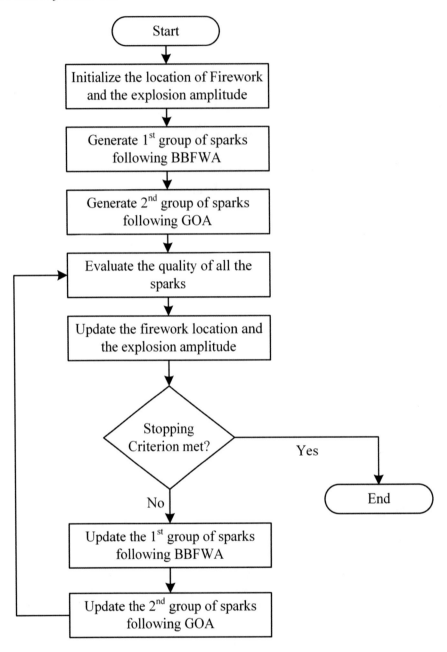

Update the location of firework (x) with the location of the ith spark
else

$$A = C_r A$$

end

$$l = 2$$

while(the stopping criterion is not satisfied)

Update deceleration coefficient (c) following equation (1)

for $i = 1$ to n_1

    Generate the location of the ith spark: $S1_i \sim U(x - A, x + A)$

end

for $i = 1$ to n_1

    Normalize the distance between grasshoppers in *[1,4]*

    Update the position of the ith search agent ($S2_i$) following equation (4)

    Bring the search agent back if it goes outside the boundaries

end

    Overall sparks: $S = \begin{bmatrix} S1 \\ S2 \end{bmatrix}$

    Overall number of sparks: $n = 2 * n_1$

    Evaluate fitness of each spark: $f(S_i)$ $(i = 1, 2, ..., n)$

if $\min(f(S_i)) < f(x)$

    Update the location of firework (x) with the location of the ith spark

else

    $A = C_r A$

end

    $l = l + 1$

end

return x

    End

MATHEMATICAL MODEL OF MICROGRID

Multiple distributed generation (DG) units are aggregated in a microgrid system. In most of the cases direct connection of these DGs to the distribution network is not suitable due to the nature of energy produced. Thus, before connecting to a bus, the DGs are associated with power electronic interfaces such as inverters (Jiayi, Chuanwen, & Rong, 2008). As a result, developing mathematical model of the inverter along with its associated controllers is important for the analysis of microgrid systems. The control strategy of an inverter coupled with an individual DG is shown diagrammatically in Figure 3. The discussion in this section describes the dynamic model of droop-controlled inverters along with the necessary load and line equations to develop the complete microgrid model. The modeling technique described in this section is based on the studies carried out in (Mueller & Kimball, 2017; Pogaku, Prodanovic, & Green, 2007; Rasheduzzaman, Mueller, & Kimball, 2014).

Inverter Model

Reference Frame Transformation

The inverter is coupled to the inverter bus through an LCL filter as shown in Figure 3. The three-phase capacitor voltage and inductor currents of the LCL filter are transformed from stationary abc reference frame to the synchronously rotating dq reference frame following the theory of Park's transformation.

Figure 3. Block diagram of control strategy of droop-controlled inverter for individual DG

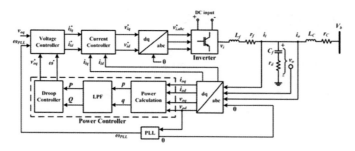

Figure 4. Relationship between abc and dq quantities

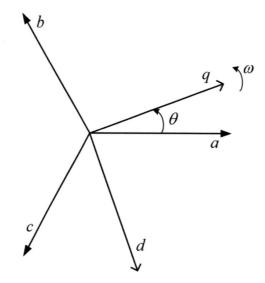

The axes of the three-phase stationary abc reference frame and the direct (d) and quadrature (q) axes of the synchronously rotating dq reference frame are shown in Figure 4, where θ represents the angle difference between the two reference frames and ε represents the rotational speed of the dq reference frame. This is accomplished using the following transformation

$$
\begin{bmatrix} v_q \\ v_d \\ v_o \end{bmatrix} = \frac{2}{3} \begin{bmatrix} \cos(\theta) & \cos(\theta - \frac{2\pi}{3}) & \cos(\theta + \frac{2\pi}{3}) \\ \sin(\theta) & \sin(\theta - \frac{2\pi}{3}) & \sin(\theta + \frac{2\pi}{3}) \\ \frac{1}{2} & \frac{1}{2} & \frac{1}{2} \end{bmatrix} \begin{bmatrix} v_a \\ v_b \\ v_c \end{bmatrix}
\tag{5}
$$

where, v_q and v_d are respectively the q-axis and d-axis components of the filter capacitor voltage and v_a, v_b and v_c are voltages in the stationary reference frame. The reference frame transformation of the filter inductor current, i_l and the output current, i_0 can be obtained using similar relationships. In equation (5), θ represents the transformation angle which is calculated by a phase locked loop (PLL). Details of this transformation technique is given in (Krause, Wasynczuk, Sudhoff, & Pekarek, 2002).

Phase Locked Loop (PLL)

A dq-based PLL is used to measure the phase and frequency. In the PLL, a proportional-integral (PI) controller is used to force the d-axis component of the capacitor voltage to become 0. This results in the steady-state voltage magnitude to be equal to its q-axis component. The PLL equations are

$$\frac{d}{dt}\phi_{PLL} = -v_{od} \tag{6}$$

$$\omega_{PLL} = -k_{p,PLL}v_{od} + k_{i,PLL}\phi_{PLL} \tag{7}$$

$$\frac{d}{dt}\theta = \omega_{PLL} \tag{8}$$

where, ϕ_{PLL} is the integrator state of the PI controller. $k_{p,PLL}$ and $k_{i,PLL}$ are respectively the proportional and integral gain, ω_{PLL} is the calculated frequency and θ is the transformation angle.

Power Controller

In the power controller, the instantaneous active (p) and reactive (q) power outputs are calculated first from the capacitor voltage and output current. Then, the droop controller generates the voltage magnitude and frequency references based on the active and reactive power values. The instantaneous active (p) and reactive (q) power outputs are given by

$$p = \frac{3}{2}(v_d i_{od} + v_q i_{oq}) \tag{9}$$

$$q = \frac{3}{2}(v_q i_{od} - v_d i_{oq}) \tag{10}$$

Average active (P) and reactive (Q) power values are calculated by passing the instantaneous power outputs through a first order low pass filter (LPF). The filter equations are

$$\frac{d}{dt}P = \omega_c p - \omega_c P \tag{11}$$

$$\frac{d}{dt}Q = \omega_c q - \omega_c Q \tag{12}$$

where, ω_c is the cut-off frequency of the low pass filter.

The P-ω and Q-V droop equations are used to generate the frequency reference, ω^* and q-axis voltage magnitude reference, v_{oq}^* respectively. The equations are

$$\omega^* = \omega_n - mP \tag{13}$$

$$v_{oq}^* = V_n - nQ \tag{14}$$

where, ω_n represents the nominal frequency set point and V_n represents the nominal set point of the q-axis output voltage. The droop constants m and n are calculated from the given range of frequency and voltage magnitude.

$$m = \frac{\omega_{max} - \omega_{min}}{P_{max}} \tag{15}$$

$$n = \frac{V_{oq,max} - V_{oq,min}}{Q_{max}} \tag{16}$$

Voltage Controllers

The voltage controller compares between the reference and measured values of frequency and voltage, and generates the reference values of the output filter inductor currents through a pair of PI controller. The voltage controller equations are

$$\frac{d}{dt}\varphi_d = \omega^* - \omega_{PLL} \tag{17}$$

$$i_{ld}^* = k_{pv,d}(\omega^* - \omega_{PLL}) + k_{iv,d}\varphi_d \tag{18}$$

$$\frac{d}{dt}\varphi_q = v_{oq}^* - v_{oq} \tag{19}$$

$$i_{lq}^* = k_{pv,q}(v_{oq}^* - v_{oq}) + k_{iv,q}\varphi_q \tag{20}$$

where, φ_d and φ_q represent the integrator states of the voltage controllers. The proportional and integral gains of the respective d-axis and q-axis controllers are represented by $k_{pv,d}$, $k_{pv,q}$, $k_{iv,d}$ and $k_{iv,q}$.

Current Controllers

The reference values of filter inductor current are compared with the measured filter inductor current using the current controllers. Voltage references are provided as outputs by these current controllers, which are used to generate switching signals for the inverter. Two PI controllers are used for this purpose. The cross-coupling terms appearing due to the reference frame transformation are also eliminated by these controllers. The current controller equations are

$$\frac{d}{dt}\gamma_d = i_{ld}^* - i_{ld} \tag{21}$$

$$v_{id}^* = k_{pc,d}(i_{ld}^* - i_{ld}) + k_{ic,d}\gamma_d - \omega_n L_f i_{lq} \tag{22}$$

$$\frac{d}{dt}\gamma_q = i_{lq}^* - i_{lq} \tag{23}$$

$$v_{iq}^* = k_{pc,q}(i_{lq}^* - i_{lq}) + k_{ic,q}\gamma_q + \omega_n L_f i_{ld} \tag{24}$$

where, γ_d and γ_q are the integrator state of the current controllers. $k_{pc,d}$, $k_{pc,q}$, $k_{ic,d}$ and $k_{ic,q}$ represent the proportional and integral gains of the d-axis and q-axis controllers respectively.

LCL Filter Equations

The inverter output is connected to the microgrid through an LC filter and coupling inductor. The filter inductor Lf, filter capacitor Cf and coupling inductor L_c collectively form the LCL filter. The parasitic resistance of these components is also considered for the inverter model as shown in Figure 3. The filter dynamics are governed by the following equations

$$\frac{d}{dt}i_{ld} = \frac{1}{L_f}(-r_f i_{ld} + v_{id} - v_{od}) + \omega^* i_{lq} \tag{25}$$

$$\frac{d}{dt}i_{lq} = \frac{1}{L_f}(-r_f i_{lq} + v_{iq} - v_{oq}) - \omega^* i_{ld} \tag{26}$$

$$\frac{d}{dt}i_{od} = \frac{1}{L_c}(-r_c i_{od} + v_{od} - v_{bd}) + \omega^* i_{oq} \tag{27}$$

$$\frac{d}{dt}i_{oq} = \frac{1}{L_c}(-r_c i_{oq} + v_{oq} - v_{bq}) - \omega^* i_{od} \tag{28}$$

$$\frac{d}{dt}v_{od} = \frac{1}{C_f}(i_{ld} - i_{od}) + \omega^* v_{oq} + R_d \frac{d}{dt}(i_{ld} - i_{od}) \tag{29}$$

$$\frac{d}{dt}v_{oq} = \frac{1}{C_f}(i_{lq} - i_{oq}) - \omega^* v_{od} + R_d \frac{d}{dt}(i_{lq} - i_{oq}) \tag{30}$$

In equations (27) and (28), v_{bd} and v_{bq} represent the bus voltages at the grid side of the coupling inductor.

Figure 5. Relationship between global reference frame and local reference frames

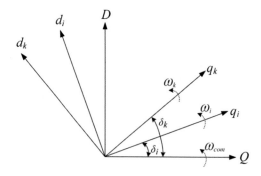

Local to Global Reference Frame Transformation

Each inverter model is developed in its own local reference frame. For modeling a microgrid system with several inverters, it is necessary to translate the values defined in the local reference frame of an inverter to a common reference frame called the global reference frame. This concept can be visualized from Figure 5, where DQ reference frame is considered to be the common reference frame and dq reference frames indicate the local reference frames of the inverters in the system. In Figure 5, i indicates the number of inverters connected in the system where, $i = 1, 2, \ldots \ldots, k$. This transformation can be achieved by

$$\begin{bmatrix} F_q \\ F_d \end{bmatrix} = R(\delta) \begin{bmatrix} f_q \\ f_d \end{bmatrix} \tag{31}$$

$$R(\delta) = \begin{bmatrix} cos\delta & -sin\delta \\ sin\delta & cos\delta \end{bmatrix} \tag{32}$$

where, δ is the angular difference between local and global reference frame and $R(\delta)$ is a transformation matrix to have obtain the local to global reference frame transformation. In equation (31), lowercase letter (f) is used to indicate a particular parameter represented in its own local reference frame and uppercase letter (F) is used to indicate the same parameter translated to the global reference frame. The angle δ is defined by

$$\frac{d}{dt}\delta = \omega - \omega_{PLL} \tag{33}$$

where, ω is the frequency of the global reference frame and ω_{PLL} is the frequency measured by PLL of a particular inverter. Often, the reference frame of the first inverter in the system is chosen as the global reference frame. In this work, we set $\omega_1 = \omega_{PLL}$ and $\delta_1 = 0$, which implies $\dot{\delta}_1 = 0$. For other inverters, $\omega \neq \omega_{PLL}$ and δ has to be calculated following equation (33).

Equations for Load and Line

To complete modeling the entire microgrid model, it is necessary to formulate the state equations for load and line in the global reference frame. Loads can be of constant impedance type which is basically a combination of resistors and inductors (RL loads) as depicted in Figure 6. The equations of RL load connected to the i_{th} bus can be described by

$$\frac{d}{dt}I_{load,d_i} = \frac{1}{L_{load_i}}(V_{bd_i} - R_{load_i}I_{load,d_i}) + \omega I_{load,q_i} \tag{34}$$

$$\frac{d}{dt}I_{load,q_i} = \frac{1}{L_{load_i}}(V_{bq_i} - R_{load_i}I_{load,q_i}) - \omega I_{load,d_i} \tag{35}$$

Line currents between two adjacent buses i and j connected through a transmission line can be described by

$$\frac{d}{dt}I_{line,d_{ij}} = \frac{1}{L_{line_{ij}}}(V_{bd_i} - V_{bd_j} - R_{line_{ij}}I_{line,d_{ij}}) + \omega I_{line,q_{ij}} \tag{36}$$

$$\frac{d}{dt}I_{line,q_{ij}} = \frac{1}{L_{line_{ij}}}(V_{bq_i} - V_{bq_j} - R_{line_{ij}}I_{line,q_{ij}}) - \omega I_{line,d_{ij}} \tag{37}$$

where, $0 \le i < j \le N$. N represents the total number of buses in the system.

Figure 6. Line configuration between two buses

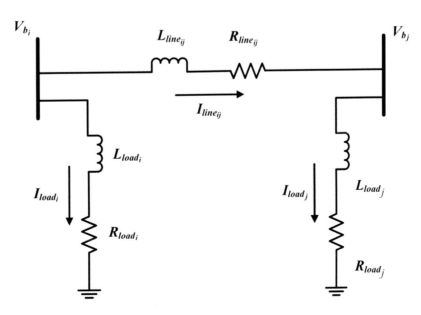

Figure 7. Line and load currents at a particular bus

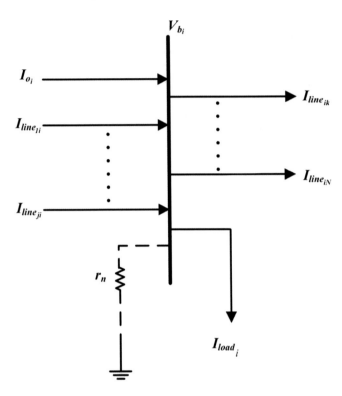

Bus Voltage Equations

The virtual resistance method can be used to find the expression of the bus voltages in the global reference frame. To determine the bus voltage at the ith bus using virtual resistance method, a high resistance connection is considered between bus i and ground. This high resistance actually represents open circuit. Ideally this resistance should be infinite, but typically a large value of resistance is considered for modeling purpose.

Bus voltage expressions are typically dependent on any incoming inverter output current, incoming or outgoing line currents and currents flowing through the connected load as shown in Figure 7. The voltage expression at bus i can be expressed as

$$V_{bd_i} = r_n \left(I_{od_i} - I_{load,d_i} + \sum_{j=1}^{i-1} I_{line,d_{ji}} - \sum_{k=i+1}^{N} I_{line,d_{ik}} \right) \tag{38}$$

$$V_{bq_i} = r_n \left(I_{oq_i} - I_{load,q_i} + \sum_{j=1}^{i-1} I_{line,q_{ji}} - \sum_{k=i+1}^{N} I_{line,q_{ik}} \right) \tag{39}$$

where, $j \leq i < k \leq N$.

Overall Microgrid Model

The equations of the inverter, load and line model described so far can be used to represent the overall microgrid model. The state vector of a droop-controlled inverter connected to the i_{th} bus can be formulated as

$$x_{inv_i} = \begin{bmatrix} \delta_i & P_i & Q_i & \varphi_{d_i} & \varphi_{q_i} & \gamma_{d_i} & \gamma_{q_i} & i_{ld_i} & i_{lq_i} & v_{d_i} & v_{q_i} & i_{od_i} & i_{oq_i} & \phi_{PLL_i} \end{bmatrix}^T \tag{40}$$

If there are total p number of inverters connected to the system, then the combined state vector of all the inverters can be represented as

$$x_{inv} = \begin{bmatrix} x_{inv_1} & x_{inv_2} & \cdots & \cdots & x_{inv_p} \end{bmatrix} \tag{41}$$

Considering the equations of the load model described from equations (31) and (32), the state vector of a load connected at the i_{th} bus is

$$x_{load_i} = \begin{bmatrix} I_{load,d_i} & I_{load,q_i} \end{bmatrix}^T \tag{42}$$

If there are total N number of buses in the microgrid system and one specific RL load is connected to each bus, then the combined state vector of all the loads will be

$$x_{load} = \begin{bmatrix} I_{load,d_1} & I_{load,q_1} & \cdots & \cdots & I_{load,d_N} & I_{load,q_N} \end{bmatrix}^T \tag{43}$$

The equations of line current from equations (33) and (34) can be used to represent the states of a line between buses i and j as

$$x_{line_{ij}} = \begin{bmatrix} I_{line,d_{ij}} & I_{line,q_{ij}} \end{bmatrix}^T \tag{44}$$

The overall state vector of all the lines can be represented as

$$x_{line} = \begin{bmatrix} I_{line,d_{1j}} & I_{line,q_{1j}} & \cdots & \cdots & I_{line,d_{kN}} & I_{line,q_{kN}} \end{bmatrix}^T \tag{45}$$

where, $1 < j \leq k \leq N$.

Based on the combined state vectors of the droop-controlled inverters, loads and lines; the states of the overall microgrid model can be described as

$$x_{mg} = \begin{bmatrix} x_{inv} & x_{load} & x_{line} \end{bmatrix} \tag{46}$$

State-space model of the whole microgrid system will have the following form

$$\dot{x}_{mg} = A_{mg}x_{mg} + B_{mg}u_{mg} \tag{47}$$

The elements of the state matrix, A_{mg} and input matrix, B_{mg} is defined by equations (6), (11), (12), (17), (19), (21), (23), (25) to (30), (33) and (34) to (37). The input vector, u_{mg} can be represented in terms of the bus voltages as

$$u_{mg} = \begin{bmatrix} V_{bd_1} & V_{bq_1} & \cdots & \cdots & V_{bd_N} & V_{bq_N} \end{bmatrix}^T \tag{48}$$

LOAD FLOW ANALYSIS

In the conventional load flow analysis, the slack bus governs the voltage and frequency of the whole system. Whereas, in case of droop-controlled islanded microgrid the voltage and frequency are regulated by droop controllers associated with each source. Due to the variation of voltage and frequency, the concept of slack bus becomes invalid in case of islanded microgrid. As a result, for an islanded microgrid with droop-controlled inverter; the system frequency has to be considered as one of the load flow variables along with the voltage magnitudes and reference angles contributed by each inverter in the system. The state variable, x can be described in terms of the load flow variables as

$$x = \begin{bmatrix} \omega & \delta_2 & \cdots & \cdots & \delta_K & v_{oq_1} & \cdots & \cdots & v_{oq_K} \end{bmatrix} \tag{49}$$

where; ω, δ and v_{oq} represents the system frequency, reference angle and voltage magnitude respectively and K represents the total number of inverters in the system. The constraints of the objective problem can be defined as

$$\omega_{min} \leq \omega \leq \omega_{max}$$
$$\delta_{min} \leq \delta \leq \delta_{max}$$
$$v_{oq}^{min} \leq v_{oq} \leq v_{oq}^{max}$$

Problem Formulation

The objective of the load flow analysis is to minimize the sum of absolute mismatch values of active and reactive power of the inverters. The objective function can be written as

$$Minimize, f(x) = \left| \sum_{i=1}^{K} \Delta P_i \right| + \left| \sum_{i=1}^{K} \Delta Q_i \right| \tag{50}$$

where; ΔP_i and ΔQ_i are the real and reactive power mismatch at the i_{th} bus. For a droop-controlled inverter, the power mismatch equations are the difference between the inverter output power calculated at the global reference frame and the reference values set by the droop controllers. For the i_{th} inverter the active and reactive power mismatch equations are

$$\Delta P_i = \frac{3}{2}(V_{od_i}I_{od_i} + V_{oq_i}I_{oq_i}) - \frac{(\omega_n - \omega)}{m_i} \tag{51}$$

$$\Delta Q_i = \frac{3}{2}(V_{oq_i}I_{od_i} - V_{od_i}I_{oq_i}) - \frac{(V_n - v_{oq_i})}{n_i} \tag{52}$$

To determine the power mismatch values, a set of equations has to be solved which involve the calculation of bus voltages and inverter output currents. For these calculations an equivalent circuit of the inverter model is considered as shown in Figure 8, where the inverter output voltage across the capacitor is considered as a voltage source behind its coupling impedance. The process of determining the power mismatch values is described in the following steps.

Step 1: First of all, following equations (31) and (32); the *d-axis* and *q-axis* components of the inverter output voltage is transformed in the global reference frame using the reference angle δ. Then, the output voltage of the ith inverter in terms of a complex quantity can be calculated as

$$V_{od_i} = sin(\delta_i)v_{oq_i} \tag{53}$$

$$V_{oq_i} = cos(\delta_i)v_{oq_i} \tag{54}$$

$$V_{o_i} = V_{od_i} + jV_{oq_i} \tag{55}$$

Step 2: Before determining the bus voltages it is required to calculate the current injected to a particular bus. For this study, only constant impedance loads are considered. So, the inverter are the only sources to inject current to their respective buses. The current injected by the inverters can be easily calculated by transforming the circuit shown in Figure 8 to its Norton equivalent as shown in Figure 9. Then, the current injected by the ith inverter is calculated as

$$I_{inj_i} = I_{SC_i} = \frac{V_{o_i}}{Z_c(\omega)} \tag{56}$$

Step 3: The bus voltages can now be calculated from the injected currents as

$$V_b = Z_{bus}(\omega)I_{inj} \tag{57}$$

For islanded microgrids the bus impedance matrix is a function of frequency and it has to be updated at each iteration. For an *N*-bus system the vector of injected currents at each bus is given by

$$I_{inj} = \begin{cases} I_{inj_p} & \text{due to inverter at bus } p \ (p \leq N) \\ 0 & \text{otherwise} \end{cases} \tag{58}$$

Step 4: After determining the bus voltages, the output current of the ith inverter can be determined by

$$I_{o_i} = \frac{V_{o_i} - V_{b_i}}{Z_c(\omega)}$$

(59)

The *d-axis* and *q-axis* components of the inverter output current in the global reference frame is given by

$$I_{od_i} = \Re\{I_{o_i}\}$$

(60)

$$I_{oq_i} = \Im\{I_{o_i}\}$$

(61)

Step 5: The equations from (53) to (61) are sufficient to calculate the active and reactive power mismatch values for each inverter by solving the equations described in (51) and (52).

Figure 8. Steady-state equivalent circuit of inverter model at bus i

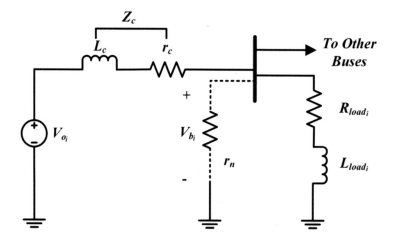

Figure 9. Norton equivalent circuit of steady-state inverter model at bus i

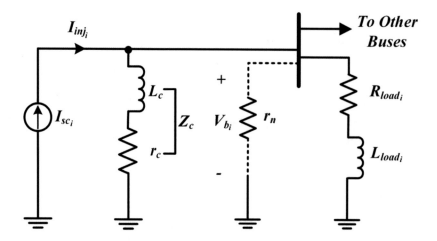

Thus, the values of the power mismatch equations can be used to evaluate the objective function as indicated in equation (50). The focus of the load flow analysis is to minimize the value of this objective function by finding an optimum solution set in terms of the load flow variables as indicated in equation (49).

Figure 10. Single-line diagram of the modified IEEE 37-bus system

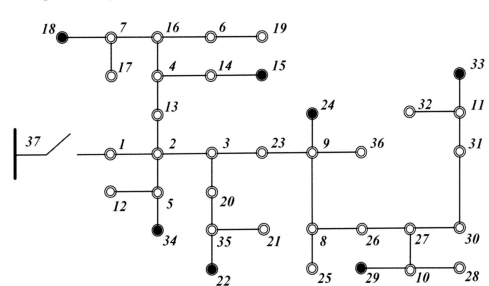

CASE STUDY

System Information

In order to conduct a comparative study between BBFWA and HBBFWA the modified IEEE 37-bus system was chosen and the load flow analysis of this system was performed using the aforementioned algorithms. The standard IEEE 37-bus system is modified by connecting seven inverters at different bus locations as indicated in (Luo & Dhople, 2014). The single line diagram of the modified IEEE 37-bus system is shown in Figure 10. In this figure, each dotted sign indicates a particular bus in the system and the location of all the 37 buses can be identified from the number associated with each dotted sign. Bus number 37 represents the utility grid and the status of the isolator switch associated with this bus indicates whether the system will operate in grid-connected mode or in islanded mode. For this study, it is considered that the isolator switch is open and the system is operating in islanded mode. The seven inverters are connected at buses 15, 18, 22, 24, 29, 33 and 34 as indicated by the black dots in Figure 10. Only constant impedance loads are considered in this case study. The branch and load parameters are considered to be the same as used in (Luo & Dhople, 2014). For all the inverters, a nominal voltage of Vn = 170 V was chosen and nominal frequency was set to ω_n = 2π60 rad/s. The maximum power ratings and the droop co-efficients for each inverter is given in Table 1.

Table 1. Inverter bus locations, power ratings and droop co-efficients (Mueller & Kimball, 2017)

i	Bus	P_{max} (kW)	Q_{max} (kVAR)	m_i^{-1}	n_i^{-1}
1	15	15	15	2387.3	1250
2	18	8	8	1273.2	666.7
3	22	10	10	1591.5	833.3
4	24	15	15	2387.3	1250
5	29	8	8	1273.2	666.7
6	33	10	10	1591.5	833.3
7	34	15	15	2387.3	1250

For the modified IEEE 37-bus system the load flow analysis was formulated as an optimization problem based on the discussion presented in the previous section. First of all, load flow analysis was performed by applying BBFWA to the modified IEEE 37-bus system following the steps involved in Algorithm 1. Later on, HBBFWA was applied to perform load flow analysis of the same system following Algorithm 3. For both algorithms, the total number of sparks was chosen to be 100. The values of amplification coefficient (Ca) and reduction coefficient (Cr) were set to 1.3 and 0.7 respectively. For this case study the following stopping criterion were considered which would terminate the optimization process once satisfied.

1. If the best fitness value is less than a pre-specified threshold (ε) value which was set to 10^{-5} for this study.
2. If the number of iterations is equal to a pre-specified value of maximum number of iterations. For this study, the maximum number of iterations was set to 100.

These algorithms operate in stochastic manner which indicates that the optimization process is associated with randomness. These algorithms start the optimization process by randomly initializing the positions of the solution variables within the boundary of pre-specified constraints. Then, a number of iterations is performed by updating the positions of each solution set through a series of random process until the optimum solution is obtained. Due to the inherent randomness of these algorithms it is most likely that the number of iterations and the execution time needed to complete the optimization process may vary for each independent run. Thus, for overall comparison among BBFWA and HBBFWA, each algorithm was executed for 30 independent runs. All the simulations were performed using a personal computer with a processor of intel core i7-8550 at 1.8 GHz and with an installed RAM of 8 GB.

Result Analysis

For each independent run, the number of iterations to reach the stopping criterion and the overall execution time were recorded. These data are summarized in Table 2 in three categories namely best, average and worst result for each algorithm. From Table 2, it can be observed that among the 30 independent runs if the best results are considered then the minimum number of iterations and the execution time required by HBBFWA to complete the load flow analysis are 60 iterations and 113.2307 sec respectively which is very much promising compared to the best results obtained by BBFWA. The convergence graph for the best result is shown in Figure 11. On the other hand, the number of iterations and the execution time required by BBFWA is less compared to HBBFWA when the worst results are considered. Nonetheless, on an average HBBFWA requires 75 iterations to complete the optimization process and the average number of iterations required by BBFWA is 85 to achieve convergence. Average execution time among the 30 independent runs is 144.3404 sec in case of HBBFWA, whereas it is 151.0586 sec in case of BBFWA. Considering the average number of iterations and computational time required by both the algorithms it can be concluded that, both the algorithms have significant difference among them and HBBFWA has the capability of achieving faster convergence compared to BBFWA. Thus, inclusion of the searching process involved in GOA along with the optimization process of BBFWA to form hybrid BBFWA (HBBFWA) has significantly improved the performance of conventional BBFWA.

Table 2. Iterations and Time required by BBFWA and HBBFWA algorithms

Parameter	Best Result		Average Result		Worst Result	
	BBFWA	HBBFWA	BBFWA	HBBFWA	BBFWA	HBBFWA
No. of Iterations	76	60	85	75	98	100
Execution Time (sec)	135.6272	113.2307	151.0586	144.3404	180.1525	197.6021

Figure 11. Convergence graph for the best results of each algorithm

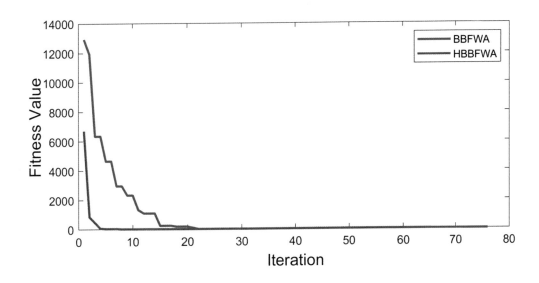

For further validation of the acquired results, SPSS statistics software was used to perform statistical analysis of the obtained data from 30 independent runs. To demonstrate the uniqueness of each algorithm, independent samples t-tests were performed to compare the means of each algorithm. Table 3 shows the t-test results based on the required number of iterations and the execution time as the comparison variables. Whenever independent samples t-test is performed in SPSS, the software also generates results of a corresponding F-test which determine whether the data sample of two groups have equal variances or not. If the p-value (significant factor) of the F-test is greater than the significance level of 0.05, then the group variances are considered to be equal. Otherwise, it is not possible to assume equal variances. Here, data sample (in terms of Number of iterations and execution time) obtained from both the algorithms does not possess equal variances as the p-value of the F-test is less than the significant level in both cases.

Table 3. Results of independent samples t-test

t-test variable	*F*-test		*t*-test for equality of means			
	F	Sig.	Mean Difference	t	df	Sig. (2-tailed)
No. of Iterations	11.013	0.002	9.600	4.005	40.959	0.000
Execution Time (sec)	9.585	0.003	6.718	1.485	41.123	0.145

For the t-test, the null hypothesis H0 assumes that the mean values of the data set are equal and the alternative hypothesis H1 assumes that the mean values of the data set are not equal. From Table 3, it can be seen that, the p-value of the t-test with respect to the required number of iterations is smaller than 0.05 which indicate that in this context there is significant difference between BBFWA and HBBFWA. On the other hand, the p-value is greater than 0.05 when the t-test is performed with respect to execution time. Thus, in terms of the execution time, the difference between the two algorithms is not that significant. However, considering the average execution time of the 30 independent runs it can be concluded that HBBFWA is 6.718 sec faster compared to BBFWA in achieving convergence for the load flow problem. Based on the studies done so far, it can be observed that HBBFWA performs relatively better compared to BBFWA considering the average number of iterations and the average execution time.

The results of the load flow analysis of the modified IEEE 37-bus system using HBBFWA is given in Table 4. Among the 30 independent runs the best result is tabulated here. The p.u. value of the steady state frequency is calculated to be 0.9962. In work of Mueller and Kimball (2017), the load flow solution of the modified IEEE 37-bus system was obtained through a quasi-Newton method. In order to make a comparison among the HBBFWA and the quasi-Newton method, the per unit (p.u.) values of the inverter output voltages at each inverter bus is tabulated in Table 5. From Table 5, it can be observed that the p.u. values of the inverter output voltages obtained through both the algorithms are very close to each other and it can also be seen that all bus voltages lie within 5% of the rated bus voltage which satisfy the IEEE standard of voltage regulation as stated in (IEEE, 2011). Furthermore, it can be observed that the p.u. values of the inverter output voltages are close to unity in case of HBBFWA which indicate that the voltages in this case are close to the nominal value. The inverter bus locations and the values of the active and reactive powers generated by each inverter in case of HBBFWA is tabulated in Table 6. These results are sufficient to calculate the voltages and phase angles at other buses of the network. The obtained load flow results can also be used to calculate steady-state operating points that can be used to linearize the non-linear equations of the system model which is necessary for control and small signal stability analysis of the system.

Table 4. Load flow results obtained by HBBFWA

Load Flow Variable	Calculated Value	Load Flow Variable	Calculated Value
ω (rad/s)	375.5577	v_{oq_1} (V)	169.911
δ_2 (deg)	-1.5659	v_{oq_2} (V)	168.486
δ_3 (deg)	-2.8722	v_{oq_3} (V)	169.937
δ_4 (deg)	1.2647	v_{oq_4} (V)	169.318
δ_5 (deg)	-0.0454	v_{oq_5} (V)	168.589
δ_6 (deg)	1.2436	v_{oq_6} (V)	162.261
δ_7 (deg)	2.0737	v_{oq_7} (V)	169.939

Table 5. Comparison among the per unit output voltages at each inverter obtained through HBBFWA and quasi-Newton method

i	Bus	Output Voltage (p.u.)	
		HBBFWA	Quasi-Newton (Mueller & Kimball, 2017)
1	15	0.9995	0.9789
2	18	0.9911	0.9601
3	22	0.9996	0.9655
4	24	0.9959	0.9844
5	29	0.9917	0.9745
6	33	0.9544	0.9673
7	34	0.9996	0.9700

Table 6. Generated active and reactive powers at each inverter in case of HBBFWA

i	Bus	Generated Power	
		Active Power (kW)	Reactive Power (kVAR)
1	15	3.226	2.089
2	18	3.310	0.275
3	22	7.032	1.407
4	24	1.348	3.693
5	29	2.908	1.149
6	33	0.439	0.562
7	34	1.274	5.346

FUTURE RESEARCH DIRECTIONS

As a future expansion of this study, other evolutionary and swarm intelligence based optimization algorithms may be merged with BBFWA to form different hybrid algorithms. Then a comparative study can be conducted among those algorithms and the HBBFWA which was employed in this chapter. Furthermore, in order to deal with multi-objective optimization problems a modified version of HBBFWA may be proposed by adding the concept of non-dominated sorting in the optimization process.

CONCLUSION

In this chapter, grasshopper optimization algorithm (GOA) was incorporated with bare bones fireworks algorithm (BBFWA) to form hybrid bare bones fireworks algorithm (HBBFWA). Then the application of this hybrid algorithm was demonstrated in obtaining efficient solution of load flow problem in case of islanded microgrids. For solving the load flow problem, an objective function was formulated based on the absolute summation of errors in the real and reactive power generations from the inverter based microgrid sources. A case study was conducted on the modified IEEE 37-bus system containing seven droop-controlled inverters. For the case study system, the objective function was solved as a minimization problem using the HBBFWA. The hybridization was performed with a view to improving the global searching capability of the conventional BBFWA in solving complex optimization problem. In order to justify the improvement, load flow analysis of the same study system was performed using BBFWA. The performance of the applied algorithms was compared through a series of statistical tests. Based on the statistical analysis HBBFWA was found to exhibit better performance compared to BBFWA in terms of the required number of iterations and the execution time. Therefore, HBBFWA can be regarded as a prospective algorithm for solving complex optimization problems and can be considered as a potential alternative to the conventional load flow methods.

REFERENCES

Abdelaziz, M. M. A., Farag, H. E., El-Saadany, E. F., & Mohamed, Y. A.-R. I. (2013). A novel and generalized three-phase power flow algorithm for islanded microgrids using a newton trust region method. *IEEE Transactions on Power Systems*, 28(1), 190–201. doi:10.1109/TPWRS.2012.2195785

Abedini, M. (2016). A novel algorithm for load flow analysis in island microgrids using an improved evolutionary algorithm. *International Transactions on Electrical Energy Systems*, 26(12), 2727–2743. doi:10.1002/etep.2231

Atashpaz-Gargari, E., & Lucas, C. (2007). Imperialist competitive algorithm: an algorithm for optimization inspired by imperialistic competition. *Proceedings 2007 IEEE congress on evolutionary computation*. 10.1109/CEC.2007.4425083

Barraza, J., Rodríguez, L., Castillo, O., Melin, P., & Valdez, F. (2018). A new hybridization approach between the fireworks algorithm and grey wolf optimizer algorithm. *Journal of Optimization, 2018*.

Chen, Y., Li, L., Zhao, X., Xiao, J., Wu, Q., & Tan, Y. (2019). Simplified hybrid fireworks algorithm. *Knowledge-Based Systems, 173*, 128–139. doi:10.1016/j.knosys.2019.02.029

Dorigo, M., & Birattari, M. (2010). *Ant colony optimization.* Springer.

Eberhart, R., & Kennedy, J. (1995). A new optimizer using particle swarm theory. *Proceedings of the Sixth International Symposium on Micro Machine and Human Science.* 10.1109/MHS.1995.494215

Elrayyah, A., Sozer, Y., & Elbuluk, M. E. (2014). A novel load-flow analysis for stable and optimized microgrid operation. *IEEE Transactions on Power Delivery, 29*(4), 1709–1717. doi:10.1109/TP-WRD.2014.2307279

Guo, J., Liu, W., Liu, M., & Zheng, S. (2019). Hybrid fireworks algorithm with differential evolution operator. *International Journal of Intelligent Information and Database Systems, 12*(1-2), 47–64. doi:10.1504/IJIIDS.2019.102326

Holland, J. H. (1992). *Adaptation in natural and artificial systems: an introductory analysis with applications to biology, control, and artificial intelligence.* MIT Press. doi:10.7551/mitpress/1090.001.0001

IEEE. (2011). IEEE Guide for Identifying and Improving Voltage Quality in Power Systems - Redline (pp. 1-70). IEEE Std 1250-2011 (Revision of IEEE Std 1250-1995): IEEE.

Ismael, S. M., Aleem, S. H. A., Abdelaziz, A. Y., & Zobaa, A. F. (2018). *Optimal Conductor Selection of Radial Distribution Feeders: An Overview and New Application Using Grasshopper Optimization Algorithm Classical and Recent Aspects of Power System Optimization* (pp. 185–217). Elsevier.

Jiayi, H., Chuanwen, J., & Rong, X. (2008). A review on distributed energy resources and MicroGrid. *Renewable & Sustainable Energy Reviews, 12*(9), 2472–2483. doi:10.1016/j.rser.2007.06.004

Kamh, M. Z., & Iravani, R. (2010). Unbalanced model and power-flow analysis of microgrids and active distribution systems. *IEEE Transactions on Power Delivery, 25*(4), 2851–2858. doi:10.1109/TPWRD.2010.2042825

Kirkpatrick, S., Gelatt, C. D., & Vecchi, M. P. (1983). Optimization by simulated annealing. *Science, 220*(4598), 671-680.

Krause, P. C., Wasynczuk, O., Sudhoff, S. D., & Pekarek, S. (2002). *Analysis of electric machinery and drive systems* (Vol. 2). Wiley Online Library. doi:10.1109/9780470544167

Li, J., & Tan, Y. (2018). The bare bones fireworks algorithm: A minimalist global optimizer. *Applied Soft Computing, 62*, 454–462. doi:10.1016/j.asoc.2017.10.046

Li, J., Zheng, S., & Tan, Y. (2014). Adaptive fireworks algorithm. *Proceedings 2014 IEEE Congress on evolutionary computation (CEC).* 10.1109/CEC.2014.6900418

Li, J., Zheng, S., & Tan, Y. (2016). The effect of information utilization: Introducing a novel guiding spark in the fireworks algorithm. *IEEE Transactions on Evolutionary Computation, 21*(1), 153–166. doi:10.1109/TEVC.2016.2589821

Li, Y., Yu, J., Takagi, H., & Tan, Y. (2019). Accelerating Fireworks Algorithm with Weight-based Guiding Sparks. *Proceedings International Conference on Swarm Intelligence.* 10.1007/978-3-030-26369-0_24

Luo, L., & Dhople, S. V. (2014). Spatiotemporal model reduction of inverter-based islanded microgrids. *IEEE Transactions on Energy Conversion, 29*(4), 823–832. doi:10.1109/TEC.2014.2348716

Mueller, J. A., & Kimball, J. W. (2017). An Efficient Method of Determining Operating Points of Droop-Controlled Microgrids. *IEEE Transactions on Energy Conversion, 32*(4), 1432–1446. doi:10.1109/TEC.2017.2719580

Mumtaz, F., Syed, M., Al Hosani, M., & Zeineldin, H. (2016). A novel approach to solve power flow for islanded microgrids using modified newton raphson with droop control of dg. *IEEE Transactions on Sustainable Energy, 7*(2), 493–503. doi:10.1109/TSTE.2015.2502482

Nikkhajoei, H., & Iravani, R. (2007). Steady-state model and power flow analysis of electronically-coupled distributed resource units. *IEEE Transactions on Power Delivery, 22*(1), 721–728. doi:10.1109/TPWRD.2006.881604

Pogaku, N., Prodanovic, M., & Green, T. C. (2007). Modeling, analysis and testing of autonomous operation of an inverter-based microgrid. *IEEE Transactions on Power Electronics, 22*(2), 613–625. doi:10.1109/TPEL.2006.890003

Rasheduzzaman, M., Mueller, J. A., & Kimball, J. W. (2014). An accurate small-signal model of inverter-dominated islanded microgrids using dq reference frame. *IEEE Journal of Emerging and Selected Topics in Power Electronics, 2*(4), 1070–1080. doi:10.1109/JESTPE.2014.2338131

Saremi, S., Mirjalili, S., & Lewis, A. (2017). Grasshopper optimisation algorithm: Theory and application. *Advances in Engineering Software, 105*, 30–47. doi:10.1016/j.advengsoft.2017.01.004

Shuai, Z., Sun, Y., Shen, Z. J., Tian, W., Tu, C., Li, Y., & Yin, X. (2016). Microgrid stability: Classification and a review. *Renewable & Sustainable Energy Reviews, 58*, 167–179. doi:10.1016/j.rser.2015.12.201

Tan, Y., & Zhu, Y. (2010, June). Fireworks algorithm for optimization. *Proceedings International Conference in Swarm Intelligence* (pp. 355-364). Berlin, Germany: Springer.

Vandoorn, T. L., Vasquez, J. C., De Kooning, J., Guerrero, J. M., & Vandevelde, L. (2013). Microgrids: Hierarchical control and an overview of the control and reserve management strategies. *IEEE Industrial Electronics Magazine, 7*(4), 42–55. doi:10.1109/MIE.2013.2279306

Yang, X.-S. (2014). *Nature-inspired optimization algorithms*. Elsevier.

Yu, C., Li, J., & Tan, Y. (2014). Improve enhanced fireworks algorithm with differential mutation. *Proceedings 2014 IEEE International Conference on Systems, Man, and Cybernetics (SMC).* 10.1109/SMC.2014.6973918

Zhang, B., Zhang, M., & Zheng, Y.-J. (2014). Improving enhanced fireworks algorithm with new gaussian explosion and population selection strategies. *Proceedings International Conference in Swarm Intelligence.* 10.1007/978-3-319-11857-4_7

Zhang, B., Zheng, Y.-J., Zhang, M.-X., & Chen, S.-Y. (2017). Fireworks algorithm with enhanced fireworks interaction. *IEEE/ACM Transactions on Computational Biology and Bioinformatics (TCBB), 14*(1), 42-55.

Zheng, S., Janecek, A., Li, J., & Tan, Y. (2014). Dynamic search in fireworks algorithm. *Proceedings 2014 IEEE Congress on evolutionary computation (CEC)*. 10.1109/CEC.2014.6900485

Zheng, S., Janecek, A., & Tan, Y. (2013). Enhanced fireworks algorithm. *Proceedings 2013 IEEE Congress on evolutionary computation*. 10.1109/CEC.2013.6557813

Zheng, Y.-J., Xu, X.-L., Ling, H.-F., & Chen, S.-Y. (2015). A hybrid fireworks optimization method with differential evolution operators. *Neurocomputing, 148*, 75–82. doi:10.1016/j.neucom.2012.08.075

ADDITIONAL READING

He, J., & Li, Y. W. (2012). An enhanced microgrid load demand sharing strategy. *IEEE Transactions on Power Electronics, 27*(9), 3984–3995. doi:10.1109/TPEL.2012.2190099

Hirsch, A., Parag, Y., & Guerrero, J. (2018). Microgrids: A review of technologies, key drivers, and outstanding issues. *Renewable & Sustainable Energy Reviews, 90*, 402–411. doi:10.1016/j.rser.2018.03.040

Hossain, M., Pota, H., Issa, W., & Hossain, M. (2017). Overview of AC microgrid controls with inverter-interfaced generations. *Energies, 10*(9), 1300. doi:10.3390/en10091300

Hossain, M. A., Pota, H. R., Hossain, M. J., & Blaabjerg, F. (2019). Evolution of microgrids with converter-interfaced generations: Challenges and opportunities. *International Journal of Electrical Power & Energy Systems, 109*, 160–186. doi:10.1016/j.ijepes.2019.01.038

Pota, H. R. (2013). Droop control for islanded microgrids. Paper presented at the 2013 IEEE Power & Energy Society General Meeting. 10.1109/PESMG.2013.6672541

Senjyu, T., Miyazato, Y., Yona, A., Urasaki, N., & Funabashi, T. (2008). Optimal distribution voltage control and coordination with distributed generation. *IEEE Transactions on Power Delivery, 23*(2), 1236–1242. doi:10.1109/TPWRD.2007.908816

Tan, Y. (2015). *Fireworks Algorithm*. Springer. doi:10.1007/978-3-662-46353-6

Tan, Y., Yu, C., Zheng, S., & Ding, K. (2013). Introduction to fireworks algorithm. [IJSIR]. *International Journal of Swarm Intelligence Research, 4*(4), 39–70. doi:10.4018/ijsir.2013100103

Yang, X.-S. (2010a). *Engineering optimization: an introduction with metaheuristic applications*. John Wiley & Sons. doi:10.1002/9780470640425

Yang, X.-S. (2010b). *Nature-inspired metaheuristic algorithms*. Luniver press.

KEY TERMS AND DEFINITIONS

Droop Controller: It is an autonomous approach for controlling frequency and voltage level of a generating unit, utilizing the *real power – frequency* and *reactive power – voltage* relationships.

Global Optimum: Global optimum solution of an optimization problem is the solution which provides the optimum (either minimum or maximum) value of the objective function compared to all possible solution sets.

Islanded Microgrid: Islanded microgrid system is disconnected from the main grid and all the distributed generator units are collectively responsible for supplying power to different loads.

Load Flow Analysis: It is a computational tool essential to determine steady state operating points of any power system. The complex voltages at all the buses, power flows from different buses and through the transmission lines can be obtained through load flow analysis.

Local Optimum: Local optimum solution of an optimization problem is the solution for which the value of the objective function is optimum (either minimum or maximum) within a small range of nearby possible solution sets.

Metaheuristic Optimization: Optimization technique where it is not required to calculate the derivative of the objective function. Rather, the optimization technique is associated with several stochastic components and the optimum solution is obtained by trial and error.

Objective Function: The function whose value is intended to be minimized or maximized through the optimization process.

Optimization: Optimization refers to a mathematical technique of obtaining the minimum or maximum value of a given function dependent on several variables. These variables depend on several constraints.

Optimum Solution: The set of decision variables for which the value of given objective function is minimum or maximum.

Chapter 14
A Fireworks–Based Approach for Efficient Packet Filtering in Firewall

Sreelaja N. K.

PSG College of Technology, India

ABSTRACT

Information protection in computers is gaining a lot of importance in real world applications. To secure the private networks of businesses and institutions, a firewall is installed in a specially designated computer separate from the rest of the network so that no incoming packet can directly get into the private network. The system monitors and blocks the requests from illegal networks. The existing methods of packet filtering algorithms suffer from drawbacks in terms of search space and storage. To overcome the drawbacks, a Fireworks-based approach of packet filtering is proposed in this chapter. Termed Fireworks-based Packet Filtering (FWPF) algorithm, the sparks generated by the fireworks makes a decision about the rule position in the firewall ruleset matching with the incoming packet. The advantage of FWPF is that it reduces the search space when compared to the existing packet filtering algorithms.

INTRODUCTION

In real world applications, information protection in computers is gaining a lot of importance. Logical security system such as firewall is made use of in such systems. To secure the private networks of businesses and institutions, firewalls are the crucial elements. A firewall is a set of related programs located at a gateway server that protects the resources of a private network from the users of the external network. A firewall is often installed in a specially designated computer separate from the rest of the network so that no incoming packet can directly get into the private network. The firewall monitors and blocks the requests from illegal networks (Sreelaja & Vijayalakshmi Pai, 2010).

Packet filtering performance of basic firewalls largely affects the throughput of a network protected by the firewall. Packet filtering (Eyadat, 2008) refers to accept or block incoming packets based on the filtering rules defined in the ruleset. A filtering rule is a multidimensional structure where each dimension

DOI: 10.4018/978-1-7998-1659-1.ch014

Copyright © 2020, IGI Global. Copying or distributing in print or electronic forms without written permission of IGI Global is prohibited.

is a set of network fields and an action field. The network field denotes source IP address, destination IP address, source port and destination port. The action field for each rule is accept or drop based on which the incoming packets are filtered. An accept action allows the packet access into the protected domain. A drop action causes a packet, in violation of the security policy, to be rejected. The filtering rules in the ruleset can be any or all of the combination of source IP address, destination IP address, source port and destination port. A filtering rule is said to be matching filter for an incoming packet if all the fields in the filtering rule matches with the corresponding fields of the incoming packet header.

In this chapter, a Fireworks based approach for filtering the incoming packets in a network based on the filtering rules in a rule set is proposed. Termed Fireworks based Packet Filtering (FWPF) algorithm, a firework is exploded at a point in the ruleset and the sparks generated by the fireworks fall at several positions on the filtering rules in the firewall ruleset. The sparks are traversed to make a decision about the rule position in the ruleset matching with the incoming packet. This approach provides an optimized search technique to find the positions of the filtering rules in the ruleset matching with the incoming packet. The advantage of FWPF algorithm is that the incoming packets are filtered strictly according to the filtering rules in the ruleset. It is shown that FWPF algorithm scales well in terms of number of searches when compared to sequential search even for a very few number of rules in the ruleset. Also, it is shown that the drawbacks in other existing packet filtering methods are overcome by FWPF algorithm.

RELATED WORK

Mohammad M. Masud, Umniya Mustafa, Zouheir Trabelsi. (2014) have proposed a data driven packet filtering approach. According to this approach, each rule in the rule set is considered a class. The training dataset contains a packet header info and the corresponding class label. Then the classifier is used to classify new incoming packets. The predicted class is checked against the packet to see if this packet really matches the predicted rule. If yes, the corresponding action of the rule is taken. Otherwise, the traditional way of matching rules is followed. The advantage of this data mining firewall is that it offers a much faster rule matching. It is proved that the classifier can achieve very high accuracy of 98% or more, thereby making firewall six times or more faster in making filtering decision.

Trabelsi, Zhang, & Zeidan, (2012, October) have proposed a Packet Filtering Optimization Using Statistical Traffic Awareness Test to improve firewall packet filtering time through optimizing the order of security policy filtering rules and rule-fields (Trabelsi, Zhang, & Zeidan, 2012). The proposed mechanism is based on reordering rules and rule-fields according to packet matching and non-matching histograms, respectively. The current and previous traffic windows statistics are used to check the system stability using Chi-Square Test. If the system stability test indicates that the firewall is stable the same current rule and/or rule-fields orders are used for filtering the next traffic window. Otherwise, an update of the rule and/or rule-fields order structures is required for filtering the next traffic window. However, there is an error precision rate according to this method and 100% classification accuracy is not possible.

Hazem Hamed, Adel El-Atawy, Ehab Al-Shaer (2006) have proposed an Adaptive Statistical Optimization Techniques for Firewall Packet Filtering that introduce a minimal overhead on the firewall processing to allow rejecting the maximum number of the packets as early as possible, thereby reducing the matching time significantly. According to this approach, the space complexity is bounded by O (n), and computational complexity is O (n log n).

Shariful Hasan Shaikot and Min Sik Kim (2010) proposed a lightweight traffic-aware packet classifier which reorganizes its internal data structure (rule tree) based on the traffic pattern to reduce the search time for the most frequently visited rules in the ruleset. According to this approach, during preprocessing stage, the rules in the ruleset are converted into intervals, which takes O(ni) where n is the number of rules and i is the number of intervals. The Internal Rule Tree construction time is O (n log n).

Kencl Schwarzer (2006) have proposed the adaptive packet filtering method which periodically introduces shortcuts into the search tree along frequently travelled paths, to reduce the number of memory accesses. The complexity of memory accesses is O (n log n), where n is the total number of nodes denoting the source or destination IP address.

Sreelaja & Vijayalakshmi Pai (2010) have proposed an Ant Colony Optimization based approach of packet filtering (ACO-PF) which is efficient in terms of memory and search time. The memory needed is similar to that of sequential search and the average number of searches to find a match is ln n where n is the number of filtering rules in the ruleset.

To further reduce the number of searches, and to reduce the computational complexity making it suitably a lightweight algorithm, a fireworks-based approach of packet filtering is found to be suitable.

BUILDING PACKET FILTERING RULES IN A FIREWALL

Firewalls has a set of logical rules programmed in by a firewall administrator. The firewall filters the data packets by comparing with the logical rules. Screening routers or packet filters are the firewalls which operate at the network or transport layer. These firewalls filter the incoming packets based on the rules defined in the ruleset (Eyadat, 2008). The IP packet header of each incoming packet has four fields namely source address, destination address, source port and destination port. In Packet filtering, the packet headers are inspected by a router or firewall and compared with the rules in the ruleset to make a decision on whether to allow the packet or deny the packet. Packet filtering is carried out by setting up an access list that includes all computers in the local network by name or IP address so that communications can flow between them and all the traffic between "trusted" hosts are allowed. There are two methods of packet filtering namely Stateless packet filtering and Stateful packet filtering. Stateless packet filtering is called static packet filtering and the packets are allowed or blocked based on several criteria. The different criteria that a Stateless Filter can be configured to use are IP header information, TCP or UDP port number being used, Internet Control Message Protocol (ICMP) message type and Fragmentation flags (e.g., ACK and SYN) (Eyadat, 2008).

Consider a network in which there is a web server, FTP server and SMTP server which is in the demilitarized zone in the organization with the IP addresses 192.168.2.32, 192.168.2.25 and 192.168.2.29 respectively as shown in (Eyadat, 2008). It has one internal filtering router with an internal IP address 172.30.1.1/24 and one external filtering router with an external IP address 192.168.1.2/24. The firewall filtering rules are designed by allowing all traffic from trusted network outside. The public network cannot access the firewall directly. SMTP data is allowed to pass through firewall and is routed to SMTP gateway. All ICMP data is denied. Public networks accessing all internal servers by Telnet is blocked. Table 1 shows the ruleset for ICMP packets. Rules that enable web access are those rules which need to cover both standard HTTP traffic on TCP Port 80 as well as Secure HTTP (HTTPS) traffic on TCP Port 443 as shown in Table 2. Table 3 shows the ruleset for DNS rules that enable external clients to access computers in the network using the same TCP and UDP ports. Table 4 shows the ruleset that enables

FTP which support two separate connections TCP Port 21 (FTP Control port) and TCP 20 (FTP Data port). Table 5 shows the ruleset for e-mail server (Eyadat, 2008).

MODEL OF THE SYSTEM

The model for packet filtering is designed such that there are separate detection units to filter the incoming packets based on Source address, destination address, source port and destination port. In the source address detection unit, the source address of the incoming packet is compared with the source address of

Table 1. Rules for ICMP packets (Eyadat, 2008)

Rule	Protocol	Transport Protocol	Source IP	Destination IP	ICMP Message	Action
1	ICMP Inbound	ICMP	Any	Any	Source Quench	Allow
2	ICMP Outbound	ICMP	192.168.2.1/24	Any	Echo request	Allow
3	ICMP Inbound	ICMP	Any	192.168.2.1/24	Echo reply	Allow
4	ICMP Inbound	ICMP	Any	192.168.2.1/24	Destination Unreachable	Allow
5	ICMP Inbound	ICMP	Any	192.168.2.1/24	Service Unavailable	Allow
6	ICMP Inbound	ICMP	Any	192.168.2.1/24	Time to Live (TTL)	Allow
7	ICMP Inbound	ICMP	Any	192.168.2.1/24	Echo request	Drop
8	ICMP Inbound	ICMP	Any	192.168.2.1/24	Redirect	Drop
9	ICMP Outbound	ICMP	192.168.2.1/24	Any	Echo reply	Drop
10	ICMP Outbound	ICMP	192.168.2.1/24	Any	TTL Exceeded	Drop

Table 2. Rules that enable web access (Eyadat, 2008)

Rule	Protocol	Transport Protocol	Source IP	Source Port	Destination IP	Destination Port	Action
1	HTTP Inbound	TCP	Any	Any	192.168.2.32	80	Allow
2	HTTPS Inbound	TCP	Any	Any	192.168.2.32	443	Allow
3	HTTP Outbound	TCP	192.168.2.1/24	Any	Any	80	Allow
4	HTTPS Outbound	TCP	192.168.2.32	Any	Any	443	Allow

Table 3. Rules that enable DNS (Eyadat, 2008)

Rule	Protocol	Transport Protocol	Source IP	Source Port	Destination IP	Destination Port	Action
1	DNS Outbound	TCP	192.168.2.31	Any	Any	53	Allow
2	DNS Outbound	UDP	192.168.2.31	Any	Any	53	Allow
3	DNS Inbound	TCP	Any	Any	192.168.2.31	53	Allow
4	DNS Inbound	UDP	Any	Any	192.168.2.31	53	Allow

Table 4. Rules that enable FTP(Eyadat, 2008)

Rule	Protocol	Transport Protocol	Source IP	Source Port	Destination IP	Destination Port	Action
1	FTP control Inbound	TCP	Any	Any	192.168.1.25	21	Allow
2	FTP Data Inbound	TCP	192.168.1.25	20	Any	Any	Allow
3	FTP PASV	TCP	Any	Any	192.168.1.25	Any	Allow
4	FTP control Outbound	TCP	192.168.1.25	Any	Any	21	Allow
5	FTP Data Outbound	TCP	Any	20	192.168.1.25	Any	Allow

Table 5. Rules that enable Email (Eyadat, 2008)

Rule	Protocol	Transport Protocol	Source IP	Source Port	Destination IP	Destination Port	Action
1	Outbound POP3	TCP	192.168.2.1/24	Any	Any	110	Allow
2	Outbound POP3 / S	TCP	192.168.2.1/24	Any	Any	995	Allow
3	Inbound POP3	TCP	Any	Any	192.168.2.1/24	110	Allow
4	Inbound POP3 / S	TCP	Any	Any	192.168.2.1/24	995	Allow
5	SMTP Outbound	TCP	192.168.2.29	Any	Any	25	Allow
6	SMTP / S Outbound	TCP	192.168.2.29	Any	Any	465	Allow
7	SMTP Inbound	TCP	Any	Any	192.168.2.29	25	Allow
8	SMTP / S Inbound	TCP	Any	Any	192.168.2.29	465	Allow

the filtering rules in the ruleset. Thus, the source address is the comparison field in the source address detection unit. Similarly, the destination address, source port, and destination port are the comparison field in the destination address detection unit, source port detection unit and destination port detection unit respectively. The filtering rules in the ruleset of each detection unit are sorted in ascending order based on the comparison field of the detection unit. The source address, destination address, source port and destination port of the incoming packet is compared for a match with the filtering rules in the source address, destination address, source port and destination port detection units respectively. The packet is accepted or dropped according to the action field in the rule. If there doesn't exist any rule match for the incoming packet in all the detection units, the packet is logged to check for an intrusion (Sreelaja & Vijayalakshmi Pai, 2010).

Preprocessing of Ruleset

The address 10.1.1.0 refers to the range of addresses from 10.1.1.1 to 10.1.1.255. The preprocessing of the source address and destination address is achieved by converting the source and the destination address into a numeric equivalent and stored in the rule set. The conversion is done in such a way that the length of the values preceding and succeeding the dot in the IP address must be three. If the length is less than 3, then zeros are added preceding the number. Table 6 shows the preprocessing of the IP address (Sreelaja & Vijayalakshmi Pai, 2010).

Table 6. Preprocessing the IPaddress

IP address	Numeric Equivalent
105.105.12.5	105105012005
12.4.4.0	012004004000

FIREWORKS ALGORITHM

Inspired by observing Fireworks explosion, a novel swarm intelligence algorithm, called Fireworks Algorithm (FA), is proposed for global optimization of complex functions. The FA is presented and implemented by simulating the explosion process of Fireworks. In the FA, two explosion (search) processes are employed and mechanisms for keeping diversity of sparks are also well designed. When a Firework is set off, a shower of sparks will fill the local space around the Firework. The explosion process of a Firework can be viewed as a search in the local space around a specific point where the firework is set off through the sparks generated in the explosion. Mimicking the process of setting Fireworks, a rough framework of the FA is depicted in Figure 1. The most recently proposed FireWorks Algorithm (FWA) is a swarm intelligence algorithm that was published by (Tan & Zhu, 2010). This algorithm is inspired by fireworks explosion at night and is quite effective at finding global optimal value. As a firework explodes, a shower of sparks is shown in the adjacent area. Those sparks will explode again and generate other showers of sparks in a smaller area. Gradually, the sparks will search the whole solution space in a fine structure and focus on a small place to find the optimal solution.

Figure 1. Framework of fireworks algorithm

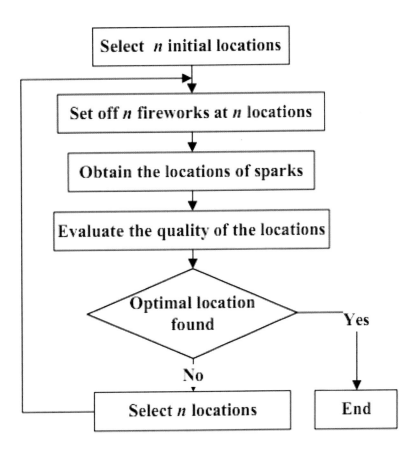

FIREWORKS BASED PACKET FILTERING ALGORITHM

A Firework based Packet Filtering (FWPF) algorithm is used to filter the incoming packets according to the filtering rules in the rule set. A firework is exploded at a point in the rule-set and the sparks fall at several positions on the filtering rules in the ruleset. The sparks are traversed to find the filtering rule matching with the incoming packet. A tabu-list denotes a dynamic memory structure. The tabu-list has a low and a high position to store the position of the rules. A matching list is used to store the filtering rule positions matching with the incoming packet. Initially the low position, high position and the matching list will be empty.

The first spark is traversed and depending on the detection unit chosen, the comparison field of the chosen filtering rule in the position denoted by the spark is compared with the corresponding incoming packet field. If the incoming packet field value is greater than the compared value of the filtering rule, the filtering rule position denoted by the spark is stored in the low position. If the incoming packet field value is less than the compared field value of the filtering rule, the filtering rule position denoted by the spark is stored in the high position. If both the values are equal, then the filtering rule position denoted by the spark is stored in the matching list. The process is repeated for the remaining sparks. The filtering rule positions stored in the low and high position denotes the range of the rules in the ruleset to be searched for a match with the incoming packet. If the high position is found, the remaining sparks following the high position are not traversed, since the matching rule does not exist in those sparks.

If the low position, high position and the matching list is not empty, the difference between the first position in the matching list and the low position is found. Also, the difference between the high position and the last position in the matching list is found. If the difference is not 1, the firework is exploded at a point between low position and first position in the matching list as well as high position and last position in the matching list and the process of finding a match with the incoming packet is repeated.

If the low and high positions are empty and the matching list is not empty, the firework is exploded at a point preceding the first position in the matching list and the process of finding a match is repeated by traversing all the sparks. The firework is also exploded at a point following the last position in the matching list and the process of finding a match is repeated until a high position is reached or all the sparks are traversed.

If the low position is empty and the high position and matching list is not empty, the firework is exploded at a point preceding the first position in the matching list and the sparks are traversed to find the matching rules. Also, the firework is exploded at a point between the last position in the matching list and high position and the process of finding a match is repeated until high position is obtained or all sparks are traversed.

If the high position is empty and the low position and matching list is not empty, the firework is exploded at a point following the last position in the matching list and the sparks are traversed to find the matching rules until a high position is reached or all sparks are traversed. Also, the firework is exploded at a point between the first position in the matching list and low position and the process of finding a match is repeated by traversing all the sparks.

The process is stopped when the difference between the low position and the first position in the matching list is 1 as well as the difference between the last position in the matching list and the high position is 1 if the matching list is not empty. If all the matching filtering rules are obtained, the other field values of the matching filtering rules are compared with the corresponding fields of the incoming packet. If a match occurs, the packet is forwarded or dropped depending on whether the status of the filtering rule is accepted or dropped respectively. If the matching list is empty and the difference between high position and low position is 1, the incoming packet does not match with the filtering rules and the incoming packet is dropped.

Algorithm

Figure 2 shows the pseudocode for FWPF algorithm.

CASE STUDY

The case study is explained for rules in a rule set in a destination address detection unit. Consider an incoming packet with the destination address 192.168.0.0 and destination port number 22. As a pre-processing technique, the destination address is represented as a number. Thus, the destination address

Figure 2. Pseudo code for FWPF algorithm

```
Procedure FWPF ( )
Low = 0 ; High = 0 ; Matching List = { }
Firework is exploded at a point in the ruleset and sparks fall at several positions ;
10:
Repeat
Traverse the first spark
if C (P) > C (RS) , low = position of spark, Matching list = { }
//C(P) is the comparison field of the incoming packet , C(RS) is the corresponding field in the ruleset.
if C (P) < C (RS) , high = position of spark, Matching list = { }
if C (P) = C (RS) ,   Matching list = { position of spark }
Traverse the next spark
Until (high position is obtained or all sparks are traversed ) ;
If  ( first position in the matching list - low position  ) = 1 and
    ( high position -  last position in the matching list ) = 1 then
Return ( Matching list )  ;
Else
If ( low position – high position ) = 1  return ( ' No match found ' ) ;
Else If ( low position < > 0 and high position < > 0  and Matching list < > empty )
Firework is exploded at a point in the ruleset between low position and first position in the Matching
list and sparks fall at several positions ;
Firework is exploded at a point in the ruleset between high position and last position in the Matching
list and sparks fall at several positions ;
Goto 10 ;
Else If ( low position = 0 and high position = 0 and Matching list < > empty )
Firework is exploded at a point preceding the first position in the Matching list and sparks fall at
several positions ;
Firework is exploded at a point following the last position in the Matching list and sparks fall at
several positions ;
Goto 10;
Else If ( low position = 0  and high position < > 0  and Matching list < > empty )
Firework is exploded at a point in the ruleset between high position and last position in the Matching
list and sparks fall at several positions ;
Firework is exploded at a point preceding the first position in the Matching list and sparks fall at
several positions ;
Goto 10;
Else If ( low position < > 0  and high position = 0  and Matching list < > empty )
Firework is exploded at a point in the ruleset between low position and first position in the Matching
list and sparks fall at several positions ;
Firework is exploded at a point following the last position in the Matching list and sparks fall at
several positions ;
Goto 10;
End FWPF ( ) ;
```

Table 7. Filtering rules in the rule set

Rule Position	Destination Address	Destination Port	Status
1	109103000000	427	ACCEPT
2	109103000000	548	ACCEPT
3	109103000000	201	ACCEPT
4	109103000000	202	ACCEPT
5	109103000000	204	ACCEPT
6	109103000000	206	ACCEPT
7	109103000000	427	ACCEPT
8	119004000000	548	ACCEPT
9	119004000001	201	ACCEPT
10	119004000002	202	ACCEPT
11	119004000003	204	ACCEPT
12	119004000003	206	ACCEPT
13	192168000000	873	ACCEPT
14	192168000000	22	ACCEPT
15	192168000000	137	ACCEPT
16	192168000000	138	ACCEPT
17	192168000000	139	ACCEPT
18	192168000000	445	ACCEPT
19	192168000001	8080	ACCEPT

192.168.0.0 is denoted as 192168000000. Since, the comparison field in a destination address detection unit is the destination address, the incoming packet's destination address 192168000000 is compared with the destination address of the rules in the rule set shown in Table 7.

According to FWPF algorithm, a firework is exploded at a point in the ruleset. The point chosen for exploding the firework is in the range of rules between 10 and 15. The sparks fall at filtering rules in the ruleset at positions 10, 11 and 15 respectively in the firewall ruleset. The destination address of the filtering rules at positions 10, 11 and 15 respectively in the ruleset are compared with the destination address of the incoming packet. The destination address of the filtering rule at position 10 is less than the destination address of the incoming packet. Thus, the position 10 is stored in the low position. The next spark is traversed and the destination address of the filtering rule at position 11 is less than the destination address of the incoming packet. Thus, the position 11 is stored in the low position. The next spark is traversed and the destination address of the filtering rule at position 15 is equal to the destination address of the incoming packet. Thus position 15 is stored in the matching list. The matching list contains the value {15}. Since the difference between the low position and the first position in the matching list is not 1, the firework is exploded between 11 and 15. The sparks fall at filtering rules at positions 12 and 13 respectively in the firewall ruleset. The spark at position 12 is traversed and the destination address of the filtering rule at position 12 is less than the destination address of the incoming packet. Thus position 12 is stored in the low position. The next spark is traversed and the destination address of the filtering rule at position 13 is equal to the destination address of the incoming packet. Thus position 13 is stored in the matching list. The matching list contains the value {13, 15}.

Since the high position is empty, the firework is exploded at a point following the last position in the matching list. The point chosen for exploding the firework is in the range of rules between 16 and 19. The sparks fall on the filtering rules in the ruleset at positions 17, 18 and 19 respectively. The sparks are traversed until a high position is obtained. It is found that the destination address of the filtering rules at the rule positions 17 and 18 are equal to the destination address of the incoming packet and are stored in the matching list. The matching list contains the values {13, 15, 17, 18}. The next spark is traversed and the destination address of the filtering rule at position 19 is found to be higher than the destination address of the incoming packet. Thus, the rule position 19 is stored in the high position. Since the difference between the low position and first position in the matching list as well as the last position in the matching list and high position is 1, the process is stopped. Thus, the destination address of the rules denoted by the rule positions in the matching list matches with the incoming destination address. The destination ports of these matching rules are compared with the incoming packet and it is found that the filtering rule at position 14 matches with the incoming packet and the packet is allowed to pass.

Lemma 1: The entire set of filtering rules in the ruleset need not be searched for filtering the incoming packets.

Proof:

Consider a set of filtering rules R1…Rn at positions 1, 2,…, n in the firewall ruleset. The rules R1…Rn are sorted in ascending order.

The firework is exploded at a point in the ruleset and the sparks S1, S2 and S3 falls on the filtering rules at positions 2, 5 and 7 respectively as shown in Figure 3. Thus, the comparison field value in the filtering rules R2, R5 and R7 are compared with the corresponding field value of the incoming packet. Since, the fields in the ruleset are sorted in ascending order, the rules in the ruleset can be written as shown in equation (1).

$$R2 < R5 < R7 .\tag{1}$$

The spark S1 is traversed and if the comparison field value in the filtering rule R2 is less than the incoming packet field value, the rule position R2 is stored in the low position. The next spark S2 is traversed and if the comparison field value in the filtering rule R5 is higher than the incoming packet field value, the rule position R5 is stored in the high position. Since the high position is obtained, the spark S3 is not traversed and the process is stopped. Therefore, the search space lies between rules R2 and R5 and the entire set of rules need not be searched. Therefore the search space lies between rules R2 and R5 and the entire set of rules need not be searched.

Lemma 2: If the value of the compared field in the rules Ri and Rj in the ruleset matches with the incoming packet field value, then the values in the compared field in the rules from positions i to j matches with the incoming packet field value.

Figure 3. Search space in the ruleset

Rules	Comparison Field	Sparks
R_1		
R_2	L	S_1
R_3		
R_4		
R_5	H	S_2
R_6		
R_7		S_3
....		
R_n		

Proof:

Consider a set of filtering rules R1…Rn at positions 1, 2,…., n in the firewall ruleset. The rules R1… Rn are sorted in ascending order. Assume there is more than one filtering rule in the ruleset matching with the incoming packet.

Figure 4. Ruleset with seven matching rules

Rules	Compared Field 1	Field 2	Sparks
R_1			
R_2	M		S_1
R_3			
R_4			
R_5			
R_6			
R_7	M		S_2
R_8	M		S_3
R_9			
...			
R_n			

The firework is exploded at a point in the ruleset and the sparks S1, S2 and S3 falls on the filtering rules at positions 2, 7 and 8 respectively as shown in Figure 4. Thus, the comparison field values in the filtering rules R2, R7 and R8 are compared with the corresponding field value of the incoming packet.

The spark S1 is traversed and if the comparison field value in the filtering rule R2 is equal to the incoming packet field value, R2 is stored in the matching list. The next spark S2 is traversed and if the comparison field value in the filtering rule R7 is equal to the incoming packet field value, R7 is stored in the matching list. The next spark S3 is traversed and if the comparison field value in the filtering rule R8 is equal to the incoming packet field value, R8 is stored in the matching list.

Since the comparison field value of the filtering rules R2, R7 and R8 are sorted in ascending order and matches with the incoming packet field value, it implies that the comparison field values of the rules R2 to R8 matches with the incoming packet field.

EXPERIMENTAL RESULTS

The experiment is repeated for the filtering rules stored in the firewall ruleset in a destination port detection unit shown in Table 8. FWPF algorithm filters the incoming packets shown in Table 9 based on the destination port in the rules in the ruleset. It is shown in Table 9 FWPF algorithm filters the packets strictly based on the rules in the ruleset. It is shown that the destination port 21 of the second incoming packet matches with 5th filtering rule in the ruleset. Since a match has occurred, the corresponding destination ip of the filtering rule is compared for a match with the destination ip of the incoming packet. Since a match does not occur, the incoming packet is dropped. Also, the eleventh incoming packet is not present in the firewall ruleset and is dropped. The experimental results prove the accuracy of FWPF algorithm is 100% which would allow only incoming packets defined by the rules in the ruleset.

Table 8. Firewall Ruleset (Eyadat, 2008)

Rule	Protocol	Transport Protocol	Source IP	Source Port	Destination IP	Destination Port	Action
1	Inbound POP3	TCP	Any	Any	192.168.2.1 / 24	110	Allow
2	Inbound POP3/ S	TCP	Any	Any	192.168.2.1 / 24	995	Allow
3	SMTP Inbound	TCP	Any	Any	192.168.2.29	25	Allow
4	SMTP / S Inbound	TCP	Any	Any	192.168.2.29	465	Allow
5	FTP control Inbound	TCP	Any	Any	192.168.1.25	21	Allow
6	DNS Inbound	TCP	Any	Any	192.168.2.31	53	Allow
7	DNS Inbound	UDP	Any	Any	192.168.2.31	53	Allow
8	HTTP Inbound	TCP	Any	Any	192.168.2.32	80	Allow
9	HTTPS Inbound	TCP	Any	Any	192.168.2.32	443	Allow

Table 9. Incoming Packets (Eyadat, 2008)

Incoming Packet	Protocol	Transport Protocol	Source IP	Source Port	Destination IP	Destination Port	Action
1	FTP control Inbound	TCP	Any	Any	192.168.1.25	21	Allow
2	FTP control Inbound	TCP	Any	Any	192.168.1.23	21	Drop
3	SMTP Inbound	TCP	Any	Any	192.168.2.29	25	Allow
4	DNS Inbound	TCP	Any	Any	192.168.2.31	53	Allow
5	DNS Inbound	TCP	Any	Any	192.168.2.31	54	Allow
6	HTTP Inbound	TCP	Any	Any	192.168.2.32	80	Allow
7	Inbound POP3	TCP	Any	Any	<u>192.168.2.1/24</u>	110	Allow
8	HTTPS Inbound	TCP	Any	Any	192.168.2.32	443	Allow
9	SMTP /S Inbound	TCP	Any	Any	192.168.2.29	465	Allow
10	Inbound POP3/S	TCP	Any	Any	<u>192.168.2.1/24</u>	995	Allow
11	HTTPS Inbound	TCP	Any	Any	192.168.2.32	67	Drop

Computational Complexity Of The System

Lemma 3: Given a sample space S and event A in the sample space, the indicator random variable I{A} associated with event A is deðned as

I {A} =1 if A occurs

I {A} =0 if A does not occur

Let XA =I {A} then E [XA] =Pr{A}

Proof:

By the definition of an indicator random variable and the definition of expected value we have

E [XA] =E [I {A}]

E [XA] =1.Pr {A} +0.Pr {A'} where A'=S−A, the complement of A.

E [XA] =Pr {A}

The system is modelled using indicator random variables and the computational complexity of the system is analysed.

Let 'n' be the total number of rules in the ruleset. A probabilistic analysis is used, since the filtering rules in the ruleset are chosen randomly for comparison with the incoming packet.

Choose a random variable X whose value equals the number of comparisons made to match an incoming packet with the rules in the ruleset. Choose an indicator random variable Xi associated with the event in which the ith rule is compared.

Xi =1 if rule i is compared with the incoming packet (2a)

Xi =0 if rule i is not compared with the incoming packet (2b)

and

X =X1 +X2 +X3 +⋯+Xn

By Lemma 3, E[Xi]=Pr {rule i is compared} (3)

The filtering rules in the ruleset are chosen in a random order for comparison with the incoming packet. Hence the first i filtering rules are chosen in a random order. Out of these first i filtering rules, one rule is equally likely to be chosen for comparison. Thus the rule i has a probability of 1/i of being chosen for comparison.

Thus E[Xi]= 1/i (4)

From (3) we have $E[X] = E[\sum_{i=1}^{n} Xi]$. (5)

Using linearity of expectation we have,

$$E[X] = \sum_{i=1}^{n} E[Xi]$$

$$E[X] = \sum_{i=1}^{n} 1/i \quad \text{from (4)}$$

Using harmonic series (Cormen, Leiserson, Rivest, & Stein, 2001) we have

E[X] = ln n + O(1) (6)

Thus, on an average the number of comparisons to be made is ln n where n is the number of filtering rules in the ruleset.

COMPARISON BETWEEN FWPF ALGORITHM AND EXISTING ALGORITHMS FOR PACKET FILTERING

FWPF algorithm is compared with the existing packet filtering algorithms in terms of search space and efficiency.

Comparison Between FWPF Algorithm and
ACOPF Algorithm for Packet Filtering

The advantage of FWPF algorithm when compared to ACOPF algorithm (Sreelaja & Vijayalakshmi Pai, 2010) is that it reduces the search space and the convergence occurs easily since the range of the rules is decided based on the sparks and the entire set of rules is not searched as in ACOPF algorithm. Also, the matching rules can be obtained simultaneously in the range of the sparks searched.

Figure 5. Comparison of FWPF, ACOPF and sequential search

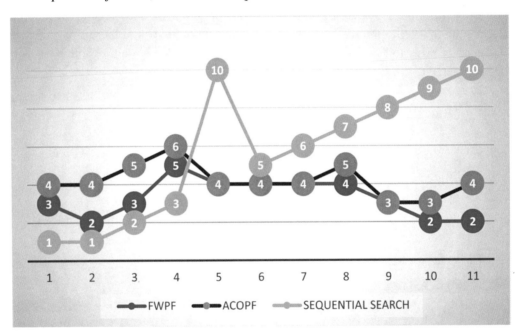

Figure 5 shows a comparison of the number of searches required for matching the incoming packets given in Table 9 for the filtering rules in the firewall ruleset in Table 8 using FWPF, ACO-PF and sequential search. It is observed from Figure 5 that FWPF algorithm has less number of searches for 7 incoming packets. Also, the number of searches for the remaining 4 incoming packets were the same using both FWPF algorithm and ACOPF algorithm. It is observed from Table 9 that the incoming packet 1 and 2 has the same destination port number. However, for the incoming packet 1, the number of searches using ACOPF algorithm and FWPF algorithm are 4 and 3 respectively whereas for the incoming packet 2, the number of searches using FWPF algorithm is 2 showing that the range of filtering rules chosen for matching plays a significant role. It is also inferred from the graph shown in Figure 5 that FWPF algorithm scales well when compared to sequential search.

Comparison of Data Driven Firewall for Faster Packet Filtering, Packet Filtering Optimization Using Statistical Traffic Awareness Test and FWPF Algorithm

Mohammad M. Masud, Umniya Mustafa, Zouheir Trabelsi. (2014) have proposed a packet filtering approach based on data mining technique. The advantage of this approach is that the speed of the classifier is rapid in making filtering decision and the classifier attains very high accuracy of 98% or more.

Trabelsi, Zhang, and Zeidan (2012) have proposed a mechanism to improve firewall packet filtering time through optimizing the order of security policy filtering rules and rule-fields. However, the drawback is that the algorithm has an error precision rate and 100% classification accuracy is not possible.

The classification accuracy is 100% in FWPF algorithm, since the filtering rules in the rule-set are compared for a match with the incoming packet as shown in Experimental Results.

Comparison of Adaptive Statistical Optimization Techniques for Packet Filtering, Lightweight Traffic-Aware Packet Classification and FWPF algorithm

Hamed et al. (2006) proposed a statistical optimization technique which rejects the maximum number of packets at an earlier stage which introduces a minimal overhead on the firewall, thereby reducing the matching time significantly. According to this approach, the space complexity is bounded by O (n), and computational complexity is O (n log n).

Shariful Hasan Shaikot and Min Sik Kim (2010) proposed a lightweight traffic-aware packet classifier which reorganizes its internal data structure (rule tree) based on the traffic pattern to reduce the search time for the most frequently visited rules in the rule-set. According to this approach, during preprocessing stage, the rules in the rule-set are converted into intervals, which takes O (ni) where n is the number of rules and i is the number of intervals. The IRT construction time is O (n log n).

The computational complexity of FWPF algorithm is O (ln n) where n is the number of filtering rules used for comparison. Thus, the computational complexity is less than the computational complexity of Adaptive Statistical Optimization Techniques and Lightweight Traffic Aware Packet Classification technique.

Comparison of FWPF Algorithm and Segment Based List Search

El-A. Adel, S. Taghrid, Al-S. Ehab, L. Hong (2007) proposed a technique called segment-based list search (SLS) in which each packet is matched against the segments one-by-one until a match takes place. Once the matching segment is identified, it is moved to the top of the list. The drawback is that the segmentation process was shown to be O (ns) where n is the number of rules, and s is the number of segments resulting and the filtering time is O(s).

In packet filtering method using FWPF algorithm, a segmentation process is not needed and the storage complexity is O (n) where n is the number of filtering rules in the ruleset. Also, a linear search is not used and the rules need not be moved after a match is found.

Comparison of FWPF Algorithm and Adaptive Packet Filtering Method

Kencl and Schwarzer (2006) proposed the adaptive packet filtering method which periodically introduces shortcuts into the search tree along frequently traveled paths, to reduce the number of memory accesses.

The complexity of memory accesses is O ($N \log N$), where N is the total number of nodes denoting the source/destination IP.

In FWPF algorithm, the complexity of storage is O (n) where n is the number of filtering rules. The average number of comparisons in the ruleset for packet filtering using FWPF algorithm is O ($\ln n$) where the value of 'n' depends on the number of filtering rules searched for comparison.

Comparison of Bilayer PSO Based Packet Filtering and FWPF Algorithm

A PSO based packet filtering method (SelvaRani & Vairamuthu, 2016) was proposed for rulesets which has large number of rules. However, it is argued in (SelvaRani & Vairamuthu, 2016) that the linear search method is effective for small number of rules in the ruleset. It is shown in Figure 5 that FWPF algorithm scales well than linear search method of packet filtering even for a very small number of rules in the ruleset.

CONCLUSION

Firewall plays an important role in ensuring security and performing packet classification based on multiple fields. This chapter deals with packet filtering in a firewall using Firework based approach. A Fireworks based Packet Filtering (FWPF) algorithm for efficient packet filtering has been proposed. The advantage of FWPF over ACOPF (Sreelaja & Vijayalakshmi Pai, 2010) is that it reduces the search space in the firewall rule-set. It is shown that FWPF algorithm has overcome the drawbacks of the existing packet filtering methods in terms of both storage and search space. The number of searches using FWPF algorithm is less when compared to sequential search method. The future work is to update the ruleset dynamically in an optimized manner.

REFERENCES

Cormen, T. H., Leiserson, C. E., Rivest, R. L., & Stein, C. (2001). Introduction to algorithms second edition. The Knuth-Morris-Pratt Algorithm, year.

El-Atawy, A., Samak, T., Al-Shaer, E., & Li, H. (2007, May). Using online traffic statistical matching for optimizing packet filtering performance. In *Proceedings IEEE INFOCOM 2007-26th IEEE International Conference on Computer Communications* (pp. 866-874). IEEE.

Eyadat, M. (2008). Fall 08 Packet Filtering. Retrieved from www.csudh.edu/eyadat/classes/CIS478/ handouts/Fall08/Packet%20Filtering.ppt

Hamed, H., El-Atawy, A., & Al-Shaer, E. (2006). Adaptive Statistical Optimization Techniques for Firewall Packet Filtering. In *Proceedings IEEE INFOCOM 2006, 25TH IEEE International Conference on Computer Communications*. 10.1109/INFOCOM.2006.129

Kencl, L., & Schwarzer, C. (2006). Traffic-adaptive packet filtering of denial of service attacks. *Proceedings of the 2006 International Symposium on World of Wireless, Mobile, and Multimedia Networks* (2006), pp. 485-489. 10.1109/WOWMOM.2006.111

Masud, M. M., Mustafa, U., & Trabelsi, Z. (2014). Comparison of a data driven firewall for faster packet filtering. In *Proceedings Fourth International Conference on Communications and Networking, ComsNet-2014.*

Rani, B. S., & Vairamuthu, S. (2016). An Intelligent Packet Filtering Based on Bi-layer Particle Swarm Optimization with Reduced Search Space. In *Proceedings of the Second International Conference on Computer and Communication Technologies* (pp. 639-647). New Delhi, India: Springer.

Shaikot, S. H., & Kim, M. S. (2010). Lightweight Traffic-Aware Packet Classification for Continuous Operation. In *Proceedings 10th Annual International Symposium on Applications and the Internet.* Academic Press.

Sreelaja, N. K., & Vijayalakshmi Pai, G. A. (2010, September). Ant Colony Optimization based Approach for efficient Packet Filtering in Firewall. *Applied Soft Computing*, *10*(4), 1222–1236. doi:10.1016/j.asoc.2010.03.009

Tan, Y., & Zhu, Y. (2010, June). Fireworks algorithm for optimization. In *Proceedings International Conference in Swarm Intelligence* (pp. 355-364). Berlin, Germany: Springer.

Trabelsi, Z., Zhang, L., & Zeidan, S. (2012, October). Firewall packet filtering optimization using statistical traffic awareness test. In *International Conference on Information and Communications Security* (pp. 81-92). Berlin, Germany: Springer. 10.1007/978-3-642-34129-8_8

334

Chapter 15
Innovative Aspects of Virtual Reality and Kinetic Sensors for Significant Improvement Using Fireworks Algorithm in a Wii Game of a Collaborative Sport

Alberto Ochoa-Zezzatti
ⓘ https://orcid.org/0000-0002-9183-6086
Universidad Autonóma de Ciudad Juárez, Mexico

Ismael Rodríguez
ⓘ https://orcid.org/0000-0001-9722-610X
Jagiellonian University, Poland

José Mejia
Universidad Autonóma de Ciudad Juárez, Mexico

Jose Peinado
Universidad Autonóma de Ciudad Juárez, Mexico

Saúl González
Universidad Autonóma de Ciudad Juárez, Mexico

Jesús Bahena
Universidad Autonóma de Ciudad Juárez, Mexico

Víctor Zezatti
Universidad Autonoma del Estado de Morelos, Mexico

ABSTRACT

A new report on childhood obesity is published every so often. The bad habits of food and the increasingly sedentary life of children in a border society has caused an alarming increase in the cases of children who are overweight or obese. Formerly, it seemed to be a problem of countries with unhealthy eating habits, such as the United States or Mexico in Latin America, where junk food is part of the diet in childhood. However, obesity is a problem that we already have around the corner and that is not so difficult to fight in children. In the present research the development of an application that reduces the problem of the lack of movement in the childhood of a smart city is considered a future problem which it is the main contribution, coupled with achieving an innovative way of looking for an Olympic sport without the complexity of physically moving to a space with high maintenance costs and considering the adverse weather conditions.

DOI: 10.4018/978-1-7998-1659-1.ch015

Copyright © 2020, IGI Global. Copying or distributing in print or electronic forms without written permission of IGI Global is prohibited.

INTRODUCTION

The increase in childhood obesity, a problem of great importance in an intelligent city, determines the challenges that must be built with respect to applications that involve Artificial Intelligence. Computer games to combat childhood obesity are very important to reduce a future problem in our society. Exergaming, computer games to exercise children increasingly play less on the street and spend more time with video games and computer games, so they lead a more sedentary life. This, together with bad eating habits, increases the cases of obese children every year. What can parents do to avoid being overweight in childhood? A bet that comes to us from the University of Western Australia, Liverpool John Mores University and the University of Swansea in the United Kingdom is the exergaming, an Anglicism that comes from joining the word "exerdizze" in Turkish (exercise in English) with gaming (game). These are games that offer consoles such as Xbox, Kinect or Wii in which you interact through physical activity in tests in which you have to run, bike, play bowling or jump fences. The researchers tested children who performed high and low intensity exergaming and measured their energy expenditure. The conclusion reached was that the exergaming generated an energy expenditure comparable to the exercise of moderate or low intensity, depending on the difficulty of the game. In addition, the game was satisfactory for the children, who enjoyed the activities they did. It is an advantage that parents can take advantage of to prevent children from spending so many hours sitting in front of the console, since it has been shown that they can obtain long-term health benefits. In any case, it must always be one of the means we can use to encourage children to do some physical activity but not the only one. Going out the street to play, run, jump, must always be on the children's agenda, as is shown in Figure 1.

Figure 1. Intelligent application using Kinect

BACKGROUND

Emotions in Children

Since the science-based child psychology emerged in the second half of the nineteenth century promised to provide a rational basis for education for the overall development of the child. This whole area developing offering new interesting proposals as the wearing of the study of children not only to child psychology but proposed the creation of a focused science to the child that went beyond child psychology (Chrisman, 1896). This thanks to William Preyer who is considered the father of child psychology and eye not the first, but if he did it with a rigorous accuracy same which is made its observations in its work by some very systematics (Siegfried, 1982).

Emotional Disorders in Children

Mental disorders of children affect many children and their families. Children of all ages, ethnic or racial backgrounds, and regions of the United States have mental disorders. According to the report by the National Research Council and Institute of Medicine in the division (Prevention of mental, emotional and behavioral disorders in young people: progress and possibilities, 2009) who gathered findings from previous studies, it is estimated that 13 to 20% of children living in the United States (up to 1 in 5) has a mental disorder in a given year, and about 247,000 million dollars a year are spent on childhood mental disorders(CDC, 2016). In the literature we find several definitions to refer to emotional, mental or behavioral problems. These days we find that they are referred to as "emotional disorders" ("emotional disturbance"). The Education Act Individuals with Disabilities Education Act ("IDEA" for short) defines the performance of emotional disorders as "that condition exhibiting a characteristic in a long time in a degree of sharpness that negatively affects boy". Immediately we list the classifications of the types of behaviors as emotional disorder (Parentcenterhub.org, 2016).

1. The lack of ability to learn that is inexplicable by intellectual, sensory or health reasons.
2. The lack of ability to maintain personal relationships on good terms with like or their teachers.
3. Inconsistent behavior or feelings under normal circumstances.
4. Is usually sadness or depression.
5. Develop physical symptoms or fears associated with personal or school problems.

- **Hyperactivity:** In this type of behavior manifest the child inattentive, easily distracted and a degree of impulsivity.
- **Assaults:** When the result of the behavior ends in wounds, either themselves or their neighbors.
- **Withdrawal:** The social life shows signs of delay or individual shows inability to relate to their environment. It includes excessive fears or anxiety.
- **Immaturity:** When you experience crying spells where it is not warranted; it is unable to adapt to changes.

- **Learning difficulties:** learning does not develop at the same pace than the average in their environment. It remains below the level below their peers. There are even more young children with serious emotional disturbances where the thought comes to distort, severe anxiety, not common motor acts, and behaviors too irritable. Sometimes diagnosed with severe psychosis or schizophrenia (Parentcenterhub.org, 2016).

Play Therapy

Play therapy is defined as a formal recognition therapeutic model and also has demonstrated effectiveness in children with problems of emotional stress contributing and being manifest in the child during normal development. Play therapy builds on the child's play as a natural means of self-expression, experimentation and communication. While the child plays the child learns about the world and their relationships tested reality, explores emotions and roles. It also gives the child the possibility to externalize his personal history, thus releasing negative feelings and frustrations, mitigating the effects of painful experiences and that he shudders, giving relief to feelings of anxiety and stress (Tomas, 2016) The play therapist is a specialized and trained in play and suitable for the various stages of child development professional technical therapeutic methods. This must grasp and understand as well as engaging in child's play to be able to create a relationship of confidence and trust for expression and handling of internal conflicts of the child are favored, also download and understanding of their emotions more entrapped making able to recognize and explore issues that affect their lives (Schaefer, 2012). The Serious game proposed does not replace ludic therapy one your therapist, but seeks to grant an auxiliary support tool and also effective as support of those who are in contact with children at some point show signs of a state of low mood. Inclusive also could be used by health professionals as part of their therapeutic tools to control emotions their patients.

Serious Games

An old definition of the 70's that so far has remained is that serious games are those that have an educational or therapeutic express purpose and not just fun. Within this definition it is where the real challenge for developers because maintaining this balance between fun and fulfill the purpose of carefully planned learning. Once the construction of the game the focus on learning or therapeutic purpose is often happens that the fun part of such an important and necessary neglected juice undermining the quality and impact of the game that should have on users. The applications are varied and range from the most common are in education, management, policy, advocacy, planning, among others (Braga & Silveira, 2015). Why games like support? The answer is simple and intuitive as these are part of the training of people. They range from individual games to games on computers, either two or three or even members of many teams. Also an important aspect of socialization and identity construction of individuals. Every culture has games that are practiced from generation to generation. Although he senses that his first games were not designed with learning or therapeutic purposes it can be seen that in addition to the fun and entertainment to the individual to his help in their physical and mental development because they fail to stimulate the individual. And to reinforce the above mentioned the time of the revolution technology that we live where practically the use of technology has become indispensable (Silveira, 2016).

Important When Building a Serious Game Elements

Within an important list of features that include a serious game we must begin by referring to the memory of the Game. This virtue is that the game must memorize the achievements or what he has learned the player, is that after the game not only the difficulty of the game is restarted at the same point as this may cause the player does not appeal to play because it will be the same to play again. But it should include a way the game remembers what the player has learned should be educational or gambling know what part of therapy player stayed this if the game was used as recovery therapy of some kind (Csikszentmihalyi, 1990). The game flow is very important to sow player loyalty. To this we must try to modulate the difficulty that not frustrating or boring into the other end to the user. For this reason what the difficulty must be carefully modulated (Csikszentmihalyi, 1990). Another very important thing is the story or narrative. The combination of history, landscape and context must be consistent with the culture and country. The narrative is a basic element which should tell graphical environment has to be immersive (immersed, submerged, tucked) so that the player feels he is in the game. As the above interactivity must be present for the player to interact as much as possible playing. We must not forget also that should provide elements consistent with reality, as an objective of the game is that the player develops and / or better their skills. Another of the most important things of a serious game is to provide some degree of adaptability, this is the game fits the style of the player to the game to respond properly and depending on the style of the you a serious game, think of the public who will play, stories that may be of interest, environments and characters with which the player will feel attracted to play are essential part of the game. The rules must be clearly defined. The player. And above all, and yet we should not let pass a serious game must by obligation be fun (Silveira, 2016).

Proposal Methodology: Fireworks Algorithm

We consider this behavior to simulate different bio-inspired algorithms evaluated in the literature, such as algorithms Cultural and Multi-Agent Systems Algorithm Fireworks, determining that the latter properly considered clustering between communities and how to visually show how social isolation increased with time in the absence of a model of social integration, and public policies for this. Inclusive we consider evaluate a model of predator-prey game to analyze the relationships between these minorities and the rest of the majority group(CDC, 2016; Parentcenterhub.org, 2016).

Fireworks Algorithm Framework

When a firework is set off, a shower of sparks will fill the local space around the firework (Chrisman, 1896; Siegfried, 1982). In our opinion, the explosion process of a firework can be viewed as a search in the local space around a specific point where the firework is set off through the sparks generated in the explosion. When we are asked to find a point xj satisfying f(xj) = y, we can continually set off 'fireworks' in potential space until one 'spark' targets or is fairly near the point xj. Mimicking the process of setting off fireworks, a rough framework of the FA is depicted in Figure 2. In the FA, for each generation of explosion, we first select n locations, where n fireworks are set off. Then after explosion, the locations of sparks are obtained and evaluated. When the optimal location is found, the algorithm stops. Otherwise, n other locations are selected from the current sparks and fireworks for the next generation of explosion. From Figure 2, it can be seen that the success of the FA lies in a good design of the explosion process and a proper method for selecting locations, which are respectively elaborated in next subsections.

Figure 2. Framework of fireworks algorithm

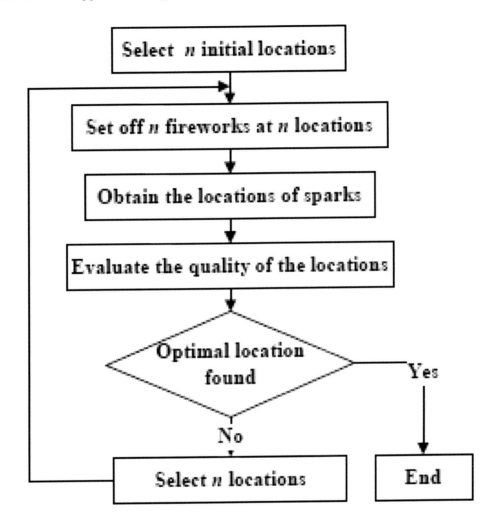

Design of Fireworks Explosion

Through observing fireworks display, we have found two specific behavior of fireworks explosion. When fireworks are well manufactured, numerous sparks are generated, and the sparks centralize the explosion center. In this case, we enjoy the spectacular display of the fireworks. However, for a bad firework explosion, quite few sparks are generated, and the sparks scatter in the space.

The two manners are depicted in Figure 3. From the standpoint of a search algorithm, a good firework denotes that the firework locates in a promising area which may be close to the optimal location. Thus, it is proper to utilize more sparks to search the local area around the firework. In the contrast, a bad firework means the optimal location may be far from where the firework locates. Then, the search radius should be larger. In the FA, more sparks are generated and the explosion amplitude is smaller for a good firework, compared to a bad one (Blanco, 2012).

Figure 3. Two types of fireworks explosion

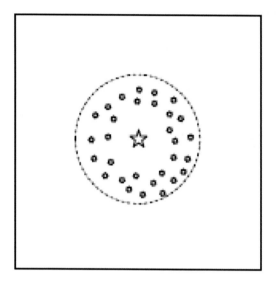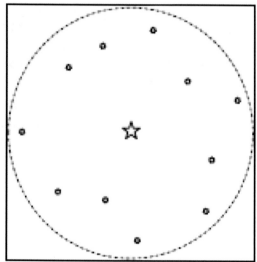

Number of Sparks

Suppose the FA is designed for the general optimization problem:

$$Minimize f(\chi) \in \mathbb{R}, \chi_{min} \leq \chi \leq \chi_{max}$$

where x = x1, x2, . . ., xd denotes a location in the potential space, f(x) is an objective function, and xmin and xmax denote the bounds of the potential space.

Then the number of sparks generated by each firework xi is defined as follows.

$$s_i = m \cdot \frac{y_{max} - f(\chi_i) + \varepsilon}{\sum_{i=1}^{n}(y_{max} - f(\chi_i)) + \varepsilon}$$

where m is a parameter controlling the total number of sparks generated by the n fireworks, ymax = max(f(xi)) (i = 1, 2, . . ., n) is the maximum (worst) value of the objective function among the n fireworks, and ξ, which denotes the smallest constant in the computer, is utilized to avoid zero-division-error.

To avoid overwhelming effects of splendid fireworks, bounds are defined for si, which is shown in Equation 3.

$$\hat{s}_i = \begin{cases} round(a \cdot m) & if s_i < am \\ round(b \cdot m) & if s_i > bm, a < b < 1 \\ round(s_i) & otherwise \end{cases}$$

where a and b are const parameters.

Amplitude of Explosion

In contrast to the design of sparks number, the amplitude of a good firework explosion is smaller than that of a bad one. Amplitude of explosion for each firework is defined as follows.

$$A_i = \hat{A} \cdot \frac{f(\chi_i) - y_{min} + \varepsilon}{\sum_{i=1}^{n} (f(\chi_i) - y_{min}) + \varepsilon}$$

where $\hat{A}$ denotes the maximum explosion amplitude, and $y_{min} = \min(f(\chi_i)) - (i = 1, 2, ..., n)$ is the minimum (best) value of the objective function among the n fireworks.

Generating Sparks

In explosion, sparks may undergo the effects of explosion from random z directions (dimensions). In the FA, we obtain the number of the affected directions randomly as follows.

$$z = round(d \cdot rand(0,1))$$

where d is the dimensionality of the location x, and rand (0, 1) is an uniform distribution over [0,1].

The location of a spark of the firework xi is obtained using Table 1.

Mimicking the explosion process, a spark's location ˜xj is first generated. Then if the obtained location is found to fall out of the potential space, it is mapped to the potential space according to the algorithm.

Table 1. Obtain the location of a spark

Algorithm 1. Obtain the location of a spark
Initialize the location of the spark: $\tilde{x}_j = x_i$;
$z = round(d \cdot rand(0,1))$;
Randomly select z dimensions of $\tilde{x}_j$;
Calculate the displacement: $h = A_i \cdot rand(-1,1)$;
for each dimension $\tilde{x}_k^j \in \{$pre-selected z dimensions of $\tilde{x}_j\}$ do
$\tilde{x}_k^j = \tilde{x}_k^j + h$;
if $\tilde{x}_k^j < x_k^{min}$ or $\tilde{x}_k^j > x_k^{max}$ then
map $\tilde{x}_k^j$ to the potential space: $\tilde{x}_k^j = x_k^{min} + \| \tilde{x}_k^j \| \%(x_k^{max} - x_k^{min})$;
end if
end for

To keep the diversity of sparks, we design another way of generating sparks — Gaussian explosion, which is show in Table 2. A function Gaussian(1, 1), which denotes a Gaussian distribution with mean 1 and standard deviation 1, is utilized to define the coefficient of the explosion. In our experiments, $\hat{m}$ sparks of this type are generated in each explosion generation.

Table 2. Obtain the location of a specific spark

Algorithm 2. Obtain the location of a specific spark

Initialize the location of the spark: $\hat{x}_j = x_i$;
$z = round(d \cdot rand(0, 1))$;
Randomly select z dimensions of $\hat{x}_j$;
Calculate the coefficient of Gaussian explosion: $g = Gaussian(1, 1)$;
for each dimension $\hat{x}_k^j \in \{$pre-selected z dimensions of $\hat{x}_j\}$ do
  $\hat{x}_k^j = \hat{x}_k^j \cdot g$;
  if $\hat{x}_k^j < x_k^{min}$ or $\hat{x}_k^j > x_k^{max}$ then
    map $\hat{x}_k^j$ to the potential space: $\hat{x}_k^j = x_k^{min} + |\hat{x}_k^j| \% (x_k^{max} - x_k^{min})$;
  end if
end for

Selection of Locations

At the beginning of each explosion generation, n locations should be selected for the fireworks explosion. In the FA, the current best location x∗, upon which the objective function f(x∗) is optimal among current locations, is always kept for the next explosion generation. After that, n − 1 locations are selected based on their distance to other locations so as to keep diversity of sparks. The general distance between a location xi and other locations is defined as follows.

$$R(\chi_i) = \sum_{j \in K} d(\chi_i, \chi_j) = \sum_{j \in K} \left\| \chi_i - \chi_j \right\|$$

where K is the set of all current locations of both fireworks and sparks.

Then the selection probability of a location xi is defined as follows.

$$p(\chi_i) = \frac{R(\chi_i)}{\sum_{j \in K} R(\chi_j)}$$

When calculating the distance, any distance measure can be utilized including Manhattan distance, Euclidean distance, Angle-based distance, and so on (Csikszentmihalyi, 1990). When d (xi, xj) is defined as | f(xi) − f(xj) |, the probability is equivalent to the definition of the immune density-based probability in (Heller, 2016).

PROTOTYPE PROPOSED

Due to the existing climate in Ciudad Juarez - A border society - where the temperature for more than three months does not allow outdoor activities, and few sports are played other than baseball and soccer, for our research we decided to choose the Water polo and help the students of basic school levels to agree to collaborate as a team, respect the rules and that the game could interconnect with other users in a model called "Cooperative Model for the resolution of problems", an innovative idea proposed In massive multiplayer online role-playing games (MMORPGs), cooperation between players to accomplish difficult tasks is often an integral mechanic of gameplay, and organized groups of players, often called guilds, clans, or factions, emerge. Sometimes the relationships players from within the game spill over into friendships or romantic relationships in the material world. In other instances, romantic partners and groups of material world friends find that playing together strengthens their bonds. We use components bought with our Project to develop our innovative model as is shown in Figure 4.

Figure 4. Components of the Wii application used and its realystic images to créate avatar in wrestling

The main idea of the Serious Game for a Wii platform, is to develop the skills associated with empathy and psychomotor skills to improve the performance of children, that is why, to build the prototype of the serious game we initially used three scenarios associated with the practice of the Waterpolo: A covered swimming pool, an Olympic pool or a delimited area in a water park. When starting our Serious Game, each player must register their name and assigned position in order for the hardware to reflect the movements required to play as a team. And determine the modality of the game, in this case, the player will select a level that goes from simple to complex. At the simplest level, the player will have the possibility to verify if the movements made are appropriate according to the FINA gift, that is why the importance of our proposal lies in that together with playing simultaneously with other players you can learn from a more appropriate way the game to go demonstrating that you can complete challenges that are proposed and, in turn, develop their skills and knowledge in the Waterpolo, that is why the Serious Game proposes to the user to demonstrate their skills and knowledge., as the serious game progresses each time the player achieves the desired objectives, a sound model is made to reward good performance in the serious game, as is shown in Figure 5.

As mentioned in this document, this project is currently in the construction phase. This prototype Serious Game has the firm intention of taking the next phase of complete and functional construction. A foundation sponsored by one of the most important children's hospitals in the city of Paso Texas in the United States. He has shown a genuine interest in the project, for which he mentioned providing the necessary support for its realization. This foundation has childcare programs and has interesting and very efficient strategies. That is why you would like to have this type of tools integrated into your programs. For this, it will soon be formalized by both parties committed to supporting the project shown in this document. In future research, we try to modify a game based on collaborative work in a group - we are choosing rugby seven - with high intensity of pressure for each child and modify the importance related to the support of this type of pressure related to the responsibility of a Collective activity, an approxima-

Figure 5. Our Wii serious game model using collaborative task to play waterpolo

tion will be related to what is implied for water polo, as shown in Figure 5. A very relevant aspect, is to consider that if someone asks why he likes to use our Serious Game, this user will be able to respond: because he has had a playful scope and of adequate selection with the avatar, so he could have empathy for our proposal. By analyzing in more detail the group of people who used our Serious Games, we determined that, like the role-play, it is a hobby that unites them and gives them opportunities to help each other and their videogame community. It is a safe environment in which you can experience social interactions, something fundamental when the weather does not allow it. This group of users of our Serious Game says that they have witnessed the personal growth of individuals in terms of their self-esteem and the expansion of their social interactions as a result of the game. This is just one of the benefits of the game. Our research showed that it was discovered that everyone can find some hours a week to "save the universe, catch the villains or solve mysteries" -including learning to practice Water polo, and that playing with the computer is as fun as any other activity in our research Playing our Serious Game can strengthen a variety of skills such as math and reading online recommendations. Increase the ability to think and speak clearly and concisely, when formulating and implementing their plans, cooperating and communicating with others, as well as increasing the ability to analyze written and verbal information. Placed on the market our Serious Game will determine that players are cohesive members of the group in multiplayer games, can help people develop leadership skills and promote cooperation, teamwork, friendship and open communication. In other studies related with this kind of Wii Serious Games, we try to compare with our colleagues of Montenegro whom propose and develop an innovative Serious Game which involve a model to Fencing practitioners, this sport is reach high popularity in these society. A representative model can be shown in the next figure 6:

What would users expect from our proposal of a Serious Game in this Wii model to learn and practice Water polo?

Improve mood player as elapsed play through the tools that will be used as background music, using music therapy techniques to lift the spirits Player (Blanco, 2012). Another element of the strategy are the colors of the stage. Through the effect of color on mood it is to have the player in a positive emotional

Figure 6. Use of Wii software to improve performance in modern pentathlon (fencing using laser spades)

state (Heller, 2016). The third element is through the sounds in the game. With each success and each failure, environmental sounds own scenario in which you are playing. And the fourth element is the recognition of achievements. Through badges, medals, trophies, scores and appointments you want the player to have feeling of satisfaction with the recognition of each achievement (Leary, 2001).

RESULTS

The scenes structured associated with the agents cannot be reproduced in general, since they only represent a little while dice in the space and time of the different societies. These represent a unique form and innovating of adaptive behavior which solves a computational problem that it does not try to clustering the societies only with a factor associated with his external appearance (phenotype), trying to solve a computational problem that involves a complex change between the existing relations with the population which practice these sports. The generated configurations can be metaphorically related to the knowledge of the behavior of the community with respect to an optimization problem (to conform to cluster social and culturally with other similar people, without being of the same sport (Parentcenterhub.org, 2016)). In the table 1 is shown a sample of seven sports described the features analyzed in each different sport and their practice required.

We try to improve the next equation 4, in this describe K as the performance of the practice each sport in the city and their respective promotion in diverse locations.

$$K = \left[C + CS + GAL \right] + CBS$$

In where:

C = represents if the sport can be practice in wherever weather, for example the Chess.

CS = represents the Symbolic Capital associated with the perspective of a society, practice Fencing is considering sophisticated.

G = is the gender of the range of population, in Juarez City the population pyramid is different to the rest of Latin America because the violence provokes deaths and exodus of the city.

AL = Playful Aspect related with the age of the children practice a sport, for example in the Trampoline the playful aspect is associated with the high promotion of this sport.

CBS = Social Benefits-Cost related with each sport, in the case to Rhythmic Gymnastics is associated with improve of healthy in sedentary children less weight because require many sport activities related with the four events: ball, club, hoop and ribbon.

Table 3. Multivariable analysis with the information of the number of spaces to recuperate to practice these virtual sports and their representations by gender (issue) –values to Male and Female respectively-, the social status by their practice, fun to use the Wii application, the weather, Improved increase health to change paradigms to sedentarism in children and finally the relationship between social cost/benefice associated with their practice. Using Fireworks Algorithm, we reorganize the real values with another future and possible scenarios.

Virtual Sport	Space Gender	Social Status	Fun	Complexity	Kinetic Adaptation	Climate	Increase Health	Cost-Benefit
Aquatic Sky	8 m-.50,f-.45	0.498	0.914	0.928	0.815	0.774	0.715	0.387
Baseball	5 m-50, f-.40	0.617	0.658	0.574	0.971	0.385	0.712	0.514
BMX Bike	3 m-.40,f- .40	0.562	0.748	0.611	0.996	0.303	0.897	0.448
Bowling	4 m-.30,f- .30	0.620	0.631	0.715	0.884	0.856	0.802	0.744
Dance Rolling	9 m-.27, f-.49	0.884	0.924	0.788	0.956	0.589	0.895	0.916
Fencing	7 m-.57, f-.37	0.912	0.815	0.478	0.914	0.487	0.914	0.872
Figure Sky	5 m-.19, f-.50	0.948	0.912	0.916	0.978	0.398	0.917	0.887
Skateboarding	7 m-.50, f-.43	0.427	0.967	0.887	0.916	0.884	0.896	0.914
Sport Climbing	3 m-.46, f-.37	0.597	0.814	0.896	0.985	0.816	0.928	0.948
Surf	1 m-.50, f-.29	0.716	0.918	0.918	0.994	0.662	0.867	0.912
Synchronized Swimming	3 f-47	0.275	0.637	0.416	0.989	0.814	0.748	0.885
Tae Kwon Do	6 m-.40,f-.30	0.857	0.714	0.628	0.914	0.851	0.879	0.568
Underwater Hockey	1 m-.37,f-.24	0.878	0.764	0.928	0.974	0.918	0.928	0.914
Waterpolo	14 m-.45,f- .40	0.578	0.784	0.925	0.997	0.627	0.914	0.879

To date, a Tool for Decision-Making is being developed to identify in graphic form the way in which violence affects a composite index to the HDI in different parts of the City and with different scenarios according to the perspective of increase or decrease of it, for this three scenarios are being built (optimistic, pessimistic and gradual progress) for the identification of changes with respect to the temporality and ubiquity of the information. The analysis and interpretation of these scenarios with respect to time should be treated with extreme care seeking to make a balance between the numerical prediction made and justified by the use of equations, being able to select an index, a composite index, a factor or an associated range.

Figure 7 shows the perspective of the proposed Decision Making Tool and its main components, including a scenario generator associated with the year of numerical prediction -which can be shown through the use of radar charts and tachometers of statistical variability., the changes in the scenarios shown, the adjustment of parameters with respect to social aspects and their relation with the year to be projected, the visualization of a map showing in color the changes in the HDI for each AGEP of the city associated with the increase in the violence and the visualization of a narrative script detailing the most important final parameters of the simulation carried out, as is possible to see in figure 7.

One of the most relevant aspects of the research carried out is the migration of the Decision-Making Tool to the site of the Social Research Center of the UACJ, so that any user can consult with respect to the associated indicators to HDI and its effect of the existing violence in the City.

Figure 7. Simulator of the decision-making tool

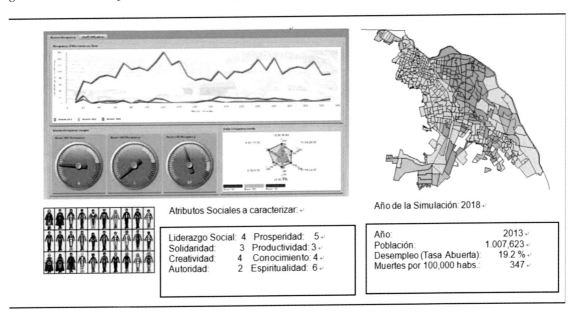

Proposed Design of Experiments

On the other hand, the specific objectives will be determined through a correlational study, where you experiment with different variables. This with the purpose of knowing the existing relationship between two or more variables to understand which variables are those that most affect the HDI such as; the design of public policies that improve the quality of life of people with issues such as insecurity, violence and kidnapping. Likewise, it is intended to analyze the degree of association between these variables.

These results will be thrown through a factorial design that tries to analyze by means of a design of experiments with orthogonal arrangement, the effect that the different independent variables have like violence, insecurity and kidnapping in different levels like age, gender and socioeconomic level, about the dependent variable that in our research is an effect associated with the quality of life reviled as HDI, or that in its case, this is not present.

In the present investigation, a design of experiments will be carried out in which different interactions of the variables to be studied will be carried out: Violence, insecurity, extortion and kidnapping, which are the control variables (Figure 8). Likewise, these variables will be studied in four levels: Geographical area, level of studies, gender and age, which are the noise variables.

Figure 8. Design of experiments proposed

				Zona Geo	1	1	1	1	2	2	2	2	3	3	3	3	4	4	4	4
				Estudios	1	2	3	4	1	2	3	4	1	2	3	4	1	2	3	4
				Genero	1	1	2	2	1	1	2	2	2	2	1	1	2	2	1	1
				Edad	1	1	2	2	2	2	1	1	1	1	2	2	2	2	1	1
A	B	C	D																	
1	1	1	1																	
1	1	1	2																	
1	2	2	1																	
1	2	2	2																	
1	1	2	1																	
1	1	2	2																	
1	2	1	1																	
1	2	1	2																	
2	1	2	1																	
2	1	2	2																	
2	2	1	1																	
2	2	1	2																	
2	1	1	1																	
2	1	1	2																	
2	2	2	1																	
2	2	2	2																	

A relevant aspect is a study with greater depth associated with sensors could properly determine how the metabolism of each child works and its process of acquiring the metabolic process through their respective golgi devices.

One of the methodological aspects that justify the scenarios for its simulation, are associated with the surveys of the perception of violence that have been carried out in the Social Research Center and that show the variables associated with various items of the state that the Society keeps with regarding the most prevalent indicators of violence.

Another aspect to be developed will be the implementation of said Decision Making Tool in Mobile Devices as proposed in (Chung et al.), Which have the ability to modify values in situations of high uncertainty such as the type of change in the Mexican dollar-peso ratio with respect to the economy and in the social part, the increase in violence in a specific month -in that category, the decrease in deaths during 2011 can be associated with the increase in extortion, kidnapping and robbery with violence.

DISCUSSIONS AND FUTURE RESEARCH

The most relevant aspect of this research is to consolidate the practice of sports in children and young people who, due to weather conditions, cannot agree to join together to practice a sport together with the self-confidence generated in the players., which allows improving their performance in other areas of their daily life through a model of emotional support in children, which entails a commitment and intrinsic complexity in their motor development. Considering that childhood is a vulnerable stage where they are also in full development and any event or occurrence may be able to cause negative effects and may leave the child permanently marked by the rest of their life (The Hospital for Sick Children, 2010). Therefore, it is very important to focus more on how to obtain results associated with group performance, sponsored by the individual. That is why the future of the Serious Game, will require a deeper investigation that allows to be of great impact by having an opportunity to help children and youth who do not have access to sports for various reasons. In the future, the Serious Games may present a natural opportunity due in large part to the acceptance that videogames have in this age and even more so with the advantage that these generations have easy access to technology. As mentioned in the present investigation, this prototype wishes to continue consolidating in order to establish diverse teams associated mainly with the avatar. This prototype in regard to the Serious Game to achieve the complete and functional construction phase. At this time and due to a project with funding from the European Union and the collaboration of FINA, we want to make a Wii application that allows being inclusive through interesting and very efficient strategies associated with mobility. FINA is very interested in this type of applications that could diversify the practice of Water polo in developing countries. In future research, we try to improve the practice of a sport associated with a game and based on collaborative work in a group with high intensity of pressure for each child as is professional tennis and modify the importance related to the support of this type of pressure related to the responsibility of a collective activity (Garciá-Mundo, Vargas, Genero, & Piattini, 2014), as shown in Figure 9.

Figure 9. A serious game based on collective activities and related with the increase of social skills

The main experiment consisted of detailing each one of the 47 sports, with 500 agents, and one condition of unemployment of 50 generations, this allowed us to generate different scenarios related with Time Horizons, which was obtained after comparing different cultural and social similarities in each community, and to determine the existing relations between each one in relation with the Mahalanobis Distance (the number of dots indicated each sport and the size of people represents the number of people which determine the magnitude related with the society).

REFERENCES

Blanco, J. (2012). Musicoterapia Como Alternativa Terapeutica En La Depresion. *Universidad de San Carlos, 1*(1), 1–76.

Braga, P. H. C., & Silveira, I. F. (2015). *A Pattern Language for semi-automatic generation of Digital Animation through hand-drawn Storyboards*. In *Proceedings of SIBGRAPI - Conference on Graphics, Patterns, and Images, 28*.

CDC. (2016). HHS of USA. Center for Disease Control and Prevention. Especiales de los CDC. Retrieved from Salud mental de los niños: Apoyo de los servicios de salud conductual para quienes los necesitan website: https://www.cdc.gov/spanish/especialesCDC/SaludMentalNinos/index.html

Chrisman, O. (1896). Paidologie: Entwurf zu einer Wissenschaft des Kindes (U. of C. Libraries, Ed.). Jena, Bernhard Vopeliu.

Csikszentmihalyi, M. (1990). *Flow: The Psychology of Optimal Experience*. New York: Harper & Row.

Garciá-Mundo, L., Vargas, J., Genero, M., & Piattini, M. (2014). Contribuye el Uso de Juegos serios a Mejorar el Aprendizaje en el Área de la Informática. *JENUI 2014-Proceedings of the XX Jornadas Sobre La Ensenaña Universitaria de La Informática*, 303–310.

Heller, E. (2016). *Psicología del color Cómo actúan los colores sobre los sentimientos y la razón* (1st ed.). Amadora: Gustavo Gill. [Psychology of Color: How Colors Affect Feelings and Reason]

Leary, M. R. (2001). Interpersonal Rejection. *Dialogues in Clinical Neuroscience, 17*(4), 435–441. PMID:26869844

Parentcenterhub.org. (2016). Center for Parent Information & Resources. Retrieved from Sobre la Ley IDEA: https://www.parentcenterhub.org/sobreidea/

Schaefer, C. E. (2012). Fundamentos de Terapia de Juego. MANUAL MODERNO. [Fundamentals of Game Therapy: Modern Manual]. Hipódromo: John Wiley & Sons.

Siegfried, J. (1982). Origins of Child Psychology: William Preyer. In *The problematic Science* (pp. 300–321). Psychology in Nineteenth-Century Thought.

Silveira, I. F. (2016). *Juegos Serios: Teoría y Práctica*. [Serious Games: Theory and Practice].

The Hospital For Sick Children. (2010). Efectos psicológicos del desastre sobre los niños [Psychological effects of the Disaster on Children]. Retrieved from https://www.aboutkidshealth.ca/Article?contentid =302&language=Spanish

Tomas, U. (2016). El Psicoasesor. [The Psychoassessor]. Retrieved from 25 poderes terapéuticos del juego website: http://elpsicoasesor.com/25-poderes-terapeuticos-del-juego/

Section 5

Innovative Applications of Swarm Intelligence and Swarm Robotics

Chapter 16
Optimization of PID Controller for a Hybrid Power System Using Particle Swarm Optimization Technique

Sandeep Bhongade

 https://orcid.org/0000-0003-0575-5093

Shri Govindram Seksaria Institute of Technology and Science, India

M. P. S. Chawla

Shri Govindram Seksaria Institute of Technology and Science, India

Bhumika Sahu

Shri Govindram Seksaria Institute of Technology and Science, India

ABSTRACT

With the advancement of technology, power demand is increasing day-by-day. Energy deficiency problem and increasing petroleum/diesel cost have resulted in severe impacts to many technical facts. Introduction of non-conventional energy sources such as wind and photovoltaic energy, which is clean and copiously present in nature, can be possible solutions to these problems. This chapter presents optimization of a Hybrid power system, with one of swarm intelligent algorithms named as particle swarm optimization (PSO). The hybrid system uses PID controllers for controlling its output. It has been done by studying various combinations of diesel engine generator, wind turbine generator, aqua electrolyzer, fuel cell, and battery. With the optimized system parameters, high-quality power supply can be delivered to the load and the frequency fluctuations can also be minimized.

DOI: 10.4018/978-1-7998-1659-1.ch016

Copyright © 2020, IGI Global. Copying or distributing in print or electronic forms without written permission of IGI Global is prohibited.

INTRODUCTION

The present era is expected to experience immense growth and challenges for power generation, supply and utilization. Now-a-days the role of renewable energy sources is increasing in an exponential rate. It is due to the reason that global awareness for the need of environment protection and requirement of reduction in dependency on fossil fuels in the field of power generation. Thus, exploration of many of the nonconventional sources and their integration to conventional sources are done to provide clean energy and supply the load demand in the most intelligent way (M. H. Nehrir et al., 2011; Chandraprabha, Namrata Singh, Shalini Thakur and Rituraj Karan, 2015).

"Hybrid Power Systems (HPS) are small set of co-operating units, generating electricity or electricity and heat, with diversified primary energy carriers (renewable and non-renewable), while the co-ordination of their operation takes place by utilization of advanced power electronics systems" (Sonali Goel and Renu Sharma, 2017). Hybrid power systems by definition have been developed for the production and utilization of electrical power. HPS are independent of central and large electricity grid and integrate numerous different kinds of sources of power. Generally, HPS can work in connection with power grid or they can work alone as standalone system to provide power to different loads, from one to several homes or farms, small industrial plants up to large local customers. When connected to grid, HPS offer electrical power generated by various sources and fed the excess power back in the grid, in case of more power generation than load demand. Main purpose of hybrid power systems is to deliver power to isolated, remote loads where the price of the connection from long distance transmission or distribution grid is very high.

Optimization plays an important role for improving systems performance and effective working. An optimization algorithm is a method of obtaining the optimum solution of a problem that can be achieved by following a technique and comparing numerous solutions iteratively. To find the best solution for large scale optimization problem, evolutionary algorithms are established. Evolutionary algorithms are population-based meta-heuristic algorithm as they are inspired by natural biological evolution or social behavior of living beings. Particle swarm optimization is one of these algorithms. It has the upsides of simple usage, stable convergence characteristics, and good computational effectiveness (Gaing, 2004).

Therefore, a hybrid power system is proposed in this paper with PID controllers optimized by particle swarm optimization technique. The proposed system can also be used in isolated small islands as a standalone system, to reduce fuel consumption of conventionally used in diesel/petrol generation systems and it is also good for global environment protection concerns.

EXISTING HYBRID POWER SYSTEM

This segment depicts the basics of proposed hybrid power system. The generation subsystems comprise wind turbine generator, diesel engine generator, aqua electrolyzer and fuel cell. Aqua electrolyzer is utilized to change over the fluctuating intensity of wind turbine generator into hydrogen and give it as a fuel to fuel cell (Lee & Wang, 2008). In this way power loss due to wind fluctuation can be minimized and system can be fully utilized.

For controlling the output of each subsystem, PID controller is used and for optimizing the controller performance particle swarm optimization (PSO) is used. The feedback gain parameters (k_r, k_{fc}, k_{deg})

are also optimized using PSO to reduce the frequency and power deviations. A series of simulation has been carried out to prove its working for different combination of generation components.

Different cases are considered for simulation as shown in Table 1. For simulation all the subsystem is considered to be in first order

Table 1. Simulation Conditions For each Case (Senjyu, Nakaji, Uezato & Funabashi, 2005)

	Case I	Case II	Case III	Case IV
Diesel Generator	Ö	Ö	Ö	Ö
Fuel Cell	-	Ö	Ö	-
Aqua Electrolyzer	-	Ö	Ö	-
Battery	-	-	-	Ö
Wind Turbine	Ö	Ö	□	Ö

Wind Turbine Generator(WTG)

The changes in speed of wind rely upon time and related to the past speed. A few models of wind speed have been established and utilized. In this paper Auto Regressive Moving Average (ARMA) model is utilized, in which the wind speed is represented by ARMA time-series which is given as (Wang & Billinton, 2001):

$$y_t = \varnothing_1 y_{t-1} + \varnothing_2 y_{t-2} + \ldots + \varnothing_n y_{t-n} + \alpha_t - \theta_1 \alpha_{t-1} - \theta_2 \alpha_{t-2} - \ldots - \theta_m \alpha_{t-m} \tag{1}$$

Where, $\varnothing_i$ is autoregressive parameter in which i varies from 1 to n. θ_j is moving average parameter in which j varies from 1 to m. α_t is noise parameter with zero mean. The simulated wind speed SW_t can be calculated using the following equation (Senjyu, Nakaji, Uezato & Funabashi, 2005):

$$SW_t = \mu_t + \sigma_t y_t \tag{2}$$

Where, μ_t is average wind speed and σ_t is standard deviation.

During power generation by wind turbine generator, the output power depends on the wind speed at that particular time. The characteristic of WTG is presented in Figure 2. Cut in speed is the minimum speed required for power generation whereas, the cut-out speed is the maximum speed of wind up to which power can be generated. Rated speed is the speed at which maximum power is generated. Above rated wind speed output power become constant.

The output power of wind turbines Pw is calculated using the following equation [30]:

$$= 0 (WS < W_{in}, WS > W_{out})$$

$$P_w = (WS - W_{in}), (W_{in} < WS < W_{rs})$$

Figure 1. System Configuration of existing hybrid power system (Senjyu, Nakaji, Uezato & Funabashi, 2005)

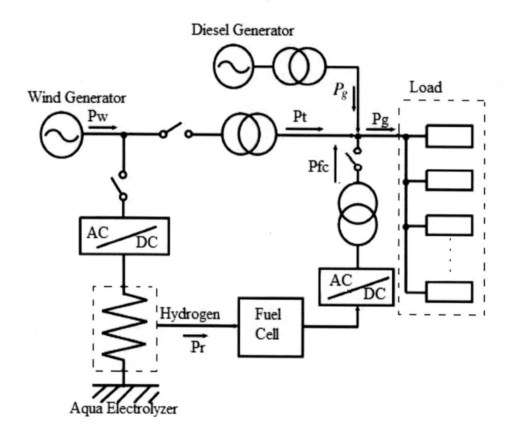

$$P_w = 1 (W_{rs} < WS < W_{out})$$

Where, W_{in} is cut in wind speed.

W_{out} is cut out wind speed.

W_{rs} *Wrs* is rated wind speed.

ε is slope of straight line which passes through points connecting cut in and rated wind speed.

Figure 2. Relationship between output power and wind speed of WTG (Nayak & Maharana, 2017)

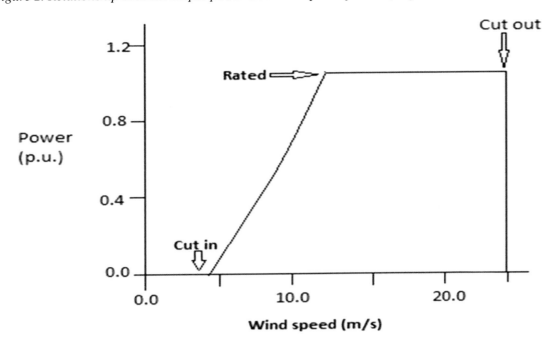

Aqua Electrolyzer (AE)

Electrolysis is used for the production of hydrogen by absorbing any fluctuations in the output power from WTG by aqua electrolyzers. The produced hydrogen is kept within the hydrogen tank and utilized by fuel cells. The requirement of the load is fulfilled by total output from WTG, DEG and FC. The transfer function of the aqua electrolyzer system is given as follows (Lee & Wang, 2008):

$$P_{AE}(s) = \frac{K_{AE}}{1 + sT_{AE}}$$

Where, K is the gain and T is time constants of system.

Fuel Cell (FC)

The fuel cell generates electric power by reverse electrolysis; that is the reaction of oxygen and hydrogen which forms water. It is similar to the oxidation/reduction process of a battery. In fuel cell, reaction takes place in fuel (not in electrodes)(Rajshetra, 2005).In the past few years, fuel cell generation have gained more attention due to the advantages, such as onsite installation, diversity of fuels, low pollution, reusability of exhaust heat and high efficiency. The transfer function of the fuel cell generation system is given as follows (Lee & Wang, 2008):

$$P_{FC}(s) = \frac{K_{FC}}{1 + sT_{FC}} \qquad (5)$$

Where, K is the gain and T is time constants of system.

Diesel Engine Generator (DEG)

A DEG consists of diesel engine and electric generator to provide electrical energy and various ancillary devices, such as control systems, circuit breakers etc. Diesel engine generator can produce steady and reliable electrical energy at required voltages and power levels (Wang, 2012). During power outages, emergency backup electrical generators powered by diesel engine provide reliable, immediate and full-strength electric power. The transfer function is given as follows:

$$P_{DEG}(s) = \frac{K_{DEG}}{1 + sT_{DEG}}$$

Where, K is the gain and T is time constants of system.

Control Strategy

The control strategy is obtained by controlling the power error which is the difference between the load demand (P_D) and net power generated (P_G) (Senjyu, Nakaji, Uezato & Funabashi, 2005).

$$P_G = P_w + P_{DEG} + P_{FC} - {}^\circ P_{AE}$$

Where, P_w is the power generated by wind turbine generator.

P_{DEG} is the power generated by diesel engine generator.

P_{FC} is the power generated by fuel cell.

P_{AE} is the power generated by aqua electrolyzer.

Hence, the net controlling power error,

$$\Delta P = P_D - P_G$$

Change in power generation affect the frequency response in power systems. For an ideal system the relation between frequency and power deviation is given as following (Lee & Wang, 2008):

$$\Delta F = \frac{\Delta P}{k}$$

Where, ΔP is the variation of generating power and k is the system frequency characteristic constant.

In a practical system, slow response is observed in the frequency. Hence equation (8) can be modified as (Senjyu, Nakaji, Uezato & Funabashi, 2005):

$$\frac{\Delta F}{\Delta P} = \frac{1}{k(1+T_s)}$$

Equation (9) can also be represented as:

$$\Delta F = \frac{1}{D+sM} \cdot \Delta P$$

Where, M is inertia constant & D is damping constant. Different parameters have been taken from T. Senjyu et al and are shown in Table 2.

Table 2. Parameters of the Hybrid System (Senjyu, Nakaji, Uezato & Funabashi, 2005).

Gain	Time Constant (sec)
$K_{DEG} = 1$	$T_{DEG} = 2$
$K_{AE} = 1$	$T_{AE} = 0.2$
$K_{FC} = 1$	$T_{FC} = 4$
$K_b = 1$	$T_b = 0.1$
$D = 0.2$	$M = 0.012$

PID Controller and Performance Index

APID controller consist the arrangement for Proportional, Integral and Derivative actions, which attempts to minimize the error between a measured process variable and a desired set point. Ttransfer function of PID controller is given as:

$$C(s) = K_p + \frac{K_i}{s} + K_d s$$

Optimization of performance of the system can be carried out by adjusting performance index. Lower value of index is preferred for running a robust system. The performance index is defined as a quantitative measure to indicate the system performance of the designed PID controller (Nayak & Maharana, 2017).

In control system, there are various performance indices viz. Integral Square Error (ISE), Integral Absolute Error (IAE), Integral Time Absolute Error (ITAE) and Integral Time Square Error (ITSE) are utilized to estimate the performance of system (Subhojit Malik, Palash Dutta, Sayantan Chakrabarti and Abhishek Barman, 2014; Stepan Ozana, 2016).Since integral square error always results in positive error and it allows to discriminate over damped system from under damped system, hence it is used as fitness function to analyze performance of PID controllers. Using ISE, power error is calculated to design optimum system,which is defined as:

$$ISE = \int_0^t e^2 dt$$

Where, e is power error obtained in the simulation time t and k isthe variable in terms of the value of K_p, K_i and K_d. Limits taken for electrolyzer, fuel cell and DEG are from zero to 1.0, 0.3 and 0.8 per unit respectively.

Particle Swarm Optimization (PSO)

Swarm intelligence is a branch of nature inspired approaches which is used for function optimization. PSO is based on the combined nature of self-structured systems. It mimics the behaviors of bird flocking (Kumar & Gupta, 2013; Kennedy & Eberhart, 1995). PSO learns from the situation and practices it for solving the optimization problems. Particle used in PSO represents single solution in search space and is analogous to the bird. Every particle has a fitness value which is estimated by optimizing the fitness function. The particles also have velocities to direct its flying and all the particles go through the search area to obtain the best result by chasing the current optimum particle (Gaing, 2004). A basic flowchart of PSO is shown in Figure 3 to explain its working.

Various steps for designing controller using PSO are:

Step1. Initialization of a population of particles is done with arbitrary position and velocities in d dimension search space. Confine the search space by specifying the lower and upper bounds of every variable. The population is initialized with the velocity and position set to the predefined range and satisfying the equality and inequality constraints.

Step 2. In each iteration, the velocities of all particles are updated according to the equation (13)

$$V_{id}^{(t+1)} = wV_{id}^{(t)} + c_1 r_1 (p_{bestid}^{(t)} - x_{id}^{(t)}) + c_2 r_2 (g_{bestd}^{(t)} - x_{id}^{(t)})$$

Where $V_{id}^{(t+1)}$: velocity of particle i in d dimensional space

$X_{id}^{(t)}$: position of particle i in d dimensional space

$p_{best\,id}^{(t)}$: best position of individual i in d dimensional space until generation t

$g_{best\,d}^{(t)}$: best position of the group in d dimension until generation t

w : inertia weight factor controlling the dynamics of flying

Figure 3. Flowchart of PSO

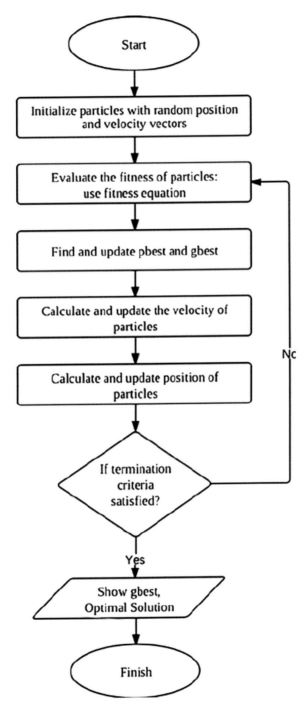

c_1 : cognitive parameter

c_2 :social parameter

r_1 and r_2 : random variables in the range [0,1]

Step 3. Every time after iteration, respective position of all particles is reorganized. This is done by using the following equation (14)

$$x_{id}^{(t+1)} = x_{id}^{(t)} + v_{id}^{(t+1)} \tag{15}$$

Step 4. Update particle best position $p_{best\ id}^{(t)}$ and globalbest position $g_{best\ d}^{(t)}$ using equation (15) and (16).

$$p_{best\ id}^{(t+1)} \leftarrow X_{id}^{(t+1)} \text{ if } f(X_{id}^{(t+1)}) < f(p_{best\ id}^{(t)}) \tag{16}$$

$$g_{best\ d}^{(t+1)} \leftarrow X_{id}^{(t+1)} \text{ if } f(X_{id}^{(t+1)}) < f(g_{best\ d}^{(t)}) \tag{17}$$

Step 5. The process continues to repeat from Step 2 to Step 4 until a sufficient good fitness is obtained. Otherwise, the process will automatically stop after reaching maximum set number of iterations. Once we get global best fitness, algorithm is then terminated.

Implementation of PSO Algorithm has been performed on different configuration of hybrid power system and parameters of PSO are given in Table 3.

Table 3. Parameters of PSO

Parameter	Value
Swarm Size	30
Maximum no. of Iteration	200
Cognitive Component	1.414
Social Component	1.414
Inertia Weight	0.8

CASE STUDIES

In this section, different case studies of hybrid power system are presented with performed simulations and results are discussed. For showing its effectiveness, a series of simulation are done to prove its working for different combinations of generation components.

Case I. This case consists of diesel generator and wind turbine generator. In order to achieve balance between generation and load, sum of both the power error and frequency error is given to PID controller. Here, PID controller is tuned using PSO for the optimization of system. Along with the parameters of PID controller, gain Kg present in the feedback loop is also optimized in algorithm. All calculations done based on per unit (pu) system.

Case II. This case consists of DEG, FC generators, WTG, and AE. Working procedure of case II is same as case I. Here, three separate PID controllers are provided for AE, FC and DEG. Also gains from frequency feedback are included in optimization process.

Case III. The components required for Case III are same as of case II. Thus, this case also consists of DEG, FC generators, WTG and AE. However, the components are connected in a different way in this case. In case III, the entire output of WTG is given to AE for electrolysis. Hence, only DEG and FC generators supply to fulfill the required load.

Case IV. In this case wind power, battery and diesel engine generators contribute to supply the load. Working procedure of system is same as explained in case I. The transfer function for battery is given below (Gaing, 2004):

$$P_b(s) = \frac{K_b}{1 + sT_b}$$

Where, K is the gain and T is time constants of system. Also, limits for controller of battery are considered as ± 0.5 per unit.

SIMULATION RESULTS

In this section, simulation results of the several studied cases and their analysis is given. Simulation time of 120 sec and sampling time is taken as 20 msec for each case. Also, power demand is constant at 1.0 per unit. For DEG a delay of 20 sec is taken as it does not respond instantaneously.

Case I. From Figure 4 it can be noticed that DEG and WTG contribute 0.4 pu and 0.6 pu power respectively so that total power generation will reach to power demand i. e. 1 pu. Also, when output from the WTG changes unexpectedly, this system is unable to provide high-quality power to the load. The reason is that diesel generators have very large time constant. Thus, DEG does not provide immediate response to load demand.

It can be seen from figure 6 that initially there is some power error. As power generation approaches power demand, error oscillates around zero. The oscillations are due to fluctuations in power generation because of variable wind speed.

An optimized values of gains K_p, K_i, K_d, and K_g has been shown in Table 4. From the graphical and tabular results, it is observed that, when the output power of the wind turbines changes unexpectedly, the system is unable to supply high-quality power to the load. The reason is that diesel generators have very large time constant and cannot respond instantly to load demand.

Figure 4. (a) Generated power, (b) Power supply error

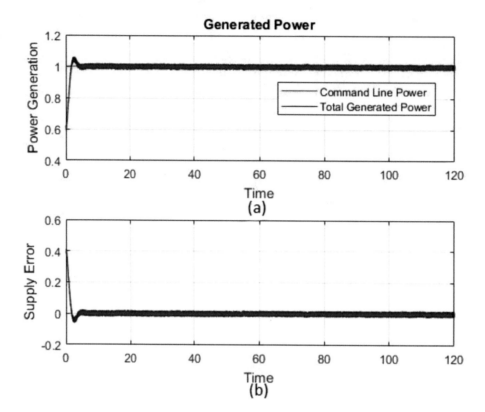

Case II. From Table 4 it can be noticed that DEG, WTG and FC contribute 0.38 pu, 0.6 pu and 0.02 pu power respectively, so that total power generation will reach to power demand i. e. 1 pu. Power generated by aqua electrolyzer is not considered, as it provides input power to fuel cell and does not contribute directly to power generation. Also, the error in the power required is huge when the power generated by WTGvaries quickly over a broad range. Though, the error in required supply turns out to be around zero and the system is able to provide sufficient power to meet required load. Time constant of aqua electrolyzers for power utilization is small so, these are used to absorb the variations in WTG output power. Thus, this system can deliver high- quality power to load when the output of wind turbines varies rapidly. In similar way, this system controls the frequency appropriately. Various results obtained from simulation are as follows:

It can be seen from Figure 7 that initially there is some power error. As power generation approaches power demand, error oscillates around zero. The oscillations are due to fluctuation in power generation due to variable wind speed.

Figure 8 shows best fitness obtained at 10.1 with respect to iteration numbers. This means that after the best fitness obtain, the algorithm works in stable region. Ideally best fitness value should be as minimum as possible.

Figure 5. Case I. (a) Total power generated, (b) Frequency Deviation, (c) Power generated by wind turbine generator, (d) Power generated by Diesel engine generator

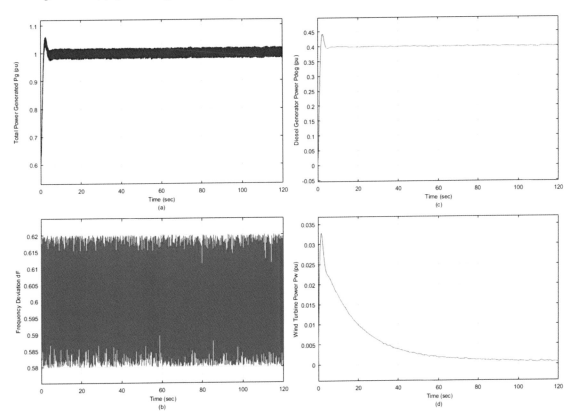

An optimized values of gains K_p, K_i, K_d, and K_g has been shown in Table 5. From above results, it is seen that the error in the supply demand is huge when the generating power of wind turbines varies all of a sudden over a wide range. In this way, the system can deliver high- quality power to load demand, when the output power of wind turbines changes suddenly.

Case III. It can be clearly seen from Table 5 that DEG and FC contribute 0.8 pu and 0.2 pu power respectively, so that total power generation will reach to power demand i. e. 1 pu. Power generated by aqua electrolyzer is not considered, as it provides input power to fuel cell and does not contribute directly to power generation. Also, there is no fluctuation in total power generation due to absence of wind effect. From above results, it can be noticed that rapid variation ingenerated power byWTG affects the error in supply demand and turn out to be zero, as entire output power ofWTG is utilized in electrolysis. Thus, for this system it is possible to provide very high-quality power to the load requirement with sudden changes in wind turbine output power.

Various results obtained from simulation are as follows:

It can be seen from figure 10 that initially there is some power error. As power generation approaches power demand, error oscillates around zero. The oscillations are due to fluctuation in power generation because of variable wind speed.

Figure 6. Best fitness obtained w.r.t iteration

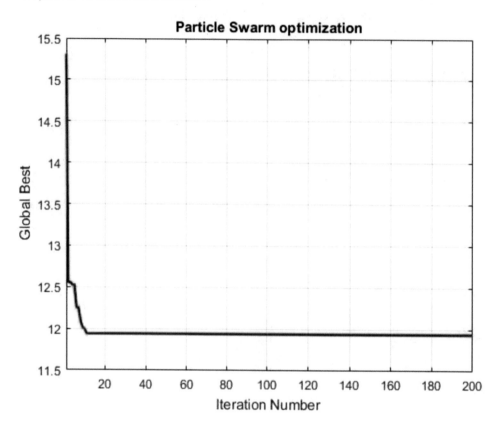

Table 4. Optimized values

	K_p	K_i	K_d	K_g
Diesel engine generator	100	1.0244	52.4615	1.2512

Figure 11 shows best fitness obtained at 112.8 with respect to iteration numbers. This means that after the best fitness obtain, the algorithm works in stable region. Ideally best fitness value should be as minimum as possible.

An optimized values of gains K_p, K_i, K_d, and K_g has been shown in Table 6. From the tabulated results, it is observed that, when the generating power of wind turbines varies suddenly over a wide range, the error in supply demand becomes zero, as the entire output power generated from wind turbine generators is used in electrolysis. Hence, for this system it is possible to supply very high-quality power to the load demand with sudden changes in wind turbine output power.

Figure 7. (a) Generated power, (b) Power supply error

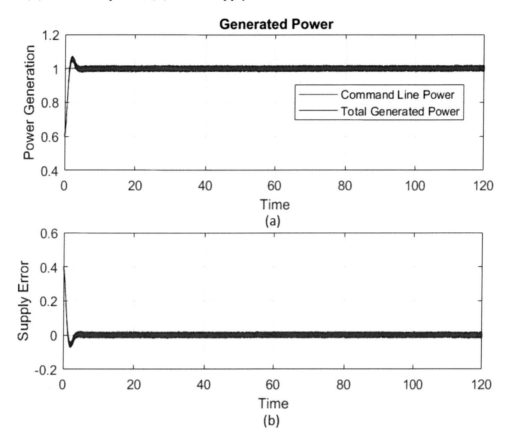

Case IV. It is observed from Table 6 that WTG and battery contribute 0.6 pu and 0.4 pu power respectively so that total power generation will reach to power demand i. e. 1 pu. Also, DEG generation reaches to zero as soon as battery supply to its maximum power. From the results, it can be noticed that this system is also able to provide good quality power to fulfill the required load, with sudden change in wind turbine generator output. But use of battery is limited by its charging/discharging capacity and inverter capacity. Here, it is considered that, if the battery power goes below 50% then it injects discharge operation and when battery power reaches above 100% it injects charge operation.

Various results obtained from simulation are as follows:

It can be seen from figure 13 that, there is no initial gradual increase in total power generation, as sufficient power is available from starting, since we battery is used in this case which can supply power from the instant it is connected to the system. As power generation approaches power demand, error oscillates around zero. The oscillations are due to fluctuation in power generation because of variable wind speed.

Figure 8. Best fitness obtained w.r.t iteration

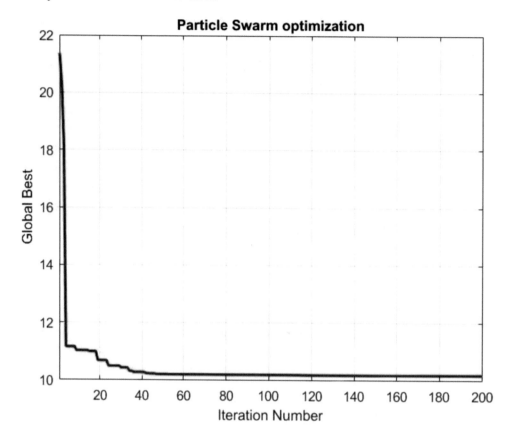

DISCUSSIONS

From the simulation results, it is clear that in Case I simulation, the system is the least expensive system in comparison to other systems but in case of sudden change in wind speed or wind turbine output power, it is unable to deliver good quality power to the load. For system of case III, it is possible to deliver very high-quality power to the load demand with sudden changes in wind turbine output power. But overall performance is not effective, as the entire output of wind generator is utilized in electrolysis. The system of case IV can provide high quality power to the load but the system is expensive as it contains battery with large capacity. The lifespan of battery is very small due to frequent charging and discharging operation. The hybrid system of case II provides high quality power in comparison to case I and it is most effective and less expensive system in comparison to case III and case IV systems. The frequency response characteristics presented in Table 4 with peak value and settling time shows that system of case II provides good frequency response with the tuning of PID controllers. Also, global best settles on minimum value in case II as compared to other cases. Hence it provides better convergence.

The frequency response characteristics presented in Table 7 with peak value and settling time shows that system of case II provides good frequency response with the tuning of PID controllers. Also, global best settles on minimum value in case II as compared to other cases. Hence it provides better convergence.

Figure 9. Case II. (a) Total power generated, (b) Frequency Deviation, (c) Power generated by diesel engine generator, (d) Power generated by wind turbine generator, (e) Power generated by fuel cell, (f) Power generated by aqua electrolyzer

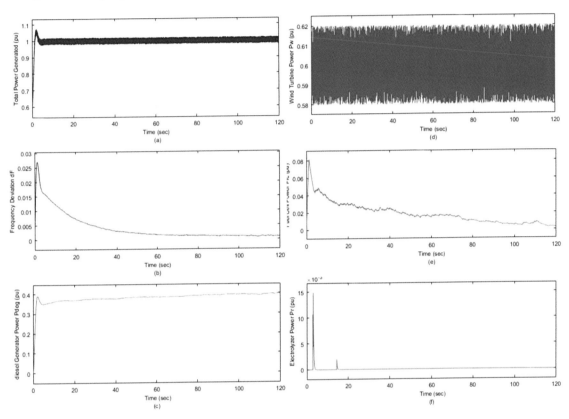

Table 5. Optimized values

	K_p	K_i	K_d	K_{FB}
Elecrolyzer	-100	-100	-5.2965	100
Fuel cell	99.5368	-6.44	-0.4740	-94.326
Diesel engine generator	100	1.1630	36.2580	7.5267

CONCLUSION

Based on results obtained, it can be concluded that, by using optimized parameters, the hybrid power system provides high quality power with minimum deviations. It is also clear that, of the four-system studied with different combinations of its subsystems, the system which uses WTG, AE, FC with DEG gives the best results and also settles faster (minimum global best) than other cases. The future work would be towards: system sizing, economic analysis, operations and maintenance practices. Hybrid power systems which would be developed are to be feasible with viable options with the added benefit of being environmentally friendly and ensured safety.

Figure 10. (a) Generated power, (b) Power supply error

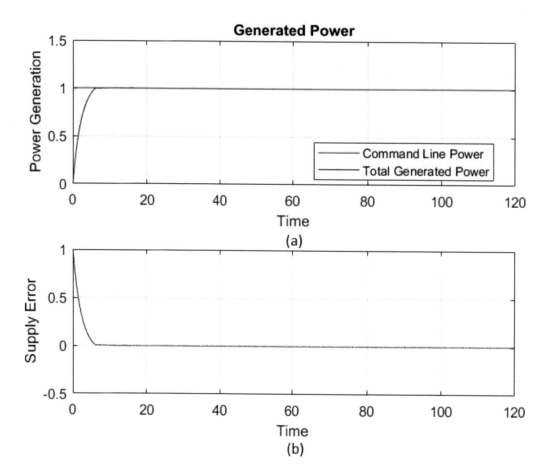

FUTURE SCOPE

Further study can be carried out using other optimization techniques, such as grey wolf optimization, fractional order PID etc. to tune the controller parameters. Energy storage devices can be added in the system to improve hybrid power system efficiency. The future work could be towards System sizing, Economic analysis, Operations and maintenance practices. Hybrid power systems which would be developed are to be feasible with viable options with the added benefits of being environmentally friendly ensuring safety.

Figure 11. Best fitness obtained w.r.t iteration

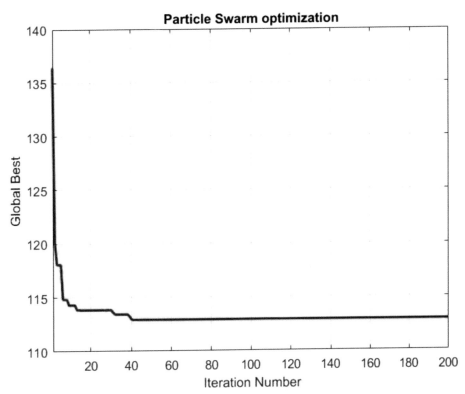

Figure 12. Case III. (a) Total power generated, (b) Frequency Deviation, (c) Power generated by diesel engine generator, (d) Power generated by fuel cell

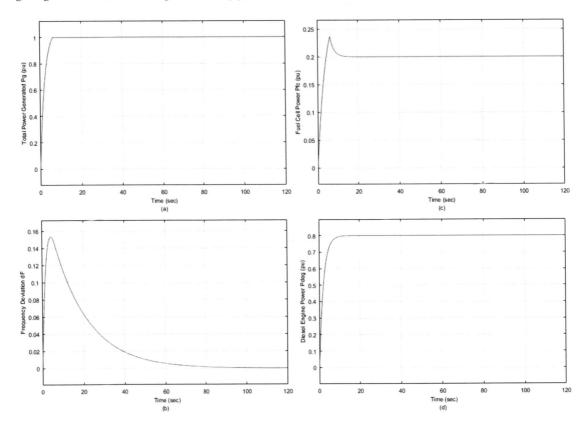

Table 6. Optimized values

	K_p	K_i	K_d	K_{FB}
Fuel cell	100	0.2582	8.1725	81.5930
Diesel engine generator	100	100	-100	11.4168

Figure 13. (a) Generated power, (b) Power supply error

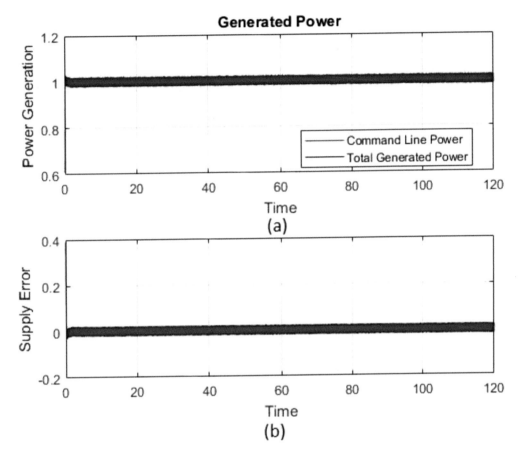

Figure 14. Case IV. (a) Total power generated, (b) Frequency Deviation, (c) Power generated by diesel engine generator, (d) Power generated by wind turbine generator, (e) Power generated by battery

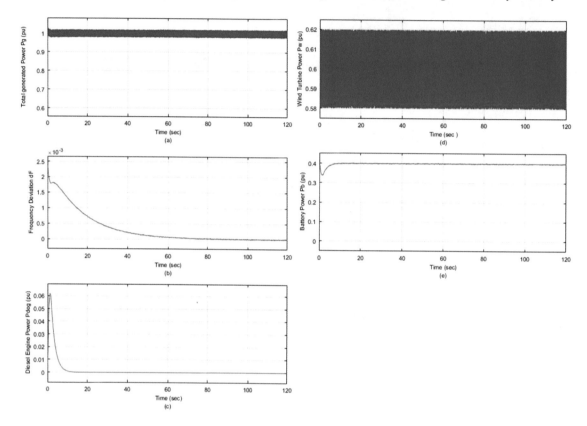

Table 7. Comparison of frequency response of all the four cases on different parameters.

	PEAK VALUE	SETTLING TIME (sec)	GLOBAL BEST
CASE I	1.64	102	11.9
CASE II	1.35	70	10.1
CASE III	7.67	110	112.8
CASE IV	0.12	80	22.5

REFERENCES

Chandraprabha, N. S., Thakur, S., & Karan, R. (2015). Current Stature and Future Outlook of Hybrid Renewable Energy System. *International Advanced Research Journal in Science, Engineering and Technology, 2*(1), 58–62.

Fathima, A. H., & Palanisamy, K. (2015). Optimization in microgrids with hybrid energy systems – A review. *Renewable & Sustainable Energy Reviews, 45*, 431–446. doi:10.1016/j.rser.2015.01.059

Gaing, Z. L. (2004). A Particle Swarm Optimization approach for optimum design of PID controller in AVR system. *IEEE Transactions on Energy Conversion, 19*(2), 384–391. doi:10.1109/TEC.2003.821821

Goel, S., & Sharma, R. (2017). Performance evaluation of stand alone, grid connected, and hybrid renewable energy systems for rural application: A comparative review. *Renewable & Sustainable Energy Reviews, 78*, 1378–1389. doi:10.1016/j.rser.2017.05.200

Kennedy, J., & Eberhart, R. (1995). Particle swarm optimization. *Proceedings of the IEEE International Conference on Neural Networks*, pp. 1942–1948 November-December1995. Perth, Australia. IEEE.

Kumar, A., & Gupta, R. (2013). Tunning of PID controller using PSO algorithm and compare results of integral errors for AVR system. *International Journal of Innovative Research and Development, 2*(4), 58–68.

Lee, D. J., & Wang, L. (2008). Small-signal stability analysis of an autonomous hybrid renewable energy power generation/energy storage system part I: Time-domain simulations. *IEEE Transactions on Energy Conversion, 23*(1), 311–320. doi:10.1109/TEC.2007.914309

Malik, S., Dutta, P., Chakrabarti, S., & Barman, A. (2014, March). Parameter Estimation of a PID Controller using Particle Swarm Optimization Algorithm. *International Journal of Advanced Research in Computer and Communication Engineering, 3*(3).

Nayak, A., & Maharana, M. K. (2017, February). Tuning of PID controller to maintain load frequency for hybrid power system. *Proceedings 2017 International Conference on Innovative Mechanisms for Industry Applications (ICIMIA)* (pp. 24-28). IEEE. 10.1109/ICIMIA.2017.7975623

Nehrir, M. H., Wang, C., Strunz, K., Aki, H., Ramakumar, R., Bing, J., ... Salameh, Z. (2011). Hybrid Renewable/Alternative Energy Systems for Electric Power Generation: Configurations, Control, and Applications. *IEEE Transactions on Sustainable Energy, 2*(4), 392–403. doi:10.1109/TSTE.2011.2157540

Ozana, S. (2016). PID Controller design based on global optimization technique with additional constraints. *Journal of Electrical Engineering, 67*(3), 160-168.

Pavani, V. S., & Kumar, G. (2017). An Analysis of Advanced Wind/Fuel Cell based Hybrid Power Generation Strategies for Microgrid Applications. *International Journal for Indian Innovative Research Engineering Streams of Technological Sciences, 1*(3), 2017.

Rajshetra, K. (2005). Hybrid fuel cell strategies for clean pwer generation. *IEEE Transactions on Industry Applications, 41*(3), 682–689. doi:10.1109/TIA.2005.847293

Senjyu, T., Nakaji, T., Uezato, K., & Funabashi, T. (2005). A hybrid power system using alternative energy facilities in isolated island. *IEEE Transactions on Energy Conversion, 20*(2), 406–414. doi:10.1109/TEC.2004.837275

Wang, L. (2012). Dynamic analysis of a microgrid system for supplying electrical loads in a sailing boat. *Proceedings of 2012 IEEE Power and Energy Society General Meeting.* Doi:10.1109/PESGM.2012.6344601

Wang, P., & Billinton, R. (2001). Reliability beneðt analysis of adding WTG to a distribution system. *IEEE Transactions on Energy Conversion, 16*(2), 134–139. doi:10.1109/60.921464

Chapter 17
A Survey on the Applications of Swarm Intelligence to Software Verification

Tsutomu Kumazawa
Software Research Associates, Inc., Japan

Munehiro Takimoto
Tokyo University of Science, Japan

Yasushi Kambayashi
Nippon Institute of Technology, Japan

ABSTRACT

Applying swarm intelligence techniques to software engineering problems has appealed to both researchers and practitioners in the software engineering community. This chapter describes issues and challenges of its application to formal verification, which is one of the core research fields in software engineering. Formal verification, which explores how to effectively verify software products by using mathematical technique, often suffers from two open problems. One is the so-called state explosion problem that verification tools need too many computational resources to make verification feasible. The other problem is that the results of verification have often too much complexity for users to understand. While a number of research projects have addressed these problems in the context of traditional formal verification, recent researches demonstrate that Swarm Intelligence is a promising tool to tackle the problems. This chapter presents how Swarm Intelligence can be applied to formal verification, and surveys the state-of-the-art techniques.

DOI: 10.4018/978-1-7998-1659-1.ch017

Copyright © 2020, IGI Global. Copying or distributing in print or electronic forms without written permission of IGI Global is prohibited.

INTRODUCTION

Evolutionary algorithms and Swarm Intelligence algorithms have gotten more and more attention to appeal both researchers and industrial practitioners. People become aware of the effectiveness and efficiency of these algorithms. Today, we have more than one hundred kinds of well-studied Swarm Intelligence algorithms (Xing & Gao, 2016; Boussaïd, Lepagnot, & Siarry, 2013), such as Genetic Algorithms (Hromkovič, 2001), Ant Colony Optimization (Dorigo & Stützle, 2004), and Fireworks Algorithms (Tan & Zhu, 2010). These algorithms share several common characteristics; they are stochastic, nondeterministic, and non-exhaustive. Although these characteristics do not guarantee that those algorithms always produce the optimal solutions, we can find good solutions for many combinatorial optimization problems (Hromkovič, 2001) that are otherwise unsolvable. Owing to the rapid improvements of these algorithms, people have successfully applied such algorithms not only to the well-known practical problems but also to the current theoretical computer science problems.

This chapter surveys a recent research field; the application of Swarm Intelligence algorithms to software engineering problems, especially to the formal software verification. Software engineering is a research area of computer science that studies the methodologies about how to create highly reliable and error-free software systems. We have yet to achieve the ultimate goal of software engineering. There are several reasons. The recent software systems are extremely complex. They run on diverse environments such as various kinds of smart devices, large factories, the Internets and safety-critical machines like robots and automobiles. Such diversity yields a lot of challenges not only in the practical fields but also theoretical field. In fact, many serious accidents relating to industrial software troubles have been reported to date. For example, Leveson analyzed several spacecraft accidents whose causes were involved with software failures (Leveson, 2004). Tamai reported the failure of software systems in financial industry in Japan, and its following lawsuit (Tamai, 2009; Tamai, 2015). These cases indicate that software accidents have high impacts not only on the specific industry and companies, but also on our entire society. Software engineers have tried to establish methodologies for developing safe and reliable systems, but it is still middle-of-the-road.

Software verification is one of the main research topics of software engineering. It aims at assuring reliability of software systems by providing methodologies for checking whether they have defects or not. In general, there are two approaches for verification; software testing and formal verification. Software testing confirms that the results of sample are the same as expected ones. Samples are representative behaviors of the target software. Each one of the samples is executed on the real system and its actual results are compared with its expected ones. If there is any difference between them, it is highly verisimilar that the target system has some problems with respect to the sample setting. Software testing is empirically known to detect serious failures efficiently and effectively. Therefore, it is widely accepted as the de facto standard in software industry. Unfortunately, software testing can show there are problems, but it fails to show the target system is flawless. On the other hand, the formal verification aims to prove the correctness of the system. Given formal descriptions of the target system and properties that are required to be true on the system, a verifier, i.e. a formal verification tool, proves that the system satisfies the properties. If the verifier can make a proof, we can conclude that the system is flawless. Research scientists have developed many methodologies that tackle with finding proofs automatically and efficiently. We focus on a formal verification technique, Model Checking (Clarke & Emerson, 1981), since it is one of the most successful formal verification techniques both in academics and in industry. A main difference between software testing and model checking is that while the former investigates only sample behaviors, the latter explores whole behaviors of the software exhaustively to guarantee the system's reliability. This chapter focuses on the researches that realize formal verification using metaheuristic Swarm Intelligence methodologies.

Although one of the advantages of model checking is its rigorousness, it is known to suffer from the state explosion problem. The problem is a situation that has too huge search space and takes too much time to check all of them. Since model checking conducts exhaustive search over a huge space that consists of the whole behaviors of the target system to prove its correctness, the verification may require unacceptable amounts of computational time and space. When the system has several concurrent and autonomous processes as in the cases of embedded systems, this situation often gets worse and verification can be infeasible because the complexity of the system's behavior increases exponentially as the number of processes increases (known as state explosion). Thus, the most important research challenge in model checking is to develop ways to overcome or at least mitigate the state explosion problem. The key observation is that exhaustive search is one of the main causes of the state explosion problem, and we expect to mitigate the problem if we employ nondeterministic and stochastic search algorithms.

Formal verification-based Swarm Intelligence algorithms have made a remarkable progress by combining with effective heuristic exploration strategies. The mitigation is achieved through the synergies between improvements of general-purpose Swarm Intelligence algorithms and vigorous studies to establish the ways of applications of them in the software engineering community. One notable example is the Search-Based Software Engineering (SBSE) (Harman, Mansouri, & Zhang, 2012). SBSE is an approach to address software engineering problems based on optimization methods such as evolutionary algorithms and various metaheuristics. The research domains of SBSE cover almost all the software engineering problems; from software design to software verification. There are a number of literatures published to date. Instead of reviewing a broad range of SBSE work, this chapter focuses on the formal verification domain. We have two reasons to do so. First, to the best of our knowledge, there has been no such work that reviews adaptations of Swarm Intelligence methodologies to the formal verification techniques. Second, the decisive ways to overcome the state explosion problem are not known, even though recent research results reveal that Swarm Intelligence is one of the most promising techniques for mitigating state explosion problem effectively.

The structure of the balance of this chapter is as follows. In BACKGROUND section, we review model checking techniques. Instead of discussing formally, we present its principle informally by a simple example to help the readers understand model checking intuitively. Then we discuss research challenges of model checking and review the existing techniques to address them. MODEL CHECKING WITH SWARM INTELLIGENCE section surveys model checking techniques using Swarm Intelligence. We focus on model checking algorithms using Ant Colony Optimization and Particle Swarm Optimization. This section emphasizes that how the model checking problem can be translated into the problem of these optimization techniques, for the sake of future researches of applications of Swarm Intelligence. We also discuss other kinds of model checking researches with Swarm Intelligence. We finally discuss the challenges for future researches of the model checking in FUTURE RESEARCH DIRECTIONS section and we summarize this chapter in CONCLUSION section.

BACKGROUND

Formal software verification techniques have been developed for decades. For example, Hoare Logic (Hoare C. A., 1969) is one of the pioneering researches of proving the correctness of programs. Deductive approaches were employed in a formal verification of reactive systems (Lamport, 1977; Manna & Pnueli, 1995). This chapter focuses on model checking, which is based on exhaustive search algorithms. This section introduces model checking informally with a simple example.

Model Checking: An Overview

Model checking (Clarke & Emerson, 1981) is one of the formal verification techniques that is widely accepted in both computer science community and industry. One of the most important contributions of model checking is to support the analysis of concurrent systems that consist of multiple autonomous entities called processes. In general, it is very difficult to analyze concurrent systems whose processes interact with each other in complicated manners. Most model checking techniques help us find faults of concurrent systems such as deadlocks and livelocks. The overview of model checking is stated as follows: Given a model of the system M that is described using some kind of graph-based formalism, and a property Æ that is a formal statement expected to hold on the system, it decides whether M satisfies Æor not (Clarke, 2008).

The inputs to model checking are the model and the property. First of all, we need specifications of software systems for verification. In the terminology of model checking, specifications are described as models of systems. Because most failures of systems are rooted in their complicated behaviors, we need to specify models of the behavioral aspects of the systems. The directed graphs are employed to formalize models such as finite automata, Kripke structures (Clarke Jr., Grumberg, Kroening, Peled, & Veith, 2018) and Labeled Transition Systems (LTSs) (Magee & Kramer, 2006). Such kinds of models are called state transition models since they are used to represent temporal transitions of system states. Kripke structures can model how the values of variables in a program changes as time goes during execution. Meanwhile, LTSs are suited to describe temporal ordering of firing system events or actions. As another approach, process algebra such as CSP (Hoare, 1985), CCS and A.Calculus (Milner, 1999) are also major formalisms of concurrent systems.

Modeling is a common and important activity in software engineering. During developing a software system, engineers abstract details of the target system and models them to understand requirements, designs, or even the software itself. Modeling and verification were traditionally studied based on the assumption that they are conducted with manual labors of engineers before implementing the software system. However, it has been said that it is difficult for practitioners to manually apply formal techniques to industrial software development because of the lack of application know-hows. Fortunately, recent researches have been improving the situation. For example, software model checking (Jhala & Majumdar, 2009) realizes the verification of software systems directly by creating models from program codes automatically.

In addition to models, engineers need to describe properties that should hold in the system. Since software development is domain-specific, there is no general grounds of the correctness of software systems. It means that we have to prepare the functional and non-functional requirements of the system in advance. In model checking, verification is reduced to checking the satisfaction of properties. Model checking provides highly expressive description languages of properties to users. Realization of property checking is an important feature of model checking as a general verification technique which can be applied to wide ranges of realistic software development.

Given a model and a property, model checking tries to prove that the former satisfies the latter mechanically. We summarize some of the advantages of model checking in accordance with the discussion in the essay written by Clarke (Clarke, 2008) as follows:

- The verification is fully automated. It inspires researchers to develop a number of model checking tools, called model checkers such as NuSMV 2 (Cimatti, et al., 2002), SPIN (Holzmann G., 2003), TLA+ and its bundling toolbox (Lamport, 2002; Wayne, 2018), and LTSA (Magee & Kramer, 2006). A more lightweight formal verification tool that is closely related to model checking is Alloy (Jackson, 2006). Model checkers do not need any support from users to complete verification.
- Model checking returns results to the users within practical time.
- Model checkers present a counterexample if they conclude that the model does not satisfy the property. A counterexample is not only an evidence of the violation, but also an effective hint for the user to understand what problems either the model or the property has.
- During the development of large-scale systems, it may be difficult for engineers to prepare the entire specifications due to the limitation of time and budgets. Model checking can be used to verify only important portions of the entire system by extracting behaviors based on the appropriate levels of abstraction.
- Model checking supports description of properties using Temporal Logic. Temporal Logic is one of the variants of modal logic. It is very useful for reasoning important temporal behaviors.

Motivating Example

In order to help the reader capture the outline of model checking intuitively, consider the following example of a system that controls railroad crossings. This simple example is cited from the textbook (Baier & Katoen, 2008).

The mission of the system is to properly control the safety gates deployed on a road where trains cross. If a train approaches to the crossing road the gate should be closed until they leave the road. While there is no train near the road, the gate should be open to let vehicles and pedestrians cross the railroad. Each train sends two kinds of signals when it approaches and leaving the gate respectively. After receiving each signal, the control system orders the gates to either close or open them in accordance with the type of the signal. What we would like to do is to show that there is no failure or fault in the control system when the system is deployed into the operation environment.

The first step is to model the behaviors of the complete system which contains the control systems and the surrounding environment, i.e., gates and trains. We can see that they are not only all concurrent and autonomous entities but also interacting with each other for coordination. Such entities are called processes. Hence, our example is regarded as a concurrent system. We model each process as a state transition model, and construct the composite process model to represent the entire behaviors.

We adopt LTSs as a formalism of state transition models. An LTS is a directed graph whose nodes and edges are called states and transitions respectively. It has the unique initial state and a set of labels (called actions) associated to edges. A trace of an LTS is defined by a sequence of actions that are obtained by passing transitions starting from the initial state. We interpret that a set of traces shows the behaviors of a process. We only consider that the length of a trace is infinite, i.e., each process executes forever without termination. From the practical point of view, it is difficult for engineers to explicitly provide state transition models to model checkers. Instead, most model checkers have formal specification languages for modeling systems. For example, PROMELA (Holzmann G., 2003) and FSP (Magee & Kramer, 2006) are specification languages employed by SPIN and LTSA respectively. We assume that our example is specified in such a specific language.

For simplicity, we make the following assumptions about the processes presented in our example:

- We abstract the behavior of each train such that it sends signals to the control system and crosses the road. We do not consider other characteristics, e.g., its speed, size, and the number of passengers. Moreover, instead of considering each distinct train, we only consider the single Train process that models representative behaviors of each one of the trains. We do not treat special cases such as the one that multiple trains approach the gate simultaneously.
- Similar to Train process, we only prepare a single Gate process although there may be several gates. The gate has two kinds of positions, i.e., the top and the bottom. The gate transits its position spontaneously without taking intermediate position.
- The role of the control system is to control the position of the gate. Signals from Train process and those to Gate process are sent without delay. We call the system Controller process.

The LTSs of Train, Gate, and Controller processes are shown in Figure 1. In the figure, Circles and arcs represent states and their transitions respectively. The initial states are depicted as arcs that do not have source states. Each label that is associated to a transition indicates an action. For example, approach in Train process is interpreted as the action that the train sends the signal of approaching to the gate. The trace of Train process is a sequence of actions starting from the initial state, i.e., approach, enter, exit, approach, ...

Figure 1. LTSs of train, gate, and controller processes are shown in diagrams. Source: (Baier & Katoen, 2008)

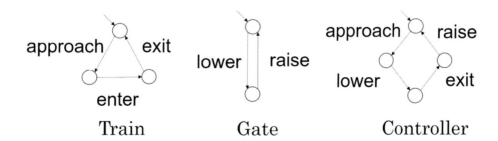

We use the parallel composition operation (Magee & Kramer, 2006) to construct the composite process in an LTS. Figure 2 shows the composite process of the system that represents its entire behavior. The principles of the parallel composition are as follows:

Figure 2. LTS of the composite process is shown in a diagram

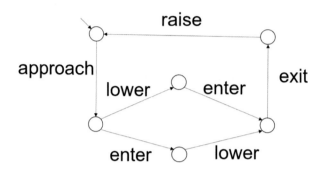

- Actions shared between multiple processes occur simultaneously (called handshaking). For example, because approach action is shared in Train and Controller processes, their state transitions should be fired at the same time. This mechanism is useful for describing interactions or communications between processes.

- Actions that appear only in a single process occur independently of the other processes. For example, enter action is declared only in Train process and it can occur between approach and exit actions. We employ the interleaving mechanism, that is, each action is atomic and only one of the actions is fired at a time. The temporal ordering of unshared actions is preserved. Unshared actions are often used to represent the internal behaviors of each process.

The second step is to prepare the property to be verified. Here we must consider that the invariant property SafeCrossing that is, when train is crossing the road, the gate is closed. SafeCrossing can be formally described using Linear Temporal Logic (LTL) (Manna & Pnueli, 1992; Giannakopoulou & Magee, 2003): $SafeCrossing = \mathbf{G}(TrainCrossing \rightarrow GateDown)$. In the formula, proposition TrainCrossing is true when the action enter occurs before exit occurs, otherwise false. It represents the state that Train is in the gate. Similarly, proposition GateDown is true when lower arises until raise occurs, otherwise false. $\mathbf{G}$ is a temporal operator defined in LTL meaning that the formula after the operator "always" holds. Finally, operator $\rightarrow$ .is an implication in the classical logic. Other kinds of Temporal Logic used for model checking are Computation Tree Logic (Clarke & Emerson, 1981), CTL* and ¼.Calculus (Clarke Jr., Grumberg, Kroening, Peled, & Veith, 2018).

The third step is to decide whether the composite process satisfies SafeCrossing or not. In this chapter, we present the outline of an automata-theoretic technique for model checking of LTL formulae (Vardi & Wolper, 1986; Holzmann G., 2003; Giannakopoulou & Magee, 2003). The idea of the automata-theoretic model checking is to search for a trace that violates the property over the composite LTS. The key insight of the algorithm is that the violating traces satisfies the negation of the property, and the intersection of the composite LTS and the set of traces satisfies the negation of the property that represents the set of violating traces. Based on the idea, the verification is conducted as follows. The negation of SafeCrossing i.e., ¬SafeCrossing is translated into the equivalent Büchi automaton (Clarke Jr., Grumberg, Kroening, Peled, & Veith, 2018), where ¬ is the negation operator. A Büchi automaton is a finite automaton that accepts a set of traces of infinite length. The automatic translation algorithms have been proposed in literature (Gastin & Oddoux, 2001; Giannakopoulou & Lerda, 2002; Giannakopoulou &

Magee, 2003). Figure 3 shows a Büchi automaton constructed from ¬SafeCrossing. In the figure, the black state is the error state, i.e., the accepting state of the automaton. We say that a trace is accepted by a Büchi automaton if it passes some accepting state infinitely many times. We omit the outgoing transitions from the accepting state for simplicity, because every trace that passes the state is always accepted in the case of ¬SafeCrossing. In other words, every finite trace that reaches the error state violates SafeCrossing.

Figure 3. Büchi automaton of ¬SafeCrossing is shown in a diagram

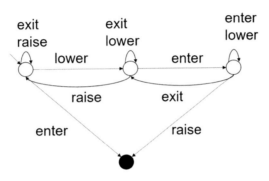

After the construction of the Büchi automaton, we compute the intersection of the composite LTS and the Büchi automaton. It can be conducted automatically by applying the parallel composition operation (Giannakopoulou & Magee, 2003). Note that the intersection represents a subset of traces of the composite LTSs that only violates SafeCrossing. Figure 4 shows the intersection. Finally, we search for a trace arriving at an error state. Because we can regard the intersection as a directed graph, we can use search algorithms over directed graphs in this step. In our example, a finite trace (approach, enter) is a violation, called a counterexample. This counterexample indicates a dangerous failure of the control system that a train can enter the crossing when the gate is open. Most model checkers return a counterexample to the user.

Figure 4. The intersection of the composite LTS and the Büchi automaton is shown in a diagram

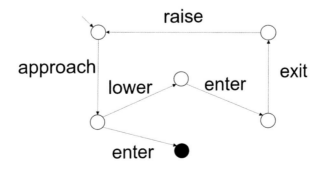

RESEARCH CHALLENGES IN MODEL CHECKING

This section discusses research challenges of model checking that are tried to deal with Swarm Intelligence. We also survey the existing researches aiming for overcoming the challenges within the field of traditional model checking.

Challenges for Model Checking

We discuss two research challenges of model checking; the state explosion problem and the problem of lengthy and incomprehensible counterexamples. Although they have been studied for decades, they are still open problems.

Most of the model checking techniques employ exhaustive search algorithms. Exhaustive search techniques are effective when the size of the search space is small. Unfortunately, search spaces in model checking tend to be huge graphs. It is generally known that as the number of processes constructing the entire target system increases linearly, the corresponding size of their composite LTS increases exponentially due to their complex interactions of shared actions and interleaving of internal unshared actions. Such exponential increase of the search spaces is called the state explosion problem. In the railroad crossing example, recall that we find a counterexample on the directed graph shown in Figure 4. If we have to distinguish each train, we have to add a model of each train, which may cause the state explosion. The problem becomes serious due to the constraints of computational resources such as running time and memories. In addition, because it is known that the complexity of LTL and CTL* model checking is PSPACE-complete (Clarke Jr., Grumberg, Kroening, Peled, & Veith, 2018), we need exploration techniques of large discrete search spaces which efficiently reduce the unnecessary parts. The state explosion problem is inevitable and many alleviation techniques have been proposed.

The other problem comes from the practical point of view of model checking. When we would like to find subtle failures hidden in a large model, the length of counterexamples is apt to be large. Because there is no general criterion about the quality of counterexamples, model checkers may find lengthy counterexamples. For example, consider the railroad crossing example again. Both the trace (approach, enter) and the trace (approach, lower, enter, exit, raise, approach, enter) are counterexamples. Which of the counterexamples should model checkers return? Human users use the counterexample to analyze the target model and property. They need a counterexample that is easy to understand and that has less superfluous information for their efficient analysis. To this end, it is highly desirable for model checkers to present counterexamples as short as possible. In our example, we conclude that the best counterexample is the trace (approach, enter). We address the problem by regarding model checking as a combinatorial optimization problem. The objective function to be minimized contains the length of counterexamples. Note that it is not necessary for human practitioners to always obtain the shortest counterexamples. Adopting the Swarm Intelligence, we realize the model checking techniques that both mitigates the state explosion problem effectively and presents short counterexamples.

Model Checking Techniques

This subsection reviews the researches of model checking in order to address the two problems discussed above.

In general, properties written in Temporal Logic formulae are categorized into several classes. One of the most widely accepted classifications is Safety and Liveness (Lamport, 1977). Safety properties state that undesirable incidents never occur. This class of properties can be described in the simple LTL formula $G\neg p$ where p denotes the formula that represents undesirable incidents. On the other hand, liveness properties state that some desirable thing eventually holds. Liveness can be formulated using LTL as Fp where F is a temporal operator meaning "eventually" or "finally", and p is the formula formalizing desirable properties. In our train crossing example, SafeCrossing is a safety property.

The distinction between safety properties and liveness properties is important when we search for counterexamples. Because a counterexample has infinite length in liveness checking and the size of search spaces is finite, it consists of a loop, i.e., a Strongly Connected Component (SCC) in the terminology in Graph Theory, and has the finite trace from the initial state to the SCC. Traditionally, the search techniques adopted by most model checkers are based on Depth First Search (DFS), such as Nested DFS (Clarke Jr., Grumberg, Kroening, Peled, & Veith, 2018; Holzmann G., 2003; Baier & Katoen, 2008). Nested DFS finds loop-shaped counterexamples by combining two DFSs. The first DFS searches the state space as usual and invokes the second DFS that detects the state already visited. The algorithms for searching for SCCs (Cormen, Stein, Rivest, & Leiserson, 2001; Tarjan, 1972) are also useful. Although they are practical, the length of counterexamples found by DFS-based techniques depends on the implementation. Safety checking can be reduced to the special case of liveness checking. Fortunately, the introduction of error states as in the case of the train crossing example makes the checking reachability analysis to error states simpler (Giannakopoulou & Magee, 2003). Hence, instead of Nested DFS, we can use DFS or the Breadth-First Search (BFS). BFS is guaranteed to detect the shortest counterexamples, but it often suffers from the state explosion problem.

Since the birth of model checking, the alleviation of state explosion problem has been considered the most important concern for researchers in model checking. Many practical alleviation techniques have been developed. We briefly discuss three kinds of such techniques: reduction of search spaces, abstraction, and efficient representations of search spaces. The first approach is to reduce unnecessary search spaces. Some researchers developed minimization techniques of state transition models (Lee & Yannakakis, 1992; Bustan & Grumberg, 2003) based on behavioral equivalence relations (Milner, 1999; Sangiorgi, 2011). Partial Order Reduction (POR) (Clarke Jr., Grumberg, Kroening, Peled, & Veith, 2018) reduces the useless temporal orderings of transitions. The second approach, abstraction, is that we create an abstract search space from the original search space first and then conduct model checking on the abstract space. Since the abstract search space is smaller than the original one, we can save the memory for model checking. Counterexample-guided Abstraction Refinement (Clarke, Grumberg, Jha, Lu, & Veith, 2003) analyzes counterexamples obtained by the model checking on the abstract space and expand the space if necessary. The third approach is to investigate search space representations as small as possible. Ordered Binary Decision Diagrams (OBDDs) (Clarke Jr., Grumberg, Kroening, Peled, & Veith, 2018) are known to be an efficient expression of search spaces. Symbolic Model Checking utilizes OBDDs to implement efficient model checking (Clarke Jr., Grumberg, Kroening, Peled, & Veith, 2018). Shuppan and Biere proposed an algorithm that finds shortest counterexamples in symbolic model checking to compute comprehensible counterexamples for users (Schuppan & Biere, 2005). Bitstate Hashing is another way of reducing the memory used for storing state information (Holzmann G., 2003).

Parallel algorithms are expected to enhance the performance of model checking and to mitigate the state explosion problem. Edelkamp and Jabbar developed a parallel and distributed algorithm of model checking (Edelkamp & Jabbar, 2006). Their technique uses heuristics for verification and can detect short counterexamples. Holzmann et al. proposed parallel algorithms for model checking (Holzmann G. J., 2012; Filippidis & Holzmann, 2014). Their techniques are based on BFS and can be used for the detection of the shortest counterexamples.

Solvers of the Boolean Satisfiability Problem (SAT) (Knuth, 2015) have been known to be effective tools for model checking. Bounded Model Checking (BMC) discusses the reduction techniques of model checking into SAT (Biere, Cimatti, Clarke, & Zhu, 1999; Schuppan & Armin, 2006). Using modern SAT solvers, we can solve model checking problems very efficiently.

As a different research direction from the deterministic approaches discussed above, model checking using heuristic search algorithms has been studied. Directed model checking adopts heuristic search algorithms based on A*, Best-First Search, Iterative Deepening A* and the improved Nested DFS (Edelkamp, Lafuente, & Leue, 2001; Edelkamp, Leue, & Lluch-Lafuente, 2004; Edelkamp, et al., 2008; Andisha, Wehrle, & Westphal, 2015). It also uses several heuristics suitable for model checking, e.g., a distance estimate to error states in safety checking. The directed model checker HSF-SPIN is developed. Groce and Visser proposed some heuristics especially appropriate for model checking of Java programs (Groce & Visser, 2004). Their main heuristics are based on various metrics of the target program. They used DFS, Best-First Search, A* and Beam Search to evaluate the proposed heuristics. Tim et al. propose a heuristic approach to implement efficient BMC (Timm, Gruner, & Sibanda, 2017). Analogously, a heuristic search is proposed for checking behavioral equivalence between formally described models (Francesco, Lettieri, Santone, & Vaglini, 2016).

Grosu and Smolka propose Monte Carlo Model Checking, which employs a random sampling approach, to curtail search spaces (Grosu & Smolka, 2005). They discuss a sampling strategy for finding short counterexamples. Parízek and Lhoták introduce an efficient randomized backtracking to the exploration of state spaces using DFS (Parízek & Lhoták, 2019).

MODEL CHECKING WITH SWARM INTELLIGENCE

Swarm Intelligence is a promising technique to solve hard optimization problems efficiently. Model checking and its challenging problems discussed above are no exception to this principle. In this section, we introduce applications of Ant Colony Optimization (Dorigo & Stützle, 2004) and Particle Swarm Optimization (Kennedy & Eberhart, 1995) to model checking. Finally, we review the recent work inspired by Swarm Intelligence techniques.

Ant Colony Optimization

Ant Colony Optimization (ACO) is a powerful Swarm Intelligence algorithm inspired by the behaviors of worker ants. In searching for food, a worker ant walks to explore their surrounding area and communicate with each other by means of a chemical substance called pheromone that they secrete. As time goes by, ants form a short path from their nest to food, which can be regarded as a convergence (Figure 5). ACO formulates the idealized process in the optimization framework. ACO is good at indirectly solving the single-source shortest path search problem on directed graphs. When it is applied to a general optimization problem, the search space is represented as a directed graph, an objective function or fitness is expressed as a distance between nodes of the graph. Unlike deterministic graph search algorithms such as Dijkstra's algorithm (Dijkstra, 1959), ACO is a stochastic and distributed optimization technique. A

Figure 5. Ants converge to the shorter path

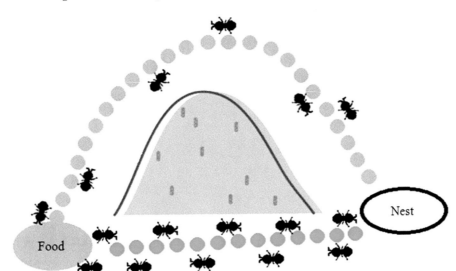

stochastic method is an effective means of avoiding the convergence to local minima. Furthermore, it takes advantage of emergence originating from interactions between many autonomous ants.

ACO consists of several components. The nest and food are the source and destination node of the graph respectively. ACO assumes that there are a number of worker ants moving on the graph. Each of the ants starts the nest and randomly moves from node to node that are connected by directed edges to search for food. Once the ant reaches the food, it goes back to the nest by passing the nodes it has visited before in the opposite direction. Here, we assume that an ant has a memory for remembering the path. Ants have a special cooperation mechanism to indirectly communicate with each other using pheromone. Typically, while returning to the nest, an ant deposits a certain degree of pheromone on the path. Pheromone contains information about the quality of paths that preceding ants passed. During the random search of food, the succeeding ants use the pheromone as a bias. The more pheromone is put on a path by an ant, the more likely the path is selected by its successors. This cooperation scheme through pheromone provokes the ants to choose some shortest path and makes ants converge to an optimal solution ultimately.

The detailed procedure of typical ACO is as follows (Dorigo & Stützle, 2004). First, we initialize pheromone for preparation of exploring the search space. The random initialization strategy is frequently employed. After the initialization phase, ants set off for exploration. The aim of this exploration phase is to make ants find solution candidates. When it selects the node to visit next, it computes the selection probability with the degrees of pheromone accumulated by preceding ants. In principle, we assign the higher probability to an edge than another if the edge has more pheromone than another. The probability that an ant $k \in A$ staying at node i selects the node j is computed as follows:

$$p_{ij}^k = \frac{[\tau_{ij}]^\alpha [\eta_{ij}]^\beta}{\sum_{l \in N_i} [\tau_{il}]^\alpha [\eta_{il}]^\beta}, \; if \; j \in N_i \#(1)$$

where A is the set of ants, N_i is the set of successor nodes of i τ_{ij} is the value of pheromone on (i,j) i.e., the edge from i to j and η_{ij} is the predetermined heuristic value. Furthermore, α and β are predefined parameters to determine the effects of τ_{ij} and η_{ij} respectively.

When several candidate solutions are found or the predefined number of steps elapses, the exploration phase ends and the update phase starts. Each degree of pheromone is updated according to the specific update strategy. One of the most widespread strategies is formulated below:

$$\tau_{ij} = (1-\rho)\tau_{ij} + \sum_{k \in A}{}^{''} \tau_{ij}^k, \#(2)$$

$$\Delta\tau_{ij}^k = \begin{cases} \dfrac{1}{L_k}, & if(i,j) \in T^k \\ 0, & otherwise \end{cases}, \#(3)$$

where $\rho(0 < \rho \le 1)$ is the constant evaporation ratio, T^k is the path explored by ant k, and L_k is the distance of T^k $"$ τ_{ij}^k represents the degree of pheromone deposited on T^k by ant k. The role of the parameter ρ is to evade the local minima because of the strong effect of the positive feedback given by $"$ τ_{ij}^k. The exploration and update phases are repeated until the termination condition holds. A converged solution, i.e., the shortest path, is an optimum solution.

The reduction of the model checking problem to ACO is realized in a straightforward manner. In principle, model checking is a search problem to find a path that is a counterexample on a directed graph. Hence, both ACO and model checking share the same assumption about the search space, i.e., directed graphs. In the terminology of ACO, the nest corresponds to the initial state of a state transition model. Similarly, food corresponds to the error state in case of safety checking. The paths found by ants are mapped to counterexamples, i.e., finite traces that reach the error state. The objective function to minimize is the length of each counterexample. This function is translated into the length of each path on the target graph directly. The remaining issue is the means of dealing with the state explosion problem. Normally, ACO assumes that the whole structure of the search space is given explicitly and that ants can find paths without any limitations of computational resources. However, due to the state explosion problem, the assumptions do not hold in general in model checking. In the following, we discuss two promising approaches to mitigate the state explosion problem.

ACO for huge graphs (ACOhg) is a variant of ACO whose target search space is a very large graphs (Alba & Chicano, ACOhg, 2007). The motivation behind ACOhg is that ACO is difficult to be applied to exploring large graphs in general. One problem of ACO is that the number of movement steps of ants tend to be large on a large graph, which will be a cause of memory shortage. What is worse, it is almost impossible to estimate the size of large graphs and computational resources necessary for conducting ACO beforehand.

The main idea of ACOhg is summarized below:

- ACOhg introduces the upper bound of the steps each ant can move for each iteration during the exploration. The exploration space is increased gradually to find food that is far from the nest (called the expansion technique). The aim of this extension is to avoid ants' moving huge search spaces at a time. ACOhg prepares an alternative way of reducing the search space (called the missionary technique). In the missionary technique, at each exploration step, each ant resumes its movement where some ant reaches at the end of last exploration step.

- The objective function used in ACOhg is defined based on the length of paths from the nest to food. The authors propose to add the specific penalty terms in order to avoid constructing the undesirable partial solutions due to the introduction of the upper bound of exploration.
- ACOhg "forgets" values of pheromone sometimes during the execution of the algorithm. This is because a large amount of memories may be necessary for storing values of pheromone during exploring large graphs. ACOhg releases the memory for pheromone values below the specific threshold.

In (Alba & Chicano, Safety, 2007), ACOhg is applied to safety checking of concurrent systems combined with several heuristics. According to the experimental result, although ACOhg sometimes fails to identify errors, it demonstrates a promising effectiveness as compared with DFS, BFS, A*, Best-First Search and GA show. ACOhg is later extended to safety checking with POR (Chicano & Alba, POR, 2008) and liveness checking (Chicano & Alba, Liveness, 2008). Through the experiments, the former algorithm showed better performance than the original ACOhg, while the latter algorithm outperforms Nested DFS respectively.

Although ACOhg detects safety violations efficiently in general, ants can move toward any directions almost randomly especially at the early stages of exploration. In order to address the problem of ants' wandering about the area far from food, Kumazawa et al. proposed Extended ACOhg (EACOhg) (Kumazawa, Yokoyama, Takimoto, & Kambayashi, 2016). EACOhg improved ACOhg by introducing another kind of pheromone, i.e., goal pheromone. Goal pheromone simply models how the smell of food in nature disseminates from food to the surroundings. Owing to the characteristics, goal pheromone induces ants to select shorter paths to food than other paths. Initially, goal pheromone is deposited on incoming transitions to food. At the end of each step of ants' exploration, goal pheromone is assigned to the surrounding transitions at random. When an ant finds goal pheromone in deciding the next state to visit, it takes priority with selecting a transition with goal pheromone over others without goal pheromone. To this end, the degree of goal pheromone is stronger than that of pheromone secreted by ants. In addition, we assume that the goal pheromone does not evaporate in order not to obliterate the guidance to food. The mechanism of goal pheromone enables the exploration of the search space to converge very quickly.

The dissemination manner of goal pheromone can be seen a backward random search algorithm. Hence, we consider EACOhg as a hybridization of ACO and the backward random search. EACOhg is expected to produce a synergistic effect of two distinct search strategy. In fact, the comparative experiments indicate that EACOhg outperforms ACOhg with respect to running time and length of counterexamples. Although EACOhg slightly needs more memories than ACOhg, the increase is complemented by its advantages of performance.

Kumazawa et al. have further improved EACOhg by adding hop count information to goal pheromone (Kumazawa, Takada, Takimoto, & Kambayashi, 2019). Hop counts are used to attract ants to food strongly to realize rapid convergence to solutions. The experimental result shows that the proposed method outperforms ACOhg and EACOhg in terms of lengths of counterexamples and running time.

Particle Swarm Optimization

Particle Swarm Optimization (PSO) is another kind of Swarm Intelligence algorithm that is used for solving nonlinear optimization problems. In PSO, a particle represents the position of a candidate solution. Each particle moves towards an optimal solution on the search space. The velocity of a particle is determined by its current velocity, and the globally and individually best solutions having found thus far. The position of the particle is computed from its current position and the velocity. Starting from the initial population, every particle explores the search space and updates its velocity and position repeatedly until the predetermined convergence criterion holds.

Ferreira et al. presented a novel technique based on PSO to find safety violations efficiently (Ferreira, Alba, Chicano, & Gómez-Pulido, 2008). They adapt PSO to model checking in the following manner:

- A particle is a path from the initial state to some state. Here, a path is the ordered set of edges on the state space. If a path reaches an error state or deadlock, it represents a counterexample.
- A technical challenge for applying PSO to model checking is how to define the velocity and position of a particle on the discrete state space. The authors addressed the problem by representing a path as a floating-point vector. The vector contains the length of the path and each edge passed by the path that is encoded to a floating-point value. The vector representation is treated as the current position of the particle on the continuous space and used for computing its velocity.
- The authors define the objective function to maximize for deadlock detection of Java programs as follows:

$$f(x)=DL \times deadlockfound + \%blocked + 1/(1+pathlen) \tag{4}$$

where DL is a predefined constant; $deadlockfound$ takes 1 if a deadlock is found, otherwise 0. $\%blocked$ is the percentage of concurrent threads blocked at the end of the path, and $pathlen$ is the length of the path. The formulation of the objective function is based on the assumption that we try to find a path that reaches a deadlock and whose length is the smallest. Furthermore, the larger the number of threads blocked at the end of the path blocked becomes, the larger value the function takes.

Ferreira et al. applied the PSO-based technique to find deadlocks of network protocols. They concluded that PSO is promising as compared with BFS, DFS and randomized DFS.

Model Checking Based on Swarm Intelligence and Metaheuristics

Swarm Intelligence algorithms and other metaheuristics have been employed to address many kinds of software engineering problems in a number of literatures of SBSE (Harman, Mansouri, & Zhang, 2012). Genetic Algorithm (GA) was mainly used in the pioneering literature of formal verification. Alba and Troya proposed the use of GA for verifying communication protocols (Alba & Troya, 1996). Their main concern is to detect deadlocks and useless state transitions. Note that one of the research motivations of model checking is to find concurrency problems such as deadlocks. Godefroid and Khurshid studied the performance of GA for exploring huge search spaces (Godefroid & Khurshid, 2002). They pointed out that heuristic search methods can help model checking applied to large systems. It indicates that the approach based on Swarm Intelligence is able to contribute to the mitigation of the state explosion problem.

More recent researches used various nondeterministic metaheuristic approaches for efficient model checking. Francesca et al. adapted ACO to deadlock detection (Francesca, Santone, Vaglini, & Luisa, 2011). In (Chicano, Ferreira, & Alba, 2011), Simulated Annealing was first adopted to model checking. The authors conducted comprehensive experimental comparisons among model checking algorithms, including the deterministic algorithms such as DFS and BFS, and nondeterministic ones such as A*, GA, ACO, PSO, Simulated Annealing, Random Search, and Beam Search. According to their experiment, nondeterministic techniques tend to show favorable performance with respect to the length of counterexamples. Staunton and Clark used Estimation of Distribution Algorithm (EDA) for model checking with the aim of mitigating the state explosion problem and finding short counterexamples (Staunton & Clark, 2010; Staunton & Clark, 2011). A variant of EDAs, which is called Bayesian Optimization Algorithm, is used for deadlock detection (Pira, Rafe, & Nikanjam, 2017). Yousefian et al. proposed a GA-based model checking of safety properties that is applied to graph transformation systems (Yousefian, Rafe, & Rahmani, 2014). Poulding and Feldt proposed a novel heuristic model checking algorithm using Monte-Carlo Tree Search (Poulding & Feldt, 2015). Milewicz and Poulding later proposed a parallel implementation of this search strategy (Milewicz & Poulding, 2017). Hybrid approaches are also studied these days. Rafe et al. adapted a hybrid metaheuristic algorithm that combines PSO with Gravitational Search Algorithm to deadlock detection (Rafe, Moradi, Yousefian, & Nikanjam, 2015). MS-ACO (Rafe, Darghayedi, & Einollah, 2019) is one of the state-of-the-art algorithms that detect violations of both safety and liveness using ACO.

FUTURE RESEARCH DIRECTIONS

The researches of model checking with Swarm Intelligence are active. This section discusses the future prospects of the researches.

Choosing Appropriate Swarm Intelligence

The existing researches have employed various kinds of methodologies of Swarm Intelligence and metaheuristics. We survey ACO-based approaches in this chapter. According to the experiments in the literatures, we expect that ACO is one of the best optimization frameworks for model checking. However, to the best of our knowledge, there is no decisive evidence of which methodology is best suited. Although some literature conducts comparative experiments, e.g., (Chicano, Ferreira, & Alba, 2011), we need more comprehensive comparisons among Swarm Intelligence algorithms. The statistical evaluation must be done from the viewpoint of runtime performance, memory consumption, and the quality of solutions. Also, the theoretical analysis of most of the aforementioned algorithms is left for future researches.

Applications to Liveness Checking

Most of the Swarm Intelligence based model checking techniques focus on the verification of safety properties, but not on that of liveness properties. Liveness properties are useful when we check stimulus-response relations of software systems, which describe relationships between inputs to the system and the corresponding outputs made by the system. The relations are typically observed in reactive systems. However, liveness checking is more difficult than safety checking in general since it needs to find a counterexample with a loop. For liveness checking, we should develop efficient ways of detecting SCCs using Swarm Intelligence. Several techniques of liveness checking are developed on the basis of ACO (Chicano & Alba, Liveness, 2008; Rafe, Darghayedi, & Einollah, 2019). The study of liveness checking leads to support the verification of full expressions of Temporal Logic.

Combinations with Optimization Methods of Model Checking

We have investigated a number of research efforts to tackle with the state explosion problem and the problem of creating short counterexamples in the community of formal verification techniques. Such methods are called optimization techniques of model checking. They have been shown to be effective not only by the experiments, but also by numerous applications to large-scaled industrial software systems. We should combine the optimization techniques of model checking with Swarm Intelligence for further improvement. A synergetic approach of safety checking supporting POR is proposed in (Chicano & Alba, POR, 2008).

Tool Support and Conducting Realistic Case Studies

We have to develop practical model checkers that use Swarm Intelligence. Tool support is necessary because we can easily evaluate the developed methods comparing with the traditional model checkers to analyze their benefits and limitations. Tools that implement new ideas can inspire use of Swarm Intelligence in state-of the-art model checking, such as model checking for infinite search spaces (Schuppan & Armin, 2006), Probabilistic Model Checking (Baier & Katoen, 2008) and Software Model Checking (Jhala & Majumdar, 2009).

Another benefit of the tool support is to promote the widespread use of the developed tools in industry. Case studies under realistic conditions help us collect know-hows and lessons learned in using Swarm Intelligence for model checking. For example, through the case studies, we will get insights about determining the appropriate values of the parameters that each Swarm Intelligence technique needs.

CONCLUSION

Formal verification is one of the important activities in software system development in order to provide reliable and correct software systems. Failures of systems can make serious effects on our society. This chapter investigated the applications of Swarm Intelligence to a kind of formal verification techniques, namely model checking. Although model checking is one of the most famous verification techniques in software engineering, there still exist challenges to address; the state explosion problem and the acquisition of comprehensible counterexamples. In order to overcome the challenges, we formulated model checking as a combinatorial optimization problem. Owing to the formulation, we can adapt Swarm Intelligence algorithms to model checking. We discussed model checking algorithms based on ACO and PSO. We also reviewed the existing researches using Swarm Intelligence. Because recent researches have shown that Swarm Intelligence is a promising technique for formal verification, we hope that the collaborative researches of Swarm Intelligence and software engineering refine verification techniques furthermore.

ACKNOWLEDGMENT

This research received no specific grant from any funding agency in the public, commercial, or not-for-profit sectors.

REFERENCES

Alba, E., & Chicano, F. (2007). ACOhg: dealing with huge graphs. In *Proceedings of the 9th Annual Conference on Genetic and Evolutionary Computation*, 10-17. Academic Press.

Alba, E., & Chicano, F. (2007). Finding safety errors with ACO. In *Proceedings of the 9th Annual Conference on Genetic and Evolutionary Computation*, 1066-1073. Academic Press.

Alba, E., & Troya, J. M. (1996). Genetic Algorithms for protocol validation. In *Proceedings of the 4th International Conference on Parallel Problem Solving from Nature, Lecture Notes in Computer Science, 1141*, 870-879. Academic Press.

Andisha, A. S., Wehrle, M., & Westphal, B. (2015). Directed Model Checking for PROMELA with Relaxation-Based Distance Functions. In *Proceedings of the 22nd International Symposium on Model Checking Software, Lecture Notes in Computer Science, 9232*, 153-159. 10.1007/978-3-319-23404-5_11

Baier, C., & Katoen, J.-P. (2008). *Principles of Model Checking*. MIT Press.

Biere, A., Cimatti, A., Clarke, E. M., & Zhu, Y. (1999). Symbolic model checking without BDDs. In *Proceedings of the 5th International Conference on Tools and Algorithms for Construction and Analysis of Systems*, 193-207. Academic Press.

Boussaïd, I., Lepagnot, J., & Siarry, P. (2013). A survey on optimization metaheuristics. *Information Sciences, 237*, 82–117. doi:10.1016/j.ins.2013.02.041

Bustan, D., & Grumberg, O. (2003). Simulation-based minimization. *ACM Transactions on Computational Logic, 4*(2), 181–206. doi:10.1145/635499.635502

Chicano, F., & Alba, E. (2008). Ant colony optimization with partial order reduction for discovering safety property violations in concurrent models. *Information Processing Letters, 106*(6), 221–231. doi:10.1016/j.ipl.2007.11.015

Chicano, F., & Alba, E. (2008). Finding liveness errors with ACO. In *Proceedings of the IEEE Congress on Evolutionary Computation 2008*, 2997-3004. 10.1109/CEC.2008.4631202

Chicano, F., Ferreira, M., & Alba, E. (2011). Comparing metaheuristic algorithms for error detection in Java programs. In *Proceedings of the Third International Symposium on Search Based Software Engineering, Lecture Notes in Computer Science, 6956*, 82-96. 10.1007/978-3-642-23716-4_11

Cimatti, A., Clarke, E. M., Giunchiglia, E., Giunchiglia, F., Pistore, M., Roveri, M., ... Tacchella, A. (2002). NuSMV 2: an opensource tool for symbolic model checking. In *Proceedings of the 14th International Conference on Computer Aided Verification*, 359-364. 10.1007/3-540-45657-0_29

Clarke, E., Grumberg, O., Jha, S., Lu, Y., & Veith, H. (2003). Counterexample-guided abstraction refinement for symbolic model checking. *Journal of the Association for Computing Machinery, 50*(5), 752–794. doi:10.1145/876638.876643

Clarke, E. M. (2008). The birth of model checking. *25 Years of Model Checking. Lecture Notes in Computer Science, 5000*, 1–26. doi:10.1007/978-3-540-69850-0_1

Clarke, E. M., & Emerson, E. (1981). Design and synthesis of synchronization skeletons using branching-time temporal logic. In *Logic of Programs* (pp. 52–71). Workshop.

Clarke, E. M. Jr, Grumberg, O., Kroening, D., Peled, D., & Veith, H. (2018). *Model Checking* (2nd ed.). MIT Press.

Cormen, T. H., Stein, C., Rivest, R. L., & Leiserson, C. E. (2001). *Introduction to Algorithms* (2nd ed.). MIT Press.

Dijkstra, E. W. (1959). A note on two problems in connexion with graphs. *Numerische Mathematik, 1*(1), 269–271. doi:10.1007/BF01386390

Dorigo, M., & Stützle, T. (2004). *Ant Colony Optimization*. MIT Press. doi:10.7551/mitpress/1290.001.0001

Edelkamp, S., & Jabbar, S. (2006). Large-scale directed model checking LTL. In *Proceedings of the 13th International Conference on Model Checking Software*, 1-18. Academic Press.

Edelkamp, S., Lafuente, A., & Leue, S. (2001). Directed explicit model checking with HSF-SPIN. In *Proceedings of the 8th International SPIN Workshop on Model Checking of Software*, 57-79. 10.1007/3-540-45139-0_5

Edelkamp, S., Leue, S., & Lluch-Lafuente, A. (2004). Directed explicit-state model checking in the validation of communication protocols. *International Journal of Software Tools for Technology Transfer, 5*(2-3), 247–267. doi:10.100710009-002-0104-3

Edelkamp, S., Schuppan, V., Bosnacki, D., Wijs, A., Fehnker, A., & Husain, A. (2008). Survey on directed model checking. In *Proceedings of the 5th International Workshop on Model Checking and Artificial Intelligence, Lecture Notes in Computer Science, 5348*, 65-89. Academic Press.

Ferreira, M., Alba, E., Chicano, F., & Gómez-Pulido, J. A. (2008). Detecting protocol errors using particle swarm optimization with Java Pathfinder. In *Proceedings of the High Performance Computing & Simulation Conference*, 319-325. Academic Press.

Filippidis, I., & Holzmann, G. J. (2014). An improvement of the piggyback algorithm for parallel model checking. In *Proceedings of the 2014 International SPIN Symposium on Model Checking of Software*, 48-57. 10.1145/2632362.2632375

Francesca, G., Santone, A., Vaglini, G., & Luisa, V. M. (2011). Ant colony optimization for deadlock detection in concurrent systems. In *Proceedings of 2011 IEEE 35th Annual Computer Software and Applications Conference*, 108-117. 10.1109/COMPSAC.2011.22

Francesco, N. D., Lettieri, G., Santone, A., & Vaglini, G. (2016). Heuristic search for equivalence checking. *Software & Systems Modeling, 15*(2), 513–530. doi:10.100710270-014-0416-2

Gastin, P., & Oddoux, D. (2001). Fast LTL to Büchi automata translation. In *Proceedings of the 13th International Conference on Computer Aided Verification*, 53-65. 10.1007/3-540-44585-4_6

Giannakopoulou, D., & Lerda, F. (2002). From states to transitions: improving translation of LTL formulae to Büchi automata. In *Proceedings of the 22nd International Conference on Formal Techniques for Networked and Distributed Systems*, 308-326. 10.1007/3-540-36135-9_20

Giannakopoulou, D., & Magee, J. (2003). Fluent model checking for event-based systems. In *Proceedings of the 9th European software engineering conference held jointly with 11th ACM SIGSOFT international symposium on Foundations of software engineering*, 257-266. Academic Press.

Godefroid, P., & Khurshid, S. (2002). Exploring very large state spaces using genetic algorithms. In *Proceedings of the 8th International Conference on Tools and Algorithms for the Construction and Analysis of Systems*, 266-280. Academic Press. 10.1007/3-540-46002-0_19

Groce, A., & Visser, W. (2004). Heuristics for model checking Java program. *International Journal of Software Tools for Technology Transfer*, 6(4), 260–276. doi:10.100710009-003-0130-9

Grosu, R., & Smolka, S. A. (2005). Monte Carlo model checking. In *Proceedings of the 11th International Conference on Tools and Algorithms for the Construction and Analysis of Systems*, 271-286.

Harman, M., Mansouri, S. A., & Zhang, Y. (2012). Search-based software engineering: trends, techniques, and applications. *ACM Computing Surveys, 45*(1), 11:1-11:61.

Hoare, C. A. (1969). An axiomatic basis for computer programming. *Communications of the ACM, 12*(10), 576–580. doi:10.1145/363235.363259

Hoare, C. A. (1985). *Communicating Sequential Processes*. Prentice-Hall.

Holzmann, G. (2003). *The Spin Model Checker: Primer and Reference Manual*. Addison-Wesley Professional.

Holzmann, G. J. (2012). Parallelizing the Spin model checker. In *Proceedings of the 19th International Conference on Model Checking Software*, 155-171. 10.1007/978-3-642-31759-0_12

Hromkovič, J. (2001). *Algorithmics for Hard Problems: Introduction to Combinatorial Optimization, Randomization, Approximation, and Heuristics*. Springer-Verlag. doi:10.1007/978-3-662-04616-6

Jackson, D. (2006). *Software Abstractions: Logic, Language, and Analysis*. MIT Press.

Jhala, R., & Majumdar, R. (2009). Software model checking. *ACM Computing Surveys, 41*(4), 21:1-21:54.

Kennedy, J., & Eberhart, R. (1995). Particle swarm optimization. In *Proceedings of International Conference on Neural Networks, 4*, 1942-1948. 10.1109/ICNN.1995.488968

Knuth, D. E. (2015). *The Art of Computer Programming, Volume 4, Fascicle 6: Satisfiability*. Addison-Wesley Professional.

Kumazawa, T., Takada, K., Takimoto, M., & Kambayashi, Y. (2019). Ant colony optimization-based model checking extended by smell-like pheromone with hop counts. *Swarm and Evolutionary Computation, 44*, 511–521. doi:10.1016/j.swevo.2018.06.002

Kumazawa, T., Yokoyama, C., Takimoto, M., & Kambayashi, Y. (2016). Ant colony optimization-based model checking extended by smell-like pheromone. *EAI Endorsed Transactions on Industrial Networks and Intelligent Systems, 3*(7).

Lamport, L. (1977). Proving the correctness of multiprocess programs. *IEEE Transactions on Software Engineering, 3*(2), 125–143. doi:10.1109/TSE.1977.229904

Lamport, L. (2002). *Specifying Systems: The TLA+ Language and Tools for Hardware and Software Engineers*. Addison-Wesley Longman.

Lee, D., & Yannakakis, M. (1992). Online minimization of transition systems (extended abstract). In *Proceedings of the twenty-fourth annual ACM symposium on Theory of Computing*, 264-274. 10.1145/129712.129738

Leveson, N. G. (2004). The role of software in spacecraft accidents. *Journal of Spacecraft and Rockets*, *41*(4), 564–575. doi:10.2514/1.11950

Magee, J., & Kramer, J. (2006). *Concurrency: State Models & Java Programs* (2nd ed.). John Wiley & Sons.

Manna, Z., & Pnueli, A. (1992). *The Temporal Logic of Reactive and Concurrent Systems*. Springer-Verlag. doi:10.1007/978-1-4612-0931-7

Manna, Z., & Pnueli, A. (1995). *Temporal Verification of Reactive Systems: Safety*. Springer-Verlag. doi:10.1007/978-1-4612-4222-2

Milewicz, R. M., & Poulding, S. (2017). Scalable parallel model checking via Monte-Carlo Tree Search. *Software Engineering Notes*, *42*(4), 1–5. doi:10.1145/3149485.3149495

Milner, R. (1999). *Communicating and Mobile Systems: the Pi-Calculus*. Cambridge University Press.

Parízek, P., & Lhoták, O. (2019). Fast detection of concurrency errors by state space traversal with randomization and early backtracking. *International Journal of Software Tools for Technology Transfer*, *21*(4), 365–400. doi:10.100710009-018-0484-7

Pira, E., Rafe, V., & Nikanjam, A. (2017). Deadlock detection in complex software systems specified through graph transformation using Bayesian optimization algorithm. *Journal of Systems and Software*, *131*, 181–200. doi:10.1016/j.jss.2017.05.128

Poulding, S., & Feldt, R. (2015). Heuristic model checking using a Monte-Carlo Tree Search Algorithm. In *Proceedings of the 2015 Annual Conference on Genetic and Evolutionary Computation*, 1359-1366. 10.1145/2739480.2754767

Rafe, V., Darghayedi, M., & Einollah, P. (2019). MS-ACO: A multi-stage ant colony optimization to refute complex software systems specified through graph transformation. *Soft Computing*, *23*(12), 4531–4556. doi:10.100700500-018-3444-y

Rafe, V., Moradi, M., Yousefian, R., & Nikanjam, A. (2015). A meta-heuristic solution for automated refutation of complex software systems specified through Graph Transformations. *Applied Soft Computing*, *33*(C), 136–149. doi:10.1016/j.asoc.2015.04.032

Sangiorgi, D. (2011). *Introduction to Bisimulation and Coinduction*. Cambridge University Press. doi:10.1017/CBO9780511777110

Schuppan, V., & Armin, B. (2006). Liveness checking as safety checking for infinite state spaces. *Electronic Notes in Theoretical Computer Science*, *149*(1), 79–96. doi:10.1016/j.entcs.2005.11.018

Schuppan, V., & Biere, A. (2005). Shortest counterexamples for symbolic model checking of LTL with Past. In *Proceedings of the 11th International Conference on Tools and Algorithms for the Construction and Analysis of Systems*, 493-509. 10.1007/978-3-540-31980-1_32

Staunton, J., & Clark, J. A. (2010). Searching for safety violations using Estimation of Distribution Algorithms. In *Proceedings of 2010 Third International Conference on Software Testing, Verification, and Validation Workshops*, 212-221. 10.1109/ICSTW.2010.24

Staunton, J., & Clark, J. A. (2011). Finding short counterexamples in Promela models using Estimation of Distribution Algorithms. In *Proceedings of the 13th Annual Conference on Genetic and Evolutionary Computation*, 1923-1930. 10.1145/2001576.2001834

Tamai, T. (2009). Social impact of information system failures. *IEEE Computer, 42*(6), 58–65. doi:10.1109/MC.2009.199

Tamai, T. (2015). Software engineering view of a large-scale system failure and the following lawsuit. *Proceedings of the 2nd IEEE/ACM International Workshop on Software Engineering Research and Industrial Practice*, 18-24. 10.1109/SERIP.2015.12

Tan, Y., & Zhu, Y. (2010). Fireworks algorithm for optimization. *Proceedings of the First International Conference on Advances in Swarm Intelligence*, 355-364.

Tarjan, R. (1972). Depth-first search and linear graph algorithms. *SIAM Journal on Computing, 1*(2), 146–160. doi:10.1137/0201010

Timm, N., Gruner, S., & Sibanda, P. (2017). Model Checking of Concurrent Software Systems via Heuristic-Guided SAT Solving. *Lecture Notes in Computer Science, 10522*, 244–259. doi:10.1007/978-3-319-68972-2_16

Vardi, M. Y., & Wolper, P. (1986). An automata theoretic approach to automatic program verification. *Proceedings of First Symposium on Logic in Computer Science*, 332-344.

Wayne, H. (2018). *Practical TLA+: Planning Driven Development*. Apress. doi:10.1007/978-1-4842-3829-5

Xing, B., & Gao, W.-J. (2016). *Innovative Computational Intelligence: A Rough Guide to 134 Clever Algorithms*. Springer Publishing Company, Inc.

Yousefian, R., Rafe, V., & Rahmani, M. (2014). A heuristic solution for model checking graph transformation systems. *Applied Soft Computing, 24*(C), 169–180. doi:10.1016/j.asoc.2014.06.055

KEY TERMS AND DEFINITIONS

Counterexample: An example violation that is returned by a model checker when verification fails.

Model: In the context of software development, a model refers to an abstract representation of the certain aspects of software systems.

Model Checking: A formal verification technology of software systems that mechanically checks whether the given models satisfies the specified properties or not.

Property: A formal description of what the target software systems are required to hold.

State Explosion Problem: A problem in observing model checking, which states that search spaces are too large to explore exhaustively.

Verification: An activity that the developed software systems or their specifications are confirmed to be correct with respect to the stakeholders' requirements.

Chapter 18
Research on the Construction of Underwater Platform Combat Deduction System Based on Service-Oriented and Multi-Agent Technology

Yuxiang Sun
Nanjing University, China

ABSTRACT

Object-oriented intelligent modeling, model management, etc. are difficult problems in the designing and development of underwater platform combat deduction system. The command and control description model based on OODA loop depicted the business process of underwater platform combat deduction using service-oriented and agent modeling technology and established an underwater platforms deduction system architecture, effectively solving the problem of intelligence, reusing, and extensibility in combat deduction modeling. The chapter has reference value in the designing and development of underwater platforms deduction systems.

INTRODUCTION

Combat deduction refers to: "Imitation of combat processes according to known or intended situations and data. Including the simulation of actual military exercises and computer combat simulation. It is usually used to research and test the combat plan, evaluate the effectiveness of combat equipment, and explore new combat theories. By means of combat deduction, both the rationality and feasibility of combat strategies and combat plans can be verified, the ability of commanders to analyze problems and deal with incidents can be trained, and new tactics can be explored in the context of combat scenarios. Therefore, research and build an underwater platform combat deduction system that is close to actual

DOI: 10.4018/978-1-7998-1659-1.ch018

Copyright © 2020, IGI Global. Copying or distributing in print or electronic forms without written permission of IGI Global is prohibited.

combat, model intelligence, reasonable structure and flexible use, and carry out combat plan exercises for underwater platforms such as underwater unmanned vehicles and submarines, plays an important role in optimizing the underwater platform combat plan and training the commander's combat ability.

Based on the OODA ring command and control description model, this paper briefly describes the business process of underwater platform combat deduction, combines service-oriented technology and Agent modeling technology, and builds an architecture of underwater platform combat deduction system based on service-oriented and multi-Agent, and discusses the implementation method of agent modeling technology.

Definition of Combat Deduction Function of Underwater Platform

The definition of the underwater platform combat deduction function is the basis for constructing the underwater platform combat deduction system. At present, different types and uses of combat deduction systems have been developed and applied domestic and abroad (Bello, 2006; Wei, Song, & Kim, 2014; Jin et al., 2017; Alexander & Kelly, 2013; Tavcar, Kaluza, Kvassay, Schneider, & Gams, 2014, August; Xiaofeng, Siguangya, Lin, 2000; Yan, Zhang, & Sun, 2008, October; Zhao, Zhang, Sun, & Yan, 2012). Among them, the Joint Warfare System (JWARS) is a simulation system supported by the US military to support joint combat operations, mainly including the problem domain, simulation domain and platform domain. The problem domain provides software for analysis purposes and describing combat functions; the simulation domain provides "engine" that drives the simulation run; and the platform domain provides system hardware and human-computer interaction interface (Chengjing & Jianing, 2015; Li, Yi, Sun, & Gong, 2012). With the function definition method of the joint war system, the typical OODA ring command and control description model (Pan Guanhua, 2015; Fusano, Sato, & Namatame, 2011, March) is adopted for the underwater platform combat process and its characteristics. The business process analysis of the underwater platform combat process is carried out, and the underwater platform combat deduction function is described.

The general working process of the underwater platform combat system is as follows: the intelligence sub-system collects the battlefield information, completes the comprehensive processing of intelligence, and forms a unified tactical situation; the command sub-system carries out underwater acoustic environment and tactical situation analysis, assists the commander to complete the offensive and defensive decision-making, and clarifies the attack and defense plan. That is to determine the type of attack and defense weapons, channels, platform occupying maneuver schemes, etc; weapon subsystems launch for shooting solution, launch control, complete weapons attack and integrated defense and other combat activities.

Taking the underwater platform as an example, according to the Observation (O) –Orientation (O) - Decision (D) - Action (A) process (Jiang, Wei, Xuanhua, 2015), the operation process of the underwater platform is mainly divided into the following stages: information collection and processing, battlefield situation generation and display, combat assistant decision-making, weapon attack and defense application, and combat effectiveness evaluation (Minghui, 2014), as shown in Figure 1.

Figure 1. Combat process model of underwater platform

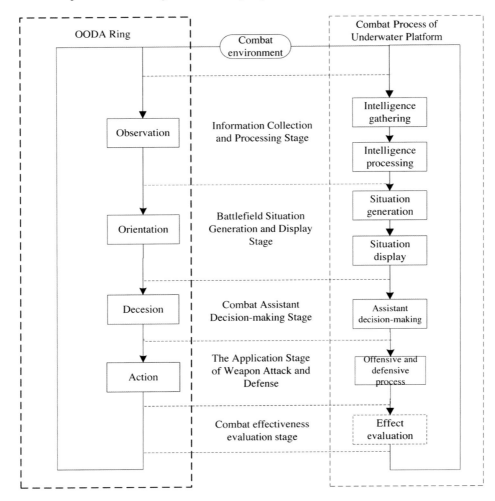

STRUCTURE CONSTRUCTION OF UNDERWATER PLATFORM COMBAT DEDUCTION SYSTEM

Basic Composition of Combat Deduction System for Underwater Platform

According to the function definition, the underwater platform combat deduction system is mainly composed of guidance and control subsystem, underwater platform model simulation subsystem, environment and force simulation subsystem, combat deduction workbench and deduction resource database. The connection relationship of each part is established by simulation service bus (SSB), as shown in Figure 2.

The guidance and control subsystem is the management and control center of the underwater platform combat deduction system. It mainly includes such functional components as scenario editing and generation, simulation operation control, deduction event generation and management, deduction effect evaluation, deduction process recording and playback, battlefield situation display, deduction data management and so on. It is used for the control and management of the whole underwater platform combat

Figure 2. Composition of combat deduction system for underwater platform

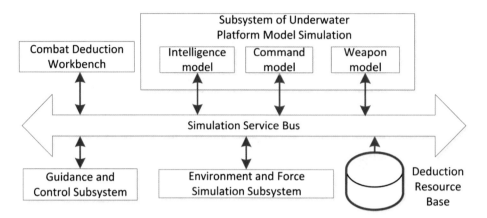

deduction by the guidance and control personnel. The simulation subsystem of underwater platform model is the core component of underwater platform combat deduction system. It mainly consists of three parts: intelligence model, command model and weapon model. It includes sonar, radar, navigation, information fusion processing, tactical situation and parameter display, assistant decision-making, target motion element solution, weapon (torpedo, missile, sonar reactance, etc.) launching and controlling and other functional components. It is used to complete the combat function simulation of underwater platform combat system.

The environment and force simulation subsystem is the basis of the underwater platform combat deduction system. It is used to generate and maintain battlefield environment and combat entities, and to provide static and dynamic information such as geographical environment and main entities of combat area.

Combat deduction workbench is a human-computer interaction interface of underwater platform combat deduction system. It is mainly used for commanders to monitor the combat situation of underwater platform in real time, and use deduction aided tools to complete command and control activities in the process of deduction.

The deduction resource base is the data and model management center of the underwater platform combat deduction system. It mainly includes environment database, combat model database, combat scenario database, protocol service library, etc. It provides data and model services for combat deduction.

Simulated Service Bus (SSB) is the interconnection and interworking part of each component of the underwater platform combat deduction system. It provides a standardized communication infrastructure for service requesters and service providers. It has the ability of discovery, routing, matching and selection, and supports dynamic interaction between services.

Agent Model Composition of Underwater Platform Combat Deduction System

One of the key tasks of the underwater platform combat deduction system is to establish a complete simulation model system that matches the problem solving (Yang, 2006). Using multi-agent modeling technology, the sub-functions of underwater platform model simulation subsystem, environment and force simulation subsystem are modeled by Agent, and the object model and integrated structure of underwater platform combat deduction system are constructed, as shown in Figure 3.

Figure 3. The agent model of underwater platform combat deduction system

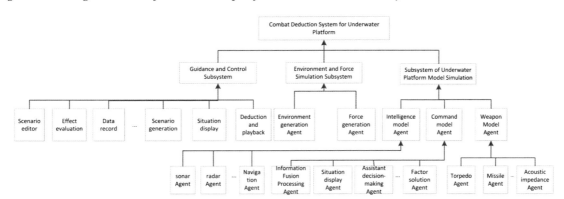

The environment and force simulation subsystem mainly simulate all the geographical environment, marine environment, meteorological environment and electromagnetic environment in the combat area. It also models the main combat entities and event entities in the combat area, and accurately simulates the battlefield environment and the counterforce behavior.

The simulation subsystem of underwater platform model includes intelligence model agent, command model agent and weapon model agent. Among them, intelligence model agent mainly collects combat information, provides basic data for estimating and analyzing combat situation, and provides information basis for combat decision-making, including sonar agent, radar agent and navigation agent, etc. Command model agent is the core component of the system, which has the ability of obtaining information from outside and certain decision-making ability, and can change its own state, and with others. Entities interact to complete the related command and control activities, including information fusion processing agent, tactical situation and parameter display agent, assistant decision-making agent, target motion element solving agent, etc. Weapon model agent cooperates with torpedo agent, missile agent, acoustic countermeasure agent to complete torpedo attack, missile attack, mine deployment and countermeasure according to the instructions issued by combat command model agent. Anti-defense and other combat processes.

Guidance and control subsystem is used to control and manage the whole underwater platform combat deduction. It is the management and control center of the underwater platform combat deduction system. Service-oriented is used to model it.

Architecture Establishment of Combat Deduction System for Underwater Platform

As a technical design tool of simulation model service system, service-oriented has good encapsulation, reusability and high integration across platforms. Literature (Wu, Li, Xiao, & Liu, 2018) proposes a framework of underwater platform combat simulation platform based on Web service, which divides different types of subsystems into modules and integrates them with Web service technology, which improves the reusability of the model. However, in essence, the integration process is based on the order of service execution provided by the process and the data transmission relationship between them. As a static application, Web service technology can only passively wait for the call, but cannot actively provide services, so it is difficult to adapt to the requirements of the underwater platform combat deduction system. Agent technology has the characteristics of autonomy, adaptability and responsiveness due to the introduction of artificial intelligence. It combines with service-oriented to form a multi-agent system based on Web service, which can complement each other.

Therefore, based on the underwater platform combat deduction model system, making full use of the advantages of service-oriented and multi-agent modeling, a service-oriented and intelligent underwater platform combat deduction system architecture is constructed, as shown in Figure 4.

Figure 4. Architecture of underwater platform combat deduction system

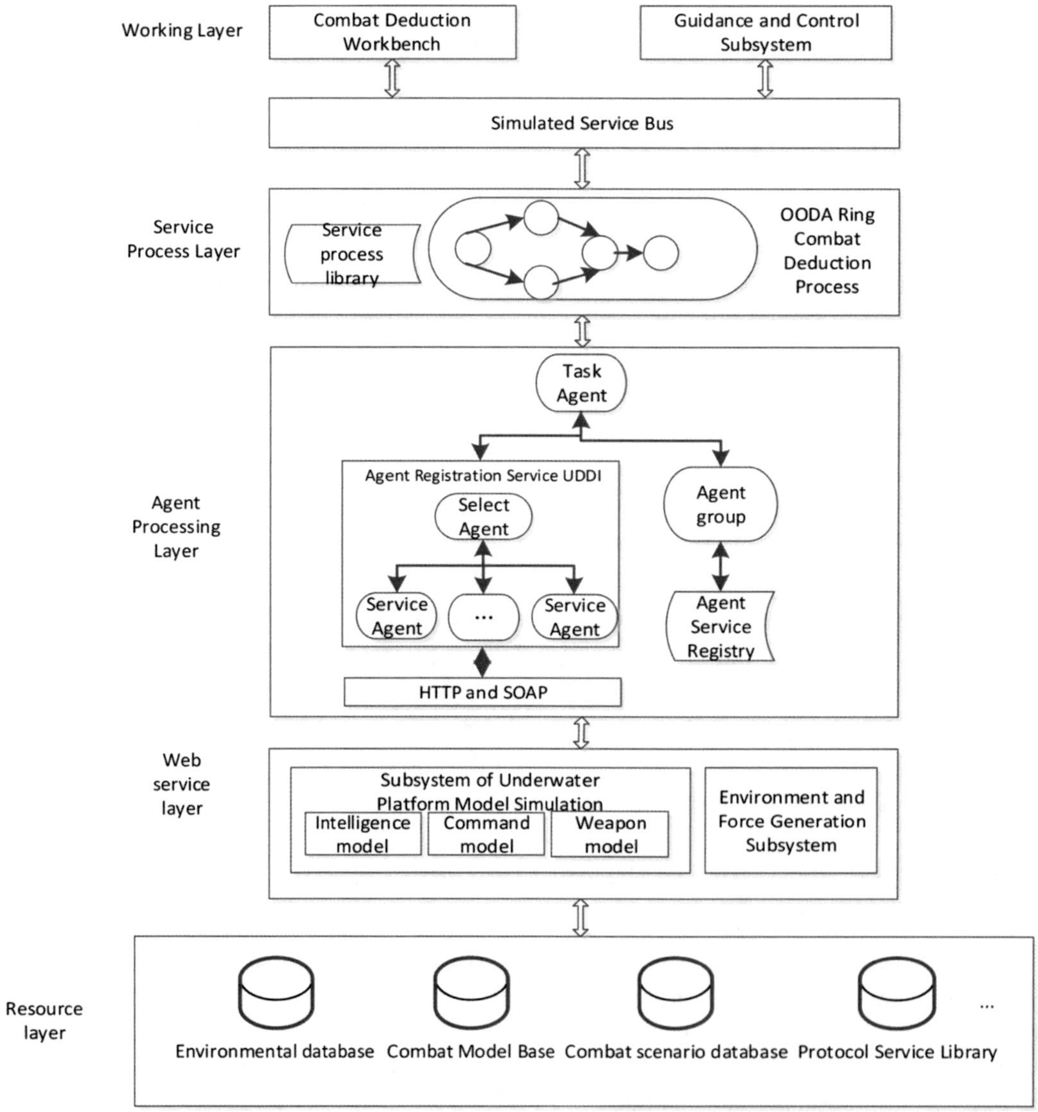

The system structure adopts a five-layer architecture including working layer, service process layer, agent processing layer, Web service layer and resource layer. Through hierarchical processing, the coupling of each module in the system is weakened and the system has stronger adaptability.

1. **Working Layer**: This layer is mainly composed of combat deduction workbench and guidance and control subsystem. It mainly provides the human-computer interaction of trainees to the combat deduction system of underwater platform and the control and management of the combat deduction system of underwater platform for trainees.
2. **Service Process Layer**: This layer provides OODA loop operation process for underwater platform combat deduction system, and stores it through service process description library. The function is to ensure that the user sends a deduction instruction to the task agent to assign tasks according to the OODA loop operation process, and then finds the Web service that is most suitable for the combat task in the Agent processing layer and feeds back to the task agent. Task Agent sends selected Web service information to service process template, and combines these service information according to the order of service process to construct new applications to meet the needs of trainees.
3. **Agent Processing Layer**: This layer is in the middle layer, which is the key part of service integration intellectualization. There are four main aspects of work: first, responsible for the communication between Web service and Agents, registering corresponding Web service for each service agent; second, publishing tasks according to the functional requirements in the service process; third, selecting the most matching services according to certain needs evaluation; fourth, selecting the best service according to certain needs evaluation; and third, selecting the best service. Good service information is bound to the process to form a new application that can meet business needs.
4. **Web Service Layer**: It is the executor of service integration system, mainly for encapsulating existing functional components and forming Web service. The encapsulation of services can not only reduce development costs and improve reusability, but also improve the flexibility of the system and facilitate the construction of new application systems. Each service in the Web service Layer is registered in the Agent Registry by a corresponding Service Agent. Instead of communicating directly between each Web service, the corresponding Service Agent is responsible for it.
5. **Resource Layer**: This layer includes environment database, battle model database, battle scenario database, protocol service library, etc. It provides data support and persistent service for underwater platform combat deduction system.

Service Agent Management Process

Service Agents mainly include "command model agent", "intelligence model agent", "weapon model agent", "environment generation agent" and "force model agent". The management includes registration and call.

Service Agent Registration Process

The registration process of the service agent is shown in Figure 5. The UDDI central node is the core position in the entire Agent service integration architecture, providing a unified discovery, service description and integration platform for the realization of the collaborative work functions of each service agent. Each service agent sends a SOAP request to the UDDI central node of Agent service. The

Figure 5. Registration flow chart of service agent

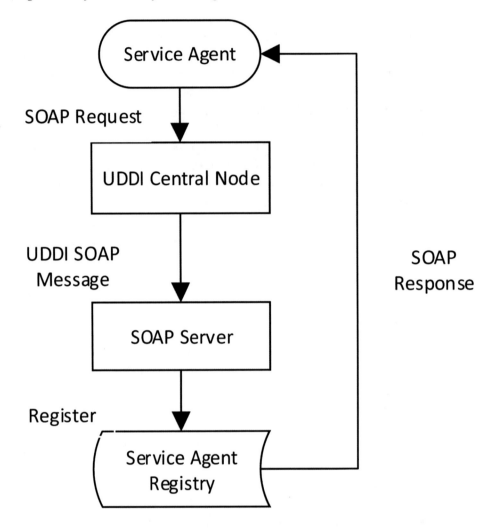

SOAP server of the registration center receives the UDDI SOAP message and processes it, registers the service agent that issued the SOAP request in the Agent service registration database, and then returns the SOAP response to the SOAP server. The service agent that issued the SOAP request. Each of the above service agents can publish its own basic information to the UDDI central node, or look up other related registered service agents from the UDDI as needed, and finally call the bound service to form an integrated architecture for collaborative work.

Service Agent Call Process

The flow chart of calling Agent service is shown in Figure 6. In this structure, the trainee can find the corresponding service flow in the service process library by inputting the demand, and send the service type required by the process to the task agent to allocate the task. After receiving the service type, the task agent goes to the UDDI center. The selection agent of the node sends a message, and the selection agent in the agent service library selects the service that best meets the user's requirement in the current service library according to the user's needs, and the task agent sends the Web service information corresponding to the selected service agent to the task agent. Service process templates, combined with service information in the order of service processes, to build new applications that meet user needs.

Figure 6. Call flow chart of service agent

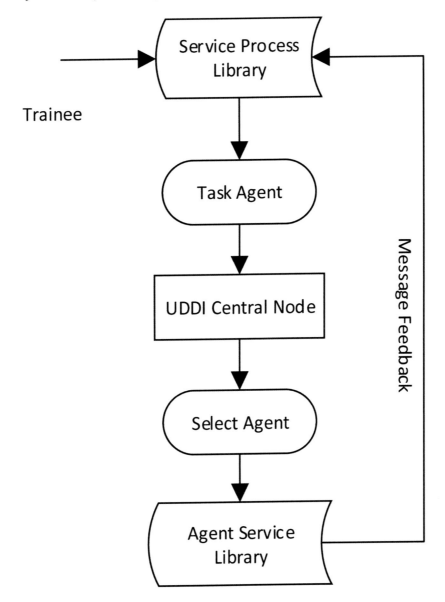

AN AGENT DESIGN EXAMPLE OF UNDERWATER PLATFORM COMBAT DEDUCTION BUSINESS MODEL

Relations and Structures of Main Business Model Agents

Business function class agent includes intelligence model agent, command model agent, weapon model agent and so on. The combat deduction model agent of underwater platform mainly includes platform model agent, intelligence model agent, command model agent, weapon model agent and so on. Its basic relationship is shown in Figure 7.

Figure 7. Basic business model Agent

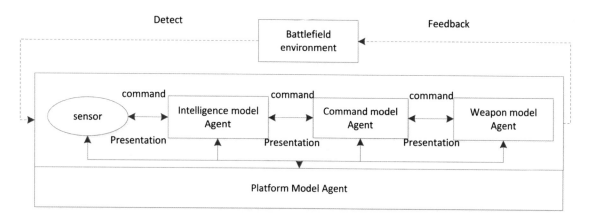

Design Example of Platform Model Agent

Taking the platform model Agent as an example, the platform model Agent is established based on the establishment of the related entity equipment model and according to the steps of business model construction. Platform model Agent is mainly composed of perception module, decision module and action module. Its structure description is shown in Figure 8.

THE SIMULATION PROCESS OF UNDERWATER PLATFORM COMBAT DEDUCTION SYSTEM BASED ON MAXSIM

Operation Flow of Combat Deduction System of Underwater Platform

Based on the MAXSim underwater platform combat deduction system architecture, and on the basis of the logical description model of business model Agent and the functional model of equipment, an underwater platform combat deduction system composed of guidance control, deduction workbench, general data blackboard, simulation model package, CGF and database is constructed, which has both automatic and semi-automatic operation modes. The system is simulated. The actual operation process is shown in Figure 9.

Figure 8. Platform model agent structure description

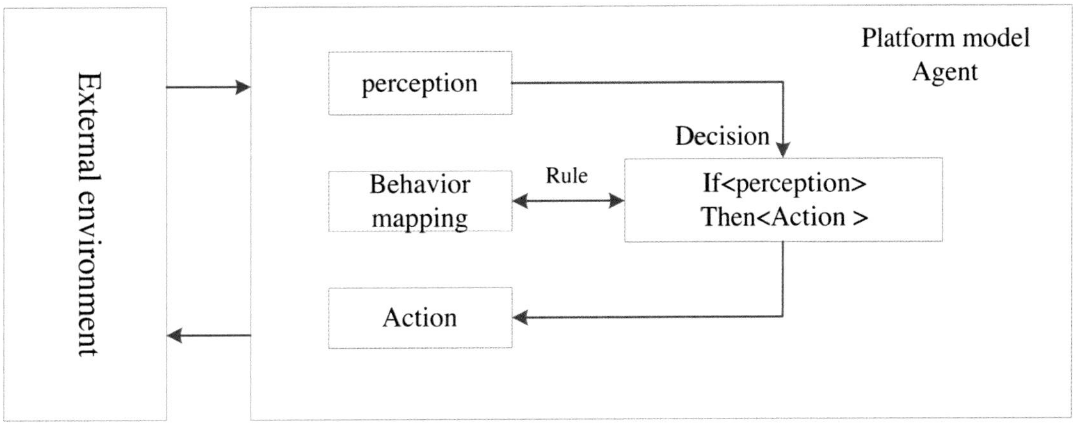

1. Preparatory stage of simulation: Start up Manager, GBB space and distributed server, load combat scenario and generate underwater platform model.
2. Simulation operation stage: underwater platform intelligence model Agent real-time observation of sea conditions, organization and configuration of sensors to implement target reconnaissance and search of sea areas. The command model Agent of underwater platform deals with information acquired by sensors, identifies targets, judges threats and so on, and generates battlefield tactical situation. The command decision model gives corresponding combat instructions according to the current situation. Weapon model agent organizes weapon channels according to combat instructions, keeps track of targets, outputs weapon firing data, or uses underwater acoustic countermeasure equipment for defense.
3. Effectiveness evaluation stage: After the simulation operation, the deduction effect evaluation information is given according to the combat deduction evaluation model of underwater platform, and the related information is archived.

Verification of the Simulation Process of the Combat Deduction System for Underwater Platforms

Operation Scenario Description of Underwater Platforms

In order to realize the combat deduction of underwater platforms, and verify the models and systems established by the models mentioned above, a simple combat scenario of underwater platforms is designed. Through this scenario, we can deduce the purpose, situation and development of both sides of the battle, and guide the whole battle deduction. The details are described as follows:

Red team and Blue team are XXX underwater platform with several torpedoes on board. They swim in a certain sea area. The Blue team underwater platform moves from distant sea to a reserved sea area. Red team underwater platform encounters Blue team underwater platform swimming in the sea area during its combat readiness patrol mission. According to the relevant rules, Red team underwater platform carries out tactical evacuation of Blue team underwater platform, and blue team underwater platform decides to leave.

Figure 9. Simulation flow of submarine combat system

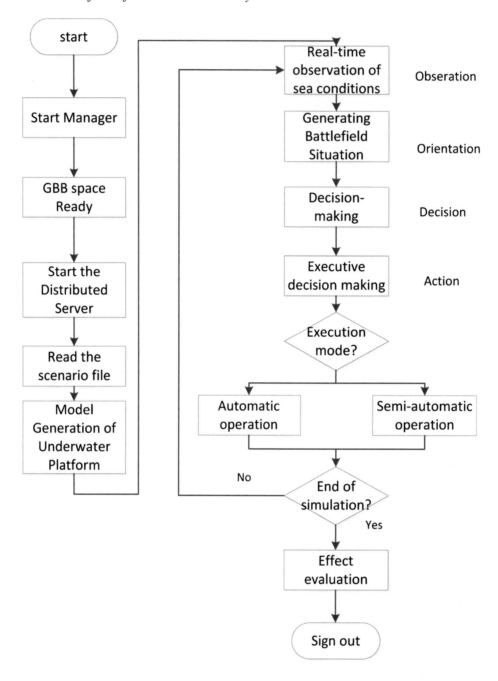

Operation Simulation Process of Underwater Platform Combat Deduction

In the process of battle deduction simulation, according to the battle scenario, the Red team underwater platform and the Blue team underwater platform carry out tactical confrontation deduction. Each business model agent is an autonomous agent. The whole battle process is simulated based on Agent, and through GBB, the two sides of the confrontation form interactive perception.

In the course of tactical confrontation deduction, the Red team underwater platform expels the Blue team underwater platform which intrudes into a certain sea area. After sensing by its sensors, the Blue team underwater platform turns its course and accelerates its departure from a certain sea area, as shown in Figure 10.

Figure 10. The red underwater platform away from blue underwater platform situation map

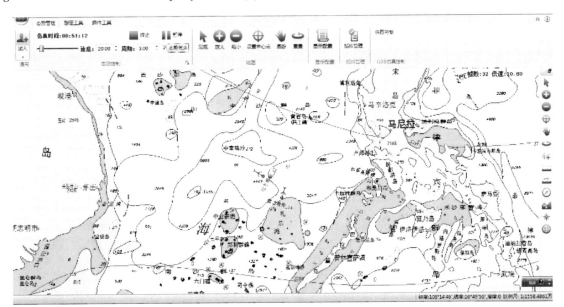

CONCLUSION

Based on the description model of OODA ring command and control, this paper analyses the business process and function of underwater platform combat deduction, and constructs an underwater platform combat deduction system based on service-oriented and Agent modeling technology. Compared with the framework of the combat simulation platform based on service-oriented, the framework of the system is characterized by the organic combination of service-oriented and Agent modeling technology, and the establishment of a service-oriented and intelligent underwater platform combat deduction system structure. It has the advantages of intelligence, reusability and scalability of the combat deduction model. The simulation process of the underwater platform combat deduction system is given and the underwater level is realized. The process simulation of the platform combat deduction system verifies the rationality of the system structure and business model Agent. It provides a feasible technical approach for the construction of intelligent and flexible underwater platform combat deduction system, and has important reference value for the agent modeling of the underwater platform combat deduction system.

REFERENCES

Alexander, R., & Kelly, T. (2013). Supporting systems of systems hazard analysis using multi-agent simulation. *Safety Science, 51*(1), 302–318. doi:10.1016/j.ssci.2012.07.006

Bello, P. (2006). *Theoretical Foundations for Rational Agency in Third Generation Wargames* (No. AFRL-IF-RS-TR-2006-2). Air Force Research Lab.

Fusano, A., Sato, H., & Namatame, A. (2011, March). Multi-agent based combat simulation from OODA and network perspective. In *2011 UkSim 13th International Conference on Computer Modelling and Simulation* (pp. 249-254). IEEE. 10.1109/UKSIM.2011.54

Hu, X., & Siguangya, W. L. (2000). SDS2000: A Qualitative and Quantitative Integrated Research and Simulation Environment for Strategic Decision. *Journal of Systems Simulation, 1*(6), 595–599.

Huang, C., & Wei, J. (2015). *Preliminary Strictness: Military Chess Deduction and Its Application.* Beijing: Aviation Industry Press.

Jiang, Wei, & Xuanhua. (2015). Combat simulation experiment based on OODA command and control loop. *Command and Control and Simulation, 37*(3), 112-115.

Jin, T., Liu, Z. W., Zhou, H., Guan, Z. H., Qin, Y., & Wu, Y. (2017). Robust average formation tracking for multi-agent systems with multiple leaders. *IFAC-PapersOnLine, 50*(1), 2427–2432. doi:10.1016/j.ifacol.2017.08.404

Li, M. (2014). *Research on deductive evaluation of underwater countermeasure effectiveness based on Monte Carlo method.* Beijing: China Ship Research Institute.

Li, N., Yi, W., Sun, M., & Gong, G. (2012). Development and application of intelligent system modeling and simulation platform. *Simulation Modelling Practice and Theory, 29*, 149–162. doi:10.1016/j.simpat.2012.08.001

Pan, G. (2015). *Principle of Integrated Command and and Control System for Ships.* Xi'an: Northwest Industrial Press.

Tavcar, A., Kaluza, B., Kvassay, M., Schneider, B., & Gams, M. (2014, August). Surrogate-agent modeling for improved training. In *Proceedings of the Twenty-first European Conference on Artificial Intelligence* (pp. 1103-1104). Academic Press.

Wei, Y., Song, K. S., & Kim, D. S. (2014). Message oriented management and analysis tool for naval combat systems. *IFAC Proceedings, 47*(3), 10524-10528.

Wu, H., Li, H., Xiao, R., & Liu, J. (2018). Modeling and simulation of dynamic ant colony's labor division for task allocation of UAV swarm. *Physica A, 491*, 127–141. doi:10.1016/j.physa.2017.08.094

Yan, B., Zhang, S., & Sun, J. (2008, October). A service-oriented air combat simulation system. In *2008 Asia Simulation Conference-7th International Conference on System Simulation and Scientific Computing* (pp. 192-199). IEEE. 10.1109/ASC-ICSC.2008.4675354

Yang, A. (2006). *A networked multi-agent combat model: Emergence explained.* University of New South Wales, Australian Defence Force Academy, School of Information Technology and Electrical Engineering.

Zhao, Z. G., Zhang, S. G., Sun, J. B., & Yan, B. (2012). Service-oriented air combat simulation architecture. *Journal of Beijing Institute of Technology, 21*(3), 408–414.

Compilation of References

Abdelaziz, M. M. A., Farag, H. E., El-Saadany, E. F., & Mohamed, Y. A.-R. I. (2013). A novel and generalized three-phase power flow algorithm for islanded microgrids using a newton trust region method. *IEEE Transactions on Power Systems*, *28*(1), 190–201. doi:10.1109/TPWRS.2012.2195785

Abdulmajeed, N. H., & Ayob, M. (2014). A firework algorithm for solving capacitated vehicle routing problem. *International Journal of Advancements in Computing Technology*, *6*(1), 79.

Abdulmajeed, N. H., & Ayob, M. (2014). A Firework Algorithm for Solving Capacitated Vehicle Routing Problem. *International Journal of Advancements in Computing Technology, Bangi, Selangor, Malaysia*, *6*(1), 79–86.

Abedini, M. (2016). A novel algorithm for load flow analysis in island microgrids using an improved evolutionary algorithm. *International Transactions on Electrical Energy Systems*, *26*(12), 2727–2743. doi:10.1002/etep.2231

Aerts, S., Lambrechts, D., Maity, S., Van Loo, P., Coessens, B., De Smet, F., ... Hassan, B. (2006). Gene prioritization through genomic data fusion. *Nature Biotechnology*, *24*(5), 537–544. doi:10.1038/nbt1203 PMID:16680138

Aladwan, F., Alshraideh, M., & Rasol, M. (2015). A Genetic Algorithm Approach for Breaking of Simplified Data Encryption Standard. *International Journal of Security and Its Applications*, *9*(9), 295–304. doi:10.14257/ijsia.2015.9.9.26

Alamaniotis, M., Choi, C. K., & Tsoukalas, L. H. (2015). Application of fireworks algorithm in gamma-ray spectrum fitting for radioisotope identification. [IJSIR]. *International Journal of Swarm Intelligence Research*, *6*(2), 102–125. doi:10.4018/IJSIR.2015040105

Alamaniotis, M., & Tsoukalas, L. H. (2018). Assessment of Gamma-Ray-Spectra Analysis Method Utilizing the Fireworks Algorithm for Various Error Measures. In *Critical Developments and Applications of Swarm Intelligence* (pp. 155–181). IGI Global. doi:10.4018/978-1-5225-5134-8.ch007

Alba, E., & Chicano, F. (2007). ACOhg: dealing with huge graphs. In *Proceedings of the 9th Annual Conference on Genetic and Evolutionary Computation*, 10-17. Academic Press.

Alba, E., & Chicano, F. (2007). Finding safety errors with ACO. In *Proceedings of the 9th Annual Conference on Genetic and Evolutionary Computation*, 1066-1073. Academic Press.

Alba, E., & Troya, J. M. (1996). Genetic Algorithms for protocol validation. In *Proceedings of the 4th International Conference on Parallel Problem Solving from Nature, Lecture Notes in Computer Science*, *1141*, 870-879. Academic Press.

Alcalá-Fdez, J., Fernandez, A., Luengo, J., Derrac, J., García, S., Sánchez, L., & Herrera, F. (2011). KEEL data-mining software tool: Data set repository, integration of algorithms and experimental analysis framework, J. Mult.-. *Valued Log. Soft Comput.*, *17*, 255–287.

Alexander, R., & Kelly, T. (2013). Supporting systems of systems hazard analysis using multi-agent simulation. *Safety Science, 51*(1), 302–318. doi:10.1016/j.ssci.2012.07.006

Aliev, R. A., Fazlollahi, B., & Aliev, R. R. (2004). *Soft computing and its applications in business and economics* (Vol. 157). Berlin, Germany: Springer. doi:10.1007/978-3-540-44429-9

Ali, H. M., Ejaz, W., Lee, D. C., & Khater, I. M. (2018). Optimising the power using firework-based evolutionary algorithms for emerging IoT applications. *IET Networks, 8*(1), 15–31. doi:10.1049/iet-net.2018.5041

Alihodzic, A. (2016, November). Fireworks algorithm with new feasibility-rules in solving UAV path planning. In *2016 3rd International Conference on Soft Computing & Machine Intelligence (ISCMI)* (pp. 53-57). IEEE. 10.1109/ISCMI.2016.33

Alihodzic, A., Hasic, D., & Selmanovic, E. (2018, August). An Effective Guided Fireworks Algorithm for Solving UCAV Path Planning Problem. In *International Conference on Numerical Methods and Applications* (pp. 29-38). Cham, Switzerland: Springer.

Alizadeh, A. A., Eisen, M. B., Davis, R. E., Ma, C., Lossos, I. S., Rosenwald, A., ... Yu, X. (2000). Distinct types of diffuse large B-cell lymphoma identified by gene expression profiling. *Nature, 403*(6769), 503–511. doi:10.1038/35000501 PMID:10676951

Alonge, F., & D'Ippolio, F. (2010). Extended Kalman Filter for Sensorless Control of Induction Motors. *Proceedings IEEE First Symposium on Sensorless Control for Electronic Drives*, pp. 107–113. 10.1109/SLED.2010.5542796

Alsofyani, I. M., Idris, N., Sutikno, T., & Alamri, Y. A. (2012). An optimized Extended Kalman Filter for speed sensorless direct torque control of an induction motor. *Proceedings 2012 IEEE International Conference on Power and Energy (PECon)*, pp. 319–324. Kota Kinabalu. 10.1109/PECon.2012.6450230

Amhaimar, L., Ahyoud, S., Elyaakoubi, A., Kaabal, A., Attari, K., & Asselman, A. (2018). PAPR Reduction Using Fireworks Search Optimization Algorithm in MIMO-OFDM Systems. *Journal of Electrical and Computer Engineering, 2018*. doi:10.1155/2018/3075890

Andisha, A. S., Wehrle, M., & Westphal, B. (2015). Directed Model Checking for PROMELA with Relaxation-Based Distance Functions. In *Proceedings of the 22nd International Symposium on Model Checking Software, Lecture Notes in Computer Science, 9232*, 153-159. 10.1007/978-3-319-23404-5_11

Angiulli, F., Cesario, E., & Pizzuti, C. (2008). Random walk biclustering for microarray data. *Information Sciences, 178*(6), 1479–1497. doi:10.1016/j.ins.2007.11.007

Arsic, A., Tuba, M., & Jordanski, M. (2016, July). Fireworks algorithm applied to wireless sensor networks localization problem. *Proceedings 2016 IEEE Congress on Evolutionary Computation (CEC)* (pp. 4038-4044). IEEE. 10.1109/CEC.2016.7744302

Atashpaz-Gargari, E., & Lucas, C. (2007). Imperialist competitive algorithm: an algorithm for optimization inspired by imperialistic competition. *Proceedings 2007 IEEE congress on evolutionary computation*. 10.1109/CEC.2007.4425083

Athar, H., Pooya, S., Ziaei, D., & Goudarzi, N. (n.d.). Artificial Intelligence for Optimal Sitting of Individual and Networks of Wind Farms. In *ASME 2019 Power Conference*. American Society of Mechanical Engineers Digital Collection.

Babu, T. S., Ram, J. P., Sangeetha, K., Laudani, A., & Rajasekar, N. (2016). Parameter extraction of two diode solar PV model using Fireworks algorithm. *Solar Energy, 140*, 265–276. doi:10.1016/j.solener.2016.10.044

Bacanin, N., Tuba, M., & Beko, M. (2015). Hybridized fireworks algorithm for global optimization. *Mathematical Methods and Systems in Science and Engineering*, 108-114.

Bacanin, N., & Tuba, M. (2015, May). Fireworks algorithm applied to constrained portfolio optimization problem. *Proceedings 2015 IEEE Congress on Evolutionary Computation (CEC)* (pp. 1242-1249). IEEE. 10.1109/CEC.2015.7257031

Bahramian-Habil, H., Azad-Farsani, E., Vahidi, B., Askarian-Abyaneh, H., & Gharehpetian, G. B. (2017). Fault Current Limiter Placement Using Multi-Objective Firework Algorithm. *Electric Power Components and Systems, 45*(17), 1929–1940. doi:10.1080/15325008.2017.1405466

Baidoo, E. (2017). Fireworks Algorithm for Unconstrained Function Optimization Problems. *Applied Computer Science, 13*.

Baier, C., & Katoen, J.-P. (2008). *Principles of Model Checking*. MIT Press.

Balamurugan, R., Natarajan, A., & Premalatha, K. (2018). A New Hybrid Cuckoo Search Algorithm for Biclustering of Microarray Gene-Expression Data. *Applied Artificial Intelligence, 32*(7-8), 644–659. doi:10.1080/08839514.2018.1501918

Bao, S., Zhang, M., Yin, J., & Cai, Z. (2019). A Research on the Order Picking Optimization for Stacker's Composite Operation of Semi-tray out of the Automated Warehouse. *Industrial Engineering Journal, 22*(1), 90.

Barraza, J., Melin, P., Valdez, F., González, C. I., & Castillo, O. (2017). Iterative fireworks algorithm with fuzzy coefficients, FUZZ-IEEE: pp. 1-6. Naples, Italy, July 9-12. doi:10.1109/FUZZ-IEEE.2017.8015524

Barraza, J., Rodríguez, L., Castillo, O., Melin, P., & Valdez, F. (2018). A New Hybridization Approach between the Fireworks Algorithm and Grey Wolf Optimizer Algorithm, *Journal of Optimization, 2018*.

Barraza, J., Rodríguez, L., Castillo, O., Melin, P., & Valdez, F. (2018). A new hybridization approach between the fireworks algorithm and grey wolf optimizer algorithm. *Journal of Optimization, 2018*.

Barraza, J., Melin, P., Valdez, F., & González, C. (2017). Fireworks algorithm (FWA) with adaptation of parameters using fuzzy logic. In *Nature-Inspired Design of Hybrid Intelligent Systems* (pp. 313–327). Cham, Switzerland: Springer. doi:10.1007/978-3-319-47054-2_21

Barraza, J., Melin, P., Valdez, F., & Gonzalez, C. (2017). Fuzzy fireworks algorithm based on a sparks dispersion measure. *Algorithms, 10*(3), 83. doi:10.3390/a10030083

Barraza, J., Melin, P., Valdez, F., & Gonzalez, C. I. (2016, July). Fuzzy FWA with dynamic adaptation of parameters. *Proceedings 2016 IEEE Congress on Evolutionary Computation (CEC)* (pp. 4053-4060). IEEE. 10.1109/CEC.2016.7744304

Barraza, J., Melin, P., Valdez, F., Gonzalez, C. I., & Castillo, O. (2017, July). Iterative fireworks algorithm with fuzzy coefficients. *Proceedings 2017 IEEE International Conference on Fuzzy Systems (FUZZ-IEEE)* (pp. 1-6). IEEE.

Barraza, J., Valdez, F., Melin, P., & González, C. (2020). Optimal Number of Clusters Finding Using the Fireworks Algorithm. In *Hybrid Intelligent Systems in Control, Pattern Recognition, and Medicine* (pp. 83–93). Cham, Switzerland: Springer. doi:10.1007/978-3-030-34135-0_7

Barthelemy, P., Bertolotti, J., & Wiersma, D. S. (2008). A Lévy flight for light. *Nature, 453*(7194), 495–498. doi:10.1038/nature06948 PMID:18497819

Basílio, D. F. F. (2018). *Approaching the Optimal Performance of Nonlinear OFDM With FWA Techniques* (Doctoral dissertation).

Batista, G., Prati, R., & Monard, M. (2004). A study of the behavior of several methods for balancing machine learning training data. *SIGKDD Explorations, 6*(1), 20–29. doi:10.1145/1007730.1007735

Batuwita, R., & Palade, V. (2009). AGm: a new performance measure for class imbalance learning. application to bioinformatics problems. *Proceedings of the 8th International Conference on Machine Learning and Applications (ICMLA 2009)*, pp. 545–550. 10.1109/ICMLA.2009.126

Bejinariu, S. I., Costin, H., Rotaru, F., Luca, R., Niță, C. D., & Lazăr, C. (2016, August). Fireworks algorithm based image registration. In *International Workshop Soft Computing Applications* (pp. 509-523). Cham, Switzerland: Springer.

Bejinariu, S. I., Luca, R., & Costin, H. (2016, October). Nature-inspired algorithms based multispectral image fusion. *Proceedings 2016 International Conference and Exposition on Electrical and Power Engineering (EPE)* (pp. 010-015). IEEE. 10.1109/ICEPE.2016.7781293

Bejinariu, S. I., Rotariu, C., Costin, H., & Luca, R. (2019, March). Image Registration using Fireworks Algorithm and Chaotic Sequences. *Proceedings 2019 11th International Symposium on Advanced Topics in Electrical Engineering (ATEE)* (pp. 1-4). IEEE. 10.1109/ATEE.2019.8725020

Bejinariu, S. I., Costin, H., Rotaru, F., Luca, R., & Niță, C. (2016). Fireworks algorithm based single and multi-objective optimization. *Bulletin of the Polytechnic Institute of Jassy. Automatic Control and Computer Science Section, 62*(3), 19–34.

Bello, P. (2006). *Theoretical Foundations for Rational Agency in Third Generation Wargames* (No. AFRL-IF-RS-TR-2006-2). Air Force Research Lab.

Ben-David, A. (2008a). Comparison of classification accuracy using Cohen's weighted kappa. *Expert Systems with Applications, 34*(February (2)), 825–832. doi:10.1016/j.eswa.2006.10.022

Ben-David, A. (2008b). About the relationship between ROC curves and Cohen's kappa. *Engineering Applications of Artificial Intelligence, 21*(September (6)), 874–882. doi:10.1016/j.engappai.2007.09.009

Biere, A., Cimatti, A., Clarke, E. M., & Zhu, Y. (1999). Symbolic model checking without BDDs. In *Proceedings of the 5th International Conference on Tools and Algorithms for Construction and Analysis of Systems,* 193-207. Academic Press.

Blanco, J. (2012). Musicoterapia Como Alternativa Terapeutica En La Depresion. *Universidad de San Carlos, 1*(1), 1–76.

Board, F. S. (2017). Artificial intelligence and machine learning in financial services. November, available at http://www. fsb. org/2017/11/artificialintelligence-and-machine-learning-in-financialservice/(accessed 30th January, 2018).

Bolaji, A. L. A., Ahmad, A. A., & Shola, P. B. (2018). Training of neural network for pattern classification using fireworks algorithm. *International Journal of System Assurance Engineering and Management, 9*(1), 208–215. doi:10.100713198-016-0526-z

Bonabeau, E., Dorigo, M., & Theraulaz, G. (1999). Swarm intelligence: from natural to artificial systems. Oxford University Press.

Bonabeau, E., Dorigo, M., Marco, D., Theraulaz, G., & Théraulaz, G. (1999). Swarm intelligence: from natural to artificial systems (No. 1). Oxford University Press.

Bouarara, H. A., Hamou, R. M., Amine, A., & Rahmani, A. (2015). A fireworks algorithm for modern web information retrieval with visual results mining. [IJSIR]. *International Journal of Swarm Intelligence Research, 6*(3), 1–23. doi:10.4018/IJSIR.2015070101

BouDaher, E., & Hoorfar, A. (2016, June). Fireworks algorithm: A new swarm intelligence technique for electromagnetic optimization. *Proceedings 2016 IEEE International Symposium on Antennas and Propagation (APSURSI)* (pp. 575-576). IEEE. 10.1109/APS.2016.7695996

Boussaïd, I., Lepagnot, J., & Siarry, P. (2013). A survey on optimization metaheuristics. *Information Sciences, 237,* 82–117. doi:10.1016/j.ins.2013.02.041

Bradley, A. P. (1997). The use of the area under the ROC curve in the evaluation of machine learning algorithms. *Pattern Recognition, 30*(7), 1145–1159. doi:10.1016/S0031-3203(96)00142-2

Braga, P. H. C., & Silveira, I. F. (2015). *A Pattern Language for semi-automatic generation of Digital Animation through hand-drawn Storyboards*. In *Proceedings of SIBGRAPI - Conference on Graphics, Patterns, and Images, 28*.

Brown, G., Wyatt, J., Harris, R., & Yao, X. (2005). Diversity creation methods: A survey and categorization. *Information Fusion, 6*(1), 5–20. doi:10.1016/j.inffus.2004.04.004

Bustan, D., & Grumberg, O. (2003). Simulation-based minimization. *ACM Transactions on Computational Logic, 4*(2), 181–206. doi:10.1145/635499.635502

Cai, Y., Qi, Y., Chen, H., Cai, H., & Hejlesen, O. (2018, May). Quantum Fireworks Evolutionary Algorithm for Vehicle Routing Problem in Supply Chain with Multiple Time Windows. In *2018 2nd IEEE Advanced Information Management, Communicates, Electronic, and Automation Control Conference (IMCEC)* (pp. 383-388). IEEE. 10.1109/IMCEC.2018.8469677

Calderaro, V., Galdi, V., Graber, G., & Piccolo, A. (2015, March). Optimal siting and sizing of stationary supercapacitors in a metro network using PSO. *Proceedings 2015 IEEE International Conference on Industrial Technology (ICIT)* (pp. 2680-2685). IEEE. 10.1109/ICIT.2015.7125493

Cano, A., Zafra, A., & Ventura. S. (2013). Weighted data gravitation classification for standard and imbalanced data. *IEEE Trans. Cybern. 43,* December (6).

Can, U., & Alatas, B. (2015). Physics based metaheuristic algorithms for global optimization. *American Journal of Information Science and Computer Engineering, 1,* 94–106.

Cao, F., Bo, L., & Dong, S. P. (2013). Image classification based on effective extreme learning machine. *Neurocomputing, 102*(2), 90–97. doi:10.1016/j.neucom.2012.02.042

Cao, H., Li, X.-L., Woon, D. Y.-K., & Ng, S.-K. (2013). Integrated oversampling for imbalanced time series classification. *IEEE Transactions on Knowledge and Data Engineering, 25*(12), 2809–2822. doi:10.1109/TKDE.2013.37

Cao, Q., Leggio, K., & Schniederjans, M. (2005). A comparison between Fama and French's model and artificial networks in predicting the Chinese stock market. *Computers & Operations Research, 32*(10), 2499–2512. doi:10.1016/j.cor.2004.03.015

CDC. (2016). HHS of USA. Center for Disease Control and Prevention. Especiales de los CDC. Retrieved from Salud mental de los niños: Apoyo de los servicios de salud conductual para quienes los necesitan website: https://www.cdc.gov/spanish/especialesCDC/SaludMentalNinos/index.html

Chandraprabha, N. S., Thakur, S., & Karan, R. (2015). Current Stature and Future Outlook of Hybrid Renewable Energy System. *International Advanced Research Journal in Science, Engineering and Technology, 2*(1), 58–62.

Chang, E., & Zak, S. (1996). *An Introduction to Optimization*. New York, NY: Wiley.

Chan, T., & Shi, K. (2011). *Applied Intelligent Control of Induction Motor Drives*. Singapore: Wiley. doi:10.1002/9780470825587

Chawla, N. V., Bowyer, K. W., Hall, L. O., & Kegelmeyer, W. P. (2002). SMOTE: Synthetic minority over-sampling technique. *Artificial Intelligence Research, 16*(1), 321–357. doi:10.1613/jair.953

Chawla, N. V., Lazarevic, A., & Hall, L. O. (2003). SMOTEBoost: improving prediction of the minority class in boosting. *Proceedings of the 7th European Conference on Principles of Data Mining and Knowledge Discovery*, pp. 107–119. 10.1007/978-3-540-39804-2_12

Chen, X., Zhang, Y., Li, K., & Huang, B. (2019, May). Path Planning of Mobile Robot Based on Improved Wolf Swarm Algorithms. *Proceedings 2019 IEEE 8th Joint International Information Technology and Artificial Intelligence Conference (ITAIC)* (pp. 359-364). IEEE. 10.1109/ITAIC.2019.8785503

Chen, A., Leung, M., & Daouk, H. (2003). Application of neural networks to an emerging financial market: Forecasting and trading the Taiwan stock index. *Computers & Operations Research, 30*(6), 901–923. doi:10.1016/S0305-0548(02)00037-0

Chena, X., Liua, S., Chena, T., Zhangb, Z., & Zhangb, H. (2012). An Improved Semi-Supervised Clustering Algorithm for Multi-Density Datasets with Fewer Constraints. *Procedia Engineering, 29*, 4325–4329. doi:10.1016/j.proeng.2012.01.665

Cheng, Y., & Church, G. M. (2000). *Biclustering of expression data.* Paper presented at the International Conference on Intelligent Systems for Molecular Biology.

Cheng, R., Bai, Y., Zhao, Y., Tan, X., & Xu, T. (2019). Improved fireworks algorithm with information exchange for function optimization. *Knowledge-Based Systems, 163*, 82–90. doi:10.1016/j.knosys.2018.08.016

Cheng, S., Qin, Q., Chen, J., Shi, Y., & Zhang, Q. (2015). Analytics on fireworks algorithm solving problems with shifts in the decision space and objective space. [IJSIR]. *International Journal of Swarm Intelligence Research, 6*(2), 52–86. doi:10.4018/IJSIR.2015040103

Cheng, S., Shi, Y., Qin, Q., Ting, T. O., & Bai, R. (2014). Maintaining population diversity in brain storm optimization algorithm. *Proceedings of the 2014 IEEE Congress on Evolutionary Computation, CEC 2014*, 3230–3237. 10.1109/CEC.2014.6900255

Chen, H., Deng, X., Yan, L., & Ye, Z. (2017, December). Multilevel thresholding selection based on the fireworks algorithm for image segmentation. *Proceedings 2017 International Conference on Security, Pattern Analysis, and Cybernetics (SPAC)* (pp. 175-180). IEEE. 10.1109/SPAC.2017.8304271

Chen, H., Yang, S., Li, J., & Jing, N. (2018). Exact and Heuristic Methods for Observing Task-Oriented Satellite Cluster Agent Team Formation. *Mathematical Problems in Engineering, 2018*, 2018. doi:10.1155/2018/2103625

Chen, J., Xie, S., Li, H., Luo, J., & Feng, K. (2015). Robot path planning based on adaptive integrating of genetic and ant colony algorithm. *International Journal of Innovative Computing, Information, & Control, 11*(3).

Chen, J., Yang, Q., Ni, J., Xie, Y., & Cheng, S. (2015, May). An improved fireworks algorithm with landscape information for balancing exploration and exploitation. *Proceedings 2015 IEEE Congress on Evolutionary Computation (CEC)* (pp. 1272-1279). IEEE. 10.1109/CEC.2015.7257035

Chen, S., Liu, Y., Wei, L., & Guan, B. (2018). PS-FW: A hybrid algorithm based on particle swarm and fireworks for global optimization. *Computational Intelligence and Neuroscience, 2018*, 2018. doi:10.1155/2018/6094685 PMID:29675036

Chen, X., Shi, C., Zhou, A., Xu, S., & Wu, B. (2018, November). A Hybrid Replacement Strategy for MOEA/D. *Proceedings International Conference on Bio-Inspired Computing: Theories and Applications* (pp. 246-262). Springer, Singapore. 10.1007/978-981-13-2826-8_22

Chen, X., You, Z.-H., Yan, G.-Y., & Gong, D.-W. (2016). IRWRLDA: Improved random walk with restart for lncRNA-disease association prediction. *Oncotarget, 7*(36), 57919. doi:10.18632/oncotarget.11141 PMID:27517318

Chen, Y., Li, L., Zhao, X., Xiao, J., Wu, Q., & Tan, Y. (2019). Simplified hybrid fireworks algorithm. *Knowledge-Based Systems, 173*, 128–139. doi:10.1016/j.knosys.2019.02.029

Chen, Y., Wang, Y., & Zhang, Y. (2017). Crustal velocity structure of central Gansu Province from regional seismic waveform inversion using firework algorithm. *Earth Science, 30*(2), 81–89. doi:10.100711589-017-0184-5

Chen, Y., Yang, W., Li, M., Hao, Z., Zhou, P., & Sun, H. (2018). Research on Pest Image Processing Method Based on Android Thermal Infrared Lens. *IFAC-PapersOnLine*, *51*(17), 173–178. doi:10.1016/j.ifacol.2018.08.083

Chicano, F., & Alba, E. (2008). Ant colony optimization with partial order reduction for discovering safety property violations in concurrent models. *Information Processing Letters*, *106*(6), 221–231. doi:10.1016/j.ipl.2007.11.015

Chicano, F., & Alba, E. (2008). Finding liveness errors with ACO. In *Proceedings of the IEEE Congress on Evolutionary Computation 2008*, 2997-3004. 10.1109/CEC.2008.4631202

Chicano, F., Ferreira, M., & Alba, E. (2011). Comparing metaheuristic algorithms for error detection in Java programs. In *Proceedings of the Third International Symposium on Search Based Software Engineering, Lecture Notes in Computer Science*, *6956*, 82-96. 10.1007/978-3-642-23716-4_11

Choe, W., Ersoy, O. K., & Bina, M. (2000). Neural network schemes for detecting rare events in human genomic DNA. *Bioinformatics (Oxford, UK)*, *16*(12), 1062–1072. doi:10.1093/bioinformatics/16.12.1062 PMID:11159325

Cho, R. J., Campbell, M. J., Winzeler, E. A., Steinmetz, L., Conway, A., Wodicka, L., ... Lockhart, D. J. (1998). A genome-wide transcriptional analysis of the mitotic cell cycle. *Molecular Cell*, *2*(1), 65–73. doi:10.1016/S1097-2765(00)80114-8 PMID:9702192

Chrisman, O. (1896). Paidologie: Entwurf zu einer Wissenschaft des Kindes (U. of C. Libraries, Ed.). Jena, Bernhard Vopeliu.

Cimatti, A., Clarke, E. M., Giunchiglia, E., Giunchiglia, F., Pistore, M., Roveri, M., ... Tacchella, A. (2002). NuSMV 2: an opensource tool for symbolic model checking. In *Proceedings of the 14th International Conference on Computer Aided Verification*, 359-364. 10.1007/3-540-45657-0_29

Clarke, E. M. (2008). The birth of model checking. *25 Years of Model Checking. Lecture Notes in Computer Science*, *5000*, 1–26. doi:10.1007/978-3-540-69850-0_1

Clarke, E. M., & Emerson, E. (1981). Design and synthesis of synchronization skeletons using branching-time temporal logic. In *Logic of Programs* (pp. 52–71). Workshop.

Clarke, E. M. Jr, Grumberg, O., Kroening, D., Peled, D., & Veith, H. (2018). *Model Checking* (2nd ed.). MIT Press.

Clarke, E., Grumberg, O., Jha, S., Lu, Y., & Veith, H. (2003). Counterexample-guided abstraction refinement for symbolic model checking. *Journal of the Association for Computing Machinery*, *50*(5), 752–794. doi:10.1145/876638.876643

Clerc, M. (2010). *Particle swarm optimization* (Vol. 93). John Wiley & Sons.

Contreras-Cruz, M. A., Ayala-Ramirez, V., & Hernandez-Belmonte, U. H. (2015). Mobile robot path planning using artificial bee colony and evolutionary programming. *Applied Soft Computing*, *30*, 319–328. doi:10.1016/j.asoc.2015.01.067

Contreras, J., Espinola, R., Nogales, F., & Conejo, A. (2003). ARIMA models to predict next-day electricity prices. *IEEE Transactions on Power Systems*, *18*(3), 1014–1020. doi:10.1109/TPWRS.2002.804943

Cormen, T. H., Leiserson, C. E., Rivest, R. L., & Stein, C. (2001). Introduction to algorithms second edition. The Knuth-Morris-Pratt Algorithm, year.

Cormen, T. H., Stein, C., Rivest, R. L., & Leiserson, C. E. (2001). *Introduction to Algorithms* (2nd ed.). MIT Press.

Cornic, D. (2010, October). Efficient recovery of braking energy through a reversible dc substation. Proceedings *Electrical systems for aircraft, railway, and ship propulsion* (pp. 1–9). IEEE. doi:10.1109/ESARS.2010.5665264

Crassidis, J. L., & Junkins, J. L. (2012). *Optimal Estimation of Dynamic Systems* (2nd ed.). Boca Raton, FL: CRC Press.

Crawford, B., Soto, R., Astudillo, G., Olguín, E., & Misra, S. (2016, July). Solving Set Covering Problem with Fireworks Explosion. *Proceedings International Conference on Computational Science and Its Applications* (pp. 273-283). Cham, Switzerland: Springer. 10.1007/978-3-319-42085-1_21

Csikszentmihalyi, M. (1990). *Flow: The Psychology of Optimal Experience.* New York: Harper & Row.

Dang, X. T., Tran, D. H., Hirose, O., & Satou, K. (2015). SPY: A Novel Resampling Method for Improving Classification Performance in Imbalanced Data. *Proceedings Seventh International Conference on Knowledge and Systems Engineering (KSE).* 10.1109/KSE.2015.24

de la Torre, S., Sánchez-Racero, A. J., Aguado, J. A., Reyes, M., & Martínez, O. (2014). Optimal sizing of energy storage for regenerative braking in electric railway systems. *IEEE Transactions on Power Systems, 30*(3), 1492–1500. doi:10.1109/TPWRS.2014.2340911

Demsar, J. (2006). Statistical comparisons of classifiers over multiple data sets. *Journal of Machine Learning Research, 7*, 1–30.

Deng, L., Zhang, Q. C., Chen, Z., Meng, Y., Guan, J., & Zhou, S. (2014). PredHS: A web server for predicting protein–protein interaction hot spots by using structural neighborhood properties. *Nucleic Acids Research, 42*(W1), W290–W295. doi:10.1093/nar/gku437 PMID:24852252

Dijkstra, E. W. (1959). A note on two problems in connexion with graphs. *Numerische Mathematik, 1*(1), 269–271. doi:10.1007/BF01386390

Ding, H., Ke, L., & Geng, Z. (2016, July). Route planning in a new tourist recommender system: A fireworks algorithm based approach. *Proceedings 2016 IEEE Congress on Evolutionary Computation (CEC)* (pp. 4022-4028). IEEE. 10.1109/CEC.2016.7744300

Ding, K., Chen, Y., Wang, Y., & Tan, Y. (2015, May). Regional seismic waveform inversion using swarm intelligence algorithms. *Proceedings 2015 IEEE Congress on Evolutionary Computation (CEC)* (pp. 1235-1241). IEEE. 10.1109/CEC.2015.7257030

Ding, K., & Tan, Y. (2015). Attract-repulse fireworks algorithm and its CUDA implementation using dynamic parallelism. [IJSIR]. *International Journal of Swarm Intelligence Research, 6*(2), 1–31. doi:10.4018/IJSIR.2015040101

Ding, K., Zheng, S., & Tan, Y. (2013, July). A GPU-based parallel fireworks algorithm for optimization. *Proceedings of the 15th annual conference on Genetic and evolutionary computation* (pp. 9-16). ACM. 10.1145/2463372.2463377

Divina, F., Pontes, B., Giráldez, R., Aguilar-Ruiz, J. S. (2012). An effective measure for assessing the quality of biclusters. *Computers in biology and medicine, 42*(2), 245-256.

Divina, F., & Aguilar-Ruiz, J. S. (2006). Biclustering of expression data with evolutionary computation. *IEEE Transactions on Knowledge and Data Engineering, 18*(5), 590–602. doi:10.1109/TKDE.2006.74

Dolicanin, E., Fetahovic, I., Tuba, E., Capor-Hrosik, R., & Tuba, M. (2018). Unmanned combat aerial vehicle path planning by brainstorm optimization algorithm. *Studies in Informatics and Control, 27*(1), 15–24. doi:10.24846/v27i1y201802

Domingos, P. (1999). MetaCost: a general method for making classifiers cost-sensitive. *Proceedings of the 5th ACM SIGKDD International Conference of Knowledge Discovery and Data Mining,* pp. 155–164. San Diego, CA. 10.1145/312129.312220

Dong, W., & Zhou, M. (2016). A supervised learning and control method to improve particle swarm optimization algorithms. *IEEE Transactions on Systems, Man, and Cybernetics Systems, 47*(7), 1135–1148. doi:10.1109/TSMC.2016.2560128

Dorigo, M., & Di Caro, G. (1999, July). Ant colony optimization: a new meta-heuristic. *Proceedings of the 1999 congress on evolutionary computation-CEC99 (Cat. No. 99TH8406)* (Vol. 2, pp. 1470-1477). IEEE. 10.1109/CEC.1999.782657

Dorigo, M., & Stutzle, T. (2004). *Ant colony optimization*. Cambridge: The MIT Press. doi:10.7551/mitpress/1290.001.0001

Dou, S. Q., Li, J. J., & Kang, F. (2019). Health diagnosis of concrete dams using hybrid FWA with RBF-based surrogate model. *Water Science and Engineering*, *12*(3), 188–195. doi:10.1016/j.wse.2019.09.002

Dou, S., Li, J., & Kang, F. (2017). Parameter identification of concrete dams using swarm intelligence algorithm. *Engineering Computations*, *34*(7), 2358–2378. doi:10.1108/EC-03-2017-0110

Duan, J., Qu, Q., Gao, C., & Chen, X. (2017, July). BOF steelmaking endpoint prediction based on FWA-TSVR. *Proceedings 2017 36th Chinese Control Conference (CCC)* (pp. 4507-4511). IEEE. 10.23919/ChiCC.2017.8028067

Dunn, O. J. (1961). Multiple comparisons among means. *Journal of the American Statistical Association*, *56*(March(293)), 52–64. doi:10.1080/01621459.1961.10482090

Dutta, R. K., Karmakar, N. K., & Si, T. (2016). Artificial neural network training using fireworks algorithm in medical data mining. *International Journal of Computers and Applications*, *137*(1), 1–5. doi:10.5120/ijca2016908726

Easton, D., Bishop, D., Ford, D., & Crockford, G. (1993). Genetic linkage analysis in familial breast and ovarian cancer: Results from 214 families. The Breast Cancer Linkage Consortium. *American Journal of Human Genetics*, *52*(4), 678–701. PMID:8460634

Eberhart, R. C., Shi, Y., & Kennedy, J. (2001). *Swarm Intelligence (Morgan Kaufmann series in evolutionary computation)*. Morgan Kaufmann Publishers.

Eberhart, R., & Kennedy, J. (1995, November). Particle swarm optimization. *Proceedings of the IEEE International Conference on Neural Networks* (Vol. 4, pp. 1942-1948). 10.1109/ICNN.1995.488968

Eberhart, R., & Kennedy, J. (1995, October). A new optimizer using particle swarm theory. *MHS'95 Proceedings of the Sixth International Symposium on Micro Machine and Human Science* (pp. 39-43). IEEE. 10.1109/MHS.1995.494215

Edelkamp, S., & Jabbar, S. (2006). Large-scale directed model checking LTL. In *Proceedings of the 13th International Conference on Model Checking Software*, 1-18. Academic Press.

Edelkamp, S., Schuppan, V., Bosnacki, D., Wijs, A., Fehnker, A., & Husain, A. (2008). Survey on directed model checking. In *Proceedings of the 5th International Workshop on Model Checking and Artificial Intelligence, Lecture Notes in Computer Science*, *5348*, 65-89. Academic Press.

Edelkamp, S., Lafuente, A., & Leue, S. (2001). Directed explicit model checking with HSF-SPIN. In *Proceedings of the 8th International SPIN Workshop on Model Checking of Software*, 57-79. 10.1007/3-540-45139-0_5

Edelkamp, S., Leue, S., & Lluch-Lafuente, A. (2004). Directed explicit-state model checking in the validation of communication protocols. *International Journal of Software Tools for Technology Transfer*, *5*(2-3), 247–267. doi:10.100710009-002-0104-3

Eisen, M. B., Spellman, P. T., Brown, P. O., & Botstein, D. (1998). Cluster analysis and display of genome-wide expression patterns. *Proc Natl Acad Sci USA*. 10.1073/pnas.95.25.14863

El-Atawy, A., Samak, T., Al-Shaer, E., & Li, H. (2007, May). Using online traffic statistical matching for optimizing packet filtering performance. In *Proceedings IEEE INFOCOM 2007-26th IEEE International Conference on Computer Communications* (pp. 866-874). IEEE.

Elrayyah, A., Sozer, Y., & Elbuluk, M. E. (2014). A novel load-flow analysis for stable and optimized microgrid operation. *IEEE Transactions on Power Delivery*, *29*(4), 1709–1717. doi:10.1109/TPWRD.2014.2307279

Erten, S., Bebek, G., Ewing, R. M., & Koyutürk, M. (2011). DADA: Degree-aware algorithms for network-based disease gene prioritization. *BioData Mining*, *4*(1), 19. doi:10.1186/1756-0381-4-19 PMID:21699738

Eusuff, M., Lansey, K., & Pasha, F. (2006). Shuffled frog-leaping algorithm: A memetic meta-heuristic for discrete optimization. *Engineering Optimization*, *38*(2), 129–154. doi:10.1080/03052150500384759

Eyadat, M. (2008). Fall 08 Packet Filtering. Retrieved from www.csudh.edu/eyadat/classes/CIS478/handouts/Fall08/Packet%20Filtering.ppt

Farswan, P., & Bansal, J. C. (2019). Fireworks-inspired biogeography-based optimization. *Soft Computing*, *23*(16), 7091–7115. doi:10.100700500-018-3351-2

Fathima, A. H., & Palanisamy, K. (2015). Optimization in microgrids with hybrid energy systems – A review. *Renewable & Sustainable Energy Reviews*, *45*, 431–446. doi:10.1016/j.rser.2015.01.059

Fernández, A., del Jesus, M. J., & Herrera, F. (2010). On the 2-tuples-based genetic tuning performance for fuzzy rule-based classification systems in imbalanced data-sets. *Inf. Sci.*, *180*(8), 1268–1291. doi:10.1016/j.ins.2009.12.014

Fernández, A., García, S., Luengo, J., Bernado-Mansilla, E., & Herrera, F. (2010). Genetics-based machine learning for rule induction: State of the art, taxonomy, and comparative study. *IEEE Transactions on Evolutionary Computation*, *14*(December (6)), 913–941. doi:10.1109/TEVC.2009.2039140

Fernandez-Rodriguez, A., Fernández-Cardador, A., Cucala, A. P., Domínguez, M., & Gonsalves, T. (2015). Design of robust and energy-efficient ATO speed profiles of metropolitan lines considering train load variations and delays. *IEEE Transactions on Intelligent Transportation Systems*, *16*(4), 2061–2071. doi:10.1109/TITS.2015.2391831

Fernández, S., García, S., del Jesus, M. J., & Herrera, F. (2008). A study of the behaviour of linguistic fuzzy rule-based classification systems in the framework of imbalanced data-sets. *Fuzzy Sets and Systems*, *159*(18), 2378–2398. doi:10.1016/j.fss.2007.12.023

Ferreira, M., Alba, E., Chicano, F., & Gómez-Pulido, J. A. (2008). Detecting protocol errors using particle swarm optimization with Java Pathfinder. In *Proceedings of the High Performance Computing & Simulation Conference*, 319-325. Academic Press.

Filippidis, I., & Holzmann, G. J. (2014). An improvement of the piggyback algorithm for parallel model checking. In *Proceedings of the 2014 International SPIN Symposium on Model Checking of Software*, 48-57. 10.1145/2632362.2632375

Fortes, E., Macedo, L. H., Martins, L. F. B., & Miotto, E. L. (2017, March). A fireworks metaheuristic for the design of PSS and TCSC-POD controllers for small-signal stability studies. In Latin American Congress on Generation, Transmission, and Distribution (CLAGTEE) (pp. 1-6).

Francesca, G., Santone, A., Vaglini, G., & Luisa, V. M. (2011). Ant colony optimization for deadlock detection in concurrent systems. In *Proceedings of 2011 IEEE 35th Annual Computer Software and Applications Conference*, 108-117. 10.1109/COMPSAC.2011.22

Francesco, N. D., Lettieri, G., Santone, A., & Vaglini, G. (2016). Heuristic search for equivalence checking. *Software & Systems Modeling*, *15*(2), 513–530. doi:10.100710270-014-0416-2

Frank, A., & Asuncion, A. (2018). UC Machine Learning Repository. Retrieved from https://archive.ics.uci.edu/ml/index.php

Friedman, M. (1937). The use of ranks to avoid the assumption of normality implicit in the analysis of variance. *Journal of the American Statistical Association*, *32*(200), 675–701. doi:10.1080/01621459.1937.10503522

Friedman, M. (1940). A comparison of alternative tests of significance for the problem of m rankings. *Annals of Mathematical Statistics*, *11*(1), 86–92. doi:10.1214/aoms/1177731944

Fusano, A., Sato, H., & Namatame, A. (2011, March). Multi-agent based combat simulation from OODA and network perspective. In *2011 UkSim 13th International Conference on Computer Modelling and Simulation* (pp. 249-254). IEEE. 10.1109/UKSIM.2011.54

Fu, Y., Ding, J., Wang, H., & Wang, J. (2018). Two-objective stochastic flow-shop scheduling with deteriorating and learning effect in Industry 4.0-based manufacturing system. *Applied Soft Computing*, *68*, 847–855. doi:10.1016/j.asoc.2017.12.009

Gaing, Z. L. (2004). A Particle Swarm Optimization approach for optimum design of PID controller in AVR system. *IEEE Transactions on Energy Conversion*, *19*(2), 384–391. doi:10.1109/TEC.2003.821821

Galar, M., Fernández, A., Barrenechea, E., Bustince, H., & Herrera, F. (2011). An overview of ensemble methods for binary classifiers in multi-class problems: Experimental study on one-vs-one and one-vs-all schemes. *Pattern Recognition*, *44*(August (8)), 1761–1776. doi:10.1016/j.patcog.2011.01.017

Galar, M., Fernandez, A., Barrenechea, E., Bustince, H., & Herrera, F. (2012). A Review on Ensembles for the Class Imbalance Problem: Bagging-, Boosting-, and Hybrid-Based Approaches. *IEEE Transactions on Systems, Man and Cybernetics. Part C, Applications and Reviews*, *42*(4), 463–484. doi:10.1109/TSMCC.2011.2161285

Gallager, R. (2013). *Stochastic Processes Theory for Application*. Cambridge, UK: Cambridge University Press. doi:10.1017/CBO9781139626514

Gao, Y., Zhang, B., Lu, M., & Ma, A. (2019, February). Game Based SBCA Cloud Resource Adjustment Method. *Proceedings 2019 21st International Conference on Advanced Communication Technology (ICACT)* (pp. 47-51). IEEE. 10.23919/ICACT.2019.8702050

Gao, H., & Diao, M. (2011). Cultural firework algorithm and its application for digital filters design. *International Journal of Modelling Identification and Control*, *14*(4), 324–331. doi:10.1504/IJMIC.2011.043157

Gao, H., & Li, C. (2015). Opposition-based quantum firework algorithm for continuous optimisation problems. *International Journal of Computing Science and Mathematics*, *6*(3), 256–265. doi:10.1504/IJCSM.2015.069747

Gao, Z., Fang, J., Zhang, Y., Jiang, L., Sun, D., & Guo, W. (2015). Control of urban rail transit equipped with ground-based supercapacitor for energy saving and reduction of power peak demand. *International Journal of Electrical Power & Energy Systems*, *67*, 439–447. doi:10.1016/j.ijepes.2014.11.019

Garciá-Mundo, L., Vargas, J., Genero, M., & Piattini, M. (2014). Contribuye el Uso de Juegos serios a Mejorar el Aprendizaje en el Área de la Informática. *JENUI 2014-Proceedings of the XX Jornadas Sobre La Enseñanza Universitaria de La Informática*, 303–310.

García, S., Fernández, A., Luengo, J., & Herrera, F. (2010). Advanced nonparametric tests for multiple comparisons in the design of experiments in computational intelligence and data mining: Experimental analysis of power. *Inf. Sci.*, *180*(May(10)), 2044–2064. doi:10.1016/j.ins.2009.12.010

García, S., Molina, D., Lozano, M., & Herrera, F. (2009). A study on the use of non-parametric tests for analyzing the evolutionary algorithms' behaviour: A case study. *Journal of Heuristics*, *15*(December (6)), 617–644. doi:10.100710732-008-9080-4

Gastin, P., & Oddoux, D. (2001). Fast LTL to Büchi automata translation. In *Proceedings of the 13th International Conference on Computer Aided Verification*, 53-65. 10.1007/3-540-44585-4_6

Ge, M., Li, A., & Wang, M. (2016). A bipartite network-based method for prediction of long non-coding RNA–protein interactions. *Genomics, Proteomics, & Bioinformatics*, *14*(1), 62–71. doi:10.1016/j.gpb.2016.01.004 PMID:26917505

Gholizadeh, S., & Milany, A. (2018). An improved fireworks algorithm for discrete sizing optimization of steel skeletal structures. *Engineering Optimization*, *50*(11), 1829–1849. doi:10.1080/0305215X.2017.1417402

Giannakopoulou, D., & Magee, J. (2003). Fluent model checking for event-based systems. In *Proceedings of the 9th European software engineering conference held jointly with 11th ACM SIGSOFT international symposium on Foundations of software engineering*, 257-266. Academic Press.

Giannakopoulou, D., & Lerda, F. (2002). From states to transitions: improving translation of LTL formulae to Büchi automata. In *Proceedings of the 22nd International Conference on Formal Techniques for Networked and Distributed Systems*, 308-326. 10.1007/3-540-36135-9_20

Godefroid, P., & Khurshid, S. (2002). Exploring very large state spaces using genetic algorithms. In *Proceedings of the 8th International Conference on Tools and Algorithms for the Construction and Analysis of Systems*, 266-280. Academic Press. 10.1007/3-540-46002-0_19

Goel, S., & Sharma, R. (2017). Performance evaluation of stand alone, grid connected, and hybrid renewable energy systems for rural application: A comparative review. *Renewable & Sustainable Energy Reviews*, *78*, 1378–1389. doi:10.1016/j.rser.2017.05.200

Goh, K.-I., Cusick, M. E., Valle, D., Childs, B., Vidal, M., & Barabási, A.-L. (2007). The human disease network. *Proceedings of the National Academy of Sciences of the United States of America*, *104*(21), 8685–8690. doi:10.1073/pnas.0701361104 PMID:17502601

Goldberg, D. E. (1989). *Genetic algorithms in search, optimization, and machine learning*. Boston, MA: Addison-Wesley Longman Publishing.

Gong, C. (2016). Chaotic adaptive fireworks algorithm. *Proceedings of the Seventh International Conference on Swarm Intelligence* (pp. 515-525). Bali, Indonesia. Academic Press.

Gong, C. (2016, June). Chaotic adaptive fireworks algorithm. *Proceedings International Conference on Swarm Intelligence* (pp. 515-525). Cham, Switzerland: Springer.

Gong, C. (2016). Opposition-based adaptive fireworks algorithm. *Algorithms*, *9*(3), 43. doi:10.3390/a9030043

Gong, C. (2019). Dynamic search fireworks algorithm with chaos. *Journal of Algorithms & Computational Technology*, *13*. doi:10.1177/1748302619889559

Gong, C. (2020). Dynamic Search Fireworks Algorithm with Adaptive Parameters. [IJACI]. *International Journal of Ambient Computing and Intelligence*, *11*(1), 115–135. doi:10.4018/IJACI.2020010107

Gonsalves, T. (n.d.). Feature Subset Optimization through the Fireworks Algorithm. *Studies*, *8*, 12.

Gonsalves, T. (2016). Two diverse swarm intelligence techniques for supervised learning. In *Psychology and mental health: Concepts, methodologies, tools, and applications* (pp. 849–861). IGI Global. doi:10.4018/978-1-5225-0159-6.ch034

González-Gil, A., Palacin, R., & Batty, P. (2013). Sustainable urban rail systems: Strategies and technologies for optimal management of regenerative braking energy. *Energy Conversion and Management*, *75*, 374–388. doi:10.1016/j.enconman.2013.06.039

Goswami, D., & Chakraborty, S. (2015). A study on the optimization performance of fireworks and cuckoo search algorithms in laser machining processes. *Journal of The Institution of Engineers (India): Series C, 96*(3), 215-229.

Goswami, D., & Chakraborty, S. (2015). Parametric optimization of ultrasonic machining process using gravitational search and fireworks algorithms. *Ain Shams Engineering Journal, 6*(1), 315–331. doi:10.1016/j.asej.2014.10.009

Gough, J., Karplus, K., Hughey, R., & Chothia, C. (2001). Assignment of homology to genome sequences using a library of hidden Markov models that represent all proteins of known structure. *Journal of Molecular Biology, 313*(4), 903–919. doi:10.1006/jmbi.2001.5080 PMID:11697912

Grewal, M. (2001). *Kalman Filtering: theory and practice using Matlab*. New York: John Wiley.

Groce, A., & Visser, W. (2004). Heuristics for model checking Java program. *International Journal of Software Tools for Technology Transfer, 6*(4), 260–276. doi:10.100710009-003-0130-9

Grosu, R., & Smolka, S. A. (2005). Monte Carlo model checking. In *Proceedings of the 11th International Conference on Tools and Algorithms for the Construction and Analysis of Systems*, 271-286.

Gu, W., Yu, Y., & Hu, W. (2017). Artificial bee colony algorithmbased parameter estimation of fractional-order chaotic system with time delay. *IEEE/CAA Journal of Automatica Sinica, 4*(1), 107-113.

Guan, J. X., Su, Q. H., Li, W., & Yu, C. (2016). A Numerical Integration Method Based on Fireworks Algorithm. DEStech Transactions on Computer Science and Engineering, (aita).

Guan, H., Dai, Z., Zhao, A., & He, J. (2018). A novel stock forecasting model based on High-order-fuzzy-fluctuation Trends and Back Propagation Neural Network. *PLoS One, 13*(2). doi:10.1371/journal.pone.0192366 PMID:29420584

Guendouz, M., Amine, A., & Hamou, R. M. (2017). A discrete modified fireworks algorithm for community detection in complex networks. *Applied Intelligence, 46*(2), 373–385. doi:10.100710489-016-0840-9

Guerreiro, J., Beko, M., Dinis, R., & Montezuma, P. (2017, September). Using the Fireworks Algorithm for ML Detection of Nonlinear OFDM. *Proceedings 2017 IEEE 86th Vehicular Technology Conference (VTC-Fall)* (pp. 1-5). IEEE. 10.1109/VTCFall.2017.8287944

Guo, J., & Liu, W. (2018, October). Enhanced Fireworks Algorithm with an Improved Gaussian Sparks Operator. *Proceedings International Symposium on Intelligence Computation and Applications* (pp. 38-49). Springer, Singapore.

Guo, J., Liu, W., Liu, M., & Zheng, S. (2019). Hybrid fireworks algorithm with differential evolution operator. *International Journal of Intelligent Information and Database Systems, 12*(1-2), 47–64. doi:10.1504/IJIIDS.2019.102326

Guo, Y., Ji, J., Ji, J., Gong, D., Cheng, J., & Shen, X. (2019). Firework-based software project scheduling method considering the learning and forgetting effect. *Soft Computing, 23*(13), 5019–5034. doi:10.100700500-018-3165-2

Gu, Q., Zhu, L., & Cai, Z. (2009). Evaluation measures of the classification performance of imbalanced data sets. *Communications in Computer and Information Science, 51*(1), 461–471. doi:10.1007/978-3-642-04962-0_53

Gu, S., Kelly, B., & Xiu, D. (2018). *Empirical asset pricing via machine learning (No. w25398)*. National Bureau of Economic Research.

Hamed, H., El-Atawy, A., & Al-Shaer, E. (2006). Adaptive Statistical Optimization Techniques for Firewall Packet Filtering. In *Proceedings IEEE INFOCOM 2006, 25TH IEEE International Conference on Computer Communications*. 10.1109/INFOCOM.2006.129

Hamosh, A., Scott, A. F., Amberger, J. S., Bocchini, C. A., & McKusick, V. A. (2005). Online Mendelian Inheritance in Man (OMIM), a knowledgebase of human genes and genetic disorders. *Nucleic Acids Research, 33*(suppl_1), D514-D517.

Hanczar, B., Hua, J., Sima, C., Weinstein, J., Bittner, M., & Dougherty, E. R. (2010). Small-sample precision of ROC-related estimates. *Bioinformatics, 26*(6), 822-830.

Hand, D. J. (2009). Measuring classifier performance: a coherent alternative to the area under the ROC curve, Mach Learn 77, pp. 103–123.

Handl, J., & Knowles, J. (2007). An evolutionary approach to multiobjective clustering. *IEEE Transactions on Evolutionary Computation, 11*(1), 56–76. doi:10.1109/TEVC.2006.877146

Hansen, N. (1996). Adapting arbitrary normal mutation distributions in evolution strategies: The covariance matrix adaptation. In *Proceedings of the 1996 IEEE International Conference on Evolutionary Computation*, pp. 312-317. Nagoya, Japan. 10.1109/ICEC.1996.542381

Han, W., Xu, J., Zhou, M., Tian, G., Wang, P., Shen, X., & Hou, E. (2015). Cuckoo search and particle filter-based inversing approach to estimating defects via magnetic flux leakage signals. *IEEE Transactions on Magnetics, 52*(4), 1–11. doi:10.1109/TMAG.2015.2498119

Han, X., Zheng, L., Wang, L., Zheng, H., & Wang, X. (2019). Fireworks algorithm based on dynamic search and tournament selection. *International Journal of Computers and Applications*, 1–12. doi:10.1080/1206212X.2019.1590034

Hao, L. (2019, October). A Fireworks-inspired Estimation of Distribution Algorithm. [IOP Publishing.]. *IOP Conference Series. Materials Science and Engineering, 631*(5). doi:10.1088/1757-899X/631/5/052053

Hao, Y., Wu, W., Li, H., Yuan, J., Luo, J., Zhao, Y., & Chen, R. (2016). NPInter v3. 0: An upgraded database of noncoding RNA-associated interactions. *Database (Oxford)*, 2016. PMID:27087310

Harman, M., Mansouri, S. A., & Zhang, Y. (2012). Search-based software engineering: trends, techniques, and applications. *ACM Computing Surveys, 45*(1), 11:1-11:61.

Hasoon, J. N., & Hassan, R. (2019). Solving Job Scheduling Problem Using Fireworks Algorithm. *Journal of Al-Qadisiyah for Computer Science and Mathematics, 11*(2), 1-8.

Haykin, S. (2010). *Neural Networks and Learning Machine*. Upper Saddle River, NJ: Pearson Education.

He, W., Mi, G., & Tan, Y. (2013, June). Parameter optimization of local-concentration model for spam detection by using fireworks algorithm. *Proceedings International Conference in Swarm Intelligence* (pp. 439-450). Berlin, Germany: Springer. 10.1007/978-3-642-38703-6_52

He, L., Li, W., Zhang, Y., & Cao, Y. (2019). A discrete multi-objective fireworks algorithm for flowshop scheduling with sequence-dependent setup times. *Swarm and Evolutionary Computation, 51*, 100575. doi:10.1016/j.swevo.2019.100575

Heller, E. (2016). *Psicología del color Cómo actúan los colores sobre los sentimientos y la razón* (1st ed.). Amadora: Gustavo Gill. [Psychology of Color: How Colors Affect Feelings and Reason]

Hilairet, M., Auger, F., & Berthelot, E. (2009). Speed and rotor flux estimation of induction machines using a two-stage extended Kalman filter. *Automatica, 5*(8), 1819–1827. doi:10.1016/j.automatica.2009.04.005

Hoare, C. A. (1969). An axiomatic basis for computer programming. *Communications of the ACM, 12*(10), 576–580. doi:10.1145/363235.363259

Hoare, C. A. (1985). *Communicating Sequential Processes*. Prentice-Hall.

Holland, J. H. (1992). *Adaptation in natural and artificial systems: an introductory analysis with applications to biology, control, and artificial intelligence*. MIT Press. doi:10.7551/mitpress/1090.001.0001

Holzmann, G. (2003). *The Spin Model Checker: Primer and Reference Manual*. Addison-Wesley Professional.

Holzmann, G. J. (2012). Parallelizing the Spin model checker. In *Proceedings of the 19th International Conference on Model Checking Software*, 155-171. 10.1007/978-3-642-31759-0_12

Hongyuan, G. A. O., Yanan, D. U., & Chenwan, L. I. (2018). Quantum fireworks algorithm for optimal cooperation mechanism of energy harvesting cognitive radio. *Journal of Systems Engineering and Electronics*, *29*(1), 18–30. doi:10.21629/JSEE.2018.01.02

Hromkovič, J. (2001). *Algorithmics for Hard Problems: Introduction to Combinatorial Optimization, Randomization, Approximation, and Heuristics*. Springer-Verlag. doi:10.1007/978-3-662-04616-6

Hu, Y., Wang, K., Wan, J., Wang, K., & Hu, X. (2018, October). Multi-Constrained Routing Based on Particle Swarm Optimization and Fireworks Algorithm. *Proceedings IECON 2018-44th Annual Conference of the IEEE Industrial Electronics Society* (pp. 5901-5905). IEEE. 10.1109/IECON.2018.8592907

Huang, M., & Yu, B. (2019, April). Demo Abstract: RPTB: Range-based Positioning TestBed for WSN. *Proceedings IEEE INFOCOM 2019-IEEE Conference on Computer Communications Workshops (INFOCOM WKSHPS)* (pp. 999-1000). IEEE.

Huang, C., & Wei, J. (2015). *Preliminary Strictness: Military Chess Deduction and Its Application*. Beijing: Aviation Industry Press.

Huang, G. B., Zhu, Q. Y., & Siew, C. K. (2006). Extreme learning machine: Theory and applications. *Neurocomputing*, *70*(1-3), 489–501. doi:10.1016/j.neucom.2005.12.126

Huang, J., & Ling, C. X. (2005). Using AUC and accuracy in evaluating learning algorithms. *IEEE Transactions on Knowledge and Data Engineering*, *17*(3), 299–310. doi:10.1109/TKDE.2005.50

Huang, X. B., Li, H. B., Zhu, Y. C., Wang, Y. X., Zheng, X. X., & Wang, Y. G. (2016, September). Transmission line icing short-term forecasting based on improved time series analysis by fireworks algorithm. *Proceedings 2016 International Conference on Condition Monitoring and Diagnosis (CMD)* (pp. 643-646). IEEE. 10.1109/CMD.2016.7757904

Hussain, S., & Abid Bazaz, M. (2016). Sensorless control of PMSM drive using extended Kalman filter and fuzzy logic controller. *International Journal of Industrial Electronics and Drives*, *3*(1), 12–19. doi:10.1504/IJIED.2016.077677

Hu, X., & Siguangya, W. L. (2000). SDS2000: A Qualitative and Quantitative Integrated Research and Simulation Environment for Strategic Decision. *Journal of Systems Simulation*, *1*(6), 595–599.

Iannuzzi, D., Ciccarelli, F., & Lauria, D. (2012). Stationary ultracapacitors storage device for improving energy saving and voltage profile of light transportation networks. *Transportation Research Part C, Emerging Technologies*, *21*(1), 321–337. doi:10.1016/j.trc.2011.11.002

IEEE. (2011). IEEE Guide for Identifying and Improving Voltage Quality in Power Systems - Redline (pp. 1-70). IEEE Std 1250-2011 (Revision of IEEE Std 1250-1995): IEEE.

Ikegami, H., & Mori, H. (2018). Development of discrete CoFFWA for distribution network reconfigurations. *Electrical Engineering in Japan*, *205*(3), 55–62. doi:10.1002/eej.23151

Iman, R. L., & Davenport, J. M. (1980). Approximations of the critical region of the Friedman statistics. *Communications in Statistics. Theory and Methods*, *9*(6), 571–595. doi:10.1080/03610928008827904

Imran, A. M., & Kowsalya, M. (2014). A new power system reconfiguration scheme for power loss minimization and voltage profile enhancement using fireworks algorithm. *International Journal of Electrical Power & Energy Systems, 62*, 312–322. doi:10.1016/j.ijepes.2014.04.034

Imran, A. M., Kowsalya, M., & Kothari, D. P. (2014). A novel integration technique for optimal network reconfiguration and distributed generation placement in power distribution networks. *International Journal of Electrical Power & Energy Systems, 63*, 461–472. doi:10.1016/j.ijepes.2014.06.011

Ismael, S. M., Aleem, S. H. A., Abdelaziz, A. Y., & Zobaa, A. F. (2018). *Optimal Conductor Selection of Radial Distribution Feeders: An Overview and New Application Using Grasshopper Optimization Algorithm Classical and Recent Aspects of Power System Optimization* (pp. 185–217). Elsevier.

Jackson, D. (2006). *Software Abstractions: Logic, Language, and Analysis*. MIT Press.

Jadoun, V. K., Shah, M. K., Pandey, V. C., Gupta, N., Niazi, K. R., & Swarnkar, A. (2016). Multi-Area Dynamic Economic Dispatch Problem with Multiple Fuels Using Improved Fireworks Algorithm.

Jadoun, V. K., Pandey, V. C., Gupta, N., Niazi, K. R., & Swarnkar, A. (2018). Integration of renewable energy sources in dynamic economic load dispatch problem using an improved fireworks algorithm. *IET Renewable Power Generation, 12*(9), 1004–1011. doi:10.1049/iet-rpg.2017.0744

Janecek, A., & Tan, Y. (2011, June). Using population-based algorithms for initializing nonnegative matrix factorization. *Proceedings International Conference in Swarm Intelligence* (pp. 307-316). Berlin, Germany: Springer. 10.1007/978-3-642-21524-7_37

Janecek, A., & Tan, Y. (2015). Swarm Intelligence for Dimensionality Reduction: How to Improve the Non-Negative Matrix Factorization with Nature-Inspired Optimization Methods. In Emerging Research on Swarm Intelligence and Algorithm Optimization (pp. 285-309). IGI Global.

Janecek, A., & Tan, Y. (2011). Swarm intelligence for non-negative matrix factorization. [IJSIR]. *International Journal of Swarm Intelligence Research, 2*(4), 12–34. doi:10.4018/jsir.2011100102

Janecek, A., & Tan, Y. (2011). Using population-based algorithms for initializing nonnegative matrix factorization. In *Proceedings of International Conference on Advances in Swarm Intelligence* (2011, pp. 307-316). Springer-Verlag.

Janecek, A., & Tan, Y. (2011, July). Iterative improvement of the multiplicative update nmf algorithm using nature-inspired optimization. *Proceedings 2011 Seventh International Conference on Natural Computation* (Vol. 3, pp. 1668-1672). IEEE. 10.1109/ICNC.2011.6022356

Jeronymo, D. C., Leite, J. V., Mariani, V. C., dos Santos Coelho, L., & Goudos, S. K. (2018, May). Spiral inductor design based on fireworks optimization combined with free search. *Proceedings 2018 7th International Conference on Modern Circuits and Systems Technologies (MOCAST)* (pp. 1-4). IEEE. 10.1109/MOCAST.2018.8376558

Jhala, R., & Majumdar, R. (2009). Software model checking. *ACM Computing Surveys, 41*(4), 21:1-21:54.

Jiang, M., Luo, Y. P., & Yang, S. Y. (2007). Particle swarm optimization-stochastic trajectory analysis and parameter selection. *Swarm intelligence, Focus on ant and particle swarm optimization*, 179-198.

Jiang, R., Gan, M., & He, P. (2011). Constructing a gene semantic similarity network for the inference of disease genes. *Proceedings BMC systems biology*. 10.1186/1752-0509-5-S2-S2

Jiang, Wei, & Xuanhua. (2015). Combat simulation experiment based on OODA command and control loop. *Command and Control and Simulation, 37*(3), 112-115.

Jiang, J., Xue, Y., Ma, T., & Chen, Z. (2018). Improved artificial bee colony algorithm with differential evolution for the numerical optimisation problems. *International Journal on Computer Science and Engineering*, *16*(1), 73–84.

Jiayi, H., Chuanwen, J., & Rong, X. (2008). A review on distributed energy resources and MicroGrid. *Renewable & Sustainable Energy Reviews*, *12*(9), 2472–2483. doi:10.1016/j.rser.2007.06.004

Jingmei, L., Lanting, L., Jiaxiang, W., & He, L. (2018, February). A CMP Thread Scheduling Strategy Based on Improved Firework Algorithm. *Proceedings 2018 4th International Conference on Computational Intelligence & Communication Technology (CICT)* (pp. 1-6). IEEE. 10.1109/CIACT.2018.8480208

Jin, T., Liu, Z. W., Zhou, H., Guan, Z. H., Qin, Y., & Wu, Y. (2017). Robust average formation tracking for multi-agent systems with multiple leaders. *IFAC-PapersOnLine*, *50*(1), 2427–2432. doi:10.1016/j.ifacol.2017.08.404

Jun, Y. U., Takagi, H., & Ying, T. A. N. (2019, June). Fireworks Algorithm for Multimodal Optimization Using a Distance-based Exclusive Strategy. *Proceedings 2019 IEEE Congress on Evolutionary Computation (CEC)* (pp. 2215-2220). IEEE.

Kalman, R. (1960). *A New Approach to Linear Filtering and Prediction Problems*. Baltimore, MD: Research Institute for Advanced Study. doi:10.1115/1.3662552

Kamh, M. Z., & Iravani, R. (2010). Unbalanced model and power-flow analysis of microgrids and active distribution systems. *IEEE Transactions on Power Delivery*, *25*(4), 2851–2858. doi:10.1109/TPWRD.2010.2042825

Karaboga, D., & Basturk, B. (2007). A powerful and efficient algorithm for numerical function optimization: Artificial bee colony (ABC) algorithm. *Journal of Global Optimization*, *39*(3), 459–471. doi:10.100710898-007-9149-x

Karimov, J., & Ozbayoglu, M. (2015, October). High-quality clustering of big data and solving empty-clustering problem with an evolutionary hybrid algorithm. *Proceedings 2015 IEEE International Conference on Big Data (Big Data)* (pp. 1473-1478). IEEE. 10.1109/BigData.2015.7363909

Karkalos, N. E., & Markopoulos, A. P. (2018). Determination of Johnson-Cook material model parameters by an optimization approach using the fireworks algorithm. *Procedia Manufacturing*, *22*, 107–113. doi:10.1016/j.promfg.2018.03.017

Kecman, V. (2006). *Learning and Soft Computing*. Upper Saddle River, NJ: Pearson Education.

Kencl, L., & Schwarzer, C. (2006). Traffic-adaptive packet filtering of denial of service attacks. *Proceedings of the 2006 International Symposium on World of Wireless, Mobile, and Multimedia Networks* (2006), pp. 485-489. 10.1109/WOWMOM.2006.111

Kennedy, J., & Eberhart, R. (1995). Particle swarm optimization. *Proceedings of the IEEE International Conference on Neural Networks*, pp. 1942–1948 November-December1995. Perth, Australia. IEEE.

Kennedy, J., & Eberhart, R. C. (2001). *Swarm intelligence*. San Francisco, CA: Morgan Kaufmann Publishers.

Khatri, P., & Drăghici, S. (2005). Ontological analysis of gene expression data: Current tools, limitations, and open problems. *Bioinformatics (Oxford, England)*, *21*(18), 3587–3595. doi:10.1093/bioinformatics/bti565 PMID:15994189

Khodaparastan, M., Dutta, O., Saleh, M., & Mohamed, A. A. (2019). Modeling and simulation of dc electric rail transit systems with wayside energy storage. *IEEE Transactions on Vehicular Technology*, *68*(3), 2218–2228. doi:10.1109/TVT.2019.2895026

Khoshgoftaar, T. M., Hulse, J. V., & Napolitano, A. (2011). Comparing boosting and bagging techniques with noisy and imbalanced data. *IEEE Transactions on Systems, Man, and Cybernetics. Part B, Cybernetics*, *41*(3), 552–568. doi:10.1109/TSMCA.2010.2084081

Khuat, T. T., & Le, M. H. (2016). An effort estimation approach for agile software development using fireworks algorithm optimized neural network. [IJCSIS]. *International Journal of Computer Science and Information Security, 14*(7).

Khuat, T. T., & Le, M. H. (2017). An application of artificial neural networks and fuzzy logic on the stock price prediction problem. *JOIV: International Journal on Informatics Visualization, 1*(2), 40–49. doi:10.30630/joiv.1.2.20

Kim, D. W., Park, G. J., Lee, J. H., Kim, J. W., Kim, Y. J., & Jung, S. Y. (2017). Hybridization algorithm of fireworks optimization and generating set search for optimal design of IPMSM. *IEEE Transactions on Magnetics, 53*(6), 1–4. doi:10.1109/TMAG.2017.2668608

Kim, Y. (1994, September). Speed Sensorless Vector Control of Induction Motor Using Extended Kalman Filter. *IEEE Transactions on Industry Applications, 30*(5).

Kirkpatrick, S., Gelatt, C. D., & Vecchi, M. P. (1983). Optimization by simulated annealing. *Science, 220*(4598), 671-680.

Knuth, D. E. (2015). *The Art of Computer Programming, Volume 4, Fascicle 6: Satisfiability.* Addison-Wesley Professional.

Köhler, S., Bauer, S., Horn, D., & Robinson, P. N. (2008). Walking the interactome for prioritization of candidate disease genes. *American Journal of Human Genetics, 82*(4), 949–958. doi:10.1016/j.ajhg.2008.02.013 PMID:18371930

Kondo, K. (2010). Recent energy saving technologies on railway traction systems. *IEEJ Transactions on Electrical and Electronic Engineering, 5*(3), 298–303. doi:10.1002/tee.20533

Kou, G., Chao, X., Peng, Y., Alsaadi, F. E., & Herrera-Viedma, E. (2019). Machine learning methods for systemic risk analysis in financial sectors. *Technological and Economic Development of Economy, §§§*, 1–27.

Krause, P. C., Wasynczuk, O., & Pekarek, S. (2012). *Electromechanical Motion Devices* (2nd ed.). Piscataway, NJ: IEEE Press. doi:10.1002/9781118316887

Krause, P. C., Wasynczuk, O., & Sudhoff, S. (2013). *Analysis of Electric Machinery and Drive Systems* (3rd ed.). Piscataway, NJ: IEEE Press. doi:10.1002/9781118524336

Krause, P. C., Wasynczuk, O., Sudhoff, S. D., & Pekarek, S. (2002). *Analysis of electric machinery and drive systems* (Vol. 2). Wiley Online Library. doi:10.1109/9780470544167

Kubat, M., Holte, R. C., & Matwin, S. (1998). Machine learning for the detection of oil spills in satellite radar images. *Machine Learning, 30*(2-3), 195–215. doi:10.1023/A:1007452223027

Kumar, A., & Gupta, R. (2013). Tunning of PID controller using PSO algorithm and compare results of integral errors for AVR system. *International Journal of Innovative Research and Development, 2*(4), 58–68.

Kumar, K., & Bhattacharya, S. (2006). Artificial neural network vs. linear discriminant analysis in credit ratings forecast. *Review of Accounting and Finance, 5*(3), 216–227. doi:10.1108/14757700610686426

Kumar, V., Chhabra, J. K., & Kumar, D. (2015). Optimal choice of parameters for fireworks algorithm. *Procedia Computer Science, 70*, 334–340. doi:10.1016/j.procs.2015.10.027

Kumazawa, T., Yokoyama, C., Takimoto, M., & Kambayashi, Y. (2016). Ant colony optimization-based model checking extended by smell-like pheromone. *EAI Endorsed Transactions on Industrial Networks and Intelligent Systems, 3*(7).

Kumazawa, T., Takada, K., Takimoto, M., & Kambayashi, Y. (2019). Ant colony optimization-based model checking extended by smell-like pheromone with hop counts. *Swarm and Evolutionary Computation, 44*, 511–521. doi:10.1016/j.swevo.2018.06.002

Kung, L., & Yu, S. (2008). Prediction of index futures returns and the analysis of financial spillovers-A comparison between GARCH and the grey theorem. *European Journal of Operational Research*, *186*(3), 1184–1200. doi:10.1016/j. ejor.2007.02.046

Lahcen, A., Mustapha, H., Ali, E., Saida, A., & Adel, A. (2019). Peak-to-Average Power Ratio Reduction Using New Swarm Intelligence Algorithm in OFDM Systems. *Procedia Manufacturing*, *32*, 831–839. doi:10.1016/j.promfg.2019.02.291

Lal, T. N., Chapelle, O., Western, J., & Elisseeff, A. (2006). Embedded methods. *Stud. Fuzziness Soft Comput.*, *207*(1), 137–165. doi:10.1007/978-3-540-35488-8_6

Lamport, L. (1977). Proving the correctness of multiprocess programs. *IEEE Transactions on Software Engineering*, *3*(2), 125–143. doi:10.1109/TSE.1977.229904

Lamport, L. (2002). *Specifying Systems: The TLA+ Language and Tools for Hardware and Software Engineers*. Addison-Wesley Longman.

Lana, I., Del Ser, J., & Vélez, M. (2017, June). A novel fireworks algorithm with wind inertia dynamics and its application to traffic forecasting. *Proceedings 2017 IEEE Congress on Evolutionary Computation (CEC)* (pp. 706-713). IEEE. 10.1109/CEC.2017.7969379

Łapa, K. (2017, September). Population-Based Algorithm with Selectable Evolutionary Operators for Nonlinear Modeling. In *International Conference on Information Systems Architecture and Technology* (pp. 15-26). Cham, Switzerland: Springer.

Łapa, K., & Cpałka, K. (2016). On the application of a hybrid genetic-firework algorithm for controllers structure and parameters selection. *Information Systems Architecture and Technology: Proceedings of 36th International Conference on Information Systems Architecture and Technology–ISAT 2015–Part I* (pp. 111-123). Cham, Switzerland: Springer.

Łapa, K., Cpałka, K., & Rutkowski, L. (2018). New Aspects of Interpretability of Fuzzy Systems for Nonlinear Modeling. In *Advances in Data Analysis with Computational Intelligence Methods* (pp. 225–264). Cham, Switzerland: Springer. doi:10.1007/978-3-319-67946-4_9

Larrañaga, P., & Lozano, J. A. (Eds.). (2001). *Estimation of distribution algorithms: A new tool for evolutionary computation* (Vol. 2). Springer Science & Business Media.

Larson, R., & Farber, B. (2003). Elementary Statistics Picturing the World, (pp. 428-433). Pearson Education.

Leary, M. R. (2001). Interpersonal Rejection. *Dialogues in Clinical Neuroscience*, *17*(4), 435–441. PMID:26869844

Le, D.-H., & Dang, V.-T. (2016). Ontology-based disease similarity network for disease gene prediction. *Vietnam Journal of Computer Science*, *3*(3), 197–205. doi:10.100740595-016-0063-3

Lee, D. C. (2016a). Designing an extended Kalman filter for estimating speed and flux of an induction motor with unknown noise covariance. *Proc. IEEE Canadian Conference on Electrical and Computer Engineering*, June. 10.1109/CCECE.2016.7726654

Lee, D. C. (2016b). Gradient-based methods of tuning noise covariance for an induction motor model. *Proc. IEEE Canadian Conference on Electrical and Computer Engineering*, June. 10.1109/CCECE.2016.7726630

Lee, D. J., & Wang, L. (2008). Small-signal stability analysis of an autonomous hybrid renewable energy power generation/energy storage system part I: Time-domain simulations. *IEEE Transactions on Energy Conversion*, *23*(1), 311–320. doi:10.1109/TEC.2007.914309

Lee, D., & Yannakakis, M. (1992). Online minimization of transition systems (extended abstract). In *Proceedings of the twenty-fourth annual ACM symposium on Theory of Computing*, 264-274. 10.1145/129712.129738

Lee, H., Jung, S., Cho, Y., Yoon, D., & Jang, G. (2013). Peak power reduction and energy efficiency improvement with the superconducting flywheel energy storage in electric railway system. *Physica. C, Superconductivity, 494*, 246–249. doi:10.1016/j.physc.2013.04.033

Lee, K. C. (2017). Inverse scattering of a conducting cylinder in free space by modified fireworks algorithm. *Progress in Electromagnetics Research, 59*, 135–146. doi:10.2528/PIERM17061101

Lee, K. C. (2018). Microwave imaging of a conducting cylinder buried in a lossless half space by modified fireworks algorithm. *Microwave and Optical Technology Letters, 60*(6), 1374–1381. doi:10.1002/mop.31159

Lei, C., Fang, B., Gao, H., Jia, W., & Pan, W. (2018, October). Short-term power load forecasting based on Least Squares Support Vector Machine optimized by Bare Bones Fireworks algorithm. *Proceedings 2018 IEEE 3rd Advanced Information Technology, Electronic, and Automation Control Conference (IAEAC)* (pp. 2231-2235). IEEE. 10.1109/IAEAC.2018.8577212

Leigh, W., Hightower, R., & Modani, N. (2005). Forecasting the New York stock exchange composite index with past price and interest rate on condition of volume spike. *Expert Systems with Applications, 28*(1), 1–8. doi:10.1016/j.eswa.2004.08.001

Lenin, K., Reddy, B. R., & Kalavathi, M. S. (2015). Reduction of Real Power Loss by Upgraded Fireworks Algorithm. *International Journal of Advanced Engineering and Science, 4*(2), 1.

Leveson, N. G. (2004). The role of software in spacecraft accidents. *Journal of Spacecraft and Rockets, 41*(4), 564–575. doi:10.2514/1.11950

Lewis, F. (1992). *Applied Optimal Control & Estimation*. New York: Prentice Hall.

Li, H., Bai, P., Xue, J. J., Zhu, J., & Zhang, H. (2015, June). Parameter estimation of chaotic systems using fireworks algorithm. *Proceedings International Conference in Swarm Intelligence* (pp. 457-467). Cham, Switzerland: Springer. 10.1007/978-3-319-20472-7_49

Li, J., Fong, S., & Zhuang, Y. (2015). Optimizing SMOTE by metaheuristics with neural network and decision tree. *Proceedings 2015 3rd International Symposium on Computational and Business Intelligence (ISCBI)*. IEEE.

Li, X., Han, S., Zhao, L., & Gong, C. (2017, November). Adaptive fireworks algorithm based on two-master sub-population and new selection strategy. *Proceedings International Conference on Neural Information Processing* (pp. 70-79). Cham, Switzerland: Springer. 10.1007/978-3-319-70093-9_8

Li, Z.-R., Lin, H. H., Han, L., Jiang, L., Chen, X., & Chen, Y. Z. (2006). PROFEAT: a web server for computing structural and physicochemical features of proteins and peptides from amino acid sequence. *Nucleic acids research, 34(suppl_2)*, W32-W37.

Liang, J. J., Qu, B. Y., Suganthan, P. N., & Chen, Q. (2014). Problem definitions and evaluation criteria for the CEC 2015 competition on learning-based real-parameter single objective optimization. Technical Report201411A, Computational Intelligence Laboratory, Zhengzhou University, China and Technical Report, Nanyang Technological University, Singapore, 29, 625-640.

Liang, J., Qu, B., Suganthan, P., & Hernandez-Diaz, A. G. (2013). Problem Definitions and Evaluation Criteria for the CEC 2013 Special Session on Real-Parameter Optimization. Technical Report 201212 (2013). Zhengzhou University, China.

Liang, J. J., Qu, B. Y., Suganthan, P. N., & Hernández-Díaz, A. G. (2013). Problem definitions and evaluation criteria for the CEC 2013 special session on real-parameter optimization. Computational Intelligence Laboratory, Zhengzhou University, China and Nanyang Technological University, Singapore. *Technical Report, 201212*(34), 281–295.

Liao, Y., Fu, C., & Mung'onya, E. M. (2019, May). 2D DOA Estimation of PR-WSF Algorithm Based on Modified Fireworks Algorithm. *Proceedings International Conference on Artificial Intelligence for Communications and Networks* (pp. 210-224). Springer, Cham. 10.1007/978-3-030-22968-9_19

Li, G., Kou, G., & Peng, Y. (2016). A group decision making model for integrating heterogeneous information. *IEEE Transactions on Systems, Man, and Cybernetics. Systems, 48*(6), 982–992. doi:10.1109/TSMC.2016.2627050

Li, H., Bai, P., Xue, J. J., Zhu, J., & Zhang, H. (2015). *Parameter Estimation of Chaotic Systems Using Fireworks Algorithm. Advances in Swarm and Computational Intelligence.* Springer International Publishing.

Lihu, A., & Holban, Ş. (2015). De novo motif prediction using the fireworks algorithm. [IJSIR]. *International Journal of Swarm Intelligence Research, 6*(3), 24–40. doi:10.4018/IJSIR.2015070102

Li, J. (2019). (Preprint). A random dynamic search algorithm research. *Journal of Computational Methods in Sciences and Engineering*, 1–14.

Li, J. Y., & Lu, C. (2016). Assembly sequence planning with fireworks algorithm. *International Journal of Modeling and Optimization, 6*(3), 195–198. doi:10.7763/IJMO.2016.V6.526

Li, J., & S. Z. (2014). *Adaptive Fireworks Algorithm. IEEE Congress on Evolutionary Computation (CEC)*, 3214-3221. Beijing, China.

Li, J., & Tan, Y. (2015, May). Orienting mutation-based fireworks algorithm. *Proceedings 2015 IEEE Congress on Evolutionary Computation (CEC)* (pp. 1265-1271). IEEE. 10.1109/CEC.2015.7257034

Li, J., & Tan, Y. (2016, July). Enhancing interaction in the fireworks algorithm by dynamic resource allocation and fitness-based crowdedness-avoiding strategy. *Proceedings 2016 IEEE Congress on Evolutionary Computation (CEC)* (pp. 4015-4021). IEEE. 10.1109/CEC.2016.7744299

Li, J., & Tan, Y. (2017). Loser-Out Tournament-Based Fireworks Algorithm for Multimodal Function Optimization. *IEEE Transactions on Evolutionary Computation, 22*(5), 679–691. doi:10.1109/TEVC.2017.2787042

Li, J., & Tan, Y. (2018). The bare bones fireworks algorithm: A minimalist global optimizer. *Applied Soft Computing, 62*, 454–462. doi:10.1016/j.asoc.2017.10.046

Li, J., & Tan, Y. (2019). A Comprehensive Review of the Fireworks Algorithm. [CSUR]. *ACM Computing Surveys, 52*(6), 121.

Li, J., Zhang, L.-H., Niu, Y., & Ren, H.-P. (2016). Model predictive control for extended Kalman filter-based speed sensorless induction motor drives. *Proc. IEEE Applied Power Electronics Conference and Exposition (APEC)*, pp. 2770–2775. 10.1109/APEC.2016.7468256

Li, J., Zheng, S., & Tan, Y. (2014, July). Adaptive fireworks algorithm. *Proceedings 2014 IEEE Congress on evolutionary computation (CEC)* (pp. 3214-3221). IEEE. 10.1109/CEC.2014.6900418

Li, J., Zheng, S., & Tan, Y. (2016). The effect of information utilization: Introducing a novel guiding spark in the fireworks algorithm. *IEEE Transactions on Evolutionary Computation, 21*(1), 153–166. doi:10.1109/TEVC.2016.2589821

Li, M. (2014). *Research on deductive evaluation of underwater countermeasure effectiveness based on Monte Carlo method.* Beijing: China Ship Research Institute.

Li, N., Yi, W., Sun, M., & Gong, G. (2012). Development and application of intelligent system modeling and simulation platform. *Simulation Modelling Practice and Theory, 29,* 149–162. doi:10.1016/j.simpat.2012.08.001

Lin, G., Jing, Z., & Liu, Z. (2014). Tuning of Extended Kalman Filter using Improved Particle Swarm Optimization for Sensorless Control of Induction Motors. *Journal of Computer Information Systems, 10.*

Liu, F. Z., Xiao, B., Li, H., & Cai, L. (2018, June). Discrete Fireworks Algorithm for Clustering in Wireless Sensor Networks. *Proceedings International Conference on Swarm Intelligence* (pp. 273-282). Cham, Switzerland: Springer. 10.1007/978-3-319-93815-8_27

Liu, J., Zheng, S., & Tan, Y. (2013, June). The improvement on controlling exploration and exploitation of firework algorithm. *Proceedings International Conference in Swarm Intelligence* (pp. 11-23). Berlin, Germany: Springer. 10.1007/978-3-642-38703-6_2

Liu, S., Gao, X., He, H., & Qi, W. (n.d.). Soft Sensor Modelling of Acrolein Conversion Based on Hidden Markov Model of Principle Component Analysis and Fireworks Algorithm. *The Canadian Journal of Chemical Engineering, 97*(12), 3052-3062.

Liu, X., Zhang, X., & Zhu, Q. (2017, April). Enhanced Fireworks Algorithm for Dynamic Deployment of Wireless Sensor Networks. *Proceedings 2017 2nd International Conference on Frontiers of Sensors Technologies (ICFST)* (pp. 161-165). IEEE. 10.1109/ICFST.2017.8210494

Liu, Z., Feng, Z., & Ke, L. (2016, June). A modified fireworks algorithm for the multi-resource range scheduling problem. *Proceedings International Conference on Swarm Intelligence* (pp. 535-543). Cham, Switzerland: Springer. 10.1007/978-3-319-41000-5_53

Liu, G., Wong, L., & Chua, H. N. (2009). Complex discovery from weighted PPI networks. *Bioinformatics (Oxford, England), 25*(15), 1891–1897. doi:10.1093/bioinformatics/btp311 PMID:19435747

Liu, J., Zheng, S., & Tan, Y. (2014, July). Analysis on global convergence and time complexity of fireworks algorithm. *Proceedings 2014 IEEE Congress on Evolutionary Computation (CEC)* (pp. 3207-3213). IEEE. 10.1109/CEC.2014.6900652

Liu, L., Luo, C., & Shen, F. (2017). Multi-Agent formation control with target tracking and navigation. *Proceedings 2017 IEEE International Conference on Information and Automation, ICIA 2017,* (July), 98–103. 10.1109/ICInfA.2017.8078889

Liu, L., Yang, S., & Wang, D. (2010). Particle swarm optimization with composite particles in dynamic environments. *IEEE Transactions on Systems, Man, and Cybernetics. Part B, Cybernetics, 40*(6), 1634–1648. doi:10.1109/TSMCB.2010.2043527 PMID:20371407

Liu, L., Zheng, S., & Tan, Y. (2015, May). S-metric based multi-objective fireworks algorithm. *Proceedings 2015 IEEE Congress on Evolutionary Computation (CEC)* (pp. 1257-1264). IEEE. 10.1109/CEC.2015.7257033

Liu, W., Shi, H., He, X., Pan, S., Ye, Z., & Wang, Y. (2018). An application of optimized Otsu multi-threshold segmentation based on fireworks algorithm in cement SEM image. *Journal of Algorithms & Computational Technology, 13.*

Liu, X. Y., Wu, J., & Zhou, Z. H. (2009). Exploratory undersampling for classimbalance learning. *IEEE Transactions on Systems, Man, and Cybernetics. Part B, Cybernetics, 39*(2), 539–550. doi:10.1109/TSMCB.2008.2007853 PMID:19095540

Liu, Z., Feng, Z., & Ke, L. (2015, May). Fireworks algorithm for the multi-satellite control resource scheduling problem. *Proceedings 2015 IEEE Congress on evolutionary computation (CEC)* (pp. 1280-1286). IEEE. 10.1109/CEC.2015.7257036

Liu, Z., Jiang, D., Zhang, C., Zhao, H., Zhao, Q., & Zhang, B. (2019). A Novel Fireworks Algorithm for the Protein-Ligand Docking on the AutoDock. *Mobile Networks and Applications,* 1–12. doi:10.100711036-018-1136-6

Li, X. G., Han, S. F., & Gong, C. Q. (2017). Analysis and improvement of fireworks algorithm. *Algorithms*, *10*(1), 26. doi:10.3390/a10010026

Li, X. G., Han, S. F., Zhao, L., Gong, C. Q., & Liu, X. J. (2017). Adaptive mutation dynamic search fireworks algorithm. *Algorithms*, *10*(2), 48. doi:10.3390/a10020048

Li, X., Ma, S., & Hu, J. (2017, July). Multi-search differential evolution algorithm. *Applied Intelligence*, *47*(1), 231–256. doi:10.1007/s10489-016-0885-9

Li, Y., & Patra, J. C. (2010). Genome-wide inferring gene–phenotype relationship by walking on the heterogeneous network. *Bioinformatics (Oxford, England)*, *26*(9), 1219–1224. doi:10.1093/bioinformatics/btq108 PMID:20215462

Li, Y., Yu, J., Takagi, H., & Tan, Y. (2019, July). Accelerating Fireworks Algorithm with Weight-based Guiding Sparks. *Proceedings International Conference on Swarm Intelligence* (pp. 257-266). Springer, Cham. 10.1007/978-3-030-26369-0_24

Loebis, D., Sutton, R., Chudley, J., & Naeem, W. (2004, December). Adaptive tuning of a Kalman filter via fuzzy logic for an intelligent AUV navigation system. *Control Engineering Practice*, *12*(12), 1531–1539. doi:10.1016/j.conengprac.2003.11.008

López-López, Á. J., Abrahamsson, L., Pecharromán, R. R., Fernández-Cardador, A., Cucala, P., Östlund, S., & Söder, L. (2014). *A variable no-load voltage scheme for improving energy efficiency in dc-electrified mass transit systems*. Proceedings *2014 Joint Rail Conference*. American Society of Mechanical Engineers Digital Collection.

López-López, A. J., Pecharromán, R. R., Fernández-Cardador, A., & Cucala, A. P. (2014). Assessment of energy-saving techniques in direct-current-electrified mass transit systems. *Transportation Research Part C, Emerging Technologies*, *38*, 85–100. doi:10.1016/j.trc.2013.10.011

Lu, C., & Li, J. Y. (2017). Assembly sequence planning considering the effect of assembly resources with a discrete fireworks algorithm. *International Journal of Advanced Manufacturing Technology*, *93*(9-12), 3297–3314. doi:10.100700170-017-0663-9

Ludwig, S. A., & Dawar, D. (2015). Parallelization of enhanced firework algorithm using MapReduce. [IJSIR]. *International Journal of Swarm Intelligence Research*, *6*(2), 32–51. doi:10.4018/IJSIR.2015040102

Luenberger, D. G. (1979). *Introduction to Dynamic Systems*. John Wiley & Sons.

Luo, C., Jan, G. E., Zhang, J., & Shen, F. (2017). Boundary aware navigation and mapping for a mobile automaton. *Proceedings 2016 IEEE International Conference on Information and Automation, IEEE ICIA 2016*, (August), 561–566. Academic Press.

Luo, C., Krishnan, M., Paulik, M., Cui, B., & Zhang, X. (2014). A novel lidar-driven two-level approach for real-time unmanned ground vehicle navigation and map building. *Intelligent Robots and Computer Vision XXXI: Algorithms and Techniques*, *9025*, 902503. International Society for Optics and Photonics.

Luo, C., Yang, S. X., Li, X., & Meng, M. Q. H. (2017). Neural-Dynamics-Driven Complete Area Coverage Navigation Through Cooperation of Multiple Mobile Robots. *IEEE Transactions on Industrial Electronics*, *64*(1), 750–760. doi:10.1109/TIE.2016.2609838

Luo, H., Xu, W., & Tan, Y. (2018, July). A Discrete Fireworks Algorithm for Solving Large-Scale Travel Salesman Problem. *Proceedings 2018 IEEE Congress on Evolutionary Computation (CEC)* (pp. 1-8). IEEE. 10.1109/CEC.2018.8477992

Luo, L., & Dhople, S. V. (2014). Spatiotemporal model reduction of inverter-based islanded microgrids. *IEEE Transactions on Energy Conversion*, *29*(4), 823–832. doi:10.1109/TEC.2014.2348716

Luo, T. (2019). Research on financial network big data processing technology based on fireworks algorithm. *EURASIP Journal on Wireless Communications and Networking*, *2019*(1), 122. doi:10.118613638-019-1443-z

Lu, Q., Gui, W., & Su, M. (2019). A Fireworks Algorithm for the System-Level Fault Diagnosis Based on MM* Model. *IEEE Access: Practical Innovations, Open Solutions*, *7*, 136975–136985. doi:10.1109/ACCESS.2019.2942336

Lyu, Z., Wei, Z., Lu, Y., Wang, X., Li, M., Xia, C., & Han, J. (2019). Multi-Node Charging Planning Algorithm With an Energy-Limited WCE in WRSNs. *IEEE Access: Practical Innovations, Open Solutions*, *7*, 47154–47170. doi:10.1109/ACCESS.2019.2909778

M., Liu, S.H., and Mernik, (2013). Exploration and exploitation in evolutionary algorithms: A survey. *ACM Computational Survey*, *45*(3), pp. 35-32. New York, NY.

Ma, T., & Xia, Z. (2017, October). A Community Detection Algorithm Based on Local Double Rings and Fireworks Algorithm. *Proceedings International Conference on Intelligent Data Engineering and Automated Learning* (pp. 129-135). Cham, Switzerland: Springer. 10.1007/978-3-319-68935-7_15

Magee, J., & Kramer, J. (2006). *Concurrency: State Models & Java Programs* (2nd ed.). John Wiley & Sons.

Malik, S., Dutta, P., Chakrabarti, S., & Barman, A. (2014, March). Parameter Estimation of a PID Controller using Particle Swarm Optimization Algorithm. *International Journal of Advanced Research in Computer and Communication Engineering*, *3*(3).

Manickam, C., Raman, G. P., Raman, G. R., Ganesan, S. I., & Chilakapati, N. (2016). Fireworks enriched P&O algorithm for GMPPT and detection of partial shading in PV systems. *IEEE Transactions on Power Electronics*, *32*(6), 4432–4443. doi:10.1109/TPEL.2016.2604279

Manimala, K., David, I. G., & Selvi, K. (2015). A novel data selection technique using fuzzy C-means clustering to enhance SVM-based power quality classification. *Soft Computing*, *19*(11), 3123–3144. doi:10.1007/s00500-014-1472-9

Manna, Z., & Pnueli, A. (1992). *The Temporal Logic of Reactive and Concurrent Systems*. Springer-Verlag. doi:10.1007/978-1-4612-0931-7

Manna, Z., & Pnueli, A. (1995). *Temporal Verification of Reactive Systems: Safety*. Springer-Verlag. doi:10.1007/978-1-4612-4222-2

Manson, K., Lee, D., Bloemink, J., & Palizban, A. (2018, November). Enhanced Fireworks Algorithm to Optimize Extended Kalman Filter Speed Estimation of an Induction Motor Drive System. *Proceedings 2018 IEEE 9th Annual Information Technology, Electronics, and Mobile Communication Conference (IEMCON)* (pp. 267-273). IEEE. 10.1109/IEMCON.2018.8614914

Mareda, T., Gaudard, L., & Romerio, F. (2017). A parametric genetic algorithm approach to assess complementary options of large scale windsolar coupling. *IEEE/CAA Journal of Automatica Sinica*, *4*(2), 260-272.

Margain, L., Ochoa, A., Padilla, T., González, S., Rodas, J., Tokudded, O., & Arreola, J. (2016). Understanding the consequences of social isolation using fireworks algorithm. In Innovations in Bio-Inspired Computing and Applications (pp. 285-295). Cham, Switzerland: Springer. doi:10.1007/978-3-319-28031-8_2

Marino, R., Tomei, P., & Verrelli, C. M. (2010). *Induction Motor Control Design*. Rome, Italy: Springer. doi:10.1007/978-1-84996-284-1

Martins, M., Costa, L., Frizera, A., Ceres, R., & Santos, C. (2014). Hybridization between multi-objective genetic algorithm and support vector machine for feature selection in walker-assisted gait. *Computer Methods and Programs in Biomedicine*, *113*(3), 736–748. doi:10.1016/j.cmpb.2013.12.005 PubMed

Masud, M. M., Mustafa, U., & Trabelsi, Z. (2014). Comparison of a data driven firewall for faster packet filtering. In *Proceedings Fourth International Conference on Communications and Networking, ComsNet-2014.*

Ma, T., & Niu, D. (2016). Icing forecasting of high voltage transmission line using weighted least square support vector machine with fireworks algorithm for feature selection. *Applied Sciences (Basel, Switzerland)*, 6(12), 438. doi:10.3390/app6120438

Matlab/Simulink website: https://www.mathworks.com/videos/series/understanding-kalman-filters.html. (2019).

Mattos, C. L., Barreto, G. A., Horstkemper, D., & Hellingrath, B. (2017, June). Metaheuristic optimization for automatic clustering of customer-oriented supply chain data. *Proceedings 2017 12th International Workshop on Self-Organizing Maps and Learning Vector Quantization, Clustering, and Data Visualization (WSOM)* (pp. 1-8). IEEE. 10.1109/WSOM.2017.8020025

Mazurowski, M. A., Habas, P. A., Zurada, J. M., Lo, J. Y., Baker, J. A., & Tourassi, G. D. (2008). Training neural network classifiers for medical decision making: The effects of imbalanced datasets on classification performance. *Neural Networks: Off. J. Int. Neural Network Soc.*, 21(2-3), 427–436. doi:10.1016/j.neunet.2007.12.031 PMID:18272329

Melián, B., & Moreno, J. (2003). Metaheuristics: A global vision. *Ibero-American Journal of Artificial Intelligence*, 19, 7–28.

Messaoudi, I., & Kamel, N. (2019). Community Detection Using Fireworks Optimization Algorithm. *International Journal of Artificial Intelligence Tools*, 28(03). doi:10.1142/S0218213019500106

Miao, Y., Ma, X., Jin, X., & Lu, H. (2018, July). Mobile Robot Odor Source Localization Based on Modified FWA. *Proceedings 2018 IEEE 8th Annual International Conference on CYBER Technology in Automation, Control, and Intelligent Systems (CYBER)* (pp. 854-860). IEEE. 10.1109/CYBER.2018.8688288

Milewicz, R. M., & Poulding, S. (2017). Scalable parallel model checking via Monte-Carlo Tree Search. *Software Engineering Notes*, 42(4), 1–5. doi:10.1145/3149485.3149495

Milner, R. (1999). *Communicating and Mobile Systems: the Pi-Calculus.* Cambridge University Press.

Mirjalili, S., Mirjalili, S. M., & Lewis, A. (2014). Grey wolf optimizer. *Advances in Engineering Software*, 69, 46–61. doi:10.1016/j.advengsoft.2013.12.007

Misra, P. R., & Si, T. (2017). Image segmentation using clustering with fireworks algorithm. *Proceedings of 11th International Conference on Intelligent Systems and Control* (pp. 97-102). Coimbatore, India. 10.1109/ISCO.2017.7855961

Mnif, M., & Bouamama, S. (2017). Firework algorithm for multi-objective optimization of a multimodal transportation network problem. *Procedia Computer Science*, 112, 1670–1682. doi:10.1016/j.procs.2017.08.189

Mnif, M., & Bouamama, S. (2017, September). A multi-objective formulation for multimodal transportation network's planning problems. *Proceedings 2017 IEEE International Conference on Service Operations and Logistics, and Informatics (SOLI)* (pp. 144-149). IEEE. 10.1109/SOLI.2017.8120985

Mo, H., & Xu, L. (2015). Research of biogeography particle swarm optimization for robot path planning. *Neurocomputing*, 148, 91–99. doi:10.1016/j.neucom.2012.07.060

Mori, H., & Ikegami, H. (2017, July). *An advanced fireworks algorithm for distribution network reconfigurations. Proceedings 2017 IEEE Power & Energy Society General Meeting* (pp. 1–5). IEEE.

Mu, B., Zhao, J., Yuan, S., & Yan, J. (2017, May). Parallel dynamic search fireworks algorithm with linearly decreased dimension number strategy for solving conditional nonlinear optimal perturbation. *Proceedings 2017 International Joint Conference on Neural Networks (IJCNN)* (pp. 2314-2321). IEEE. 10.1109/IJCNN.2017.7966136

Mueller, J. A., & Kimball, J. W. (2017). An Efficient Method of Determining Operating Points of Droop-Controlled Microgrids. *IEEE Transactions on Energy Conversion, 32*(4), 1432–1446. doi:10.1109/TEC.2017.2719580

Mumtaz, F., Syed, M., Al Hosani, M., & Zeineldin, H. (2016). A novel approach to solve power flow for islanded microgrids using modified newton raphson with droop control of dg. *IEEE Transactions on Sustainable Energy, 7*(2), 493–503. doi:10.1109/TSTE.2015.2502482

Natarajan, N., & Dhillon, I. S. (2014). Inductive matrix completion for predicting gene-disease associations. *Bioinformatics (Oxford, England), 30*(12), 60–68. doi:10.1093/bioinformatics/btu269 PMID:24932006

Nayak, S. C., Misra, B. B., & Behera, H. S. (2013, September). Hybridzing chemical reaction optimization and artificial neural network for stock future index forecasting. *Proceedings 2013 1st International Conference on Emerging Trends and Applications in Computer Science* (pp. 130-134). IEEE. 10.1109/ICETACS.2013.6691409

Nayak, S. C., Misra, B. B., & Behera, H. S. (2018). ACFLN: artificial chemical functional link network for prediction of stock market index. Evolving Systems, 1-26.

Nayak, A., & Maharana, M. K. (2017, February). Tuning of PID controller to maintain load frequency for hybrid power system. *Proceedings 2017 International Conference on Innovative Mechanisms for Industry Applications (ICIMIA)* (pp. 24-28). IEEE. 10.1109/ICIMIA.2017.7975623

Nayak, S. C., & Misra, B. B. (2018). Estimating stock closing indices using a GA-weighted condensed polynomial neural network. *Financial Innovation, 4*(1), 21. doi:10.118640854-018-0104-2

Nayak, S. C., Misra, B. B., & Behera, H. S. (2014). Impact of data normalization on stock index forecasting. *Int. J. Comp. Inf. Syst. Ind. Manag. Appl, 6*, 357–369.

Nayak, S. C., Misra, B. B., & Behera, H. S. (2016). An adaptive second order neural network with genetic-algorithm-based training (ASONN-GA) to forecast the closing prices of the stock market. [IJAMC]. *International Journal of Applied Metaheuristic Computing, 7*(2), 39–57. doi:10.4018/IJAMC.2016040103

Nayak, S. C., Misra, B. B., & Behera, H. S. (2016). Efficient forecasting of financial time-series data with virtual adaptive neuro-fuzzy inference system. *International Journal of Business Forecasting and Marketing Intelligence, 2*(4), 379–402. doi:10.1504/IJBFMI.2016.080132

Nayak, S. C., Misra, B. B., & Behera, H. S. (2017). Artificial chemical reaction optimization based neural net for virtual data position exploration for efficient financial time series forecasting. *Ain Shams Engineering Journal*.

Nayak, S. C., Misra, B. B., & Behera, H. S. (2017). Artificial chemical reaction optimization of neural networks for efficient prediction of stock market indices. *Ain Shams Engineering Journal, 8*(3), 371–390. doi:10.1016/j.asej.2015.07.015

Nayak, S. C., Misra, B. B., & Behera, H. S. (2017). Efficient financial time series prediction with evolutionary virtual data position exploration. *Neural Computing & Applications*, 1–22.

Nayak, S. C., Misra, B. B., & Behera, H. S. (2017). Exploration and incorporation of virtual data positions for efficient forecasting of financial time series. *International Journal of Industrial and Systems Engineering, 26*(1), 42–62. doi:10.1504/IJISE.2017.083179

Neagu, B. C., Ivanov, O., & Gavrilaş, M. (2017, October). A comprehensive solution for optimal capacitor allocation problem in real distribution networks. *Proceedings 2017 International Conference on Electromechanical and Power Systems (SIELMEN)* (pp. 565-570). IEEE. 10.1109/SIELMEN.2017.8123388

Nehrir, M. H., Wang, C., Strunz, K., Aki, H., Ramakumar, R., Bing, J., ... Salameh, Z. (2011). Hybrid Renewable/Alternative Energy Systems for Electric Power Generation: Configurations, Control, and Applications. *IEEE Transactions on Sustainable Energy, 2*(4), 392–403. doi:10.1109/TSTE.2011.2157540

Nerurkar, P., Shirkeb, A., Chandanec, M., & Bhirudd, S. (2018). *A Novel Heuristic for Evolutionary Clustering*, Kurukshetra, India. *Procedia Computer Science, 125*, 780–789. doi:10.1016/j.procs.2017.12.100

Newman, M. E. (2004). Fast algorithm for detecting community structure in networks. *Physical Review. E, 69*(6). doi:10.1103/PhysRevE.69.066133 PMID:15244693

Nie, Z., Yang, X., Gao, S., Zheng, Y., Wang, J., & Wang, Z. (2016). Research on autonomous moving robot path planning based on improved particle swarm optimization. *2016 IEEE Congress on Evolutionary Computation, CEC 2016*, 2532–2536. 10.1109/CEC.2016.7744104

Nikkhajoei, H., & Iravani, R. (2007). Steady-state model and power flow analysis of electronically-coupled distributed resource units. *IEEE Transactions on Power Delivery, 22*(1), 721–728. doi:10.1109/TPWRD.2006.881604

Niu, S., Ding, Y., & Liang, Z. (2015, August). Study on Distribution Network Reconfiguration with Various DGs. *Proceedings International Conference on Materials Engineering and Information Technology Applications (MEITA 2015)*. Atlantis Press. 10.2991/meita-15.2015.140

Ogata, K. (2010). *Modern Control Engineering, 5*. Upper Saddle River, NJ: Prentice Hall.

Ong, C.-M. (1997). *Dynamic Simulation of Electric Machinery*. Prentice Hall.

Oong, T. H., & Isa, N. A. M. (2011). Adaptive Evolutionary Artificial Neural Networks for Pattern Classification. *IEEE Transactions on Neural Networks, 22*(11), 1823–1836. doi:10.1109/TNN.2011.2169426 PubMed

Ozana, S. (2016). PID Controller design based on global optimization technique with additional constraints. *Journal of Electrical Engineering, 67*(3), 160-168.

Pallone, M., Pontani, M., & Teofilatto, P. (2018). Performance evaluation methodology for multistage launch vehicles with high-fidelity modeling. *Acta Astronautica, 151*, 522–531. doi:10.1016/j.actaastro.2018.06.012

Pandey, V. C., Jadoun, V. K., Gupta, N., Niazi, K. R., & Swarnkar, A. (2018). Improved Fireworks algorithm with chaotic sequence operator for large-scale non-convex economic load dispatch problem. *Arabian Journal for Science and Engineering, 43*(6), 2919–2929. doi:10.100713369-017-2956-6

Pan, G. (2015). *Principle of Integrated Command and and Control System for Ships*. Xi'an: Northwest Industrial Press.

Panigrahi, S., Kundu, A., Sural, S., & Majumdar, A. K. (2009). Credit card fraud detection: A fusion approach using Dempster–Shafer theory and Bayesian learning. *Information Fusion, 10,* pp. 354-363.

Panwar, L. K., Reddy, S., & Kumar, R. (2015). Binary fireworks algorithm based thermal unit commitment. [IJSIR]. *International Journal of Swarm Intelligence Research, 6*(2), 87–101. doi:10.4018/IJSIR.2015040104

Parentcenterhub.org. (2016). Center for Parent Information & Resources. Retrieved from Sobre la Ley IDEA: https://www.parentcenterhub.org/sobreidea/

Parízek, P., & Lhoták, O. (2019). Fast detection of concurrency errors by state space traversal with randomization and early backtracking. *International Journal of Software Tools for Technology Transfer, 21*(4), 365–400. doi:10.100710009-018-0484-7

Pavani, V. S., & Kumar, G. (2017). An Analysis of Advanced Wind/Fuel Cell based Hybrid Power Generation Strategies for Microgrid Applications. *International Journal for Indian Innovative Research Engineering Streams of Technological Sciences, 1*(3), 2017.

Pavão, L. V., Costa, C. B. B., Ravagnani, M. A. D. S. S., & Jiménez, L. (2017). Large-scale heat exchanger networks synthesis using simulated annealing and the novel rocket fireworks optimization. *AIChE Journal. American Institute of Chemical Engineers, 63*(5), 1582–1601. doi:10.1002/aic.15524

Pei, Y., Zheng, S., Tan, Y., & Takagi, H. (2012, October). An empirical study on influence of approximation approaches on enhancing fireworks algorithm. *Proceedings 2012 IEEE International Conference on Systems, Man, and Cybernetics (SMC)* (pp. 1322-1327). IEEE. 10.1109/ICSMC.2012.6377916

Pei, Y., Zheng, S., Tan, Y., & Takagi, H. (2015). Effectiveness of approximation strategy in surrogate-assisted fireworks algorithm. *International Journal of Machine Learning and Cybernetics, 6*(5), 795–810. doi:10.100713042-015-0388-8

Pekdemir, H., & Topcuoglu, H. R. (2016, July). Enhancing fireworks algorithms for dynamic optimization problems. *Proceedings 2016 IEEE congress on evolutionary computation (CEC)* (pp. 4045-4052). IEEE.

Pekdemir, H., & Topcuoglu, H. R. (2016, July). Enhancing fireworks algorithms for dynamic optimization problems. Proceedings 2016 IEEE congress on evolutionary computation (CEC) (pp. 4045-4052). IEEE. doi:10.1109/CEC.2016.7744303

Peng, L., Zhang, H., Yang, B., & Chen, Y. (2014). A new approach for imbalanced data classification based on data gravitation. *Information Sciences, 288*, pp. 347-373.

Peri, S., Navarro, J. D., Amanchy, R., Kristiansen, T. Z., Jonnalagadda, C. K., Surendranath, V., ... Gronborg, M. (2003). Development of human protein reference database as an initial platform for approaching systems biology in humans. *Genome Research, 13*(10), 2363–2371. doi:10.1101/gr.1680803 PMID:14525934

Peterson, L. (2009). K-nearest neighbor. Scholarpedia, 4(2), 1883. doi:10.4249/scholarpedia.1883

Pholdee, N., & Bureerat, S. (2014). Comparative performance of meta-heuristic algorithms for mass minimisation of trusses with dynamic constraints. *Advances in Engineering Software, 75*, 1–13. doi:10.1016/j.advengsoft.2014.04.005

Pira, E., Rafe, V., & Nikanjam, A. (2017). Deadlock detection in complex software systems specified through graph transformation using Bayesian optimization algorithm. *Journal of Systems and Software, 131*, 181–200. doi:10.1016/j.jss.2017.05.128

Pogaku, N., Prodanovic, M., & Green, T. C. (2007). Modeling, analysis and testing of autonomous operation of an inverter-based microgrid. *IEEE Transactions on Power Electronics, 22*(2), 613–625. doi:10.1109/TPEL.2006.890003

Poulding, S., & Feldt, R. (2015). Heuristic model checking using a Monte-Carlo Tree Search Algorithm. In *Proceedings of the 2015 Annual Conference on Genetic and Evolutionary Computation*, 1359-1366. 10.1145/2739480.2754767

Prelić, A., Bleuler, S., Zimmermann, P., Wille, A., Bühlmann, P., Gruissem, W., ... Zitzler, E. (2006). A systematic comparison and evaluation of biclustering methods for gene expression data. *Bioinformatics (Oxford, England), 22*(9), 1122–1129. doi:10.1093/bioinformatics/btl060 PMID:16500941

Price, K., Storn, R., & Lampinen, J. (2005). *Differential evolution: a practical approach to global optimization*. Berlin, Germany: Springer.

Qian, Z., & Hu, C. (2019, March). Optimal Path Selection for Fault Repair Based on Grid GIS Platform and Improved Fireworks Algorithm. *Proceedings 2019 IEEE 3rd Information Technology, Networking, Electronic, and Automation Control Conference (ITNEC)* (pp. 2452-2456). IEEE. 10.1109/ITNEC.2019.8729359

Qiao, Z., Ke, L., Wang, X., & Lu, X. (2019, June). Signal Control of Urban Traffic Network Based on Multi-Agent Architecture and Fireworks Algorithm. *Proceedings 2019 IEEE Congress on Evolutionary Computation (CEC)* (pp. 2199-2206). IEEE.

Qiu, M., Xie, X., Tao, X., Xu, K., & Liu, Y. (n.d.). Research on Container Cloud Task Classification Algorithm based on Improved Random Forest. doi:10.1109/CEC.2019.8790300

Quinlan, J. R. (1996). Bagging, boosting, and C4. 5, AAAI/IAAI, 1.

Rafe, V., Darghayedi, M., & Einollah, P. (2019). MS-ACO: A multi-stage ant colony optimization to refute complex software systems specified through graph transformation. *Soft Computing, 23*(12), 4531–4556. doi:10.100700500-018-3444-y

Rafe, V., Moradi, M., Yousefian, R., & Nikanjam, A. (2015). A meta-heuristic solution for automated refutation of complex software systems specified through Graph Transformations. *Applied Soft Computing, 33*(C), 136–149. doi:10.1016/j.asoc.2015.04.032

Rahmani, A., Amine, A., Hamou, R. M., Rahmani, M. E., & Bouarara, H. A. (2015). Privacy preserving through fireworks algorithm-based model for image perturbation in big data. [IJSIR]. *International Journal of Swarm Intelligence Research, 6*(3), 41–58. doi:10.4018/IJSIR.2015070103

Rajaram, R., Palanisamy, K., Ramasamy, S., & Ramanathan, P. (2014). Selective harmonic elimination in pwm inverter using firefly and fireworks algorithm. [IJIRAE]. *International Journal of Innovative Research in Advanced Engineering, 1*, 55–62.

Rajasekaran, S., & Pai, G. A. V. (2007). *Neural Networks, Fuzzy Logic and Genetic Algorithms Synthesis and Application.* Delhi, India: PHI Learning Private Limited.

Rajshetra, K. (2005). Hybrid fuel cell strategies for clean pwer generation. *IEEE Transactions on Industry Applications, 41*(3), 682–689. doi:10.1109/TIA.2005.847293

Rani, B. S., & Vairamuthu, S. (2016). An Intelligent Packet Filtering Based on Bi-layer Particle Swarm Optimization with Reduced Search Space. In *Proceedings of the Second International Conference on Computer and Communication Technologies* (pp. 639-647). New Delhi, India: Springer.

Rasheduzzaman, M., Mueller, J. A., & Kimball, J. W. (2014). An accurate small-signal model of inverter-dominated islanded microgrids using dq reference frame. *IEEE Journal of Emerging and Selected Topics in Power Electronics, 2*(4), 1070–1080. doi:10.1109/JESTPE.2014.2338131

Ratniyomchai, T., Hillmansen, S., & Tricoli, P. (2013). Recent developments and applications of energy storage devices in electrified railways. *IET Electrical Systems in Transportation, 4*(1), 9–20. doi:10.1049/iet-est.2013.0031

Ratniyomchai, T., Hillmansen, S., & Tricoli, P. (2015, June). Energy loss minimisation by optimal design of stationary supercapacitors for light railways. *Proceedings 2015 International Conference on Clean Electrical Power (ICCEP)* (pp. 511-517). IEEE. 10.1109/ICCEP.2015.7177538

Rayyam, M., & Zazi, M. (October 2018). Particle Swarm Optimization of a Non Linear Kalman Filter for Sensorless Control of Induction Motors. *Proceedings 7th International Conference on Renewable Energy Research and Applications*, pp. 1016-1020. Paris, France.

Reddy, S., Panwar, L. K., Panigrahi, B. K., & Kumar, R. (2016, March). Optimal demand response allocation in resource scheduling with renewable energy penetration. *Proceedings 2016 IEEE 6th International Conference on Power Systems (ICPS)* (pp. 1-6). IEEE.

Reddy, K. S., Mandal, A., Verma, K. K., & Rajamohan, G. (2016). Fitting of Bezier curves using the fireworks algorithm. *International Journal of Advances in Engineering and Technology, 9*(3), 396.

Reddy, K. S., Mandal, A., Verma, K. K., & Rajamohan, G. (2016). Fitting of Bezier surfaces using the fireworks algorithm. *International Journal of Advances in Engineering and Technology, 9*(3), 421.

Reddy, K. S., Panwar, L. K., Kumar, R., & Panigrahi, B. K. (2016). Binary fireworks algorithm for profit based unit commitment (PBUC) problem. *International Journal of Electrical Power & Energy Systems, 83*, 270–282. doi:10.1016/j.ijepes.2016.04.005

Reddy, K. S., Panwar, L. K., Kumar, R., & Panigrahi, B. K. (2016). Distributed resource scheduling in smart grid with electric vehicle deployment using fireworks algorithm. *Journal of Modern Power Systems and Clean Energy, 4*(2), 188–199. doi:10.100740565-016-0195-6

Reddy, K. S., Panwar, L., Panigrahi, B. K., & Kumar, R. (2018). Low carbon unit commitment (LCUC) with post carbon capture and storage (CCS) technology considering resource sensitivity. *Journal of Cleaner Production, 200*, 161–173. doi:10.1016/j.jclepro.2018.07.195

Refaeilzadeh, P., Tang, L., & Liu, H. (2008). *Cross-Validation*. Arizona State University.

Ren, J., Ren, B., Zhang, Q., & Zheng, X. (2019). A Novel Hybrid Extreme Learning Machine Approach Improved by K Nearest Neighbor Method and Fireworks Algorithm for Flood Forecasting in Medium and Small Watershed of Loess Region. *Water (Basel), 11*(9), 1848. doi:10.3390/w11091848

Ren, Y. T., Qi, H., He, M. J., Ruan, S. T., Ruan, L. M., & Tan, H. P. (2016). Application of an improved firework algorithm for simultaneous estimation of temperature-dependent thermal and optical properties of molten salt. *International Communications in Heat and Mass Transfer, 77*, 33–42. doi:10.1016/j.icheatmasstransfer.2016.06.012

Roch-Dupré, D., Cucala, A. P., Pecharromán, R. R., López-López, Á. J., & Fernández-Cardador, A. (2018). Evaluation of the impact that the traffic model used in railway electrical simulation has on the assessment of the installation of a Reversible Substation. *International Journal of Electrical Power & Energy Systems, 102*, 201–210. doi:10.1016/j.ijepes.2018.04.030

Roch-Dupré, D., Cucala, A. P., Pecharromán, R. R., López-López, Á. J., & Fernández-Cardador, A. (2020). Simulation-based assessment of the installation of a Reversible Substation in a railway line, including a realistic model of large traffic perturbations. *International Journal of Electrical Power & Energy Systems, 115*. doi:10.1016/j.ijepes.2019.105476

Roch-Dupré, D., López-López, Á. J., Pecharromán, R. R., Cucala, A. P., & Fernández-Cardador, A. (2017). Analysis of the demand charge in DC railway systems and reduction of its economic impact with Energy Storage Systems. *International Journal of Electrical Power & Energy Systems, 93*, 459–467. doi:10.1016/j.ijepes.2017.06.022

Rodriguez, L., Castillo, O., & Soria, J. (2016). *Grey Wolf Optimizer (GWO) with dynamic adaptation of parameters* (pp. 3116–3123). Vancouver, Canada: IEEE CEC.

Rodríguez, L., Castillo, O., & Soria, J. (2017). *A Study of Parameters of the Grey Wolf Optimizer Algorithm for Dynamic Adaptation with Fuzzy Logic* (pp. 371–390). Berlin, Germany: Nature-Inspired Design of Hybrid Intelligent Systems.

Roy, D., Maitra, M., & Bhattacharya, S. (2017). Study of formation control and obstacle avoidance of swarm robots using evolutionary algorithms. *2016 IEEE International Conference on Systems, Man, and Cybernetics, SMC 2016 - Conference Proceedings*, 3154–3159. IEEE.

Rubio, E., & Castillo, O. (2017). *Interval Type-2 Fuzzy Possibilistic C-Means Optimization Using Particle Swarm Optimization* (pp. 63–78). Switzerland: Nature-Inspired Design of Hybrid Intelligent Systems. doi:10.1007/978-3-319-47054-2_4

Salman, I., Ucan, O., Bayat, O., & Shaker, K. (2018). Impact of metaheuristic iteration on artificial neural network structure in medical data. *Processes (Basel, Switzerland)*, 6(5), 57. doi:10.3390/pr6050057

Salvatore, L., Stasi, S., & Tarchioni, L. (1993, October). A new EKF-based algorithm for flux estimation in induction machines. *IEEE Transactions on Industrial Electronics*, 40(5), 496–504. doi:10.1109/41.238018

Sanchez, M. A., Castillo, O., Castro, J. R., & Melin, P. (2014). Fuzzy granular gravitational clustering algorithm for multivariate data. *Information Science, 279*, 498–511. *Amsterdam, The Netherlands*. doi:10.1016/j.ins.2014.04.005

Sangeetha, K., Babu, T. S., & Rajasekar, N. (2016). Fireworks algorithm-based maximum power point tracking for uniform irradiation as well as under partial shading condition. In *Artificial Intelligence and Evolutionary Computations in Engineering Systems* (pp. 79–88). New Delhi, India: Springer. doi:10.1007/978-81-322-2656-7_8

Sangiorgi, D. (2011). *Introduction to Bisimulation and Coinduction*. Cambridge University Press. doi:10.1017/CBO9780511777110

Saravanan, B., Kumar, C., & Kothari, D. P. (2016). A solution to unit commitment problem using fire works algorithm. *International Journal of Electrical Power & Energy Systems, 77*, 221–227. doi:10.1016/j.ijepes.2015.11.030

Saremi, S., Mirjalili, S., & Lewis, A. (2017). Grasshopper optimisation algorithm: Theory and application. *Advances in Engineering Software, 105*, 30–47. doi:10.1016/j.advengsoft.2017.01.004

Schaefer, C. E. (2012). Fundamentos de Terapia de Juego. MANUAL MODERNO. [Fundamentals of Game Therapy: Modern Manual]. Hipódromo: John Wiley & Sons.

Schuppan, V., & Armin, B. (2006). Liveness checking as safety checking for infinite state spaces. *Electronic Notes in Theoretical Computer Science, 149*(1), 79–96. doi:10.1016/j.entcs.2005.11.018

Schuppan, V., & Biere, A. (2005). Shortest counterexamples for symbolic model checking of LTL with Past. In *Proceedings of the 11th International Conference on Tools and Algorithms for the Construction and Analysis of Systems*, 493-509. 10.1007/978-3-540-31980-1_32

Schutte, J. F., & Groenwold, A. A. (2005). A study of global optimization using particle swarms. *Journal of Global Optimization, 31*(1), 93–108. doi:10.100710898-003-6454-x

Seiffert, C., Khoshgoftaar, T. M., Van Hulse, J., & Napolitano, A. (2010). Rusboost: A hybrid approach to alleviating class imbalance. *IEEE Trans. Syst. Man Cybern. Part A, 40*(1), 185–197. doi:10.1109/TSMCA.2009.2029559

Senjyu, T., Nakaji, T., Uezato, K., & Funabashi, T. (2005). A hybrid power system using alternative energy facilities in isolated island. *IEEE Transactions on Energy Conversion, 20*(2), 406–414. doi:10.1109/TEC.2004.837275

Shadbolt, N. (2004). Nature-Inspired Computing. *IEEE Intelligent Systems, 19*(1), 2–3. doi:10.1109/MIS.2004.1265875

Shaikot, S. H., & Kim, M. S. (2010). Lightweight Traffic-Aware Packet Classification for Continuous Operation. In *Proceedings 10th Annual International Symposium on Applications and the Internet*. Academic Press.

Sheskin, D. J. (2007). *Handbook of Parametric and Nonparametric Statistical Procedures*. London, UK: Chapman & Hall.

Shi, C., Ren, Z., & He, X. (2016, September). Research on Load Balancing for Software Defined Cloud-Fog Network in Real-Time Mobile Face Recognition. *Proceedings International Conference on Communications and Networking in China* (pp. 121-131). Cham, Switzerland: Springer. Academic Press.

Shi, J., Xu, B., Zhu, P., & Lu, M. (2016, October). Multi-task firework algorithm for cell tracking and contour estimation. *Proceedings 2016 International Conference on Control, Automation, and Information Sciences (ICCAIS)* (pp. 27-31). IEEE. 10.1109/ICCAIS.2016.7822430

Shi, J., Xu, B., Zhu, P., Lu, M., Zhang, W., Xu, L., & Zhang, J. (2015, October). Multiple cells tracking by firework algorithm. *Proceedings 2015 International Conference on Control, Automation, and Information Sciences (ICCAIS)* (pp. 508-511). IEEE.

Shi, K., Chan, T., Wong, Y., & Ho, S. (2000). Speed Estimation of an Induction Motor Drive Using an Extended Kalman Filter. *2000 IEEE Power Engineering Society Winter Meeting, Conference Proceedings (Cat. No.00CH37077)*, 1, pp. 243–248, Singapore, 2000. 10.1109/PESW.2000.849963

Shi, K., Chan, T., Wong, Y., & Ho, S. L. (2002, February). Speed Estimation of an Induction Motor Drive Using an Optimized Extended Kalman Filter. *IEEE Transactions on Industrial Electronics*, 49(1), 124–133. doi:10.1109/41.982256

Shi, Y. (2001, May). Particle swarm optimization: developments, applications and resources. *Proceedings of the 2001 congress on evolutionary computation (IEEE Cat. No. 01TH8546)* (Vol. 1, pp. 81-86). IEEE. 10.1109/CEC.2001.934374

Shi, Y. (2014). Developmental swarm intelligence: Developmental learning perspective of swarm intelligence algorithms. [IJSIR]. *International Journal of Swarm Intelligence Research*, 5(1), 36–54. doi:10.4018/ijsir.2014010102

Shi, Y., & Eberhart, R. C. (2001, May). Fuzzy adaptive particle swarm optimization. In *Proceedings of the 2001 congress on evolutionary computation (IEEE Cat. No. 01TH8546)* (Vol. 1, pp. 101-106). IEEE. 10.1109/CEC.2001.934377

Shuai, Z., Sun, Y., Shen, Z. J., Tian, W., Tu, C., Li, Y., & Yin, X. (2016). Microgrid stability: Classification and a review. *Renewable & Sustainable Energy Reviews*, 58, 167–179. doi:10.1016/j.rser.2015.12.201

Si, T., & Ghosh, R. (2015, March). Explosion sparks generation using adaptive transfer function in firework algorithm. *Proceedings 2015 3rd International Conference on Signal Processing, Communication, and Networking (ICSCN)* (pp. 1-9). IEEE. 10.1109/ICSCN.2015.7219917

Siegfried, J. (1982). Origins of Child Psychology: William Preyer. In *The problematic Science* (pp. 300–321). Psychology in Nineteenth-Century Thought.

Silveira, I. F. (2016). *Juegos Serios: Teoría y Práctica*. [Serious Games: Theory and Practice].

Simoes, M., Bose, K., & Spiegel, J. (1997). Fuzzy Logic Based Intelligent Control of a Variable Speed Cage Machine Wind Generation System. *IEEE Transactions on Power Electronics*, 12(1), 87–95. doi:10.1109/63.554173

Simon, D. (2008). Biogeography-based optimization. *IEEE Transactions on Evolutionary Computation*, 12(6), 702–713. doi:10.1109/TEVC.2008.919004

Si, T. (2016). Grammatical Evolution Using Fireworks Algorithm. *Proceedings of Fifth International Conference on Soft Computing for Problem Solving* (pp. 43-55). Springer, Singapore.

Sokolova, M., & Lapalme, G. (2009). A systematic analysis of performance measures for classification tasks. *Information Processing & Management*, 45(4), 427–437. doi:10.1016/j.ipm.2009.03.002

Soler, J., Tenc'e, F., Gaubert, L., & Buche, C. (2013). Data Clustering and Similarity. *Proceedings of the Twenty-Sixth International Florida Artificial Intelligence Research Society Conference*, pp. 492-495. Academic Press.

Song, B., Xu, J., & Xu, L. (2018, July). PSO-based Extended Kalman Filtering for Speed Estimation of an Induction Motor. *Proceedings of the 37th Chinese Control Conference*, Wuhan, China, pp. 3803-3807. 10.23919/ChiCC.2018.8482581

Song, X., Gao, S., Chen, C., & Gao, Z. (2019). Enhanced Fireworks Algorithm-Auto Disturbance Rejection Control Algorithm for Robot Fish Path Tracking. *International Journal of Computers, Communications, & Control, 14*(3), 401–418. doi:10.15837/ijccc.2019.3.3547

Soto, J., & Melin, P. (2015). *Optimization of the Fuzzy Integrators in Ensembles of ANFIS Model for Time Series Prediction: The case of Mackey-Glass*. Paris, France: IFSA-EUSFLAT.

Sreeja, N. K. (2019). A weighted pattern matching approach for classification of imbalanced data with a fireworks-based algorithm for feature selection. *Connection Science, 31*(2), 143–168. doi:10.1080/09540091.2018.1512558

Sreelaja, N. K., & Vijayalakshmi Pai, G. A. (2010, September). Ant Colony Optimization based Approach for efficient Packet Filtering in Firewall. *Applied Soft Computing, 10*(4), 1222–1236. doi:10.1016/j.asoc.2010.03.009

Staunton, J., & Clark, J. A. (2010). Searching for safety violations using Estimation of Distribution Algorithms. In *Proceedings of 2010 Third International Conference on Software Testing, Verification, and Validation Workshops*, 212-221. 10.1109/ICSTW.2010.24

Staunton, J., & Clark, J. A. (2011). Finding short counterexamples in Promela models using Estimation of Distribution Algorithms. In *Proceedings of the 13th Annual Conference on Genetic and Evolutionary Computation*, 1923-1930. 10.1145/2001576.2001834

Storn, R., & Price, K. (1997). Differential evolution–a simple and efficient heuristic for global optimization over continuous spaces. *Journal of Global Optimization, 11*(4), 341–359. doi:10.1023/A:1008202821328

Strumberger, I., Tuba, E., Bacanin, N., Beko, M., & Tuba, M. (2018, July). Bare bones fireworks algorithm for the RFID network planning problem. *Proceedings 2018 IEEE Congress on Evolutionary Computation (CEC)* (pp. 1-8). IEEE. 10.1109/CEC.2018.8477990

Sturges, H. A. (1926). The Choice of a Class Interval. *Journal of the American Statistical Association, 21*(153), 65–66. doi:10.1080/01621459.1926.10502161

Su, T. J., Tsou, T. Y., Wang, S. M., Hoang, V. M., & Pin, K. W. (2016). A hybrid control design of FOPID and FWA for inverted pendulum systems.

Suksri, S., & Kimpan, W. (2016, December). Neural Network training model for weather forecasting using Fireworks Algorithm. *Proceedings 2016 International Computer Science and Engineering Conference (ICSEC)* (pp. 1-7). IEEE.

Sun, L., & Wu, Z. (n.d.). Distribution System Reconfiguration Based on FWA and DLF with DGs. doi:10.1109/ICSEC.2016.7859952

Sun, Y. F., Wang, J. S., & Song, J. D. (2016). An improved fireworks algorithm based on grouping strategy of the shuffled frog leaping algorithm to solve function optimization problems. *Algorithms, 9*(2), 23. doi:10.3390/a9020023

Sun, Y., Kamel, M., Wong, A., & Wang, Y. (2007). Cost-sensitive boosting for classification of imbalanced data. *Pattern Recognition, 40*(12), 3358–3378. doi:10.1016/j.patcog.2007.04.009

Sun, Y., Wong, A. K. C., & Kamel, M. S. (2009). Classification of imbalanced data: A review. *International Journal of Pattern Recognition and Artificial Intelligence, 23*(4), 687–719. doi:10.1142/S0218001409007326

Suo, G., Song, L., Dou, Y., & Cui, Z. (2019, November). Multi-dimensional Short-Term Load Forecasting Based on XGBoost and Fireworks Algorithm. *Proceedings 2019 18th International Symposium on Distributed Computing and Applications for Business Engineering and Science (DCABES)* (pp. 245-248). IEEE. 10.1109/DCABES48411.2019.00068

Su, T. J., Li, T. Y., Wang, S. M., Hoang, V. M., & Chen, Y. F. (2016). A novel method for controller design in engineering education. *World Trans. Eng. Technol. Educ, 14*(2), 288–294.

Su, T. J., Wang, S. M., Li, T. Y., Shih, S. T., & Hoang, V. M. (2016). Design of hybrid sliding mode controller based on fireworks algorithm for nonlinear inverted pendulum systems. *Advances in Mechanical Engineering, 9*(1).

Swider, D. J., & Weber, C. (2007). Extended ARMA Models for Estimating Price Developments on Day- ahead Electricity Markets. *Electric Power Systems Research, 77*(5-6), 583–593. doi:10.1016/j.epsr.2006.05.013

Szklarczyk, D., Gable, A. L., Lyon, D., Junge, A., Wyder, S., Huerta-Cepas, J., ... Bork, P. (2018). STRING v11: Protein–protein association networks with increased coverage, supporting functional discovery in genome-wide experimental datasets. *Nucleic Acids Research, 47*(D1), D607–D613. doi:10.1093/nar/gky1131 PMID:30476243

Taidi, Z., Benameur, L., & Chentoufi, J. A. (2017). A fireworks algorithm for solving travelling salesman problem. *International Journal of Computational Systems Engineering, 3*(3), 157–162. doi:10.1504/IJCSYSE.2017.086740

Takagi, R. (2012). Preliminary evaluation of the energy-saving effects of the introduction of superconducting cables in the power feeding network for DC electric railways using the multi-train power network simulator. *IET Electrical Systems in Transportation, 2*(3), 103–109. doi:10.1049/iet-est.2011.0048

Tamai, T. (2009). Social impact of information system failures. *IEEE Computer, 42*(6), 58–65. doi:10.1109/MC.2009.199

Tamai, T. (2015). Software engineering view of a large-scale system failure and the following lawsuit. *Proceedings of the 2nd IEEE/ACM International Workshop on Software Engineering Research and Industrial Practice*, 18-24. 10.1109/SERIP.2015.12

Tan, Y. (2015). Fireworks algorithm introduction. China/Beijing State: Science Press.

Tan, Y. (2019). *Forum of fireworks algorithms*. Retrieved from https://www.cil.pku.edu.cn/fwa/index.htm

Tan, Y. (2019). Python implementation of fireworks algorithms. Retrieved from https://github.com/cilatpku/firework-algorithm

Tan, Y., & Zheng, S. (2014). *Dynamic Search in Fireworks Algorithm*. Evolutionary Computation (CEC 2014), Beijing, China. Academic Press.

Tan, Y., & Zhu, Y. (2010). Fireworks Algorithm for Optimization. *Proc. First International Conference of Advances in Swarm Intelligence, ICSI 2010*, June 12-15.Beijing, China.

Tan, Y., & Zhu, Y. (2010). Fireworks algorithm for optimization. *Proceedings International Conference in Swarm Intelligence*, (pp. 355-364). Berlin, Germany: Springer.

Tan, Y., & Zhu, Y. (2010). Fireworks algorithm for optimization. *Proceedings of the First International Conference on Advances in Swarm Intelligence*, 355-364.

Tan, Y., & Zhu, Y. (2010, June). Fireworks algorithm for optimization. In *Proceedings International Conference in Swarm Intelligence* (pp. 355-364). Berlin, Germany: Springer.

Tan, Y., & Zhu, Y. (2010, June). Fireworks algorithm for optimization. *Proceedings International conference in swarm intelligence* (pp. 355-364). Berlin, Germany: Springer.

Tan, Y., & Zhu, Y. (2010, June). Fireworks algorithm for optimization. *Proceedings International Conference in Swarm Intelligence* (pp. 355-364). Berlin, Germany: Springer.

Tan, Y., Tan, Y., & Zhu, Y. (2015). *Fireworks Algorithm for Optimization Fireworks Algorithm for Optimization.* (December), 355–364.

Tang, P., Lang, L., Hu, F., & Zhu, D. (2017, July). The design of two-fold redundancy linear arrays in aperture synthesis radiometers. *Proceedings 2017 IEEE International Symposium on Antennas and Propagation & USNC/URSI National Radio Science Meeting* (pp. 149-150). IEEE. 10.1109/APUSNCURSINRSM.2017.8072117

Tang, Y., Zhang, Y. Q., & Chawla, N. (2009). SVMS modeling for highly imbalanced classification. *IEEE Transactions on Systems, Man, and Cybernetics. Part B, Cybernetics, 39*(1), 281–288. doi:10.1109/TSMCB.2008.2002909 PMID:19068445

Tanweer, M. R., Suresh, S., & Sundararajan, N. (2015). Self-regulating particle swarm optimization algorithm. *Information Sciences, 294*, 182–202. doi:10.1016/j.ins.2014.09.053

Tan, Y. (2015). *Fireworks Algorithm.* Heidelberg, Germany: Springer. doi:10.1007/978-3-662-46353-6

Tan, Y., Yu, C., Zheng, S., & Ding, K. (2013). Introduction to fireworks algorithm. [IJSIR]. *International Journal of Swarm Intelligence Research, 4*(4), 39–70. doi:10.4018/ijsir.2013100103

Tan, Y., & Zhu, Y. (2010). *Fireworks Algorithm for Optimization* (pp. 355–364). Berlin, Germany: Springer-Verlag.

Tan, Y., & Zhu, Y. (2010). Fireworks Algorithm for Optimization. *Proceedings of International Conference on Advances in Swarm Intelligence* (2010, pp. 355-364). Springer-Verlag. 10.1007/978-3-642-13495-1_44

Tan, Y., & Zhu, Y. (2010, June). Fireworks algorithm for optimization. *Proceedings International conference in swarm intelligence* (pp. 355-364). Springer, Berlin, Germany.

Tan, Y., & Zhu, Y. C. (2010). Fireworks algorithm for optimization. *Proceedings of The First International Conference on Swarm Intelligence* (pp. 355-364). Beijing, China.

Taowei, C., Yiming, Y., Kun, Z., & Duan, Z. (2018, October). A Membrane-Fireworks Algorithm for Multi-Objective Optimization Problems. *Proceedings 2018 11th International Congress on Image and Signal Processing, BioMedical Engineering and Informatics (CISP-BMEI)* (pp. 1-6). IEEE. 10.1109/CISP-BMEI.2018.8633082

Tao, Y., & Zhao, L. (2018). A novel system for WiFi radio map automatic adaptation and indoor positioning. *IEEE Transactions on Vehicular Technology, 67*(11), 10683–10692. doi:10.1109/TVT.2018.2867065

Tarjan, R. (1972). Depth-first search and linear graph algorithms. *SIAM Journal on Computing, 1*(2), 146–160. doi:10.1137/0201010

Tavcar, A., Kaluza, B., Kvassay, M., Schneider, B., & Gams, M. (2014, August). Surrogate-agent modeling for improved training. In *Proceedings of the Twenty-first European Conference on Artificial Intelligence* (pp. 1103-1104). Academic Press.

Telescaa, L., Bernardib, M., & Rovellib, C. (2005). *Intra-cluster and inter-cluster time correlations in lightning sequences.* Amsterdam, The Netherlands: Physica A, 356, pp. 655–661.

The Hospital For Sick Children. (2010). Efectos psicológicos del desastre sobre los niños [Psychological effects of the Disaster on Children]. Retrieved from https://www.aboutkidshealth.ca/Article?contentid=302&language=Spanish

Tian, G., Liu, C., & Jiang, H. (2019, May). Scheduling Strategy of Space-based Satellite Based on Fireworks Algorithm under Cloud Computing. *Proceedings of the 2019 4th International Conference on Big Data and Computing* (pp. 91-96). ACM. 10.1145/3335484.3335511

Tian, G., Ren, Y., & Zhou, M. (2016). Dual-objective scheduling of rescue vehicles to distinguish forest fires via differential evolution and particle swarm optimization combined algorithm. *IEEE Transactions on Intelligent Transportation Systems*, *17*(11), 3009–3021. doi:10.1109/TITS.2015.2505323

Tian, G., Zhou, M., & Chu, J. (2013). A chance constrained programming approach to determine the optimal disassembly sequence. *IEEE Transactions on Automation Science and Engineering*, *10*(4), 1004–1013. doi:10.1109/TASE.2013.2249663

Tian, G., Zhou, M., Chu, J., Qiang, T., & Hu, H. (2014). Stochastic cost-profit tradeoff model for locating an automotive service enterprise. *IEEE Transactions on Automation Science and Engineering*, *12*(2), 580–587. doi:10.1109/TASE.2013.2297623

Tian, G., Zhou, M., Li, P., Zhang, C., & Jia, H. (2016). Multiobjective optimization models for locating vehicle inspection stations subject to stochastic demand, varying velocity and regional constraints. *IEEE Transactions on Intelligent Transportation Systems*, *17*(7), 1978–1987. doi:10.1109/TITS.2016.2514277

Tian, Z., Guo, M., Wang, C., Xing, L., Wang, L., & Zhang, Y. (2017). Constructing an integrated gene similarity network for the identification of disease genes. *Journal of Biomedical Semantics*, *8*(1), 32. doi:10.118613326-017-0141-1 PMID:29297379

Timm, N., Gruner, S., & Sibanda, P. (2017). Model Checking of Concurrent Software Systems via Heuristic-Guided SAT Solving. *Lecture Notes in Computer Science*, *10522*, 244–259. doi:10.1007/978-3-319-68972-2_16

Ting, D. X., Ming, L. C., & Hua, H. Z. (2018, July). Fireworks Explosion Algorithm for Hybrid Flow Shop Scheduling and Optimization Problem1. [IOP Publishing.]. *IOP Conference Series. Materials Science and Engineering*, *382*(3). doi:10.1088/1757-899X/382/3/032005

Ting, K. M. (2002). An instance-weighting method to induce cost-sensitive trees. *IEEE Transactions on Knowledge and Data Engineering*, *14*(3), 659–665. doi:10.1109/TKDE.2002.1000348

Tizhoosh, H. R. (2005). Opposition-Based Learning: A New Scheme for Machine Intelligence. In *Proceedings of International Conference on Computational Intelligence for Modelling, Control & Automation, & International Conference on Intelligent Agents, Web Technologies, & Internet Commerce.* Vienna, Austria. Academic Press.

Tomas, U. (2016). El Psicoasesor. [The Psychoassessor]. Retrieved from 25 poderes terapéuticos del juego website: http://elpsicoasesor.com/25-poderes-terapeuticos-del-juego/

Tomek, I. (1976). Two modifications of CNN. *IEEE Transactions on Systems, Man, and Cybernetics. Part B, Cybernetics*, *6*(11), 769–772.

Trabelsi, Z., Zhang, L., & Zeidan, S. (2012, October). Firewall packet filtering optimization using statistical traffic awareness test. In *International Conference on Information and Communications Security* (pp. 81-92). Berlin, Germany: Springer. 10.1007/978-3-642-34129-8_8

Tuba, E., Dolicanin, E., & Tuba, M. (2017, July). Guided Fireworks Algorithm Applied to the Maximal Covering Location Problem. *Proceedings International Conference on Swarm Intelligence* (pp. 501-508). Cham, Switzerland: Springer. 10.1007/978-3-319-61824-1_55

Tuba, E., Jovanovic, R., Beko, M., Tallón-Ballesteros, A. J., & Tuba, M. (2018, November). Bare Bones Fireworks Algorithm for Medical Image Compression. *Proceedings International Conference on Intelligent Data Engineering and Automated Learning* (pp. 262-270). Cham, Switzerland: Springer. 10.1007/978-3-030-03496-2_29

Tuba, E., Strumberger, I., Bacanin, N., & Tuba, M. (2018, June). Bare bones fireworks algorithm for capacitated p-median problem. *Proceedings International Conference on Swarm Intelligence* (pp. 283-291). Cham, Switzerland: Springer. 10.1007/978-3-319-93815-8_28

Tuba, E., Strumberger, I., Zivkovic, D., Bacanin, N., & Tuba, M. (2018, May). Rigid Image Registration by Bare Bones Fireworks Algorithm. *Proceedings 2018 6th International Conference on Multimedia Computing and Systems (ICMCS)* (pp. 1-6). IEEE. 10.1109/ICMCS.2018.8525968

Tuba, E., Tuba, I., Dolicanin-Djekic, D., Alihodzic, A., & Tuba, M. (2018, March). Efficient drone placement for wireless sensor networks coverage by bare bones fireworks algorithm. *Proceedings 2018 6th International Symposium on Digital Forensic and Security (ISDFS)* (pp. 1-5). IEEE. 10.1109/ISDFS.2018.8355349

Tuba, E., Tuba, M., & Beko, M. (2016, September). Node localization in ad hoc wireless sensor networks using fireworks algorithm. *Proceedings 2016 5th International Conference on Multimedia Computing and Systems (ICMCS)* (pp. 223-229). IEEE. 10.1109/ICMCS.2016.7905647

Tuba, M., Bacanin, N., & Alihodzic, A. (2015, April 21-22). *Multilevel image thresholding by fireworks algorithm.* Paper presented at the 2015 25th International Conference Radioelektronika (RADIOELEKTRONIKA).

Tuba, M., Bacanin, N., & Alihodzic, A. (2015, April). Multilevel image thresholding by fireworks algorithm. *Proceedings 2015 25th International Conference Radioelektronika (RADIOELEKTRONIKA)* (pp. 326-330). IEEE. 10.1109/RADIOELEK.2015.7129057

Tuba, M., Bacanin, N., & Beko, M. (2015, April). Fireworks algorithm for RFID network planning problem. *Proceedings 2015 25th International Conference Radioelektronika (RADIOELEKTRONIKA)* (pp. 440-444). IEEE. 10.1109/RADIOELEK.2015.7129049

Tuba, V., Alihodzic, A., & Tuba, M. (2017, March). Multi-objective RFID network planning with probabilistic coverage model by guided fireworks algorithm. *Proceedings 2017 10th International Symposium on Advanced Topics in Electrical Engineering (ATEE)* (pp. 882-887). IEEE. 10.1109/ATEE.2017.7905125

Tuba, E., Jovanovic, R., Hrosik, R. C., Alihodzic, A., & Tuba, M. (2018, June). Web Intelligence Data Clustering by Bare Bone Fireworks Algorithm Combined with K-Means. *Proceedings of the 8th International Conference on Web Intelligence, Mining, and Semantics* (p. 7). ACM. 10.1145/3227609.3227650

Tuba, E., Jovanovic, R., & Tuba, M. (2020). Multispectral Satellite Image Classification Based on Bare Bone Fireworks Algorithm. In *Information and Communication Technology for Sustainable Development* (pp. 305–313). Singapore: Springer. doi:10.1007/978-981-13-7166-0_30

Tuba, E., Strumberger, I., Bacanin, N., Jovanovic, R., & Tuba, M. (2019, June). Bare bones fireworks algorithm for feature selection and SVM optimization. *Proceedings 2019 IEEE Congress on Evolutionary Computation (CEC)* (pp. 2207-2214). IEEE. 10.1109/CEC.2019.8790033

Tuba, E., Strumberger, I., Bacanin, N., Zivkovic, D., & Tuba, M. (2019, July). Acute Lymphoblastic Leukemia Cell Detection in Microscopic Digital Images Based on Shape and Texture Features. *Proceedings International Conference on Swarm Intelligence* (pp. 142-151). Springer, Cham. 10.1007/978-3-030-26354-6_14

Tuba, E., Tuba, M., & Beko, M. (2016, June). Support vector machine parameters optimization by enhanced fireworks algorithm. *Proceedings International Conference on Swarm Intelligence* (pp. 526-534). Springer, Cham. 10.1007/978-3-319-41000-5_52

Tuba, E., Tuba, M., & Dolicanin, E. (2017). Adjusted fireworks algorithm applied to retinal image registration. *Studies in Informatics and Control*, 26(1), 33–42. doi:10.24846/v26i1y201704

Tuba, E., Tuba, M., & Simian, D. (2016, September). Wireless sensor network coverage problem using modified fireworks algorithm. *Proceedings 2016 International Wireless Communications and Mobile Computing Conference (IWCMC)* (pp. 696-701). IEEE. 10.1109/IWCMC.2016.7577141

Tuba, E., Tuba, M., Simian, D., & Jovanovic, R. (2017, June). JPEG quantization table optimization by guided fireworks algorithm. *Proceedings International Workshop on Combinatorial Image Analysis* (pp. 294-307). Springer, Cham. 10.1007/978-3-319-59108-7_23

Tung, K. T., & Loan, N. T. B. (2016). Applying Artificial Neural Network Optimized by Fireworks Algorithm for Stock Price Estimation. *ICTACT Journal on Soft Computing, 6*(3).

Ullah, Z., Xu, Z., Zhang, L., Zhang, L., & Ullah, W. (2018). RL- and ANN-based modular path planning controller for resource-constrained robots in the indoor complex dynamic environment. *IEEE Access: Practical Innovations, Open Solutions, 6*, 74557–74568. doi:10.1109/ACCESS.2018.2882875

Ulrich, I., & Borenstein, J. (1998). VFH+: Reliable obstacle avoidance for fast mobile robots. *Proceedings IEEE International Conference on Robotics and Automation, 2*, 1572–1577. doi:10.1109/ROBOT.1998.677362

Van Driel, M. A., Bruggeman, J., Vriend, G., Brunner, H. G., & Leunissen, J. A. (2006). A text-mining analysis of the human phenome. *European Journal of Human Genetics, 14*(5), 535–542. doi:10.1038j.ejhg.5201585 PMID:16493445

Vandoorn, T. L., Vasquez, J. C., De Kooning, J., Guerrero, J. M., & Vandevelde, L. (2013). Microgrids: Hierarchical control and an overview of the control and reserve management strategies. *IEEE Industrial Electronics Magazine, 7*(4), 42–55. doi:10.1109/MIE.2013.2279306

Vanunu, O., Magger, O., Ruppin, E., Shlomi, T., & Sharan, R. (2010). Associating genes and protein complexes with disease via network propagation. *PLoS Computational Biology, 6*(1). doi:10.1371/journal.pcbi.1000641 PMID:20090828

Vardi, M. Y., & Wolper, P. (1986). An automata theoretic approach to automatic program verification. *Proceedings of First Symposium on Logic in Computer Science*, 332-344.

Vasant, P. (2013). *Meta-heuristics optimization algorithms in engineering, business, economics, and finance.* Information Science Reference. doi:10.4018/978-1-4666-2086-5

Wang, B., Xia, X., Meng, H., & Li, T. (2017). Bad-scenario-set robust optimization framework with two objectives for uncertain scheduling systems. *IEEE/CAA Journal of Automatica Sinica, 4*(1), 143-153.

Wang, C., Wang, Y., Yan, L., Ye, Z., Cai, W., & Wu, P. (2019, September). Financial Early Warning of Listed Companies Based on Fireworks Algorithm Optimized Back-Propagation Neural Network. *Proceedings 2019 10th IEEE International Conference on Intelligent Data Acquisition and Advanced Computing Systems: Technology and Applications (IDAACS)* (Vol. 2, pp. 927-932). IEEE. 10.1109/IDAACS.2019.8924376

Wang, C., Wu, P., Yan, L., Zhou, F., & Cai, W. (2018, September). Image retrieval based on fireworks algorithm optimizing convolutional neural network. In *2018 IEEE 4th International Symposium on Wireless Systems within the International Conferences on Intelligent Data Acquisition and Advanced Computing Systems (IDAACS-SWS)* (pp. 53-56). IEEE. 10.1109/IDAACS-SWS.2018.8525760

Wang, D. D., Kai, Y., He, Z. J., Yuan, Y. Q., & Zhang, J. (2018). Application Research Based on GA-FWA in Prediction of Sintering Burning Through Point. DEStech Transactions on Computer Science and Engineering, (ccme).

Wang, L. (2012). Dynamic analysis of a microgrid system for supplying electrical loads in a sailing boat. *Proceedings of 2012 IEEE Power and Energy Society General Meeting.* Doi:10.1109/PESGM.2012.6344601

Wang, S., & Yao, X. (2009). Diversity analysis on imbalanced data sets by using ensemble models. *Proceedings of IEEE Symposium Series on Computational Intelligence and Data Mining (IEEE CIDM 2009)*, pp. 324–331. 10.1109/CIDM.2009.4938667

Wang, J., Pan, B., Tang, C., & Ding, Q. (2019). Construction Method and Performance Analysis of Chaotic S-Box Based on Fireworks Algorithm. *International Journal of Bifurcation and Chaos in Applied Sciences and Engineering, 29*(12). doi:10.1142/S021812741950158X

Wang, L., Liu, J., & Qian, F. (2019). A New Modeling Approach for the Probability Density Distribution Function of Wind power Fluctuation. *Sustainability, 11*(19), 5512. doi:10.3390u11195512

Wang, P., & Billinton, R. (2001). Reliability beneðt analysis of adding WTG to a distribution system. *IEEE Transactions on Energy Conversion, 16*(2), 134–139. doi:10.1109/60.921464

Wang, P., Ding, Z., Jiang, C., Zhou, M., & Zheng, Y. (2015). Automatic web service composition based on uncertainty execution effects. *IEEE Transactions on Services Computing, 9*(4), 551–565. doi:10.1109/TSC.2015.2412943

Wang, S., Li, Y., & Yang, H. (2017). Self-adaptive differential evolution algorithm with improved mutation mode. *Applied Intelligence, 47*(3), 1–15. doi:10.1007/s10489-017-0914-3

Wang, X., Peng, H., Deng, C., Li, L., & Zheng, L. (2018, October). An Improved Firefly Algorithm Hybrid with Fireworks. *Proceedings International Symposium on Intelligence Computation and Applications* (pp. 27-37). Springer, Singapore.

Wang, X., Peng, H., Deng, C., Li, L., & Zheng, L. (2019). An improved firefly algorithm hybrid with fireworks. *Proceedings of 10th International Symposium on Intelligence Computation and Applications* (pp. 27-37). Jiujiang, China. 10.1007/978-981-13-6473-0_3

Wang, Y., & Liu, J. (2019, June). A Sparse Fireworks Algorithm for Gene Regulatory Network Reconstruction based on Fuzzy Cognitive Maps. *Proceedings 2019 IEEE Congress on Evolutionary Computation (CEC)* (pp. 1188-1194). IEEE. 10.1109/CEC.2019.8790068

Wang, Y., Zhang, M. X., & Zheng, Y. J. (2017, July). A hyper-heuristic method for UAV search planning. *Proceedings International Conference on Swarm Intelligence* (pp. 454-464). Springer, Cham. 10.1007/978-3-319-61833-3_48

Wang, Z., Yu, G., Kang, Y., Zhao, Y., & Qu, Q. (2014). Breast tumor detection in digital mammography based on extreme learning machine. *Neurocomputing, 128*(5), 175–184. doi:10.1016/j.neucom.2013.05.053

Wang, Z., Zhu, Q., Huang, M., & Yang, B. (2017). Optimization of economic/environmental operation management for microgrids by using hybrid fireworks algorithm. *International Transactions on Electrical Energy Systems, 27*(12). doi:10.1002/etep.2429

Wayne, H. (2018). *Practical TLA+: Planning Driven Development.* Apress. doi:10.1007/978-1-4842-3829-5

Wei, Y., Song, K. S., & Kim, D. S. (2014). Message oriented management and analysis tool for naval combat systems. *IFAC Proceedings, 47*(3), 10524-10528.

Wei, X., Liu, L., Wang, Y., & Yang, Y. (2018). Reentry trajectory optimization for a hypersonic vehicle based on an improved adaptive fireworks algorithm. *International Journal of Aerospace Engineering, 2018*, 2018. doi:10.1155/2018/8793908

Wei, Z., Wang, L., Lyu, Z., Shi, L., Li, M., & Wei, X. (2018, June). A multi-objective algorithm for joint energy replenishment and data collection in wireless rechargeable sensor networks. *Proceedings International Conference on Wireless Algorithms, Systems, and Applications* (pp. 497-508). Springer, Cham. 10.1007/978-3-319-94268-1_41

Wilson, D. R., & Martinez, T. R. (2000). Reduction techniques for instance-based learning algorithms. *Machine Learning*, *38*(3), 257–286. doi:10.1023/A:1007626913721

Wolpert, D. H., & Macready, W. G. (1997). No free lunch theorems for optimization. Evolutional Computational, pp. 67–82. Piscataway, NJ: IEEE Trans. doi:10.1109/4235.585893

Wu, B. Y. (2006). On the intercluster distance of a tree metric. Theoretical Computer Science, 369, pp. 136–141. Amsterdam, The Netherlands: Elsevier. doi:10.1016/j.tcs.2006.07.056

Wu, H., Li, H., Xiao, R., & Liu, J. (2018). Modeling and simulation of dynamic ant colony's labor division for task allocation of UAV swarm. *Physica A*, *491*, 127–141. doi:10.1016/j.physa.2017.08.094

Xia, C., Wei, Z., Lyu, Z., Wang, L., Liu, F., & Feng, L. (2018, October). A novel mixed-variable fireworks optimization algorithm for path and time sequence optimization in WRSNs. *Proceedings International Conference on Communications and Networking in China* (pp. 24-34). Springer, Cham.

Xia, H., Chen, H., Yang, Z., Lin, F., & Wang, B. (2015). Optimal energy management, location and size for stationary energy storage system in a metro line based on genetic algorithm. *Energies*, *8*(10), 11618–11640. doi:10.3390/en81011618

Xiang, Z., Yang, Y., Ma, X., & Ding, W. (2003). Microarray expression profiling: Analysis and applications. *Current Opinion in Drug Discovery & Development*, *6*(3), 384–395. PMID:12833672

Xiao, Y., Zhang, J., & Deng, L. (2017). Prediction of lncRNA-protein interactions using HeteSim scores based on heterogeneous networks. *Scientific Reports*, *7*(1), 3664. doi:10.103841598-017-03986-1 PMID:28623317

Xiao, Z., Tian, B., & Lu, X. (2019). Locating the critical slip surface in a slope stability analysis by enhanced fireworks algorithm. *Cluster Computing*, *22*(1), 719–729. doi:10.100710586-017-1196-6

Xie, M., Hwang, T., & Kuang, R. (2012). Prioritizing disease genes by bi-random walk. *Proceedings Pacific-Asia Conference on Knowledge Discovery and Data Mining*. Berlin, Germany: Springer.

Xie, C., Yuan, J., Li, H., Li, M., Zhao, G., Bu, D., ... Zhao, Y. (2013). NONCODEv4: Exploring the world of long noncoding RNA genes. *Nucleic Acids Research*, *42*(D1), D98–D103. doi:10.1093/nar/gkt1222 PMID:24285305

Xie, S., Li, H., Yang, C., & Yao, S. (2018). Crashworthiness optimisation of a composite energy-absorbing structure for subway vehicles based on hybrid particle swarm optimisation. *Structural and Multidisciplinary Optimization*, *58*(5), 2291–2308. doi:10.100700158-018-2022-3

Xing, B., & Gao, W.-J. (2016). *Innovative Computational Intelligence: A Rough Guide to 134 Clever Algorithms*. Springer Publishing Company, Inc.

Xin, J., Chen, G., & Hai, Y. (2009, April). A particle swarm optimizer with multi-stage linearly-decreasing inertia weight. *Proceedings 2009 International Joint Conference on Computational Sciences and Optimization* (Vol. 1, pp. 505-508). IEEE. 10.1109/CSO.2009.420

Xiong, J., Cheng, Z., Gao, J., Wang, Y., Liu, L., & Yang, Y. (2019, June). Design of LPV Control System Based on Intelligent Optimization. *Proceedings 2019 Chinese Control and Decision Conference (CCDC)* (pp. 2160-2165). IEEE. 10.1109/CCDC.2019.8832439

Xue, Y., Zhuang, Y., Meng, X., & Zhang, Y. (2013). Self-adaptive, learning-based ensemble algorithm for solving matrix eigenvalues.

Xue, J. J., Wang, Y., Li, H., Meng, X. F., & Xiao, J. Y. (2016). Advanced fireworks algorithm and its application research in PID parameters tuning. *Mathematical Problems in Engineering*, *2016*, 2016. doi:10.1155/2016/2534632

Xue, J. J., Wang, Y., Li, H., & Xiao, J. Y. (2016, June). Discrete fireworks algorithm for aircraft mission planning. *Proceedings International Conference on Swarm Intelligence* (pp. 544-551). Springer, Cham. 10.1007/978-3-319-41000-5_54

Xue, J., Wang, Y., & Xiao, J. (2017). Uncertain bilevel knapsack problem and its solution. *Journal of Systems Engineering and Electronics, 28*(4), 717–724. doi:10.21629/JSEE.2017.04.11

Xue, Y., Zhao, B., & Ma, T. (2016). Performance analysis for clustering algorithms. *International Journal of Computing Science and Mathematics, 7*(5), 485. doi:10.1504/IJCSM.2016.080089

Xue, Y., Zhao, B., & Ma, T. (2016, October). Classification based on fireworks algorithm. *Proceedings International Conference on Bio-Inspired Computing: Theories and Applications* (pp. 35-40). Springer, Singapore.

Xue, Y., Zhao, B., Ma, T., & Liu, A. X. (2018). An evolutionary classification method based on fireworks algorithm. *IJBIC, 11*(3), 149–158. doi:10.1504/IJBIC.2018.091747

Xue, Y., Zhao, B., Ma, T., & Pang, W. (2018). A Self-Adaptive Fireworks Algorithm for Classification Problems. *IEEE Access : Practical Innovations, Open Solutions, 6*, 44406–44416. doi:10.1109/ACCESS.2018.2858441

Xue, Y., Zhao, B., Ma, T., & Pang, W. (2018). A self-adaptive fireworks algorithm for classification problems. *IEEE Access: Practical Innovations, Open Solutions, 6*, 44406–44416. doi:10.1109/ACCESS.2018.2858441

Yan, B., Zhang, S., & Sun, J. (2008, October). A service-oriented air combat simulation system. In *2008 Asia Simulation Conference-7th International Conference on System Simulation and Scientific Computing* (pp. 192-199). IEEE. 10.1109/ASC-ICSC.2008.4675354

Yang, A. (2006). *A networked multi-agent combat model: Emergence explained.* University of New South Wales, Australian Defence Force Academy, School of Information Technology and Electrical Engineering.

Yang, J., Wang, W., Wang, H., & Yu, P. (2002). /spl delta/-clusters: capturing subspace correlation in a large data set. *Proceedings 18th International Conference on Data Engineering.* 10.1109/ICDE.2002.994771

Yang, S. X., & Luo, C. (2004). A Neural Network Approach to Complete Coverage Path Planning. *IEEE Transactions on Systems, Man, and Cybernetics. Part B, Cybernetics, 34*(1), 718–725. doi:10.1109/TSMCB.2003.811769 PMID:15369113

Yang, W., & Ke, L. (2019). An improved fireworks algorithm for the capacitated vehicle routing problem. *Frontiers of Computer Science, 13*(3), 552–564. doi:10.100711704-017-6418-9

Yang, W., Zhang, C., & Mu, B. (2015). Data-intensive service mashup based on game theory and hybrid fireworks optimization algorithm in the cloud. *Informatica (Vilnius), 39*(4).

Yang, X.-S. (2010). *Nature-inspired metaheuristic algorithms.* Luniver Press.

Yang, X.-S. (2014). *Nature-inspired optimization algorithms.* Elsevier.

Yang, X., & Tan, Y. (2014, October). Sample index-based encoding for clustering using evolutionary computation. *Proceedings International Conference in Swarm Intelligence* (pp. 489-498). Springer, Cham. 10.1007/978-3-319-11857-4_55

Yan, M., Handong, Z., & Wei, Z. (2019). Research on Intelligent Minefield Attack Decision Based on Adaptive Fireworks Algorithm. *Arabian Journal for Science and Engineering, 44*(3), 2487–2496. doi:10.100713369-018-3159-5

Ye, W., & Wen, J. (2017, December). Adaptive fireworks algorithm based on simulated annealing. *Proceedings 2017 13th International Conference on Computational Intelligence and Security (CIS)* (pp. 371-375). IEEE. 10.1109/CIS.2017.00087

Ye, S., Ma, H., Xu, S., Yang, W., & Fei, M. (2017). An effective fireworks algorithm for warehouse-scheduling problem. *Transactions of the Institute of Measurement and Control, 39*(1), 75–85. doi:10.1177/0142331215600047

Yet, X., Li, J., Xu, B., & Tan, Y. (2018, July). Which Mapping Rule in the Fireworks Algorithm is Better for Large Scale Optimization. *Proceedings 2018 IEEE Congress on Evolutionary Computation (CEC)* (pp. 1-8). IEEE.

Yin, X., Li, X., Liu, L., & Wang, Y. (2017, July). Improved fireworks algorithm and its application in PID parameters tuning. *Proceedings 2017 36th Chinese Control Conference (CCC)* (pp. 9841-9846). IEEE. 10.23919/ChiCC.2017.8028926

Ying, T., & Zhu, Y. (2010). Fireworks Algorithm for Optimization. Proceedings Advances in Swarm Intelligence, First International Conference, ICSI 2010, Part I. Beijing, China, June 12-15.

Yin, L., Qiu, J., & Gao, S. (2018). Biclustering of gene expression data using Cuckoo Search and genetic algorithm. *International Journal of Pattern Recognition and Artificial Intelligence, 32*(11). doi:10.1142/S0218001418500398

Yin, X., Wei, X., Liu, L., & Wang, Y. (2018). Improved hybrid fireworks algorithm-based parameter optimization in high-order sliding mode control of hypersonic vehicles. *Complexity, 2018*, 2018. doi:10.1155/2018/9098151

Yongge, W. U. (2013). Function of lncRNAs and approaches to lncRNA-protein interactions. *Science China. Life Sciences, 56*(10), 876–885. doi:10.100711427-013-4553-6 PMID:24091684

Yousefian, R., Rafe, V., & Rahmani, M. (2014). A heuristic solution for model checking graph transformation systems. *Applied Soft Computing, 24*(C), 169–180. doi:10.1016/j.asoc.2014.06.055

Yu, C., Kelley, L. C., & Tan, Y. (2015, May). Dynamic search fireworks algorithm with covariance mutation for solving the CEC 2015 learning based competition problems. *Proceedings 2015 IEEE Congress on Evolutionary Computation (CEC)* (pp. 1106-1112). IEEE. 10.1109/CEC.2015.7257013

Yu, C., Kelley, L. C., & Tan, Y. (2016, July). Cooperative framework fireworks algorithm with covariance mutation. *Proceedings 2016 IEEE Congress on Evolutionary Computation (CEC)* (pp. 1196-1203). IEEE. 10.1109/CEC.2016.7743923

Yu, C., Kelley, L., Zheng, S., & Tan, Y. (2014, July). Fireworks algorithm with differential mutation for solving the CEC 2014 competition problems. *Proceedings 2014 IEEE Congress on Evolutionary Computation (CEC)* (pp. 3238-3245). IEEE. 10.1109/CEC.2014.6900590

Yu, C., Li, J., & Tan, Y. (2014, October). Improve enhanced fireworks algorithm with differential mutation. *Proceedings 2014 IEEE International Conference on Systems, Man, and Cybernetics (SMC)* (pp. 264-269). IEEE. 10.1109/SMC.2014.6973918

Yu, C., & Tan, Y. (2015, May). Fireworks algorithm with covariance mutation. *Proceedings 2015 IEEE Congress on Evolutionary Computation (CEC)* (pp. 1250-1256). IEEE. 10.1109/CEC.2015.7257032

Yu, G., Li, F., Qin, Y., Bo, X., Wu, Y., & Wang, S. (2010). GOSemSim: An R package for measuring semantic similarity among GO terms and gene products. *Bioinformatics (Oxford, England), 26*(7), 976–978. doi:10.1093/bioinformatics/btq064 PMID:20179076

Yu, J., & Takagi, H. (2017, July). Acceleration for fireworks algorithm based on amplitude reduction strategy and local optima-based selection strategy. *Proceedings International Conference on Swarm Intelligence* (pp. 477-484). Springer, Cham. 10.1007/978-3-319-61824-1_52

Yu, J., Takagi, H., & Tan, Y. (2018). Multi-layer Explosion Based Fireworks Algorithm. *J Swarm Intel Evol Comput, 7*(173), 2.

Yu, J., Takagi, H., & Tan, Y. (2018). Multi-layer Explosion-Based Fireworks Algorithm. *International Journal of Swarm Intelligence and Evolutionary Computation, 7*(3), 1–9. doi:10.4172/2090-4908.1000173

Yu, J., Takagi, H., & Tan, Y. (2018, June). Accelerating the Fireworks Algorithm with an Estimated Convergence Point. *Proceedings International Conference on Swarm Intelligence* (pp. 263-272). Springer, Cham. 10.1007/978-3-319-93815-8_26

Yu, J., Takagi, H., & Tan, Y. (2019). Fireworks Algorithm for Multimodal Optimization Using a Distance-based Exclusive Strategy. *Proceedings of 2019 IEEE Congress on Evolutionary Computation* (pp. 2216-2221). Wellington, New Zealand. 10.1109/CEC.2019.8790312

Yu, J., Tan, Y., & Takagi, H. (2018, July). Scouting strategy for biasing fireworks algorithm search to promising directions. *Proceedings of the Genetic and Evolutionary Computation Conference Companion* (pp. 99-100). ACM. 10.1145/3205651.3205740

Yu, L., Wang, S., & Lai, K. K. (2009). A neural-network-based nonlinear metamodeling approach to financial time series forecasting. *Applied Soft Computing*, *9*(2), 563–574. doi:10.1016/j.asoc.2008.08.001

Yu, X., Binping, Z., & Tinghuai, M., & X., L. A. (2018). An evolutionary classification method based on fireworks algorithm. *International Journal of Bio-inspired Computation*.

Zadeh, L. A. (1989). Knowledge Representation in Fuzzy Logic. *IEEE Transactions on Knowledge and Data Engineering*, *1*(1). doi:10.1109/69.43406

Zadrozny, B., & Elkan, C. (2001). Learning and making decisions when costs and probabilities are both unknown. *Proceedings of the 7th International Conference on Knowledge Discovery and Data Mining (KDD01)*, pp. 204–213. 10.1145/502512.502540

Zadrozny, B., Langford, J., & Abe, N. (2003). Cost-sensitive learning by cost-proportionate example weighting. *Proceedings of the 3rd International Conference of Data Mining*, pp. 435–442. Melbourne, FL. 10.1109/ICDM.2003.1250950

Zalasiński, M., Łapa, K., & Cpałka, K. (2018). Prediction of values of the dynamic signature features. *Expert Systems with Applications*, *104*, 86–96. doi:10.1016/j.eswa.2018.03.028

Zambrano-Bigiarini, M., Clerc, M., & Rojas, R. (2013). Standard particle swarm optimization 2011 at CEC2013: a baseline for future PSO improvements. In *Proceedings of the 2013 IEEE Congress on Evolutionary Computation*, pp. 2337-2344, Cancun, Mexico. 10.1109/CEC.2013.6557848

Zhan, D., & Xie, C. (2018). An Improved Multi-Objective Fireworks Algorithm. *Proceedings of 9th International Symposium on Intelligence Computation and Applications* (pp. 204-218). Guangzhou, China.

Zhang, B., Zheng, Y.-J., Zhang, M.-X., & Chen, S.-Y. (2017). Fireworks algorithm with enhanced fireworks interaction. *IEEE/ACM Transactions on Computational Biology and Bioinformatics (TCBB)*, *14*(1), 42-55.

Zhang, J., & Zhang, H. (2018, July). An Improved Back Propagation Neural Network Forecasting Model Using Variation Fireworks Algorithm for Short-time Traffic Flow. *Proceedings 2018 13th World Congress on Intelligent Control and Automation (WCICA)* (pp. 1085-1090). IEEE. 10.1109/WCICA.2018.8630368

Zhang, T., Yue, Q., Zhao, X., & Liu, G. (n.d.). An improved firework algorithm for hardware/software partitioning. Applied Intelligence, 49(3), 950–962.

Zhang, B., Zhang, M. X., & Zheng, Y. J. (2014, July). A hybrid biogeography-based optimization and fireworks algorithm. *Proceedings 2014 IEEE Congress on Evolutionary Computation (CEC)* (pp. 3200-3206). IEEE. 10.1109/CEC.2014.6900289

Zhang, B., Zhang, M., & Zheng, Y. J. (2014, October). Improving enhanced fireworks algorithm with new gaussian explosion and population selection strategies. *Proceedings International Conference in Swarm Intelligence* (pp. 53-63). Springer, Cham. 10.1007/978-3-319-11857-4_7

Zhang, B., Zheng, Y. J., Zhang, M. X., & Chen, S. Y. (2017). Fireworks algorithm with enhanced fireworks interaction. [TCBB]. *IEEE/ACM Transactions on Computational Biology and Bioinformatics, 14*(1), 42–55. doi:10.1109/TCBB.2015.2446487 PMID:28182542

Zhang, H., Kou, G., & Peng, Y. (2019). Soft consensus cost models for group decision making and economic interpretations. *European Journal of Operational Research.*

Zhang, J., & Li, W. (2019, July). Last-Position Elimination-Based Fireworks Algorithm for Function Optimization. *Proceedings International Conference on Swarm Intelligence* (pp. 267-275). Springer, Cham. 10.1007/978-3-030-26369-0_25

Zhang, J., Li, Z., Wang, C., Zang, D., & Zhou, M. (2016). Approximate simulation budget allocation for subset ranking. *IEEE Transactions on Control Systems Technology, 25*(1), 358–365. doi:10.1109/TCST.2016.2539329

Zhang, J., Wang, C., Zang, D., & Zhou, M. (2015). Incorporation of optimal computing budget allocation for ordinal optimization into learning automata. *IEEE Transactions on Automation Science and Engineering, 13*(2), 1008–1017. doi:10.1109/TASE.2015.2450535

Zhang, J., Wang, C., & Zhou, M. (2014). Fast and epsilon-optimal discretized pursuit learning automata. *IEEE Transactions on Cybernetics, 45*(10), 2089–2099. doi:10.1109/TCYB.2014.2365463 PMID:25415995

Zhang, J., Xu, L., Li, J., Kang, Q., & Zhou, M. (2014, October). Integrating particle swarm optimization with learning automata to solve optimization problems in noisy environment. *Proceedings 2014 IEEE International Conference on Systems, Man, and Cybernetics (SMC)* (pp. 1432-1437). IEEE. 10.1109/SMC.2014.6974116

Zhang, J., Zhang, L., Wang, C., & Zhou, M. (2016). Approximately Optimal Computing Budget Allocation for Selection of the Best and Worst Designs. *IEEE Transactions on Automatic Control, 62*(7), 3249–3261. doi:10.1109/TAC.2016.2628158

Zhang, J., Zhu, S., & Zhou, M. (2017, July). From Resampling to Non-resampling: A Fireworks Algorithm-Based Framework for Solving Noisy Optimization Problems. *Proceedings International Conference on Swarm Intelligence* (pp. 485-492). Springer, Cham. 10.1007/978-3-319-61824-1_53

Zhang, L., & Wang, C. (2019, June). A Spectrum Allocation Algorithm Based on Non-cooperative Game. [IOP Publishing.]. *Journal of Physics: Conference Series, 1213*(3). doi:10.1088/1742-6596/1213/3/032026

Zhang, M., Yuan, Y., Wang, R., & Cheng, W. (2018). Recognition of mixture control chart patterns based on fusion feature reduction and fireworks algorithm-optimized MSVM. *Pattern Analysis & Applications*, 1–12.

Zhang, Q., & Li, H. (2007). MOEA/D: A multiobjective evolutionary algorithm based on decomposition. *IEEE Transactions on Evolutionary Computation, 11*(6), 712–731. doi:10.1109/TEVC.2007.892759

Zhang, S., Zhou, Y., Li, Z., & Pan, W. (2016). Grey Wolf optimizer for unmanned combat aerial vehicle path planning. *Advances in Engineering Software, 99*, 121–136. doi:10.1016/j.advengsoft.2016.05.015

Zhang, T., Ke, L., Li, J., Li, J., Li, Z., & Huang, J. (2016, July). Fireworks algorithm for the satellite link scheduling problem in the navigation constellation. *Proceedings 2016 IEEE Congress on Evolutionary Computation (CEC)* (pp. 4029-4037). IEEE. 10.1109/CEC.2016.7744301

Zhang, T., & Liu, Z. (2017). Fireworks algorithm for mean-VaR/CVaR models. *Physica A, 483*, 1–8. doi:10.1016/j.physa.2017.04.036

Zhang, W., Qu, Q., Zhang, Y., & Wang, W. (2018). The linear neighborhood propagation method for predicting long non-coding RNA–protein interactions. *Neurocomputing, 273*(1), 526–534. doi:10.1016/j.neucom.2017.07.065

Zhang, X., & Hu, Y. (2019, June). Multiconstrained routing based on artificial bee colony algorithm and dynamic fireworks algorithm. [IOP Publishing.]. *Journal of Physics: Conference Series, 1237*(2). doi:10.1088/1742-6596/1237/2/022058

Zhang, Y., Lei, X., & Tan, Y. (2017). Firefly Clustering Method for Mining Protein Complexes. *Proceedings International Conference on Swarm Intelligence.* 10.1007/978-3-319-61824-1_65

Zhang, Y., Liu, J., Zhou, H., Guo, K., & Tang, F. (n.d.). Intelligent Reconfiguration for Distributed Power Network with Multivariable Renewable Generation. *Proceedings* 2018 *Asian Conference on Energy, Power, and Transportation Electrification (ACEPT)* (pp. 1-5). IEEE. 10.1109/ACEPT.2018.8610870

Zhao, H., Zhang, C., & Ning, J. (n.d.). A core firework updating information guided dynamic fireworks algorithm for global optimization. *Soft Computing*, 1-27.

Zhao, N., Roberts, C., Hillmansen, S., Tian, Z., Weston, P., & Chen, L. (2017). An integrated metro operation optimization to minimize energy consumption. *Transportation Research Part C, Emerging Technologies, 75*, 168–182. doi:10.1016/j.trc.2016.12.013

Zhao, X., Li, R., Zuo, X., & Tan, Y. (2017, July). Elite-Leading Fireworks Algorithm. *Proceedings International Conference on Swarm Intelligence* (pp. 493-500). Springer, Cham.

Zhao, Y., Chen, S., & Chen, T. (2017). K-means clustering method based on artificial immune system in scientific research project management in universities. *International Journal of Computing Science and Mathematics, 8*(2), 129–137. doi:10.1504/IJCSM.2017.083746

Zhao, Z. G., Zhang, S. G., Sun, J. B., & Yan, B. (2012). Service-oriented air combat simulation architecture. *Journal of Beijing Institute of Technology, 21*(3), 408–414.

Zheng, S., & Tan, Y. (2013, March). A unified distance measure scheme for orientation coding in identification. *Proceedings 2013 IEEE Third international conference on information science and technology (ICIST)* (pp. 979-985). IEEE. 10.1109/ICIST.2013.6747701

Zheng, S., Li, J., Janecek, A., & Tan, Y. (2017). A cooperative framework for fireworks algorithm. *IEEE/ACM Transactions on Computational Biology and Bioinformatics (TCBB), 14*(1), 27-41.

Zheng, S., Janecek, A., Li, J., & Tan, Y. (2014, July). Dynamic search in fireworks algorithm. *Proceedings 2014 IEEE Congress on evolutionary computation (CEC)* (pp. 3222-3229). IEEE. 10.1109/CEC.2014.6900485

Zheng, S., Janecek, A., & Tan, Y. (2013, June). Enhanced fireworks algorithm. *Proceedings 2013 IEEE Congress on evolutionary computation* (pp. 2069-2077). IEEE.

Zheng, S., Janecek, A., & Tan, Y. (2013, June). Enhanced fireworks algorithm. *Proceedings 2013 IEEE Congress on evolutionary computation* (pp. 2069-2077). IEEE. 10.1109/CEC.2013.6557813

Zheng, S., Li, J., Janecek, A., & Tan, Y. (2017). A cooperative framework for fireworks algorithm. [TCBB]. *IEEE/ACM Transactions on Computational Biology and Bioinformatics, 14*(1), 27–41. doi:10.1109/TCBB.2015.2497227 PMID:26552094

Zheng, S., Li, J., & Tan, Y. (2014). Adaptive fireworks algorithm. In *Proceedings of the 2014 IEEE Congress on Evolutionary Computation* (2014, pp. 3214-3221). Beijing, China.

Zheng, S., Liu, L., Yu, C., Li, J., & Tan, Y. (2014, October). Fireworks algorithm and its variants for solving ICSI2014 competition problems. *Proceedings International Conference in Swarm Intelligence* (pp. 442-451). Springer, Cham. 10.1007/978-3-319-11897-0_50

Zheng, S., Yu, C., Li, J., & Tan, Y. (2015, May). Exponentially decreased dimension number strategy based dynamic search fireworks algorithm for solving CEC2015 competition problems. *Proceedings 2015 IEEE Congress on Evolutionary Computation (CEC)* (pp. 1083-1090). IEEE. 10.1109/CEC.2015.7257010

Zheng, W., Qian, Y., & Lu, H. (2013). Text categorization based on regularization extreme learning machine. *Neural Computing & Applications*, 22(3-4), 447–456. doi:10.100700521-011-0808-y

Zheng, Y. J., Song, Q., & Chen, S. Y. (2013). Multiobjective fireworks optimization for variable-rate fertilization in oil crop production. *Applied Soft Computing*, 13(11), 4253–4263. doi:10.1016/j.asoc.2013.07.004

Zheng, Y. J., Xu, X. L., Ling, H. F., & Chen, S. Y. (2015). A hybrid fireworks optimization method with differential evolution operators. *Neurocomputing*, 148, 75–82. doi:10.1016/j.neucom.2012.08.075

Zheng, Y., Wang, L., & Xi, P. (2018, August). Improved Ant Colony Algorithm for Multi-Agent Path Planning in Dynamic Environment. *Proceedings 2018 International Conference on Sensing, Diagnostics, Prognostics, and Control (SDPC)* (pp. 732-737). IEEE. 10.1109/SDPC.2018.8664885

Zhou, X., Zhao, Q., & Zhang, D. (2019, July). Discrete Fireworks Algorithm for Welding Robot Path Planning. [IOP Publishing.]. *Journal of Physics: Conference Series*, 1267(1). doi:10.1088/1742-6596/1267/1/012003

Zhou, Z. H., & Liu, X. Y. (2006). Training cost-sensitive neural networks with methods addressing the class imbalance problem. *IEEE Transactions on Knowledge and Data Engineering*, 18(1), 63–77. doi:10.1109/TKDE.2006.17

Zhu, Q. B., Wang, Z. Y., & Huang, M. (2016). Fireworks algorithm with gravitational search operator. *Kongzhi yu Juece/ Control and Decision, 31*(10), 1853-1859. (in Chinese).

Zhu, R., Li, G., Liu, J.-X., Dai, L.-Y., & Guo, Y. (2019). ACCBN: ant-Colony-clustering-based bipartite network method for predicting long non-coding RNA–protein interactions. *BMC Bioinformatics*, 20(1), 16. doi:10.118612859-018-2586-3 PMID:30626319

Zong, W., & Huang, G. B. (2011). Face recognition based on extreme learning machine. *Neurocomputing*, 74(16), 2541–2551. doi:10.1016/j.neucom.2010.12.041

About the Contributors

Ying Tan is a full professor of Peking University, director of Computational Intelligence Laboratory at Peking University, and the inventor of Fireworks Algorithm (FWA). He worked as a professor of Faculty of Design, Kyushu University, Japan, in 2018, at Columbia University as senior research fellow in 2017, and at Chinese University of Hong Kong as research fellow, and at University of Science and Technology of China in 2005-2006 as a professor under the 100-talent program of CAS. He serves as the Editor-in-Chief of IASEI Transactions on Swarm Intelligence, and International Journal of Computational Intelligence and Pattern Recognition (IJCIPR), the Associate Editor of IEEE Transactions on Cybernetics (CYB), IEEE Transactions on Neural Networks and Learning System (NNLS), Neural Networks, International Journal of Swarm Intelligence Research (IJSIR), etc. He also served as an Editor of Springer's Lecture Notes on Computer Science (LNCS) for 40+ volumes, and Guest Editors of several referred Journals, including IEEE/ACM Transactions on Computational Biology and Bioinformatics, Information Science, Neurocomputing, Natural Computing, Swarm and Evolutionary Optimization, etc. He is the founder general chair of the ICSI International Conference series since 2010 and the DMBD conference series since 2016. He won the 2nd-Class Natural Science Award of China in 2009 and 2nd-Class Natural Science Award of Ministry of Education of China in 2019 and many best paper awards. His research interests include swarm intelligence, fireworks algorithm, machine learning and data mining, intelligent information processing for information security and financial prediction, etc. He has published more than 350+ papers in refereed journals and conferences in these areas, and authored/co-authored 13 books, including "Fireworks Algorithm" by Springer in 2015, and "GPU-based Parallel Implementation of Swarm Intelligence Algorithms" by Morgan Kaufmann (Elsevier) in 2016, and received 5 invention patents.

Saad Mohammad Abdullah received his BSc Engineering and MSc Engineering degree in Electrical and Electronic Engineering from Islamic University of Technology (IUT), Gazipur, Bangladesh in the years 2016 and 2019, respectively. He is serving as a Lecturer in the Department of EEE, IUT since 2017. His research interests include nature-inspired optimization algorithms, power system stability and control, microgrid systems, renewable energy integration and wireless power transfer.

* * *

Ashik Ahmed completed his MSc and PhD in Electrical and Electronic Engineering (EEE) from King Fahd University of Petroleum and Minerals, Dharhan, Saudi Arabia, and Islamic University of Technology (IUT), Gazipur, Bangladesh in the years 2010 and 2016, respectively. He completed his undergraduate level of study from the EEE department of IUT, Gazipur, Bangladesh in 2003. He joined the university as a Lecturer in the department of EEE in 2004 and got promoted to Professor in January 2020 where he is serving currently. Till date, he has published 15 peer-reviewed journal articles and several conference papers. He has been working as a member of the reviewer panels of several SCI/SCI-E indexed journals since 2012.

John Ball is an Associate Professor and Robert D. Guyton Endowed Chair of Teaching Excellence in the Department of Electrical and Computer Engineering, Mississippi State University.

Juan Barraza is a student of the Computer Science Department of Tijuana Institute of Technology. Also, he is a graduate student in Computer Science and her thesis was conducted under the supervision of Patricia Melin. His research interests are in Neural Networks, Optimization Algorithms and Fuzzy Logic. He has published seven research papers.

Sandeep Bhongade (1974) received M.E. degree in Electrical Engineering from V.J.T.I. Mumbai, Mumbai University (India) in 2003 and Ph. D degree from IIT Roorkee in 2012. Presently, he is a faculty member in the Electrical Engineering Department at Shri G.S Institute of Technology & Science, Indore (M.P) -India. His research interests include power system & control, power system simulation and optimization, and deregulated electricity market. He is a Senior IEEE Member.

Zhuming Bi is a Professor of Mechanical Engineering at the Department of Civil and Mechanical Engineering, Purdue University Fort Wayne, USA. He served as a Senior Engineer at National Institute of Standards and Technology (NIST) of USA (2016), a Senior Project Engineer at Northern Ireland Technology Centre, Queen's University Belfast of UK (2007 – 2009), a Research Scientist at the Integrated Manufacturing Technologies Institute of National Research Council Canada (2003 – 2007), a NSERC Postdoctoral Fellow at Simon Fraser University, Burnaby, BC, Canada (2002 – 2003), and a Visiting Scholar to Nanyang Technological Uni-versity (2001) and City University of Hong Kong (1997-1998). He was as an Associ-ate Professor at the Department of Manufacturing Engineering, Nanjing University of Science and Technology in China (1996 -1999). He received a Ph.D. degree in Design and Manufacturing from the University of Saskatchewan in Saskatoon of Canada (2002), and a Ph.D. degree in Mechatronic Control and Automation from Harbin Institute of Technology in China (1994). Dr. Bi's research interests are Robotics and Automation, Internet of Things (IoT), Enterprise Systems, and Sustainable Manufacturing. He has published 110 international journal articles with 1749 times of citations by others in Web of Science in these research fields. He is the only awardee for the 'Outstanding Faculty in Research' and 'Featured Faculty in Research Endeavors' at Purdue University Fort Wayne in 2016-2017. He received IEEE Region 4 Outstanding Professional Award in 2018.

Subhranginee Das is a research scholar currently pursuing Ph.D. (Computer Science Engineering) at Kalinga Institute of Industrial Technology, Bhubaneswar, India. She has received Gold medal in Mathematics (2004) from Utkal University, Bhubaneswar. She also was the University topper in M. Tech in Computer Science (2009) at Utkal University, Bhubaneswar. She has 7 years of teaching experience. Her area of research interest includes Data mining, Soft computing, Evolutionary computation & Financial time series forecasting. She has numerous publications in various journals and conferences of national repute.

David Roch-Dupré was born in Madrid in 1992. He obtained the Degree in Electromechanical Engineering (Electronics specialty) from Comillas Pontifical University (Madrid, Spain) in 2014 and the Official Master's Degree in Industrial Engineering and the Official Master's Degree in Research in Engineering Systems Modeling from the same university in 2016. From September 2013 to June 2016 he was visiting student in the Railway Systems Research Group of the Institute for Applied Research (IIT) at Comillas Pontifical University, developing his Final Degree project and his Master's Thesis. Currently he is a FPU predoctoral researcher at IIT, where he is doing the PhD in the Railway Systems Research Group. His research interests include railway electrification, energy efficiency, control systems and nature-inspired optimization techniques.

Tad Gonsalves obtained the B.Sc degree in theoretical Physics in 1990 and the MSc degree in Astrophysics in 1992 from the Poona University, India. He received the PhD degree in Intelligent Systems from Sophia University, Tokyo in 2004. Currently he is Professor in the Department of Information & Communication Sciences, Sophia University, Tokyo. His research interests include design of Expert Systems, Fuzzy Systems, Evolutionary Computation, Machine Learning, Computational Linguistics, autonomous driving of ground and aerial vehicles. He is the author of the book, "Artificial Intelligence: A non-technical Introduction".

Claudia I. Gonzalez received the Ph.D. in Computer Science from UABC University in Tijuana, Mexico (2016) and the Masters Degree in Computer Science from Tijuana Institute of Technology (2005). Currently she is a Professor of Computer Science in the Division of Graduate Studies and Research of Tijuana Institute of Technology, where she lectures at the undergraduate and graduate levels. Her research interests are Type-2 Fuzzy Logic, Artificial Vision, Pattern Recognition, Modular Neural Networks and Deep Learning techniques.

Shoufei Han received the B.S. degree in computer science from the Hefei University, Hefei, China, in 2012, and the M.S. degree in computer science from Shenyang Aerospace University, Shenyang, China, in 2018. He is currently pursuing the Ph.D. degree in computer science at Nanjing University of Aeronautics and Astronautics, Nanjing, China. His current research interests include machine learning, intelligent algorithm, extreme learning machine, and evolutionary computation.

Yasushi Kambayashi is an associate professor in the Department of Computer and Information Engineering from the Nippon Institute of Technology. He worked at Mitsubishi Research Institute as a staff researcher before joining the Institute. His research interests include theory of computation, theory and practice of programming languages, and political science. He received his PhD in Engineering from the University of Toledo, his MS in Computer Science from the University of Washington, and his BA in Law from Keio University. He has written a number of articles related to multi-agent systems. He was a committee member of the Japan Information-Technology Engineers Examination, a Fellow of IARIA, a committee member of various international conferences including INSTICC, and a member of ACM, IEEE Computer Society, Tau Beta Pi, IPSJ, JSSST, IEICE System Society, IADIS, and Japan Flutist Association.

Tsutomu Kumazawa received Ph.D. from the University of Tokyo in 2011. In 2011 he was hired as the software engineer by Software Research Associates, Inc., Tokyo, Japan. Until 2019, he joined various kinds of software development projects as a member of industrial software development teams. He has experienced mainly design, implementation, and testing phases in a number of software systems development. He is currently a researcher at Key Technology Laboratory in Software Research Associates, Inc. His research interests are Software Engineering and Computer Science, in particular, the development and implementation of formal software verification and analysis techniques and their applications.

Daniel C. Lee received the Ph.D. and S.M. degrees from the Massachusetts Institute of Technology in Electrical Engineering & Computer Science. He received a B.S. degree in Electrical Engineering with honors and a B.S. degree in Mathematics from the University of Maryland at College Park. From 1993 to 1998, Dr. Lee devoted his research to the systems engineering of networks and communication systems at the U.S. Naval Research Laboratory (NRL) in Washington, DC. Dr. Lee's academic career began in 1998 as he joined the faculty of Electrical Engineering Department at the University of Southern California. He is currently a Professor in the School of Engineering Science at Simon Fraser University, in British Columbia, Canada. His main research interests have been optimization and resource allocation issues in systems and networks. Applications of his research include smart city, smart grid, wireless communications and networking, sensor networks, optical networks, broadcasting, and internet multimedia.

Tingjun Lei is a Ph.D. student in the Department of Electrical and Computer Engineering, Mississippi State University.

Xiujuan Lei received the Ph.D. from Northwestern Polytechnical University, Xi'an, China, in 2005. She was a visiting scholar in Department of Computer Science and Engineering, State University of New York at Buffalo, USA from 2009 to 2010. She is currently a professor of Shaanxi Normal University. Her current research interests include bioinformatics, intelligent computing, pattern recognition and data mining.

Chaomin Luo received his Ph.D. degree in electrical and computer engineering in the Department of Electrical and Computer Engineering at the University of Waterloo, Waterloo, Ontario, Canada in 2008, where he was awarded Postgraduate Scholarship (PGS) from the Natural Sciences and Engineering Research Council (NSERC) of Canada; received the Best Student Paper Presentation Award at the SWORD'2007 Conference, and was a recipient of the 2003-2005 Graduate Incentive Award and the 2005-2006 President's Graduate Scholarship. He earned his M.Sc. degree in engineering systems and computing at the University of Guelph, Guelph, Ontario, Canada, in which he was awarded several Ontario Graduate Scholarships (OGS), and his B.Eng. degree in electrical engineering from the Southeast University, Nanjing, China. After he received his Ph.D., he was an Assistant Professor in the Graduate Institute of Electrical Engineering, College of Electrical Engineering and Computer Science, the National Taipei University, in 2008, and then an Associate Professor, in the Department of Electrical and Computer Engineering, at the University of Detroit Mercy, Michigan, USA. He is currently an Associate Professor, Department of Electrical and Computer Engineering, at the Mississippi State University, Mississippi State, MS 39762, USA. He received the Best Paper Award in the IEEE International Conference on Information and Automation (IEEE ICIA2017). He is Associate Editor in 2019 IEEE/RSJ International Conference on Intelligent Robots and Systems (IROS 2019). He is Tutorials Co-Chair in The 2020 IEEE Symposium Series on Computational Intelligence. Dr. Luo is selected in the Marquis Who's Who in America, 2019-2020 edition. His research interests, of cross-disciplinary and multi-disciplinary, lie in two areas. One is in Robotics, Autonomous Systems, Control Systems, Applied Artificial Intelligence and Machine Learning for Autonomous Systems and Robotics, Intelligent Systems, and Mechatronics and Automation. The other is in VLSI/FPGA CAD, Optimization of VLSI, and Embedded Systems for Robotics and Autonomous Systems. He was an early researcher to apply semi-definite programming and second order cone programming into VLSI optimization design. He was the first researcher to successfully develop biologically inspired neural dynamics model for complete coverage robot motion planning. Dr. Luo has extensive industry experience in Canada, Singapore and China in embedded systems, intelligent instrument, automation, control and mechatronics. His industry experience includes working as an electronics engineer, hardware designer and a director of the embedded systems and intelligent instrument Lab. Dr. Luo is an INFORMS, IEEE and ASEE member. He has shown his leadership nationally and internationally on his research field. He was the Panelist in the Department of Defense, USA, 2015-2016, 2016-2017 NDSEG Fellowship program and Panelist in 2017 NSF GRFP Panelist program. He was the General Co-Chair of the 1st IEEE International Workshop on Computational Intelligence in Smart Technologies (IEEE-CIST 2015), and Journal Special Issues Chair, IEEE 2016 International Conference on Smart Technologies (IEEE-SmarTech), Cleveland, OH, USA. He was the Program Co-Chair in 2018 IEEE International Conference on Information and Automation (IEEE-ICIA'2018). He was the Plenary Session Co-Chair in the 2019 and 2018 International Conference on Swarm Intelligence, and he was the Invited Session Co-Chair in the 2017 International Conference on Swarm Intelligence. He was the Publicity Chair in the 2011 IEEE International Conference on Automation and Logistics. He was on the Conference Committee in the 2012 International Conference on Information and Automation and International Symposium on Biomedical Engineering and the Publicity Chair in the 2012 IEEE International Conference on Automation and Logistics. Also, he was Chair and Vice Chair of IEEE SEM - Computational Intelligence Chapter and was a Chair of IEEE SEM - Computational Intelligence Chapter and Chair of Education Committee of IEEE SEM. Dr. Luo serves as the Editorial Board Member of Journal of Industrial Electronics and Applications, and International Journal of Complex Systems – Computing, Sensing and Control, Associate Editor of International journal of Robotics and Automation, and Associate Editor of International Journal of Swarm Intelligence Research (IJSIR). He has organized and chaired several special sessions on topics of Intelligent Vehicle Systems and Bio-inspired Intelligence in reputed international conferences such as IJCNN, IEEE-SSCI, IEEE-CEC, IEEE-CASE, and IEEE-Fuzzy, etc. He has extensively published in reputed journals and conference proceedings, such as IEEE Transactions on Industrial Electronics, IEEE Transactions on Neural Networks and Learning Systems, IEEE Transactions on SMC, IEEE Transactions on Cybernetics, IEEE-ICRA, and IEEE-IROS, etc.

Katherine Manson received her B.Sc. in electrical engineering and B.Sc. in computer science from the University of Saskatchewan in 1991. She received her M.A.Sc. in Engineering Science at Simon Fraser University in 2019. In 2011 she was hired as an instructor at the British Columbia Institute of Technology and is currently the program head of the Electrical Power and Industrial Control option of the Electrical and Computer Engineering Technology program. She researches in the area of application of evolutionary algorithms to electrical power technology. She is the co-author of several other papers related to Enhanced Fireworks Algorithms applied to using the extended Kalman filter for speed sensing induction motor control, electrical protection and smart grid optimization.

Patricia Melin holds the Doctor in Science degree (Doctor Habilitatus D.Sc.) in Computer Science from the Polish Academy of Sciences. She is a Professor of Computer Science in the Graduate

Division, Tijuana Institute of Technology, Tijuana, Mexico, since 1998. In addition, she is serving as Director of Graduate Studies in Computer Science and head of the research group on Hybrid Neural Intelligent Systems (2000-present). She is past President of NAFIPS (North American Fuzzy Information Processing Society) 2019-2020. Prof. Melin is the founding Chair of the Mexican Chapter of the IEEE Computational Intelligence Society. She is member of the IEEE Neural Network Technical Committee (2007 to present), the IEEE Fuzzy System Technical Committee (2014 to present) and is Chair of the Task Force on Hybrid Intelligent Systems (2007 to present) and she is currently Associate Editor of the Journal of Information Sciences and IEEE Transactions on Fuzzy Systems. She is member of NAFIPS, IFSA, and IEEE. She belongs to the Mexican Research System with level III. Her research interests are in Modular Neural Networks, Type-2 Fuzzy Logic, Pattern Recognition, Fuzzy Control, Neuro-Fuzzy and Genetic-Fuzzy hybrid approaches. She has published over 300 journal papers, 10 authored books, 22 edited books, and more than 300 papers in conference proceedings with h-index of 63. She has served as Guest Editor of several Special Issues in the past, in journals like: Applied Soft Computing, Intelligent Systems, Information Sciences, Non-Linear Studies, JAMRIS, Fuzzy Sets and Systems. She has been recognized as Highly Cited Researcher in 2017 and 2018 by Clarivate Analytics because of having multiple highly cited papers in Web of Science.

B. B. Misra has completed his B. Text. degree in 1984 from Kanpur University, M. Tech. (Computer Science) in 2002 from Utkal University, and Ph.D. (Engineering) in 2011 from Biju Pattanaik University of Technology. He has done his Post Doctoral Research during 2013-14, at AJOU University, South Korea under the Technology Research Program for Brain Science, headed by Prof. Sung-Bae cho, Yonsei university, South Korea. His areas of research include data science, machine learning, and computational intelligence. He has edited two books one for IGI Global and the other for the Springer, published one monograph for the Lambert Academic Publishing, Germany, six book chapters, and more than 90 papers in different journals and conferences of National and International repute. Presently he is continuing as a Professor of the Department of Computer Science and Engineering at Silicon Institute of Technology, Bhubaneswar.

Sreeja N. K. is an Assistant Professor (Senior Grade) in the Department of Applied Mathematics and Computational Sciences at PSG College of Technology, Coimbatore, India. She obtained her Master's Degree in Computer Applications awarded by Avinashilingam Deemed University, Coimbatore, India in 2003 and Ph.D Degree in Computer Applications awarded by Anna University, Chennai, India in 2016. Her Research interests span Machine Learning, Soft Computing and Pattern Recognition. She has around 11 publications in various Journals, Edited Book chapters and International/National Conference Proceedings. She is a Gold medal recipient awarded by Bharathiar University, Coimbatore, India for academic excellence in Under Graduate level.

Sreelaja N. K is an Assistant Professor (Selection grade) in the Department of Applied Mathematics and Computational Sciences, PSG College of Technology, Coimbatore, India. She obtained her Ph.D in Computer Applications awarded by Anna University, India.She has published many papers in the areas of swarm intelligence and computer security in peer reviewed international journals and conferences. Her research interests include Security in Computing, Swarm Intelligence and Machine learning. She serves as an Editorial Board member of Information Processing in Agriculture, published by Elsevier. She has served as a reviewer for many international journals and conferences.

Sarat Chandra Nayak holds a Ph.D. degree in Computer Engineering from VSSUT, Burla, India and M. Tech. in Computer Science from Utkal University, Bhubaneswar, India. His research interests are Data Mining, Soft Computing, Predictive Systems, Financial Time Series Forecasting, Computational Intelligence, Evolutionary Computation, and Classification. He has more than 45 research articles in reputed International journals and conferences, and 5 book chapters in his credit. He has 10 years of experience in teaching and research. Dr. Nayak currently associated with computer science and engineering department as a Professor at CMR College of Engineering & Technology (Autonomous), Hyderabad, India.

Alberto Ochoa makes a postdoctoral stay during his sabbatical year, in the Information Technology Management (GTI) of the National Institute of Electricity and Clean Energies (INEEL). Carlos Alberto's interest in coming to stay at our Institute was mainly due to the fact that he has known Yasmín Hernández and Gustavo Arroyo, researcher and Information Technology Manager, for several years, respectively, during which time they shared research results. in small collaborations, which has corroborated that they have similar interests. On the other hand, says Carlos, the problem addressed by INEEL is an excellent application niche for its area of expertise. Working at the GTI also allows you to meet more research staff. It should be noted that the project in which Carlos works is related to the design and implementation of an intelligent logistics model for transport, using a Bio-Inspired algorithm (a solution offered by nature) and Mutiating Systems to establish the best route, considering a set of restrictions. The idea is to generate a catalog of solutions for companies that need to transport products and optimize the load and transfer. Initially there are contacts in Petróleos Mexicanos (PEMEX) and with the company Baxter, with whom meetings and agreements have already been held. It is expected that the generated models can be applied to other industries and companies. In addition to his research, Carlos Alberto collaborates in the creation of a Thematic Network of Smart Cities of CONACYT. Likewise, it is proposing to propose joint projects under the CONACYT funds scheme and the thesis management as a whole. At the end of his sabbatical year, he will return to his work center, the Autonomous University of Ciudad Juárez and will continue collaborating in the Applied Computing Master, where he currently directs four Doctorate students in Technology. For all those interested in coming to make their sabbatical year at INEEL, Carlos recommends approaching the different Managements to structure a project proposal, in such a way that both parties obtain a work benefit, as well as propose projects that are not only high impact on technology, but are applications to solve specific problems of the energy sector. Carlos Alberto is a level II researcher and has a Doctorate in Advanced Technology from the National Polytechnic Institute (IPN) in 2004, an Academic Postdoctorate at Unicamp, in Brazil in 2006, and a Postdoctorate in the CIATEC Industry Center CONACYT in 2009. He was part of the third generation of the Training Program in Technological Research of the Institute in 1994, experience that allowed him to know different aspects of the research in this sector. The current research stay will allow him, he says, to contribute new ideas and know first-hand, timely solutions in the country's energy sector.

Bhumika Sahu is doing his master's in Power Electronics from the Department of Electrical Engineering, at Shri G.S Institute of Technology & Science, Indore (M.P)-India. His areas of interest include microgrid, control system application in different areas, power system.

Hideyuki Takagi received the degrees of Bachelor and Master from Kyushu Institute of Design in 1979 and 1981, and the degree of Doctor of Engineering from Toyohashi University of Technology in 1991. He was a researcher at Panasonic Central Research labs in 1981 - 1995, was an Associate Professor of Kyushu Institute of Design in 1995 - 2003, and is a Professor of Kyushu University now. He was a visiting researcher at UC Berkeley in 1991-1993 hosted by Prof. L. A. Zadeh. He has been a volunteer for IEEE Systems, Man, and Cybernetics (SMC) Society. Some of his contributions are: Vice President in 2006 - 2009: a member of Administrative Committee/Board of Governors in 2001 - 2010, and 2016 - 2018: Chair of SMC Japan Chapter in 2014 - 2017: Technical Committee (TC) Coordinator in 2004 - 2005: Chair of TC on Soft Computing in 1998 - 2004 and since 2008: Distinguished Lecturer in 2006 - 2011: Associate Editor of IEEE Transactions on SMC, Part B / Cybernetics since 2001.

Munehiro Takimoto is a professor in the Department of Information Sciences at Tokyo University of Science. His research interests include the design and implementation of programming languages. He received his undergraduate, postgraduate, and doctoral degrees in engineering from Keio University. He is a member of ACM, IEEE Computer Society, IPSJ, JSST, and IEICE System Society.

Fevrier Valdez is a researcher of the National System of Researchers Level 1 in Mexico recognized by CONACYT. My main interests are Intelligence Computing, Swarm Intelligence, Bio-Inspired Computing, Evolutionary Computing, Fuzzy Logic, Neural Networks, Intelligence Control and Parallel Computing. Actually the Phd Fevrier Valdez is developing research in the bio inspired and nature computing. This researching is of great relevance to international level which had allowed an international recognition. Is professor-researcher of full time in the Tijuana Institute of Technology.

Yu Xue is a member of IEEE (92058890), ACM (2270255), and CCF (E200029023M). He received the Ph. D. degree from School of Computer Science and Technology, Nanjing University of Aeronautics \& Astronautics, China, in 2013. He is an associate professor in the School of Computer and Software, Nanjing University of Information Science and Technology. He is a visiting scholar of the Department of Computer Science and Engineering, Michigan State University, East Lansing, U.S. He was a visit scholar of School of Engineering and Computer Science at Victoria University of Wellington. His research interests include Evolutionary Computation, Machine Learning and Data Mining.

Jun Yu received a Bachelor degree from Northeastern University, China in 2014, and a Master degree and a doctorate from Kyushu University, Japan in 2017 and 2019, respectively. He is currently an Assistant Professor of Niigata University, Japan. His research interests include evolutionary computation, multi-modal optimization, and machine learning.

JunQi Zhang received the Ph.D. degree in computing science from Fudan University, Shanghai, China, in 2007.He became a Post-Doctoral Research Fellow and a Lecturer with the Key Laboratory of Machine Perception, Ministry of Education in Computer Science, Peking University, Beijing, China, in 2007. He is currently a full professor with Department of Computer Science and Technology, Tongji University, Shanghai. He has over 10 papers in IEEE TRANSACTIONS. His current research interests include firework algorithm, particle swarm optimization, intelligent and learning automata, machine learning, high-dimensional index, and multimedia data management. Dr. Zhang was a recipient of the Outstanding Post-Doctoral Award from Peking University.

Yuchen Zhang received the bachelor's degree in Xi'an Technological University, Xi'an, China, in 2015. He is currently pursuing the Ph.D. degree in School of Computer Science, Shaanxi Normal University, Xi'an, China. His current research interests include intelligent computing and bioinformatics.

Index

Purchase Print, E-Book, or Print + E-Book

IGI Global's reference books are available in three unique pricing formats:
Print Only, E-Book Only, or Print + E-Book.
Shipping fees may apply.

www.igi-global.com

Recommended Reference Books

ISBN: 978-1-5225-5912-2
© 2019; 349 pp.
List Price: $215

ISBN: 978-1-5225-8176-5
© 2019; 2,218 pp.
List Price: $2,950

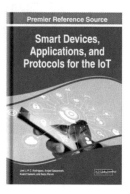

ISBN: 978-1-5225-7811-6
© 2019; 317 pp.
List Price: $225

ISBN: 978-1-5225-7268-8
© 2019; 316 pp.
List Price: $215

ISBN: 978-1-5225-7455-2
© 2019; 288 pp.
List Price: $205

ISBN: 978-1-5225-8973-0
© 2019; 200 pp.
List Price: $195

Do you want to stay current on the latest research trends, product announcements, news and special offers?
Join IGI Global's mailing list today and start enjoying exclusive perks sent only to IGI Global members.
Add your name to the list at **www.igi-global.com/newsletters.**

Publisher of Peer-Reviewed, Timely, and Innovative Academic Research

www.igi-global.com   Sign up at www.igi-global.com/newsletters   facebook.com/igiglobal   twitter.com/igiglobal   linkedin.com/igiglobal

Ensure Quality Research is Introduced to the Academic Community

Become an IGI Global Reviewer for Authored Book Projects

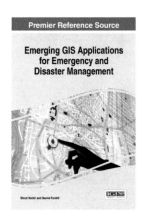

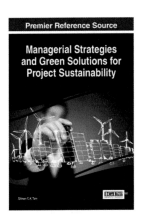

The overall success of an authored book project is dependent on quality and timely reviews.

In this competitive age of scholarly publishing, constructive and timely feedback significantly expedites the turnaround time of manuscripts from submission to acceptance, allowing the publication and discovery of forward-thinking research at a much more expeditious rate. Several IGI Global authored book projects are currently seeking highly-qualified experts in the field to fill vacancies on their respective editorial review boards:

Applications and Inquiries may be sent to:
development@igi-global.com

Applicants must have a doctorate (or an equivalent degree) as well as publishing and reviewing experience. Reviewers are asked to complete the open-ended evaluation questions with as much detail as possible in a timely, collegial, and constructive manner. All reviewers' tenures run for one-year terms on the editorial review boards and are expected to complete at least three reviews per term. Upon successful completion of this term, reviewers can be considered for an additional term.

If you have a colleague that may be interested in this opportunity, we encourage you to share this information with them.

IGI Global Proudly Partners With eContent Pro International

Receive a 25% Discount on all Editorial Services

Editorial Services

IGI Global expects all final manuscripts submitted for publication to be in their final form. This means they must be reviewed, revised, and professionally copy edited prior to their final submission. Not only does this support with accelerating the publication process, but it also ensures that the highest quality scholarly work can be disseminated.

English Language Copy Editing

Let eContent Pro International's expert copy editors perform edits on your manuscript to resolve spelling, punctuaion, grammar, syntax, flow, formatting issues and more.

Scientific and Scholarly Editing

Allow colleagues in your research area to examine the content of your manuscript and provide you with valuable feedback and suggestions before submission.

Figure, Table, Chart & Equation Conversions

Do you have poor quality figures? Do you need visual elements in your manuscript created or converted? A design expert can help!

Translation

Need your documjent translated into English? eContent Pro International's expert translators are fluent in English and more than 40 different languages.

Hear What Your Colleagues are Saying About Editorial Services Supported by IGI Global

"The service was very fast, very thorough, and very helpful in ensuring our chapter meets the criteria and requirements of the book's editors. I was quite impressed and happy with your service."

– Prof. Tom Brinthaupt,
Middle Tennessee State University, USA

"I found the work actually spectacular. The editing, formatting, and other checks were very thorough. The turnaround time was great as well. I will definitely use eContent Pro in the future."

– Nickanor Amwata, Lecturer,
University of Kurdistan Hawler, Iraq

"I was impressed that it was done timely, and wherever the content was not clear for the reader, the paper was improved with better readability for the audience."

– Prof. James Chilembwe,
Mzuzu University, Malawi

Email: customerservice@econtentpro.com   **www.igi-global.com/editorial-service-partners**

www.igi-global.com

Celebrating Over 30 Years of Scholarly
Knowledge Creation & Dissemination

InfoSci®-Books

A Database of Over 5,300+ Reference Books Containing Over 100,000+ Chapters Focusing on Emerging Research

GAIN ACCESS TO **THOUSANDS** OF REFERENCE BOOKS AT **A FRACTION** OF THEIR INDIVIDUAL LIST **PRICE**.

InfoSci®-Books Database

The **InfoSci®-Books** database is a collection of over 5,300+ IGI Global single and multi-volume reference books, handbooks of research, and encyclopedias, encompassing groundbreaking research from prominent experts worldwide that span over 350+ topics in 11 core subject areas including business, computer science, education, science and engineering, social sciences and more.

Open Access Fee Waiver (Offset Model) Initiative

For any library that invests in IGI Global's InfoSci-Journals and/ or InfoSci-Books databases, IGI Global will match the library's investment with a fund of equal value to go toward **subsidizing the OA article processing charges (APCs) for their students, faculty, and staff** at that institution when their work is submitted and accepted under OA into an IGI Global journal.*

INFOSCI® PLATFORM FEATURES

- No DRM
- No Set-Up or Maintenance Fees
- A Guarantee of No More Than a 5% Annual Increase
- Full-Text HTML and PDF Viewing Options
- Downloadable MARC Records
- Unlimited Simultaneous Access
- COUNTER 5 Compliant Reports
- Formatted Citations With Ability to Export to RefWorks and EasyBib
- No Embargo of Content (Research is Available Months in Advance of the Print Release)

*The fund will be offered on an annual basis and expire at the end of the subscription period. The fund would renew as the subscription is renewed for each year thereafter. The open access fees will be waived after the student, faculty, or staff's paper has been vetted and accepted into an IGI Global journal and the fund can only be used toward publishing OA in an IGI Global journal. Libraries in developing countries will have the match on their investment doubled.

To Learn More or To Purchase This Database:
www.igi-global.com/infosci-books

eresources@igi-global.com • Toll Free: 1-866-342-6657 ext. 100 • Phone: 717-533-8845 x100

www.igi-global.com

Printed in the United States
By Bookmasters